Reassessing the Employment Relationship

MANAGEMENT, WORK AND ORGANISATIONS

Series editors: **Gibson Burrell**, The Management Centre, University of Leicester
Mick Marchington, Manchester Business School
Paul Thompson, Department of Human Resource Management,
University of Strathclyde

This series of new textbooks covers the areas of human resource management, employee relations, organisational behaviour and related business and management fields. Each text has been specially commissioned to be written by leading experts in a clear and accessible way. The books contain serious and challenging material, take an analytical rather than prescriptive approach and are particularly suitable for use by students with no prior specialist knowledge.

The series is relevant for many business and management courses, including MBA and post-experience courses, specialist masters and postgraduate diplomas, professional courses and final-year undergraduate courses. These texts have become essential reading at business and management schools worldwide.

Published

Emma Bell
READING MANAGEMENT AND ORGANIZATION IN FILM

Paul Blyton and Peter Turnbull
THE DYNAMICS OF EMPLOYEE RELATIONS (3rd edn)

Paul Blyton, Edmund Heery and Peter Turnbull (eds)
REASSESSING THE EMPLOYMENT RELATIONSHIP

Sharon C. Bolton
EMOTION MANAGEMENT IN THE WORKPLACE

Sharon C. Bolton and Maeve Houlihan (eds)
SEARCHING FOR THE HUMAN IN HUMAN RESOURCE MANAGEMENT

Peter Boxall and John Purcell
STRATEGY AND HUMAN RESOURCE MANAGEMENT (2nd edn)

J. Martin Corbett
CRITICAL CASES IN ORGANISATIONAL BEHAVIOUR

Susan Corby, Steve Palmer and Esmond Lindop
RETHINKING REWARD

Ian Greener
PUBLIC MANAGEMENT

Keith Grint
LEADERSHIP

Irena Grugulis
SKILLS, TRAINING AND HUMAN RESOURCE DEVELOPMENT

Geraldine Healy, Mike Noon and Gill Kirton (eds)
EQUALITY, INEQUALITIES AND DIVERSITY

Damian Hodgson and Svetlana Cicmil (eds)
MAKING PROJECTS CRITICAL

Marek Korczynski
HUMAN RESOURCE MANAGEMENT IN SERVICE WORK

Karen Legge
HUMAN RESOURCE MANAGEMENT: anniversary edition

Patricia Lewis and Ruth Simpson (eds)
GENDERING EMOTIONS IN ORGANIZATIONS

Patricia Lewis and Ruth Simpson (eds)
VOICE, VISIBILITY AND THE GENDERING OF ORGANIZATIONS

Stephen Proctor and Frank Mueller (eds)
TEAMWORKING

Pullen et al (eds)
EXPLORING IDENTITY

Helen Rainbird (ed.)
TRAINING IN THE WORKPLACE

Jill Rubery and Damian Grimshaw
THE ORGANISATION OF EMPLOYMENT

Harry Scarbrough (ed.)
THE MANAGEMENT OF EXPERTISE

Hugh Scullion and Margaret Linehan (eds)
INTERNATIONAL HUMAN RESOURCE MANAGEMENT

Adrian Wilkinson, Mick Marchington, Tom Redman and Ed Snape
MANAGING WITH TOTAL QUALITY MANAGEMENT

Colin C. Williams
RETHINKING THE FUTURE OF WORK

Diana Winstanley and Jean Woodall (eds)
ETHICAL ISSUES IN CONTEMPORARY HUMAN RESOURCE MANAGEMENT

For more information on titles in the Series please go to www.palgrave.com/business/mwo

Reassessing the Employment Relationship

Edited by

Paul Blyton
Professor of Industrial Relations and Industrial Sociology, Cardiff University, UK

Edmund Heery
Professor of Employment Relations, Cardiff University, UK

Peter Turnbull
Professor of Human Resource Management and Labour Relations, Cardiff University, UK

First published 2011 by
PALGRAVE MACMILLAN

Palgrave Macmillan in the UK is an imprint of Macmillan Publishers Limited,
registered in England, company number 785998, of Houndmills, Basingstoke,
Hampshire RG21 6XS.

Palgrave Macmillan in the US is a division of St Martin's Press LLC,
175 Fifth Avenue, New York, NY 10010.

Palgrave Macmillan is the global academic imprint of the above companies
and has companies and representatives throughout the world.

Palgrave® and Macmillan® are registered trademarks in the United States,
the United Kingdom, Europe and other countries.

ISBN 978–0–230–22172–7

This book is printed on paper suitable for recycling and made from fully
managed and sustained forest sources. Logging, pulping and manufacturing
processes are expected to conform to the environmental regulations of the
country of origin.

A catalogue record for this book is available from the British Library.

A catalog record for this book is available from the Library of Congress.

10   9   8   7   6   5   4   3   2   1
20 19 18 17 16 15 14 13 12 11

Printed and bound in Great Britain by
CPI Antony Rowe, Chippenham and Eastbourne

Contents

List of tables

List of figures

Acknowledgements

The editors acknowledge The University of North Carolina Press for permission to reproduce the Table 2.1 on page 24, and Palgrave Macmillan for permission to reproduce the Table 17.1 on page 406.

In bringing this collection together, we wish to acknowledge the help we have received from various quarters. First, our thanks to all the contributors who not only agreed to fit this task into their already busy schedules but also to respond willingly to comments on drafts that helped create a more cohesive collection than would otherwise have been the case. Second, thanks to Penny Smith at Cardiff University who was involved in the volume's early stages, and to Angela Cox who played an important role in keeping track on where we were up to, as drafts move back and forth. Our thanks too to Ursula Gavin and her colleague Mark Cooper at Palgrave Macmillan, for their enthusiasm and their patience.

Contributors

At the time the writing for this collection started, all the contributors were members of the HRM Section at the Cardiff Business School, Cardiff University. Since that time, Sukanya Sengupta has joined Warwick Business School.

1

Reassessing the employment relationship: An introduction

Paul Blyton, Edmund Heery and Peter Turnbull

It's 20 years since members of the Human Resource Management (HRM) section at Cardiff Business School came together to produce *Reassessing Human Resource Management* (Blyton and Turnbull, 1992). The spur for writing that volume was the evident lack of reflection on the extent to which HRM represented essentially a re-labelling exercise for Personnel Departments or signalled something more fundamental in the management of labour. By examining HRM from several different perspectives, we endeavoured to cast a critical eye on the subject and explore various tensions and contradictions that were apparent among the different elements and policy goals contained within HRM.

The book seemingly struck a chord with many readers and at different times the editors were encouraged to produce a new edition. But what became increasingly clear in the intervening period was the need for a more wide-ranging reconsideration of the employment relationship. Issues of HRM form one part of that picture, but events unfolding over the past two decades call for a broader reassessment of employment and labour management within contemporary work organizations. These events and developments have been occurring at different levels, ranging from the ubiquitous – the gathering pace of globalization and the growing influence of financial markets on the operation of firms, for example – to the more specific emergence of new business models and new forms of work in particular industry sectors, many of these a direct reflection of advances in information technology. Substantial changes are evident too in the way that work is regulated, by governments, employers and representatives of employees, and more broadly in the thinking and discussion about the norms and standards that are appropriate in relation to people at work. The intensity of debate over phrases such as 'decent work', 'ethical behaviour', 'social responsibility' and 'work–life balance' signals some of the ways in which previous understandings about employment relationships are being subject to greater questioning and challenge.

The employment relationship lies at the heart of work organizations. The aim of this volume is to explore the ways that this relationship, the contexts within which it occurs, and more broadly the ways in which the employment relationship might be studied and thought about, have changed over the recent period and the implications of those changes. To achieve this we have kept to the model that served us well in our earlier 'Reassessment' volume: to draw on contributors with a range of perspectives and fields of expertise, to analyse the changes taking place, and the drivers of change, at different levels. Lying at the heart of relations between capital and labour, the employment relationship figures prominently in the fields of employment relations, HRM and industrial/organizational sociology. Members of the HRM Section at Cardiff are well placed to comment from the viewpoint of these different perspectives. Much expanded since the time of our earlier volume, the editors have been able to draw on over 20 members of the Section to cover the much broader canvas represented by the present volume.

Before giving an overview of the nature of these individual contributions, however, this introduction needs to touch briefly on two other areas. First it is important to say something more about the focus of our enquiry: the employment relationship and both its continued centrality in work organizations and its enduring contested and indeterminate nature. Second, it is worthwhile noting some of the main developments impacting upon the employment relationship, many of which are considered in more detail in individual chapters. These developments encapsulate not only changes in the broad context of work, but also the emergence of new forms and new ideas about the employment relationship and the way current discussions over work standards raise complex questions about future employment.

What is the employment relationship?

The 'relationship' to which the employment relationship refers is that between employer and employee. At its heart is an exchange between the buyers and sellers of labour (Coyle-Shapiro and Conway, 2004). The terms of this exchange are broadly defined in the contract of employment between the two central parties (Deakin and Njoya, 2008). This contract 'is the outcome of a transaction that encompasses both the entitlements and the obligations of the employee' (Brown et al., 2000: 616). Yet while the contract of employment represents the 'cornerstone' of the employment relationship (Kahn-Freund, 1954: 45) the relationship as a whole has a far more complex structure. To continue the metaphor, while a cornerstone acts as a key component of a structure, it is also the basis on which the rest of that structure is built. In the same way, while the contract of employment establishes the general terms of the exchange of labour for a reward, this 'market exchange' typically is an exchange of labour power (rather than a precisely defined labour output) for a wage, and thus is indeterminate in the *precise amount* of labour being purchased in the exchange. That labour power – often quantified in terms of the hours that the provider of labour must commit to the employer – requires translation into productive labour by means of a managerial process of organizing, directing and controlling.

The specific ways in which management achieves this translation of labour power into actual labour are crucial for both parties. On the one hand, the effective deployment of labour lies at the heart of competitive success; in recent years this has been exemplified in the importance attributed to securing workforce commitment to achieve high performance (Appelbaum et al., 2000). As we have discussed elsewhere (Blyton and Turnbull, 2004), management relies not only on securing worker compliance, but also on active workforce cooperation to provide discretionary labour (that is labour above a minimum requirement) to achieve high performance levels. Arguably, in sectors experiencing intensified competition (see below), the employer's reliance on employees willingly deploying their skills, initiative and talent is even more important today than it was a generation ago. On the other hand, the managerial process is also a critical factor in employees' overall experience of work: their access to rewarding and fulfilling jobs, being treated fairly and equitably, being involved in decision-making and having scope to use and develop their skills; or alternatively, being subject to unreasonable levels of work intensity, direction and control. These experiences hinge crucially on how management organizes its workforce and conducts the process of securing productive labour. In capitalist societies, management's actions are underpinned by substantial power resources (and far greater power resources than labour can draw upon) to define the process of productive activity. However, management does not enjoy an unrestricted prerogative. The law, the professional standards set by bodies (such as the Chartered Institute of Personnel and Development) in relation to people management, agreements with trade unions and counter-controls applied by workers, all act to constrain managerial action. And as we discuss in the next section, this 'governance regime' has been undergoing significant transformation in latter years, making a reassessment of the employment relationship particularly timely.

Whilst it is true to say that the employment relationship rests on an exchange between employer and employee, it also comprises a structure of 'rights, obligations, formal and informal social relationships' on which the daily experience of work is shaped (McGovern et al., 2007: 12). The majority of day-to-day interactions are based on a host of unwritten rules, assumptions and expectations on both sides. It has become common practice to refer to key elements of these assumptions and expectations as part of a 'psychological contract', of reciprocal obligations between employees and their work organizations (Rousseau, 1995). The term itself has proven controversial: not least over whether there is sufficient 'shared understanding' or congruence of view between employers and employees that could be said to constitute a 'contract' (Morrison and Robinson, 2004). Nevertheless, this discussion further underlines the point that the formal contract of employment covers only certain dimensions of the employment relationship, and that the behaviour of both parties – together with their beliefs, expectations and understandings – constitute important elements in the overall relationship between employers and employees.

Just as the employment relationship is crucial for management in their efforts to extract profitable work from employees, it is also central in the overall lives of those employees. The terms on which that relationship is constructed – the income it provides, the duration and arrangement of working hours and the degree of job security embedded in different forms of employment contract – all importantly shape people's ability to organize, plan and successfully fulfil their lives outside work. These features of employment – whether it provides decent pay, reasonable work hours, some degree of job security – are all indicators of the overall quality of jobs. The broader point here, however, is that paid work is much more than an effort–reward exchange. It has important implications for health, personal development, families and communities (Sisson, 2008: 6). Indeed, the nature of the employment relationship is central to how we, as individuals, are able to construct the rest of our lives, and develop and maintain our sense of meaning and identity in contemporary society.

Further, while employees establish individual contracts of employment with an employer, the experience of work for the majority of employees is as an inherently shared, cooperative and collective endeavour. Indeed, this act of working with others is what many employees commonly report as one of the most valued aspects of their employment. Thus, in the study of work it is vital to recognize these collective and shared interests among employees; that is, to understand employees and analyse the employment relationship from a collective as well as an individual perspective.

Changes in the context of employment relationships

So far, we have dwelt more on continuities embodied in the employment relationship (its indeterminate nature for example, its composition of formal and informal aspects and its importance for both employers and employees) than on changes occurring within work and capitalist societies more generally. The continuities are important and are sometimes lost from sight, but to answer the question of why reassess the employment relationship now, we need to acknowledge the marked extent of changes that have been taking place in recent years and their deep-seated impact on employment. These changes have been occurring at different levels and at different speeds, and many are interlinked. It is sufficient here to note some of the most prominent, for many aspects of these changes are examined in more detail in forthcoming chapters.

At the most generalized level, different writers and researchers trace many of the far-reaching developments in employment relationships back to the changing ways in which capitalist activity is being conducted. The continued growth of more globalized systems of goods and service production, together with the deepening influence of financial markets on the way that enterprises behave, can be seen to have introduced a step change in the conduct of capitalism amounting, over the past generation, to the creation of a new economic order. Several chapters in this volume consider particular aspects of these developments. However, an overarching effect of the twin forces of globalization and financialization – between them incorporating a range of developments from rapid industrialization of economies such as Brazil, Russia, India and China to spreading trade liberalization and deregulation – is an intensification of competition and an accelerated drive to maximize (short-term) returns, partly through securing lower costs and particularly, lower labour costs (Cappelli, 1999; Sennett, 2006).

One way these forces potentially impact on extant employment relationships is by the methods employers seek to obtain labour at a lower price than represented by their regular workforce. These methods include, among others, expanding non-standard forms of employment contract, and greater use of agency workers, sub-contractors and outsourcing arrangements

(Marchington et al., 2005). As a consequence, internal employees in an ever-expanding range of occupations and sectors have increasingly been subject to intensified market pressures, with standard employment contracts, stable pay and benefits, opportunities for promotion and a degree of job security giving way to more insecure and less predictable jobs, with 'no long term' the watchword of these new employment conditions (Sennett, 1998).

The extent and pace at which contractual relations are altering is subject to dispute on both sides of the Atlantic (Cappelli, 1999; Jacoby, 1999; McGovern et al., 2007). The picture is a varied one – significant change evident in some areas (such as the use of outsourcing and agency workers) but also the widespread persistence of long-term employment and continuing contracts (Doogan, 2001, 2009; McGovern et al., 2007). What is also clear, however, is that while some aspects of employment contracts have remained highly standardized (Brown et al., 2000) other elements have been subject to a far greater degree of differentiation, particularly in relation to work hours, in a managerial endeavour to deploy labour more flexibly (Anxo, et al., 2004; Blyton, 2008).

As noted earlier, it is evident too that one outcome of the greater emphasis on competitiveness has been an increased focus on achieving 'high performance' (Frost, 2008). Nowhere is this more evident than in the field of Human Resource Management and a concern with which (and in what ways) human resource (HR) measures contribute to improved performance. This focus impacts directly on employment relationships and the ways that different HR measures – from appraisals and job evaluation to teamworking and performance-related pay – shape managerial expectations of employees at work. Much discussion has taken place in recent years over whether (and to what extent) jobs have become more demanding (Green, 2006) and employer expectations inflated over what constitutes 'a fair day's work'. The view that expectations placed on employees are inexorably rising over time has been captured in such phrases as 'greedy organisations' (Coser, 1967) and more recently by what Van Dyne and Ellis term *job creep* 'the slow and subtle expansion of employee job duties' (2004: 181). It has also been suggested that this trend is exacerbated by 'effort-biased technical change' (Green, 2006: 69); that is, the increased use of e-mail, mobile phones and other devices that erode the boundaries between work and leisure and contribute to time pressure (Bittman et al., 2010).

These conditions alone – changes in the nature of capitalist activity, managerial responses to increased competition and the search for lower labour costs – would be sufficient to warrant a fundamental reconsideration of the employment relationship. But a series of other (and in important respects related) developments give further weight to these changes. Prominent among these is the changing nature of regulation of the employment relationship, most clearly evidenced in the marked contraction of collective regulation by employers and trade unions in many countries, and the corresponding rise in unilateral regulation by employers (Brown and Nash, 2008; Kersley et al., 2006; Milner, 1995). In the UK, along with the US, several decades of union membership decline have left trade unions much weakened in their ability to protect members' interests and influence patterns of job control and work organization (Brown et al., 1998; Kolins Givan, 2007). This decline in union membership and influence has been reflected in a much reduced ability to assert the necessity for regulation by collective bargaining. A corresponding increase in (employer-sponsored) non-union channels of representation, and growth in relationships with unionized groups based on consultation rather than negotiation, further underline the important ways in which the regulation of the employment relationship has been reconstituted, particularly in liberal market economies (Howell, 2004). Added to this, the state too has amended its regulatory approach. While certain collective rights have received additional statutory support (in relation to rights to information and consultation for example), overall the state's emphasis has been to promote individual statutory rights within the employment relationship, covering issues such as protection against various kinds of discrimination and rights to information regarding different terms of the contract (Brown et al., 2000). Crucially, however, the evidence (ibid.: 623) points to the importance of a collective, trade union presence in ensuring these individual employment rights are upheld: compliance is significantly higher where union representation remains in place. Thus, the widespread dismantling of the collective regulation of the employment relationship not only diminishes the collective employee voice within the workplace, but also raises doubts about whether individual statutory protections will be fully upheld. The ramifications of the decline in collective employee voice, and the ability of employees collectively to resist managerial actions which they find unacceptable, resonate across many of the chapters in the present volume as authors explore the changing nature of the employment relationship in the contemporary workplace.

Two further factors also need incorporating into our claim regarding the timely nature of reassessing the employment relationship. First, the growing heterogeneity of the labour force, both in terms of the diversity of the workforce and the contractual arrangements they are employed under, raises important questions about how different individuals and groups are subject to different forms of employment relationship. The diversity of an organization's workforce at any one time (for example, in terms of gender and ethnicity as well as the mix of regular and temporary employees, agency workers, self-employed sub-contractors, consultants and so on) means that employment relationships within single organizations will often be far more varied than hitherto. This overall diversity in the employment experience is further heightened by the growth of new sectors and occupations, many in the 'knowledge' sector linked to continued developments in information and communications technology.

The second factor is the growing attention being given to normative issues relating to the employment relationship (for example, Budd, 2004; Pinnington et al., 2007). With increasing frequency, writers are posing the questions: what should employment relationships look like in the twenty-first century, and in what ways are current normative standards and assumptions no longer adequate to ensure that all parties conduct themselves appropriately? Here we can witness, among other things, the increased role that ethical discussions are playing within business and business education, and the links to issues such as 'corporate responsibility', 'dignity at work', 'justice' and 'fairness'. So when writers – including a number of those contributing to the present volume – are contemplating such questions as 'what constitutes ethical behaviour at work', what comprises a 'decent' job and 'what encompasses fairness, equality and justice at work', it is important not only to consider the nature of this normative discussion, but also to locate it within the changing nature of employment relationships more broadly.

The structure of the book

Many of the themes and issues noted above are reflected in the chapters that follow. The eighteen chapters are grouped into four sections. Given the approach taken by a number of the contributors, the structure is of necessity a relatively broad one: several chapters could happily sit in more than one section. Nevertheless, the different sections give an indication of the various approaches that the contributors have taken in their task of reassessing important aspects of the employment relationship. In the first part, six chapters consider different perspectives that can be used to study the employment relationship. In the investigation of work and employment over the past decade, a focus on HRM has been prominent and in Chapter 2, Rick Delbridge offers a critique of the main paths that much of this HRM research has taken. The author asserts that much of that research has adopted too readily a management-derived agenda towards the workforce, leading in turn to an overly conservative approach to research agenda setting. In his critique, the author draws both on Michael Burawoy's discussion of the public role of academics and on the research avenues being explored by those associated with Critical Management Studies. Delbridge argues the case for a more critical and theorized approach to HRM research, a greater independence from practitioner interests and less willingness to accept managerial orthodoxies regarding management–worker relations.

A key aim of management's approach to the employment relationship is to use forms of control which simultaneously secure a disciplined workforce whilst at the same time yielding committed and productive workers. This need for management to secure active workforce cooperation, rather than mere compliance makes control a critical aspect of management but at the same time, a problematic one to achieve. In Chapter 3, Mike Reed evaluates the extent to which new control regimes are replacing former structures. He portrays vertical, bureaucratized control mechanisms progressively giving way to more diverse or hybrid control systems. These combine a wide variety of factors – from target-setting and performance management, to teamworking structures, customer service priorities and professional work ethics – to generate a web of control elements. As the author elaborates, many aspects of these 'micromechanics of control' are based on inculcating employees with a particular subjective understanding of their work roles and responsibilities. In opening up this discussion of the changing nature of managerial control in the workplace, the author sheds valuable light on an aspect of the employment relationship that is not fully defined by the employment contract but requires management to translate the labour potential it has purchased into productive effort.

The legal regulation of the employment relationship is the area considered in Chapter 4 by Edmund Heery. He examines developments in the law which he argues amount to a 'progressive juridification' of the employment relationship since the 1960s. The particular focus of the chapter is how scholars have debated four issues of concern to the development of this legal role: its desirability, potential to shape the nature of employment relations, the role of different actors *vis-à-vis* the effective implementation of the law in the workplace and the law's relationship with other means of regulating the employment relationship, such as through collective bargaining. The chapter delineates the different sides of the debate in each of these aspects. In so doing the author makes important points about the relative strengths and weaknesses (or successes and failures) of the law in regulating the employment relationship, and the extent to which legal rights can take the place of institutions in decline, most notably trade unions. The growing significance of legal regulation is clearly demonstrated and this represents an important change to the employment relationship and the terms on which labour is hired and managed.

In Chapter 5, Sukanya Sengupta and Keith Whitfield return to the recent literature on HRM and offer a critique of studies that explore links between HRM practices and organizational performance. Their chapter not only highlights the continuing methodological problems in establishing causal relationships between the two, but also points to the overly narrow way in which performance is perceived. They argue the case for a substantial broadening of the performance measure to incorporate outcomes that reflect different stakeholder interests – not only shareholders and senior management, but also employees, customers, suppliers and the broader community. The last of these, for example, would include measures relating to the organization's social and environmental responsibilities. In this way, the authors argue, a multidimensional measure of performance will yield a more accurate view of how effectively people are managed within an organization.

Issues of corporate responsibility also form part of Mike Marinetto's discussion in Chapter 6, which considers the employment relationship from the viewpoint of ethical theory. As the author notes, despite the early development of industrial relations scholarship being closely associated with the promotion of a just and ethical treatment of employees, current research approaches concerned directly with the ethics of the employment relationship are rare. Further, when discussion of ethics is included, the range of ethical perspectives drawn upon is generally narrow; for example, there is a persistent emphasis on consequentialist arguments, seen in the repeated deployment of the 'business case' to support progressive management practice. In his discussion, Marinetto explores the potential contribution of a variety of philosophical schools and, notably draws on the existentialist philosophy of Sartre and Heidegger. His purpose is to consider alternative ways of evaluating specific policies and practices in the management of labour. One outcome of this broadening of scope is seen to be a more explicit consideration of ethical issues underpinning specific aspects of the employment relationship.

In the final chapter in Part 1, Robyn Thomas and Annette Davies explore the relevance of identity research for analysing the employment relationship. One of their starting points is the way in which more turbulent economic conditions potentially undermine traditional identity 'anchors' – the established structures of working lives in terms of places and forms of work and work communities. To illustrate the value of an identity perspective, Thomas and Davies draw on a study of the changing experience of middle managers involved in social work in the UK. Their enquiry identifies the increasing pressures faced by social workers to align their professional identities more closely with bureaucratic and managerial expectations in regard to the regulation, accountability and measurement of their work. The case highlights the scope that these employees found to resist attempts to control their work identity. More broadly, the chapter highlights further ways in which the employment relationship is a contested space, with competing discourses vying to define the roles and responsibilities of the parties involved.

Part 2 focuses on the ways in which different kinds of development are re-shaping the contexts within which employment relationships are created and maintained. In Chapter 8, Marco Hauptmeier analyses how developments in markets are impacting upon employment relations (ER). He argues that in comparison with other governance mechanisms (for example, the law and collective bargaining) the relative weight of markets in shaping ER has increased. Changes in market conditions (the liberalization of markets and increased competition, for example) are examined in terms of the changes they have triggered in the context and content of employment relations. Within firms, market-oriented ER practices such as temporal flexibility and performance-related pay are seen, in part, as the result of companies mimicking successful features of competitors that link employment practices with product market conditions. Any convergent ER tendencies within this pattern, however, are seen to be mediated by continued variation within different market segments.

In Chapter 9, Jean Jenkins and Peter Turnbull also consider the impact of changing market conditions, particularly the implications of increasing globalization for labour. Their focus is the extent to which (and conditions under which) workers can exert influence over their terms and conditions of employment, rather than be subject to a 'race to the bottom', as employers pursue lower labour cost options in different parts of the world. What their discussion illustrates is the differentiated position of labour in the face of globalization, with workers in some sectors exposed to the full forces of globalization, while others are engaged in sectors where capital is more geographically restricted and where labour thus has more scope to exercise influence. The authors draw on studies in the clothing and port transport sectors to illustrate their argument. In the former, highly mobile capital, the dominance of lead firms and the potential to draw on a largely feminized and weakly protected labour force represent especially adverse conditions for labour to develop an effective response to protect its interests. In the port transport case, in contrast, the need for capital to be located close to markets is shown to be a key factor in the ability of workers successfully to block the introduction by employers of alternative (non-union) labour.

In Chapter 10, David Nash examines links between governance structures, sources of finance and employment outcomes. From a starting point of the

Varieties of Capitalism typology, the author explores the ways that firms operate under different institutional arrangements. Sources of capital, and in particular whether those sources exert a short- or long-term influence on management behaviour, are seen to exercise various influences on labour management, ranging from forms of employment contract and training and development opportunities, to employee representation and collective bargaining structures. However, Nash cautions against seeking to 'read off' labour management practices from national institutional arrangements; within 'varieties of capitalism', firms retain a freedom to manoeuvre in deciding precisely how they will manage the workforce. Nevertheless, the argument underlines the value of understanding particular management behaviours within a broader context of financial and regulatory structures.

In the final chapter in Part 2, Hugh Willmott demonstrates the value of broadening the view of how labour markets and employment relationships are regulated. For both providers and purchasers of labour, certificates and qualifications act as indicators of competence. With the proliferation of educational establishments providing qualifications, an important differentiator in sectors such as higher education, and more specifically business schools, is whether particular courses of the institution have been accredited by one of the main accreditation bodies. Both business schools and those studying at them have an interest in securing accreditation as a badge of quality. An effect of this is to place those private accrediting bodies in positions of considerable power in the business education market. The author explores this growing influence and the suitability of placing greater regulatory powers into the hands of private organizations.

The contributions to Part 3 address substantive developments in the employment relationship. In Chapter 12, Peter Turnbull and Victoria Wass examine the acceleration of earnings inequality in the UK over the past 30 years, which has been marked by those at the top (the 'super-rich') doing especially well while those at the bottom of the income distribution have 'fallen away'. The dominant economic explanation, which focuses on the demand for skilled labour, can explain the former but not the latter; nor can it fully explain the widening of income inequality within particular occupational groups. In evaluating alternative explanations, the authors explore the impact of social institutions. This broader perspective highlights the role of trade unions and collective bargaining, and the apparent willingness of UK citizens to accept employment relationships characterized by ever greater income inequality.

In Chapter 13, Paul Blyton focuses on another major concern: changes in working time arrangements and associated developments in work–life balance provision. The author traces the changing nature of regulation of working time, and the increase in the unilateral regulation by management of many aspects of work time. One result has been a decline in standardized work time patterns in regard to both the duration and timing of work. Blyton examines this in terms of the differentiated experience of working time and access to work–life balance provisions, with those in more senior organizational positions enjoying considerable advantages in these areas compared to their lower-level counterparts. The chapter underlines the extent to which statutory regulation relating to work time and work–life balance has so far worked to the benefit of some (already advantaged) groups much more than others. The chapter reinforces the case for rehabilitating social class as a key determinant of the differentiated experience of work, a feature that it shares with other recent contributions to the analysis of the employment relationship (e.g. McGovern et al., 2007).

In Chapter 14, Deborah Foster with Laura Williams examine the ways in which equality law, policy and practice have evolved in Britain. The chapter underlines the significance of recent developments compared to past approaches, in particular the widening scope of equality law, to encompass a multiplicity of equality strands (gender, ethnicity, age, disability, sexual orientation and religion and belief) and the recognition that people potentially demonstrate multiple equality concerns that straddle two or more of these potential bases for unequal treatment. The authors give a historical account of anti-discrimination employment law, highlighting the key role of social movements and campaigns in that development. In the subsequent exploration of legal developments, the role of EU equalities policy is examined, alongside its significance in extending the grounds on which unfair discrimination in employment can be claimed. In their review of developments at workplace level, the contribution of statutory rights, collective agreements and individual litigation are explored, with the authors emphasizing the continuing contribution of trade unions to the further development of equal opportunities policies and practices within the workplace.

In the final chapter in Part 3, Edmund Heery examines aspects of employee representation within work organizations. His twin starting points are, on the one hand, a belief in the fundamental importance of workers' interests being represented at work, and on the other hand, the experience of three decades of union decline and an associated rise in other, non-union forms of employee representation. The chapter offers an overview of how scholars in the field have considered these trends, in particular: how unions should seek to reverse their decline; and whether the rise of alternative forms of representation pose a threat to, or are a potential opportunity for, trade union revitalization. Following a review and critique of the different stands of argument, the author presents an 'interest framework', a set of normative principles that can be used to assess institutions of worker representation. This framework underscores the continuing importance of trade unions as representatives of worker interests, but also the ways in which this role can be supplemented through the activities of other representation channels, such as statutory systems of worker participation, employer-sponsored programmes of employee involvement and civil society organizations that campaign on particular issues, or on behalf of particular groups, within the workforce (such as carers, people with disabilities or migrants).

The final part of the book deals with issues relating to specific employment groups and work settings. In Chapter 16, Emmanuel Ogbonna considers research on front-line service workers. His starting point is that service interactions between customers and employees have been a research focus both among marketing and employment studies academics. However, as the author details, the two sets of studies have rarely acknowledged one another or the potential for collaboration and cross-fertilization. While marketing researchers have been firmly focused on customer satisfaction aspects of the service encounter, employment studies specialists have focused primarily on the employment experience of service workers, and in particular the ways that management seek to regulate and control the employees' behaviour, and the scope that those workers have to resist these managerial efforts and thereby exert some control over their work process. In the final part of the chapter the author explores potential areas for more collaborative research on service encounters, for example through greater recognition of the significance of the customer in influencing both the work experience of the service employees and the way that they deliver the service involved.

In Chapter 17, Tim Edwards provides a critical review of the debate surrounding the growth of 'knowledge work' and the extent to which this is associated with fundamental economic change and a different form of employment relationship. Many previous writers have characterized knowledge workers as significantly different in their approach to work, compared with those in more traditional work roles: the knowledge work group being portrayed as placing a high value upon autonomy, interesting work and an opportunity to develop new skills, in return for which they are willing to provide high levels of commitment and performance. In practice, however, as the author demonstrates, the rhetoric surrounding the growth of knowledge work has created a view of a 'new' economy, new workforce and new worker–management relationship which is overstated and oversimplified. Edwards argues the case for a more careful and nuanced examination of what different forms of knowledge work exist, the different contexts in which these are developing and the degree to which in practice they are associated with a new pattern of worker–management relations, and thus a significantly distinct employment relationship.

In the final chapter, Rachel Ashworth and Tom Entwistle examine aspects of employment in the public services in the light of several initiatives designed to reform public management practice, with the aim of securing improved performance and higher levels of control. The chapter outlines the range of reform initiatives that have been taken and considers the depth of change that the various reforms in practice represent, compared to extant practices of service provision. Their particular focus is on the extent to which this reform agenda has substantially changed the work processes that public service workers undertake. Ashworth and Entwistle are sceptical about claims that there has been a wholesale transformation of the public sector employment relationship, driven by the rise of New Public Management. Echoing some of the findings of the case reported by Thomas and Davies in Chapter 6, they show the extent to which employees are able to deflect, modify and adjust the pressure for change in their work activities. A result has been that public employment has retained many of its traditional characteristics.

Together, therefore, the chapters provide a wide-ranging examination of the issues impacting on the contemporary employment relationship. They identify too a series of questions and avenues of enquiry regarding the future development of this central aspect of work organizations. These questions and discussions also act to underline the continuing importance of the employment relationship as a focus of attention for all those concerned with the changing nature of work.

References

Anxo, D., Fagan, C., McCann, D., Lee, S. and Messenger, J.C. (2004) 'Introduction: working time in industrialized countries', in J.C. Messenger (ed) Working Time and Workers' Preferences in Industrialized Countries: Finding the Balance, London: Routledge, pp. 1–9.

Appelbaum, E., Bailey, T., Berg, P. and Kalleberg, A.L. (2000) Manufacturing Advantage: Why High Performance Work Systems Pay Off, Ithaca, NY: Cornell University Press.

Bittman, M., Brown, J.E. and Wacjman, J. (2010) 'The mobile phone, perpetual contact and time pressure', Work, Employment and Society, 23 (4): 673–92.

Blyton, P. (2008) 'Working time and work-life balance', in P. Blyton, N. Bacon, J. Fiorito and E. Heery (eds) The Sage Handbook of Industrial Relations, London: Sage, pp. 513–28.

Blyton, P. and Turnbull, P. (eds) (1992) Reassessing Human Resource Management, London: Sage.

Blyton, P. and Turnbull, P. (2004) The Dynamics of Employee Relations, 3rd edition, Houndmills: Palgrave Macmillan.

Brown, W. and Nash, D. (2008) 'What has been happening to collective bargaining under New Labour? Interpreting WERS 2004', Industrial Relations Journal, 39 (2): 91–103.

Brown, W., Deakin, S., Hudson, M., Pratten, C. and Ryan, P. (1998) *The Individualisation of Employment Contracts in Britain*, London: DTI.

Brown, W., Deakin, S., Nash, D. and Oxenbridge, S. (2000) 'The employment contract: from collective procedures to individual rights', *British Journal of Industrial Relations*, 38 (4): 611–30.

Budd, J. (2004) *Employment with a Human Face: Balancing Efficiency, Equity and Voice*, Ithaca and London: ILR Press.

Coser, L.A. (1967) 'Greedy organisations', *European Journal of Sociology*, 8: 196–215.

Cappelli, P. (1999) 'Career jobs are dead', *California Management Review*, 42: 146–66.

Coyle-Shapiro, J. A-M., and Conway, N. (2004) 'The employment relationship through the lens of social exchange', in J. A-M. Shapiro, L.M. Shore, M.S. Taylor and L.E. Tetrick (eds) *The Employment Relationship: Examining Psychological and Contextual Perspectives*, Oxford: Oxford University Press, pp. 5–28.

Deakin, S. and Njoya, W. (2008) 'The legal framework of employment relations', in P. Blyton, N. Bacon, J. Fiorito and E. Heery (eds) *The Sage Handbook of Industrial Relations*, London: Sage, pp. 284–304.

Doogan, K. (2001) 'Insecurity and long-term employment', *Work, Employment and Society*, 15 (3): 419–41.

Doogan, K. (2009) *New Capitalism?: The Transformation of Work*, Cambridge: Polity.

Frost, A.C. (2008) 'The high performance work systems literature in industrial relations', in P. Blyton, N. Bacon, J. Fiorito and E. Heery (eds) *The Sage Handbook of Industrial Relations*, London: Sage, pp. 420–33.

Green, F. (2006) *Demanding Work: The Paradox of Job Quality in the Affluent Economy*, Princeton and Oxford: Princeton University Press.

Howell, C. (2004) 'Is there a third way for industrial relations?', *British Journal of Industrial Relations*, 42 (1): 1–22.

Jacoby, S. (1999) 'Are career jobs heading for extinction?', *California Management Review*, 42: 123–45.

Kahn-Freund, O. (1954) 'Legal framework', in A. Flanders and H.A. Clegg (eds) *The System of Industrial Relations in Great Britain: Its History, Law, and Institutions*, Oxford: Basil Blackwell, pp. 42–127.

Kersley, B., Alpin, C., Forth, J., Bryson, A., Bewley, H., Dix, G. and Oxenbridge, S. (2006) *Inside the Workplace: Findings from the 2004 Workplace Employment Relations Survey*, Abingdon: Routledge.

Kolins Givan, R. (2007) 'Side by side we battle onwards? Representing workers in contemporary America', *British Journal of Industrial Relations*, 45 (4): 829–55.

McGovern, P., Hill, S., Mills, C. and White, M. (2007) *Market, Class and Employment*, Oxford: Oxford University Press.

Marchington, M., Grimshaw, D., Rubery, J. and Willmott, H. (2005) *Fragmenting Work: Blurring Organisational Boundaries and Disordering Hierarchies*, Oxford: Oxford University Press.

Milner, S. (1995) 'The coverage of collective pay-setting institutions in Britain, 1895–1990', *British Journal of Industrial Relations*, 33 (1): 69–91.

Morrison, E.W. and Robinson, S.L. (2004) 'The employment relationship from two sides: incongruence in employees' and employers' perceptions of obligations', in J. A-M. Shapiro, L.M. Shore, M.S. Taylor and L.E. Tetrick (eds) *The Employment Relationship: Examining Psychological and Contextual Perspectives*, Oxford: Oxford University Press, pp. 161–80.

Pinnington, A., Macklin, R. and Campbell, T. (eds) (2007) *Human Resource Management: Ethics and Employment*, Oxford: Oxford University Press.

Rousseau, D. (1995) *Psychological Contracts in Organizations*, Thousand Oaks, CA: Sage.

Sennett, R. (1998) *The Corrosion of Character*, New York: Norton.

Sennett, R. (2006) *The Culture of New Capitalism*, New Haven: Yale University Press.

Sisson, K. (2008) *Putting the Record Straight: Industrial Relations and the Employment Relationship*, Warwick Papers in Industrial Relations, No. 88, University of Warwick: IRRU.

Van Dyne, L. and Ellis, J.B. (2004) 'Job creep: a resistance theory perspective on organizational citizenship behaviour as overfulfillment of obligations', in J. A-M. Shapiro, L.M. Shore, M.S. Taylor and L.E. Tetrick (eds) *The Employment Relationship: Examining Psychological and Contextual Perspectives*, Oxford: Oxford University Press, pp. 181–205.

part 1

Perspectives on the employment relationship

2

The critical future of HRM

Rick Delbridge

In this provocation I advance a view on how HRM researchers should address certain weaknesses in the field through engagement more directly and productively with proximate social science disciplines and, in particular, critical management studies. This is necessary in my view to respond to at least two concerns with the current nature of much HRM research: its conservatism and its irrelevance. I will argue that a more critical and social scientific approach to the study of the managerial actions and management practices of HRM that places the employment relationship at its heart is required in order to shift mainstream HRM research from its currently narrow, managerialist and performance-obsessed state and that in making these steps a more vibrant, diverse and impactful stream of HRM research can be delivered.

Currently, and notwithstanding the efforts of leading critical HRM scholars such as Legge (1978, 1995) and Keenoy (1990, 1999), HRM research is generally conservative in its objectives, its definitions of appropriate subjects and in the knowledge that is produced. This was demonstrated empirically by a major review of HRM papers in leading academic journals which found that only a tiny minority challenged the dominant managerialist consensus. The authors concluded that there was an 'explicit strategy by journals to publish in a way that privileges theoretical perspectives that support the dominant discourse in HRM (i.e. prescriptive, positivist, managerial, functionalist and strategic)' (Keegan and Boselie, 2006: 1506), that 'mainstream management journals have largely ignored critical perspectives on HRM' (Keegan and Boselie, 2006: 1467) and that as a consequence those critical HRM studies that do exist have had a lack of impact on mainstream HRM research. Recent observations by Boselie et al. (2009: 464) reinforce that point, 'The HRM and performance stream of research and the critical HRM stream represent two completely different worlds that, generally, have little interaction'. In the absence of sustained dialogue with critical HRM researchers, the mainstream has become increasingly consensual, narrow and managerialist; and as a consequence, I argue, enfeebled.

The limitations of much HRM research have fundamental roots. In following Weber, I understand the primary purpose of social science research to be the explanation of social phenomena. I would contend that too much HRM research, both qualitative and quantitative in nature, contents itself with description. As Hesketh and Fleetwood (2006) have argued in a forthright critique of positivist research into the HR-performance link, the presenting of statistical associations does not constitute the identification of causal relationships and without clear and careful theorization of those statistical characteristics, presentation of these data represents description at best. And this is also true of under-analysed and poorly theorized accounts produced on the basis of interviews or other qualitative research methods. In producing what Geertz (1973) accurately and positively labelled 'thick description', qualitative researchers must offer more than journalistic accounts. They must meet the standards of carefulness and thoroughness in data collection, analysis and theorization expected of social science to produce an understanding of the causal relationships that explain those data (while recognizing how corrigible and provisional these explanations may prove to be).

The weaknesses of much current mainstream HRM research have rendered it largely irrelevant both to researchers in proximate disciplines that have overlapping interests in aspects of work, organization and management in contemporary capitalism and to the actors that populate these fields of activity, even the managers that are generally the focus of HRM research. Research that presents descriptive accounts or untheorized statistical relationships is no more useful to practitioners engaged in 'practising HRM' (or those constituting the wider field experiencing this) than it is to academics or policy makers seeking insights and explanations of employment relationships. Indeed, despite widespread claims to relevance and impact by HRM researchers, managers have generally remained much less convinced. An HR consultant has observed, 'Practitioners have pressed on regardless, in the justified belief that what the academics were writing about had little relevance to their day to day lives as they wrestle with the realities of organisational life ... HRM cannot be blamed or given credit for changes that were taking place anyway. For example, it is often alleged to have inspired a move from a pluralism to unitarism in industrial relations. But newspaper production was moved from Fleet Street to Wapping by Murdoch, not because he had read a book about HRM but as a means of breaking the print unions' control' (Armstrong, 2000: 577–8). In developing research that both documents and influences the practice of HRM, scholars will need to record and interpret these 'organizational realities' and the context of employment relationships within which they are embedded as central features.

To begin, this chapter builds on Michael Burawoy's recent work in sociology to explicate and then develop an articulation of critical HRM. From this, a brief review of the key characteristics of the diverse forms of critical management studies is presented and their implications for the development of a critical HRM are considered. I am far from alone in having drawn some of these conclusions about the current state of HRM research and in the third main section of the chapter I briefly consider some important recent contributions from researchers both more and less mainstream in approach before concluding with some final remarks on the future prospects of HRM.

Burawoy's division of sociological labour

It is some years now since Burawoy (2004) first advanced his argument for public sociology as a way of addressing the perceived divide between 'ivory tower academics' and their publics. This notion has found considerable traction within sociology and beyond and Burawoy has developed his arguments in a number of ways, including to contend that a shift in focus from the labour process to labour movement in the study of employment relations has advanced sociologists' engagement with labour organizations (Burawoy, 2008). The challenge of engaging audiences beyond academia is central in addressing the charge of irrelevance that I have made against HRM (and which could, and has, been levelled at many other areas of the academy). Before turning to that specifically, however, I want to review the typology from which Burawoy develops his public sociology. Burawoy distinguishes public sociology from three other types – professional, policy and critical sociologies – and this is useful for HRM is in need of a critical orientation before it can expect to achieve, to coin the cliché, rigour and relevance.

Burawoy builds his typology on the answers to two fundamental questions through which researchers 'can problematize our place in society': First, for whom is knowledge produced? And secondly, to what ends will that knowledge be used? He conceives the first question as, 'If we are going to talk to others, which others and how shall we do it?' (Burawoy, 2004: 1606) and differentiates between academic and extra-academic audiences. In addressing the second question, Burawoy draws on Weber to distinguish between technical rationality and value rationality, either or both of which might underpin the production of knowledge. Burawoy (2004: 1606) explains:

> Do we take the values and goals of our research for granted, handed down to us by some external (funding or policy) agency? Should we only concentrate on providing solutions to predefined problems, focusing on the means to achieve predetermined ends, on what Weber called technical rationality and what I shall call *instrumental knowledge*? In other words, should we repress the question of ends and pretend that knowledge and laws spring spontaneously from the data, if only we can develop the right methods? Or should we be concerned explicitly with the goals for which our research may be mobilized, and with the values that underpin and guide our research? Like Weber, I believe that without value commitments there can be no sociology, no basis for the questions that guide our research programs. Without values social science is blind. We should try to be clear about those values by engaging in what Weber called value discussion, leading to what I will refer to as *reflexive knowledge*.

This identification of the values of research, of the politics of the production of knowledge as it were, is a fundamental starting point in the articulation of a critical HRM. Burawoy uses these distinctions between types of knowledge and different audiences to elaborate a 2 × 2 table. As he notes, these are not watertight distinctions but ideal types that are internally complex. There are 'fractals' within each type that may display the character of other types but they are subordinate to the underlying *raison d'etre* within that type. He also makes clear that these are types of sociology, not sociologist, and individuals can simultaneously inhabit more than one of the cells (Table 2.1).

Table 2.1 Burawoy's sociologies

	Academic audience	Extra-academic audience
Instrumental knowledge	Professional sociology	Policy sociology
– Knowledge	Theoretical/empirical	Concrete
– Legitimacy	Scientific norms	Effectiveness
– Accountability	Peers	Clients/patrons
– Pathology	Self-referentiality	Servility
– Politics	Professional self-interest	Policy intervention
Reflexive knowledge	Critical sociology	Public sociology
– Knowledge	Foundational	Communicative
– Legitimacy	Moral vision	Relevance
– Accountability	Critical intellectuals	Designated publics
– Pathology	Dogmatism	Faddishness
– Politics	Internal debate	Public dialogue

Source: From Burawoy, 2004: 1607.

Professional sociology provides the basis for the other sociologies, without it critical sociology has nothing to critique. This is the domain of mainstream academic enterprise informed by norms of locally, socially constructed 'scientific legitimacy' and peer influence. Public and policy sociology speak to audiences beyond academia. Policy sociology refers to where there is a specific problem defined by a client – the relation is instrumental since the research terrain is not defined by the sociologist. Public sociology is the domain of 'public intellectualism' and engages audiences beyond the academy in dialogue on matters of political and moral concern. As Burawoy notes, public sociology must be relevant without falling into the trap of faddishness and subservience to publics. Critical sociology provides the critique that is necessary to counterbalance the pathologies of the other sociologies; it examines the implicit and explicit, normative and descriptive foundations of the research programmes of professional sociology, the values under which research in policy sociology is conducted and the moral commitments of public sociological research. It is 'the conscience of professional sociology' (Burawoy, 2004: 1609). The sociologies are reciprocally interdependent, 'the flourishing of each depends on the flourishing of all'.

Burawoy's sociologies give a framework through which the twin weaknesses of HRM – conservatism and irrelevance – can be assessed and suggestions developed for how they might be addressed. His explicit reference to the audience for which knowledge is produced provides a basis for evaluating the engagement of HRM researchers with various different practice and policy communities that work in, advise on or in some way are a part of the employment relationships and management practices within the broad sphere of HRM. The issue of the ends to which the research is put raises the further question of what has become termed 'impact', particularly in higher education policy circles and in debates about the 'value' of research. While distinct from the focus of Burawoy's own primary concerns, his expectation that knowledge will be used anticipates that it will have impact in some form and this speaks to my charge of the irrelevance of much HRM research. Beyond the twin concerns of for whom knowledge is produced and to what purposes it may be used, we can extend our consideration to build further reflection on related matters regarding the assumptions that underpin research, the types of research conducted, the topics under investigation and the forms of knowledge that are produced. In so doing we can put these further aspects of much current HRM research under the spotlight.

For the purposes of this essay, let me consider HRM researchers in the conduct of academic enquiry as exemplifying the 'professional' category within Burawoy's division of labour. The established dominant paradigm of HRM research reflects assumptions of unitarism, individualization, performativity and decontextualization (Keegan and Boselie, 2006). That is, mainstream HRM assumes superordinate, managerially determined corporate goals, individual rather than collective employment relations, the autonomy of managers in individual workplaces and organizations without reflecting the relevant contests and contexts of these settings and is obsessed with seeking to demonstrate the performance effects of HR practices. Within the space constraints of this chapter, and in keeping with the spirit of provocation, the reader will have to allow for this sweeping characterization. Suffice to say some or all of these observations have been made by numerous commentators on HRM research from both within and beyond the field (Boxall et al., 2007; Janssens and Steyaert, 2009; Keegan and Boselie, 2006; Keenoy, 2009; Paauwe, 2009). These mainstream assumptions are the focus for a critical HRM.

Building on critical management studies

Critical HRM has the opportunity to draw on the intellectual resources of a number of proximate social science fields including critical management studies, the sociology of work and organizations and industrial relations. These are themselves somewhat intertwined and overlapping subsets of the social sciences. In this chapter I will concentrate primarily on the connections and productive engagement that may be encouraged through reflection upon the central characteristics of the diverse range of work conducted under the label 'critical management studies' (CMS). Given HRM is itself a subset of management research, CMS provides the most direct example of how the assumptions of HRM may be challenged.

The CMS is a broad church but it is possible to identify some common themes and underlying concerns across its range of research and theorizing. In important ways, CMS has an espoused agenda that directly confronts the weaknesses of conservatism and irrelevance of which I have accused the bulk of HRM research. CMS has an explicit expectation to make a difference, that is, an agenda for change; research is typically undertaken with the espoused intention to radically transform management practices and organizational systems. It must be accepted that the evidence on the impact of CMS is much less compelling than the aspirations of its most spirited advocates. Nonetheless, research is conducted in ways that speak to alternatives to the prevalent assumptions of mainstream HRM, for example, in situating social phenomena in their political, social and economic contexts. Management practices and organizational structures are analysed and critiqued with a recognition of their embeddedness in wider historical contexts and this includes recognition of their positioning as part of, and within, broader patterns of relations of domination. Thus a politicized agenda of change is a central motif of CMS which stands it in sharp distinction with much HRM research. As Burawoy (2004: 1612) comments, 'One function of critical sociology is to show that the world does not have to be the way it is'.

A central feature of a critical approach to understanding management (and critical social science more generally) is conceptualizing power and its relationships to knowledge and action. CMS strongly argues the position that the apparent neutrality of knowledge works to obscure processes of enduring domination and power asymmetries. Critical researchers have shown how processes of rationalization and objectification in formal organizing make techniques of control possible (Hasselbladh and Kallinikos, 2000). In addressing issues of power, knowledge and organizational control, CMS builds upon and extends what Greenwood and Hinings (2002: 411) identified as a sociological approach to organization theory which is concerned with 'who controls and the consequences of that control'. This they contrasted with 'management theory' with its concern with efficiency and 'how to understand and thus design efficient and effective organizations'. This mirrors concerns with HRM researchers' fixation with issues of performance and their predilection for normative arguments over explanations founded on a recognition of the wider social characteristics and contexts of contemporary organization. However, rather than juxtaposing power and efficiency, CMS researchers see these as inextricably linked aspects of capitalism (Clegg et al., 2006). A critical HRM will provide analysis and explanation that connects questions of power with issues of 'efficiency' that extend beyond managerial definitions.

Various attempts have been made to distil the essence of CMS, especially given the range of ontological and epistemological approaches that are loosely grouped under the label. Drawing on the work of Fournier and Grey (2000) and Adler et al. (2007), it is possible to identify a number of key themes that are common to work in the broad school of CMS. The themes are: the questioning of the taken-for-granted; moving beyond instrumentalism and assumptions of performativity; the concern for reflexivity and meanings in research; and the challenging of structures of domination. I will briefly review each of these and their implications for a critical HRM.

Questioning the taken-for-granted

CMS challenges the assumptions and conventions of managerialist thinking. In this regard it both meets the defining criterion of Burawoy's critical domain and also confronts the first of the dominant assumptions of mainstream HRM. CMS questions the purpose and effects of management and problematizes assumptions of managers as experts holding legitimate positions of authority. In doing this, CMS highlights the social construction and institutionalization of these conventions and thus opens them up to critique. By challenging unitarist assumptions of shared corporate goals and functionalist concerns with efficiency, the critical management theorist focuses on the power relations of contemporary capitalist organizations, making transparent the inequalities of such roles, and questioning the rationales and consequences of capitalist conventions. This recognition of the plurality of interests and potential for conflict within employment relations places control at the centre of understanding and explaining management. Critical HRM (CHRM) is necessarily therefore concerned with the role that HR practices play in achieving and sustaining managerial control, and concomitantly, how those practices are experienced by employees.

In questioning conventions, the best CMS research engages with the context and history of employment relations. Much early critical work concentrated on the profound differences of discretion, opportunity and material rewards that resulted from the increasing industrialization of economies (for example, Marglin, 1974). In particular, critical scholars such as Fox (1974) rejected conventional views that technologies and organization develop in ways that are necessary or appropriate to the demands of the 'neutral' economic conditions of the time. Fournier and Grey (2000: 18) describe this as the 'denaturalization' project of CMS. By this they refer to the 'unmasking' of mainstream management theory which has constructed particular versions of appropriateness in terms of management practices and organizational systems while obscuring these in a language of science, rationality and 'naturalness'. CMS, and therefore CHRM, work to deconstruct these projections of particular organizational realities and inevitabilities.

CMS draws attention to the power and influence of discourses that construct and sustain 'techniques of control' (Hasselbladh and Kallinikos, 2000). In so doing CMS challenges the apparent self-evidence of a specific, orthodox way of representing the world (e.g. organizations have particular structures and specific goals); the argument that there is no alternative (TINA) works as a powerful conservative influence in favour of the status quo (see Adler et al., 2007). The denaturalization project of CMS has thus centred on the *apparently* neutral language of both mainstream organization theory and management practice. A central objective of CMS is to challenge these institutionalized forms of understanding and hold these to critical account. This is one of the opportunities for CHRM. For example, over the past two decades HRM research has played a significant role in promoting arguments in favour of *inter alia* teamworking, flexibility and 'high commitment' HR practices. Research seeking to evaluate and explain the implications of these features in workplace relations must both unpack and interrogate the objectives of managers and provide an understanding of the contextual circumstances of the introduction and operation of these practices rather than promote these as universal 'best practices' (for an early example, see Delbridge and Turnbull, 1992).

For critical social scientists it is not just language that cannot be neutral. Resonant with Burawoy's (2004) advocacy of 'value discussion' and discussions of knowledge for whom and knowledge for what, critical theorists hold that knowledge and its creation is not neutral. Moreover, as Jermier (1998: 238) contends, the processes of denaturalization that are central to critical research include uncovering the partiality of researchers and this adds a further inescapable question for social scientists: 'Whose side are you on?' This is particularly prescient in current policy contexts where academic researchers are expected to show the value of their research to society on the basis of its impact, particularly when this is anticipated to be measured in economic terms. As Burawoy's framework helps make explicit, researchers must ensure they and/or their agendas are not captured by sponsors.

In challenging assumptions (including the inevitability of globalization and its consequences and the dominance of 'market forces') and problematizing conventions (including those of neutrality and objectivity in research), CMS focuses research on management and organization on questions of control, power, knowledge and legitimacy. In so doing it seeks to unpack the unitarism of mainstream theories and introduce a fundamental recognition of the negotiated orders and structured antagonisms of capitalism that define the character of the field of study.

We can extend this argument for CHRM by building here also on the contributions of industrial relations and political science in examining the institutions of capitalist political economy. The mainstream HRM approach has focused on the individual employee and their employment relationship and in so doing accepted the economistic approaches and dominant market discourses of neo-liberalism found to varying degrees in advanced Western economies. Indeed, Keenoy (2009) suggests that the spread of the discourse of HRM has been intimately associated with the political adoption of neo-liberal economic policies. But industrial relations and political science continue to demonstrate the constraining and enabling influences of various national and international institutions in explaining workplace relations and organizational systems. CHRM must place at the heart of its analyses the collective employment relationships still to be found within the corporation and institutional structures beyond if it is to offer compelling explanations of how HR practices are negotiated ('formally' and 'informally'), put into practice and experienced by both those commonly understood as 'managers' and those they manage.

Beyond instrumentalism and performative intent

HRM researchers have been accused of being obsessed with the 'Holy Grail' of seeking to prove a link between HR practices and organizational performance (Keenoy, 2009). This stems at least in part from the managerialism of HRM and is also connected to the distinction Burawoy (2004) draws between instrumental and reflexive knowledge. This obsession should not be confused with demonstrable practical relevance since numerous critics have observed that HR practitioners remain largely sceptical of the value of HRM research despite this dominant orientation and focus on performance (for example, Hesketh and Fleetwood, 2006).

CMS has taken the wider field of management studies to task for similarly instrumental and performative predilections. Fournier and Grey (2000: 17) describe this emphasis on performance outcomes in general and instrumental notions of efficiency in particular in the following terms:

> A performative intent ... means the intent to develop and celebrate knowledge which contributes to the production of maximum output for minimum input; it involves inscribing knowledge within means-ends calculation. Non-critical management study is governed by the principle of performativity which serves to subordinate knowledge and truth to the production of efficiency. In non-critical management study, performativity is taken as an imperative towards which all knowledge and practice must be geared ....

A critical approach to HRM challenges the exclusive emphasis given to material, and in particular, financial measurements of inputs and outputs and encourages a wider range of issues and outcomes to be considered. Past studies in mainstream HRM have included concerns with standard measures of individual employees' well-being, job satisfaction and so on but CHRM could also connect the study of HRM more directly with wider concerns regarding, for example, skills development and workplace learning in connection with initiatives taken by organized labour or the state, or issues of stress and medical care as part of a more holistic analysis of work/extra-work relationships. At the same time, it should be noted that CHRM would not eschew any interest in economic measures and business performance. Clearly these are important aspects of the corporate context of HRM and the financialization of contemporary capitalism has had direct impact at the workplace (Thompson, 2003).

In times of global economic recession, these concerns are ever more pressing and the evidence that HRM research can contribute meaningfully and positively to tackling these challenges is particularly thin on the ground.

Reflexivity, meaning and difference

CMS is a broad, some might say disparate, collection of researchers with assorted interests and objectives; a wide range of ontological assumptions, epistemologies and research methodologies are to be found. The breadth of approaches and the conflicts between them have recently been recognized as a potential strength of CMS with productive advances in theorizing and understanding seen to be the result of both these contests and the constructive engagement of advocates' of each in the interstices of their positions (see Fournier and Grey, 2000; Delbridge and Ezzamel, 2005). Similarly, Burawoy (2004: 1612) counteracts the lamentations of those who bemoan the fragmentation of sociology to anticipate the prospect of 'a unity based on diversity – a unity that incorporates a plurality of perspectives'.

For this to be realized, CHRM will have to be home to an ongoing set of debates that inquire as to the strengths, weaknesses and implications of researchers' assumptions and positions. CMS explicitly advocates the reflexive consideration of both researchers' philosophical assumptions about the nature of the social world they are researching (ontology) and how knowledge of that world may be acquired (epistemology). As has been discussed, such concerns have not resulted in homogeneity in research approach, ontological assumptions, epistemologies or methods across the CMS community, far from it. But they do require a sensitivity and reflexivity to their implications.

While critics have bemoaned the dominance of positivism and quantitative research methods in mainstream HRM, there is no necessary assumption that any particular approaches and methods might be found in critical HRM. What will be required in CHRM is an explicit reflection upon the limitations and implications of any research approach and the recognition that the currently dominant HRM paradigm presents a naturalizing discourse around positivism and 'scientific methods' that must be unpacked and examined. Much CMS is founded on a research approach that seeks to get close to a subject of study and make sense of the social phenomena under investigation on the terms of the research participants. This allows greater access to understanding of the practise of management practices and their unpredictable and emergent properties, to the multiple interests and multi-vocality of workplaces and to an evaluation of the outcomes of the structured antagonisms of capitalism. That said, CHRM will also look to make sense of the history and context of these social settings. In revealing the socio-economic conditions of the corporation and through describing aggregate patterns of developments, survey work will have its place. CHRM researchers will also become familiar with the challenges of interpreting micro-level observational data in their wider contexts and in seeking to explain more macro-levels of activity on the basis of the analysis of micro-data, though this discussion lies beyond our concerns in this chapter.

Challenging structures of domination

The final weakness of mainstream HRM identified above is that of decontextualization. For robust explanation of the local and contingent, it is necessary for analysis to be situated in its meaningful context and history. In critical social science there are long-standing traditions of, for example, the assessment and evaluation of the historical developments of management control in capitalist economies (for example, Edwards, 1979; Marglin, 1974) and critique of the dehumanized, depersonalized and alienating nature of work in many capitalist organizations. Jermier (1998) suggests that two key themes across critical social science are the misuse of power in society, resulting in the mistreatment of some individuals and groups, and the justification for aligning science with the interests of the mistreated. There have been significant differences in how members of the broad church of CMS have understood and responded to these themes. Some CMS scholars have advocated a radical and even revolutionary commitment to change which is expressly 'anti-management', rejecting engagement and discussion with managers and seeking to undermine and destabilize management through critique. From this perspective, notions of 'better management' are rejected, 'The argument is that management is irredeemably corrupt since its activity is inscribed within performative principles which CMS seeks to challenge' (Fournier and Grey, 2000: 24).

Given that the pathology of critical sociology is identified by Burawoy (2004) as dogmatism, it is incumbent upon CHRM to be reflexive in regard to the preferences and priorities to which it subscribes. While I am not suggesting that CMS and CHRM should be coterminous, CHRM researchers are likely to find their objectives align with those CMS researchers who have opted to engage in contingent and localized interaction with managers in order to contribute to the amelioration of the negative effects of the inequalities of the capitalist workplace and the promotion of 'better' management. Better management is generally understood in terms of it and its effects becoming less oppressive or socially divisive (for example, Alvesson and Willmott, 1996; Fournier and Grey, 2000; Watson, 1994) with the wider intention of challenging the structures of domination within capitalism and hence lessening the distortion of its asymmetrical power relations. In this approach, there is a consistent commitment to engagement *with* management practitioners in order to seek change and some form of transformation of systems and structures. There is also recognition of the heterogeneity of 'management' and that managers are themselves managed and thus subject to control and potential exploitation. This approach provides the platform and orientation from which CHRM can aspire to relevance while simultaneously throwing off the conservative cloak of the mainstream.

Ways forward: the opportunities of plurality

CHRM will place analysis and explanation of managerial action, management practices and the nature of employment relations at its centre but do so in ways that acknowledge the multiple interests and multi-vocality of workplaces which are in turn understood to be embedded within the structured antagonisms of capitalist economies. This research agenda will require researchers to engage with a wider variety of organizational and institutional actors than is currently the case in mainstream research. Trade unionists and other employee representatives, policy makers, charities and non-governmental organizations, professional bodies and associations, lobbyists and political organizations all help constitute the world within which HRM is constructed and enacted. In turn, the complex new challenges implied in this approach to HRM research will require a diversity of theoretical lenses and a much broader range of topics will need to be studied.

The plurality in this research agenda will need to be matched by new ways of engaging and debating within academic circles. As I proceed to outline below, there has been recent attention to the processes of dialogue within and across the academy which suggests that careful attention to ensure the constructive nature of such discussions is vital if positions are not to remain fragmented and polarized. Taking the opportunities of plurality will require care, heightened reflexivity and a willingness to engage across perceived boundaries in constructive ways. Put simply, CHRM will imply changes in both who HRM researchers talk with and how those discussions take place.

There are reasons for cautious optimism. The weaknesses of HRM research have not gone without recent comment both from within and beyond the field. Perhaps most significantly, well-established mainstream HRM researchers from within the community have begun to voice concerns. Most notable amongst these is the recent argument put forward by Boxall et al. (2007) for a move to 'analytical HRM' in their opening chapter to the *Oxford Handbook of Human Resource Management*. Boxall et al. (2007: 4) commence by stating,

> We use the notion of 'analytical HRM' to emphasize that the fundamental mission of the academic management discipline of HRM is not to propagate perceptions of 'best practice' in 'excellent companies' but, first of all, to identify and explain what happens in practice. Analytical HRM privileges explanation over prescription. The primary task of analytical HRM is to build theory and gather empirical data in order to account for the way management actually behaves in organizing work and managing people across different jobs, workplaces, companies, industries, and societies.

They do not engage in a detailed critique of the field but they do argue against claims for universal applicability of HR practices and cite Pfeffer as a prime offender in this regard. They also observe that too little attention has been paid to context in much HRM research, although by this they appear to primarily be referring to the goals and politics of the wider organization rather than the socioeconomic and institutional contexts of employment relations more generally. They also comment that too many HRM researchers have sought to justify HR policies and practices in narrowly defined terms around the profit-orientated bottom line, 'This misunderstands the plurality of organizational effectiveness' (Boxall et al., 2007: 5).

Boxall and colleagues (2007: 7) advance three important characteristics of analytical HRM: first, it is concerned with what management does and explaining why; second, it is concerned with how processes of HRM work; and 'third, it is interested in questions of "for whom and how well", with assessing the outcomes of HRM, taking account of both employee and managerial interests, and laying a basis for theories of wider social consequence'. This takes us close to some of the arguments advanced by critical social scientists and CMS scholars. In important ways, therefore, we can see similarities in the position advocated by these mainstream authors and the position put forward in this chapter, though this is not to deny major differences in the values, commitments and approaches that would be expected in the undertaking of these research agendas. There is a further important point of connection with the arguments made here. Along with advancing a view that more 'analytical', theoretical and pluralistic approach to HRM research would lead to 'better research', Boxall and colleagues also recognize that this research will be of greater relevance to its audiences: 'Education founded on an analytical conception of HRM should help practitioners to understand relevant theory and develop analytical skills which can then be applied in their specific situation and that do not leave them flat-footed when they move to a new environment'

(Boxall et al., 2007: 4). Watson (2007: 123) in the same Handbook echoes this in his call for theorizing which is critical and social scientific, breaking free from 'its earlier managerialist anchor and its concern with making organizations more effective or competitive'. As he proceeds to affirm 'in no way whatsoever is this to argue for HRM research and writing which lacks relevance for people with a practical involvement in HRM ... In the final analysis, good theory tells us about "how things work in the world".'

Paauwe (2009) is another leading HRM researcher to recently argue for a wider and 'more balanced approach' to HRM research that pays greater attention to the concerns and well-being of employees (a broadening of the 'stakeholders' of HRM) and takes a more multi-dimensional perspective on performance. Paauwe offers a 'contextually based theory of human resources' and seeks to extend attention to the factors that shape HR policies and practices in specific organizational contexts and wider institutional systems. Thus, in a similar fashion and form to the 'analytical HRM' proposed by Boxall and colleagues, Paauwe has from *within* the HRM field begun to enunciate fundamental concerns with the dominant approaches and frameworks of analysis. Having said this, Paauwe is in some ways more conservative in his summary. He appears to seek to sidestep criticism of the attempts to identify the linkage between performance and HRM when commenting that 'criticizing the efforts currently being made in the area is of course possible and legitimate, but without offering a serious alternative it is of limited value, often simply ending up in a rather sterile mantra-like rejection of the positivist paradigm' (Paauwe, 2009: 134). In their rejoinder to Paauwe, Janssens and Steyaert note that this view is 'unfortunate as it does not grasp the full potential of critiques to further develop a field' (2009: 143), though they themselves acknowledge that oppositional stances often fail to provide for constructive engagement. This highlights the importance of intertwining a new research agenda with novel ways of engaging in academic practice.

The increasing awareness of the limitations of current HRM research from within the mainstream is a promising development and offers the possibility that CHRM may begin to enjoy increased presence in, and greater influence on, the field than in the past. However, considerable attention must be paid to the nature of dialogue and engagement if constructive and productive discussions are to result. As Burawoy (2004: 1609) argues, it is incumbent on professional sociology to recognize the value of critique and to engage with critical sociology, 'A flourishing professional sociology always has to find space for such critical engagement, for open discussion of what we are up to. Indeed, one might argue, it is this reflexivity that makes sociology an intellectual as well as a professional enterprise.' But engaging professional HRM also places responsibilities and expectations on critical HRM, particularly with regard to the form of reflexive engagement that is pursued. Forms of reflexive engagement have recently been the subject of conceptual work within critical management studies (Alvesson et al., 2008) and Janssens and Steyaert (2009) build very productively on that conceptual work to articulate what they term a 'plea for reflexivity in HRM studies'.

Rather than attempting synthesis or proposing a radical alternative – with the attendant danger that the debates are polarized and nothing productive emerges – Janssens and Steyaert (2009) draw on Alvesson et al.'s (2008) summary of forms of reflexivity to advocate a R(econstructive)–reflexivity approach. This stands for reconstructing and reframing by bringing in alternative issues, perspectives, paradigms and political values in order to illuminate the field and in particular draw attention to what has been marginalized or left out. Janssens and Steyaert argue that in only resisting, critical commentaries of HRM run the risk of remaining within the existing frame and reinforcing the positivist HRM research agenda in a reactive way. This results in a failure to re-set that agenda and a concomitant inability to meaningfully contribute to the development of that field. In contrast, they suggest that R-reflexivity 'provides alternative descriptions, interpretations, vocabularies and voices that could be taken into account, aiming to open up new avenues, paths and lines of interpretations that produce "better" research ethically, politically, empirically and theoretically' (Janssens and Steyaert, 2009: 144). This approach thus seeks to connect different perspectives rather than synthesizing or displacing one with another. It thus exhibits what I call here the 'opportunity of plurality' and have elsewhere described as 'the strength of difference' that can be found when incompatible approaches find ways to constructively engage (Delbridge and Ezzamel, 2005).

Along with constructive comments on the nature of dialogue, Janssens and Steyaert (2009) also highlight issues with the substance of Paauwe's position, in particular his advancement of a stakeholder approach. Their concerns include that only powerful stakeholders will be given attention, power issues remain ignored and that 'employees' are understood only as a single homogeneous stakeholder and their diverse interests are not considered. From a CHRM viewpoint, Paauwe does not go far enough in challenging the mainstream approach and its attendant economistic conception of 'performance' and he thus runs the risk of continuing to overlook the effects of HRM practices on society. Janssens and Steyaert conclude that 'if HRM wants to stop reinforcing a top management perspective, it will have to let go of its privileged association with strategic management . . . only by replacing performance by a broader concept of outcome, will HRM consider its societal embeddedness and the long-term impact it has on stakeholders in society' (Janssens and Steyaert, 2009: 148).

Janssens and Steyaert (2009) offer a number of correctives or points of connection to Paauwe's (2009) argument from critical perspectives which overlap and complement the future research agenda for CHRM advanced in this chapter. The first of these is the call for the incorporation of employee perspectives to be on a basis that acknowledges the political nature of the employment relationship; a more pluralist line of interpretation is thus advanced which seeks to accommodate the complexity of the employment relationship and notes that goals and interests may be conflicting as well as shared. Second, Janssens and Steyaert argue that HRM researchers might direct their attention to researching social issues connected to employees' rights in ways that impact on how practitioners undertake the management of these, 'Such analyses of the practice of HRM may further provide ways that allow professionals to develop more skilled approaches to balancing inherent tensions in the employment relationships' (2009: 146). Such a line of reasoning embraces the suggestion that HRM research can be both 'critical' and 'relevant'. Third, they argue that studies of HRM should consider patterns of power and inequality at broader political–economic levels as well as at organizational levels: 'understanding how work is currently organized and managed cannot be done without relating HRM to broader patterns of culture, power and inequality' (Janssens and Steyaert, 2009: 146). Thus contrary to the views of at least some mainstream researchers, Janssens and Steyaert (2009: 146–7) argue that attention to the political nature of employment relationships will produce 'better' research, commenting that:

> Opportunities for new problematizations and theoretical development will occur if HRM devotes more attention to underlying conflicts at work, focuses more explicitly on the implications of new forms of work for employees without assuming a harmony of interests, and considers the broader political–economic forces influencing the way work is managed.

Finally, they highlight that more attention needs to be paid to the way that HRM affects the nature of managerial work and the complexities and tensions this brings about for managers in dealing with the interests of employees. Management practices are now widely understood as being constituted through discourses, micro-practices and rhetorical strategies (Whittington, 2006). Understanding HRM as processes of ongoing enactment and social production recognizes that HRM is 'continuously performed' and allows for the reflexive engagement of actors in their contexts. This potentially continues to connect HRM research with that conducted in Strategic Management but it is now re-conceived in the forms and discourses of 'strategy-as-practice' which has become increasingly prevalent in that domain of research.

Concluding remarks

In this chapter I have advanced an argument for CHRM which both locates employment relations at the heart of the HRM research agenda and advocates a more reflexive and constructive engagement between those interested in researching the actors, practices and consequences of HRM and others with related interests across the social science spectrum, in particular critical management studies. In my view, this will have implications for *both* mainstream and critical researchers in terms of the work that they conduct and the manner in which they engage with various audiences. To realize the positives of plurality, researchers will need to engage in reconstructive reflexivity, that is to participate in all aspects of scholarship in ways that seek new directions or interpretations in order to develop more robust explanation of HRM phenomena and thus 'better research'. This is to develop new theory on the basis of difference rather than to contribute to sterile and conflictual arguments from fixed positions of antagonism. The positive prospect for HRM is that this offers a way forward that can result in research that is both robustly theorized and has meaningful practical implications that are less readily dismissed or ignored.

This is not to suggest that combining critical and public HRM will be straightforward; the evidence from within CMS indicates that scholars often feel engagement comes at the expense of critique (Delbridge and Thomas, 2009). Much work to promote the contexts for, and discourses of, meaningful dialogue remains.

Too much of the debate regarding academic relevance and the 'impact of research' is currently being conducted in ignorance of Burawoy's crucial distinction between policy sociology – where researchers attend to a problem that has been defined by the sponsor – and public sociology which seeks to be relevant without subservience to any particular sponsor or interest group. In advocating that research be rigorous and relevant, it is important not to be seen to provide the context wherein only research projects deemed of 'economic value' and conducted in response to the concerns of the elites of society are considered legitimate. In seeking engagement, CHRM researchers must avoid being captured by their sponsors.

Speculation on the substance of the research themes of CHRM lies outside the limits of this brief chapter but one would anticipate that research will extend beyond the individual and the corporation, deploy numerous different approaches and methods, place aspects of power and control at the heart of analysis and provide explanation that speaks to significant societal concerns. A key aspect of communicating the findings of CHRM must be their incorporation in educational materials of various forms. This is perhaps the area where mainstream research has been influential in promoting the dominant managerialist discourse and CHRM researchers will need to disseminate their findings through educational materials in order to influence the normative development of both students and HR professionals. This has wider implications for the debate surrounding impact as well. Too often, the ways researchers engage with students is overlooked or trivialized in discussions of how theoretically informed research can have impact beyond academic audiences. And, to reiterate, the opportunity of plurality must also be understood as referring to the variety of actors and organizations that constitute the multiplicity of the HRM research agenda. Engagement with charities, nongovernmental organizations, trade unions and other public sector and third sector organizations will contribute to the development of a CHRM that is both robust and relevant and that can make a positive difference to society and the individuals within our organizations who comprise the world of 'human resource management'.

References

Adler, P., Forbes, L. and Willmott, H. (2007) 'Critical Management Studies: Premises, Practices, Problems and Prospects', *Annals of the Academy of Management*, 1: 119–80.

Armstrong, M. (2000) 'The Name has Changed but has the Game Remained the Same?', *Employee Relations*, 22: 576–89.

Alvesson, M. and Willmott, H. (1996) *Making Sense of Management: A Critical Introduction* (London: Sage).

Alvesson, M., Hardy, C. and Harley, B. (2008) 'Reflecting on Reflexivity: Reflexive Textual Practices in Organization and Management Theory', *Journal of Management Studies*, 45 (3): 480–501.

Boselie, P., Brewster, C. and Paauwe, J. (2009) 'In Search of Balance – Managing the Dualities of HRM: An Overview of the Issues', *Personnel Review*, 38(5): 461–71.

Boxall, P., Purcell, J. and P. Wright (2007) 'Human Resource Management: Scope, Analysis, and Significance', in P. Boxall, J. Purcell and P. Wright (eds) *The Oxford Handbook of Human Resource Management* (Oxford: Oxford University Press).

Burawoy, M. (2004) 'Public Sociologies: Contradictions, Dilemmas, and Possibilities', *Social Forces*, 82(4): 1–16.

Burawoy, M. (2008) 'The Public Turn: From Labor Process to Labor Movement', *Work and Occupations*, 35: 371–87.

Clegg, S., Courpasson, D., and Phillips, N. (2006) *Power and Organizations* (London: Sage).

Delbridge, R. and Ezzamel, M. (2005) 'The Strength of Difference: Contemporary Conceptions of Control', *Organization*, 12(5): 603–18.

Delbridge, R and Thomas, R. (2009) 'After the Fall: The Critical Future of HRM and Management Research', presentation at Academy of Management Meeting, Chicago.

Delbridge, R. and Turnbull, P. (1992) 'Human Resource Maximisation: The Management of Labour under a JIT System', in P. Blyton and P. Turnbull (eds) *Reassessing Human Resource Management* (London: Sage).

Edwards, R. (1979) *Contested Terrain: The Transformation of the Workplace in the Twentieth Century* (London: Heinemann).

Fournier, V. and Grey, C. (2000) 'At The Critical Moment: Conditions and Prospects for Critical Management Studies', *Human Relations*, 53(1): 7–32.

Fox, A. (1974) *Beyond Contract* (London: Faber and Faber).

Geertz, C. (1973) *The Interpretation of Cultures* (New York: Basic Books).

Greenwood, R. and Hinings, C. R. (2002) 'Disconnects and Consequences in Organization Theory?' *Administrative Science Quarterly*, 47: 411–21.

Hasselbladh, H. and Kallinikos, J. (2000) 'The Project of Rationalization: A Critique and Reappraisal of Neo-institutionalism in Organization Studies', *Organization Studies*, 21(4): 697–720.

Hesketh, A. and Fleetwood, S. (2006) 'Beyond Measuring the Human Resources Managemennt-Organizational Performance link: Applying Critical Realist Meta-Theory', *Organization*, 13: 677–700.

Janssens, M. and C. Steyaert (2009) 'HRM and Performance: A Plea for Reflexivity in HRM Studies', *Journal of Management Studies*, 46: 1, 143–55.

Jermier, J. (1998) 'Introduction: Critical Perspectives on Organizational Control', *Administrative Science Quarterly*, 43: 235–56.

Keegan, A. and Boselie, P. (2006) 'The Lack of Impact of Dissensus Inspried Analysis on Developments in the Field of Human Resource Management', *Journal of Management Studies*, 43: 1491–511.

Keenoy, T. (1990) 'Human Resource Management: Rhetoric, Reality and Contradiction', *International Journal of Human Resource Management*, 3(1): 363–84.

Keenoy, T. (1999) 'HRM as Hologram: A Polemic', *Journal of Management Studies*, 36(1): 1–23.

Keenoy, T. (2009) 'Human Resource Management', in M. Alvesson, T. Bridgman and H. Willmott (eds) *The Oxford Handbook of Critical Management Studies* (Oxford: Oxford University Press).

Legge, K. (1978) *Power, Innovation and Problem-Solving in Personnel Management* (New York: McGraw-Hill).

Legge, K. (1995) Human Resource Management: Rhetorics and Realities (London: Macmillan).

Marglin, S. (1974) 'What Do Bosses Do? The Origins and Functions of Hierarchy in Capitalist Production', *Review of Radical Political Economics*, 6(2): 60–112.

Paauwe, J. (2009) 'HRM and Performance: Achievements, Methodological Issues and Prospects', *Journal of Management Studies*, 46: 1, 129–42

Thompson, P. (2003) 'Disconnected Capitalism: Or Why Employers Can't Keep Their Side of the Bargain', *Work, Employment & Society*, 17(2): 359–78.

Watson, T. (1994) *In Search of Management* (London: Routledge).

Watson, T. (2007) 'Organization Theory and HRM', in P. Boxall, J. Purcell and P. Wright (eds) *The Oxford Handbook of Human Resource Management* (Oxford: Oxford University Press).

Whittington, R. (2006) 'Completing the Practice Turn in Strategy Research', *Organization Studies*, 27: 613–34.

3

Control in contemporary work organizations

Mike Reed

Control relations are fundamental to the organization of work processes within any socio-economic order. This is in part due to the technical need for co-ordinating mechanisms that, at least in theory, will ensure that work gets done in ways that are appropriate to the organization's requirements (Berry et al., 1995). But it is also due to the political need for forms of regulation and surveillance that manage the conflicts that necessarily pervade the work organization. Work is a 'contested terrain' in which the 'frontier of control' within and between work groups is a dynamic process subject to the complex and shifting power relations in which these groups are embedded (Edwards, 1979; Fox, 1971; Goodrich, 1975; Thompson, 1989). Thus, any particular form or regime of workplace control is located within a wider political economy of power relations within which its distinctive organizational logic and architecture will emerge and take on a not insignificant degree of institutional continuity and resilience (Burawoy, 1985). Organizational control, therefore, is viewed in this chapter as consisting of *a complex and dynamic configuration of mechanisms and practices through which the regulation and monitoring of work performance is contested by groups or 'corporate agents' (Archer, 2000, 2003) embedded in institutionalized power relations.*

The key institutionalized power relation in which organizational control mechanisms and practices are located is the employment relationship because it is an enduring and ubiquitous institution of all advanced capitalist political economies. As such, 'organizational control' is always embedded within a wider set of 'social control' relations and mechanisms geared to the maintenance of social order (Innes, 2003). They interact with each other in highly complex ways to form dynamic patterns of power relations between the major 'corporate agents' within advanced capitalist societies who have the organizational capacities to shape institutional outcomes.

Consequently, the control logics and forms that become established within work organizations emerge out of the interplay between the constraints and opportunities made available by prevailing power structures and the ways in which these are creatively exploited by employers and employees in pursuit of their collective interests and values. Organizational control regimes emerge from the attempts of certain groups to design and impose certain principles and mechanisms of 'regulative surveillance' on other groups who are engaged with them in struggles to dominate the process through which resources are allocated and the distributional outcomes which it reproduces. As corporate agents, groups will possess and deploy varying organizational capacities required to engage in power struggles over the mechanisms through which control can be secured, maintained and challenged. In this respect, control systems within work organizations are necessarily dynamic entities that develop in ways that are indelibly shaped by ongoing power struggles within the workplace and the wider economy and polity in which it is located (Elger and Smith, 2005). Thus, the degree of internal consistency that the former achieve is limited by the extremely broad range of stakeholder interests and values which they have to accommodate and regulate.

The chapter will review and evaluate the thesis that a form of organizational control has been in the process of developing since the late 1980s that signifies a radical transformation in the way through which effective 'regulative surveillance' over work had been achieved for most of the twentieth century. *This 'new control logic' is seen to combine electronic surveillance, cultural engineering and political management to form a hybridized control regime that fundamentally breaks with the core features of the conventional, 'neo-Weberian' control model/regime* (Reed, 1999; Sewell, 2001, 2005; Thompson and Warhurst, 1998). By recombining more advanced information and communication technologies with indirect and implicit cultural and political management techniques, organizational elites are now able, it is argued, to implement modes of regulative surveillance that dispense with much of the, relatively inefficient and ineffective, control infrastructure on which the orthodox model/regime relied (Castells, 2000; Sennett, 2006; van Dijk, 1999). Control has become leaner, internalized, flexible and mobile within advanced capitalist societies and business corporations that operate in globalized political economies characterized by extreme instability and uncertainty. The major focus of control has moved away from the design and monitoring of standardized work tasks towards the management of highly complex informational, human and material 'flows' that are inherently resistant to the orthodox control technologies embedded in bureaucratic hierarchies. In their place, a new morphology of 'network-based' control forms has emerged in which hybridized control regimes, selectively combining principles and elements drawn from complementary and competing control logics, are fast becoming the norm – both in the private and public sectors of all advanced capitalist political economies (Clegg et al., 2006). Some economic sectors and institutional fields – such as informatics, pharmaceuticals and the creative industries – may be more advanced and radical in restructuring their control regimes than others – such as mass catering, clothing manufacture and retailing. But the underlying 'direction of travel', it is contended by many influential researchers and commentators (Castells, 2000; Barker, 1999; Davidow and Malone, 1993; Heckscher and Donellon, 1994; Kanter, 1990), is driving towards a hybridized form of 'network control' that will come to dominate increasing areas of socio-economic life in the twenty-first century.

The next section of the chapter will review the key features of the orthodox, neo-Weberian control model/regime and its putative strengths and weaknesses under prevailing socio-economic conditions. This will be followed by a consideration of research on organizational control that has given much greater emphasis to the cultural forms through which regulative surveillance over work is achieved. In turn, this will lead into a review of more recent work on contemporary organizational surveillance and discipline that draws extensively on Foucault's analysis of 'capillary power and control' in modern societies (Burrell, 2006; Foucault, 1976a, b, 2003). The latter refers to more finely grained, horizontal or web-like forms of control that go about their business in much less transparently coercive and authoritarian ways than more orthodox control regimes. Research on 'therapeutic' or 'disciplinary' forms of control has provided both theoretical and empirical inspiration for those researchers who have identified the key features of the new control model/regime as it has emerged in response to much more subtle forms of regulative surveillance focused on issues such as commitment, emotion, identity and mobility. It also resonates with the analyses of those researchers who, rather more ambitiously and perhaps unwisely, have attempted to construct prognoses of the generic forms of organizational control that will become dominant in twenty-first century capitalist economies and societies as they attempt to cope with the extreme discontinuities and uncertainties endemic in global geo-political systems and structures. A concluding section will provide an overview discussion and assessment of the key themes and debates elaborated in previous sections.

Neo-Weberian control

Much of the history of work and work organization during the twentieth century can be viewed as the gradual emergence, development and refinement of a control model/ regime that most closely approximated to the core structural and cultural elements of rational bureaucratic administration as identified by the German sociologist, Max Weber (Beniger, 1986; Child, 2005; Clegg, 1990; Edwards, 1979; Heckscher and Donellon, 1994; Jacques, 1996; McAuley et al., 2007; Morgan, 1990; Perrow, 1986; Reed, 1999; Thompson, 1989). This control model/regime takes the primary features of bureaucratic control – functional specialization, process standardization and hierarchical co-ordination – and builds relatively unobtrusive and indirect, but vital, 'secondary control mechanisms' on to these core structural elements. In this way, more sophisticated processes of cognitive and normative control can be 'grafted on' to the primary structural control mechanisms that bureaucratic organization relies on to achieve effective behavioural regulation within the workplace through formalized rule systems and standardized operating procedures (Perrow, 1986: 119–56). As a result, neo-Weberian control is seen to facilitate the development of a much more integrated and continuous form of regulative surveillance than is possible under the more direct and fragmented forms of workplace control practised and legitimated by Taylor's Scientific Management and Fordist mass production regimes (Littler, 1985). The latter generate highly personalized, diffuse and often relatively confrontational forms of supervision over work performance, while the former permits a much more remote, depersonalized, well-integrated and unobtrusive form of regulative surveillance to emerge.

Within a 'neo-Weberian' control regime, employees are more likely to submit voluntarily to control instruments – such as rule systems – focused on the cognitive and normative processes through which basic 'behavioural premises and patterns' are set. Of course, to some extent, this focus on the need for primary structural control mechanisms to be complemented by more subtle and unobtrusive secondary control mechanisms – that frame the tacit assumptions and premises on which work behaviour is routinely based – anticipates the much greater emphasis that Foucauldian scholars and researchers give to internalized discipline and self-surveillance at work (Barker, 1999; Burrell, 2006; McKinlay and Starkey, 1998; Townley, 1994, 1999, 2004, 2008). But the neo-Weberian control model also speaks to the growing emphasis on informal workplace control mechanisms – such as Burawoy's (1979) study of 'shop-floor games' and Knights et al.'s (1985) anthology on the micro-politics of technological and organizational change – that has emerged from over three decades of workplace research carried out within the labour process tradition, beginning with the publication of Braverman's (1974) classic study.

Throughout the 1980s and 1990s, the labour process tradition intellectually energized research on and debate over the inherent complexity of organizational control regimes that mediated between political economy and work designs within advanced capitalist economies (Knights and Willmott, 1990; Knights et al., 1985; Thompson, 1989). By focusing on the dynamic combinations of structural, technological and ideological mechanisms through which management struggle to sustain control in the face of endemic worker resistance, in all its multifarious forms, labour process research illuminated the multi-dimensional nature of regulative surveillance at 'the organizational coalface' (Burawoy, 1985; Child, 1985; Littler and Salaman, 1982; Reed, 1989, 1990; Salaman, 1979). Yet, it could not shake off the criticism that its 'realist' ontology and 'objectivist' methodology sustained a form of analysis that 'drastically underestimates the knowledgeability and capability of workers faced with a range of management imperatives.... What is lacking is an adequate discussion of the reactions of the workers, as themselves knowledgeable and capable agents, to the technical division of labour and Taylorism' (Giddens, 1982: 40). Thus, an emerging critique of labour process studies of organizational control that crystallized around the theme of the 'missing subject' (Casey, 1995; Knights and Willmott, 1985, 1989, 1990) identified a substantive concern and a theoretical-cum-methodological problem that would increasingly resonate with the 'cultural turn' in studies of work organizations and control regimes in the 1990s. A sustained analytical and empirical focus on 'worker subjectivity', including the subjectivity of managerial, technical and professional workers, was maintained within labour process research on changing control regimes over a period of two decades or more. But the latter found itself under continual pressure to develop a 'sociology of management knowledge' that provided a more coherent exposition of how new control theories and techniques come to be fabricated, implemented and revised. For many researchers and commentators (Reed, 1989, 1990; Watson, 1994; Whitley, 1984; Whittington, 1994; Willmott, 1987), this search for a 'sociology of management knowledge' that would enable us to better understand the complexities of 'control in practice' would only be feasible if the more deterministic predilections of a quasi-Marxist labour process tradition were to be succeeded by a neo-Weberian control model in which managerial and worker agency played a central role. In this way, it was argued, Weber's analytical interests in the structural architecture through which bureaucratic control is formally realized – through functional specialization, process standardization and hierarchical co-ordination – could be complemented by a substantive interest in the managerial agency through which these control mechanisms become operationalized.

Thus, both Weber and Braverman, starting from very different ideological and methodological premises, were seen to be guilty of presenting highly abstract analyses of organizational control that needed to be substantially revised in the light of empirical findings and theoretical developments focused on 'real world control strategies and practices'. Consequently, the growing emphasis on 'worker subjectivity and agency' throughout the 1980s stimulated the emergence of approaches in which corporate culture and organizational symbolism were to take a much more centre stage role in the understanding of control within work organizations. These approaches would reject the highly rationalistic and deterministic assumptions on which both neo-Weberian theory and labour process analysis had reportedly rested (Turner, 1990). In their place, the former would offer conceptions of 'organizational control' in which themes such as identity, emotion, insecurity and ethnicity would play a much more central substantive and theoretical role than they had ever enjoyed within the once dominant neo-Weberian and neo-Marxist approaches (Casey, 1995, 2002; Collinson, 2003).

Cultural control

From the mid-1980s onwards, the increasing emphasis on culturally based forms of organizational control – in which symbolically mediated modes of regulation, monitoring and disciplining at work became the major concern – was embedded within a wider 'cultural turn' in the study of work organizations (Martin, 2002; Martin and Frost, 1996; Reed, 2005). In part, the latter signalled an intellectual movement in support of general theoretical approaches – such as social phenomenology, post-modernism, post-structuralism and neo-institutionalism – that attached fundamental importance to the status of 'work organizations' as socially constructed entities. The latter had no existence or meaning apart from that given to them by, and continually reconfirmed through, the cultural processes and practices that made them possible in the first place (Alvesson, 2002; Hassard and Parker, 1993; Parker, 2000; Smircich, 1983, 1985; Westwood and Linstead, 2001). But it also reflected the growing influence of particular research methodologies and tools – such as discourse analysis, institutional ethnography, organizational sensemaking and actor-network theory and analysis – that derived intellectual inspiration from these wider theoretical movements. These new and innovative approaches aspired to provide interpretive studies of control processes grounded in detailed understandings of the linguistic, symbolic and discursive practices through which they were generated and reproduced (Alvesson and Karreman, 2000; Grant et al., 1998, 2004; Law and Hassard, 1999; Phillips and Hardy, 2002; Smith, 2005; Thompson, 2003; Weick, 1995).

Taken as a complete package, these general theoretical approaches and the specific research programmes and practices that they promote hold out the promise of a revitalized cultural sociology of organizational control (Du Gay and Pryke, 2002; Ray and Sayer, 1999). The latter would equip researchers to identify precise patterns of compliance and commitment within the workplace that are seen to emerge out of delicate and ambiguous negotiations as to meaningful collective interpretations and the modes of social intervention that they sanction. Instead of viewing control relations as institutionalized social entities that exert a considerable degree of continuous structural constraint over the interpretive options available to social actors and the courses of social interaction potentially flowing from them, cultural researchers, who prioritize the symbolic, linguistic and discursive antecedents of control relations, re-assert the latter's essentially open, contingent and transitory nature.

For cultural researchers, 'control' is, by its very nature, open to multiple linguistic and discursive interpretations as to its meaning, status and relevance within shifting organizational settings. These interpretations defy the lazy imposition of pre-determined theoretical categories relating to 'political economy' or 'social structure' or 'labour market' on the part of the analyst – who is then presumed to have privileged access to a level and degree of understanding unavailable to the actors involved in that situation. Thus, for these cultural researchers, our theoretical understanding of control processes within work organizations is necessarily parasitic upon the primary understandings and accounts of them constructed by those who make and remake them (Smith, 2005). As cultural researchers, our central role is to explicate the narrative storylines that organizational members construct and communicate about their understanding of control practices in their everyday organizational lives. If the cultural researcher wishes to re-interpret these narrative storylines through a wider theoretical lens, then this must be done with extreme care and humility typical of the 'reflexive researcher' in order that the complex iterative relationship between 'theoretical' and 'everyday' forms of understanding may be properly maintained and appreciated (Smith, 2005).

But the turn towards control as an inherently reflexive cultural process and practice, rather than an objectified material artefact and entity, also signalled a growing interest in forms of organizational control in which the 'management of meanings' was coming to dominate both academic research and public debate about 'the future of work' (Casey, 1995; Handy, 1984; Keat and Abercrombie, 1991; Leadbeater and Lloyd, 1987; Pettigrew and Fenton, 2000).

As advanced capitalist political economies began to undergo a conceptual metamorphosis into 'knowledge economies', the focus of research attention in the study of organizational control turned towards the 'knowledge-intensive-organizations' which were now seen to constitute the leading edge of dramatic innovations in control regimes and their supporting cultural technologies (Alvesson, 2004; Child, 2005; Thrift, 1999, 2005). These were typically forms of work organization in which relatively large numbers of professional, managerial and technical workers were employed. They also required even more complex forms of regulative surveillance attuned to the self-managed working environments in which such categories of 'expert labour' were used to performing their highly complex and ambiguous work tasks (Fincham, 2009; Reed, 1996; Robertson and Swan, 2003). Within 'knowledge-intensive-organizations', the focus for managerial control strategies and practices was seen to be moving even further away from the external imposition of standard-ized and formalized routines towards the 'the manufacture of commitment and consent' through the manipulation of corporate cultures that contained components of paternalistic ideology, team-based working, competitive indi-vidualism, performance management and professional work ethics (Alvesson, 2004; Alvesson and Willmott, 2002; Barley and Kunda, 1992; Casey, 1995; Courpasson, 2000; Karreman and Alvesson, 2004; Kunda, 1992; Robertson and Swan, 2003, 2004; Thompson and Warhurst, 2001). Selected elements of this culturally based control regime were also seen to be emerging in relation to certain categories of lower-level employees who were formally outside the 'core employment group' of professional, managerial and technical staff but whose skills and expertise are regarded as critical to the success of high qual-ity, high performance work regimes in which the quality of 'customer service' is the overriding concern (Barker, 1999; Ezzamel and Willmott, 1998; Frenkel et al., 1999; Knights and McCabe, 2003; Korczynski, 2003; Sewell, 1998; Sturdy and Fineman, 2001).

Over a period of time, this growing body of work – focusing on organiza-tional control as a socio-cultural process in which employers and managers strive to shape, if not transform, the subjective understandings that employ-ees have of their work roles and their wider significance for the corpora-tion's long-term viability – sensitized researchers to the endemic resistance of workplace cultures to managerial manipulation (Ackroyd and Thompson, 1999; Albrow, 1997; Fineman, 1993; Kunda, 1992; Pettigrew, 1985; Martin, 1992, 2005; Morgan and Sturdy, 2000; Strati, 2000). As Knights and McCabe (2003: 79) have, more recently, reflected, 'management deployed the discourse of re-engineering and culture change to signify a shift away from bureaucratic, hierarchical control and towards autonomy, responsibility, and self-discipline. For us, re-engineering signifies a change toward a process-based, rather than a functional, approach to the organization of work'. However, as Knights and McCabe's research – in organizational settings as diverse as call centres, automobile manufacture and financial services – also demonstrates, these cultural re-engineering programmes could not disguise *the political reality of management's continued preoccupation with long-term profitability and the constraints that this unavoidably imposed on culture change initiatives within the workplace.* It also highlighted the fact that whereas the repackaging of previously isolated and relatively mundane culture change techniques and experiments – such as total quality management, business process engineering and project team working – was relatively new and innovative, they still contained structurally embedded tensions and contradictions that inevitably generated unintended consequences that severely limited their longer-term impact. Pre-existing structural inequalities in power and authority, between and within various managerial, professional, technical and operational groups, continued to exert a disproportional impact on the effects that such cultural re-engineering strategies and programmes had on institutionalized control relations. This did not mean to say that they had no long-term impact on organizational control regimes but that their effects were mediated by a complex range of structural factors that are often underestimated, if not ignored, by researchers who tend to overplay the theoretical importance and practical influence of culturally based forms of explanation (Westwood and Linstead, 2001).

Indeed, by the second half of the 1990s something of a theoretical and political backlash was beginning to be expressed on the part of more mainstream organizational control researchers who felt that the 'cultural turn' had itself 'spun out of control' in ways that were having a deleterious effect on their capacity to identify long-term continuities in control strategies and forms (Ackroyd and Thompson, 1995; Reed, 1999, 2005; Thompson and McHugh, 1995). The pre-occupation with culturally based forms of control – in both private and, especially, public sector work organizations (Ferlie et al., 1996; Newman, 2001; Pollitt, 1993) – seemed to be generating a form of discursive reductionism or determinism in which an obsession with linguistic practices and symbolic forms marginalized, if not excluded, any concern with the underlying socio-material conditions in which they are grounded and which indelibly influence their organizational impact.

Also, 'the cultural turn' seemed to be supporting the promulgation of highly contentious generalizations about the growing influence of various 'cultural control narratives' – such as 'the culture of the customer' (Du Gay, 1996; Du

Gay and Salaman, 1992) or 'emotional labour' (Fineman, 1996; Fineman and Sturdy, 1999; Hochschild, 1983) – which, at the very least, were in need of conceptual clarification and empirical specification (Fournier and Grey, 1999; Korczynski, 2003). Thus, the overwhelming emphasis given to the role of discursive practices in shaping control strategies and relations came to be seen as counterproductive for many mainstream researchers. This was the case insofar as it analytically marginalized the key link between structural movements in the wider political economy of contemporary capitalism and changing forms and patterns of control at the level of capitalist work organization. It also encouraged the widespread adoption of an underlying conception of expert or 'knowledge work' in which more orthodox – that is, materially and structurally based – forms of control were seen to be 'genetically incapable' of being effectively mobilized and implemented (Thompson and Ackroyd, 2005). In turn, this tended to reinforce modes of analysis that seemed to be fixated with putative 'paradigm shifts' in control regimes where there is assumed to be system-wide transformations in control logics and patterns. As a result, the critics argued, these modes of, culturally based, analysis were ill-equipped to accommodate the emerging social and organizational reality of complex combinations of hybridized control systems that displayed much greater continuity with the neo-Weberian control model/regime than could ever be envisaged by more 'epochal-type' analysis (Thompson and Warhurst, 1998).

Nevertheless, 'the cultural turn' imprinted itself on the study of organizational control logics and regimes in ways that were to influence the field up until the present time. This was particularly the case as increasing numbers of researchers and commentators within the field began to draw on the work of the French philosopher/historian of ideas and organizational practices, Michele Foucault, for intellectual inspiration and insight into the increasing importance of 'capillary power and control' in modern societies and organizations.

Capillary control

As Burrell (2006) has recently noted, there has been something of an ideological and theoretical polarization in relation to how Foucault's work has been received and assimilated into mainstream studies of work organization. There is no doubting the theoretical and methodological impact of his work on the study of organizations over the last couple of decades or so. But the ways in which it has been evaluated has attracted a diversity of interpretive interventions. For some, Foucault is the unthreatening pluralist whose core ideas and claims can be incorporated into more orthodox approaches towards the sociology of work without too much fuss and disruption (Grint, 1991; McKinlay and Starkey, 1998). For others, his work has provided vital intellectual inspiration for an expanding body of post-modern/post-structuralist theorizing about new forms of disciplinary surveillance and control within contemporary work organizations that fundamentally questions, indeed radically undermines, the philosophical foundations, theoretical coherence and knowledge claims associated with more mainstream approaches such as labour process theory and neo-Weberian institutional theory (Clegg et al., 2006; Knights, 2009; Sewell, 2001, 2005; Willmott, 2005). For a third group of interlocutors, the distinctions, indeed divisions, between Foucault and, say, Marx and Weber have been grossly overemphasized such that the materialist ontological foundations and structural analytical sensitizers of Foucault's work on the historical development of micro-level organizational control technologies and practices have been illegitimately obscured and marginalized (Marsden, 1999; Pearce and Woodiwiss, 2001; Rawlinson et al., 2002). As a result, this third interpretation contends Foucault's potential contribution to our understanding of the internal dynamics and contextual embedding of organizational control technologies has remained a largely untapped resource that is still awaiting its full exploitation.

Whatever interpretive gloss we put on Foucault's work and its implications for research on emerging control regimes in contemporary work organizations, we can identify three, interrelated, areas in which his work has been extensively and productively drawn upon to provide new insights into changing control relations and the endemic contradictions and tensions that they embody.

First, it entails a decisive break with theoretical approaches to the study of organizational control that continue to overemphasize the significance of vertical control systems at the expense of horizontal, 'web-like' or multi-stranded capillary forms of control that do not conform to the institutional logic of bureaucratic rationality and authority. In this respect, Foucault and his followers are much more interested in the informal, internalized forms of disciplinary control that are evident, for example, in team-working- or peer-review-based quality management systems than in more formalized regulatory control institutions such as collective bargaining (Foucault, 2003; McKinlay and Starkey, 1998). These forms of 'disciplinary control' seem to become even more significant where new information and communication technologies provide 'certain information about subordinate behaviour while eliminating the necessity for face-to-face engagement. They can transmit the presence of the omnipresent observer and so induce compliance without the messy, conflict-prone exertions of reciprocal relations' (Zuboff, 1988: 323).

Second, the attention that Foucault and those who have followed him – sometimes labelled as the 'governmentalists' (Dean, 1999; Miller and Rose, 2008; Rose, 1989, 1999) – give to the more complex, 'bottom-up' or network-based forms of control that have emerged in contemporary neoliberal political economies and societies is seen to be contextualized by the development of new forms of 'governmentality' within the workplace. The latter are thought to embody new ways of thinking about and practicing 'governance' – that is, the actual conduct of governing – in an era when established forms of highly centralized 'command and control' systems typical of large-scale corporate bureaucracies can no longer cope with the complexity and instability inherent in global capitalism (Castells, 2000; Thompson, 2003; van Dijk, 1999).

Finally, each of these innovations in control – that is the increasing significance of workplace capillary control within network-based forms of governance – seems to suggest the more widespread diffusion of *hybridized forms of organizational control*. The latter usually combine competing design principles and operational processes within much more loosely integrated and informally co-ordinated control regimes that radically depart from the core axioms and overarching rationale of the neo-Weberian model. As a result, the state is afforded much less theoretical and empirical significance in accounting for changing control regimes because it is no longer able, or prepared, to take on the range of responsibility and detailed accountability entailed in the notion of 'sovereign power'. Indeed, 'the state' is seen to be increasingly differentiated and fragmented into more specialized and diverse political agencies than can no longer be contained within centralized 'command and control' systems (Cerny, 2005). This 'dispersed state' may be called upon to intervene in situations that potentially threaten the underlying cohesion and stability of the established socio-economic order – such as the recent financial crisis and current economic recession. But this is unlikely to lead to the reconstruction of the 'sovereign state', with all its panoply of centralized command and control systems, because the process of structural hybridization has simply gone too far for such a reversion to the neo-Weberian form to be politically and organizationally feasible.

Following the example that Foucault set in *Discipline and Punish* (1976) and in other publications, such as *The Birth of the Clinic* (1976) and *Society must be Defended* (2003), the overriding focus for the 'governmentalists' has been the practical technologies through which modern organizations, and their administrative, professional and managerial elites have designed and implemented control regimes that have the socio-psychological internalization of work discipline at their very core. Throughout the work of those researchers and scholars who have followed Foucault's lead, there is a sustained analytical focus on *how continuous control* of workplace mentalities, practices and relations is realized through the fabrication and application of *seemingly mundane techniques and systems* such as timetables/schedules, delegated supervision, team-working, performance benchmarking, individualized staff selection and appraisal, spatial segregation and enclosure and remote monitoring (Barker, 1993, 1999; Clegg et al., 2006; Frenkel et al., 1999; Garrahan and Stewart, 1992; Reed, 1999; Sewell, 1998, 2001, 2005; Sewell and Wilkinson, 1992; Sturdy and Fleming, 2003; Taylor et al., 2002; Tomaney, 1994). While much of this kind of research has been concerned with relatively standardized and rationalized work in factories, call centres and mass consumption outlets, attention has also been directed at higher level, 'knowledge work and organizations' in which expert labour of various kinds – managerial, technical and professional – is subject to similar, if somewhat more elaborate and indirect, control techniques that combine cultural, technological and organizational mechanisms (Courpasson, 2000; Deem et al., 2007; Grey, 1994; Robertson and Swan, 2003, 2004; Townley, 1994). Within this research setting, theoretical and empirical attention shifts towards the discursive construction of workers as 'disciplined subjects' and the panoply of symbolic and cultural processes through which occupational and organizational identities are selectively managed (Alvesson and Robertson, 2006; Alvesson and Willmott, 2002; Casey, 1995; Collinson, 2003; Jacques, 1996; Kondo, 1990). Indeed, it is this point that the detailed focus on the mundane control practices and techniques through which everyday regulative surveillance within the workplace is routinely achieved gives way to wider questions about new forms of 'governmentality' and 'governance' at work that are implicit within Foucault's ideal typical model of 'panopticon control' (Dean, 1999; Edwards, 2006; Miller and Rose, 2008; Zuboff, 1988).

Sewell (2001, 2005), among others (Barker, 1999; Burrell, 1988; Clegg et al., 2006; Townley, 1994, 1999, 2004), has argued that Foucault's forensic analysis of 'panopticon control' – that is, the detailed, intrusive, continuous and remote surveillance and disciplining of behaviour typical of the modern prison – provides an analytically and interpretively powerful metaphor for understanding the control regimes emerging across modern organizations. Based on Bentham's ideal typical model (Edwards, 2006) of the organizing principles that should inform the architectural design and administrative operation of the modern prison, Foucault's concept of 'panopticon' facilitates a deeper understanding of the cultural and discursive control mechanisms that shape everyday organizational life. This is so to the extent that it gives us insight into the complex 'micro-circuits and techniques of control' within contemporary organizations that are much more difficult to pin down and contest than the externally imposed and structurally fixed control logic and technology inherent in orthodox neo-Weberian control. 'Panopticon control' is more opaque, pervasive and insidious because it subjects individuals and groups within work organizations to mundane techniques of appraisal, categorization, treatment, enumeration and segmentation that are extremely difficult to identify, much less contest and resist, because they have become accepted as 'normal' and 'taken-for-granted'. As Sewell (2001: 191) argues, 'never before in the workplace have we been subjected to such a degree of enumeration and classification through the application of surveillance and performance measurement, undertaken by superiors and peers alike ... However, these are not presented as instruments of power and control. Rather, they constitute a reformatory therapy enacted through behavioural normalization'. Once these normalizing and disciplining techniques are brought together and eventually integrated within a general regime of surveillance that facilitates the continuous monitoring of all movements and flows within the work organization, then we have a form of 'generative discipline and control' as 'a potent, creative and powerful social force, difficult for us to resist' (Barker, 1999: 42).

In practice, this may take some considerable time to come to fruition and the degree of overall integration achieved between the various control techniques may be more unstable and fragile than the theoretical, ideal typical, model of 'panopticon control' suggests (Edwards, 2006). Additionally, the extent to which certain employees willingly participate in such disciplinary control regimes – because they derive material advantage from their involvement and/or their values and beliefs predispose them to identify with the regulatory norms that such regimes inculcate – should not be underestimated. Nevertheless, the 'governmentalists' are convinced that Foucault's analysis of 'panopticon control' precisely and systemically identifies the complex combination of discursive, technical and organizational mechanisms and practices through which contemporary control systems 'become manifest in actual day-to-day organizational activity as a method for doing good work in the organization' (Barker, 1999: 42). Within modern work organizations, control becomes 'embedded in the various means whereby we "shape" ourselves. Through this process, we necessarily surrender some of our autonomy to the will of the organization ... many organizational disciplines undoubtedly are overt and tangible ... most times, however, disciplines work beyond the perception of an organization's members ... we surrender our autonomy in a number of ways that appear to us as natural occurrences' (Barker, 1999: 42–3).

As already indicated, 'panopticon control' seems particularly well-suited to contemporary forms of 'governmentality' and 'governance' that demand much more flexible, adaptable, mobile and sophisticated control systems than those typically associated with neo-Weberian control regimes – within both the private and public sectors of most modern capitalist political economies (Barney, 2004; Castells, 2000; Ezzamel and Reed 2008; Farrell and Morris, 2003; Newman, 2001; Stalder, 2006; Thompson, 2003). Thus, contemporary debates around the type of control regime most closely associated with the 'post-bureaucratic organization' (Child and McGrath, 2001; Heckscher and Donnellon, 1994; Pettigrew and Fenton, 2000; Reed, 2005, 2010 forthcoming) seem to indicate that network-based, 'stakeholder' or 'participative' forms of governance, operating within and between different levels of socio-political decision-making (Crouch, 2005; Ezzamel and Reed, 2008), require dynamic combinations of control mechanisms and processes that cannot be accommodated within the linear design logic on which neo-Weberian control is premised. Standardization, formalization and centralization of control processes and relations are increasingly seen to be at odds with intensifying ideological demands for devolved and dispersed forms of political, economic and social organization that are responsive to the need to do something about the 'democratic deficits' inherent in modern capitalist societies and workplaces. They are also seen to be increasingly inconsistent with the much more elaborate, indeed 'seductive', control systems required in knowledge-intensive organizations which require their employees to exercise much higher levels of decision-making autonomy and discretion than is usually the case in conventional bureaucratic structures (Alvesson, 2004; McKinlay, 2005; Sewell, 2005).

Thus, new forms of governance at work can be seen as a response to intensifying political demands for forms of organizational democracy that give employees, customers, clients and citizens a substantial role on the co-production and co-evaluation of public services (Clarke et al., 2007). They also reflect escalating economic demands for forms of organizational management that are sensitive to the need for 'high trust/low control' employment systems in which core 'knowledge workers' will only fully exercise their specialist expertise if they are convinced that they are properly recognized and protected by the corporate culture. Consequently, the organizational capacity of orthodox control regimes to meet these demands and expectations is seriously in doubt because they lack the openness, transparency and flexibility associated with network-based forms of political and economic governance (Ezzamel and Reed, 2008).

However, 'governmentalists' remain pessimistic about the potential of these new forms of governmentality and governance to achieve anything approaching the political ideal of 'participative democracy' in contemporary organizational forms or practices within the workplace or beyond. Indeed, they see 'panopticon control' as symptomatic of the increasing ideological domination and discursive pervasiveness of a form of neoliberal doctrine and practice in which rationalities and programmes of government are shaped by 'indirect mechanisms and techniques' linked to the new and dispersed centres of power emerging in advanced liberal economies and democracies (Miller and Rose, 2008). At the core of these 'indirect mechanisms and techniques' of government lie *new practices and relations for calculating* how individuals, groups and organizations are to be administered and controlled in ways that are consistent with a new ethic of individual choice and personal responsibility under the unstable and uncertain conditions inherent in advanced liberal economies and democracies. Within this unstable and changing context, a plethora of expert techniques and skills are required to develop, apply and legitimate the new mechanisms and practices through which organizational control can, potentially at least, be realized at work, at play, at home and in public life. As Miller and Rose (2008: 24) describe the current situation:

> 'Advanced liberal rule depends upon expertise in a different way, and connects experts differently into technologies of rule. It seeks to de-governmentalize the state and to de-statize practices of government, to detach the substantive authority of expertise from the apparatuses of political rule, relocating experts within a market governed by the rationalities of competition, accountability and consumer demand. It seeks to govern not through "society", but through the regulated choices of individual citizens, now construed as subjects of choices and aspirations to self-actualization and self-fulfilment .... As an autonomizing and pluralizing formula of rule, this form of rule is dependent upon the proliferation of little regulatory instances across a territory and their multiplication, at a "molecular" level, through the interstices of our present experience. It is dependent, too, upon a particular relation between political subjects and expertise, in which the injunctions of the experts merge with our own projects for self-mastery and the enhancement of our lives'.

(Miller and Rose 2008: 24)

At the level of the work organization, this regime of advanced liberal rule leads to a proliferation of control technologies that are increasingly difficult to combine, much less integrate, into cohesive 'control regimes'. The latter seem to oscillate, often wildly, between the desire of organizational elites to re-assert control as a route to securing compliance and to delegate control as a means to achieving commitment and trust from employees. However, the increasingly dispersed, fragmented and disconnected levels of institutional governance, within contemporary capitalist political economies and societies, also makes it increasingly difficult for macro-level political managers and micro-level organizational administrators to co-ordinate effectively their control strategies and practices in ways that sustain coherent narratives of change and innovation (Crouch, 2005; Thompson, 2003; Whitley, 1999, 2003). The proliferation and elaboration of 'post-bureaucratic' intra-organizational control regimes (Johnson et al., 2009) – whether through more sophisticated cultural mechanisms and information technologies or through simpler, even cruder, modes of coercive imposition and punishment or through, rather tentative and fragile, combinations of both the 'old' and 'new' – seems to generate an underlying process of 'hybridization' in which control management becomes even more precarious and contingent.

Control hybrids

Control hybrids have been an increasingly influential theme in research on organizational control over the last decade or so. This is so for a number of reasons. First, the process of hybridization – that is, the socio-political processes through which organizations develop more complex, multi-dimensional and multi-level control systems based on combinations of components drawn from a diverse range of institutional logics and forms that often conflict with each other – raises fundamental questions about the dynamics of organizational change and innovation in an increasingly 'hyper-competitive' and 'uncontrollable' environments (Castells, 2000; Clegg et al., 2006; Ferlie et al., 1996; Pettigrew and Fenton, 2000). Second, the increasing prevalence and significance of hybrid control regimes also prompts difficult debates over the theoretical frameworks, models and methodologies that organizational researchers and analysts need to understand and explain these, relatively new and innovative, organizational forms and practices. Much of mainstream organizational theorizing and analysis is based on typologically based forms of classification and categorization, premised on clear, coherent and consistent 'logics of differentiation and identification', which may no longer pertain in the radically unstable and uncertain global world in which we now live. Finally, the putative move towards hybrid control logics and forms provokes serious and difficult questions about 'the distribution of power and privileges within organizational boundaries . . . a hybrid is not a smooth organizational combination of contradictory principles but a new creation, a singular model capable of challenging the very nature of bureaucracies' (Clegg et al., 2006: 333).

As complex, intermediary organizational forms based on contradictory, and often competing if not conflicting, logics, control hybrids can be seen as a response to intensifying levels of socio-economic, political and cultural complexity and instability within the wider environment. They are also 'condemned' to struggle with the deep-seated discontinuities and disruptions that the latter inevitably generates. In this respect, hybridization can be interpreted as an organizational strategy for attempting to manage the deepening structural inequalities, political divisions and cultural contestations that advanced 'informational capitalism' (Castells, 2000) necessarily throws up and reproduces. Insofar as they are expected to juggle with the competing demands of market rationality, political expediency, social inclusivity, administrative conformity and legal integrity, contemporary work organizations, and their managerial elites, are forced to come to terms with an unmanageable range and diversity of social values and interests – while also managing to maintain their own power base and legitimacy. Hybridization, potentially at least, offers an organizational means for 'managing the unmanageable' insofar as it facilitates the segmentation, containment and regulation of fundamental economic, political and cultural conflicts – what Weber called the 'warring gods' – that cannot, in any meaningful or practical sense, be effectively eradicated.

Considered in this light, the increasing prevalence and relevance of control hybrids within contemporary work organizations might be interpreted as a new solution to an old problem – that is, the evolution of pluralistic organizational forms that offer real prospects for achieving the incremental resolution of deep-seated conflicts through the expansion of more transparent forms of 'communicative rationality' in which closed circuits of decision-making are opened up to wider participation (Ray and Reed, 1994). At the same time, control hybrids may also offer increasingly hard-pressed and insecure organizational elites a viable strategy for sustaining their power and legitimacy within a socio-historical context when traditional cultural sources of political legitimacy, such as bureaucratic rationality and authority, seem obsolete. This is achieved through a more broadly based and inclusive systems of oligarchic rule – in which middle-tier and lower-level elite groups, closer to the 'chaotic messiness' of operational control, are more coherently aligned with strategic decision-making circles and circuits – combined with more substantial decentralization and delegation of the practical conduct of governance than is usually the case within conventional bureaucratic hierarchies (Clegg et al., 2006).

Practical organizational examples of hybrid control forms can be identified across the full spectrum of contemporary private and public sector corporations – from 'high performance work systems', 'flexible labour markets', 'knowledge-creating companies' and 'network production and distribution systems' (Applebaum et al., 2006; Grimshaw et al., 2005; Nohria and Berkley, 1994; Nonaka and Takeuchi, 1995; Peck, 1996) within the former to 'multi-agency partnerships', 'primary care networks', 'foundation hospitals' and 'public–private partnerships' within the latter (Ferlie et al., 1996; Massey and Pyper, 2005; McLaughlin et al., 2002; Miller, 2005; Newman, 2001). All of these organizational forms involve significant dispersal and delegation of control in order to stimulate enhanced participation by and accountability to 'citizen consumers' (Clarke et al., 2007) in ways that facilitate the co-production and co-evolution of the new governance structures and systems which they will require. But, at the same time, they are overlaid by 'panopticon-style' systems of surveillance and discipline – such as auditing regimes, performance management technologies, market-testing reviews and individualized behavioural competence assessments – that are designed and tested by middle-tier, professional experts, deployed by lower-level operational managers and legitimated by policy-making elites as strategically vital to the organization's survival in a hyper-competitive global market. In turn, 'softer', culturally and discursively based, control techniques are also extensively and intensively deployed as mechanisms geared to anticipating and containing the inevitable resistance, in all its manifest variety, which these, relatively new and innovative, control systems will face (Courpasson, 2000; Thrift, 2005).

In these respects, structural contradictions and the socio-political tensions that they inevitably generate are built into the very design principles and mechanisms on which control hybrids are developed. Hence, instability, fragmentation, disputation and ambiguity are necessary, rather than contingent, features of control hybrids insofar as they reflect and mediate, in their institutional form and operational logic, the situational conditions and contexts within which they emerged and from which they take their cultural legitimacy and political authority. Thus, the 'structural and cultural inheritances' (Archer, 2000, 2003) that control hybrids draw upon for their political authority and cultural legitimacy entail capacities and constraints that simultaneously empower and limit their ability to shape the socio-historical contexts in which they are embedded and the material conditions under which they operate. Domination – that is, institutionalized structures of power relations – remains highly concentrated around a relatively small and cohesive set of strategic elites or oligarchs that 'strive to build a democratic plurality of actors while reinforcing, unobtrusively, the power of the inner circle' (Clegg et al., 2006: 338). A much wider range of social, political and economic interests are accommodated within this, still highly concentrated, power structure, through various forms of control dispersal, delegation and devolution to a more inclusive range of stakeholders than would usually be the case under mono-organizational forms – such as 'command and control' systems. Yet, the structural backbone of hybrid control forms, underpinning the combinations of diverse elements from which they are constructed and maintained, is provided by the substantial power inequalities between strategic elites, who determine 'the rules of the game' that will indelibly shape how such hybrids are designed and function, and subordinate groups who are required to follow, and ideally internalize, these rules. While the inclination of subordinate groups to follow elite-determined 'rules of the game' will be highly variable, and their capacity to resist, subvert and avoid such rules will be highly contingent, hybrid control forms are likely to remain just as much 'contested terrains' as their organizational predecessors and the 'structural and cultural inheritances' that they, in turn, were bequeathed by their organizational forebears.

Discussion and conclusion

Previous exposition and evaluation in this chapter clearly indicates that more recent analyses of changing forms of organizational control have been intellectually dominated by, broadly speaking, Foucauldian analytical perspectives and models that highlight the 'delicate mechanisms' through which workplace discipline and surveillance are routinely achieved within modern societies. Indeed, they have closely followed Foucault's (2003: 30) injunction to make an ascending analysis of control which 'begins with its infinitesimal mechanisms, which have their own history, their own trajectory, their own techniques and tactics, and then look how these mechanisms of power, which have their solidity and, in a sense, their own technology, have been and are invested, colonized, used, inflected, transformed, displaced, extended and so on by increasingly general mechanisms and forms of overall domination'. This dedicated focus on the 'micromechanics of control', and the material operations, technical instrumentation and expert knowledge through which they are mobilized, has provided crucial intellectual sustenance to contemporary researchers who are intent on mapping the mundane techniques through which organizational discipline can be achieved in particular settings. They are primarily interested in *'how' control works* in a wide range of localized organizational contexts and, tentatively, exploring the wider implications of these analyses of 'practical control' for more generalized forms of domination in modern societies. The fact that organizational control always works imperfectly should not obscure the reality of contemporary control regimes that recombine selected elements of both 'old' and 'new' technologies of regulative surveillance in ways that mark a distinct shift in the art and practice of governance in advanced liberal societies.

There is little doubt that these 'localized and ascending' analyses of changing organizational control regimes, once they are connected to more generalized and globalized forms of power and domination – as is the case in the work of the 'governmentalists' discussed in an earlier section of this chapter – have been highly productive for the study of work and work organizations. They have made us more sensitive to the 'micromechanics of control', in all their contemporary complexity, and their problematic intersections with macro-level domination structures and elite control strategies that have been the major research interest for succeeding generations of Marxist and Weberian scholars in the sociology of work and organization studies. In addition, this work on the 'micromechanics of control' has helped us to better understand the internal dynamics and external trajectories of emerging control hybrids as they struggle to manage and contain the conflicting imperatives – for commitment and compliance, for participation and regulation, for quality and efficiency, for individualism and collectivism and for dispersal and concentration – that initially created them and now sustains them within highly unstable and threatening geo-political environments.

In these respects, this increasingly influential body of work on control hybrids seems to resonate very powerfully with wider debates over transformations in contemporary political economies where the putative shift towards 'post-bureaucratic' or 'network-based' state structures – within which power and control become much more widely dispersed and elongated than under conventional hierarchical structures – dovetails with intensifying political demands for greater 'democratization' within the workplace and its radical implications for intra-organizational control regimes (Castells, 2000; Mulgan, 1997; Reed, 2005; Thompson, 2003). Yet, previous discussion within this chapter also indicates that it would be a fundamental error to assume that the increasing prevalence and importance of micro-level hybridized control regimes necessarily entails the widespread dilution of concentrated hierarchical power and control – that is, structures of domination that provide ruling minorities located within the top command positions of political, economic and cultural hierarchies (Scott, 2001, 2008) with the institutional capacity to shape the strategic mechanisms through which intermediate and lower level control is secured.

Previous discussion also indicates that the growing significance of 'soft power and control' – that is culturally and discursively based rather than materially and structurally based forms of power and control (Clegg et al., 2006; Lukes, 2005; Nye, 2004) – within hybridized control regimes should not be taken to imply that 'hard power and control' are, in effect, redundant. *It is the, increasingly complex, combinations of 'hard' and 'soft' control within contemporary work organizations and within the wider structures of domination in which they are embedded that provides the analytical key to explaining the dynamics and trajectories of change in contemporary control regimes* (Perrow, 2002, 2008). In this respect, concentrations of elite power and control, embedded within and supported by structures of domination, remain far more resilient and significant than many theorists of the hybridized control regimes emerging under the conditions presented by 'informational capitalism' have assumed. As Harrison (1994: 171–88) has argued in relation to the increasing reliance of capitalist corporations on networked production systems in which a core of powerful, elite firms dominate a wider ring of subordinate producers and suppliers:

'the evolving global system of joint ventures, supply chains, and strategic alliances in no sense constitutes a reversal – let alone a negation – of the 200-year-old tendency towards *concentrated control* within industrial capitalism, even if the actual production activity is increasingly being decentralized and dispersed . . . . downsizing, outsourcing, and mass layoffs are creating fear and insecurity among a large and growing fraction of the population. In the brave new world of lean production, there are winners, but there are also a growing number of losers. Such is the *dualistic* nature of networked production systems; what I call the dark side of flexibility'.

Relocated within this wider political economy – in which concentrated elite firm power and dualistic labour market structures and employment management strategies remain dominant – the move towards hybrid control regimes at the level of capitalist work organization can now be interpreted as part of a wider attempt, on the part of corporate elites, to shift the economic burden of radical corporate restructuring and related organizational change on to those least able to protect themselves from its consequences (Thompson, 2003). Thus, the move towards intra-organizational control hybrids, across both the private and public sectors within advanced capitalist political economies and societies, can now be seen as *a key component of a continuing bureaucratization of the employment relationship in which concentrated strategic control by political and economic elites is, however tentatively and tendentiously, more effectively aligned with dispersed forms of operational control at the local level*. The continuing bureaucratization of the capitalist employment relationship entails the development of more elaborate 'secondary control mechanisms' (referred to earlier on in this chapter) in which employees, particularly 'knowledge workers', are discursively reconstructed as 'disciplined subjects' that internalize, at least to some degree, the more extensive normative requirements of their working lives under the new, hybridized intra-organizational control regimes that networked capitalism generates. Pressures to develop an infrastructure of more elaborate 'secondary control mechanisms', at least for those who remain in employment and especially for those that are assigned 'core' status, are likely to become even more pronounced in conditions of globalized economic recession. Increasing differentiation, if not polarization, between what Castells (2000) calls the 'core workforce' and the 'generic disposable workforce' predisposes management towards more hybridized intra-organizational control regimes leading 'workers to experience multiple sources of loyalty, identity and commitment, as well as feelings of insecurity and destabilization' (Grimshaw et al., 2005: 29). In turn, limited improvements in worker empowerment and autonomy made possible under control hybridization may be threatened by the much tighter product and labour market conditions that economic recession imposes (Hyman, 2006). This is particularly the case for those professional occupational groups and knowledge workers worst hit by the employment impact of economic recession and its deleterious effects on their labour market power and organizational status (Percival, 2009). Much depends, as always, on where employees are structurally located within the power and control hierarchies that continue to shape network-based forms of organizing and the political skill with which they deploy whatever room for manoeuvre this positioning affords to them.

This re-interpretation of the shift towards hybrid control – as a further elaboration, rather than reversal, of bureaucratization by extension of the 'secondary control mechanisms' that certain key groups of employees experience – is entirely consistent with the analyses that researchers, such as Thompson (2003) and Clegg et al. (2006), have recently formulated of the much more fragmented and disconnected, yet concentrated and streamlined, power structures through which advanced capitalist political economies are currently managed. Thus, the more extensive reliance on intra-organizational control regimes based on the deployment of 'soft power' and inter-organizational governance structures that are much more market-based and decentralized than those characteristic of neo-corporatist style industrial/ managerial capitalism can be seen as two sides of the same political coin – that is, an attempt on the part of coalitions of top-level elite groups, operating under the chronic instabilities and uncertainties endemic to advanced 'informational capitalism', to delegate operational control to middle/lower-level elites much more substantially than ever before while retaining strategic control at the centre. This *dualistic control strategy* may have worked, in a fashion, for much of the neoliberal dominated 1980s and 1990s during which the economic, political and cultural costs of radical institutional and organizational restructuring were, largely, borne by traditional blue-collar groups located in the primary and manufacturing sectors of the economy. Whether or not it can survive the latest global financial crisis of 'fast capitalism' (Dale and Burrell 2008; Grey, 2009; Sennett, 2006; Thrift, 2005) is a moot point, given that it is the 'high value end' of the manufacturing and service sectors – in which 'knowledge-intensive-firms' and their 'knowledge workers' are most prominent – where the employment consequences of the latest 'shake-out' are likely to be most dramatic and where the underlying cultural legitimacy of new control regimes are likely to be most severely tested. For those within the 'core group' that remain in employment, the material and cultural advantages that they derive from a dualistic control strategy and the hybridized control regimes that it engenders may be considerable. But this is likely to be of little consolation to those 'generic workers' or 'knowledge workers' who are regarded as 'surplus to requirements' within a much harsher economic climate in which work organizations and their managers can no longer afford the luxury of hoarding and protecting relatively scarce expert labour from the vicissitudes of a global economic downturn.

References

Ackroyd, S and Thompson, P. (1999). *Organizational Misbehaviour*. London: Sage.

Albrow, M. (1997). *Do Organizations Have Feelings?* London: Routledge.

Alvesson, M. (2002). *Understanding Organizational Culture*. London: Sage.

Alvesson, M. (2004). *Knowledge Work and Knowledge-Intensive Firms*. Oxford: Oxford University Press.

Alvesson, M. and Karreman, D. (2000). 'Varieties of Discourse: On the Study of Organization through Discourse'. *Human Relations*, 53 (9): 1125–49.

Alvesson, M. and Willmott, H. (2002). 'Identity Regulation as Organizational Control: Producing the Appropriate Individual'. *Journal of Management Studies*, 39 (5): 619–44.

Alvesson, M. and Robertson, M. (2003). 'The Best and the Brightest: The Construction, Significance and Effects of Elite Identities in Consulting Firms'. *Organization*, 13 (2): 195–224.

Applebaum, E., Bailey, T., Berg, P. and Kalleberg, A. L. (2000). *Manufacturing Advantage: Why High Performance Work Systems Pay Off*. Ithaca. New York: ILR Press.

Archer, M. (2000). *Being Human: The Problem of Agency*. Cambridge: Cambridge University Press.

Archer, M. (2003). *Structure, Agency and the Internal Conversation*. Cambridge: Cambridge University Press.

Barker, J. R. (1993). 'Tightening the Iron Cage: Concertive Control in Self-Managing Teams'. *Administrative Science Quarterly*, 38: 408–37.

Barker, J. R. (1999). *The Discipline of Teamwork: Participation and Concertive Control*. Thousand Oaks, California: Sage Publications.

Barley, S. R. and Kunda, G. (1992). 'Design and Devotion: Surges of Rational and Normative Ideologies of Control in Managerial Discourse'. *Administrative Science Quarterly*, 41: 404–41.

Barney, D. (2004). *The Network Society*. Cambridge: Polity Press.

Beniger, J. R. (1986). *The Control Revolution: Technological and Economic Origins of the Information Society*. Cambridge. Mass: Harvard University Press.

Berry, A. J., Broadbent, J. and Otley, D. (1995). *Management Control: Theories, Issues and Practices*. London: Macmillan.

Braverman, H. (1974). *Labour and Monopoly Capital: The Degradation of Work in the Twentieth Century.* New York: Monthly Review Press.

Burawoy, M. (1979). *Manufacturing Consent: Changes in the Labour Process Under Monopoly Capitalism.* Chicago: University of Chicago Press.

Burawoy, M. (1985). *The Politics of Production.* London: Verso.

Burrell, G. (1988). 'Modernism, Post Modernism and Organizational Analysis 2: The Contribution of Michel Foucault'. *Organization Studies,* 9 (2): 221–35.

Burrell, G. (2006). 'Foucauldian and Postmodern Thought and the Analysis of Work' in M. Korczynski, R. Hodson and P. Edwards (eds). *Social Theory at Work.* Oxford: Oxford University Press, 155–81.

Casey, C. (1995). *Work, Self and Society: After Industrialism.* London: Routledge.

Casey, C. (2002). *Critical Analysis of Organizations: Theory, Practice, Revitalization.* London: Sage.

Castells, M. (2000). *The Rise of Network Society.* Second Edition. Oxford: Blackwell.

Cerney, P. (2005). The *Changing Architecture of Politics.* London: Sage.

Child, J. (1985). 'Managerial Strategies, New Technology, and the Labour Process' in D. Knights, H. Willmott and D. Collinson (eds). *Job Redesign: Critical Perspectives on the Labour Process.* Aldershot: Gower, 107–41.

Child, J. (2005). *Organization.* Oxford: Blackwell.

Child, J and McGrath, R. (2001). 'Organizations Unfettered: Organizational Form in an Information-Intensive Economy'. *Academy of Management Journal,* 44 (6): 43–76.

Clarke, J., Newman, J., Smith, N., Wilder, E. and Westmarland, L. (2007). *Creating Citizen-Consumers.* London: Sage.

Clegg, S. (1990). *Modern Organizations: Organization Studies in the Post-Modern World.* London: Sage.

Clegg, S. R. Courpasson, D. and Phillips, N. (2006). *Power and Organizations.* London: Sage.

Collinson, D. (2003). 'Identities and Insecurities: Selves at Work'. *Organization,* 10 (3): 527–47.

Courpasson, D. (2000). 'Managerial Strategies of Domination: Power in Soft Bureaucracies'. *Organization Studies,* 21 (1): 142–61.

Crouch, C. (2005). *Capitalist Diversity and Change: Recombinant Governance and Institutional Entrepreneurs.* Oxford: Oxford University Press.

Dale, K. and Burrell,G. (2008). *The Spaces of Organisation and the Organisation of Space.* London: Palgrave Macmillan.

Davidow, W. and Malone, M. (1993). *The Virtual Corporation: Structuring and Revitalizing the Organization for the 21st Century.* New York: Harper Collins.

Dean, M. (1999). *Governmentality: Power and Rule in Modern Society.* London: Sage.

Deem, R., Hillyard, S. and Reed, M. (2007). *Knowledge, Higher Education and the New Managerialism.* Oxford: Oxford University Press.

Du Gay, P. (1996). *Consumption and Identity at Work.* London: Sage.

Du Gay, P. and Salaman, G. (1992). 'The Cult(ure) of the Customer'. *Journal of Management Studies,* 29 (5): 615–34.

Du Gay, P. and Pryke, M. (eds) (2002). *Cultural Economy.* London: Sage.

Edwards, R. (1979). *Contested Terrain: The Transformation of the Workplace in the Twentieth Century.* London: Heinemann.

Edwards, P. (2006). 'Power and Ideology in the Workplace: Going Beyond even the Second Version of the Three-Dimensional View'. *Work, Employment and Society,* 20 (3): 571–81.

Elger, T. and Smith, C. (2005). *Assembling Work: Remaking Factory Regimes in Japanese Multinationals in Britain.* Oxford: Oxford University Press.

Ezzamel, M. and Willmott, H. (1998). 'Accounting for Teamwork: A Critical Study of Group-Based Systems of Organizational Control'. *Administrative Science Quarterly,* 43: 333–67.

Ezzamel, M. and Reed, M. (2008). 'Governance: A Code of Many Colours'. *Human Relations*, 61 (5): 597–615.

Farrell, C. and Morris, J. (2003). 'The Neo-Bureaucratic State: Professionals, Managers and Professional Managers in Schools, General Practices and Social Work'. *Organization*, 10 (1): 129–56.

Ferlie, E., Pettigrew, A., Ashburner, L. and Fitzgerald, L. (1996). *The New Public Management in Action*. Oxford: Oxford University Press.

Fincham, R. (2009). 'A New(ish) Model of Professional Work' Unpublished paper, 24th Employment Relations Unit (ERU) Annual Conference, 3/4th September, Cardiff Business School.

Fineman, S. (ed.) (1993). *Emotion in Organizations*. London: Sage.

Fineman, S. (1996). 'Emotion and Organizing' in S. R. Clegg, C. Hardy and W. Nord (eds). *Handbook of Organization Studies*. London: Sage, 543–64.

Fineman, S. and Sturdy, A. (1999). 'The Emotions of Control'. *Human Relations*, 52 (5): 631–63.

Fournier, V. and Grey, C. (1999). 'Too Much, Too Little, and Too Often: A Critique of Du Gay's Analysis of Enterprise'. *Organization*, 6 (1): 107–28.

Foucault, M. (1976a). *The Birth of the Clinic*. London: Tavistock Publications Ltd.

Foucault, M. (1976b). *Discipline and Punish: The Birth of the Prison*. Harmondsworth: Allen Lane.

Foucault, M. (2003). *Society Must be Defended*. London: Allen and Lane.

Fox, A. (1971). *A Sociology of Work in Industry*. Collier Macmillan.

Frenkel, S., Korczynski, M., Shire, K. A. and Tam, M. (1999). *On the Frontline of Work in the Information Economy*. Ithaca and London: Cornell University Press.

Garrahan, P. and Stewart, P. (1992). The *Nissan Enigma: Flexibility at Work in a Local Economy*. London: Cassell.

Giddens, A. (1982). 'Power, the Dialectic of Control and Class Structuration' in A. Giddens and G. Mackenzie (eds). *Social Class and the Division of Labour*. Cambridge: Cambridge University Press, 29–45.

Goodrich, C. L. (1975). *The Frontier of Control: A Study in British Workshop Politics*. London: Pluto Press.

Grant, D., Keenoy, T. and Oswick, C. (eds) (1998). *Discourse and Organization*. London: Sage.

Grant, D., Hardy, C., Oswick, C. and Putnam, L. (eds) (2004). *The Sage Handbook of Organizational Discourse*. London: Sage.

Grey, C. (1994). 'Career as a Project of the Self and Labour Process Discipline'. *Sociology*, 28: 479–98.

Grey, C. (2009). *A Very Short, Fairly Interesting and Reasonably Cheap Book about Studying Organizations*. Second Edition. London: Sage.

Grimshaw, D., Marchington, M., Rubery, J. and Willmottt, H. (eds) (2005). *Fragmenting Work: Blurring Organizational Boundaries and Disordering Hierarchies*. Oxford: Oxford University Press.

Grint, K. (1991). *The Sociology of Work in Industry*. Cambridge: Polity Press.

Handy, C. B. (1984). *The Future of Work*. Oxford: Blackwell.

Harrison, B. (1994). *Lean and Mean*. London: The Guilford Press.

Hassard, J. and Parker, M. (eds) (1993). *Postmodernism and Organizations*. London: Sage.

Heckscher, C. and Donnellon, A. (eds) (1994*). The Post-Bureaucratic Organization: New Perspectives on Organizational Change*. London: Sage.

Hochschild, A. R. (1983). *The Managed Heart*. Berkeley: University of California Press.

Hyman, J. (2006). 'The Remaking of Work: Empowerment or Degradation?' in G. Wood and P. James (eds). *Institutions, Production, and Working Life*. Oxford: Oxford University Press, 185–202.

Innes, M. (2003). *Understanding Social Control: Deviance, Crime and Social Order*. Berkshire: Open University Press.

Jacques, R. (1996). *Manufacturing the Employee: Management Knowledge from the 19th to 21st Centuries*. Thousand Oaks CA: Sage.

Johnson, P., Wood, G., Brewster, C. and Brookes, M. (2009). 'The Rise of Post-Bureaucracy: Theorists' Fancy or Organizational Praxis?'. *International Sociology*, 24 (1): 37–61.

Kanter, R. M. (1990). *When Giants Learn to Dance*. London: Unwin Hyman.

Karreman, D. and Alvesson, M. (2004). 'Cages in Tandem: Management Control, Social Identity, and Identification in a Knowledge-Intensive Firm'. *Organization*, 11 (1): 149–74.

Keat, R. and Abercrombie, N. (eds) (1991). *Enterprise Culture*. London: Routledge.

Knights, D. (2009). 'Power at Work in Organizations' in M. Alvesson, T. Bridgman and H. Willmott (eds), *The Oxford Handbook of Critical Management Studies*, Oxford: Oxford University Press, 144–165.

Knights, D. and Willmott, H. (1985). 'Power and Identity in Theory and Practice'. *Sociological Review*, 33 (1): 22–46.

Knights, D. and Willmott, H. (1989). 'Power and Subjectivity at Work: From Degradation to Subjugation in Social Relations'. *Sociology*, 23 (4): 535–58.

Knights, D. and Willmott, H (eds) (1990). *Labour Process Theory*. London: Macmillan.

Knights, D. and McCabe, D. (2003). *Organization and Innovation: Guru Schemes and American Dreams*. Berkshire: Open University Press.

Knights, D., Willmott, H. and Collinson, D. (eds) (1985) *Job Redesign: Critical Perspectives on the Labour Process*. Aldershot. Gower.

Kondo, D. K. (1990). *Crafting Selves: Power, Gender, and Discourses of Identity in a Japanese Workplace*. Chicago: University of Chicago Press.

Korczynski, M. (2003). 'Communities of Coping: Collective Emotional Labour in Service Work'. *Organization*, 10 (1): 55–79.

Kunda, G. (1992). *Engineering Culture: Control and Commitment in a High-Tech Corporation*. Philadelphia: Temple University Press.

Law, J. and Hassard, J. (eds) (1999). *Actor Network Theory and After*. Oxford: Blackwell.

Leadbeater, C. and Lloyd, J. (1987). *In Search of Work*. Harmondsworth: Penguin.

Littler, C. R. (1985). *The Development of the Labour Process in Capitalist Societies*. London: Heinemann.

Littler, C. R. and Salaman, G. (1982). 'Bravermania and Beyond'. *Sociology*, 16 (2): 251–69.

Lukes, S. (2005). *Power: A Radical View*. Second Edition. London: Macmillan.

Marsden, R. (1999). *The Nature of Capital*. London: Routledge.

Martin, J. (1992). *Cultures in Organizations; Three Perspectives*. Oxford: Oxford University Press.

Martin, J. (2002). *Organizational Culture: Mapping the Terrain*. Thousand Oakes. CA: Sage Publications.

Martin, J. and Frost, P. (1996). 'The Organizational Culture War Games: A Struggle for Intellectual Dominance' in S. R. Clegg, C. Hardy and W. R. Nord (eds). *Handbook of Organization Studies*. London: Sage, 599–621.

Massey, A. and Pyper, R. (2005). *Public Management and Modernization in Britain*. Basingstoke: Palgrave Macmillan.

McAuley, J., Duberley, J. and Johnson, P. (2007). *Organization Theory: Challenges and Perspectives*. Englewood Cliffs. NJ: Prentice Hall.

McKinlay, A. (2005). 'Knowledge Management' in S. Ackroyd, R. Batt, P. Thompson and P. Tolbert (eds). *The Oxford Handbook of Work and Organization*. Oxford: Oxford University Press.

McKinlay, A. and Starkey, K. (eds) (1998). *Foucault, Management and Organization Theory*. London: Sage.

McLaughlin, K., Osborne, S. and Ferlie, E. (eds) (2002). *New Public Management: Current Trends and Future Prospects*. London: Routledge.

Miller, D. (2005). 'What is Best "Value"? Bureaucracy, Virtualism and Local Governance' in P. Du Gay (ed.). *The Values of Bureaucracy*. Oxford: Oxford University Press, 233–54.

Miller, P. and Rose, N. (2008). *Governing the Present: Administering Economic, Social and Personal Life*. Cambridge: Polity.

Morgan, G. (1990). *Organizations in Society*. Basingstoke: Macmillan.

Morgan, G. and Sturdy, A. (2000). *Beyond Organizational Change: Structure, Discourse and Power in UK Financial Services*. Basingstoke: Macmillan.

Mulgan, G. (1997). *Connexity: How to Live in a Connected World*. Boston. Mass: Harvard Business School Press.

Newman, J. (2001). *Modernizing Governance: New Labour, Policy and Society*. London: Sage.

Nohria, N. and Berkley, J. D. (1994). 'The Virtual Organization: Bureaucracy, Technology and the Implosion of Control' in C. Hecksher and A. Donnellon (eds). *The Post-Bureaucratic Organization: New Perspectives on Organizational Change*. Thousand Oaks. CA: Sage, 108–28.

Nonaka, I. and Takeuchi, H. (1995). *The Knowledge-Creating Company: How Japanese Companies Create the Dynamics of Innovation*. Oxford: Oxford University Press.

Nye, J. S. (2004). *Soft Power: The Means to Success in World Politics*. New York: Public Affairs.

Parker, M. (2000). *Organizational Culture and Identity*. London: Sage

Pearce, F. and Woodiwiss, T. (2001) 'Reading Foucault as a Realist' in J. Lopez and G. Potter (eds). *After Postmodernism: An Introduction to Critical Realism*. London: The Athlone Press, 51–62.

Peck, J. (1996). *Workplace: The Social Regulation of Labour Markets*. London: The Guilford Press.

Percival, J. (2009). 'Architect Job Losses Sore as Crunch Hits Construction'. *The Guardian*. Friday 20th March, p. 13.

Perrow, C. (1986). *Complex Organizations: A Critical Essay*. Third Edition. New York: Random House.

Perrow, C. (2002). *Organizing America: Wealth, Power, and the Origins of Corporate Capitalism*. Princeton: Princeton University Press.

Perrow, C. (2008). 'Conservative Radicalism'. *Organization*, 15 (6): 915–21.

Pettigrew, A. M. (1985). *The Awakening Giant: Continuity and Change in ICI*. Oxford: Blackwell.

Pettigrew, A. M. and Fenton, E. M. (2000). *The Innovating Organization*. London: Sage.

Phillips, N. and Hardy, C. (2002). *Discourse Analysis: Investigating Processes of Social Construction*. Newbury Park, CA: Sage.

Pollittt, C. (1993). *Managerialism and the Public Services*. Second Edition. Oxford: Blackwell.

Rawlinson, M., Carter, C. and McKinlay, A. (eds) (2002). 'Themed Section on Foucault, Management and History'. *Organization*, 9 (4): 515–56.

Ray, L. and Sayer, A. (1999). *Culture and Economy: After the Cultural Turn*. London: Sage.

Ray, L. J. and Reed, M. (eds) (1994). *Organizing Modernity: New Perspectives on Work, Organization and Society*. London: Routledge.

Reed, M. (1989). *The Sociology of Management*. London: Harvester.

Reed, M. (1990). 'The Labour Process Perspective on Management Organization: A Critique and Reformulation' in J. Hassard and D. Pym (eds). *The Theory and Philosophy of Organizations: Critical Issues and New Perspectives*. London: Routledge, 63–82.

Reed, M. (1996). 'Organizational Theorizing: A Historically Contested Terrain' in S. R. Clegg, C. Hardy and W. R. Nord (eds). *Handbook of Organization Studies*. London: Sage, 31–56.

Reed, M. (1999). 'From the "Cage" to the "Gaze"? The Dynamics of Organizational Control in Late Modernity' in G. Morgan and L. Engwall (eds). *Regulation and Organizations: International Perspectives*. London: Routledge, 17–49.

Reed, M. (2005). 'Beyond the iron Cage? Bureaucracy and Democracy in the Knowledge Economy and Society' in P. Du Gay (ed.). *The Values of Bureaucracy*. Oxford: oxford University Press, 115–40.

Reed, M. (2010 forthcoming). 'The Post-Bureaucratic Organization and the Control Revolution' in M. Harris (ed.). *Managing Modernity*. Oxford: Oxford University Press.

Robertson, M. and Swan, J. (2003). 'Control – What Control? Culture and Ambiguity Within a Knowledge – Intensive Firm'. *Journal of Management Studies*, 40 (4): 831–58.

Robertson, M. and Swan, J. (2004). 'Going Public: The Emergence and Effects of Soft Bureaucracy within a Knowledge-Intensive Firm'. *Organization*, 11 (1): 123–48.

Rose, N. (1989). *Governing the Soul: The Shaping of the Private Self*. London: Routledge.

Rose, N. (1999). *Powers of Freedom*. Cambridge: Cambridge University Press.

Salaman, G. (1979). *Work Organizations: Resistance and Control*. London: Longman.

Scott, J. (2001). *Power*. Cambridge: Polity.

Scott, J. (2008). 'Modes of Power and the Re-conceptualization of Elites' in M. Savage and K. Williams (eds). *Remembering Elites*. Oxford: Blackwell, 27–43.

Sennett, R. (2006). *The Culture of the New Capitalism*. New Haven: Yale University Press.

Sewell, G. (1998). 'The Discipline of Teams: The Control of Team-Based Industrial Work through Electronic and Peer Surveillance'. *Administrative Science Quarterly*, 41: 397–429.

Sewell, G. (2001). 'The Prison-House of Language: the Penitential Discourse of Organizational Power' in R. Westwood. and S. Linstead (eds). *The Language of Organization*. London: Sage, 176–98.

Sewell, G. (2005). 'Nice Work? Re-thinking Managerial Control in an Era of Knowledge Work'. *Organization*, 12 (5): 685–704.

Sewell, G. and Wilkinson, B. (1992). 'Someone to Watch Over Me: Surveillance, Discipline and Just-in-Time Labour Processes'. *Sociology*, 26: 271–89.

Smircich, L. (1983). 'Concepts of Culture and Organizational Analysis'. *Administrative Science Quarterly*, 28: 339–59.

Smircich, L. (1985). 'Is the Concept of Culture a Paradigm for Understanding Organizations and Ourselves?' in P. Frost, L. Moore, M. Louis, C. Lundberg and J. Martin (eds). *Organizational Culture*. Beverly Hills. CA: Sage, 55–72.

Smith, D. (2005). *Institutional Ethnography: A Sociology for People*. New York: Rowan and Littlefield.

Stalder, F. (2006). *Manuel Castells: The Theory of the Network Society*. Cambridge: Polity.

Strati, A. (2000). *Theory and Methods in Organization Studies*. London: Sage.

Sturdy, A. J. and Fineman, S. (2001). 'Struggles for Control of Affect' in A. J. Sturdy, I. Grugulis and H. Willmott (eds). *Customer Service: Empowerment and Entrapment*. Basingstoke: Palgrave.

Taylor, P., Mulvey, G., Hyman, J. and Bain, P. (2002). 'Work Organization, Control and the Experience of Wok in Call Centres'. *Work, Employment and Society*, 16 (1): 133–50.

Thompson, G. (2003). *Between Hierarchies and Markets: The Logic and Limits of Network Forms of Organization*. Oxford: Oxford University Press.

Thompson, P. (1989). *The Nature of Work: An Introduction to Debates on the Labour Process*. London: Macmillan.

Thompson, P. (2003). 'Disconnected Capitalism: Or Why Employers Can't Keep their Side of the Bargain'. *Work, Employment and Society*, 17 (2): 359–78.

Thompson, P. and Ackroyd, S. (1995). 'All Quiet on the Workplace Front: A Critique of Recent Trends in British Industrial Sociology'. *Sociology*, 29 (4): 610–33.

Thompson, P. and Warhurst, C. (eds) (1998). *Workplaces of the Future*. Basingstoke: MacMillan.

Thompson, P. and Ackroyd, S. (2005). 'A Little Knowledge is Still a Dangerous Thing: Some Comments on the Indeterminacy of Graham Sewell'. *Organization*, 12 (5): 705–10.

Thompson, P. and McHugh, D. (2005). *Work Organization: A Critical Introduction*. Third Edition. London: Macmillan.

Thrift, N. (1999). 'The Rise of Soft Capitalism'. *Cultural Values*, 1: 29–57.

Thrift, N. (2005). *Knowing Capitalism*. London: Sage.

Tomaney, J. (1994). 'A New Paradigm of Work Organization and Technology' in A. Amin (ed.). *Post-Fordism: A Reader*. Oxford: Blackwell, 157–94.

Townley, B. (1994). *Reframing Human Resource Management: Power, Ethics and the Subject at Work*. London: Sage.

Townley, B. (1999). 'Performance Appraisal and Practical Reason'. *Journal of Management Studies*, 36: 287–306.

Townley, B. (2004). 'Managerial Technologies, Ethics and Management'. *Journal of Management Studies*, 41: 415–45.

Townley, N. (2008). *Reason's Neglect: Rationality and Organizing*. Oxford: Oxford University Press.

Turner, B. (1990). 'The Rise of Organizational Symbolism' in J. Hassard and D. Pym (eds). *The Theory and Philosophy of Organizations: Critical Issues and New Perspectives*. London: Routledge, 83–96.

Van Dijk, J. (1999). *The Network Society*. London: Sage.

Watson, T. J. (1994). *In Search of Management: Culture, Chaos and Control in Managerial Work*. London: Routledge.

Weick, K. (1995). *Sensemaking in Organizations*. Thousand Oaks CA: Sage Publications.

Westwood, R. and Linstead, S. (eds) (2001). *The Language of Organization*. London. Sage.

Whittingon, R. (1994). 'Sociological Pluralism, Institutions and Managerial Agency' in J. Hassard and M. Parker (eds). *Towards a New Theory of Organizations*. London: Routledge, 53–74.

Whitley, R. (1984). 'The Fragmented State of Management Studies: Reasons and Consequences'. *Journal of Management Studies*, 21 (3): 331–48.

Whitley, R. (1999). *Divergent Capitalisms: The Social Structuring and Change of Business Systems*. Oxford: Oxford University Press.

Whitley, R. (2003). 'From the Search for Universal Correlations to the Institutional Structuring of Economic Organizations and Change: The Development and Future of Organization Studies'. *Organization*, 10 (3): 481–501.

Willmott, H. (1987). 'Studying Managerial Work: A Critique and a Proposal'. *Journal of Management Studies*. 24: 249–70.

Willmott, H. (2005). 'Theorizing Contemporary Control: Some Post-Structuralist Responses to Some Critical Realist Questions'. *Organization*, 12 (5): 747–80.

Zuboff, S. (1988). *In the Age of the Smart Machine: The Future of Work and Power*. Oxford: Heinemann.

4

Debating employment law: responses to juridification

Edmund Heery

Introduction

For much of the twentieth century, Britain possessed an essentially voluntarist system of job regulation. The terms of the employment relationship were set primarily through voluntary collective bargaining that generated non-binding collective agreements between employers and trade unions. The function of employment law within this system was 'auxiliary' (Davies and Freedland, 1993: 29) in two distinct senses. On the one hand, collective employment law provided a framework that allowed voluntary collective bargaining to take place; principally by endowing trade unions with immunity from civil action by employers when they took strike action in furtherance of a trade dispute. On the other hand, individual employment law provided legal protection for vulnerable groups within the labour market who found it difficult to unionize and avail themselves of the benefits of collective bargaining. Protective legislation of this kind regulated the employment of women and young workers and was a notable feature of low-wage industries, where statutory wages councils set terms and conditions of employment (Deakin and Morris, 2005: 13–4).

Since the 1960s, this voluntarist system has been swamped by a flood of statutory regulation (Davies and Freedland, 1993: 59; Dickens and Neal, 2006: 4–8). Beginning with the Contracts of Employment Act 1963, there has been a progressive juridification of the employment relationship as legal regulation has encompassed more and more aspects of the wage–work bargain

(Deakin and Morris, 2005: 25–6). Recent expressions of this trend in the period since the election of the Labour Government in 1997 have included the creation of a universal statutory minimum wage, regulations setting maximum working hours, the extension of anti-discrimination law to the issues of age, religion and belief and sexual orientation and new statutory protections and entitlements to those with non-standard employment contracts, such as part-time and fixed-term workers, and those who combine paid work with caring responsibilities (Davies and Freedland, 2007). There has also been a comprehensive refashioning of collective employment law, which has included legislation on trade union democracy and governance, a statutory procedure through which employers can be required to recognize trade unions and collective rights for workers to be informed and consulted by their employers even when trade unions are absent (Davies and Freedland, 2007). Much, though not all of this legislation, has originated from the European Union but, whatever its provenance, in combination it has transformed Britain's traditional system of industrial relations.

The purpose of this chapter is to examine how academic Industrial Relations (IR)[1] has responded to this progressive juridification of its field of study, arguably the most significant change in the real world of work since the establishment of IR as an academic field after the Second World War. In doing so, four issues are considered, all of which have loomed large in recent discussion of law. The first is the desirability of law and the extent to which increased regulation promotes both equity and efficiency in the employment relationship. The focus here is the contest between 'deregulationists' critical of the spread of law and their 'regulationist' opponents who believe that employment law imports both fairness and efficiency into the labour market. The second is the efficacy of law and the degree to which statute has proved to be a potent means of shaping employment relations, especially when compared with other potential influences such as markets or the institutional matrix of different 'varieties of capitalism'. A key division here is between IR traditionalists who have long identified 'limits to the law' as a causal factor (Weekes et al., 1975) and other commentators, such as the American sociologist, Dobbin (Dobbin and Sutton, 1998), who claim that even weak law can have potent effects, shaping workforce management. The third, related issue concerns the implementation of law and the role of different institutional actors in ensuring law is effectively 'mediated' at the level of the workplace (Dickens, 1989: 170–1). The central question here concerns the conditions under which rights inscribed in statute have genuine effect at work, with different commentators ascribing differential significance to the mediating role of trade unions, employers, state agencies and social movement organizations. The final issue concerns the relationship of law to other means of regulating the employment relationship and the extent to which the increased volume of statute law has substituted for or complemented regulation through collective bargaining, long the centrepiece of industrial relations. For some commentators, employment law stands at the centre of a new 'employment rights regime' that, at least in the USA, has largely displaced industrial relations based on trade unions and collective bargaining (Piore and Safford, 2006). Others, in contrast, have identified a new hybrid in which legal regulation is fused with collective bargaining and trade unions use the law as a resource within a post-voluntarist system of interest representation (Heery and Conley, 2007).

Desirability of law

Opposition to the growth of employment law was once a characteristic of the political left and centre in Britain, among those committed to preserving the voluntarist settlement (Deakin and Morris, 2005: 28). In more recent times, however, opposition has tended to come from the political right and to be articulated principally by economists of a neoliberal stamp who claim that legal regulation inhibits the free working of the labour market and so generates a series of sub-optimal effects. Writers starting from this position typically oppose the introduction of new law and have mounted an intellectual case for 'deregulation'; that is for the removal of law or, when this is not possible, its weakening so that the legal burden on business is reduced. Where law is unavoidable, writers in this camp tend to argue that it should take the form of 'soft law', relying on voluntary adherence rather than coercive enforcement and incorporate exemptions and exclusions, such that laws do not apply to small enterprises or to young workers, those with non-standard contracts or without a minimum period of service.

The arguments of deregulationists conform to a long tradition of conservative opposition to progressive change, the core elements of which have been identified by Hirschman (1991). According to Hirschman, conservative opponents of reform have repeatedly deployed three rhetorical tropes. They have argued that reform generates perverse effects, rebounding against the very groups it is intended to help; that it is often futile, falling short of its objective of improving conditions; and that it jeopardizes other desirable states and conditions such as liberty or efficiency. These same three arguments from perversity, futility and jeopardy run like red lines through the deregulationist case against employment law. They can be illustrated by the attack on the introduction of Britain's National Minimum Wage, perhaps the most significant legal reform of the UK labour market of recent times.

The most frequent attack on the minimum wage by opponents has been on the grounds of perversity. Minimum wages, it is claimed, artificially raise the wage of low-productivity workers above the rate at which the labour market will clear and so contribute to falling demand for labour and a higher rate of unemployment. A reform of the labour market intended to improve conditions for the poor, therefore, acts in precisely the reverse way to what is intended and pushes low-wage workers out of employment and into dependence on benefits (Minford and Haldenby, 1999: 18; Oi, 1997). Women and minorities, moreover, the very groups that well-meaning reformers most want to aid, will suffer the severest perverse effect (Forrest and Dennison, 1984: 24–5).

This unintended, job-destroying capacity of minimum wages, and indeed other labour laws, is the most common but not the sole argument used by deregulationists. They have also claimed that minimum wage laws are futile, failing in their declared goal of reducing poverty and inequality. This may simply be because minimum wage law can be avoided, with workers and their employers colluding in non-compliance through cash-in-hand and other informal arrangements (Hatton, 1997: 24; Hevia and Schwartz, 1997: 16). Minimum wage law may provide a stimulus to the growth of the informal economy. Futility may also arise because the minimum wage is a blunt instrument for dealing with poverty. Many of its recipients, critics have pointed out, are married women or young workers living in multi-earner households whose standard of living is not related directly to their own level of earnings (Forrest and Dennison, 1984: 44–7; Lal, 1995). Instead of artificially raising the pay of those not in the direst need, it is suggested, the benefit system should be used to target those on lowest incomes. For deregulationists, wages should be set through the labour market, with additional, income support being made available to those whose earnings are so low they cannot experience an adequate standard of living.

Deregulationists have also deployed the rhetoric of jeopardy. Two basic types of this argument can be identified. It is suggested that employment law can jeopardize ethically desirable states or conditions; for example, by constraining the liberty of property owners or by reducing the self-reliance of workers in the labour market. It is also suggested that law imposes a burden on business, adds to costs and so reduces efficiency. In a context of a globalizing economy, this effect can result in reduced competitiveness: the sclerosis which is often said to characterize European economies when compared with more lightly regulated competitors in North America and Asia. It is the jeopardy to business efficiency that features most strongly in the argument against the minimum wage. In the debate surrounding the passage of the National Minimum Wage Act it was claimed by critics that the minimum wage would raise costs, generate inflation and reduce profits and that these effects would be exacerbated by increased earnings for the lower paid working their way up the pay structure through coercive comparisons (Minford and Haldenby, 1999: 18). This magnified wage hike was seen as a major blow that threatened to halt the UK economic recovery and reduce competitiveness.

'Regulationist' position

Standing in opposition to the deregulationists is an equally entrenched camp that looks favourably on employment law. Adherents of this 'regulationist' position believe that labour law is essential to guarantee the just treatment of workers and serves as a counterweight within the employment relationship to the greater economic power of the employer. Increasingly, this social justice argument for law has been allied to a 'business case', which holds that regulation can enhance business efficiency, principally by providing incentives for business to upgrade human resource systems. Regulationists advocate the passing of new law to solve problems and generally are keen reformists, presenting a critique of existing law and urging it be strengthened and supported by more robust measures of enforcement. They also often argue that law should be supplemented by other pressures on business, such as trade unionism; that 'social regulation' can complement the law and make it more effective (Dickens, 1999).

The arguments of regulationists are as similarly recurrent as those of their opponents and once again can be seen in the debate over minimum wages. Contrary to the futility thesis, regulationists believe that minimum wage law can help lift the working poor out of poverty and reduce inequality; they believe that law is effective (Brown, 2006: 64–6). For these benefits to occur, however, minimum wage law must be effectively enforced and must be integrated with the tax and benefit system so that additional income received through the wage is not lost through higher tax or reduced benefits (Croucher and White, 2007; Millar and Gardiner, 2004; Simpson, 2001). More generally, regulationists have tended to mount the case for employment law on the argument of 'market failure'; that unregulated business tends to produce sub-optimal effects within the labour market. Thus, the main economic justification for minimum wage law advanced by regulationists is the theory of monopsony (Manning, 2003; see also Edwards and Gilman, 1999). Essentially, this claims that the dominant position of employers in low-wage labour markets enables them to hire labour at rates below the competitive, market-clearing wage. If wages are raised to this rate through minimum wage law the effect will be to increase, not reduce employment. Moreover, by attracting workers into the labour market the minimum wage has the capacity to lessen dependence on benefits and boost the employment rate, a primary objective of labour market policy (Davies and Freedland, 2007: 182).

Another recurrent argument of regulationists is that law can exert a 'beneficial constraint' (Streeck, 1997) on business, leading to the more effective management of labour with consequent gains in economic performance. In the context of minimum wages it has been argued that the 'shock' of their introduction can prompt employers to improve work and employment systems. This argument is essentially the reverse of the 'deregulationist' claim for perverse effects. Minimum wages, the regulationists argue, can have benign, unanticipated side-effects. Although introduced for social justice reasons, they can stabilize employment, reduce turnover, provide employers with an incentive to train and prompt the replacement of workers with technology (Deakin and Wilkinson, 1996; Sachdev and Wilkinson, 1998). Following this line of reasoning, one would expect efficiency wage gains from minimum wages and a stimulus to productivity growth.

The UK minimum wage has been in place for a decade now and there has been an extensive evaluation of its effects, which permits an assessment of the competing claims of deregulationists and their opponents. The balance of evidence supports the regulationist case and it is notable that the neoliberal critique of the minimum wage in Britain has more or less fallen silent in recent years. The main story that emerges from the research is as follows (see Metcalf, 2008). Despite some non-compliance the minimum wage has increased the earnings of about 2 million low-wage workers in Britain (9.7 per cent) with a consequent tempering of wage inequality and a reduction in the gender wage gap. The broader impact on the incidence of poverty, however, has been slight (Millar and Gardiner, 2004: 11). The benefit to the low-paid has not been paid for by higher unemployment and the main thrust of evidence is that the minimum wage has been neutral with regard to job growth. There is evidence of a modest positive effect on productivity in low-wage sectors, much of which seems attributable to increased training. The cost of the minimum wage though has been a slight rise in prices and a slight fall in profits in these same sectors. This set of findings confounds the wilder predictions of disaster from deregulationists but also disappoints the more confident hopes of the regulationist camp.[2] The minimum wage emerges as a modest but benign labour market reform.

Efficacy of law

Within IR it is common to claim that law lacks efficacy when compared with other forces shaping the employment relationship. The classic statement of this position was Weekes et al.'s (1975) critique of the failed Industrial Relations Act 1971. This ambitious piece of legislation, introduced by the Conservative Government of Edward Heath, was intended to provide a new framework for the conduct of industrial relations in Britain but failed almost completely and was largely repealed by Harold Wilson's incoming Labour Government of the mid-1970s. The key to its failure was that the main actors in industrial relations, trade unions and employers declined to make use of the new legal framework and maintained their traditional pattern of interaction based on voluntary collective bargaining. The Trades Union Congress (TUC), in particular, organized a very effective boycott of most of the Act's provisions. Essentially, the parties to the employment relationship disregarded the new law and so killed it stone dead.

The failure of the Industrial Relations Act is a particularly graphic example but IR literature is replete with other cases of laws falling short of their objectives or failing to change the behaviour of workers, managers, trade unions and employers. This phenomenon often calls forth a policy response, with commentators urging the reform of law or stronger means of enforcement (Dickens, 2007). Another response is theoretical. In this case, commentators claim essentially that employment law is a secondary or at best mediating influence on the pattern of employment relations, which is shaped more powerfully by other causal forces. To illustrate this response we can look at two examples, one dealing with collective employment law, which emphasizes the primary influence of markets, and the other dealing with individual law, which emphasizes the greater relative influence of national systems of pay determination.

In a series of articles, Brown and colleagues have charted the impact of recent changes in collective employment law on the extent and quality of collective bargaining in Britain (Brown and Nash, 2008; Brown et al., 2001; Oxenbridge et al., 2003). Examining principally the statutory recognition procedure, introduced by the Employment Relations Act 1999, they demonstrate that the legislation has failed to halt the decline of trade union membership and collective bargaining coverage, despite its coinciding with a seemingly favourable context characterized by high levels of employment. They also argue that the nature of bargaining has continued to change during the period of the new law, with declining influence of unions over pay, a narrowing of the bargaining agenda and a shift towards consultation, rather than, negotiation, as the primary process through which union–employer relations are conducted. Because of the latter shift, Brown and colleagues were initially hopeful that another piece of collective employment law, the Information and Consultation Regulations 2004, would have a greater impact, diffusing consultative machinery within the UK economy. The latest analysis, however, by Brown and Nash (2008), points to failure in this regard as well, with joint consultation seemingly declining alongside bargaining.

The main explanation given for the failure of law to revive collective bargaining is the influence of adverse conditions within product markets and, indeed, in Brown's work there has been a persistent emphasis on the role of product markets in shaping employment relations (Brown, 2008). The causal effect of product markets in cancelling the influence of employment law, it is argued, operates in two main ways. On the one hand, the internationalization of markets has undermined employer solidarity and led to a collapse of multi-employer bargaining in most industries, the basis for high levels of bargaining coverage for much of the Twentieth Century. The function of multi-employer bargaining was to regulate competition within national product markets but as the spatial reach of markets has extended beyond national borders so this function has become redundant. On the other hand, the increasing intensity of competition, including the exposure of public services to competitive pressure, has raised the incentive for employers to resist unionization and sapped the bargaining power of trade unions. This is most notable with regard to wage bargaining, where the capacity of unions to capture economic rents on behalf of their members has collapsed in the face of more intense competition. The incentive for workers to seek union protection has consequently diminished and, where unions survive, their role in determining wages has been whittled away. Increasingly, for Brown and colleagues, collective bargaining is an empty-shell and changing market forces have not only eroded bargaining coverage but reduced the significance of what was once the primary regulatory institution of the UK labour market. In the face of this deep-seated, structural change, the introduction of weak provisions to help unions secure recognition or require employers to consult with worker representatives has been insufficient to turn the historical trend.

The other example concerns equality law and the provisions that exist to secure equal pay for women. In the UK, there has been legislation to combat pay discrimination since the Equal Pay Act 1970 but despite this there is a persistent gender pay gap in the labour market and Britain has a larger gap than many other developed countries.[3] This poor relative performance in eliminating pay discrimination presents something of an empirical puzzle because public policy commitment to tackling the gender pay gap has been at least as strong as that elsewhere in Europe, especially over the last decade. Moreover, there is a seeming acceptance by many managers, at least in the corporate sector, of the business case for eliminating discrimination and the UK has a trade union movement that has increasingly pressed for action on equal pay (Colling and Dickens, 2001). One response to this puzzle has been to argue that the commitment of government, employers and unions to eliminating unequal pay is shallow and that a stronger regulatory framework is required. A central demand in this regard is for all employers to be given a statutory duty to promote pay equality through the medium of equal pay audits (Fredman, 2008: 211–8; Hepple et al., 2000: 72–9).

Another response has been to seek structural explanations that can account for Britain's particular, relative failure in eliminating pay discrimination. The main structural influence that has been identified is the national system of pay determination. A number of empirical studies into the gender pay gap across national economies have shown that the gap is larger where the system of pay determination is fragmented and decisions on pay are taken primarily at the level of the enterprise (Almond and Rubery, 1998; Blau and Kahn, 1992; Whitehouse, 1992). Where pay determination is centralized and conducted at a multi-employer level, wage inequality tends to be reduced and the earnings of the low-paid are protected by minimum rates, secured by using the bargaining strength of better-organized workers with labour market power. Because women disproportionately tend to be in lower-paid occupations, this system operates to their relative benefit and reduces the gender pay gap, as part of a general reduction of inequality.

Equal pay law does not have this broad reach. It is based on the principle of comparison with a named comparator doing the same work or work of equal value *in the same employment*. While it can lead to the overhaul of company pay practices and the upgrading of women workers who work alongside men, vertical and horizontal segregation in the labour market mean that for many women finding a comparator is not possible. It follows, that there will always be limits to the efficacy of equal pay law. For writers, who accept the institutional explanation of pay inequality, therefore, further progress towards equal pay is 'dependent on much more than the enactment of equal opportunity legislation' (Whitehouse, 1992: 83). Rubery and colleagues have called for the 'mainstreaming of gender pay equity across different levels of policy-making' (Grimshaw and Rubery, 2001: iv; see also Rubery et al., 1999: 250) and consideration of the impact on equal pay of a broad set of labour market policies. They are particularly concerned to maintain and strengthen centralized institutions of wage determination.

The strength of weak law

While an emphasis on the 'limits to the law' has been one theme in the response to juridification, another has been to stress law's efficacy. A prime exponent of this view has been Dobbin and his colleagues who, in a series of empirical studies of the impact of American employment law, have argued that the 'employment rights revolution' of the early 1970s was a key turning point, stimulating the creation of the contemporary system of human resource management in the USA (Dobbin and Sutton, 1998; Kelly and Dobbin, 1999; Sutton et al., 1994; see also Edelman, 1990; Piore and Safford, 2006). New laws in the areas of equal opportunity, pensions and benefits and health and safety, they argue, stimulated the growth of specialist functions within business to monitor and ensure compliance with these laws, formal procedures to regulate conflict arising from law within the workplace and novel policies, such as those providing for maternity leave. The continuing elaboration of law through case law, the issuing of administrative regulations and new Congressional statutes have provided an impulse for the extension of policy and practice in all of these areas. Moreover, the empirical tests conducted by Dobbin and his co-researchers indicate that other potential sources of change, such as the feminization of the workforce or the growing size of business organizations, have less effect than does the impact of law. For these writers, employment law is the primary causal factor generating the development of human resource systems.[4]

This effect of law is puzzling, particularly in the case of the USA, where the federal state is typically regarded as weak and legal intervention in business activity is often fiercely contested. Dobbin and colleagues argue that the weakness of American law, paradoxically, has helped it exert influence. They note that the ambiguity and complexity of the law has encouraged employers to develop their own compliance mechanisms, based on specialist management functions, while the susceptibility of the law to challenge leads to its continuing elaboration and the need for continuous monitoring and adaptation. They also note that managers and other professional groups have seized on the opportunity presented by law to carve out positions within business based on interpreting the law and ensuring compliance. 'The uncertainties raised by legal reform created opportunities for ambitious personnel managers to expand their purview', note Dobbin and Sutton, 'and contributed to the rise of the HRM paradigm' (1998: 442). Once ensconced, moreover, these

HR professionals 'retheorized' their role 'with business and market rationales'; that is, systems of management that were originally created to ensure compliance with law came to be interpreted as functional for the business enterprise in their own terms. This change in the justification of HR systems has helped sustain law-induced innovation over time, particularly in periods when legal enforcement mechanisms were weakened, such as the Reagan presidency of the 1980s.

There are different interpretations of the impact of juridification, therefore, which on the one hand emphasize the limits to the law and on the other stress its efficacy in comparison with other causal forces. In this case, however, the division between opposing sides is not as sharply drawn as that between regulationists and deregulationists; it is more a difference of emphasis. Thus, those who stress the limits of the law do not deny that it can have significant effects (Whitehouse, 1992: 66) and those who stress its efficacy concede that its impact is patchy and contingent (Dobbin and Sutton, 1998: 470). In both cases, moreover, there are arguments as to why the effects of law are contingent and variable, which in principle are complementary rather than competing. For the first camp, law's efficacy depends essentially on the degree to which legal incentives for particular forms of behaviour reinforce or contradict those emanating from markets and the institutional patterns of different national business systems. Theirs is an argument about structural complementarity and the degree to which law is integrated with other powerful forces shaping the employment relationship: 'The success of any legislation depends to a large extent on how far it goes with the grain of underlying societal changes and thereby steers rather than forces the process of adjustment' (Brown and Nash, 2008: 300). In the two cases of collective bargaining and equality law the argument is that this complementarity was lacking.

For the second camp, the variable impact of law depends on the degree to which compliance is diffused across the economy. This analysis is rooted in neo-institutionalism with its central objective of explaining isomorphism across organizational fields (Edelman and Suchman, 1997). Receptiveness to diffusion may partly be a function of organizations, such as their proximity to the public sphere, but is also critically dependent on the mediating role of managerial and professional groups within and across organizations who interpret the law and formulate standards of compliance. This is a more actor-centred explanation of the contingent effect of law: the latter depends on the presence and activities of mediating agents. This process of mediation, and the involvement of different IR actors within it – the third theme in the debate over juridification – is considered directly in the next section.

Mediating law

The concept of 'mediating' employment law was developed by Dickens (1989) and refers to processes initiated by actors within employing organizations that serve to translate legal regulations into changes in workplace practice or, alternatively, frustrate that translation. 'Positive mediation' in Dickens' terms involves ensuring compliance with the law but also guaranteeing that the objectives of law are secured; and that equality law results in equal treatment, that collective rights result in joint regulation. 'Negative mediation', in contrast may involve outright flouting of the law but in many cases takes the form of seeming compliance with attempts to circumvent or blunt the effect of legislation. According to some of the American institutionalist writers discussed above, mediation by professional managers often takes this latter form. The law is used to promote the interest of the professional occupational group but the compliance procedures put in place may carry only a modest benefit for the workers they are ostensibly meant to benefit (Edelman, 1990).

Debate on mediating institutions is concerned centrally with judgements of this kind and hinges on the question of which mediating institution or actor is most effective in translating law into substantive outcomes within the workplace. The default position for many IR academics in Britain is that trade unions are the most effective mediating agent. Accordingly, we first consider the nature and some evidence on the union mediating effect for individual employment law in Britain.[5] Not all commentators accept the positive, mediating effect of unions or believe it is sufficient to translate law into desirable outcomes, however, and we also consider their critique and the alternative mediating agents they have proposed.

Research on the mediating function of unions has identified three types of effect. First, trade unions alter the substantive elements of the employment contract to ensure that there is legal compliance with regulations and often provision of contractual terms that exceed statutory minima (Brown et al., 2000). Second, unions are associated with the presence of procedural rules and formal policies which are designed to ensure compliance with the law (Anderson et al., 2004; Saundry and Antcliff, 2006). Partly for this reason, union members may be less likely to have recourse to external legal procedures to enforce their rights, at least for certain types of law (Hayward et al., 2004).[6] Finally, unions are associated with a number of outcomes, which legislation was introduced to achieve. Thus, the gender wage gap is narrower in unionized establishments, there is a better health and safety record and less recourse to dismissal (Knight and Latreille, 2000; Metcalf, 2005).

Why do unions exercise this seemingly positive mediating effect? Surprizingly little has been written about this issue but we can suggest a number of reasons why unions positively mediate individual employment law. Part of the explanation is that unions are a primary institution advocating the introduction and strengthening of law in Britain and so are committed to making law work at the workplace. Moreover, unions educate workers about their employment rights and, through their lay and paid representatives, provide access to expertise and representation; unions have representatives *in situ* who can interpret the law for workers. Finally, unions scrutinize employer policy and exert bargaining power to press managers to comply with law and institute policies and procedures that give effect to statutes. To a degree, there is an elective affinity between trade unionism and employment law in that both seek to regulate management decision-making and import formality into the employment relationship.

Despite the evidence pointing to a positive union effect, critics have identified two weaknesses. One flows simply from union decline. As union presence has diminished, particularly in the private sector, then there is a need to identify alternative mediating agents who can ensure employment law has genuine effect at the workplace. The argument here is simply that a declining trade union movement lacks the capacity to translate law into real change. The other criticism is more acute and identifies union failure even when capacity is present. This argument has been particularly applied with regard to equality law and rests on the claim that unions are dominated by male and majority interests and so fail systematically to mediate law framed in the interests of women and minority groups (Cockburn, 1989; Virdee and Grint, 1994). On this view, there is a failure of will, as well as of capacity. The solution though is the same: there is a need to identify alternative mediating agents who can better represent interests neglected by unions.

Mediation by non-union actors

Three main alternatives to unions have been identified in the IR literature: human resource managers, voluntary, advocacy and identity-based organizations and government inspectors. Although the relationship to the law of HR specialists is a neglected topic in the UK, there is evidence that they perform an important mediating function. In the area of equality, for example, Hoque and Noon (2004) have shown that equal opportunities policy is likely to have more substance and to embody the spirit as well as the letter of anti-discrimination law where HR specialists are in place. This effect, moreover, is stronger than the impact of trade unions.

Others have commented on the particularly significant role played by dedicated equality specialists and have identified the important part played by senior managers in supporting HR initiatives (Cockburn, 1989). Notwithstanding these positive findings, there is continuing scepticism about the role of HR managers in mediating employment law, with the issues of variable capacity and commitment being identified once more. HR specialists often lack power within the management team and studies of equal opportunities have observed the unravelling of positive attempts at mediation as HR lost influence to other management groups (Colling and Dickens, 1998). The need for HR managers to demonstrate the business relevance of their initiatives can also affect mediation of the law, leading to a stronger commitment to action where the business case is more apparent. For example, in the area of equality, it has been argued that policy often focuses on women or minority employees in senior positions while neglecting the needs of more disadvantaged groups in low-skilled or marginal employment (Richards, 2001).

Another mediating institution, one that has attracted increasing interest from researchers in recent years, is the voluntary sector, composed of advisory, advocacy and campaigning organizations. One aspect of the work of this type of institution involves interpreting the law for workers. There are voluntary organizations that inform people of their employment rights, offer advice and act as advocates before courts and tribunals. The best known institution of this kind in Britain is *Citizens Advice*, which provides an employment advisory service to the general population through its local bureaux (Abbott, 2004). Other, smaller organizations offer services dedicated to particular categories of worker, such as ethnic minorities, migrants or homeworkers. Voluntary organizations have also sought to mediate the law by targeting employers. Stonewall, the gay rights organization, for example, operates a Diversity Champions programme, which accredits employers on the basis of their adherence to a set of employment standards and which is reinforced by an award scheme that celebrates the achievements of 'gay-friendly' employers. Other organizations, concerned with older workers or the disabled, have launched similar initiatives. The background to these programmes is the introduction of equality law which outlaws discrimination against the identity groups served by bodies like Stonewall. Their aim though is to go beyond mere compliance with the law and foster voluntary adherence to best practice on the basis of the 'business case' for diversity management.

Voluntary organizations may have a number of positive features as an institution mediating employment law. They are often possessed of high legitimacy, allowing them to exert significant pressure on employers can contact and articulate the interests of unorganized, vulnerable and other groups neglected by other representative agents and have specialist knowledge in dealing with the needs of their particular constituency (Fine, 2006; Freeman, 2005; Holgate, 2009; Holgate and Wills, 2007). US research on living wage ordinances indicates that they have a greater impact on the earnings of low-wage workers when voluntary organizations are involved in monitoring and implementation (Luce, 2004). Despite these benefits commentators have identified weaknesses in the role of voluntary organizations. It has been argued that the lack of a workplace presence reduces the capacity of voluntary organizations effectively to represent workers, confining their role to after-the-fact advocacy. Thus, Pollert (2007: 35) notes that, 'External, individual remedy is no substitute for union representation and organization which can prevent injustice, rather than attempting to rectify it in a piecemeal fashion'.[7] Moreover, attempts to mediate the law by appealing to the 'business case' may suffer from the typical drawbacks of this approach: that only a proportion of employers are receptive, while the emphasis on working in cooperation with business militates against challenging those that are not.

A final mediating agent that has attracted renewed attention from both policy and academic commentators in recent years is government enforcement agencies (Dickens, 2008). The principle of enforcing employment statutes through inspection is long established in UK employment law and is a feature of the law of many other countries. In the UK, there is a variety of enforcement agencies with powers of inspection related to particular bodies of employment law. They include the Health and Safety Executive, the Employment Agencies Standards Inspectorate, the Gangmasters Licensing Authority and HM Revenue and Customs, which has responsibility for enforcing the National Minimum Wage (BERR, 2008). The mediating role of these agencies incorporates two broad approaches. On the one hand, they seek to ensure that employers and workers are aware of the law. All operate dedicated helplines and Web pages that both convey information and allow workers and third parties to make complaints about contravention of the law. On the other hand, they engage in targeted inspection, based on an assessment of risks. This work is backed by a range of sanctions that can be deployed against employers, including issuing notices for improvement and prohibition, prosecuting employers for breaking the law, requiring restitution to workers and, in the case of the Gangmasters Licensing Authority, the withdrawal of a license to operate.

The value of this method is that it uses the sovereign authority of the state to mediate law and can be targeted at those employers that are least likely to comply with law; often the same employers who are beyond the reach of other mediating agents such as trade unions and professional HR managers. It also removes the burden of enforcing rights from individual workers through application to an Employment Tribunal. The latter is an enterprise fraught with risk for individuals and research indicates that many with legitimate grievances refrain from seeking to enforce their rights (Dickens, 2008). The use of inspection-based enforcement, alongside individual application, has been identified as one of the main factors underpinning the successful implementation of the National Minimum Wage (Brown, 2006).

Nevertheless, there are criticisms of enforcement agencies. In periods of unsympathetic government the number of inspectors has tended to fall and the adequacy of the resource committed to inspection has been questioned (Dickens, 2008). Inspection, moreover, is often conducted with a light touch and, even with targeting, the risk to bad employers of facing inspection is low (Metcalf, 2008). These criticisms imply a reform, not an abandoning of the system of inspection and calls for the extension and strengthening of the system have been a notable theme in recent public policy (Citizens Advice, 2008; CoVE, 2008). Partly in response to the latter, the Government has announced the creation of a single telephone gateway to all existing enforcement agencies and the creation of a Fair Employment Enforcement Board to integrate their activities (BERR, 2008). Pressure for further action is likely. As unions have declined so commentators and pressure groups have urged the creation of a general labour inspectorate for Britain that will enforce all employment rights, in the manner of similar inspectorates in other countries (Brown, 2004; Citizens Advice, 2008).

Debate on the role of mediating agents attests to a significant change in the structure of interest representation within the British system of employment relations. In the past, trade unions were the predominant institution of worker representation but union decline has been accompanied by the increased prominence of other institutions that offer representation to working people. There is now a more complex, multiform set of arrangements for representing the interests of people at work that embraces voluntary organizations, employer-sponsored systems of voice and state agencies, alongside trade unions. Assessments of the mediating role of these institutions often differ sharply (cf. Abbott, 2004; Pollert, 2007), with writers expressing clear preferences for particular mediating institutions. Much of the debate over mediation is not highly polarized, however, and many commentators are ready to concede the distinct but complementary contribution of different institutions (e.g. Brown, 2004; Dickens, 1999). Indeed, a major theme in academic commentary, but also in policy, is the need for cooperation between mediating agents. Thus, unions have worked with voluntary organizations to disseminate awareness of new employment rights (Heery, 1998), voluntary organizations, like Stonewall, have tried to forge partnerships with professional managers through programmes like Diversity Champions and state enforcement agencies are committed to working with unions, business and voluntary organizations to improve compliance and identify bad employers (BERR, 2008). Coalition, not competition, has become the watchword in mediating the law.

An employment rights regime?

The fourth and final area of debate concerns the implications of juridification for the traditional system of job regulation, based on trade unions and collective bargaining. The division here lies between those who perceive a progressive displacement of bargaining by legal regulation and those who believe that a recombination of the two methods is both possible and occurring in practice. The displacement thesis has been developed most forcefully by Piore and Safford (2006) with reference to change in American industrial relations though their argument could be applied equally well to Britain. At its heart is the claim that the New Deal system of industrial relations, founded in the mid-twentieth century and based on collective bargaining, has collapsed and been replaced by an 'employment rights regime'.

Piore and Safford's argument has three main components. First, they identify the distinguishing features of the new regime. At its heart lies a framework of 'substantive employment rights', the most important elements of which are equality and anti-discrimination statutes introduced since the early 1960s. This framework of law has stimulated the growth of HRM in American business, as professional managers have developed compliance procedures, and has generated major changes in labour market outcomes, including a narrowing of gender inequality, an enhancement of the relative position of older workers and improvements in the treatment of the disabled and ethnic minorities. Second, they identify the origins of the regime, which they locate in 'a shift in the axes of social mobilization'. The strategic actor that has created the employment rights regime is the new social movements, grounded in identities formed beyond the economy narrowly conceived; the Civil Rights movement, the women's movement and more latterly movements of older people, the disabled, carers and gays and lesbians. Within this new system, social movement organizations at national level propose law, federal and state governments legislate, HR managers ensure compliance and network groups of the same social movements mediate the law at workplace level and generate upwards pressure for further change. The third element is a 'fundamental shift' in the 'nature of industrial society', which has simultaneously eroded the structural supports of the old, collective bargaining system and provided a context in which new social movements could flourish and create the employment rights regime. Among the changes identified are an erosion of the once sharp boundaries between the economic and other institutional domains, the associated collapse of the breadwinner family and the feminization of the workforce and a shift from a Fordist to a flexible economy. The new network economy, characterized by project working, sub-contracting and contingent work, provides an inhospitable habitat for trade unions but not for the new social movements, which themselves adopt fluid, network-based forms of organization.

This is a bold argument but viewed from a British perspective it has a number of problematic features. Taking the elements in reverse order, Piore and Safford exaggerate structural change in society and economy: in Britain, we have a modified breadwinner economy in which men still account for the majority of working time, most workers continue to be engaged in a conventional employment relationship with traditional forms of work organization and contingent work remains a minority phenomenon (Green, 2006; Hakim, 2004; Nolan and Wood, 2003; White et al., 2004).[8] They also ignore counter-mobilization by employers and state – what might loosely be described as the Reagan or Thatcher effect – in prompting the decline of the traditional, union-based system. The claim about the shift in axes of social mobilization is also exaggerated. In the UK, there has been an intertwining of the labour movement with newer social movements and the latter have colonized trade unions to a substantial degree and used them as vehicles to pursue change. The growth of equality and other substantive employment law in Britain has in many regards been driven by union pressure, as women's committees, black workers' sections and other groups have come to influence union activity (Bradley and Healy, 2008: 100–17; Colgan and Ledwith, 2002). Finally, while there is no denying the decline of trade union membership and collective bargaining, it is not certain that the growth of substantive employment law is implicated in this development – in several European countries an extensive labour code has existed alongside high levels of union membership for much of the past century – and there is evidence that the two forms of regulation can support one another, as is indicated by the evidence on union mediation of employment law discussed above.

Recombination

It is this theme of the mutual support of different methods of job regulation that stands at the heart of the opposing position in the debate; what might be termed the 'recombination thesis'. The starting point for this position is the observation, noted above, that for much of the twentieth century, UK unions were at best lukewarm about legal regulation and preferred to regulate the employment of their members through voluntary, non-binding collective agreements. From the mid-1970s, however, unions became major advocates of the extension of legal regulation in the UK labour market and, as we have seen, have also played an important role in mediating the law at workplace level. The critical point, however, is that this embrace of legal regulation has occurred alongside continuing commitment to collective bargaining and unions have devised means of fusing the two methods. For example, the development of union policy on part-time work has been marked by the sponsorship of strategic cases, the positive judgements from which have been diffused across the economy through collective bargaining (Heery and Conley, 2007). In the area of equal pay, unions have also used favourable judgements and the threat of further cases to open up negotiations with employers (Jackson et al., 1993: 94–5). Statutory employment rights, moreover, have often provided the agenda for collective bargaining with unions using negotiations to secure concessions above statutory minima (Brown et al., 2000; Heery, 2006). In these cases, substantive law has not displaced collective bargaining but has been incorporated within it as a precedent, sanction and standard. In combination they point to British trade unions developing a post-voluntarist system of interest representation.[9]

The fusion of law and bargaining has not just occurred on the union side, it has also been promoted by legislators. Since the 1970s, both European and UK legislation has tied bodies of substantive law to a procedural obligation on employers to consult with worker representatives; who principally are trade unionists in a UK context. This linkage exists in health and safety law and the law on collective redundancies and transfer of undertakings. More recently, the growth of what is termed 'reflexive regulation' (McCrudden, 2007) has provided further opportunities for unions to shape the application of substantive law. European statutes, such as the directive on working time, allow derogation through agreement with worker representatives, while the positive equality duties imposed on public authorities in the UK impose a requirement to consult stakeholders, including trade unions. Much of this law is weak (Jaffe et al., 2008) and does not provide a duty to bargain on employers but it nevertheless affords an opportunity for unions to exert pressure and fuse the application of law with their established function as collective representatives of the workforce.

It is this emphasis on fusion, the creation of hybrid forms of regulation from the old and the new, that is characteristic of the 'recombination thesis'. Its elements have been expressed in abstract form by Crouch (2005), who argues that endogenous change within societies (i.e. change that is not accounted for by external shocks) is invariably 'recombinant', as 'entrepreneurs' create hybrids from existing institutional forms. Institutional entrepreneurs in the labour movement and the legal system, we have argued, have acted in precisely this manner by creating hybrids from the institutions of collective bargaining and substantive, individual employment law. These hybrids are characteristic of the post-voluntarist system of interest representation that we see in contemporary Britain. This model of change, with its assumption of social complexity, is very different from that advanced by Piore and Safford. Here systems of regulation march through a succession of stages, each conforming to a common, unitary set of principles, driven by deep-seated change in the structure of economy and society. The debate about the 'employment rights regime' is ultimately therefore about social theory. Its adherents conceive of society as an expressive totality, with different institutions expressing common principles, while its opponents stress complexity; the jamming together of institutions based on competing principles in a single society.

Conclusion

The growth of legal regulation is arguably the single most important trend in the real world of industrial relations of recent decades. From the 1960s onwards, we have witnessed a progressive juridification of the employment relationship as an increasing volume of statutory employment law has set the terms on which labour is hired, performed and managed. The purpose of this chapter has been to examine how academic work within IR has responded to this development. It has done so by seeking to move beyond the perennial discussion of particular laws – how good or bad they are and what effects they generate – to examine more general areas of debate over law. Four such areas of debate have been identified: the debate over the desirability of law with its contest between rival anti- and pro-regulation positions; the debate over the limits of the law with its focus on the causal power of law as a force within industrial relations; the debate over the mediation of the law and the degree to which law is given effect by different industrial relations actors; and the debate over the relationship between legal regulation and regulation through trade unions and collective bargaining, which has polarized around the claims of displacement and recombination. Other areas of debate could have been included, such as that over the desirability of particular forms of law, such as soft law or the reflexive regulation mentioned above, but have had to be excluded for reasons of space. The underlying purpose of the chapter has been to draw attention to debate *per se*. Academic fields are composed of contending voices, competing normative and theoretical positions. They tend to be at their most vital when debate is intense and these competing positions clash. Theory is often developed to defend a particular position from attack and the best research projects launched to gather evidence against rival interpretations. In bringing to the surface debates that are often submerged, the aim has been to identify fault-lines of contention and point to areas where industrial relations scholarship remains vital.

Acknowledgement

I would like to thank the following for providing very helpful comments on an earlier draft of this article: Brian Abbott, Paul Blyton, William Brown, Trevor Colling, Hazel Conley, Linda Dickens, Paul Edwards and Peter Turnbull.

Notes

1. For the purpose of this chapter 'Industrial Relations', or 'Employment Relations' as it is increasingly called, is described broadly as the academic study of work and employment relations (Frege, 2007: 1). In what follows, there is consideration of the work of human resource management scholars, employment lawyers, industrial sociologists and labour economists as well as those who unambiguously fall under the IR heading.
2. As a consequence, regulationists have entered reform-mode and called for the strengthening of the minimum wage (Simpson, 2001). There has also been the emergence of a 'living wage' movement, based around a more ambitious wage target (Holgate and Wills, 2007).
3. In 2006, women's hourly average earnings in the UK were 82 per cent of those of men and the UK ranked 18th out of a list of 28 European countries in terms of degree of success in narrowing the gender pay gap (Carley, 2007; see also Grimshaw and Rubery, 2001: 15–9).
4. Edelman contrasts her explanation of change in HR systems that identifies the legal environment as the central causal mechanisms with others that stress the contribution of HR procedures to business efficiency or worker control: 'The theory . . . considers the legal environment a central determinant of organizational change; it emphasizes legitimacy and survival over efficiency and control as the imperatives that define the form of organizational governance' (1990: 1401–3).
5. Our focus is on individual employment law but it has also been argued that union mediation is important to ensure the translation of collective employment law. The effective functioning of works councils, for example, may rest on the degree to which they are 'captured' by trade unions who offer training and support to union members who stand as works councillors (Jenkins and Blyton, 2008: 348).

6. Although unions may help resolve employment disputes without recourse to formal legal procedures, they can also have a contrary effect. Unions inform people of their rights and can assist them in taking cases and this support is particularly important where the law is complex and difficult to use. In the area of discrimination, for instance, applicants to tribunals in the UK are more likely to be union members (Peters et al., 2006).
7. Partly to rectify this problem, identity-based organizations, such as Stonewall, are keen to establish network groups in the organizations employing their members. The effectiveness of these networks in positively mediating the law, however, remains uncertain. Most are dependent on the employer and operate under an obligation to cooperate with management (Healy and Oikelome, 2007: 47–8).
8. This is not to say that no significant changes have occurred in the structure of the family, economy, enterprise or workforce. Among the fundamental changes that have occurred has been the globalization of economic activity, the shift to services, the intensification of work, the rise of part-time employment and inwards migration and widening income inequality. It is rather that the changes identified in Piore and Safford's 'grand narrative' are not as great as they claim.
9. A less positive assessment of trade union use of the law is offered by Colling (2006). Nevertheless, his account includes examples of unions initiating strategic cases to set important precedents and of law being used in negotiations as a means to secure concessions from employers.

References

Abbott, B. (2004) 'Worker representation through the citizens' Advice Bureaux', in G. Healy, E. Heery, P. Taylor and W. Brown (eds) *The Future of Worker Representation*, Basingstoke, Palgrave: 245–63.

Almond, P. and Rubery, J. (1998) 'The gender impact of recent trends in pay determination', *Work, Employment and Society*, 12, 4: 675–93.

Anderson, T., Millward, N. and Forth, J. (2004) *Equal Opportunities Policies and Practice at the Workplace: Secondary Analysis of WERS98*, Employment Relations Research Series No. 30, London, DTI.

BERR (2008) *Vulnerable Worker Enforcement Forum: Final Report and Government Conclusions*, London, Department for Business Enterprise and Regulatory Reform.

Blau, F.D. and Kahn, L.M. (1992) 'The gender earnings gap: learning from international comparisons', *American Economic Review*, 82, 2: 533–9.

Bradley, H. and Healy, G. (2008) *Ethnicity and Gender at Work: Identity, Careers and Employment Relations*, Basingstoke and New York, Palgrave MacMillan.

Brown, W. (2004) 'The future of collectivism in the regulation of industrial relations', *Human Resources and Employment Review*, 2, 4: 196–201.

Brown, W. (2006) 'The Low Pay Commission', in L. Dickens and A.C. Neal (eds) *The Changing Institutional Face of British Employment Relations*, The Netherlands, Kluwer Law International: 63–78.

Brown, W. (2008) 'The influence of product markets on industrial relations', in P. Blyton, N. Bacon, J. Fiorito and E. Heery (eds) *The Sage Handbook of Industrial Relations*, London, Sage: 113–28.

Brown, W., Deakin, S., Hudson, M. and Pratten, C. (2001) 'The limits of statutory trade union recognition', *Industrial Relations Journal*, 32, 3: 180–94.

Brown, W., Deakin, S., Nash, D. and Oxenbridge, S. (2000) 'The employment contract: from collective procedures to individual rights', *British Journal of Industrial Relations*, 38, 4: 611–29.

Brown, W. and Nash, D. (2008) 'What has been happening to collective bargaining under New Labour? Interpreting WERS 2004', *Industrial Relations Journal*, 39, 2: 91–103.

Carley, M. (2007) *Pay Developments – 2006*, Dublin, European Foundation for the Improvement of Living and Working Conditions, http://www.eurofound.europa.eu/eiro/studies/tn0704029s [Accessed 10 August 2010].

Citizens Advice (2008) *Rooting Out the Rogues: Why Vulnerable Workers and Good Employers Need a 'Fair Employment Commission'*, London, Citizens Advice.

Cockburn, C. (1989) 'Equal opportunities: the short and long agenda', *Industrial Relations Journal*, 20, 3: 213–25.

Colgan, F. and Ledwith, S. (2002) 'Gender, diversity and mobilization in UK trade unions', in F. Colgan and S. Ledwith (eds) *Gender, Diversity and Trade Unions*, London, Routledge: 154–85.

Colling, T. (2006) 'What space for unions on the floor of rights? Trade unions and the enforcement of statutory individual employment rights', *Industrial Law Journal*, 35, 2: 140–60.

Colling, T. and Dickens, L. (1998) 'Selling the case for gender equality: deregulation and equality bargaining', *British Journal of Industrial Relations*, 36, 3: 389–412.

Colling, T. and Dickens, L. (2001) 'Gender equality and trade unions: a new basis for mobilization?', in M. Noon and E. Ogbonna (eds) *Equality, Diversity and Disadvantage in Employment*, Basingstoke, Palgrave: 136–55.

CoVE (2008) *Hard Work, Hidden Lives: The Full Report of the Commission on Vulnerable Employment*, London, Trades Union Congress.

Crouch, C. (2005) *Capitalist Diversity and Change: Recombinant Governance and Institutional Entrepreneurs*, Oxford, Oxford University Press.

Croucher, R. and White, G. (2007) 'Enforcing a national minimum wage: the British case', *Policy Studies*, 28, 2: 145–61.

Davies, P. and Freedland, M. (1993) *Labour Legislation and Public Policy*, Oxford, Clarendon Press.

Davies, P. and Freedland, M. (2007) *Towards a Flexible Labour Market: Labour Legislation and Regulation since the 1990s*, Oxford, Oxford University Press.

Deakin, S. and Morris, G. (2005) *Labour Law*, fourth edition, Oxford and Portland Oregon, Hart Publishing.

Deakin, S. and Wilkinson, F. (1995) *Labour Standards – Essential to Economic and Social Progress*, London, The Institute of Employment Rights.

Dickens, L. (1989) 'Women – a rediscovered resource?', *Industrial Relations Journal*, 20, 3: 167–75.

Dickens, L. (1999) 'Beyond the business case: a three-pronged approach to equality action', *Human Resource Management Journal*, 9, 1: 9–19.

Dickens, L. (2007) 'The road is long: thirty years of equality legislation in Britain', *British Journal of Industrial Relations*, 45, 3: 463–94.

Dickens, L. (2008) *Legal Regulation, Institutions and Industrial Relations*, Warwick Papers in Industrial Relations No.89, Coventry: Industrial Relations Research Unit.

Dickens, L. and Neal, A. (2006) 'Changing times, changing needs: institutional development through three decades', in L. Dickens and A.C. Neal (eds) *The Changing Institutional Face of British Employment Relations*, The Netherlands, Kluwer Law International: 1–12.

Dobbin, F. and Sutton, J.R. (1998) 'The strength of a weak state: the rights revolution and the rise of human resource management divisions', *American Journal of Sociology*, 104, 2: 441–76.

Edelman, L.B. (1990) 'Legal environments and organizational governance: the expansion of due process in the American workplace', *The American Journal of Sociology*, 95, 6: 1401–40.

Edelman, L.B. and Suchman, M.C. (1997) 'The legal environments of organizations', *Annual Review of Sociology*, 23: 479–515.

Edwards, P. and Gilman, M. (1999) 'Pay equity and the National Minimum Wage: what can theories tell us?', *Human Resource Management Journal*, 9, 1: 20–38.

Fine, J. (2006) *Worker Centers: Organizing Communities at the Edge of the Dream*, Ithaca and London, ILR Press.

Forrest, D. and Dennison, S.R. (1984) *Low Pay or No Pay?*, Hobart Paper 101, London, Institute of Economic Affairs.

Fredman, S. (2008) 'Reforming equal pay laws', *Industrial Law Journal*, 37, 3: 193–218.

Freeman, R. (2005) 'Fighting for other folks' wages: the logic and illogic of living wage campaigns', *Industrial Relations*, 44, 1: 14–31.

Frege, C.M. (2007) *Employment Research and State Traditions: A Comparative History of Britain, Germany and the United States*, Oxford, Oxford University Press.

Green, F. (2006) *Demanding Work*, Princeton NJ, Princeton University Press.

Grimshaw, D. and Rubery, J. (2001) *The Gender Pay Gap: A Research Review*, Research Discussion Series, Manchester, Equal Opportunities Commission.

Hakim, C. (2004) *Key Issues in Women's Work*, second edition, London, The Glasshouse Press.

Hatton, T.J. (1997) 'Trade Boards and minimum wages, 1909–39', *Economic Affairs*, 17, 2: 22–8.

Hayward, B., Peters, M., Rousseau, N. and Seeds, K. (2004) *Findings from the Survey of Employment Tribunal Applications 2003*, Employment Relations Research Series No. 33, London, DTI.

Healy, G. and Oikelome, F. (2007) 'Equality and diversity actors: a challenge to traditional industrial relations?', *Equal Opportunities International*, 26, 1: 44–65.

Heery, E. (1998) 'Campaigning for part-time workers', *Work, Employment and Society*, 12, 2: 351–66.

Heery, E. (2006) 'Bargaining for balance: union policy on work-life issues in the United Kingdom', in P. Blyton, B. Blundon, K. Reed and A. Dastmalchian (eds) *Work-Life Integration: International Perspectives on the Balancing of Multiple Roles*, Basingstoke, Palgrave MacMillan: 42–62.

Heery, E. and Conley, H. (2007) 'Frame extension in a mature social movement: British trade unions and part-time work', *The Journal of Industrial Relations*, 48, 1: 5–29.

Hepple, B., Coussey, M. and Chaudhury, T. (2000) *Equality: A New Framework. Report of the Independent Review of the Enforcement of UK Anti-discrimination Legislation*, Oxford and Portland, Oregon, Hart Publishing.

Hevia, I.G. and Schwartz, P. (1997) 'Minimum wages in Spain', *Economic Affairs*, 17, 2: 15–21.

Hirschman, A.O. (1991) *The Rhetoric of Reaction: Perversity, Futility, Jeopardy*, Cambridge MA and London, The Belknap Press of Harvard University Press.

Holgate, J. (2009) 'Contested terrain: London's living wage campaign and the tensions between community and union organizing', in J. McBride and I. Greenwood (eds) *Community Unionism: A Comparative Analysis of Concepts and Contexts*, Basingstoke, Palgrave MacMillan: 49–74.

Holgate, J. and Wills, J. (2007) 'Organizing labor in London: lessons from the campaign for a living wage', in L. Turner and D.B. Cornfield (eds) *Labor in the New Urban Battlegrounds: Local Solidarity in a Global Economy*, Ithaca and London, ILR Press: 211–23.

Hoque, K. and Noon, M.A. (2004) 'Equal opportunities policy and practice in Britain: evaluating the empty-shell hypothesis', *Work, Employment and Society*, 18, 3: 481–506.

Jackson, M., Leopold, J.W. and Tuck, K. (1993) *Decentralization of Collective Bargaining*, New York, St Martin's Press.

Jaffe, M., McKenna, B. and Venner, L. (2008) *Equal Pay, Privatization and Procurement*, Liverpool, The Institute of Employment Rights.

Jenkins, J. and Blyton, P. (2008) 'Works councils', in P. Blyton, N. Bacon, J. Fiorito and E. Heery (eds) *The Sage Handbook of Industrial Relations*, Los Angeles and London, Sage: 346–57.

Kelly, E. and Dobbin, F. (1999) 'Civil rights law at work: sex discrimination and the rise of maternity leave policies', *The American Journal of Sociology*, 105, 2: 455–92.

Knight, K.G. and Latreille, P.L. (2000) 'Discipline, dismissals and complaints to Employment Tribunals', *British Journal of Industrial Relations*, 38, 4: 533–55.

Lal, D. (1995) *The Minimum Wage: No Way to Help the Poor*, Occasional Paper 95, London, Institute of Economic Affairs.

Luce, S. (2004) *Fighting for a Living Wage*, Ithaca and London, ILR Press.

Manning, A. (2003) *Monopsony in Motion: Imperfect Competition in Labour Markets*, Princeton NJ, Princeton University Press.

McCrudden, C. (2007) 'Equality legislation and reflexive regulation: a response to the discrimination law review's consultative paper', *Industrial Law Journal*, 36, 3: 255–66.

Metcalf, D. (2005) 'Trade unions: resurgence or perdition? An economic analysis', in S. Fernie and D. Metcalf (eds) *Trade Unions: Resurgence or Demise?*, London, Routledge: 83–117.

Metcalf, D. (2008) 'Why has the British National Minimum Wage had little or no impact on employment?', *Journal of Industrial Relations*, 50, 3: 489–512.

Millar, J. and Gardiner, K. (2004) *Low Pay, Household Resources and Poverty*, New York, The Joseph Rowntree Foundation.

Minford, P. and Haldenby, A. (1999) *The Price of Fairness: The Costs of the Proposed Labour Market Reforms*, London, Centre for Policy Studies.

Nolan, P. and Wood, S. (2003) 'Mapping the future of work', *British Journal of Industrial Relations*, 41, 2: 175–95.

Oi, W. (1997) 'The consequences of minimum wage legislation', *Economic Affairs*, 17, 2: 5–14.

Oxenbridge, S., Brown, W., Deakin, S. and Pratten, C. (2003) 'Initial responses to the statutory recognition provisions of the Employment Relations Act 1999', *British Journal of Industrial Relations*, 41, 2: 315–34.

Peters, M., Seeds, K. and Harding, C. (2006) *Findings from the Survey of Claimants in Race Discrimination Employment Tribunal Cases*, Employment Relations Research Series No. 54, London, DTI.

Piore, M.J. and Safford, S. (2006) 'Changing regimes of workplace governance: shifting axes of social mobilization and the challenge to industrial relations theory', *Industrial Relations*, 45, 3: 299–325.

Pollert, A. (2007) *The Unorganized Vulnerable Worker: The Case for Union Organizing*, Liverpool, The Institute for Employment Rights.

Richards, W. (2001) 'Evaluating equal opportunity initiatives', in M. Noon and E. Ogbonna (eds) *Equality, Diversity and Disadvantage in Employment*, Basingstoke, Palgrave: 15–31.

Rubery, J., Smith, M. and Fagan, C. (1999) *Women's Employment in Europe: Trends and Prospects*, London, Routledge.

Sachdev, S. and Wilkinson, F. (1998) *Low Pay, the Working of the Labour Market and the Role of a Minimum Wage*, London, The Institute of Employment Rights.

Saundry, R. and Antcliff, V. (2006) *Employee Representation in Grievance and Disciplinary Matters – Making a Difference?*, Employment Relations Research Series No. 69, London, DTI.

Simpson, B. (2001) *Building on the National Minimum Wage*, London, The Institute of Employment Rights.

Streeck, W. (1997) 'Beneficial constraints: on the economic limits of rational voluntarism', in J.R. Hollingsworth and R. Boyer (eds) *Contemporary Capitalism: The Embededdness of Institutions*, Cambridge, Cambridge University Press: 197–218.

Sutton, J.R., Dobbin, F., Meyer, J.W. and Scott, W.R. (1994) 'The legalization of the workplace', *The American Journal of Sociology*, 99, 4: 944–71.

Virdee, S. and Grint, K. (1994) 'Black self-organization in trade unions', *Sociological Review*, 42, 2: 202–26.

Weekes, B., Mellish, M., Dickens, L. and Lloyd, J. (1975) *Industrial Relations and the Limits of the Law: The Industrial Effects of the Industrial Relations Act 1971*, Oxford, Basil Blackwell.

White, M., Hill, S., Mills, C. and Smeaton, D. (2004) *Managing to Change? British Workplaces and the Future of Work*, Basingstoke, MacMillan.

Whitehouse, G. (1992) 'Legislation and labour market inequality', *Work, Employment and Society*, 6, 1: 65–86.

5

Ask not what HRM can do for performance but what HRM has done to performance

Sukanya Sengupta and Keith Whitfield

Introduction

The rise of Human Resource Management over the last quarter of a century has intensified the focus on the relationship between differing approaches to the management of people and the performance of the organizations in which they work. This is, in part, because those working in the area of people management have increasingly felt the need to justify their existence in terms that suggest that they are generators of revenue rather than simply centres of cost. The evidence seems to suggest that this is indeed the case (Paauwe, 2009), though there are substantial doubts about the methodologies deployed to generate this body of findings (Edwards and Sengupta, 2010).

To a considerable extent, this development represents a change of focus for both the practice of people management and research thereon. Bottom-line performance has moved to the centre stage of the subject-area, and has tended to crowd out other more welfare-related concerns that characterized the subject-area when the generic term for people management was 'Personnel Management'. Such a change is ironic given the contemporaneous increase in concerns about corporate social responsibility and employee well-being (Anand and Sen, 2000; Green and Whitfield, 2009). It also highlights the broader impact of the advent of HRM on the criteria used to judge whether given approaches to people management are deemed to be good or bad, fair or foul.

There is now a voluminous literature on the relationship between HRM and organizational performance, involving numerous empirical analyses of the relationship. Increasing numbers of papers are critical of the main approaches taken and sceptical of the (overwhelmingly positive and positivist) results generated (Fleetwood and Hesketh, 2007; see also Delbridge this volume). The main thrust of this literature has been to cast doubt on the proxies for HRM adopted and the modelling approaches deployed. Less attention has been paid to the proxy for performance that is used. Where there has been debate in this area, it has either centred on the limited nature of the proxy for performance used or on the adequacy of its construction.

While such criticisms are valid, they fail to address many of the contemporary debates about firm performance, most notably those relating to the broader impact of the organization on its external environment, that is, society, economy and the physical environment. Moreover, this narrowing of focus to concentrate on financial performance is inherent within the emergence of HRM itself as an area of practice, particularly for HR managers who use the linkage between HRM and bottom-line performance in a bid to gain greater legitimacy at the workplace.

Building on the work of Sen (1997, 2000), we suggest the need for both practitioners and researchers to take a broader notion of performance that involves factors that go beyond those of interest to the organization's financial shareholders, and which simultaneously allows the devotion of greater attention to the physical environmental, welfare and humanitarian concerns that have been either lost or devalued in the so-called HRM revolution of recent times. In taking this stance, we implicitly accept the position articulated by Ulrich in his 1997 paper that measurement of the relationship between human resources and performance is both feasible and desirable, but considerably more complex than most studies suggest. Our position is therefore in contrast to that taken by Pfeffer (1997) in the same volume that such measurement not only diverts attention from difficult-to-measure factors that are much more important for organizational success, but also enfeebles HR managers in their power struggles with others in their organizations, especially financial managers.

After a broad introduction setting out its main themes and the context in which it is sited, the chapter will examine some of the key papers in the HRM–performance literature, with particular emphasis on the measures of performance that they deploy. Each measure will be evaluated in relation to a variety of criteria and, most importantly, related to the stakeholders to whose interests it predominantly relates. Thereafter, the chapter will suggest alternative measures of performance that might have been deployed, and will consider why these have not been more widely used. It will conclude with a number of implications for future work on the HRM–performance link, and for the development of HRM as an area of practice. In particular, it will contend that future HRM and performance research should incorporate a new concept for performance that incorporates the wider aspects of differential performance that are of increasing importance in contemporary society.

HRM and performance: key developments and debates

Over the past two decades, HRM research has been consumed with seeking to establish a causal relationship between 'HRM' and 'performance'. Though the issue of causality remains largely unresolved, the conceptual and empirical work surrounding HRM and performance has progressed enough to suggest that HR practices are at least weakly correlated with performance. In fact, much of the evidence points to a positive and significant association between so-called high performance work systems (HPWS) involving sophisticated HRM policies and practices and performance (Bryson et al., 2005; Delaney and Huselid, 1996; Guest et al., 2003; Huselid, 1995; Patterson et al., 2004; Pfeffer, 1996). However, exactly how this happens and the extent of the impact of HRM *per se* on performance continues to be a matter of debate. Becker and Gerhart (1996) point out that the extant literature suggests that HR practices have considerable economic potential, but that there is little consensus as to how to achieve this potential. Therefore, the evidence is greeted with scepticism in some quarters due to a perception that the undertaking of more and more quantitative studies has resulted in the production of simply more data rather than greater knowledge (Edwards and Sengupta, 2010).

Theoretical underpinnings

The lack of any comprehensive theory to explain the link between HRM and performance (Guest, 1997) is partly responsible for this scepticism. However, it has been noted (for example Paauwe, 2009) that the field has advanced from rather simplistic models in which HR practices were simply shown to correlate directly with rather distant (financial) indicators to more advanced ways of theorizing and modelling HRM and performance relationships. It is argued that the presence of certain HRM practices or a combination of such practices contribute to behavioural and attitudinal outcomes of employees at the individual level which, in turn, affect Aggregated-level behaviour or HRM outcomes, such as labour productivity and employee turnover, which subsequently might impact upon organizational- or firm-level outcomes (Paauwe, 2009: 134).

Yet another significant development is that recent theoretical arguments have embraced the possibility that HRM influences organizational outcomes directly, unmediated by any HRM-related outcomes. For example, interventions in training, job design and performance management may improve employee effectiveness – whether through simply removing task-related obstacles to better performance or through enhancing employees' technical knowledge, skills and abilities (KSAs) – while leaving their HRM-related attitudes and behaviours, such as motivation and intention to leave, unchanged (Boselie et al., 2005: 79).

An increasingly popular approach is the AMO framework (Paauwe and Boselie, 2005). The elegance of the AMO theoretical framework is that it encompasses mediating changes in employee abilities (A), motivations (M) and opportunities to participate (O). Motivation is the explicitly 'HR-related' mediator here; the other two may be considered 'direct' influences on performance. Thus it combines both the direct and the indirect influences of HRM on performance.

A further refinement to the theoretical arguments is provided by the labour process critique which argues that while a HPWS may provide enhancements in discretion, these come to employees at the cost of stress, work intensification and job strain (Thompson and Harley, 2007). This is often cited as a factor underpinning the widespread increase in job stress witnessed in Western industrialized countries in recent years (Green and Whitfield, 2009).

Methodological limitations

One of the key methodological limitations in the HRM/performance literature has been the inability to address sufficiently the issue of causality. It is still open to debate as to whether high performing firms adopt high performance work practices or whether high performing firms owe their success to the adoption of these practices. Even though the issue of causality was recognized as being important more than a decade ago, little has been done to address this concern. The most common research design continues to be the quantitative survey based on cross-sectional analysis (Boselie et al., 2005; Ichniowski et al., 1997). These studies achieve generalizability at the cost of establishing the direction of causality. Since most studies focus primarily on the manufacturing sector, the generalizability of the findings has been questioned as well. Furthermore, many of the studies have been labelled as post-predictive because they measure HR practices after the performance period, resulting in those practices actually predicting past performance (Wright et al., 2005: 412). A few recent studies (Guest et al., 2003; Patterson et al., 2004; Truss, 2001) that have attempted to address the issue of causality by using longitudinal analysis have yielded divergent results. The results vary from showing no performance changes (Guest et al., 2003) to some negative outcomes (Truss, 2001) to mixed results with certain practices yielding performance benefits (Patterson et al., 2004).

While longitudinal studies may assist in establishing the direction of causality, they are not devoid of limitations. Many such studies are limited in that they have not resolved the issue of a time lag and the issue of attribution. For example, it is unclear as to how much time should elapse in order to realistically capture the effect of HRM on performance. If the time lag is long, one may be measuring the effects of factors other than HRM, whereas too short a time lag may result in understating the positive HRM and performance link, since the performance effects may not yet be evident. There is still debate as to what is the appropriate time in which to measure the performance effects of HRM since HRM benefits may not be realized for several years (Huselid and Becker, 1996) or performance may dip immediately following a change in HRM (Pil and Macduffie, 1996).

There is no easy answer to this question since the time lag could be influenced by a number of factors, such as the industry (manufacturing and public sector enterprises would typically have longer timescales whereas the services sector may have shorter timescales) and the nature of HR practices under consideration. For example, employee involvement schemes may have a more indirect effect on labour productivity in comparison to training and development which are likely to affect skill levels and have a more immediate effect on employee efficiency and productivity and ultimately financial performance. Furthermore, not all dimensions of performance may be affected at the same time by the various HR practices. For example, it is argued that HR practices have a more immediate effect on labour productivity in comparison to financial performance. Consequently, different timescales have to be considered in order to effectively capture the effect of HRM practices on these two dimensions of performance. Finally, not all HPWS practices may be introduced at the same time posing further dilemmas as to at what point of time performance should be measured to capture the effects of these practices. This problem is especially relevant in a study involving a group of companies implementing HPWS at various points of time. Given that different research methods have their own limitations, the way forward would be to embrace a multi-method study or one involving a triangulation of different methods.

Conceptual issues: HRM

Advances have recently been made with respect to the conceptualization of HRM. These developments suggest that there is some agreement on a working definition of HRM as the management of employees, rather than a distinct approach to workforce management, and there is growing consensus as to the broad areas covered by HRM (Heery, 2008). At the core there exists a set of practices that are considered to be essential for good practice across all organizations. These include sophisticated selection, appraisal, training, teamwork, communication, job design, empowerment, participation, performance-related pay, promotion, harmonization of employment status and employment security (Wall and Wood, 2005). Furthermore, terms such as high performance work systems (HPWS), high performance work practices (HPWP) and high involvement management (HIM) have been coined to refer to a set of practices which, when implemented, contributes to high performance in an organization. However, this is where the consensus ends.

The fundamental debate about whether HRM exists as a set of universal best practices ('universalist' or 'best practice' perspective) or as an integrated and coherent bundle of mutually reinforcing practices (Wall and Wood, 2005: 73) tailored to the strategy and organizational context ('contingency' or 'best fit' perspective) has matured. The empirical evidence leans towards the best practice approach (Bryson et al., 2005; Delaney and Huselid, 1996; Guest et al., 2003; Patterson et al., 2004; Pfeffer, 1996). However, there is a lack of consensus as to what constitutes a high performance HR strategy. Studies of so-called high performance work systems vary significantly as to the practices included and sometimes even as to whether a practice is likely to be positively or negatively related to high performance (Pfeffer, 1996: 784). As a consequence, the recent trend has been to move away from the universal best practice view and instead there is a dominance of contingency frameworks, whereby HRM is viewed in relation to the external environment or to organizational strategy (Barney, 1991). There is some evidence in support of the best fit approach (Harney and Dundon, 2006; Kinnie et al., 2005). However, there is a lack of consensus as to what is the most effective combination of HR practices, which bundles work best together and what are the key contextual factors that affect the HRM/performance relationship.

In some sense, the 'best practice' and 'best fit' perspectives need not be alternatives and there may be a place for both. At one level, there may be a set of universal best/good practices that benefit all organizations. At another level, the practices may need to be tailored to the specific needs of the organization, the strategy, the employees and the organizational and environmental context (Edwards and Sengupta, 2010). This is demonstrated in the work of Kinnie et al. (2005) who identified the need to tailor HR practices to fit with the expectations and needs of employees, but also suggested that there is a set of policies that are important for all groups of employees regardless of context (Kinnie et al., 2005: 24). For workers, rewards and recognition, communication, openness and work–life balance were of primary importance. This suggests that in addition to the tailored policies, there is an underpinning layer of generic HR practices associated with identity and recognition that are desirable for all types of employees. Along similar lines, Godard (2004) suggested that it makes sense to adopt good management practices with some alternative work practices grafted on top. Thus, it may be more helpful to resolve this 'best practice' versus 'best fit' debate by viewing HRM practices in terms of 'hygiene' factors and 'motivators'. There is a set of universal 'good' or 'best practices' that would benefit all organizations. While their presence may not guarantee higher performance, their absence would lead to loss of performance and costs in terms of an unhappy and dissatisfied workforce, low commitment and poor working conditions. Therefore, the presence of these practices can be advocated as being essential for organizational well-being. It can be noted though that currently no accepted theory exists that might classify different practices into 'obligatory' and 'optional', 'hygiene' factors and 'motivators' (Boselie et al., 2005: 73).

While there is some consensus as to what practices constitute a high performance work system, there is some debate about how they should be measured. There has been some development in this respect. The mere presence of practices does not determine that they are in fact used. What matters is the quality of implementation in terms of effectiveness and procedural justice. This realization has implications for the conceptualization and measurement of HRM. Measures of HRM should include provisions for looking at the implementation of HRM practices. A HPWS can be measured in three ways: its presence, its coverage (proportion of workforce covered) and its intensity (degree to which an individual employee is exposed to the practice or policy) (Boselie et al., 2005: 74). A majority of studies have relied on presence, few have used coverage (Guest et al., 2003; Huselid, 1995) and only one has examined intensity (Truss, 2001).

Conceptual issues: organizational performance

While there has been some advance in the conceptualization of HRM, the performance measure has been relatively neglected. A very simplistic view of performance has been typically adopted. The tendency has been to focus on financial measures of performance to the neglect of other performance dimensions (Boselie et al., 2005). Guest (1997) has questioned the use of this performance indicator because of the causal distance between HRM inputs and outputs based on financial performance. So many other variables, both internal and external, affect an organization's financial performance that this direct linkage strains credibility. Use of more 'proximal' outcome indicators, particularly those over which the workforce may enjoy some influence, is both theoretically more plausible and methodologically easier (Boselie et al., 2005: 75). Oddly, given how HRM's impact on performance is typically depicted as being refracted through changes in employee attitudes and behaviours, measures of employees' experiences are somewhat rare. The need for more proximal measures has resulted in the broadening of the performance measure to include behavioural outcomes, such as employee turnover and absence rates, and employee attitudes (e.g. job satisfaction, commitment). The most popular indicators are hard measures, such as employee turnover and absenteeism.

Most studies continue to rely on the subjective assessment of a single respondent (typically the manager) while measuring HRM practices and/or hard objective performance outcomes such as financial performance, labour productivity, turnover and absenteeism. Often the use of multiple respondents is advocated in order to minimize single respondent bias when subjective measures of performance are used. However, this can prove to be very expensive and time consuming, and hence the use of single respondents is more prevalent. Therefore, practical considerations often supersede conceptual refinements in research design.

Until recently, the credibility of subjective measures of performance had been questioned primarily because of the tendency for respondents to exaggerate performance effects. While the desirability of having a blend of subjective and objective performance measures is stressed (Paauwe and Richardson, 2001), there has been wide acceptance of the credibility of the subjective performance measures as a reliable estimate of company performance. Wall et al. (2004) combined findings from two studies (Michie et al., 2003; Patterson et al., 2004) and three samples to examine the validity of self-report measures of company financial performance. The first study looked at 80 UK firms in the manufacturing sector and the second was based on a stratified sample of publicly quoted UK manufacturing and service sector firms with more than 50 employees. Based on the findings, Wall et al. (2004) concluded that the subjective performance measures were shown to be related to the objective performance measures. The degree of equivalence between the findings for subjective and objective measures means we can have some confidence in findings from studies so far that have been based on subjective performance criteria. Correspondingly, the findings support the use of subjective performance measures in future studies where objective ones may not be feasible; for instance in certain sectors of the economy. Support was also provided by Machin and Stewart (1996) who argued that subjective measures are defensible on the grounds that objective measures are often socially constructed, are subject to manipulation and previous workplace surveys have shown that those establishments where respondents report poor performance subsequently have lower chances of survival. In a study of 366 companies in the manufacturing and the services sector, Guest et al. (2003) found that the use of HRM was associated with higher performance irrespective of whether a subjective or objective measure of performance was used.

Increasingly the emphasis is on recognizing the multidimensionality of the performance construct. Guest (1997) advocated the concept of a balanced scorecard, which was originally devised by management theorists David Kaplan and Richard Norton who recognized that organizations often focused too much on financial criteria, thereby neglecting other features that help to deliver competitive advantage (Heery and Noon, 2008: 21). The balanced scorecard was conceived as a template that would allow managers to measure their broader vision by balancing the financial perspective with three other, equally important perspectives: the customer, the internal process and innovation and learning. At best, the balanced scorecard provides alternative ways to measure different dimensions of a very narrow view of performance focused on maximizing competitive advantage. In so doing, it reinforced the managerialist view that has dominated the field of HRM over two decades, and failed to take into account the perspectives of other key stakeholders.

This gap was addressed by Rogers and Wright (1998) who introduced the Performance Information Market (PIM) system to allow organizations to be evaluated on their stated objectives and allow stakeholders to evaluate both the organizational objectives themselves and how well the organization is achieving them. Four distinct performance information markets were proposed: (1) the financial market, (2) the labour market, (3) the consumer (product) market and (4) the political (social) market. They argued that organizations compete in all four markets for success though with different preferential weights of importance. In so doing, they introduced a dynamic element to the performance mechanism. Rogers and Wright (1998) argue that recognizing different PIMs allows a relaxation of the need for singularity of time period in the performance construct because the four markets can use different time bases. For example, the financial information market is primarily driven by investor time preferences. The labour market clearly looks beyond quarterly performance to career management and long-term equity development (intellectual asset appreciation). Environmental and social concerns may be operationalized on an even longer time frame (Rogers and Wright, 1998: 327). Not only did Rogers and Wright identify the key stakeholder groups, they acknowledged that, depending on the organization structure and purpose, the weighting of the PIMs will vary. These weightings will also change with time and circumstance (e.g. the Exxon Valdez oil spill accident raised Exxon's relative importance in the Political/Social market). This framework of PIMs may provide a mechanism to integrate and quantify organizational objectives to build a multidimensional dynamic construct for organizational performance.

Therefore, these models laid the foundations for a development of a future performance index based on different stakeholder perspectives by defining who the key stakeholders are, and suggesting that their relative importance would be context dependent. However, they provided no indication of what the key stakeholder interests were and how to measure them. Isolated efforts have been made in that direction by Business in the Community, Kinder, Lyndenberg and Domini Research & Analytics, Inc. (KLD) and independent retailers such as Wal-Mart. These different organizations have attempted to develop performance measures and sustainability indexes to represent the interest of the different stakeholder groups and changing societal expectations. Our proposed stakeholder-based performance index, presented below, builds on the balanced scorecard model and the PIM system, as well as the existing sustainability indices to develop a multidimensional framework for measuring performance.

Advances have been made in theory whereby the human dimension has been recognized as an outcome of interest, but the assumption is predominantly that it is a precursor to financial performance rather than an end in itself, thereby still ascribing greatest importance to financial performance rather than placing the human dimension on an equal footing. For example, the Guest model (1997) suggests that human resource-based performance outcomes contribute to higher financial performance. However, this is not always the case; in fact, higher labour productivity may sometimes mean lower financial performance. For example increases in labour productivity may be accompanied by higher wage costs thereby resulting in lower profits (Freeman and Medoff, 1984). Furthermore, the production of higher quality goods and services is often achieved at the expense of higher costs, and this may cut into the profit margin. Therefore, by placing financial performance as the final performance indicator one is still serving the managerialist agenda. Similarly, lower employee turnover may contribute to greater productivity in some firms, but in others holding onto inefficient employees may actually result in lower productive efficiency and possibly lower profits. Some industries are more suited to holding on to key employees and yielding productive efficiencies through developing an internal labour market. Others, particularly creative and media firms, thrive on high employee turnover to remain efficient, lean and flexible (Sengupta et al., 2009).

Paauwe (2009) recognized the need to move beyond a purely economic focus and argued that HRM is in need of studies that reconsider the conceptualization and measurement of performance. A broader, multiple stakeholder conceptualization of HRM and performance is advocated, that takes into account performance in terms of flexibility, agility and legitimacy (Boxall and Purcell, 2003), as well as various aspects of employee well-being such as satisfaction, stress, health and safety and job security (Godard, 2004; Guest, 2002). Others advocate an even broader perspective which goes beyond the stakeholders within organizational boundaries. Janssens and Steyaert (2009) argue that, by focusing on performance outcomes, even if operationalized in a multidimensional way, HRM seems to consider only stakeholders within the organizational boundaries, overlooking the impact of HRM practices on society. A broader notion of outcome would consider the long-term impact on different stakeholders in society by embracing an economic, social and ecological dimension. Such a broad notion of performance typified not only much work in the Personnel Management tradition, but also work in the early HRM tradition associated with the so-called Harvard School (Beer et al., 1985).

Thus, the concept of the multidimensionality of the performance construct raises several larger questions. Do we conceptualize organizational performance in terms of the overall well-being of the key stakeholders in the organization (employees, customers, shareholders, suppliers), or do we go beyond the stakeholders within organizational boundaries to include other actors? Which stakeholders should we consider? Will all stakeholders' needs be given equal weight? How can we measure the key dimensions of performance? Are there standardized measures for assessing the different performance dimensions, or are these context-specific?

A new performance paradigm: moving beyond financial performance

A strong case exists for developing a multidimensional performance measure that looks beyond financial performance. First, financial indicators tend to have a short-term focus. The time constraints of financial information markets are a commonly cited obstacle to achieving more robust measures of organizational performance (Rogers and Wright, 1998).

Second, when researchers focus exclusively on financial or market performance, they tend to ignore the bigger picture, and whether high financial performance is being achieved at the cost of other stakeholders or indeed the organization's long-term future. For example, efficiency and cost-cutting measures may prove to be beneficial for shareholders and customers, but are not as appealing to employees, who may have to accept lower levels of pay or lesser health benefits. Organizations that score highly on financial performance indicators may not be doing equally well on other types of metric that focus on other stakeholders. Conversely, an organization that is not performing well financially may be performing well from another stakeholder's perspective (Colakoglu et al., 2006). A general point that can be made here is that firms can destroy trust and goodwill, among other things, through cost-cutting. This may be good for short-term financial outcomes but bad for the social capital of the organization and potentially damaging to its long-term viability.

Third, organizational performance means different things to different people and it is simplistic to assume that all organizations are guided purely by the need to maximize shareholder wealth. Indeed, Colakoglu et al. (2006) argue that while financial performance metrics are certainly critical for organizational success, it may be too simplistic to focus primarily on the financial performance of organizations as an indication of the effectiveness of HR initiatives or as an indication that they are capable of sustaining that performance. Internally, employees vary with respect to their contribution to the core business of an organization (Huselid et al., 2005) and, externally, organizations vary on the relative importance of their obligations to different stakeholder groups (Jones and Wicks, 1999). Furthermore, different organizations vary with respect to how they define performance. To some, it may be short-term profit maximization, while others such as public utility services may have a more long-term focus of capturing a large market share or building a strong customer base. Therefore, it is important to acknowledge that certain performance measures may mean more or less to different organizations depending on their strategic objectives and definition of success.

A link can be made here to best fit models of HRM. If the objective is to be the lowest cost producer with strong financial returns, the measures of performance and the HR practices will be very different from an organization with, say, innovation as its key objective. Moreover, in relation to the question of the relevant time frame for the analysis, this will be short for the cost minimizer, and longer for the innovator. Furthermore, HR practices will work very directly on employee productivity in the cost minimizing firm, but more indirectly in the innovator with its need to build trust, a willingness to experiment and take risks without fear of retribution. This is illustrated in Table 5.1.

The need for a broader performance measure is increasingly acknowledged by HR researchers (Keegan and Boselie, 2006). This view fits with the mounting pressures on organizations to behave ethically and responsibly towards society rather than being blindly guided by financial motives. Thus, in July 2002, the UK Government published a White Paper, *Modernising Company Law*, which recommended that UK companies should be required to prepare and publish an Operating and Financial Review (OFR), including material items relating to social, community and environmental performance (BITC, 2009). The recent interest and rise in corporate social responsibility (CSR) in the hierarchy of issues that businesses are encouraged to address draws attention to additional non-financial performance indicators. These include the physical environment, human rights and fair trade. Evidently, there is an international trend towards companies and public authorities becoming more interested in 'ethically' and 'socially' responsible corporate behaviour (Sachdev, 2006).

Advocates of CSR view it as introducing an ethical code to guide the conduct of business. This is seen to involve the striking of a balance between the needs for efficiency, and the upholding of decent labour standards and

Table 5.1 Business strategies, time frames, performance measures and HR strategies and policies

Business strategies	Cost minimization	Quality	Innovation
Time frame for HR polices to have effect on employee performance	Short term	Short/medium term	Medium/long term
Performance measures	Financial	Financial plus customer-focused (e.g. satisfaction, loyalty, complaints)	New products/patents, market growth, customer measures plus employee outcomes
Human Resource Strategy	HR policies expected to work in isolation	Key combinations of HR policies (e.g. teams and group pay/bonus systems)	High Performance Work System/ everything has to work together or the company will not perform

Table 5.1 (Continued)

Business strategies	Cost minimization	Quality	Innovation
Human Resource Policies	Fixed and explicit job descriptions; narrowly designed jobs and career paths; short-term, results-oriented performance appraisals; close monitoring of market pay levels for compensation decisions; minimal training and development	Fixed and explicit job descriptions; high levels of employee participation in decision-making relevant to immediate concerns; mix of individual and group criteria for performance appraisal; relatively egalitarian treatment of employees and guarantees of employment security; extensive and continuous training	Jobs that require close interaction and coordination; performance appraisals that reflect longer-term and group achievements; jobs that allow employees to develop a wide range of skills; compensation that emphasizes internal equity; low pay-rates and a wide mix of other components; broad career paths

Source: Based on Schuler and Jackson (1987).

environmental and societal responsibilities. Sceptics, in contrast, consider CSR either to be a fig leaf to enhance business reputation (Klein, 2000), or a wasteful distraction from the proper activities of a firm (Henderson, 2001). Those who adopt the latter position often quote Friedman's (1993) statement that, 'there is one and only one social responsibility of business – to use its resources and engage in activities designed to increase its profits so long as it stays within the rules of the game'. Indeed, some businesses are openly hostile to the concept of CSR; the chairman and chief executive of ExxonMobil, Lee Raymond, declared that, 'we don't invest to make social statements at the expense of shareholder return' (cited in McNulty, 2003).

Despite claims of this kind, there is a strong economic argument for considering the interests of stakeholders other than the shareholders. Orlitzky et al. (2003) conducted a meta-analysis of 52 studies from 1970 to 2003, and their 'conservative estimates' strongly support their hypothesis that higher corporate social performance leads to better financial performance (Arora and Petrova, 2009). Additional support was provided by a recent study based on data from 695 companies that have been continuously rated on social performance for the years 2001–2005 by the firm Kinder, Lyndenberg and Domini (KLD). The findings indicate that proactive policies with respect to employees and diversity are the policies most strongly related to financial performance. In addition, a combination of employee and environment policies seemingly help firms further improve their financial performance (Arora and Petrova, 2009).

Given these concerns, it is surprising that Sen's (1987) Human Development Index (HDI) has not been adapted to consider organizational performance. The HDI measures the development of a country based on a mix of measures reflecting the quality of life of individuals, such as life expectancy, literacy, educational attainment and traditional economic measures such as GDP per capita. Essentially, the HDI recognizes the need for a more balanced measure of country performance by factoring in the human component. In doing so, the HDI has revolutionized the way in which the performance/development of countries is measured. This index has become an important alternative to the traditional uni-dimensional measure of development based on gross domestic product. Although the index still fails to include any ecological considerations, it has redefined what constitutes development. A similar index could be developed for evaluating company performance, particularly as the field of HRM professes to recognize the human dimension by virtue of its definition. Prior to developing a similar index for evaluating company performance, two key questions need to be addressed. First, what should be the key dimensions of the multidimensional performance measure? Second, how do we measure the different performance dimensions or the new standards of performance?

Conceptualization of the performance measure: key dimensions

While there is a compelling case for adopting a performance measure based on a multiple stakeholder perspective, it is not clear as to who should be the key stakeholders or whether each stakeholder should be given equal weight. This is an important dilemma since there can be a huge range of potential stakeholders; anyone who has a stake/interest in the company's performance. Hence, the stakeholders can range from employees, customers and suppliers to local government, society and the physical environment. Balancing the diverse interests of the multiple stakeholders is also challenging. By definition, stakeholders have diverse and potentially conflicting interests. If there is a pie to be shared by different stakeholders, it may be the case that each stakeholder group desires to increase its share at the cost of other stakeholders.

Given the wide range, to what extent can/should the performance dimension factor in the interests of all stakeholders? One view is to restrict consideration only to those stakeholders who fall within organizational boundaries, such as employees (Paauwe, 2004). The alternative is to cast the net more broadly and consider impacts on external stakeholders, including the wider society and natural environment (Janssens and Staeyart, 2009).

One way of exploring this issue further is through the concept of resource dependence, which suggests that different stakeholders have varying salience for firm performance because of the difference in resources that they offer and contribute. On this view, the employees and the capital owners have the greatest stake both in terms of their contribution to the firm as well as their dependence on it. They are critical to the organization's performance for several reasons. First, they offer three of the fundamental factors of production, that is, labour, capital and enterprise. They have the maximum stake in the organization in terms of time, money, effort and sense of identity. While the contribution of the capital owners to the business is widely recognized, the critical contribution of employees is often overlooked. Recent research (e.g. Heskett et al., 2003; Zaltman and Zaltman, 2008), however, has suggested that employees are the critical link in the corporate social performance/financial performance relationship. Zaltman and Zaltman (2008) suggest that only satisfied employees can create a satisfied consumer base and lifelong profits. This is consistent with Barnett's (2007) position. He asserts that employees are vital in improving the firm's relationship with all other stakeholders. His concept of stakeholder-influence capacity assigns a pivotal role to the employees in developing the organization's relationships with other stakeholders. These relationships are likely to translate into long-term sustained profits and thereby sustainable performance. Furthermore, employees control a resource critical to firm performance: their knowledge, skills and attitudes. They often also work in close geographical or psychological proximity, have access to decision-makers and thus have the capacity to significantly influence firms' short-term and long-term performance (Arora and Petrova, 2009). The interests of employees and shareholders are given the greatest weight in our proposed stakeholder-based performance index.

Consumers too are quintessential for the survival of the business. Empirical evidence indicates that firms with satisfied customers enjoy premium prices, higher levels of cash flow and less price volatility (Luo and Bhattacharya, 2006), and thus superior overall market value (Fornell et al., 2006). However, customer dependence on the firm varies and is not as high as in the case of the capital owners and employees. Customers have less at stake because they can turn to another company if they do not like a product, or if the company fails to deliver. The level and direction of dependency depends upon whether it is a monopoly or perfectly competitive market. In a monopoly situation, the dependency relationship changes whereby the customer is dependent upon the organization, but in cases of perfect competition the power resides with the customer. Even so, there are sufficient political pressures and a sound legislative framework in most regulated markets to protect the consumer interest in a monopoly situation. Responsibility towards customers does not lie entirely with the firm. Therefore, firms have a relatively weaker obligation towards upholding the interests of their customers. Hence, there is a compelling practical argument in favour of developing a performance index which embraces customer satisfaction, while regarding this as less critical than employee well-being and shareholder value.

In an institutional environment where firms are under strong pressure to adopt proactive environmental policies to minimize their carbon footprint, prevent damage to the environment and be more concerned about climate change, the resource dependence perspective propositions that organizations can enhance their legitimacy and social fit by responding to these salient social concerns and normative pressures. However, the empirical evidence on proactive environmental protection and firm profitability is rather scarce. While Russo and Fouts (1997) reported a positive relationship between environmental performance and profitability, Halme and Niskanen (2001) found that the immediate stock market reaction to announcements of environmental investments was negative (Arora and Petrova, 2009). King and Lenox (2002: 289) found strong evidence that waste prevention leads to financial gain, but they also found no evidence for increased firm profitability from 'reducing pollution by other means'. Based on the evidence, we decide that physical environmental factors are important but are lower in the hierarchy, except in the case of industries that produce goods and services which have a direct negative bearing on the physical environment, such as tobacco and petroleum. These organizations could counteract negative effects by engaging in activities that benefit society and the physical environment (e.g. via developmental projects or by paying higher taxes).

Finally, there are a number of other social performance activities often termed as 'community service', such as making philanthropic contributions, supporting human rights, protecting minorities and so on. While often laudable in nature, the theoretical argument and empirical evidence as to why these activities will lead to superior firm financial performance are weak for two reasons. First, from a resource dependence perspective, these stakeholders do not have much to contribute to firm performance (Arora and Petrova, 2009). Second, much of the philanthropic activity is concentrated locally and hence these activities do not directly touch the lives of much the firms' consumer base, and therefore cannot be expected to yield direct and significant payoffs. Empirical evidence also suggests that such social issue participation may not help the firm improve its financial performance (Hillman and Keim, 2001).

Therefore, based on the resource dependency view, it could be argued that capital owners, employees and customers form the core stakeholders followed by environmental considerations. It follows that our proposed stakeholder-based performance index should have indicators for measuring employee well-being, product quality/customer satisfaction and environment-friendly production processes.

Measurement

In constructing a broader measure of performance, there are numerous alternatives from which we can choose. Assuming that shareholder interest is reflected in maximizing financial performance, we can use a range of short-term and long-term financial indicators. For this, Return on Assets (ROA) is a common measure of operating performance as suggested by Arora and Petrova (2009). The Market to Book Ratio (MBR) is a good measure for market-based performance and is chosen because it is a measure that captures the relative success of firms in maximizing shareholder value through efficient allocation and management of scarce resources. In order to capture a dimension of sustainable economic growth productivity would be a useful indicator. Productivity is measured using the Gross Value Added per worker, data for which is readily available (Yakovieva et al., 2009).

For corporate social performance indicators, we rely on the Business in the Community report, *Winning with Integrity* (WWI) and the Workplace Employment Relations Survey 2004 data set. The WWI framework provides businesses with insights into measuring and reporting social and environmental performance. It was developed and tested by a group of 20 Business in the Community (BITC) member companies. The philosophy underlying the WWI framework is that responsible businesses are built on certain principles which take into consideration the interests of key stakeholders. These include:

- To treat employees fairly and equitably
- To operate ethically and with integrity
- To respect basic human rights
- To sustain the environment for future generations

The *Winning with Integrity* (WWI) reporting framework has proved to be robust and comprehensive. It is certainly one of the best tested reporting frameworks currently available (BITC, 2009).

Employee well-being depends upon the fulfilment of certain basic physical needs (pay, working time arrangements, work–life balance and clean, safe and secure working environment); higher motivation needs (sense of achievement and fulfilment from the job itself); and emotional well-being based on notions of fairness. Within HRM, well-being is commonly believed to involve promoting employee commitment, job satisfaction and satisfaction with work–life balance and lowering anxiety (Wood, 2008). Aspects like commitment are often manifest in behavioural outcomes, such as intention to remain and employee turnover. Employee satisfaction with various aspects of the job, such as pay, working conditions, work–life balance, work–time regulations and training received, provide further useful indicators of employee well-being.

Therefore, aspects of employee well-being are captured using a range of indicators from HR outcomes, such as low levels of employee turnover and absenteeism and employee expressions of satisfaction and commitment, as well as a low number of grievances. The workforce profile by gender, race, age and disability are useful indicators of the quality and diversity policy in the organization. The degree of compliance with basic health and safety procedures and the recordable incidence of breaches thereof, as well as the presence of grievance handling procedures, are reflective of the HR support available to employees. Finally, company investment in human capital in terms of value of training and development are indicative of opportunities for growth and development.

Most customers expect good quality products and or services at reasonable prices. For some, the quality or the perceived quality supersedes cost considerations, while others are guided primarily by cost. Irrespective of the particular preferences of customers there is one common goal they all seek – satisfaction. Therefore, customer satisfaction is often reflected in a customer satisfaction index or in the market shares captured by the company. Brand loyalty and market growth are some of the other indicators of customer responsiveness. Therefore, customer interests are captured through a range of indicators such as customer complaints about products and services, customer satisfaction levels, upheld cases of anti-competitive behaviour and provision for customers with special needs (BITC, 2009). Furthermore, a high score on the customer satisfaction index would indicate that the organization has the ability to hold onto its existing market share and even expand its share.

A key stakeholder whose interests have not been represented in any of the existing performance indices is the supplier. This is surprising since a good relationship with the supplier is often key to attaining performance targets. A healthy relationship with suppliers will ensure the timely and regular supply of good quality goods and services at reasonable prices, thus enabling the production process to run smoothly and customer demands to be met. This, in turn, will contribute to greater customer satisfaction, a ready market and a steady revenue stream. A supplier satisfaction index would be a good indicator of the nature of the supplier relationship. This index can be built along the lines of a customer satisfaction index since the nature of the relationship is very similar, even though the roles are reversed. The business becomes the customer and the supplier becomes the provider.

Finally, the environmental dimension is captured by using indicators that measure the extent to which the organization uses key natural resources, such as energy and water, and adversely affects the environment through carbon emissions and waste generation.

The different performance indicators, relating to all of the main stakeholders – investors, employees, customers, suppliers and the environment – are summarized in Table 5.2. Extending the dependent variable in studies of HRM and performance to embrace all of these additional measures of potential impacts, we feel, will enrich and reinvigorate the tradition and HRM and performance research.

Table 5.2 Stakeholder-based sustainable performance indicators

Stakeholders	Objective	Indicators
Core/Primary Stakeholders		
Shareholder	Maximize returns on capital investment	ROA
	Promotion of Economic Growth	MBR
		Productivity/Gross Value Added per workforce
Employee/Management	Fair and equitable working conditions	*Pay*
		Average pay relative to industry standards
		Equality and Diversity
		Workforce profile by Gender, Race, Disability and Age
		Health and Safety
		Number of legal non-compliances on health and safety legislation
		Number of recordable incidents (fatal and non-fatal)

		including sub-contractors
		Fairness
		Existence of confidential grievance procedures for workers
		Upheld cases of corrupt or unprofessional Behaviour
		Human Capital Development
		Value of training and development provided to staff
		Employee Satisfaction/Well-being indicators
		Perception measures of the company by its employees
		Staff absenteeism
		Staff Turnover rate
		Number of staff grievances
		Staff turnover
Customer	Provide good quality products at competitive prices	Customer complaints about products and services
		Customer satisfaction levels
		Upheld cases of anti-competitive behaviour
		Provision for customers with special needs
Supplier	Offer competitive prices for goods and services procured	Levels of supplier satisfaction
Environment	Reduction of resource use and protection of the natural environment	Overall energy consumption
		Water usage
		Solid waste produced by weight
	Reduce Energy consumption	Upheld cases of prosecution for environmental offences
	Reduce Water Consumption	CO_2/greenhouse gas emissions
	Minimize wastage	Other emissions (e.g. Ozone, Radiation, SOX, NOX etc.)
		Net CO_2/ greenhouse gas measures and offsetting effect

Table 5.2 (Continued)

Stakeholders	Objective	Indicators
Community	Minimize negative externalities and maximize positive externalities to the wider community	Cash value of company support as % of pre-tax profit
		Individual value of staff time, gifts in kind and management costs
		Perception of the company's performance on human rights by the local community

Conclusion

To date, the study of the impact of HRM on performance has been dominated by short-term financial considerations. It is argued in this chapter that it is time that the Human element in HRM took the lead, by contributing to the debate about what constitutes good and effective performance rather than how HRM can be modified to fit into the narrow managerialist definition of performance. HRM in its current form is consumed with pleading for or trying to justify its legitimacy in the workplace by showing how it can assist managers in fulfilling their profit maximizing objectives. In so focusing itself, it has lost touch with a set of broader issues that were central to Personnel Management and related to the non-financial aspects of an organization's performance. It is our view that these must be brought back towards the centre of the people management stage.

References

Anand, S. and Sen, A. (2000). 'Human development and economic sustainability,' *World Development*, 28 (12), 2029–49.

Arora, P. and Petrova, M. (2009). 'Corporate social performance, stakeholder coalitions, corporate governance and performance', *Social Science Research Network Working Paper Series*, June.

Barnett, M. (2007). 'Stakeholder influence capacity and the variability of financial returns to corporate social responsibility', *The Academy of Management Review (AMR)* 32, 794–816.

Barney, G. (1991). 'Firm resources and sustained competitive advantage', *Journal of Management*, 17 (11), 99–120.

Becker, B. and Gerhart, B. (1996). 'The impact of human resource management on organizational performance: progress and prospects', *Academy of Management Journal*, 39, 779–801.

Beer, M., Spector, B., Lawrence, P., Mills, D., Walton, R. (1985). *Human Resource Management: A General Manager's Perspective*. New York, Free Press.

Bolton, S. and Houlihan, M. (2007). *Searching for the Human in Human Resource Management*. London: Palgrave Macmillan.

Boselie, P., Dietz, G. and Boon, C. (2005). 'Commonalities and contradictions in HRM and performance research, *Human Resource Management Journal*, 15 (3), 67–94.

Boxall, P. and Purcell, J. (2003). *Strategy and Human Resource Management*. Basingstoke: Palgrave.

Bryson, A., Forth, J., Kirby, S. (2005). 'High-performance practices, trade union representation and workplace performance in Britain', *Scottish Journal of Political Economy*, 53 (3), 451–91.

Business in the Community (BITC). (2009). *The Indicators that Count: Social and Environmental Indicators – A Model for Reporting Impact*, http//:www.bitc.org.uk [Accessed 7 January 2010].

Colakoglu, S., Lepak, D. and Hong, Y. (2006). 'Measuring HRM effectiveness: considering multiple stakeholders in a global context, *Human Resource Management Review*, 16, 209–18.

Delaney, J.T., and Huselid, M.A. (1996). 'The impact of human resource management practices on performance in for-profit and non-profit organizations', *Academy of Management Journal*, 39 (4), 949–69.

Edwards, T. and Rees, C. (2006). *International Human Resource Management: Globalisation, National Systems and Multinational Companies*, London: Pearson.

Edwards, P. and Sengupta, S. (2010). 'Industrial relations and economic performance', in Colling, T. and Terry, M. (eds), *Industrial Relations: Theory and Practice, Third edition*, Oxford: Blackwell Publishing.

Fleetwood, S. and Hesketh, A. (2007). 'HRM-performance research: under-theorised and lacking in explanatory power,' *International Journal of Human Resource Management*, 17 (12), 1977–93.

Fornell, C., Mithas, F., Morgeson, III, and Krishnan, M. (2006). 'Customer satisfaction and stock prices: high returns, low risk, *Journal of Marketing*, 70, 3–14.

Freeman, R. and Medoff, J. (1984). *What Do Unions Do?*, New York: Basic Books.

Friedman, M. (1993, 1973). 'The social responsibility of business is to increase its profits', in Chryssides, G. and Kaler, J. (eds), *An Introduction to Business Ethics*, London: Thompson Business Press.

Godard, J. (2004). 'A critical assessment of the high-performance paradigm', *British Journal of Industrial Relations*, 42 (2), 349–78.

Green, F. and Whitfield, K. (2009). 'The employees' experience of work', in Brown, W., Bryson, A., Forth, J. and Whitfield, K. (eds), *The Evolution of the Modern Workplace*. Cambridge: Cambridge University Press.

Guest, D. (1997). 'Human resource management and performance: a review and research agenda', *International Journal of Human Resource Management*, 8 (3), 263–76.

Guest, D. (2002). 'Human resource management, corporate performance and employee well-being: building the workers into HRM', *Journal of Industrial Relations*, 44 (3), 335–58.

Guest, D., Michie, J., Conway, N. and Sheehan, M. (2003). 'Human resource management and corporate performance in the UK', *British Journal of Industrial Relations*, 41 (2), 291–314.

Halme, M., and Niskanen, J. (2001). 'Does corporate environmental protection increase or decrease shareholder value? The case of environmental investments, *Business Strategy and the Environment*, 10, 200–14.

Harney, B. and Dundon, T. (2006). 'Capturing complexity: An integrated approach to analyzing HRM in SMEs', *Human Resource Management Journal*, (16) 1, 48–73.

Heery, E. (2008). 'Runt Redux: the rise of human resource management as a field of study', *Work and Occupations*, 35 (3), 351–7.

Heery, E. and Noon, B. (2008). *A Dictionary of Human Resource Management*, Second edition. Oxford: Oxford University Press.

Henderson, D. (2001). 'The case against corporate social responsibility', *Policy*, 17 (2), 28–32.

Heskett, J., Sasser, W. and Schlesinger, L. (2003). *The Value Profit Chain: Treat Employees Like Customers and Customers Like Employees*. New York: The Free Press.

Hillman, A. and Keim, G. (2001). 'Shareholder value, stakeholder management, and social issues: what's the bottom line?', *Strategic Management Journal*, 22, 125–39.

Hoskisson, R., Hitt, M. and Hill, C. (1991). 'Managerial risk taking in diversified firms: an evolutionary perspective', *Organizational Science*, 23, 296–314.

Huselid, M. (1995). 'The impact of human resource management practices on turnover, productivity and corporate financial performance', *Academy of Management Journal*, 38 (4), 635–72.

Huselid, M. and Becker, B. (1996). 'Methodological issues in cross-sectional and panel estimates of the human resource – firm performance link', *Industrial Relations*, 35 (3), 400–22.

Huselid, M., Becker, B. and Beatty, R. (2005). *The Workforce Scorecard: Managing Human Capital to Execute Strategy*. Boston, MS: Harvard Business School Publishing.

Ichniowski, C., Shaw, K. and Prennushi, G. (1997). 'The effects of human resource management on productivity: a study of steel finishing lines', *American Economic Review*, 87 (3), 291–313.

Janssens, M. and Steyeart, C. (2009). 'HRM and performance: A plea for reflexivity in HRM studies', *Journal of Management Studies*, 46 (1), 143–55.

Jones, T. and Wicks, A. (1999). 'Convergent stakeholder theory', *Academy of Management Review*, 24, 206–21.

Keegan, A., and Boselie, P. (2006). 'The lack of impact of dissensus inspired analysis on developments in the; field of human resource management', *Journal of Management Studies*, 43 (7), 1492–511.

Kinnie, N., Hutchinson, S., Purcell, J., Rayton, B. and Swart, J. (2005). 'Satisfaction with HR practices and commitment to the organisation: why one size does not for all', *Human Resource Management Journal*, 15 (4), 9–29.

King, A., and Lenox, M. (2002). 'Exploring the locus of profitable pollution reduction', *Management Science*, 48, 289–99.

Klein, N. (2000). *No Logo*. London: Flamingo.

Luo, X., and Bhattacharya, C. (2006). 'Corporate social responsibility, customer satisfaction, and market value', *Journal of Marketing*, 70, 1–18.

Machin, S. and Stewart, M. (1996). 'Trade unions and financial performance', *Oxford Economic Papers*, 48 (2), 213–41.

McNulty, S. (2003). 'The oil company the greens love to hate', *Financial Times*, 11 June.

Michie, J., Conway, N. and Sheehan, M. (2003). 'Human resource management and performance in the UK', *British Journal of Industrial Relations*, 41 (2), 291–314.

Orlitzky, M., Schmidt, F.L. and Rynes, S. (2003). 'Corporate social and financial performance: a meta-analysis', *Organization Studies*, 24, 403.

Paauwe, J. (2004). *HRM and Performance: Unique Approaches for Achieving Longterm Viability*. Oxford: Oxford University Press.

Paauwe, J. (2009). 'HRM and performance: achievements, methodological issues and prospects', *Journal of Management Studies*, 46 (1), 129–42.

Paauwe, J. and Richardson, R. (2001). 'Editorial introduction: HRM and performance: confronting theory and reality', *International Journal of Human Resource Management*, 27 (1), 1985–091.

Paauwe, J. and Boselie, P. (2005). 'HRM and performance: what next?', *Human Resource Management*, 15 (4), 68–83.

Patterson, M.G., West, M.A. and Wall, T.D. (2004). 'Integrated manufacturing, empowerment and company performance', *Journal of Organizational Behavior*, 25 (4), 641–65.

Pfeffer, J. (1996). *Competitive Advantage Through People*, Boston: Harvard Business School Press.

Pfeffer, J. (1997). 'Pitfalls on the road to measurement: the dangerous liaison of human resources with the ideas of accounting and finance', *Human Resource Management*, 36 (3), 357–65.

Pil, F.K. and MacDuffie, J.P. (1996). 'The adoption of high involvement work practices', *Industrial Relations*, 35 (3), 423–55.

Rogers, E.W. and Wright, P.M. (1998). 'Measuring organizational performance in strategic human resource management: problems, prospects and performance information markets', *Human Resource Management Review*, 8 (3), 311–30.

Russo, M. and Fouts, P. (1997). 'A resource-based perspective on corporate environmental performance and profitability', *Academy of Management Journal*, 40, 534–59.

Sachdev, S. (2006). 'International corporate social responsibility and employment relations', in Edwards, T. and Rees, C. (eds), *International Human Resource Management: Globalization, National Systems and Multinational Companies*. Harlow, UK: Financial Times Prentice Hall, pp. 262–84.

Schuler, R. and Jackson, S. (1987). 'Linking competitive strategies with human resource management practices', *The Academy of Management Executive*, 1, 207–19.

Sen, A. (1987) *On Ethics and Economics*, Oxford: Basil Blackwell.

Sen, A. (1997). 'From income inequality to economic inequality', *Southern Economic Journal*, 2, 384–401.

Sen, A. (2000). 'A decade of human development,' *Journal of Human Development*, 1 (1), 17–23.

Sengupta, S., Edwards, P. and Tsai, C. (2009). 'The good, the bad and the ordinary: work identities in "good" and "bad" jobs in the UK', *Work and Occupations*, 36 (1), 26–55.

Thompson, P. and Harley, B. (2007). 'HRM and the worker: labor process perspectives', in Boxall, P., Purcell, J., Wright, P. (eds), *Oxford Handbook of Human Resource Management*. Oxford, New York: Oxford University Press, pp. 147–65.

Truss, K. (2001). 'Complexities and controversies in linking HRM with organizational outcomes', *Journal of Management Studies*, 38 (8), 1121–49.

Ulrich, D. (1997). 'Measuring human resources: an overview of practice and a prescription for results', *Human Resource Management*, 36 (3), 303–320.

Wall, T.D., Michie, J., Patterson, M., Wood, S.J., Sheehan, M., Clegg, C.W. and West, M.A. (2004). 'On the validity of subjective measures of company performance', *Personnel Psychology*, 57 (1), 95–118.

Wall, T.D., and Wood, S.J. (2005). 'The romance of human resource management and business performance, and the case for big science', *Human Relations*, 58, 429–62.

Wood, S. (2008). 'Job characteristics, employee voice and well-being in Britain', *Industrial Relations Journal*, 39 (2), 153–68.

Wright, P., Gardner, T., Moynihan, L. and Allen, M. (2005). 'The HR–performance relationship: examining causal direction', *Personnel Psychology*, 58, 409–46.

Yakovieva, N., Sarkis, J. and Sloan, T. (2009). 'Sustainable benchmarking of food supply chains', *GPMI Working Papers*, No. 2009-02.

Zaltman, G., and Zaltman, L. (2008). *Marketing Metaphoria: What Deep Metaphors Reveal About the Minds of Consumers*. Cambridge, MA: HBS Business Press.

Ethics, philosophy and the employment relationship

Mike Marinetto

Introduction: business ethics in a post-2/12 world

After some 4,000 years in the making, ethics has, at last, been embraced by business. So wholehearted has been this embrace that it seems business practitioners as well as management educators are ditching Tom Peters, Michael Hammer and Peter Drucker for Plato, Xenophon and Socrates. Long-cherished management doctrines like Business Re-Engineering or Total Quality Management (TQM) belong to the past. Now Aristotelian Nicomachean ethics or Kantian deontology is all the rage around corporate boardrooms. Diogenes may even be making a comeback too. The latter may be an exaggeration of sorts. Ethical codes of conduct and social policies for businesses are not seen as optional niceties. The Friedmanite view that the sole responsibility of business is profit-making belongs to a bygone era. It belonged to a time when ruthless CEO behemoths like Jack Welsh were bestriding the corporate planet. The Gordon Gekko[1] mantra that 'greed is good' has little credence in a post-2/12 world. Of course 2/12 is a reference to the 2nd December 2001 (the World Trade Center attacks were not the only epoch defining event of that year) when Enron, once the world's largest electricity and natural gas trader, filed for Chapter 11 bankruptcy protection. This was the biggest single bankruptcy in history.

Academics have followed these developments on the ground. Business schools in both the UK and the USA, especially, are providing courses in corporate social responsibility (CSR), while academics churn out chapters and papers on business ethics. The cultural turn is *passé*, business and management academics are looking to the *ethical turn*. Now, ethical theory and moral philosophy have been applied to various business mechanisms, practices and operations: human resource management, employment relations, marketing, finance, operational supply chains, customer relations, the production process, environmentalism, investment and financial reporting.

The employment relationship contains several ethical implications. The first part of this chapter examines the extent to which ethical theory and ideas have been adopted in studies of the employment relationship. Authors using ethical theory to explore the employment relationship have generally confined themselves to the classical field of normative ethics. These ethical investigations have been dominated by discussions of non-consequentialism, where the emphasis is on justice and equality, and consequentialism, where the onus is on balancing the needs of various interests. This chapter will underline both the importance of the classical tradition of ethics and its limitations. At the same time, there exist philosophical horizons beyond the consequentialism and non-consequentialism debate. The second half of this chapter considers existential philosophy and its application to the field of employment relations, especially the function of management. Here, thinkers such as Heidegger and Sartre, who may not seem at first glance like natural commentators on ethics, will be considered. Before heading into ethics and ethical theory, there is the spectre of modern capitalism and the role of employment relations to be considered.

Capitalism and industrial relations: ethical-free zones?

Unfortunately, we have to inhabit the real world. And in the real world, capitalism is likely to be with us in the short, medium and long term – or any other temporal category you could care to mention. To use the neo-Marxist terminology of Antonio Gramsci, managerial capitalism can be described as a hegemonic system, meaning it is all conquering and dominant. Some thinkers, such as Francis Fukuyama in his bestselling book from 1992, *The End of History*, go even further. For Fukuyama, there may be shifts and changes in this dominant economic system but capitalism remains the summit, it is the absolute horizon beyond which there are no other views. Even Slavoj Žižek, the

Slovenian intellectual dubbed the Elvis of modern philosophy, is resigned to the fact that *capitalism is indestructible*: '...Mao's attempt, in the Cultural Revolution, to wipe out the traces of capitalism, ended up in its triumphant return' (2007: 7). With some degree of irony Žižek notes that we should possibly wait for some form of divine intervention – a radical revolutionary spin on Heidegger's assertion: *Nur noch ein Gott kann uns retten*, which is translated as 'only a God can save us'.

As well as the nature of employment, large corporations are different from their small and medium enterprise (SME) counterparts in terms of ownership and governance. The governance structures of modern corporations are dominated by institutional shareholders (banks, investment companies, other corporations, pension funds, insurance companies), who now effectively form an ownership oligarchy. When did the corporate revolution take place? By the start of the twentieth century, the most significant areas of the American economy were under the auspices of corporate-owned industrial combines. Here, corporate-owned companies covered a broad constituency of business sectors. At this point in time, corporate ownership in Britain was confined to heavy industry (Hannah, 1983: 22). This changed very suddenly. The munitions programme that accompanied the First World War, as well as the threat of hostile takeovers by foreign corporations, sealed the fate of the family-owned enterprise in Britain. After the 1920s, the shareholder-owned joint stock enterprise had become a generalized feature of the British economy (Tawney, 1920). The changing face of corporate ownership during the interwar years was indicated by the growing number of firms quoted on the London Stock Exchange (LSE): in 1907, there were 569 domestic manufacturing and distribution firms quoted on the LSE; by 1924, the number had grown to 719, and in 1939, the figure stood at 1,712 quoted companies (Hannah, 1983: 61). Several family-owned businesses used their investments in the securities market to expand their operations. In 1919, 30 years after being floated on the stock market, the textile company, J & P Coats, became one of the first family-owned enterprises to gain corporate status. Ten years later, it was joined by the likes of Unilever, Imperial Tobacco, ICI, Courtaulds and Guinness. Although large corporate entities had existed before the 1920s, the interwar corporate merger boom in Britain covered a diverse range of industries and business interests. To make this point, Scott writes: 'By the Second World War "big business" was a more diverse, and more powerful, sector of activity, and it was increasingly determining the conditions under which smaller enterprises had to operate' (1985: 200).

For certain social scientists, the rise of the corporation was the harbinger of a brave new, and progressive, world. American scholars of repute – sociologists

Adolf Berle and Daniel Bell, as well as the economist Carl Kaysen – led the clarion call of this new corporate age. Such writers noted how the expansion of corporations and institutional share ownership during the first half of the twentieth century introduced a new phenomenon: the minority owned company in which shares are so widely dispersed that no single shareholder has an outright stake. The minority owned corporation became commonplace, which according to writers like Berle and Kaysen created a separation between ownership and control. The separation led to the non-partisan, managerial specialist taking the helm within companies. These specialists were not shackled to class or propertied interests and as such aspired to ideals of social responsibility. For Carl Kaysen, the corporate manager had the interest of the public, rather than shareholders, at heart:

> Its responsibilities to the general public are widespread: leadership in local charitable enterprises, concern with factory architecture and landscaping, provision of support for higher education, and even research in pure science, to name a few.

(1957: 313)

Adolf Berle (1959) made a similar point, arguing that the separation of ownership and control ensured the private company was accountable to a broad range of interests. This included the interests of employees as well as the public.

One of the few British academics to test the claims made by the likes of Kaysen and Berle was Theo Nichols (1969), in a study of businessmen from 'Northern City'. The study was based on a survey of 65 business managers selected from 15 companies located in Northern City. The respondents in Nichols' study showed a marginal, or rather a non-existent, concern about social responsibility or business ethics. Rather the businessmen surveyed were motivated by long-term company goals and professional advancement. The identification of an ethical, non-partisan cadre of corporate managers seemed premature. On closer inspection, the spectre of progressive management, supposedly ushered in by the corporate age, relied on naïve, Pollyannaish optimism than proper analysis. Nichols concluded that 'the conception of social responsibility held by most Northern City businessmen was some distance removed from that advocated or implied in much management literature' (1969: 239). This was to be expected as managers operated within organizations where the interests of certain stakeholders were prioritized above all others. Since Nichols' study, not a great deal has changed. The reasons why corporate managers came to embrace narrow instrumental goals will be explored below.

Corporate governance and the ethics of industrial and employment relations

The historic function of the corporation is different to that envisaged by the likes of Berle and Kaysen. As corporations came under a diffuse system of governance in the early twentieth century, distinct objectives and institutional structures came to the fore. What the nascent corporation stood for in these years became evident during notable court actions taken by shareholders in both America and Britain. The most significant cases pitted the interests of the owners (effectively the shareholders) against those of employees. For example, the *Hutton v. West Cork Railway Company* lawsuit of 1883 established an early legal precedent over the fiduciary responsibilities of company directors and managers; it set limits on how managers could expend company finances. The legal action was taken by shareholders, specifically, to decide whether a company, or rather its directors, had the mandate 'to expend a portion of its funds in gratuities to servants', that is, employees (Law Reports, 1883: 654). This legal ruling held major implications for any gratuitous payments to employees, particularly following insolvency. In his summary, Lord Justice Bowen maintained that charity is not the responsibility of business; directors were thus denied the freedom to make assistive payments to employees who found themselves embroiled in an insolvent company.[2]

Another seminal case came before the Supreme Court of Michigan, involving *Dodge v. Ford Motor Company*. In this case, the Ford Motor Company shareholders legally challenged the decision of the Ford directors to forgo the payment of special dividends. Henry Ford, the company president and major shareholder at the time, wanted to abandon special dividend payments from the surplus capital accumulated through the success of the Model T. Instead, he wanted to reinvest the surplus capital into building up the Ford brand and business. Specifically, Ford, who was known more for intensifying car production than for enlightened work practices, wanted to employ greater numbers. The rationale being that more workers would have the opportunity of sharing the benefits of the Ford factory system, helping them, in Ford's words, to 'build up their lives and their homes' (and to afford a Model T, more accurately) (Henry Ford, 1919, cited in Banerjee, 2007: 13). As with the Hutton case in Britain, the court sided with the shareholders at the expense of employees: 'Directors cannot shape and conduct the affairs of a corporation for the mere incidental benefit of shareholders and for the primary purpose of benefiting others' (*Dodge v. Ford Motor Company 1919*, cited in Banerjee, 2007: 13). The Michigan Supreme Court was not making CSR illegal, as such. The case, however, ensured that company directors would operate in a narrow remit, where the focus on profit margins and the interests of shareholders ruled supreme (Banerjee, 2007). To use the language employed in strategic management, the shareholder in the corporate world became the key stakeholder. And this had important repercussions for the employment relationship and scholarly research on this and other relationships within and beyond the corporation.

Owing to its size and economic reach, the modern corporation absorbed a variety of different stakeholders. American business ethics expert Edward Freeman defines 'stakeholders' as any group that is affected or can, in turn, influence the firm (1984: 25–6). And the various rulings outlined above ensured that propertied interests prevailed over those of other key stakeholder groups in the emerging corporation, namely: employees, suppliers, communities, customers. The modern corporation became the institutional embodiment of propertied interests: that the primary and only responsibility of the company is to shareholders who provide the financial resources to initiate and then maintain a business. But the primacy of property did not go unchallenged.

The political and economic development of the labour movement in both America and Britain from the 1800s onwards asserted the interest of employees against those of the propertied class. As the propertied interest was challenged within the nascent corporation, the academic community in the US responded with the formation of a new disciplinary field: industrial relations. Kaufman argues how industrial relations as a formal field of study emerged in the early 1920s, involving the analysis of labour–management relations and personnel management (2004: 24). Early industrial relations scholarship, Kaufman argues, had a strong normative dimension and promoted ethical principles about how work arrangements should be managed. In terms of ethics, corporate capitalism was seen to be inhumane, lacking in democracy in the workplace and the proper treatment of employees, whose interests are overlooked and subordinate to those of capital. For the likes of Sumner Slichter, John D. Rockefeller and John R. Commons, who devised the first university course of study in industrial relations at the University of Wisconsin, the unethical treatment of employees under the capitalism should be addressed through a sustained programme of reform; these reformist interventions would restore a semblance of justice for employees.

The ethical principles embraced and promoted by the founding fathers continued to hold sway among contemporary academic practitioners of industrial relations. In fact, one of the leading figures in the field, Thomas Kochan, argued that the normative assumptions about the workplace, which underlined the field of industrial relations, distinguished it from other cognate sub-disciplines (Kochan, 1998: 37). If anything, the normative assumptions of contemporary industrial relations theorists shifted more definitely in favour of trade unions and employee interests. By the same token, criticisms of management intensified. Although the contemporary academic literature emerging from industrial relations has a definite ethical worldview, morality and ethics is rarely addressed, according to Kaufman: 'the modern industrial relations literature is relatively slim when it comes to explicit attention to the ethical foundation of the field' (2005: 48). The exceptions to this rule are two prominent American academic figures: the late Jack Barbash and of course Kochan, both of whom addressed the ethical concerns of industrial relations. In fact, Barbash began studying employment ethics in the 1970s (see Barbash and Barbash, 1989; Kochan, 1998). The neglect of ethics can be explained in terms of the disciplinary influences within industrial relations. The intellectual tools used to explore industrial relations largely borrow from, and are influenced by, social science disciplines, especially economics and sociology. Ethical philosophy is less apparent. Karl Marx has been more the order of the day than Aristotle, Kant or Bentham. In fact, as professional academia has become increasingly specialized, we are less willing to take risks by synthesizing diverse approaches to knowledge. However, recent developments within the academic community of industrial relations scholars have created potential openings for more synthesized forms knowledge. Such developments are potentially more open to ethical philosophy.

The established way of doing things within the academic study of industrial relations is being challenged from within and without. The modern day workplace in the twenty-first century has witnessed a significant shift from manufacturing to the service sector and the concomitant decline of trade union membership and collective bargaining. There is also the feminization of the workforce to consider and related issues about the encroachment of work time and pressures into the domestic sphere. The changing spectre of employment and work has forced something of what Thomas Kuhn would term, 'a paradigm revolution' within the industrial relations field. Historically, the focus of industrial relations has been on trade unions and the regulation of collective bargaining within institutional settings. The consensus in the academic peer community, and this book is a testimony to this paradigmatic shift, is that industrial relations has to broaden its scope: to go beyond the old time religion of unions and collective bargaining and to focus more explicitly on the employment relationship within institutional settings (Sisson, 2008: 5–6). One contribution that set an early trend was Blyton and Turnbull's 1994 text, *The Dynamics of the Employment Relationship*. As well as reflecting changes within the workplace, the shift from industrial relations to the employment relationship has been partly driven by internal machinations within the social sciences. There is the ongoing, some would say circular, debate about critical realism, which has opened up new theoretical and methodological possibilities. Indeed, research on the employment relationship has increasingly adopted a multi-level and multi-disciplinary approach (see Heery, 2005). In addition, the dogged class-based perspective of industrial relations has been challenged by gender and race theory. The argument, here, is that not all forms of oppression and inequality, even in the workplace, can be reduced to, and explained by, social class (see Roscigno, 2007). Hence, developments in the workplace and changing intellectual fashions are reshaping industrial relations.

The employment relationship is concerned with a broad range of issues, many of which have definite ethical repercussions. For example: human resources, new social movements and industrial relations, state regulations of the employment relationship in a fragmented workplace, payment systems, workplace surveillance, employee participation, whistle-blowing, work–life balance and corporate governance. Indeed, modern management practices in the corporate milieu have made ethical considerations a matter of urgency and paramount importance. Schumann (2001) outlines a number of ethical issues relating to modern human resource management: should companies relocate to countries where regulation and pay are both low? Are employers morally obliged to deal with discrimination and harassment? Then there is the matter of pay. Larry Burkett, the conservative Christian ethicist, considers how employers should go about determining or setting a standard of 'just pay'. His answer boils down to empathy: put yourself in the shoes of your employees and see if you can live on their earnings (1998: 160). The conclusion is that there is certainly no shortage of grist for the ethical mill when it comes to the employment relationship. But to what extent has ethical philosophy and theory been preferred over social science models in order to understand these problems and dilemmas?

Employment ethicists: consequentialism versus non-consequentialism and beyond

Ethical theory has undoubtedly made some inroads into the academic study of the employment relationship within the modern workplace. Here are some examples worth mentioning. Budd (2004) used Kant, Rawls and Aristotelian ethics to examine the ethical standards of the employment relationship. Bowie

(1999) studied the Kantian repercussions of modern day employment practices. Winstanley (2000) adopted a humanistic model, informed by Kantian ethics, to evaluate performance management. In another notable study, Provis (2000) considered the ethical repercussions of deceptive negotiations between employers and employees. Schumann (2001) employed five complementary ethical frameworks – utilitarian, rights ethics, distributive justice ethics, care ethics and virtue ethics – to judge human resource management. While the study of employment relations has been more open to ethical analysis, the reach and influence of ethical theory is still limited in the academic study of industrial relations and human resources. We would expect, because of its focus, that the study of human resource management (hereafter, HRM) to be an exception, to make up for the limited deployment of ethical theory. But even here, according to Winstanley and Woodall, 'ethical issues have been of marginal significance to the academic debates around HRM' (2000: 4). Paradoxically, the authors argue, contemporary management research has diverted attention away from ethics and towards issues such as the strategic function and effectiveness of HRM. Budd and Scoville (2005) also weigh in, arguing that scholarship on the ethics of the employment relationship is rare. As well as the paucity of ethical coverage in employment analysis, there are other residual concerns.

Employment analysts, who have put their heads above the ethical parapet, tend to rely on a narrow range of ethical perspectives. Despite some of the exotic labels and names mentioned above, studying the ethical implications of the employment relationship has revolved around the classical theories of normative ethics. This has much to do with the fact that employment ethicists, for want of a better term, have been drawn in to making normative evaluations of practices in the workplace. As such, ethical analysis of the employment relationship is mainly synonymous with passing judgements about whether the managerial treatment of employees is moral or immoral, right or wrong (often it is the latter). The normative tradition in continental philosophy has been one dominated by two theoretical approaches that were popularized during the course of the eighteenth century: consequentialism and non-consequantialism. In terms of evaluating whether certain work-based practices are ethical or not, both traditions, as will be shown, provide distinct measures of how to reach these normative judgements.

Utilitarianism offers a flexible approach to ethics. This is clearly spelt out in the works of its classical founders, from the sixteenth century ideals, or lack of them, of Niccolò Machiavelli to the British political philosophers of the seventeenth century, Hobbes and Locke. It is flexible because the principles that guide morality are a movable feast. Here, what matters are the interests of the majority, even if this requires us to occasionally overlook, or deliberately undermine, the prospects of certain minorities. How do we translate these abstract concerns into moral guides for action? According to classical utilitarian thinkers like Mill and Bentham, an action is morally right if the greatest good for the greatest number is achieved. As such, the focus is on the consequences of action: you judge the ethical value of behaviours according to its consequences. Another way of putting this is that the ends justify the means. A notable example of a utilitarian calculus in practice within the field of employment is the theory and practice of HRM. The formative Michigan Business School model of HRM (see Fombrun et al., 1984) offers what Storey (1987) describes as a utilitarian instrumentalist approach to managing people. Here, the emphasis is on achieving a close strategic fit between the management of employees and corporate objectives. This means managerial practices such as training and recruitment are geared towards controlling and monitoring the performance of employees. The utilitarian pay-off in this low-trust approach towards managing people is clear: what is good for the organization is also good for employees, in the form of secure employment and higher rewards. In practice, though, human resource policies, even when they attempt to achieve a strategic fit, emerge as incoherent and full of contradictions (Legge, 1995).

The philosophical arch-enemy of the utilitarian ethical tradition is the eighteenth century German idealist philosopher, Immanuel Kant. Two works in particular, *Grundlegung zur Metaphysik der Sitten* (or *Groundwork of the Metaphysics of Morals*, 1785) and the second volume of his critique triptych, *Critique of Practical Reason* (1788), redefined the study of ethics. In Kant's ethical theory, what matters is that people act out of duty and sacrifice, even when to do so would militate against their own interests and not result in best outcomes for their own selves. Rather it is the intentions and motives which guide behaviour that are crucial in reaching normative judgements. Kant designed what are termed 'categorical imperatives' or 'maxims' – ethical commands – to decide whether the intentions that inform action can be regarded as truly ethical. And herein is another key departure with utilitarianism, for these maxims in Kant's ethical philosophy are to be applied as universal laws or commands. There are to be no ethical adjustments in accordance with calculations about net gain and so on. Possibly the key maxim, and the one which is most relevant to the employment relationship, centres upon what can be termed the *formula of humanity*. This particular Kantian formula orders that humanity should never be treated as a means to an end: 'man and generally any rational being exists as end in himself, not merely as a means to be arbitrarily used by this or that will, but in all his actions . . . must be always regarded at some time as an end' (Kant, 2008: 45). Of course, Kant does not rule out, absolutely, the possibility that we can treat people as means towards our own ends (Wood, 1999: 183). Living a normal life would be impossible otherwise. Rather it is the humanity within people, the ability to act rationally and to act independently and autonomously, which must be consistently treated as an end in its own right. In the employment relationship, the International Labour Organisation's (ILO) Declaration of Philadelphia of 1944, though it may not have explicitly drawn from the Kantian canon, applies the humanity formulae to the realm of labour. Here, the ILO declared that labour is not a commodity and should not be treated as such. A glaring example of how this principle can be infringed without thought in the modern workplace was revealed in Michael Moore's recent film, *Capitalism: A Love Story*. Moore looks at what is known as 'Dead Peasants Insurance', practiced by several high profile corporations like Wal-Mart and Bank of America. This involves companies taking out life insurance on employees without their consent or knowledge, which means they make a profit when the employee dies.

While setting out clear normative measures for distinguishing immoral from moral behaviour, these classical theories have their detractors. For critics, normative ethical theories, especially Kantian non-consequentialism and utilitarian consequentialism, provide a less than ideal starting point when trying to assess business processes and functions such as management. One such ethico-sceptic is John Kaler (1999), for whom business and management academics should maintain a clear distance from ethical theories. He is well qualified to make such arguments, having taught, and written a textbook on, business ethics. Such theories, he suggests, are of limited use in solving ethical problems in business or management. Why? Put simply, Kant and his utilitarian enemies are too reductionist for Kaler's taste. And there are reasonable grounds for this view. These established approaches are too reductionist in the sense that they define what is ethical according to very specific forms of behaviour or aspects of morality. Thus judging between right and wrong may be reduced to securing happiness *or* pleasure for others. Because of this, such theories, especially Kantian non-consequentialism, seem unworkable in the real world. When it comes to real life issues in the workplace, the normative benchmarks of utilitarians and Kantians have us going around in ever decreasing ethical circles. Moreover, applying these long-established ethical theories to complex issues can, with some theoretical sleight of hand, produce the same conclusions. Or they can provide the sort of answers that fit with a commentator's own predilections. In fact, for Kaler, ethical theories have become increasingly redundant, because business ethics textbooks and courses just pay lip service to 'the classics'.

From virtue ethics to existentialism

There is an alternative to the ethical caprices of eighteenth century philosophers. For students of the employment relationship who cannot ideologically stomach the libertarian ethos of utilitarianism, yet find Kantian ethics too punitive and restrictive, Aristotle's take on ethics has been a favoured option. Indeed, Kaler's rejection of classical ethical theory leads him to fall back on Aristotelian virtue ethics, with a hint, as he acknowledges, of utilitarianism thrown in for good measure (see Kaler, 1999: 211–12). Morality is equated with minimizing harm and promoting benefits for human beings. The main principle to be followed when, 'attempting to solve ethical problems is the extent to which the common good is or is not being served' (Kaler, 1999: 211). The business and philosophy scholar, Robert Solomon, in his 1992 book *Excellence and Ethics* acknowledges that Kant, the utilitarians and modern ethical philosophers like John Rawls are intriguing in their own way. But these normative theories are 'oblivious to the concrete business context and indifferent to the very particular roles people play in business' (1992: 99). Instead, Solomon advocates an Aristotelian approach to business, one relevant to both the institutional machine and to the cog-like human elements that make up businesses. Solomon argues that the Aristotelian virtues in business management would help 'cultivate whole human beings, not just jungle fighters, efficiency automatons, or "good soldiers"' (1992: 180). However, the institutional demands for economic returns create a fragmented and alienated humanity. Solomon notes how the search for an Aristotelian type of wholeness extends to the business organization. The Aristotelian virtue of holism, which looks at the bigger picture beyond sectional interests, requires companies to embrace a broader constituency of stakeholders: not just a narrow concern with shareholders but also a variety of affected groups, from communities to the environment. And Solomon is optimistic both about the ability of business to change and about the present ethical standing of corporations, arguing that there are a lot fewer corrupt corporations and lot greater managerial integrity than pessimists would have us believe. In fact, he goes on to argue how the search for success will depend on Aristotelian virtues rather than cut-throat, 'greed is good' Gekko virtues (1992: 266). All this is admirable but to an extent it is misplaced. And much of the fault lies with Aristotle.

Aristotle focused on good or bad agents rather than actions, and therefore considered the long-term progress of human character towards virtue. As Louden (1989) notes, the Aristotelian ethical schema is therefore unable to consider properly the occasional (and often inevitable) tragic outcomes of human existence; these are seen as mere blips or temporary aberrations and out of character (1989: 315). Solomon simply extends the developments towards virtue to corporate entities. But contrary to this position, critics would argue that the very governance structures of modern corporations promote vice rather than virtue. Joel Bakan (2005) argues that the corporation has the personality disorder of a psychopath, who values personal gain and profit at any cost. The mindless exploitation of labour in the developing world is a testament to this psychopathology. And this brings us back again to normative theories of ethics.

For all their dogmatic and formulaic approach to ethics, consequentialist and non-consequentialist approaches attempt to focus on what truly matters when it comes to ethics and morality. This is no bad thing. When we begin to consider issues from an ethical point of view, it creates more difficulties for us than straightforward solutions. Scientific or academic judgements are certainly less problematic. Ethics which is how we treat others in our conduct is a messy business, to say the least. It creates all sorts of quandaries and dilemmas. At least ethical theories tell us what matters in the dilemmas and complexities that we face, especially involved in the employment relationship. According to Jones et al. (2005), classical ethicists – Kant, Bentham, Mill and so on – identify key complaints or problems that we have with the world around us. These insights about what is missing from our world are relevant to the realms of work and management: 'Ethical theories describe what should be of fundamental importance in society and provide a rigorous avenue for evaluating specific HRIR [human resource and industrial relations] practices and outcomes' (Budd and Scoville, 2005: 17). The authors acknowledge that we should not abandon the intellectual vernacular of classical approaches to ethics. What should be discarded, instead, is their obsession with 'moral perfection and moral exemplarity'. Jones et al. argue that the fields of business and management studies should look to ethical theories that offer greater philosophical and practical insights (Jones et al., 2005: 140).

One possibility of a more analytical approach to ethics in the workplace is post-modern analysis. For example, Alexander Styhre's (2002) study of empowerment and the Kaizen system in Swedish companies was conducted through the prism of post-modern theory, specifically Michel Foucault's later work on ethics. Although post-modern analysis has its moments of real insight, there is a concern that something really essential is missing: the onus on social construction, fragmentation and a confluence of forces opens up a whole new world of excuses (see Robert Solomon in the Richard Linklater film, Waking Life). A philosophical tradition that confronts such excuses head on is existentialism. In fact, Robert Solomon in his later works, after earlier dismissing this tradition (1992: 252), notes how the existential school of philosophy has much to offer in terms of our understanding of the human condition (see Solomon, 2006). However, existential thought has largely fallen out of favour and fashion within the academic firmament. The *outré* status of existentialism has less to do with its intellectual qualities and insights. It has more to do with the whims and fancies of what is currently fashionable in academe. The existential tradition constitutes a shift away from a strict adherence to normative judgements towards analytical evaluations of ethics. It rises above the platitudes of Aristotle and the abstractions of post-modern theory which seem detached from everyday existence. Here, existentialism is less about making normative or prescriptive judgements than enabling us to understand and explore ethical behaviour in an analytical but also practical sense. In particular, this continental tradition penetrates how individuals grapple with ethical and normative judgements in their everyday, quotidian existence.

Upon first thought, it would appear that existentialism has little to offer in terms of ethics or a system of morality. In fact, it could be argued that existentialism would be wholly antithetical to such exercises. If we consider the philosophical antecedents of existentialism, such figures as Søren Kierkegaard and Friedrich Nietzsche sought to debunk Christian ethics. For example, in the *Genealogy of Morality*, Nietzsche shows how the ability to distinguish between right and wrong is a privilege of the powerful – it has nothing to do with actual truth. The oxymoronic status of existential ethics is given further support by two of existentialism's most celebrated philosophical exponents, Martin Heidegger and Jean-Paul Sartre.

The dense and evocative *tour de force* that is *Sein und Zeit* (1927) – or *Being and Time* – revolutionized the dominant philosophical tradition of Husserlian phenomenology at the turn of the twentieth century, placing existentialism at the forefront of continental philosophy. But Heidegger's *Being and Time* seemed to reject the notion of ethics out of hand. His inquiries, he would claim, are to do with what it means 'to be' in our normal everyday existence – and nothing to do with metaphysical ethics. The potential contribution that Heidegger could make to our understanding of ethics was further undermined by his personal life. He was a committed and paid up member of Hitler's Nazi Party, only relinquishing his membership in 1945. But Joanna Hodge (1995) questions whether Heidegger truly rejected ethics, with his ethical concerns focusing more on philosophy and less on metaphysics. Heidegger's phenomenological philosophy sought nothing more than a radical overhaul of the Western philosophical tradition, an ambition which had significant implications for ethics. The key contention is that, for Heidegger, there is no such thing as a fixed human essence; the old Aristotelian belief in the essence of man as a rational animal was debunked for good. Our existence as human beings comes before any essence – we are faced with different possibilities and the freedom to determine what it means to be or to exist. In *Being and Time*, he observes: 'Yet man's *substance* is not spirit as a synthesis of soul and body; it is rather *existence*' (1962: 153). What does existence involve? Essentially, human existence is one of radical rootlessness or ungroundedness. And this is why, according to Heidegger, we plunge into conformist, everyday activities to give our lives stable meaning (Dreyfus, 1991: 37).

For many, Jean-Paul Sartre was the paradigm of the modern *über* intellectual – a playwright, novelist, philosopher, activist and meteorologist, to boot. The intended audience for his challenging phenomenological credo was the general public rather than specialist philosophers. Indeed, Sartre's existentialism was a philosophy intended for all humanity. His existential message, greatly influenced by Heidegger and the phenomenology of Edmund Husserl, was an uncompromising call to personal and political revolution: to accept the responsibilities of individual freedom and to secure the overthrow of capitalism. As an independent and radical intellectual, he railed against establishments in both his own country and abroad. In his philosophy, especially that outlined and detailed in 1943's *L'Etre et le Neant* (*Being and Nothingness*), Sartre was accused of promoting a quiet desperation. Partly in response to such accusations, Sartre gave a lecture in 1945 in which he outlined existentialism as a constructive, humanist philosophy of action. The lecture was subsequently published and titled *Existentialism and Humanism* (1948), but the original title of the essay was 'existentialism is a humanism'. Although the essay has been criticized, even by Sartre, it provides some useful pointers for assessing management. His brand of existentialism offers a practical philosophy for those that find themselves facing moral and ethical quandaries, as those who have to manage the employment relationship often do. For Sartre, all of us have to face up to our moral responsibilities and this is often the cause of existential anxiety and torment, regardless of rank or position.

What follows attempts to use the insights from the existential philosophy of Martin Heidegger and John-Paul Sartre. Specifically, the intention here is to use these ideas to explore the ethics of management and the experience of being a manager of employees. Management oversees different aspects of the employment relationship, whether the setting of pay, intervening in discrimination cases or organizing redundancies. And there are significant ethical implications that arise from management which can be placed under existential scrutiny.

Management as a humanism: existentialism, ethics and managing the employment relationship

Managers, especially those occupying seats in human resource or personnel departments, will have to face morally unpalatable choices. There is a good reason for this. Modern organizations, especially those in the private sector, are ethical-unfriendly milieus. Businesses seem like ethical no-go areas because of the institutional drive to maximize profits for shareholders. As much of the advice for improving the ethics of the employment relationship requires a more equal sharing of profits, tensions exist between this ethical impulse and the partisan inclination towards profits found in most companies. So should we ditch the illusion that managers do have ethical choices? Lafer offers the following insight: 'beyond the straightforward financial conflict, there is still a wide range of employment practices that might be conducted in a more ethical manner' (2005: 280). Even if managers cannot change wage structures or the focus on profits, there are work-based employment practices that can make for a more ethical form of management. For example, the workplace can become less authoritarian or centralized. In fact, Ackers notes how managers are integral to building ethical considerations into the 'very structures and processes of economic life' (Ackers, 2009: 457). But if research is anything to go by managers, when it comes to the employment relationship, disregard such ethical discretion. Why? The existential ideas of Sartre and Heidegger provide useful insights into how managers deal with moral and ethical choices. As well as helping to develop an ethical assessment of management, existentialism furnishes practical advice on how mangers should approach ethically sensitive problems of the employment relationship.

Towards the end of *Being and Nothingness*, Sartre hints that he would look to write a substantive theory of ethics. Warnock notes how it has been suggested that Sartre's positive approach to moral philosophy was outlined in his lecture, turned essay, 'Existentialism is a Humanism' (Warnock, 2003: xvii). Sartre's 1945 lecture portrays existentialism as a positive system of thought because individual human beings are seen as responsible for their own destiny. Even if we find ourselves in the direst or extreme circumstances, we still have certain choices and freedoms at our disposal. For Sartre, as a committed atheist, without God and a system of metaphysical rules people are responsible for their entire existence (1973: 29). To be ethical means to take responsibility for one's actions, to decide for ourselves. Of course, individuals in trying to decide for themselves will face various constraints: 'every human purpose presents itself as an attempt either to surpass these limitations, or to widen them, or else to deny or to accommodate oneself to them' (1973: 4). So what we have with Sartre's existentialism is a philosophy which insists on the near limitless scope of human freedom. This is what he means when he wrote, in *Being and Nothingness*, 'man is condemned to be free'. It is the realization of this freedom which causes anguish, despair even or what Sartre terms *la nausée* – nausea.

The simpler, less nauseating, course of action would be to deny our freedom and passively accept what happens as fated or inescapable. Much of Sartre's *opus magnum*, *Being and Nothingness*, is given over to understanding why people deny themselves such freedom. Hence, there is a deep, subterranean pessimism running through this work – frustration, disappointment and unfulfilled potential are regarded as inevitable. In this philosophical masterwork, the concept of *mauvaise foi* is introduced and elaborated (see Sartre, 1989: 47–70). *Mauvaise foi* or *bad faith* is a philosophical concept which points to how individuals deny their total freedom by deceiving or lying to themselves and choose to live instead like inanimate objects, with their functions and character already determined. Much of this bad faith is down to the fact that we live and operate as being-for-others. The fundamental mode of our existence is that we define ourselves and behave in conformity with the expectations of other people. Hence, Sartre's play *No Exit* contains the immortal line: 'Hell is other people'. The concept of bad faith is relevant to how Sartre's existentialism can be deployed to construct an ethical appreciation of management.

There is an *a priori* tendency in critical management thought to regard the manager negatively, as the vessel for capitalist exploitation. Sartre would be loath to pre-judge individuals according to their status or position in life. He would be mindful of making such moral judgements against managers or other people in high status positions: 'man may be born a slave in a pagan society, or may be a feudal baron, or a proletarian. But what never may vary are the necessities of being in the world, of having to labour and to die there' (1973: 46). Regardless of our status, we all have to exist and be responsible for how we live our lives. Where does moral judgement come into this? Of course, the Kantian and Marxist within Sartre would have problems with corporate management and managerial doctrines such as HRM, especially because of their utilitarian approach to employees. But what matters ethically from a Sartrean perspective is how managers or other leaders respond to situations. In particular, do they fall into deception and repudiate their own freedom. In the face of organizational and professional parameters, restrictions and demands, it seems that managers within modern corporate business organizations are guilty of *Bad Faith*. Certainly research seems to suggest this is the case.

In terms of studying UK managers, James Hine (2007) conducted in-depth interviews with managers from the banking and drinks industry. He conducted the interviews to gauge levels of ethical responsiveness to different issues. He found that managers did bring moral convictions into their work; they are especially aware of ethical issues relating to commercial activities. But they lacked the autonomy to freely act on their ethical convictions. Hine calls this *moral heteronomy*. Hine outlines organizational factors that constrain the ethical decision-making of managers. Firstly, the influence of the market economy, which by law prioritizes shareholder value, means economic objectives win out over moral duties and obligations. In addition, managers overlook ethical dilemmas because of their livelihood and career prospects. The idea is that if you as a manager want to get on in your career, you do not rock the boat, even if it means compromising on your personal ethical standards. This is what Sartre would have to say about Hines' findings: 'Since we have defined the situation of man as one of free choice . . . any man who takes refuge behind the excuse of his passions, or by inventing some deterministic doctrine, is a self-deceiver' (1973: 51). It could be argued that managers have no choice but to do what is expected of them, and put any personal concerns to one side. But, argues Sartre, this is a moral error. In doing so, we deny our humanity and become a living paradox. 'I say that it is also a self-deception if I choose to declare that certain values are incumbent upon me; I am a contradiction with myself if I will these values and at the same time say that they impose themselves upon me' (51).

Existential thinkers such as Sartre would argue that blaming the chain of command for not taking an ethical stand, or relying on moral guidelines, only amount to a denial of our freedom and therefore humanity. The point is that, even with morally difficult choices, we should not abrogate our responsibility to others or to doctrines or institutional rules and expectations. Sartre provides a useful illustration of what he means by this in his essay, *Existentialism and Humanism*. He recounts the story of a pupil taught by Sartre. This pupil's father was inclined to be a German collaborator and his brother was killed in the German offensive of 1940. The pupil's mother lived alone with her remaining son, deeply affected by her husband's treason and her elder son's death. Her only consolation was the company of her younger son – Sartre's pupil. But Sartre's pupil burned with hatred against the German regime and wanted to revenge his brother's death. He was left with a decision to make: the choice between going to England to join the Free French Forces or of staying in Paris to look after his mother. He went to Sartre in the hope of being advised over what would be the right, that is, most ethical, thing to do in this situation. The unethical course of action would be to rely on a philosophical system of rules like Kantian maxims or a religious belief system like Catholicism. The decision would have been made for Sartre's pupil. The truly ethical action and the advice Sartre ends up giving to the pupil was this: 'You are free, therefore choose – that is to say, invent. No rule of general morality can show you what you ought to do: no signs are vouch-safed in this world' (1973: 38). Doing what is expected from you just amounts to bad faith. Indeed, the practice of modern management is a vast edifice to bad faith, with managers fulfilling the expectations of what systems and institutions require of them.

From an existential point of view, mangers have to assume an ethical responsibility for how they act, embracing the fact that they have greater freedom than they imagined. They cannot just blame the structural obsession with shareholder value. The process of management cannot be spirited away. Management will not disappear. Managers will continue acting and behaving as they have always done. But for existentialists the crucial difference is this: how they choose to manage, and go about performing routine management tasks should be different. The first step in moving towards a more distinct form of management that embraces humane objectives is to realize that much of our professional existence in the workplace is characterized by what Heidegger, in his dense yet rich *magnum opus*, *Being and Time* (1967), describes as inauthentic existence. Central to Heidegger's existential position developed in *Being and Time* is what it means 'to be' or exist. As we have already noted, for Heidegger, what it means to be human is not set in stone – there is no absolute human essence. *Being and Time* develops this key proposition. To capture this existential form of existence, Heidegger devised a specific term: 'Dasein'. If translated, it basically means 'being there', referring to being in the world. That is, we as individuals do not simply infer the world from a position of isolated mental cognition. Rather we are in the world, among other people, among objects, within physical spaces, among images, in language and so on. And herein is a problem. The immense possibility that there is no real fixed human essence creates a sense of being without foundation. Instead of being a source of liberation, the sense of groundlessness leads us to actively plunge ourselves further into, and routinely identify with, our immediate world. We become so involved in what we are doing that we do not stand back and ask ourselves a simple question: 'Why am I doing this?' In other words, we are so busily immersed in the practical, everyday world *of doing* that we overlook our true existence or nature of being, which leads to an inauthentic existence. The inauthentic life is one in which existence is dissolved in the public environment; it is dissolved into 'the Being of the Others'; it is, to use Sartre's concept, an existence rooted in bad faith. Our existence, it seems, is not our own, for 'the real dictatorship of the "they" is unfolded. We take pleasure and enjoy ourselves as *they [man]* take pleasure; we read, see, and judge about literature and art as *they* see and judge' (1962: 164). Heidegger goes on to observe: 'The Self of everyday Dasein is the *they-Self*, which we distinguish from the authentic Self – that is, from the Self which has been taken hold of in its own way' (1962: 167). A good example of an authentic existence, of a self which has taken hold of it own way, in the context of management is found in Karen Legge's (1978) early study of personnel management and the idea of deviant innovation.

For Legge, the deviant innovator challenges dominant, often material or economic, values about personnel management and the management process in general. The deviant innovator 'attempts to change this means/ends relationship by gaining acceptance for a different set of criteria for the evaluation of organizational success' (1978: 85). Thus deviant innovators will embrace broader humanistic and social values. The humanistic approach may define organizational effectiveness in terms of job satisfaction or cultivating opportunities for self-fulfilment and autonomy. In contrast, the 'conformist innovator' accepts the conventional bottom-line measures of success and seeks ways of managing people to meet these objectives. The dominant practice of management stresses the need to become partisans of profit, thereby treating employees as malleable, and often disposable, assets. Therefore, a personnel manager displays the characteristics of a deviant innovator when he/she adopts strategies for managing human resources that challenge prevailing management norms. This may include practices such as stress management, equal opportunities, shorter working hours and empowerment. Contemporary research demonstrates how these 'deviant' practices are potentially beneficial. Green and Whitfield (2009) suggest how even minor democratization of the workplace, through work teams or involvement strategies, has shown some evidence of improved job satisfaction and security (2009: 227). Be that as it may. The deviant innovator is often a lone operator and is forced to look outside their own organization for support. As Legge points out, the deviant manager looks to 'an external reference group for the evaluation of his own and the organization's activities' (1978: 86). One external support mechanism is identified by Kochan (2007), writing about US human resource professionals. He pinpoints how codes of conduct, endorsed by professional bodies, can bolster the position and distinctive contribution of HR professionals, even though they are ultimately the employees and representatives of management. Without a professional reference group, these practitioners leave themselves vulnerable. With a strong body of professional norms and standards, HR managers are in a position to challenge the prevailing ideologies and values of the employing firm and its senior executives. Kochan's advice has some resonance with existential theory. The collective resource of the professional body allows individual personnel managers to resist conformity to the 'dictatorship of the corporate-located they'. Do managers enjoy the 'psychological space' from which to become deviant innovators or 'existential operators', musing on the ethical meaning of their choices and decisions? The daily pressures and responsibilities of seniority, according to Moberg (2000), produce inertia or indifference. As such, managers often do not have the inclination or the time to reflect on the ethical repercussions of their decisions. But there is something that can jolt managers out of their time-induced moral inertia. Research and philosophical reflection are informative on this matter.

One such piece of research, conducted by the American commentator Robert Jackall, examined the moral dilemmas and compromises that corporate managers have to make. Based on extensive interviews with managers at every level of two industrial firms and of a large public relations agency, Jackall's *Moral Mazes* (1989) opens the lid on the moral complexities and intricacies of the corporate world. Jackall found that corporate managers were far from being an amoral bunch of ruthless capitalists. Corporate managers often felt a moral uneasiness in pursuing business goals, especially if they were incompatible with their moral convictions. This moral uneasiness could result in depression, reliance on alcohol, anger or self-disgust. The managers in Jackall's research were displaying a heavy dose of existential angst or anxiety. According to Heidegger, anxiety that often emerges in moments of dread, or when death is certain, reveals the 'ownmost potentiality-for-Being – that is, its Being-free for the freedom of choosing itself and taking hold of itself' (1962: 232). In other words, anxiety brings existence face-to-face with the freedom to achieve authenticity, for such authenticity is always a distinct possibility. Anxiety achieves this by breaking not a psychological but a social illusion. According to one of the world's foremost experts on *Being and Time*, Herbert Dreyfus, anxiety draws us away from roles and patterns of behaviour which have been assigned. Anxiety reveals these roles and expectations to be 'a cultural conspiracy to provide the illusion of some ultimate meaning-motivating action'. For the openly angst-ridden, '[S]ocial action now appears as a game which there is no point in playing since it has no intrinsic meaning' (1991: 180). The same could be said of modern management.

Concluding thoughts: the slide towards ethical solipsism or existential standards?

The great high priests of modern existentialism knew very well the gaps in their defences that would invite condemnation from critics. It seems that existentialism's 'first principle' is also its great vulnerability. As shown above, people first exist and they come to define themselves by how they encounter the world. In other words, existentialism begins from the subjective. For Sartre, the first principle of existentialism is that individuals are what they make of themselves. There is nothing of eternal or universal value, everything is subjective and voluntary. And it is this first principle of subjectivity in existentialism which can expose it to the criticism that it slides towards ethical solipsism: each individual decides on what the truth is and how to live the good life. It therefore logically follows that: 'Everyone can do what he likes and will be incapable . . . of condemning either the point of view or action of anyone else' (Sartre, 1973: 24). In terms of the employment relationship, why should we condemn mass redundancies by management or the dubious practice of 'dead peasants insurance' or management's tacit cultivation of presenteeism? Executives or managers are simply defining their own existence, after all.

Both Sartre and Heidegger anticipated that existentialism's subjectivism would expose it to the intellectual ridicule of solipsism. Even though Heidegger described his view as existential 'solipsism' in *Being and Time*, he is referring here to how extreme anxiety can individualise or isolate existence. Elsewhere in his 1923 lectures he is very clear about the fact that 'Dasein as its own does not mean an isolating relativization to . . . the individual (*solus ipse*)' (cited in Dreyfus, 1991: 243). Existentialism's adversaries, argued Sartre, caricatured its claims, especially those concerning subjectivity. Existential subjectivism focuses on the freedom of the individual and his/her ability to shape their existence. Although this idea can fall foul of relativism, Sartre and other existentialists are, at the same time, making a deeply ethical demand. It is an ethical assertion that has fallen out of fashion in both the social sciences and wider society. It is a rather simple demand: we as human beings have a responsibility, regardless of our position or status, for our own lives – we should not shirk from this responsibility by looking to parents, senior colleagues or ethical theories for that matter. But we do not practice our responsibilities in isolation, for existential subjectivism has another meaning, according to Sartre. This encompasses a deeper, more general, and dare I say it more collective and interdependent, definition of human subjectivity: 'When we say that man chooses himself, we do mean that every one of us must choose himself; but that by that we also mean that in choosing himself he chooses for all men' (Sartre, 1974: 29). Existential responsibility is much greater than often portrayed, as it concerns the whole of human kind. To illustrate the point, Sartre, rather appropriately for this book, considers the vexed question of trade union membership. He notes that if a worker decides to join a Christian rather than a more radical Communist trade union, the person is endorsing a position of compliance and resignation. Clearly industrial politics was very different in Sartre's day. The choice was between different ideological unions, whereas in today's workplace the choice is between joining a union and not being a member – complete apathy, in other words. Nevertheless, the point still stands. By endorsing the compliant union or no trade union membership at all, an individual endorses resignation and futility not only for himself but also for fellow employees, and humanity as a whole. Sartre notes: 'I am thus responsible for myself and for all men' (1974: 30). Thus if there is to be an existential ethical standard in the workplace, it is one that revolves around the issue of responsibility: a duty not only to determine our own existence but also the existence of others in a way that promotes freedom, exuberance and autonomy. At the same time, the existential standard acknowledges that in the workplace, we have to grapple with the fact that hell, sometimes, really is other people.

Notes

1. Gordon Gekko is the ruthless merchant banker played by Michael Douglas in the film *Wall Street* (1987), directed by Oliver Stone. In one infamous scene, Gekko declares in a speech that: 'Greed, for want of a better word, is good'. This is a perfect summation of the Gekko philosophy. Gekko is set to return in *Wall Street: Money Never Sleeps*.
2. Employees in the UK did not get a legal right to compensation in the event of redundancy until the mid-1960s.

References

Ackers, Peter (2009), 'Employment ethics', in Tom Redman (ed.), *Contemporary Human Resource Management: Text and Cases*, 3rd edition (Harlow: FT Prentice).
Bakan, Joel (2005), *The Corporation: The Pathological Pursuit of Profit and Power* (London: Constable).
Banerjee, Subhabrata B. (2007), *Corporate Social Responsibility: The Good, the Bad and the Ugly* (Northampton, MA: Edward Elgar).
Barbash, Jack and Barbash, Kate (eds) (1989), *Theories and Concepts in Comparative Industrial Relations* (Columbia: South Carolina University Press).
Berle, Adolf A. (1959), *Power Without Property: A New Development in American Political Economy* (New York: Harcourt, Brace and Company).
Blyton, Paul and Turnbull, Pete (1994), The *Dynamics of Employee Relations* (Basingstoke: Macmillan).
Budd, J.W. (2004), *Employment with a Human Face: Balancing Efficiency, Equity and Voice* (Ithaca and London: Cornell University Press).
Budd, J.W. and Scoville, J.G. (2005) 'Moral philosophy, business ethics and the employment relationship', in J.W. Budd and J.G. Scoville (eds), *The Ethics of Human Resources and Industrial Relations* (Champaign Il.: Labor and Employment Relations Association), pp. 1–22.
Dreyfus, Hubert L. (1991), *Being-in-the-World: a Commentary on Heidegger's Being and Time*, Division I (Cambridge, Mass.: MIT Press).
Fombrun, C.J., Tichy, N.M. and Devanna, M.A. (1984) *Strategic Human Resource Management* (New York, Wiley).

Green, Francis and Whitfield, Keith (2009), 'Employees' experience of work', in William Brown, Alex Bryson, John Forth and Keith Whitfield (eds), *The Evolution of the Modern Workplace* (Cambridge: Cambridge University Press).

Hannah, Leslie (1983), *The Rise of the Corporate Economy*, 2nd edition (London: and New York: Methuen).

Heery, Edmund (2005), 'The British journal of industrial relations: position and prospect', *British Journal of Industrial Relations*, vol. 43, no. 1, pp. 1–9.

Heidegger, Martin (1976), 'Nur noch ein Gott kann uns retten,' *Der Spiegel*, 30 May 1976, pp. 193–219.

Heidegger, Martin (1996), *Being and Time*; translated by John Macquarrie and Edward Robinson (Oxford: Blackwell).

Hine, James A. H. S. (2007), 'The Shadow of Macintyre's Manager in the Kingdom of Conscience Constrained', *Business Ethics: A European Review*, vol. 16, no. 4, pp. 358–71.

Hodge, J. (1995), *Heidegger and Ethics* (London: Routledge).

Jackall, Robert (1988), *Moral Mazes: the World of Corporate Managers* (New York: Oxford University Press).

Jones, Campbell, Parker, Martin and ten Bos, Rene (2005), *For Business Ethics* (London and New York: Routledge).

Kaler, John (1999), 'What's the good of ethical theory?', *Business Ethics: A European Review*, vol. 8, no. 4, pp. 206–13.

Kant, Immanuel (1785), *Groundwork for the Metaphysics of Morals*, trans. by Arnulf Zweig and edited by Thomas E. Hill, Jr. and Arnulf Zweig (2002) (Oxford: Oxford University Press).

Kant, I. (2008) *The Critique of Practical Reason*, translated by T.K. Abbott, Forgotten Books. http//:www.forgottenbooks.org/info/9781451010077 [Accessed 14 August 2010].

Kaysen, Carl (1957), 'The social significance of the modern corporation', *American Economic Review*, vol. 47, no. 2, pp. 311–19.

Kochan, Thomas A. (1998), 'What is distinctive about industrial relations research?', in Keith Whitfield and George Strauss (eds), *Researching the World of Work: Strategies and Methods in Studying Industrial Relations* (Ithaca, NY: Cornell University Press).

Kochan, Thomas A. (2007), 'Social legitimacy of the HRM profession: a US perspective', in Peter Boxall, John Purcell, and Pat Wright (eds), *The Oxford Handbook of Human Resource Management* (Oxford; New York: Oxford University Press).

Lafer, Gordon (2005), 'The critical failure of workplace ethics', in John W. Budd and James G. Scoville (eds), *The Ethics of Human Resources and Industrial Relations* (Illionois: LERA/University of Illionois).

Law Reports (1883), 'Hutton vs. West Cork railway', *Company, Law Reports*, vol. 23, Chancery Division, pp. 654–84 (London: Council of Law Reporting).

Legge, Karen (1978), *Power, Innovation, and Problem-Solving in Personnel Management* (London: McGraw-Hill Book Company).

Legge, K. (1995), *Human Resource Management: Rhetorics and Realities* (Basingstoke: MacMillan Business).

Legge, Karen (1998), 'The morality of HRM', in Christopher Mabey, Denise Skinner and Timothy Clark (eds), *Experiencing Human Resource Management* (London: Sage Publications).

Louden, Robert (1989), 'Some vices of virtue ethics', in Louis Pojman (ed.), *Ethical Theory Classic and Contemporary Readings*, 1st edition (Belmont: Wadsworth).

Moberg, Dennis J. (2000), 'Time pressure and ethical decision making: a case for moral readiness', *Business and Professional Ethics Journal*, vol. 19, no. 2, pp. 41–67.

Nichols, Theo (1969), *Ownership, Control and Ideology: An Enquiry into Certain Aspects of Modern Business Ideology* (London: George Allen and Unwin).

Nietzsche, Friedrich (2007), *On the Genealogy of Morality*; edited by Keith Ansell Pearson; translated by Carol Diethe (Cambridge, New York: Cambridge University Press).

Provis, Chris (2000), 'Ethics, deception, and labor negotiation', *Journal of Business Ethics*, vol. 28, no. 2, pp. 145–58.

Roscigno, Vincent (2007), *The Face of Discrimination: How Race and Gender Impact Work and Home Lives* (Lanham: Rowan and Littlefield).

Sartre, Jean-Paul (1973), *Existentialism and Humanism*, translated by Philip Mairet (London: Methuen Publishing).

Sartre, Jean-Paul (1989), *Being and Nothingness: An Essay on Phenomenological Ontology*; translated by Hazel E. Barnes (London: Routledge).

Schumann, Paul L. (2001), 'A moral principles framework for human resource management ethics', *Human Resource Review*, vol. 11, pp. 93–111.

Scott, John (1985), *Corporations, Classes and Capitalism*, 2nd edition (London: Hutchinson).

Sisson, Keith (2008), 'Putting the record straight: industrial relations and the employment relationship'. *Warwick papers in Industrial Relations*, no. 88 Coventry: Industrial Relations Research Unit, University of Warwick.

Solomon, Robert C. (1992), *Ethics and Excellence: Cooperation and Integrity in Business* (New York and Oxford: Oxford University Press).

Solomon, Robert C. (2006), *Dark Feelings, Grim Thoughts: Experience and Reflection in Camus and Sartre* (Oxford/New York: Oxford University Press).

Storey, John (1987), 'Developments in the management of human resources: an interim report'. *Warwick Papers in Industrial Relations*, 17. IRRU, School of Industrial and Business Studies, University of Warwick.

Styhre, Alexander (2002), 'Kaizen, ethics, and care of the operations: management after empowerment', *Journal of Management Studies*, vol. 38, no. 6, pp. 795–810.

Tawney, Richard H. (1920), *The Acquisitive Society* (New York: Harcourt Brace Jovanovich).

Warnock, Mary (2003), 'Introduction', in Jean-Paul Sartre (ed.), *Being and Nothingness: an Essay on Phenomenological Ontology*, 2nd edition (London: Routledge).

Winstanley, D. (2000) 'Conditions of worth and the performance management paradox', in D. Winstanley and J. Woodall (eds), *Ethical Issues in Contemporary Human Resource Management* (Basingstoke, MacMillan Business), pp. 189–207.

Winstanley, D. and Woodall, Jean (2000), 'Introduction', in Diana Winstanley and Jean Woodall (eds), *Ethical Issues in Contemporary Human Resource Management* (Basingstoke: Palgrave).

Wood, Allen W. (1999), *Kant's Ethical Thought* (Cambridge: Cambridge University Press).

Žižek, Slavoj (2007), 'Resistance is Surrender', *London Review of Books*, vol. 29, no. 22 (November), p. 7.

Reassessing identity: the relevance of identity research for analysing employment relations

Robyn Thomas and Annette Davies

Introduction

Questions of identity arise with increasing regularity in the media, policy and academic debates. Gendered identities, cultural identities, national identities, racial identities, online identity, identity theft... it seems that identity has never received as much attention. This concern over identity is equally apparent in the study of work organizations, where identity, and the related concepts of subjectivity, identification, dis-identification, identity work, organizational identities and occupational identities, pepper contemporary debates in the literature. Despite this fascination with identity in studies on work organizations, however, a brief scan of the more influential academic journals in employment relations and the sociology of work reveals only a few articles, over the past decade, that principally focus on the dynamic relations of power and individual identity within the employment relationship.[1] We aim to show in this chapter that concerns over how we construct our identities within – and through – work should form a prominent analytical concern in contemporary debates on employment relations.

Of course, a concern over the self, seen as a coherent and autonomous entity, has been an enduring concern in the sociology of work, dating back to Durkheim and Marx with their critiques over the damage to the individual from capitalist relations of production. Where identity has been of interest, in both functionalist and radical structuralist approaches to the study of work, it has been understood as being a unified and essentialized[2] – a fixed phenomenon. From a functionalist perspective, for example, the importance of an individual's identity has been the focus of attention for as long as the field has existed, where the concern has been to encourage individuals to define themselves in relation to the organization, so as to achieve greater congruence between individual and organization's identity, thus enhancing commitment, loyalty, motivation and job satisfaction (Haslam et al., 2003). In radical structuralist analysis, conversely, the worker's identity is viewed as an expression of class relations. Individuals are viewed as the 'personification of economic categories' (Marx, 1976: 92), where agency is structurally determined by the location in the sphere of production. In Marxian analysis, work provided the principal source of identity and the relationship between the two was seen as key to understanding social solidarity, power and historical change (Leidner, 2006).

Contemporary theorizing on identities, however, has tended to take constructionist, particularly poststructuralist approaches to the concept, where identity is understood as contested and contingent. The conceptualization of identity has thus shifted to a more processual understanding; identity is something that is crafted on an ongoing basis, in interaction with social–linguistic and institutionalized patterns of being and knowing. This suggests that identities are much more pluralistic, complex, contradictory and fluid than has been traditionally conceived (Collinson, 2003). Appreciating identities in this manner also raises attention to enduring debates within the study of work organizations on the role of agency and structure, where the dynamics of identity construction and contestation can be understood as surface manifestations of deeper expressions of the agency–structure relationship (Ybema et al., 2009). Identity can be usefully conceptualized as a dynamic struggle between various subject positions within discourse,[3] vying for our attention and our active human agency. Thus individuals are situated in social contexts that both constrain and sustain identity (Thomas, 2009). As Ybema et al. (2009: 307) conclude, the self–other dynamic of identity construction 'can be seen to refract the agency-structure dialectic *in action*, for it shows in plain words how selves and sociality are mutually implicated and mutually co-constructed' (emphasis in the original).

The paucity of studies in the sociology of work and employment relations that focus directly on personal identities as a focus for political struggle in the workplace can be partly explained by the considerable antipathy, ambivalence, even strong animosity among some scholars towards poststructuralist conceptualizations of identity, power and agency, with identity research being equated with 'political conservatism, individualism and/or failure to consider resistance' (McCabe, 2007: 244). When identity is discussed, especially within the more traditional employment relations literature, considerable attention is given to a narrow range of collective social identities that are occupational, union or class based. This narrow focus is beginning to be criticized from within the discipline, with emphasis being given to identities formed outside of the workplace or to the complex intersections between multiple and competing identities (Briskin, 2008; Holgate et al., 2006; Piore and Safford, 2006). Despite this, however, the empirical and analytical promise of a poststructuralist understanding of individual identity remains underappreciated. This chapter aims to address this neglect drawing attention to some of the ways in which poststructuralist approaches to identity might inform the analysis of work organizations.

The chapter is structured as follows. First, we locate our argument within the context of contemporary configurations of capitalism, drawing from debates that suggest that questions over identities have become more prominent, prescient and pressing than for the previous generation. We consider the implications of this for current employment relations in Western socio-economic contexts. Following this, the main body of the chapter, in making a case for taking an 'identities-turn' in employment relations, draws attention to the ways that employees, in responding to management interventions, critically reflect on their selves, as members of different collectives, and in the context of particular constraints on their subjectivity. In doing so, we draw on empirical research that explores the reform agenda in 'modernizing' the UK public services and the experiences of social work professionals–managers. Finally, in the discussion section, we critically explore and address the ambivalence and hostility by some scholars over the 'identities-turn' in studies of work organizations, focusing on debates over agency, structure and political adequacy.

Identity uncertainty

A widely-held belief among academic commentators, the media and the public at large is that we are facing a new configuration of capitalistic relations, termed variously as 'new capitalism' (Sennett, 2006); a 'new spirit of capitalism' (Boltanski and Chiapellio, 2006); 'casino capitalism' (Strange, 1986); 'liquid modernity' (Bauman, 2004), 'reflexive modernisation' (Beck et al., 1994) and the 'network society' (Castells, 1996). With different emphasis and interests, the theoretical skeleton common to these accounts is that the dynamic of capitalism is facing significant and intensified change, marked by increases in the speed of movement of people and capital across national borders, together with changes in production and consumption. The consequences for individuals are greater experiences of turbulence in our lives, where many traditional 'identity anchors', the established structures in our working lives, places and forms of work and communities, that inform us who we are and who we might be, are increasingly being undermined.

Emphasizing both the constraints on and possibilities for identity, Bauman's (2004) 'liquid modernity' thesis, for example, argues that the collapse of many of the stable pillars of society has left us more questioning and anxious about our selves. Greater choices of identities (offering new spaces for being) and demands to be certain identities (with the potential for oppression) arise from the ambivalence and ambiguity of the concept in contemporary society. This suggests the need for greater mental identity-maintenance work, or 'identity work', that is reflexive reordering of an understanding of self, stimulated by heightened anxiety, uncertainty, unfamiliarity and insecurity over who we are and who we might be. In some contexts, individuals are pressured to undertake almost constant reinvention. Thus we see pressures to become 'future oriented' selves (Sennett, 2006), discarding temporary 'cloakroom identities' (Bauman, 2004) on an ongoing basis.

While labour force statistics from both the UK and US throw doubt over the transformation of work and the emergence of a new employment relations characterized by insecurity (Doogan, 2009), and there is a significant debate within the academic literature over the nature and extent of change (du Gay, 2007; Webb, 2006), this discourse of 'new capitalism' can be seen to represent a persuasive and powerful ideological reference within society, which has material effects on employment relations. In other words, despite labour force statistics pointing to the contrary (Doogan, 2009), the discourse of new capitalism has powerful effects, stimulating heightened feelings of insecurity, anxiety and uncertainty over self-identity. As Grey (2009) observes, the power effects of the discourse of fast capital direct us to act upon it in ways that makes its effects, to a certain extent, a self-fulfilling prophesy.

Furthermore, the discourse of new capitalism extends to the workplace. Opportunistic cost-cutting through restructuring organizations, downsizing, de-layering, contracting out, off-shoring and other methods of 'corporate liposuction' (Burrell, 1997) have delivered greater pressures, an intensification of work and greater uncertainty over job security, while attempting to maintain low costs, high quality and customer service. This has resulted in the need to put greater efforts into encouraging identification with the organization, where a climate of downsizing and delayering fosters cynicism and detachment among the survivors (Thomas and Dunkerley, 1999). The demands of global financial markets and mobile capital (Froud et al., 2006) have also contributed to the relentless consumption of management fads, change and restructuring programmes and mergers and rationalizations to achieve short-term gains in share value in an insatiable beauty contest to financial communities (Froud et al., 2006; Webb, 2006). The changing composition of the workforce, with the greater concentration of professional, technical and managerial workers, requiring higher levels of discretion and tacit skills, calls out for control strategies that facilitate self-autonomy and flexibility. Attempts to encourage employees to identify with the organization take on greater urgency as workforces become more geographically dispersed, mobile and diverse, requiring strategies to engender feelings of coherence among workers connected via virtual offices. Together, these changes suggest that identities have become a location for struggle in contemporary work organizations.

Within the public sector, the discourse of change has been embraced, with neo-liberalist calculative rationality driving endless change initiatives over the past two decades under the reform agenda of New Public Management (NPM), 'marketisation' and 'governance' (Ferlie et al., 2007; Thomas and Davies, 2005a; Webb, 2006). Although there are debates concerning the coherence and impact of this reform agenda (Clarke et al., 2000; McLaughlin et al., 2002), the period has been marked by a panoply of initiatives directed at improving cost-effectiveness, efficiency and performance in public service organizations. In pursuing these aims there has been the adoption of a range of management practices such as the use of performance indicators and targets, strong attempts to engender a 'customer' focus, decentralization and increased individualization of the employment relationship (Farnham et al., 2003; Horton, 2003; Truss, 2008). This programme of ideological and cost-driven changes can be seen as being targeted directly at public service professionals' understanding of professional service, and collective, professional and personal self-understandings, suggesting that questions of identity are at the epicentre of political struggles in public services employment relations.

In this chapter we direct our focus on an area of the public services that has faced considerable challenge over the past few decades, that of social work. We present empirical material drawn from part of a wider study on restructuring and change in the UK public services, commencing in 2001 and involving professionals–managers from three sectors: education, police and social services (Davies and Thomas, 2008; Thomas and Davies, 2005a, b). The social workers presented in the analysis are employed in two English local authorities and are located at the middle management level. These professional social workers and 'team leaders' are positioned at the focal point of struggles over meanings of professional practices and identities in the context of wider changes in the public services. There has been reluctance in the past to consider managers as subjects of capitalist relations of production within employment relations. More often they are narrowly conceived as the architects of control and the agents of capital (Willmott, 1997). However, there are studies that have focused on a managerial labour process, and the dynamics of control and resistance among this group (Alvesson and Willmott, 1996; Gottfried, 1994; LaNuez and Jermier, 1994; Thomas and Dunkerley, 1999; Willmott, 1997). It is notable that middle managers, in both the public and private sectors, have been under considerable attack from the discourses of change over the past two decades (Ehrenreich, 2006; Heckscher, 1995; Thomas and Dunkerley, 1999; Thomas and Linstead, 2002). Ehrenreich's (2006) documentation of a 'white collar underclass' of jobless former middle managers in the US, and Sennett's (1998) detailed analysis of the material consequences of the identity crisis of middle management from flexible capitalism, are both illustrative of a range of studies that highlight the declining status, power, career prospects and control for this group in contemporary capitalist economies.

For social work middle managers, legislation and executive powers have both attempted to impose change agendas such that a once professionally regulated service is now increasingly subject to external regulation and output controls (Jones, 1999; Lawler and Hearn, 1995). As with other parts of the public services, social work reform has been directed at cost control, performance monitoring and the marketization of services (Ackroyd et al., 2007; Farnham and Horton, 1996; Pollitt, 1993). The NHS and Community Care Act (1990) intensified the pressures to implement more explicit management systems into social service departments. A mixed economy of welfare was introduced breaking up the monopoly of service provision by local authorities, now recast as enablers (Farrell and Morris, 2003; Harris, 1998). Significantly, underlying all these changes, the need to cut the public spending budget has been as much a driver for change as policy-initiated change. Thus the emphasis on effective service delivery is entwined with economic measures of performance. For example, in one of the local authorities involved in the research presented in this chapter, budgets had been reduced by £10 million over a 3-year period with the concomitant pressure to cut staff numbers.

The consequences of declining resources, efficiency measures and frequent changes to policy and practice for social work professionals have been profound. This has led to frequent suggestions that we are now witnessing a crisis in social work, pointing to evidence of change fatigue, stress and frustration, rising levels of long-term sickness and absenteeism, declining job satisfaction and increased questioning over long-term career commitment among the profession (Carey, 2003; Dominelli, 1996; Jones, 2001). Problems with recruitment and retention are extreme, with one in seven social worker posts remaining unfilled. Unison, the union representing 40,000 social workers, has described the recruitment crisis as a 'ticking time bomb' (Mulholland, 2009).

'There's a kind of party line': identity control at work

Thus, emerging configurations of capitalist relations have had profound effects on organizing, with new patterns of employment relations, a changing composition and character of the workforce and a move towards more flexible, fragmented and individualized forms of work. These developments are themselves located in the dominant discourse of neo-liberalism, of consumption, consumerism, calculative rationality and individualism. They suggest that for individuals in work organizations, identity is increasingly problematic: open to challenge and scrutiny. It is in relation to this that there has been considerable interest in the role of change discourses in targeting an individual's sense of self. It is the heightened feelings of insecurity and vulnerability, together with the loss of traditional identity anchors such as class, community and religion, that render individuals more open to the appeals of corporate identifications (Alvesson and Willmott, 2002).

There has been considerable interest during the past couple of decades over managerial attempts at regulating, even prescribing, the self-identities of employees, so as to align the individual's self-conceptions with organizationally inspired discourses (Alvesson and Willmott, 2002; Alvesson et al., 2008; Casey, 1995; Kunda, 1992; McCabe, 2007; Musson and Duberley, 2007) with the aim of increasing levels of commitment and flexibility, as part of the rewriting of the wage–effort bargain. Contemporary discourses of empowerment, leadership, teamworking, customer orientation and so on are aimed at capturing the 'hearts and minds' (Deetz, 1992) of the employee. Thus identity colonization is a critical element in the lexicon of control strategies available to management. Identity control can be understood as part of normative control in the organization, defined as the 'more or less intentional effects of social practices upon processes of identity construction and reconstruction' to produce the 'appropriate individual' (Alvesson and Willmott, 2002: 629). Attempts at identity control are more likely to be successful if the management discourses resonate with, or complement, other salient sources of identification for the individual, or if they are seen to satisfy a feeling of uncertainty or incompleteness in the individual's identity make-up.

Attempts to regulate the identities of public service professionals within the discourses of reform are clearly identifiable (du Gay, 1996; Halford and Leonard, 1999; Llewellyn, 2004; Meyer and Hammerschmid, 2006). Specifically, a range of 'disciplinary technologies'[4] have been targeted at a public service professional cadre seen to be out of line with the subject position promoted in the neo-liberalist discourse. The UK public services were depicted by the New Right architects of reform to be run by self-interested and largely unmanaged professionals who had been able to exercise considerable control over service delivery (Ackroyd et al., 2007). Consequently, on the back of this discourse, concerted efforts by successive governments over the past few decades have been made to reign in professional autonomy, to establish greater control over the nature and form of service delivery and to make public service professionals more accountable for their performance. Consequently, there has been a marked rise in initiatives to encourage and cajole public service professionals to recast their professional identities away from notions of welfarism and professional discretion, and towards entrepreneurial, competitive and individualist understandings (Clarke and Newman, 1997; du Gay, 2007, 1996; Townley, 1993b). This has meant that across the public services there have been struggles over the meaning of performance, public service work, professional and personal identities.

For social workers, the reform agenda has presented profound challenges over the meaning and practice of social work (Farrell and Morris, 2003; Jones, 1999). There has been a marked increase in techniques of individual accountability, particularly through forms of codifying, calculating and standardizing decision-making and care practice, with the proliferation of rules, procedures and checklists (Ackroyd et al., 2007). The language of customer rights has been promoted over professional discretion and direction, seen as a direct challenge to professional control (Smith, 2001). The day-to-day activities of middle-raking social workers have been increasingly configured around line management duties, budget management and contract negotiation (Causer and Exworthy, 1999). These bureaucratic controls interface with normative controls (e.g. identity and cultural) (Alvesson and Kärreman, 2004), such that they operate also at the symbolic level, prescribing a managerial, entrepreneurial and competitively individualized social worker identity.

Attempts at fundamental reforms of social worker practice thus involve challenging and redirecting deeply-held understandings on what it means to be a social worker. The extent to which the reform agenda over the past two decades has resulted in institutionalizing new understandings and forms of identification over social work performance is open to question. From our research in two social work case study local authorities, however, attempts at identity regulation and the struggles around the meanings of professional practice were very apparent.[5] For example, Sebastian, a services manager reflects on the increased accountability and value-for-money targets, along with a new more explicitly managerial identity. He comments on this change:

> ...now having to be much more of a separate manager and not so much managing the professional, having to manage the professional work of the teams, but also *at the same time* meeting targets. And those targets weren't there before. So that's the difference. We used to manage the service, we ran the services as well as we could, now as well as managing the services *we've also got to meet targets*...So whereas what we were doing was the best job we could do to help people get into employment we've also now got to *prove that*, prove that we've actually saved the money.

Others referred to the ways that the social worker professional identity was being reconstructed to be more dispassionate, bureaucratized and obedient. Rob, a manager in children services, explains the increased pressures he experiences, arising largely from having to keep up with new compliance procedures, together with a wide range of other bureaucratic tasks that he is now expected to perform:

> The amount of knowledge that we're meant to have as a front line practitioner in this job, plus the amount of management things that we're doing in terms of looking at effectiveness and things like that...I mean I've got a whole row of procedure manuals over there, and I can't possibly know the entire contents of that procedures manual, you know, because the social work manual is three inches thick and there's a health and safety manual too that we're now accountable for.

Greater accountability and increased responsibility for a large number of tasks have gone hand-in-hand with attempts to curtail levels of professional trust and discretion. As Joe, a team manager working with disabled children, stated:

> I mean it's almost like you need less and less bright people doing social work because actually what you don't want them to do is to kind of really think too much about the wider issues, the wider aspects of what they're doing, what you want them to do really is to do what they're told.

We also see how these social work professional–managers are struggling to maintain their understandings of professional practice in the face of severe resource constraints and demands to be more dispassionate. Sally, a team manager with disabled children, stated:

> I think there's certain professional standards and I think probably the most important one is when we come to, sort of, funding issues and what resources we've got. And there's a kind of a party line about what we can and can't do which is very

difficult for me because I'd like to give everything to everybody. I mean particularly when you work with families with disabled children who are under immense stress and have had some very traumatic and difficult lives and you actually, your heart goes out to them and you actually want to do as much as you possibly can . . . And that's really, really difficult and sometimes, you know, it grates a bit and you feel that you can't provide those things for people.

An overwhelming message from the research participants was that there was an explicit attempt to promote a more ruthless, calculative and target-oriented managerial identity that complemented the climate of strong performance, cost-consciousness and individual accountability: 'it's everyone for themselves', 'a dog eat dog culture', that there had to be 'zero defects' and, from one participant, the observation that 'they will crucify you if something goes wrong'.

The scale and nature of change has led a number of critical scholars to argue that we are witnessing de-professionalization within social services, with an increasingly fragmented and commodified profession being controlled by externally imposed compliance procedures, resulting in the demise of the 'autonomous reflective practitioner' (Ackroyd et al., 2007; Dominelli, 1996). Following Ferlie et al.'s (1996) classification of 'winners' and 'losers' in public service restructuring, Farrell and Morris (2003: 142) also suggest a de-professionalization thesis; this arising from the 'burdens of greater legislation, increased accountability, surveillance and financial pressures'. However, despite these unquestionable demands for change, what we also observe, in studying the way these public service professionals respond to the discourses and disciplinary technologies of change, is that the de-professionalization thesis is too broad-brush and sweeping, failing to capture and appreciate the complexities of change as it is played out in practice. Crucially, however, we also argue here that the de-professionalization thesis under-appreciates the agency of social work professionals.

'I am what I am': agency, dis-identification and the crafting of selves

Management discourses are not the only, or necessarily most salient, source of identity for individuals, nor are employees passive consumers of management discourses. The subject 'is not hailed in a passive sense' (Benwell and Stokoe, 2006: 32) by disciplinary discourses but is *actively engaged*, investing in some subject positions, while reflexively resisting, renegotiating and re-crafting others. Therefore, attempts by management to produce the 'appropriate individual' can be understood as part of the processes of identity struggle, that is, a dynamic and ongoing interaction between managerial-inspired discourses and personal and collective identities. Drawing from theoretical insights from political philosophies of activism of feminism(s) (Butler, 1992; Weedon, 1987), post-colonialism (Bhabha, 1994; Said, 1979; Spivak, 1987) and queer theory (Sedgwick, 1990, 1999), identity can be understood as both a target of control and a source of resistance within employment relations (Kondo, 1990; Meyerson and Scully, 1995; Thomas and Davies, 2005a; Thomas et al., 2004). While the contested nature of change is recognized in studies on changing employment relations in the workplace (Arrowsmith et al., 2003; Edwards, 1986), an analysis of identities, as a key focus of such contestation, remains under-explored.

In studies on work organizations, there has been a focus on *dis-identification*, why and how individuals are compelled to resist attempts at identity regulation at the level of the individual subject. Studies on dis-identification have focused on how individuals pitch their understandings of themselves in opposition to the identity positions offered or prescribed in work organizations. Such research emphasizes the complexities and ambiguities around the dynamics of identity construction, highlighting how power can create and constrain identities (Kondo, 1990). Dis-identification is thus a key element in the processes of crafting *who we are* (Holmer-Nadesan, 1996; Sveningsson and Alvesson, 2003; Thomas and Davies, 2005a; Thomas and Linstead, 2002), with identity being understood as the temporary reflexive understanding gained from a complex interweaving of identification and dis-identification, emphasizing the dynamics of agency and discourses, in context (Kondo, 1990; Thomas and Davies, 2005a). The critical focus therefore, in advocating an 'identities-turn' in employment relations, is that it affords in-depth insights into the ways that employees, in responding to management interventions, consider who they are, as members of different collectives, and in the context of particular constraints on their subjectivity.

Thus, returning to our case on social work professional–managers, this complexity around the interrelationship of identity construction and contestation is apparent. The social workers involved in the research are seen to be dis-identifying and identifying with salient discourses as they struggle to craft their identities and to construct an understanding of social work practice. These struggles, in turn, reflect – and are located within – a wider matrix of discourses. An understanding of social worker agency and struggle, at this level of analysis, can offer greater nuance and appreciation of the dynamics of micro-political resistance. Such insights, we argue, may be overlooked with more broad-brush portrayals of de-professionalization and a professional cadre experiencing psychological withdrawal. Rather, through processes of dis-identification, social workers, in a critical engagement with the new social worker subject position promoted in the neo-liberal discourse of reform, can be seen to be reinterpreting and rewriting attempts at transforming the meanings of professionalism and practice. This can be illustrated with Dave's reflections. Dave is the head of a unit for young offenders. He highlights how he constantly questions and challenges the attempts to re-craft understandings of social work care and what it means to be a social worker. Drawing on an identity constructed around images of professional care, Dave illustrates how this provides him with a critical platform from which to challenge the many ways in which the service is being reduced to a series of 'boxes to be ticked'. So, despite the fact that he is *swamped by paperwork*, he often refuses to privilege such tasks as a priority as they clash with his fundamental understanding of himself as a social worker in delivering *care*, an understanding that is grounded in his ethical and strongly emotional constructions of being a public service professional. As he comments, new requests for recording and accounting for daily work are 'a complete waste of time' and 'totally pointless'. Joe, another team manager, likewise, highlights the daily struggles over the meanings of service, drawing attention to the conflict between a caring and cost-conscious subjectivity:

> These are the areas where I kick against, if you like. Where you're being asked, because of some sort of policy or some sort of head counting, that I consider to be bad practice – or they could do things in a better way, which is a better service to disabled children and their families.

Other social work managers also highlighted the myriads of ways in which they refused to take on what was seen to be a finance-driven, single-minded, calculative managerial subjectivity. However, in their refusal of this subjectivity we see how this subjectivity is rewritten to incorporate notions of professional discretion. Margaret, a team leader in elderly services, while recognizing some of the benefits of being more accountable, was actively challenging the new disempowered social worker subject position, drawing on a professionally empowered identity to shape her sense of self and performance priorities:

> I think accountability is, should be there...So in 1997 the split was implemented and I became provider only and that makes my accountability to someone else, rather than to myself, so that makes sense. But it means we, instead of someone coming to me like used to happen saying 'could we give Mrs X some extra help, she's poorly today', I have to go through a system of sending a piece of paper to a care manager to explain why I think Mrs X needs some extra help. And if they decide not to action it then I'm left waiting and Mrs Smith's left waiting because I can't spend their money. I can't take the risk and say 'I'm going to put it in anyway'. Though,

saying that – I do! We send a bit of paper saying in the meantime, 'awaiting your reply, I am supporting this' . . . we've decided that we would loosen procedures up a bit and benefit the service user – and ourselves really.

Dis-identification also arises from a subjectivity of 'the caring and supportive colleague'. We also see how these managers, in dealing with demands to work harder and suffering from long working hours and increased pressure from higher caseloads and fewer staff, are attempting to redefine the meaning of the service they can provide. Frances, a team manager in adult care, is candid about what she can and cannot achieve in performing her role and draws on a collegial and caring subject position in the way she manages her team and appraises their performance. She comments: 'I tell the staff that all time. I say "Look, you know, don't let yourself feel responsible"'.

These social work professional–managers clearly demonstrate a strong emotional attachment and investment in their work, especially in an occupational identity underpinned by the discourse of client (and colleague) care and public service. Attempts at reconfiguring meanings and identities around a calculative and codified way of being and acting have had mixed success, given the clash between these new meanings and individual social work professional–managers' preferred interests (Weedon, 1987). These 'caring' professionals have invested considerable energy in identifying with a social work profession and social service institution that has traditionally celebrated welfare provision and care unfettered in principle by questions of cost, and determined by the discretion of the ethically oriented practitioner. This forms a relatively enduring and appealing identity for many social workers. Judy, for example, is adamant when she says: '*I am what I am, I'm a caring person*'. Other research has also emphasized how a caring and service identity remains 'surprisingly robust' (Morgan et al., 2000) in social work, with attempts to instil new meanings of calculative rationality being viewed as 'insensitive, inappropriate and vulgar' (Carey, 2003: 133). This ethical and caring identity serves as a powerful resource that some of the social workers in our study drew on in challenging and destabilizing these new meanings. However, this is not the only identity resource drawn on by the social workers in challenging attempts to conjoin social workers' sense of their self with the neo-liberalist discourse. Mary, a team manager in adult services, for example, draws on professional expertise and discretion in asserting her identity as a skilled and knowledgeable professional–manager:

> I'm experienced and knowledgeable and professional in my job and this job cannot be reduced to tick boxes, which in any case aren't about the quality of service, they're just about covering your back.

So, shifting the spotlight of analysis to the micro-political highlights that underneath the few expressions of overt antagonism to managerialism is a persistent struggle over attempts to rewrite the meanings of effective service. It is the 'passionate attachment' (Butler, 1997) and the considerable and ongoing investment in alternative identity positions that provide both the site of this struggle and the source of its resistance.

Discussion: the relevance of identity research

In this chapter, we draw on poststructuralist theorizing on identity to argue for a more nuanced understanding of individual agency in the changing context of employment relations. In this discussion section, we wish to return to our observations raised at the start of the chapter over the neglect of individual identity within the discipline. Burrell (2006) wryly observes, the 'meteorite' of postmodernist thinking left a very small crater in employment relations and, further, where there has been any impact on debates by the ideas promoted in these 'Parisian fashions', the 'response teams swept into action'. (Burrell, 2006: 175). Certainly, poststructuralist-influenced approaches to appreciating the interrelations between power relations and identity at work have had little take up among researchers in the sociology of work and employment relations literature. What is more, there has been ambivalence at best and more often explicit hostility, by some critical scholars towards work that has focused on individual identities at work (Martinez Lucio and Stewart, 1997; Thompson and Ackroyd, 1995). The nature of this criticism is twofold: that such approaches promote an individualized understanding of the worker at the expense of collective identities; and that it is politically inadequate, offering an etiolated notion of agency and resistance and thereby removing the base from which to analyse and challenge the dynamics of employment relations. Drawing on our own research and others that have examined the dynamics of identity construction and contestation at work, we will now consider this critique and conclude by highlighting some of the analytical promise offered by focusing on the dynamics of power, identities and agency in contemporary debates on work organizations and employment relations.

McCabe (2007) notes the strong suspicion in critical realist critiques that a focus on the individual equates to a promotion of individualism. The accusation is that the 'celebration of the individual' leads to an individualistic and myopic focus, with a concomitant failure to appreciate the wider structures of power that shape the actual identities that are available to individuals in organizations and who is able to occupy them, within historical and cultural contexts, and material relations (Fairclough, 2005; Thompson, 2005). This reflects a mistaken conflation of individualism with identity. Further it is also suggested that it is only through collective activity that increased control in workplaces can be challenged and an emphasis on identity reduces the opportunities for the more informed to be able to transform the social world in ways that eliminates such restrictions (Bain and Taylor, 2000). For example, Blyton and Turnbull (1998: 9) are keen to emphasize that it is the 'collective aspects of relations between workforce and management that we take as our focal point'.

Focusing on the individual does not suggest that we are ignoring or discounting wider structures (dominant and deep-seated discourses), power relations, agency, material conditions nor historical development (McCabe, 2007). Moreover, it is precisely the criticism of the individualistic tendencies of contemporary discourses of change and how these attempt to seduce and entice us into processes of individualization that provides the motivation to challenge and critique among those interested in subjectivity (Alvesson and Willmott, 2002; Bergström and Knights, 2006; Collinson, 2003; Hodgson, 2005; Holmer-Nadesan, 1996; McCabe, 2007; Meriläinen et al., 2004; Thomas and Davies, 2005a).

In addition, an emphasis on subjectivity does not mean resorting to either determinism on the one hand or naïve humanism on the other. Ironically, it was attempts to bring back the 'missing subject' (Newton, 1998) in labour process theory, drawing insights from Foucault (1982), that can be seen as pivotal in putting issues of identity, subjectivity and the subject at the forefront of debates over control, agency and resistance at work (Knights and Willmott, 1989). In particular, labour process theory was viewed as being unable to fully appreciate how processes of individualization, fragmentation and intensification of work in contemporary capitalist employment relations had profound implications for self-identity (Casey, 1999; du Gay, 1996; Grey, 1994; Knights and Morgan, 1991; Sewell and Wilkinson, 1992; Willmott, 1993). However, appropriation of Foucault's (1977) ideas into the labour process debate, with the so-called manufacturing of subjectivity thesis, was viewed as being too deterministic, suggesting a 'docile body', a mere throughput for management-inspired discourses, with the impression being that the individual was more 'done to' than 'doing' (Newton, 1998). Consequently, battle lines have been drawn and theoretical positions defended, resulting in a polarized debate around questions of structure and agency in workplace power relations. These debates have centred on the problem of an *under socialized* or *over socialized* understanding of the subject, with both approaches resting on the assumption of a human being as a 'little world in himself'

(Elias, 1968: 249, cited in du Gay, 2007: 24), that is, someone who is viewed as having insufficient or too much agency.

Of course, the issue of structure versus agency has long been debated within the study of work organizations (Reed, 2003). Rather than stalling in dualistic thinking over agency and structure, however, we argue that it is conceptually fruitful to focus on the mutual cohabitation of the self and the social, whereby identity can be usefully conceived of as arising from the *interactions* between forms of identity regulation (located in often deeply entrenched discourses) and human agency, rather than one or other being an overriding influence (Bergström and Knights, 2006). Such an approach usefully locates the individual in social and temporal contexts that both constrain and sustain identity construction.

Thus, in the example of social work professional–managers presented in this chapter, there is an active engagement – a struggle – over the discourses that both constrain and sustain identities. Changes in the employment relationship for social work professionals have contributed to increased pressure of work, greater accountability, demands for a diverse range of managerial skills, longer working hours, greater insecurity and stress. However, the impact of these changes cannot be viewed in a deterministic way. Rather, the effect is to provide the context of struggle, manipulation and mediation by these public service professionals. Given their equivocal positions as both recipients and bearers of control (Willmott, 1997), these middle-raking social work professionals can be regarded as 'central political actors' (Laine and Vaara, 2007) whose agency can be targeted at challenging and reinterpreting meanings within the ideological project of new public management. As Laine and Varra argue (2007: 53) 'they can act as agents creating new discursive and social practices'. This is where challenge becomes meaningful for them: in engaging in the struggle around meanings, they can have considerable effects in further destabilizing the discourses of change.

The focus of this research was on the way that individuals exercise power in positioning themselves in a dynamic relationship with the discourses of change. In exerting their influence, these individuals drew on the collective occupational identity of the social work professional or public service manager, although no reference was made to any union-based identity or to collective action in response to the pressures of change. While it could be argued that a collective response may provide a more powerful means of transforming behavioural norms (McNay, 2000), the emphasis within this chapter has been on the way that individual identity performances also have important, albeit more subtle, effects in shifting and transforming meanings and understandings within work organizations.

Thus, we can see how, by focusing on the struggle around identities, in the analysis of changing employment relations, we are able to present an alternative critique of power–knowledge relations in organizations, gaining insights into how and why individuals challenge the meanings within discourses, rendering them less robust and unified. Taking a micro-political approach (Thomas and Davies, 2005a), we have shown how social work professionals are able to subvert, resist and re-inscribe attempts to re-craft their identities and the meanings of effective performance that are prescribed within the reform agenda. We see how they exercise power in the ways they position themselves when faced with tensions within their employment relationship. Through a process of challenging and (re)constructing meanings within social work practice, they exploit the contradictions within the discourses of change, drawing on different meanings around public service, managerial efficiency, personal survival and support for front-line staff. This detailed understanding of the ways that employees respond to change, focusing on identity work in dynamic interaction with the power of subjectivizing forces, provides an important account of human agency in the employment relationship. As Jermier et al. (1994) note, power relations in employment relations occur in more complex ways than can be understood in simple all or nothing polarized categories: 'most employees in advanced capitalist societies are neither class-conscious revolutionaries nor passive docile automatons' (Jermier et al., 1994: 9). Such neat bounded categories bear little reflection on our lived experiences. We need to appreciate that questions of 'who we are?' dynamically interact with 'who our organization wants us to be?' and that responses to such questions are many and varied. Therefore, a detailed understanding of the dynamics of control and agency in analysing work and employment relations is crucial.

Notes

1. We reviewed the following journals for the period 1999–2009: Sociology; The Sociological Review; Work, Employment and Society; British Journal of Industrial Relations; European Journal of Industrial Relations; Industrial Relations; Industrial Relations Journal and Employee Relations. For each journal we searched abstracts and key words for the terms 'identity' and/or 'subjectivity'. Overall, very little attention was given to individual identity, although collective identity was a strong focus in the articles. In addition, where individual identity was of concern, this was in the sociology of work journals rather than those more directly focused on industrial/employment relations.
2. Essentialism here refers to the assumption that all those identifying, or being identified, with a particular social category (e.g. gender) display common characteristics and have a common existence.
3. We take a critical understanding of discourses, whereby they are seen not only to constitute meanings of terms and practices, but also they engender personal identities. Discourses are thus 'historically and culturally variable ways of specifying knowledge

and truth' (Meriliäinen et al., 2004). Discourses thus 'do not identify objects, they constitute them and in the practice of doing so conceal their own invention' (Foucault, 1972: 49).

4. A Foucauldian term, disciplinary technologies are targeted at producing a 'docile body' necessary for the smooth operation of capitalism (Foucault, 1977). For example, HRM can be seen as a comprising a set of disciplinary technologies by which individuals come to know themselves, through a range of techniques designed to label, classify, delineate, rank and elicit self-confessions (Townley, 1993a).

5. In this research, we view the interview as an arena for critical reflexive engagement between the interviewer and interviewee, with the interview texts being constructed collectively by both parties. Taking a constructionist approach, where meaning is constituted in language and social action, our presentation of material in this chapter represents our constructions of the social workers' constructions of their struggles around identities, power and agency (Thomas and Linstead, 2002).

References

Ackroyd, S., Kirkpatrick, I. and Walker, R. M. (2007) 'Public management reform in the UK and its consequences for professional organization: a comparative analysis', *Public Administration*, 85, 1: 9–26.

Alvesson, M., Ashcraft, A. and Thomas, R. (2008) 'Identity matters', *Organization*, 15, 1: 5–28.

Alvesson, M. and Kärreman, D. (2004) 'Interfaces of control. Technocratic and socio-ideological control in a global management consultancy firm', *Accounting, Organizations and Society*, 29: 423–44.

Alvesson, M. and Willmott, H. (2002) 'Identity regulation as organizational control: producing the appropriate individual', *Journal of Management Studies*, 39, 5: 619–44.

Alvesson, M. and Willmott, H. (1996) *Making Sense of Management: A Critical Introduction*. London: Sage.

Arrowsmith, J., Gilman, M. W., Edwards, P. and Monder, R. (2003) 'The impact of the national minimum wage in small firms', *British Journal of Industrial Relations*, 41, 3: 435–56.

Bain, P. and Taylor, P. (2000) 'Entrapped by the "electronic panoptican"? Worker resistance in the call centre', *New Technology, Work and Employment*, 15, 1: 2–18.

Bauman, Z. (2004) *Identity*. Cambridge: Polity Press.

Beck, U., Giddens, A. and Lash, S. (1994) *Reflexive Modernisation: Politics, Tradition and Aesthetics in the Modern Social Order*. Stanford, CA: Stanford University Press.

Benwell, B. and Stokoe, E. (2006) *Discourse and Identity*. Edinburgh: Edinburgh University Press.

Bergström, O. and Knights, D. (2006) 'Organizational discourse and subjectivity: subjectification during processes of recruitment', *Human Relations*, 59, 3: 351–77.

Bhabha, H. (1994) *The Location of Culture*. London: Routledge.

Blyton, P. and Turnbull, P. (1998) *Dynamics of Employee Relations*. Second Edition. Basingstoke: Macmillan.

Boltanski, L. and Chiapello, E. (2007) *The New Spirit of Capitalism*. London: Verso.

Briskin, L. (2008) 'Cross-constituency organizing in Canadian unions', *British Journal of Industrial Relations*, 46, 2: 221–47.

Burrell, G. (1997) *Pandemonium: Towards a Retro-Organization Theory*. London: Sage.

Burrell, G. (2006) 'Foucauldian and postmodern thought and the analysis of work', in M. Korczynski, R. Hodson and P. Edwards (eds) *Social Theory at Work*. Oxford: Oxford University Press.

Butler, J. (1997) *The Psychic Life of Power*. Stanford: Standford University Press.

Butler, J. (1992) 'Contingent foundations: feminism and the question of "postmodernism"', in J. Butler, and J. W. Scott (eds) *Feminists Theorize the Political*. London: Routledge.

Carey, M. (2003) 'Anatomy of a care manager', *Work, Employment and Society*, 17, 1: 121–35.

Casey, C. (1995) *Work, Self and Society: After Industrialism*. London: Routledge.

Casey, C. (1999) ' "Come, join our family": discipline and integration in corporate organizational culture', *Human Relations*, 52, 2: 155–78.

Castells, M. (1996) *The Rise of the Network Society*. Oxford: Blackwell.

Causer, G. and Exworthy, M. (1999) 'Professionals as managers across the public sector', in M. Exworthy, and S. Halford (eds) *Professionals and the New Managerialism in the Public Sector*. Milton Keynes: OU Press.

Clarke, J. and Newman, J. (1997) *The Managerial State*. London: Sage.

Clarke, J., Gerwitz, S. and McLaughlin, E. (2000) 'Reinventing the welfare state', in J. Clarke, S. Gerwitz and E. McLaughlin (eds) *New Managerialism, New Welfare?* London: Sage.

Collinson, D. (2003) 'Identities and insecurities: selves at work', *Organization*, 10: 527–47.

Davies, A. and Thomas, R. (2008) 'Dixon of Dock Green got shot! Policing identity work and organizational change', *Public Administration*, 86: 627–42.

Deetz, S. (1992) *Democracy in an Age of Corporate Colonization*. Albany NY: Albany State University of New York Press.

Dominelli, L. (1996) 'Deprofessionalising social work: anti-oppressive practice, competencies and postmodernism', *British Journal of Social Work*, 26, 2: 153–75.

Doogan, K. (2009) *New Capitalism? The Transformation of Work*. London: Polity Press.

du Gay, P. (1996) *Consumption and Identity at Work*. London: Sage.

du Gay, P. (2007) *Organizing Identity*. London: Sage.

Edwards, P. (1986) *Conflict at Work*. Oxford: Blackwell.

Ehrenreich, B. (2006) *Bait and Switch: The Futile Pursuit of the Corporate Dream*. London: Granta Books.

Elias, N. (1968) *The Civilizing Process, Vol. 1*. Oxford: Basil Blackwell.

Fairclough, N. (2005) 'Critical discourse analysis, organizational discourse, and organizational change', *Organization Studies*, 26: 915–39.

Farnham, D. and Horton, S. (1996) *Managing People in the Public Services*. Hampshire: Macmillan.

Farnham, D., Horton, S. and White, G. (2003) 'Organisational change and staff participation and involvement in Britain's public services', *International Journal of Publics Sector Management*, 16, 6: 434–45.

Farrell, C. and Morris, J. (2003) 'The "neo-bureaucratic state": professionals, managers and professional managers in schools, general practices and social work', *Organization*, 10, 1: 129–56.

Ferlie, E., Ashburner, L., Fitzgerald, L. and Pettigrew, A. (1996) *The New Public Management in Action*. Oxford: Oxford University Press.

Ferlie, E., Lynn, L. E. Jr. and Pollitt, C. (2007) Introductory Remarks, in E. Ferlie, L. E. Lynn Jr. and C. Pollitt (eds) *The Oxford Handbook of Public Management*. Oxford: Oxford University Press.

Foucault, M. (1972) *The Archaeology of Knowledge & The Discourse on Language*. New York: Pantheon Books/Tavistock.

Foucault, M. (1977) *Discipline and Punish: The Birth of the Prison*. London: Allen Lane.

Foucault, M. (1982) 'The subject and power', in H. L. Drefus and P. Rabinow (eds) *Beyond Structuralism and Hermeneutics*. Brighton: Harvester.

Froud, J., Sukhdev, J., Leaver, A. and Williams, K. (2006) *Financialization and Strategy: Narrative and Numbers*. Abingdon, Oxon: Routledge.

Gottfried, H. (1994) 'Learning the score: the duality of control and everyday resistance in the temporary help service industry', in John M. Jermier, David Knights, and Walter R. Nord (eds) *Resistance and Power in Organizations*. 102–27, London: Routledge.

Grey, C. (1994) 'Career as a project of self and labour process discipline', *Sociology*, 28, 2: 479–97.

Grey, C. (2009) *A Very Short, Fairly Interesting and Reasonably Cheap Book about Organizations* (second edition). London: Sage.

Halford, S. and Leonard, P. (1999) 'New Identities? Professionalism, managerialism and the construction of self', in M. Exworthy and S. Halford (eds) *Professionals and the New Managerialism in the Public Sector*. Buckingham: Open University Press.

Harris, J. (1998) 'Scientific management, bureau professionalism, new managerialism: the labour process of state social work', *British Journal of Social Work*, 28: 839–62.

Haslam, S. A., Eggins, R. A. and Reynolds, K. J. (2003) 'The ASPIRe model: actualizing social and personal identity resources to enhance organisational outcomes', *Journal of Organisational and Occupational Psychology*, 76: 83–113.

Heckscher, C. (1995) *White Collar Blues*. New York: Basic Books.

Hodgson, D. E. (2005) 'Putting on a professional performance': performativity, subversion and project management', *Organization*, 12, 1: 51–68.

Holgate, J., Hebson, G. and McBride, A. (2006) 'Why gender and "difference" matters: a critical appraisal of industrial relations research', *Industrial Relations Journal*, 37, 4: 310–28.

Holmer-Nadesan, M. (1996) 'Organizational identity and space of action', *Organization Studies*, 17, 1: 49–81.

Horton, S. (2003) 'Participation and involvement: the democratisation of new public management, *International journal of Public Sector Management*, 16, 6: 403–11.

Jermier, J. M., Knights, D. and Nord, W. R. (1994) 'Introduction', in J. M. Jermier, D. Knights, and W. R. Nord (eds) *Resistance and Power in Organizations*. London: Routledge.

Jones, C. (1999) 'Social work: regulation and managerialism', in M. Exworthy and S. Halford (eds) *Professionals and the New Managerialism in the Public Sector*. Milton Keynes: OU Press.

Jones, C. (2001) 'Voices from the front line: state social workers and new labour', *British Journal of Social Work*, 31: 547–62.

Knights, D. and Willmott, H. (1989) 'Power and subjectivity at work', *Sociology*, 23: 535–58.

Knights, D. and Morgan, G. (1991) 'Corporate strategy, organisations and subjectivity: a critique', *Organization Studies*, 12: 251–73.

Kondo, D. (1990) *Crafting Selves: Power, Gender and Discourses of Identity in a Japanese Workplace*. Chicago: University of Chicago Press.

Kunda, G. (1992) *Engineering Culture. Control and Commitment in a High-Tech Corporation*. Philadelphia: Temple University Press.

Laine, P-M. and Vaara, E. (2007) 'Struggling over subjectivity: a discursive analysis of strategic development in an engineering group', *Human Relations*, 60, 1: 29–58.

LaNuez, D. and. Jermier, J. M. (1994) 'Sabotage by managers and technocrats: neglected patterns of resistance at work', in John M. Jermier, David Knights and Walter R. Nord (eds) *Resistance and Power in Organizations*. 219–51, London: Routledge.

Lawler, J. and Hearn, J. (1995) 'UK public service organizations: the rise of managerialism and the impact of change on social services departments', *International Journal of Public Sector Management*, 8, 4: 7–16.

Leidner, R. (2006) 'Identity and work', in M. Korczynski, R. Hodson and P. Edwards (eds) *Social Theory at Work*. Oxford: Oxford University Press.

Llewellyn, N, (2004) 'In search of modernization: the negotiation of social identity in organizational reform', *Organization Studies*, 25, 6: 947–68.

Martinez Lucio, M. and Stewart, P. (1997) 'The paradox of contemporary labour process theory: the rediscovery of labour and the disappearance of collectivism', *Capital and Class*, 62: 49–77.

Marx, K. (1976) *Capital: A Critique of Political Economy*. Harmondsworth: Penguin.

McCabe, D. (2007) 'Individualization at work? subjectivity, teamworking and anti-unionism', *Organization*, 14, 2: 243–66.

McLaughlin, K., Osborne, S. P. and Ferlie, E. (2002) (eds) *New Public Management: Current Trends and Future Prospects*. London: Routledge.

McNay, L. (2000) *Gender and Agency: Reconfiguring the Subject in Feminist and Social Theory*. Cambridge: Polity.

Meriliänen, S., Tienari, J., Thomas, R. and Davies, A. (2004) 'Management consultant talk: a cross-cultural comparison of normalising discourse and resistance', *Organization*, 11, 2: 539–64.

Meyer, R. and Hammerschmid, G. (2006) 'Public management reform: an identity project', *Public Policy and Administration*, 21, 1: 99–115.

Meyerson, D. E. and Scully, M. A. (1995) 'Tempered radicalism and the politics of ambivalence and change', *Organization Science*, 6, 5: 585–600.

Morgan, P. Allington, N. and Heery, E. (2000) 'Employment insecurity in the public services', in E. Heery and J. Salmon (eds) *The Insecure Workforce*. London: Routledge.

Mulholland, H. (2009) 'Tories warn of social work recruitment crisis', *Guardian Newspaper*, Guardian.co.uk, Tuesday 3rd February 2009.

Musson, G. and Duberley, J. (2007) 'Change, change or be exchanged: the discourse of participation and the manufacture of identity', *Journal of Management Studies*, 44, 1: 143–64.

Newton, T. (1998) 'Theorizing subjectivity in organizations: the failure of foucauldian studies', *Organization Studies*, 19, 3: 415–47.

Piore, M. J. and Safford, S. (2006) 'Changing regimes of workplace governance, shifting axes of social mobilization, and the challenge to industrial relations theory', *Industrial Relations*, 45, 3: 299–325.

Pollitt, C. (1993) *Managerialism and the Public Services*. Oxford: Blackwell.

Reed, M. (2003) 'The agency/structure dilemma in organization theory: open doors and brick walls', in H. Tsoukas and C. Knudsen (eds) *The Oxford Handbook of Organization Theory: Meta-Theoretical Perspectives*. Oxford: Oxford University Press.

Said, E. (1979) *Orientalism*. London: Routledge.

Sedgwick, E. K. (1990) *Epistemologies of the Closet*. Berkley, CA: University of California Press.

Sedgwick, E. K. (1999) *A Dialogue on Love*. New York: Beacon Press.

Sennett, R. (1998) *The Corrosion of Character*. New York: Norton.

Sennett, R. (2006) *The Culture of the New Capitalism*. New Haven: Yale University Press.

Sewell, G. and Wilkinson, B. (1992) 'Someone to watch over me: surveillance, discipline and the just-in-time labour process', *Sociology*, 26, 2: 271–91.

Smith, C. (2001) 'Trust and confidence: possibilities for social work in high modernity', *British Journal of Social Work*, 31, 2: 287–316.

Spivak, G. C. (1987) *In Other Worlds: Essays in Cultural Politics*. New York: Methuen.

Strange, S. (1986) *Casino Capitalism*. Oxford: Blackwell.

Sveningsson, S. and Alvesson, M. (2003) 'Managing managerial identities: organizational fragmentation, discourse and identity struggle', *Human Relations*, 56 (10): 1163–93.

Thomas, R. and Dunkerley, D. (1999) 'Careering downwards? middle management in the downsized organization', *British Journal of Management*, 10, 2: 157–69.

Thomas, R. and Linstead, A. (2002) 'Losing the plot? middle managers and identity', *Organization*, 9, 1: 71–93.

Thomas, R., Mills, A. J. and Helms-Mills, J. (2004) 'Introduction: resisting gender, gendering resistance', in R. Thomas, A. J. Mills and J. Helms-Mills (eds) *Identity Politics at Work*. London: Routledge.

Thomas, R. and Davies, A. (2005a) 'Theorising the micro-politics of resistance: discourses of change and professional identities in the UK public services', *Organization Studies*, 26, 5: 683–706.

Thomas, R. and Davies, A. (2005b) 'What have the feminists done for us? feminist theory and organizational resistance', *Organization*, 12, 5: 711–40.

Thomas, R. (2009) 'Critical studies on identities: mapping the Terrain', in M. Alvesson, T. Bridgman and H. Willmott (eds) *The Oxford Handbook of Critical Management Studies*. 166–85, Oxford: Oxford University Press.

Thompson, P. and Ackroyd, S. (1995) 'All quiet on the workplace front? a critique of recent trends in british industrial sociology', *Sociology*, 29, 4: 615–33.

Thompson, P. (2005) 'Brands, boundaries and bandwagons: a critical reflection on critical management studies', in C. Grey and H. Willmott (eds) *Critical Management Studies: A Reader*. Oxford: Oxford University Press.

Townley, B. (1993a) 'Foucault, power/knowledge, and its relevance for human resource management', *Academy of Management Review*, 18, 3: 518–45.

Townley, B. (1993b) 'Performance appraisal and the emergence of management', *Journal of Management Studies*, 30, 2: 221–38.

Truss, C. (2008) 'Continuity and change: The role of the HR function in the modern pubic sector', *Public Administration*, 86, 4: 1071–88.

Webb, J. (2006) *Organisations, Identities and the Self*. Basingstoke: Palgrave.

Weedon, C. (1987) *Feminist Practice and Poststructuralist Theory*. Oxford: Blackwell.

Willmott, H. (1993) 'Strength is ignorance; slavery is freedom: managing culture in modern organizations', *Journal of Management Studies*, 30, 4: 515–52.

Willmott, H. (1997) 'Rethinking management and managerial work: capitalism, control and subjectivity', *Human Relations*, 50, 11: 1329–59.

Ybema, S., Keenoy, T., Oswick, C., Beverungen, A., Ellis, N. and Sabelis, I. (2009) 'Articulating identities', *Human Relations*, 62, 3: 299–322.

part 2

Contextual influences shaping the employment relationship

Reassessing markets and employment relations

Marco Hauptmeier

Introduction

Markets are both a central institution and a source of turbulence in capitalist societies. The emergence and decline of markets, competition in markets and the contraction of markets are powerful social and economic processes that have a profound impact on employment relations. Weber (1948) described the competition in markets as a struggle between people without war. For Schumpeter (1942), the rise and fall of companies in markets were part of capitalism's creative destruction. Commons (1909) pointed to the 'competitive menace' in markets that drove down the living standards of workers while Polanyi (1944) regarded markets as grinding 'satanic mills' that destroy social relations if they are not embedded in social institutions. In addition, a variety of authors have linked globalization and the related expansion and liberalization of markets to the decline in labour standards and labour rights (Jenkins and Turnbull this volume; Moody, 1997; Tilly, 1995).

In a recent important article, Piore and Safford (2006) question the importance of markets for employment relations. They strongly rebut the thesis that changes in employment relations are driven by market forces, and instead suggest that they can be attributed to the rise of new identity groups and the mobilization of individual rights at the workplace. They observe a change from a collective bargaining regime to an employment rights regime based on shifting social identities. The collective bargaining regime was underpinned by class-based worker identities and labour unions that negotiated the terms of employment relations through collective bargaining. The decline of class-based identities and the rise of groups based on gender, sexuality, disability and other forms of identity underpinned the emergence of the new employment rights regime. These identity groups mobilized individual rights such as equal opportunity and anti-discrimination laws and thereby changed employment relations. Emphatically, according to Piore and Safford, changes in employment relations have not been 'produced by the increasing encroachment of the competitive market and the growing hegemony of neo-liberal ideology that has championed market-oriented reforms' (Piore and Safford, 2006, p. 300).

In contrast to Piore and Safford, this chapter seeks to demonstrate the importance of markets for changes in employment relations by identifying different mechanisms through which markets shape employment relations (see also Brown, 2008). In addition, the chapter provides evidence for the thesis that the impact of markets on employment relations has increased. This twofold purpose of the chapter is developed in six steps. First, states have focused on extending and liberalizing markets with the effect that markets have become more important in shaping employment relations compared to other governance mechanisms, such as law, associations and hierarchies. Second, the rise of a neo-liberal ideology has increased the legitimacy of markets in governing societies and employment relations. Third, the scope of many markets has broadened, exposing firms to greater competition. Fourth, increasing product-market competition and changing government regulations have created space for the mimicking of employment relations practices within sectors, a process that is described as a product-market-driven isomorphism. Fifth, management has segmented employment relations to reflect market niches. Sixth, and finally, management has introduced practices within firms, such as working time flexibility and performance-based remuneration, to link the employment relationship to market conditions.

This chapter interrogates the impact of markets on employment relations from the macro to the micro level, but also points to the relationships between factors and different levels. Changing government regulation and the rise of a neo-liberal ideology are initially discussed at the national level. The discussion of the scope of markets encompasses both local and global markets. Product-market isomorphism and segmentation are processes that work at the sectoral level, while the last section of the chapter focuses on market-oriented employment relations practices on the firm level. In order to specify the link between employment relations and markets, the chapter draws on political science, economic sociology and employment relations. In doing so, the focus is on developments in western democracies, in particular the United Kingdom,

Germany, Spain and the United States, based on secondary data and the author's own research (Hauptmeier, 2009).

The changing axis of governance – the extension of the market mechanism

Economic activities and employment relations in modern societies are organized by at least four governance mechanisms: the law, markets, hierarchies and associations (Campbell et al., 1991; Hollingsworth et al., 1994). States govern societies by law. Markets coordinate the exchange and allocation of goods, services and employees. Management organizes economic activity and employment relations through hierarchical decisions (Williamson, 1983). Associations such as labour unions and employers' associations engage in collective bargaining and regulate the substantive and procedural terms and conditions of employees.

The state plays a central role in constructing and legitimizing these different governance mechanisms. States engage in both market-making and market-constraining activities (Scharpf, 1999). They establish and liberalize markets, but at the same time, state-sanctioned governance mechanisms such as laws, hierarchies and associations constrain markets. Despite the continuing dual role of states in market-making and market constraining, states have increasingly focused on promoting and extending markets in comparison to other governance mechanisms, which has afforded markets greater weight in coordinating and shaping economic activities and employment relations.

The four governance mechanisms mentioned above exist in all market economies. However, the foundation and relative weight of each governance mechanism varies across countries. Hall and Soskice (2001), in their 'varieties of capitalism' thesis, point to the organization of economic activities beyond the market via associations in coordinated market economies, while the role of markets is more prevalent in liberal market economies. Esping-Andersen (1990) earlier pointed to variation in the degree to which people are dependent on selling their labour power in the labour market under different types of welfare regime. In neo-liberal welfare states, labour is largely a commodity, while the provision of alternative income streams and social benefits 'de-commodifies' labour in continental and Scandinavian welfare states. In all economies, the relative weight of the different governance mechanisms is influenced by historical compromises. Crouch (1993) pointed to the crucial role associations played during the formation of modern states. If associations supported state actors in their quest to rule the new nation states against church and crown, they permanently secured an influential role in the governance of economies. After World War II, the Western industrialized countries renegotiated economic order on the national and international levels and struck a balance between the governance of markets, states and employer associations and management hierarchies. Ruggie (1982) called the emerging social and economic post-war order 'embedded liberalism'.

Within embedded liberalism, the state sanctioned the role of associations, such as labour unions and employers' associations, in the governance of the economy and employment relations. These intermediary organizations between state and citizens relieved the state from the task of regulating a complex and conflict-prone area of society (Streeck and Schmitter, 1985). In addition, it was suggested that associations were closer to and better informed about the specific features of the employment relationship than were distant state bureaucracies. Over the last three decades, however, the pattern of relationships between state and associations has changed and two novel state approaches towards associations have emerged. On the one hand, centre–right governments in liberal states such as the United States and the United Kingdom attacked labour unions and sought to diminish their role in regulating employment relations. Subsequent centre–left governments in these countries did little to re-establish the role of labour unions. In continental coordinated economies, states did not attack labour unions, but they stopped proactively promoting the governance of employment relations via employers' associations and labour unions. States included employers' associations and labour unions in social pacts in a number of European countries in the 1990s (Ebbinghaus and Hassel, 2000; Hassel, 2009), but these states relied less on social pacts in the following decade. Employers' associations and labour unions continued to play an important role in training regimes in coordinated market regimes such as Germany. However, there are few examples of legislation that strengthened the regulatory capacity of labour unions and employers' associations. While western states stopped pro-actively promoting the governance of employment relations via associations, they pro-actively promoted markets.

National governments expanded markets and liberalized trade by negotiating bilateral and multilateral trade agreements (General Agreement on Tariffs and Trade) and through international organizations (e.g. the World Trade Organization) (Dicken, 2007). An important vehicle for the liberalization of markets became regional economic integration. In Europe, the European Union created common European markets by enforcing the freedom of movement of employees, goods, services and capital (Jabko, 2006). In North America, the North-American Free Trade Agreement (NAFTA) liberalized product markets. The liberalization of markets increased trade, e.g.

the volume of world exports increased from $59 billion in 1948, to $1.838 billion in 1983 and reached $13.619 billion in 2007 (WTO, 2008). Furthermore, states privatized state-owned companies and exposed a greater part of the economy to market competition. The countries of the European Union agreed in the run-up to the introduction of the euro to privatize state-run companies in sectors such as telecommunications, postal services and transport. Beyond Europe, the International Monetary Fund (IMF) forced states to privatize state-run companies when countries called upon the IMF during economic and financial crises (Stiglitz, 2002). The unilateral or multilateral market making of states has been far-reaching and informed by liberal economic ideologies (see next section).

States continue to govern societies by law. Proponents of neo-liberalism and globalization often proclaim the retreat of the state and underestimate the visible hand of the state (e.g. Friedman, 2007). The more interesting question is how the hand of the state intervenes in the political economy. On the one hand, states have cut different social benefits, but social expenditure measured as a percentage of GDP did not decrease markedly in many western states (this is to some extent related to skyrocketing health care costs) (Pierson, 2001). On the other hand, there is clear evidence that states liberalized labour markets. States lowered employment protection and alternative income streams such as unemployment benefits (Bosch and Weinkopf, 2008; Salverda et al., 2008). Employment relations continue to be regulated by substantive laws, and Piore and Safford (2006) point to equal opportunity and anti-discrimination laws as examples. But not all employment laws work to constrain markets (e.g. in the way that minimum wage legislation establishes a 'floor' under cost competition in the market). Equal opportunity legislation, for example, gives particular categories of workers a 'level playing field' to compete in the market for jobs without discrimination. Many employment laws are Janus-faced, inasmuch as they both constrain and enable labour market competition.

Managers govern firms and their employment relations through hierarchical relationships and decision-making (Williamson, 1983). However, the governance of companies and employment relations via management hierarchies is constrained by laws, associations and markets. For example, states enforce health and safety laws, environmental standards and labour laws, setting limits for management decision-making. Collective bargaining agreements bind management action to commonly agreed contractual terms and norms with labour unions. Coase's initial formulation of management hierarchies emphasized that firms integrate production to bypass markets in order to avoid transactions costs (that occur through the need to negotiate exchange, to ensure compliance and to market finished goods). Companies can avoid such transaction costs 'by forming an organization and allowing some authority (an 'entrepreneur') to direct the resources [efficiently]' (Coase, 1937, p. 390; cited in Hamilton and Feenstra, 1995). Thus, while firms sometimes create markets they also attempt to avoid transaction costs and limit competition (Marchington and Parker, 1990).

There are numerous interrelationships between the different governance mechanisms identified thus far. For the purpose of this chapter, the relationship between governance by markets and associations is of particular importance. The impact of product-market competition on collective bargaining has been well-documented through the regular Workplace Employment Relations Surveys (WERS) in the United Kingdom (Kersley, 2006). Based on this data, Brown and his collaborators found a strong relationship between the level of product-market competition and the coverage of collective bargaining – increasing competition drove the decline of collective bargaining measured in successive WERS (Brown et al., 2009).

Over recent decades, the axis of governance has changed in employment relations. In the United Kingdom and elsewhere, employment relations continue to be governed by laws and management hierarchies, but the liberalization of markets and privatization of companies exposed employment relations to the pressure and competition of markets to a far greater degree. And this, in turn, helped decrease collective bargaining coverage and the regulating capacity of labour unions and employers' associations.

Ideas and markets: the rise of neo-liberal ideologies

The rise of neo-liberal ideologies in the 1970s and 1980s (Harvey, 2005) encouraged policy makers to pursue the liberalization of markets. But what was the source of this ideological shift? In the first part of this section, it is argued that capitalist crisis has been a major driver of ideological change, including the rise of neo-liberalism. The second part then discusses how collective actors adapted to neo-liberal ideas and the expansion of markets.

Major economic crises tend to lead to fundamental changes of ideology. They are historical junctures that have the potential to change world views and set the evolution of economies and employment relations on different trajectories. Subsequent developments seem to follow a path-dependent logic (Hay, 2006). As Weber explained: 'Not ideas, but material and ideal interests, directly govern men's conduct. Yet very frequently the world images that have been created by ideas, like a switchman, have determined the tracks along which action has been pushed by the dynamic of interest' (Weber et al., 1948, p. 280). The account presented here emphasizes the importance of major economic crises in switching world views, which set action on different tracks. Research on deep economic crises indicates that ideological changes follow a similar pattern (Blyth, 2002; Gamble, 2009). They trigger not only economic but also ideological turbulences. The previously dominant economic paradigm becomes discredited and is blamed for the economic crisis. Actors associated with the previous economic paradigm lose power, while during and in the aftermath of the crisis soul-searching takes place and new economic ideas are explored and developed. These ideas have to be a viable alternative to the previous paradigm and offer solutions for overcoming the crisis (Hall, 1989). This section describes the ideological shifts following the world economic crisis in 1929 and the economic crisis of the 1970s in a stylized form. The conclusion returns to this theme and discusses the possibilities of ideological change following the 2008/2009 financial and economic crisis.

In the wake of the world economic crisis in 1929, the previously dominant *laissez-faire* economic ideology and policies became discredited (Galbraith, 1955). It became accepted that reliance on free markets had led to the social and economic catastrophe of the 1930s and that *laissez-faire* policies could no longer address social and economic problems. In the search for new ideas, John Maynard Keynes (1936) contributed crucially to the articulation of a new economic ideology, which suggested a stronger role for states in governing the economy. A key economic idea was that governments should actively take part in the governance of society and improve the functioning of markets via anti-cyclical state intervention. The changing ideological economic ideas contributed to Roosevelt's New Deal. Keynesian economic ideas also informed the re-forming of western states after World War II (Hall, 1989). Henceforth, state intervention in the economy, via collective regulation of employment relations and welfare state legislation, constrained markets.

The Keynesian economic paradigm came under pressure during the economic crises of the 1970s (Blyth, 2002; Gamble, 2009). Rising unemployment and inflation now appeared to be permanent problems. Keynesian economic policies focused on limiting the rise of unemployment through increased spending, which however also drove up the debt of governments fuelling higher inflation. An increasing number of economists and politicians argued that Keynesian economic policies caused the economic malaise and a new set of economic ideas slowly rose to prominence throughout the 1970s, promising to address the economic problems of the time. Milton Friedman and the Chicago School of Economics argued that it was the foremost task of governments to keep inflation rates stable, but otherwise governments should not interfere with self-regulating markets (Friedman, 1962). This neo-liberal ideology sees markets as the most important and effective governance mechanism for the coordination and organization of economic activities. The 'invisible hand' of the market, the exchange mechanism of supply and demand, would allocate resources, people and products most efficiently and produce the greatest welfare for society if states would only interfere as little as possible. The gradual change towards this neo-liberal paradigm gained momentum when Thatcher and Reagan came to power in the United Kingdom and United States (Harvey, 2005).

While the 1980s marks a general shift towards neo-liberalism, Gamble (2009) differentiates between different types of liberal market ideologies. Market fundamentalists regarded markets as the panacea for solving economic problems, while more moderate neo-liberal ideologies acknowledged the role of states in establishing functioning markets or mitigating some of their adverse social effects through welfare and other policies. Despite these ideological differences, the idea that markets are an efficient and legitimate mechanism for governing economies and employment relations became stronger across the board. The market idea was further strengthened through the collapse of communism in the late 1980s and early 1990s. This alternative ideology and way of governing societies was decisively weakened. The triumph of market capitalism led some observer to declare the end of history and of ideological differences (Fukuyama, 1992).

The spread of neo-liberal ideologies and interrelated material changes, such as the expansion and liberalization of markets, changed the context if not the content of employment relations. As management and unions adapted to this changing socio-economic context, their own ideologies changed over time; in particular they accepted the idea that markets are a legitimate and efficient governance mechanism.

Sabel has argued that 'workers, like the rest of us, can change themselves and the world by defending their interpretation of it' (Sabel, 1984, p. 132). The broad ideological changes seen within the labour movement, however, suggest the opposite: unions defended themselves by changing their interpretation of the world. There were two aspects to this process of adaptation. Firstly, radical union ideology that contested the hegemony of market mechanisms receded and in its place an increasing number of unions became more market oriented. This orientation, in its turn, led unions to engage in 'productivity coalitions' with management (Windolf, 1989), in which unions accepted the goal of management to maintain competitiveness and traded concessions in order to enhance the performance of firms in which their members worked. The ideological basis was an exchange between management and labour: workers participated in the effort to increase productivity while management would attempt to protect jobs. Others within the union movement retained a more radical ideology (Ancel and Slaughter, 2005) and urged resistance to neoliberalism through increased use of the strike weapon. This call to arms failed to resonate, however, and strike rates across western democracies have plummeted (Gall, 1999). A primary response of unions to expanding markets was to gradually reformulate their ideologies and to become more market oriented.

The attack on unions by the Reagan and Thatcher governments in the United States and the United Kingdom encouraged management to take on labour unions and resist the collective regulation of employment relations. It is not clear if this was initially an ideological change or if the previous truce had only been based on the power of unions and subdued anti-union sentiments. In any case, the idea of resisting unions and collective regulation became stronger in the 1980s. In addition, the orientation of Human Resource Management (HRM) emerged and there was a shift in the function of labour departments in large organizations from managing discontent to developing employee commitment and performance (Jacoby, 2004). As markets became more legitimate, management increasingly linked employment relations practices to market forces through devices such as performance-related pay and working time flexibility. The latter are specific manifestations of the market ideology permeating the workplace, to which we return in the last section.

The scope of product markets and employment relations

The relationship between the scope of product markets and employment relations is well-captured in Commons' (1909) classic article on the Philadelphia shoemakers. Initially, the shoemakers' union secured a stable income by organizing all producers in the local shoe market. However, the expansion of the product market to other cities increased competitive pressure. Rising sales of shoes produced with low-wage labour put downward pressure on wages. Only after the shoemakers expanded their union to the scope of the product market and organized all companies within it did they secure their income and standard of living. This was a key insight: workers or their unions had to take wages out of competition in order to prevent their income falling and rising along with the fluctuations of the market (Ulman, 1966). In fully union-organized product markets, producers would compete over the quality and price of the product, better service or more efficient work organization, but not over paying workers lower wages and benefits.

After Second World War product markets and employment relations institutions were delineated by the borders of the nation state. The scope of product markets and employment relations institutions broadly matched one another. National producers focused on national markets, while they were sealed-off from foreign competition through trade barriers. Based on national employment relations institutions, unions were able to establish multi-employer and sectoral collective bargaining not only in countries with a corporatist tradition but also in liberal economies (Sisson, 1987). However, the gradual removal of trade barriers and liberalization of markets by states has extended the scope of the product market beyond national borders and the reach of union organization. Unions early on recognized the need to expand their organization beyond national borders and founded global unions, but these lacked the power and capacity to take wages out of competition (Gordon and Turner, 2000). In Europe, the attempts by European trade unions to coordinate wages across borders have not been successful (Gollbach and Schulten, 2000).

The changing scope of product markets has also influenced employer strategies. In national product markets, unions tended to have more power. Militant unions at one company could push for higher wage levels, which encouraged unions at other companies to follow suit. Companies could compete with each other over paying higher wages. Taking part in multi-employer and sectoral collective bargaining protected individual employers against militant unions and upward wage competition. Delegating the negotiations to a higher bargaining level took contentious issues out of the workplace (Sisson, 1987). For bigger companies multi-employer or sectoral collective bargaining could be a cheap solution. They tended to have a higher productivity compared to small- and medium-sized companies. As the average productivity increase was an important guideline for wage increases, the rise in wage cost was often lower than the rise in productivity in large companies. But the expansion of product markets beyond national boundaries changed the logic for employers. Competition in international markets constrained union demands and employers were to a lesser degree dependent on protection against high wage demands by unions. In an open economy, unions were aware that market share could be picked up by foreign companies with lower wages, which would undercut the economic base of a company and lead to job losses and pressure on wages. When developing wage demands, unions would increasingly keep an eye on the wage levels of competitors. In addition, in international product markets, management potentially had the option to exit and could relocate production to low-wage countries (cf. Hirschman, 1970). Management's exit option and the threat to use it increased the bargaining power of employers *vis-à-vis* labour.

Despite the gradual, greater openness of economies, the extent of product-market expansion has been exaggerated by advocates of the strong globalization thesis (Friedman, 2007). Only some truly global markets have emerged, other markets remained regional, national or local in scope (Dicken, 2007). The level of competition that impacts on employment relations can be assessed by differentiating between sheltered and exposed sectors (Scharpf and Schmidt, 2000). The latter sectors are exposed to international competition, while the former are sheltered from it. Typical sheltered sectors include the public sector and health care as they cannot easily be relocated to other countries. Manufacturing tends to be exposed to international competition. The degree of competition is correlated with the required skill levels. The lower skill levels in textiles for example, made it one of the first sectors to be relocated to low-wage economies (see Jenkins and Turnbull this volume). Manufacturing producers dependent on high-skills (e.g. the automotive sector) began to relocate production at a much later stage. The level of competition is also influenced by how easily products can be transported; it is cheap to ship T-shirts around the globe while it is comparably expensive to transport cars. Not all exposed sectors are global sectors though. Trade and market liberalization have a strong regional focus as in Europe, North-American and recently in East Asia. Trade barriers have been removed within these regions but continue to exist for countries outside each regional bloc.

Despite these qualifications with respect to the expansion of markets, the scope of many markets has increased. The expansion of markets beyond borders and national employment relations institutions has weakened the unions' capacity to limit competition and to regulate the employment relationship. The regulating capacity of unions has remained stronger in sheltered sectors, which in many countries are now the main redoubt of union membership and organization, but the overall trend for unions has been adverse.

Product-market-driven isomorphism of employment relations

The expansion of markets, the declining capability of collective organizations to set standardized rules and the trans-national integration of companies has created more space for the diffusion of employment relations practices across countries (Edwards, 1998). By drawing on the institutional literature in sociology, this section argues that the spread of employment relations across countries can be described and understood as a product-market-driven isomorphism (DiMaggio and Powell, 1983).

Markets are organizational fields that are based on regulatory rules enforced by states (e.g. property rights, contract laws), a role structure that includes incumbent and challenging companies and a shared understanding of what the action in markets mean (e.g. market actors are aware that a continuous failure in the product market means the extinction of a company) (Fligstein, 1996, 2001). In constantly changing markets, it is difficult for companies to identify the best course of action. Managers have incomplete information, no clear knowledge about means–end relationships and they do not have the rational capacity to compute best practices. Organizations face two principal sources of uncertainty, namely (i) productive uncertainty in its own ability to develop and utilize human resources and new technologies, and (ii) competitive uncertainty in its product market which, unless the firm is a monopolist, is inherent in the ability of its rivals to respond with their own business strategies (Lazonick, 1991). One way to deal with such economic uncertainty is to mimic practices from competitors that are perceived to be successful (DiMaggio and Powell, 1983). On a more specific level, the transnational integration of companies, global production and HRM systems, standardization, benchmarking, coercive comparisons and whipsawing are vehicles for the spread of employment relations practices between competitors.

Multinational companies have been described as a trans-national space (Morgan et al., 2001). This suggests that multinational firms have some degree of freedom to develop similar employment relations practices. There are numerous examples of companies that have standardized and integrated production and work organization across borders. For example in the auto industry, car producers mimicked lean production practices from Japanese competitors that threatened the market share of established producers. Toyota developed the original lean production system. Later other producers developed their own equivalents; for example General Motors launched its Global Manufacturing System. The latter defines work standards and production principles (e.g. in the area of health and safety) which General Motors seeks to implement at all of its plants worldwide. Multinational companies in the service sector, such as Starbucks and McDonald's, have also developed standardized work organization systems, which they have sought to implement worldwide. In addition, a number of multinational companies have developed global HR strategies that guide employment relations practices across countries (Ferner et al., 2006).

Benchmarking is a crucial instrument or mechanism for the implementation of standardized work and employment relations practices (Sisson et al.,

2003). Management benchmarks the degree of implementation of their global programmes and performance on a variety of indicators such as labour costs or the productivity of subsidiaries. Benchmarking can have a number of different functions. It provides management with differentiated information about the business and helps to identify subsidiaries that are underperforming as well as demonstrating best practices. Positively identified employment relations practices can be implemented at other plants. Different authors point to the coercive aspect of benchmarking in the employment relationship as underperforming plants are threatened with disinvestment or plant closure (Marginson et al., 1995; Mueller and Purcell, 1992). Such forcing strategies can be used to overcome local idiosyncrasies and resistance, and help to advance the implementation of standardized employment relations practices.

Dominance effects might help to understand the direction for the spread of employment relations practices across companies and countries (Elger and Smith, 2005). Companies mimic employment relations practices from dominant economic countries and from companies that are perceived as leaders in a particular product market. These business practices are not always based on rational considerations. Abrahamson has pointed to management fads and fashions that can lead to the gradual adaptation and spread of new business practices (Abrahamson, 1991; Abrahamson and Eisenman, 2008).

In identifying product-market-driven isomorphism we do not wish to advance a convergence argument. There is a wide range of factors that limit convergence and shape particularities in employment relations, including national institutions, culture, plant histories, union resistance and the socio-economic local and regional context (on the latter, see Locke, 1992). However, a number of employment relations practices have spread and diffused across different countries, a development which requires explanation. Katz and Darbishire (2000) found that four different employment relations patterns have spread within such diverse countries as the United States, Germany, Australia, United Kingdom, Sweden and Japan, despite very different national institutional frameworks. In my own research on the auto industry I found that a wide range of employment relations practices have spread across countries including outsourcing, night work, whipsawing, benchmarking, working time flexibility, performance-based pay systems, two-tier wage systems, common health and safety standards and lean production principles (Hauptmeier, 2009). The international research group GERPISA makes the case that the transfer of production models and best practices requires an adaptation to the local and national context, which leads to the hybridization of production models (Boyer, 1998).[1] Even though the particularities of some employment relations practices vary across countries, they can broadly function equivalently (Locke and Thelen, 1995). For example, two-tier wage systems in the United States, Spain and Germany are adapted to the institutional context, but pursue similar goals such as the introduction of lower-tier wages for newly employed workers. The degree to which employment relations practices can spread across countries varies. Training, employment protection and worker representation structures continue to be more strongly shaped by national contexts. Previous literature in this area does not identify a clear logic or set of factors that explain the particular employment relations or HRM practices that are more amenable to diffusion across countries and which are more heavily influenced by country effects.

Market segmentation of employment relations

Beyond isomorphic processes in product markets, employment relations vary within product markets. There is evidence that employment relations differ systematically across market segments. Product-market segmentation, the identity of companies in product markets and the image sensitivity of companies in markets differentiate employment relations and working standards. Traditionally, labour unions sought to standardize employment relations and working conditions within product markets, but the decline of unions and decreasing scope of collective bargaining has given management more leeway to differentiate employment relations practices in line with the characteristics and competitive condition of market segments.

Pine suggests that the 'basics of market-driven management are to segment, target, position and create. *Segment* your customers and potential customers into meaningful groups that have homogenous needs within each group. *Target* those market segments that match the capabilities of the firm and have the highest business potential ... *Position* your firm and its existing and potential products and services in each of the market segments ... Finally, *create* the product and services that meet the requirements of your target market segment' (Pine, 1993, p. 223). In the field of HRM contributors to the *matching model* emphasize that HRM practices need to meet organizational objectives (Fombrun et al., 1984). Schuler and Jackson have elaborated on the 'strategic fit' theme and argue that the implementation of different organizational strategies require different 'role behaviours' on the part of employees (Schuler and Jackson, 1987). Batt (2000, 2001) shows that call centres in the United States targeted four market segments: operator services, residential, small businesses and middle market. Each market segment correlated systematically with a set of work and employment relations practices, including types and level of compensation, discretion to influence work methods, skill requirements and type of interaction with the customer. Another study of service sectors, including banking and hotels, found differences between lower and upper market segments (Keltner and Finegold, 1999). Service firms pursuing an *efficiency-oriented strategy* minimized labour input, invested little in skill development and kept work tasks simple and repetitive in order to increase volume. Service firms pursuing a *high-quality strategy*, in contrast, favoured more labour intensive services that matched customer needs and invested more resources in recruiting, training and career development.

The sociology of markets provides a different account for explaining differences between market segments. White (1981) suggests that companies do not orient themselves towards consumers as neo-classical economics would suggest, but towards each other. Firms observe each other and look for market niches that are not overcrowded. Markets are a social structure, in which companies adopt different roles or identities (Aspers, 2006a, 2006b), and in this sense, companies can influence their own exposure to competition (Marchington and Parker, 1990). This approach has not been widely adopted in employment relations, but a relationship between the identity of companies and employment relations seems to exist. For example, high-end market producers in the German auto industry such as Daimler and Porsche produce most parts of their vehicles in-house, while mass-producers outsource a larger proportion of their production.

In addition, the image sensitivity of companies in markets can differentiate labour standards. Companies that are highly dependent on their image in the market are susceptible to consumer campaigns and can be forced by social movement pressure to comply with core labour standards and adopt social codes of conduct. Social movement organizations can deploy less pressure on companies that are not so dependent on a high reputation with consumers (e.g. companies in the middle of the supply chain). This suggests a differentiation of social and labour standards between companies that are image sensitive and those that are not. Consumer campaigns in the 1990s targeted labour rights and human rights violations of companies such as Nike and Reebok (Ross, 1997). These companies quickly realized that the use of child and forced labour hurt their image, sales and profits. The companies reacted to campaigns by introducing social codes that defined minimum social and working standards for plants producing for these brands. Nike introduced monitoring teams that regularly inspect production sites (Locke and Romis, 2007; Locke et al., 2007). To what extent consumer pressure and corporate responsibility change business behaviour is, however, contested in the literature. Jones and colleagues (2005) argue that this pressure leads to significant changes in working standards if stakeholders are included in the enforcement of social codes of conduct, while Baneerjee (2007) regards social codes of conduct as mere window-dressing to obscure exploitive business practices.

Market-driven employment relations practices on the company level

The liberalization and extension of product markets increased competition. One management strategy to cope with increasing competitive pressure has been to bring the market mechanism into the company by linking employment relations practices within firms to the product market beyond. This section discusses market-oriented employment relations practices such as working time flexibility, within-company markets for the allocation of production, contingent pay and outsourcing.

Working time flexibility is an employment relations instrument that links the working time of employees to swings in the market. During peak demand, employees work more, while they work less in times of low demand. Such an adaptation of working time can respond to daily, weekly or even annual changes in demand. For example, call centres try to adapt to daily fluctuations, retailers to weekly variation including high demand on weekends and car producers to annual changes in demand as people buy more cars in the summer compared to winter. Under competitive pressure, increasing working time flexibility can save costs and increase productivity in various ways. Working time flexibility decreases the total volume of labour at slack times, decreases the costs of inventories, while some measures circumvent the payment of overtime premiums. Working time flexibility is determined within national institutional frameworks, but this leaves significant scope for more flexible working time at the firm level. In the German auto industry, for example, management and unions jointly introduced various working time flexibility measures to cope with the impact of the recessions of the European auto market in 1993. The head of labour relations at Volkswagen sought to promote working time flexibility with the metaphor of 'the breathing company' – production and working time were supposed to breath in line with the ebbs and flows of the market (Hartz, 1996). Unionists in Germany agreed to working time flexibility earlier than unions in other European countries because it was a way to defend comparatively high wages and jobs. Companies such as Ford, General Motors and Volkswagen then sought to introduce the same working time flexibility measures in other European countries such as Spain. However, Spanish unions resisted working time flexibility fiercely in the 1990s and only agreed to concessions in the following decade (Hauptmeier, 2009).

Another practice that links employment relations to product markets is the introduction of within-company markets for the distribution of production (Greer and Hauptmeier, 2008). General Motors was one of the first companies to develop this strategy. This management strategy is a development of the earlier use of whipsawing and coercive comparisons (Mueller and Purcell, 1992). General Motors has used a formal bidding process to offer the manufacture of a new product or production volumes to various plants, which are supposed to hand in a competitive tender that includes production costs and productivity estimates for the planned production. The rationale is not only to assign production to the most productive and cost-effective plants but to control local management and labour. Labour unions feel pressured to make concessions in the context of production assignments in terms of wages or greater flexibility, as only sufficient production and high utilization of plants secures employment levels and wages in tight and competitive product markets.

Pay has also become more insecure and dependent on the performance of the organization (Cappelli, 1999). Increasing competition has encouraged managers to use contingent pay and the decline of unions has provided more scope to do so. Management's strategy for contingent pay is to provide incentives for employees to increase their performance and to shift market risks to employees by withholding pay if the company is not performing well (Brown and Heywood, 2002). The regular WERS surveys allow assessment of the evolution of contingent pay for the United Kingdom. For example, collective payment by results increased from 15 per cent to 29 per cent of private United Kingdom workplaces between 1984 and 2004 (Pendleton et al., 2009). In particular, the increase of profit-related pay schemes is significant, which grew from 20 per cent to 45 per cent in private sector companies. The evidence of the WERS surveys shows a clear relationship between product competition and contingent pay. The higher the product competition, the greater the propensity of companies to use contingent pay (Pendleton et al., 2009). Contingent pay has also increased in coordinated market economies such as Germany (Kurdelbusch, 2002).

The outsourcing or vertical disintegration of production is another instrument that links employment relations to the pressure of markets (Doellgast and Greer, 2007; Greer, 2008, p. 20). Vertical disintegration is typically described as the making of new intermediate markets in previously integrated production processes (Jacobides, 2005). This can include outsourcing of production to another company, the foundation of independent sub-sidiaries and the use of temporary employment agencies. These developments have introduced markets for the sourcing of people, parts and services in com-parison to the governance of integrated production processes via management hierarchies. The changing boundaries of the firm and creation of new markets has also made it more difficult for unions to cover workers through collec-tive agreements. Vertical disintegration has contributed to the segmentation of employment relations with lower wages and working standards driven by greater market exposure at the periphery of the firm compared to the core (Doellgast and Greer, 2007).

Conclusion

This chapter has challenged Piore and Safford's (2006) thesis that changes in employment relations have been primarily shaped by law, judicial opin-ions and administrative rulings and the mobilization of these norms by identity groups over the last 30 years, rather than by markets. It is argued that Piore and Safford underestimate the impact of markets, which have become a more prevalent force in shaping employment relations as they have unfolded via various mechanisms. States have changed the axis of gov-ernance. Market economies and employment relations are coordinated and organized by the four governance mechanisms: laws, markets, hierarchies and associations. States – unilaterally and multilaterally – focussed on liberaliz-ing labour and product markets and privatizing state-run companies. This has exposed employment relations to greater market competition and has led to the decline of collective bargaining (Brown et al., 2009). To be sure, the governance of employment relations by laws, hierarchies and associa-tions continues to be significant, but the relative weight of markets in shaping employment relations in comparison to the other governance mechanisms has increased. These changes in the regulatory and material context of employ-ment relations are closely intertwined with the rise of neo-liberal ideologies. As the actors in employment relations adapted to a changing socio-economic context, they became more market oriented and markets became a more legiti-mate reference point and governance mechanism in employment relations. An increasing number of unions gradually took on a greater responsibility for the competitiveness of companies, while more radical union ideologies and strikes declined. Managers segmented employment relations and aligned them with the competitive characteristics of market segments, linked flexible working time to fluctuating demand in markets and made part of the income of employees dependent on the company's performance in markets. Outsourcing and vertical disintegration created new markets and shifted employees from previously integrated production and service companies to more precarious forms of employment. In addition, increasing market competition and declining coverage of collective bargaining gave more space for isomorphic processes in product markets that contributed to the spread of employment relations practices between competitors.

The changing axis of governance towards markets, the decline in collective bargaining and the rise of market-oriented employment relations practices can be traced back to the economic crisis of the 1970s. Major capitalist crises tend to trigger ideological change. In the wake of the economic crisis of the 1970s, the gradually unfolding shift from the Keynesian to the neo-liberal economic paradigm paved the way for the expansion and increasing legitimacy of markets in governing economies and employment relations. The big question today is whether the 2008/2009 economic crisis will similarly lead to far-reaching ideological changes. As in previous major economic crises, the current crisis has led not only to economic but also to ideological turbulence. Previous economic ideas have become discredited and new ideas are emerging. Confidence in the efficiency of self-regulating markets has been shaken to the core. The notion that states should play a significant role in ensuring the functioning of markets has become more popular following decisive state intervention in financial markets to avoid collapse. Before recent developments, it would have seemed absurd to many that governments would bail out private companies and put them under state control. In addition, the G20 has now developed the shared belief that financial markets need more regulation and common action seems possible.

At present, ideas seem to be in a state of flux and no coherent new paradigm is on the horizon. One might argue that the slightly improved economic situation in 2010 and the intention of governments to reduce budget deficits with accompanying cuts in social benefits and public services is a return to the previous economic orthodoxy. However, the ideological changes following the major economic crises in 1929 and in the 1970s were also not immediate and only unfolded gradually. Roosevelt implemented the New Deal in 1937 and neo-liberalism only became a more popular currency after the elections of Thatcher and Reagan in 1979 and 1980. If history is an indicator, the current capitalist crisis will lead to ideological change. This may shift the axis of governance once again and, in turn, reshape employment relations.

Note

1. GERPISA stands in French for *Groupe d' Etudes et de Recherches Permanent sur l' Industrie et les Salariés de l' Automobile*. In English, the group's name has been summarized as the International Network of the Automobile (web page: http://gerpisa.org/en).

References

Abrahamson, E. 1991. 'Managerial fads and fashions: the diffusion and refection of innovations'. *Academy of Management Review*, 16 (3): 586–612.

Abrahamson, E. and Eisenman, M. 2008. 'Employee-management techniques: transient fads or trending fashions?' *Administrative Science Quarterly*, 53 (4): 719–44.

Ancel, J. and Slaughter, J. 2005. *A Troublemaker's Handbook 2: How to Fight Back Where You Work – and win!* Detroit, Mich.: Labor Notes, pp. vi, 372 p.

Aspers, P. 2006a. *Markets in Fashion: A Phenomenological Approach*, London and New York: Routledge, p. 240.

Aspers, P. 2006b. 'The sociology of markets'. In Beckert, J. and Zafirovski, M. (eds) *International Encyclopedia of Economic Sociology*, London: Routledge, pp. 427–32.

Banerjee, S.B. 2007. *Corporate Social Responsibility: The Good, The Bad and the Ugly*, Cheltenham: Edward Elgar, pp. vii, 211 p.

Batt, R. 2000. 'Strategic segmentation in front-line services: matching customers, employees and human resource systems'. *International Journal of Human Resource Management*, 11 (3): 540–61.

Batt, R. 2001. Explaining wage inequality in telecommunications services: customer segmentation, human resource practices, and union decline. *Industrial & Labor Relations Review*, 54 (2): 425–49.

Blyth, M. 2002. *Great Transformations: Economic Ideas and Institutional Change in the Twentieth Century*. Cambridge, New York: Cambridge University Press, p. 284.

Bosch, G. and Weinkopf, C. 2008. *Low-Wage Work in Germany*, New York: Russell Sage Foundation, pp. vii, 327 p.

Boyer, R. 1998. *Between Imitation and Innovation: The Transfer and Hybridization of Productive Models in the International Automotive Industry*, Oxford, New York: Oxford University Press, p. 394.

Brown, W. (2008) 'The influence of product markets on industrial relations'. In P. Blyton, N. Bacon, J. Fiorito and E. Heery (eds) *The Sage Handbook of Industrial Relations*, Los Angeles, Sage Publications: 113–28.

Brown, M. and Heywood, J.S. 2002. *Paying for Performance: An International Comparison*, Armonk, NY: M.E. Sharpe, pp. xiv, 298 p.

Brown, W., Bryson, A. and Forth, J. 2009. 'Competiton and the retreat from collective bargaining'. In Brown, W. et al. (eds) *The Evolution of the Modern Workplace*, Cambridge: Cambridge University Press, pp. 22–47.

Campbell, J.L., Rogers Hollingworth, J. and Lindberg, L.N. (eds). 1991. *Governance of the American Economy*, Cambridge, New York: Cambridge University Press, p. 462.

Cappelli, P. 1999. *The New Deal at Work: Managing the Market-Driven Workforce*, Boston: Harvard Business School Press, p. 307.

Coase, R.H. 1937. 'The nature of the firm'. *Economica*, 4: 386–405.

Commons, J.R. 1909. 'American shoemakers, 1648–1895: A sketch of industrial evolution'. *The Quarterly Journal of Economics*, 24 (1): 39–84.

Crouch, C. 1993. *Industrial Relations and European State Traditions*. Oxford, New York: Clarendon Press and Oxford University Press, pp. xx, 407 p.

Dicken, P. 2007. *Global Shift: Mapping the Changing Contours of the World Economy*, London: SAGE. pp. xxiii, 599 p.: ill., maps; 525 cm.

DiMaggio, P.J. and Powell, W.W. 1983. 'The iron cage revisited: institutional isomorphism and collective rationality in organizational fields'. *American Sociological Review*, 48 (2): 147–60.

Doellgast, V. and Greer, I. 2007. Vertical disintegration and the disorganization of German industrial relations. *British Journal of Industrial Relations*, 45(1): 55–76.

Ebbinghaus, B. and Hassel, A. 2000. Striking deals: concertation in the reform of continental European welfare states. *Journal of European Public Policy*, 7 (1): 44–62.

Edwards, T. 1998. Multinationals, labour management and the process of reverse diffusion: A case study. *International Journal of Human Resource Management*, 9 (4): 696–709.

Elger, T. and Smith, C. 2005. *Assembling Work: Remaking Factory Regimes in Japanese Multinationals in Britain*, Oxford: Oxford University Press, p. viii, 414 p.

Esping-Andersen, G. 1990. *The Three Worlds of Welfare Capitalism*, Princeton, NJ: Princeton University Press, p. 248.

Ferner, A, Quintinilla, J. and Sánchez-Runde, C. (eds). 2006. *Multinationals, Institutions and the Construction of Transnational Practices: Convergence and Diversity in the Global Economy*. Basingstoke, New York: Palgrave Macmillan, p. 270.

Fligstein, N. 1996. Markets as politics: A political-cultural approach to market institutions. *American Sociological Review*, 61 (4): 656–73.

Fligstein, N. 2001. *The Architecture of Markets: An Economic Sociology of Twenty-First-Century Capitalist Societies*. Princeton: Princeton University Press, p. 274.

Fombrun, C.J., Tichy, N.M. and Devanna, M.A. 1984. *Strategic Human Resource Management*, New York and Chichester: Wiley, pp. xv, 499 p.

Friedman, M. 1962. *Capitalism and Freedom*, Chicago: University of Chicago Press, p. 202.

Friedman, T.L. 2007. *The World is Flat: A Brief History of the Twenty-First Century*, New York: Farrar, Straus and Giroux, p. 660.

Fukuyama, F. 1992. *The End of History and the Last Man*, London: Hamilton, p. xxiii, 418 p.

Gall, G. (1999) 'A review of strike activity in Western Europe at the end of the second millennium'. *Employee Relations*, 21(4), 357–77.

Galbraith, J.K. 1955. *The Great Crash, 1929*, Boston: Houghton Mifflin, p. 212.

Gamble, A. 2009. *The Spectre at the Feast: Capitalist Crisis and the Politics of Recession*, Basingstoke: Palgrave Macmillan, pp. xi, 184 p.

Gollbach, J. and Schulten, T. 2000. 'Cross-border collective bargaining networks in Europe'. *European Journal of Industrial Relations*, 6 (2): 161.

Gordon, M.E. and Turner, L. 2000. *Transnational Cooperation Among Labor Unions*, Ithaca, NY: ILR Press, p. 310.

Greer, I. 2008. 'Organised industrial relations in the information economy: the German automotive sector as a test case'. *New Technology, Work & Employment*, 23(3), 181–96.

Greer, I. and Hauptmeier, M. 2008. Political entrepreneurs and co-managers: Labour transnationalism at four multinational auto companies. *British Journal of Industrial Relations*, 46 (1): 76–97.

Hamilton, G.G. and Feenstra, R.C. 1995. Varieties of hierarchies and markets: An introduction. *Industrial & Corporate Change*, 4 (1): 51–91.

Hall, P.A. 1989. *The Political Power of Economic Ideas: Keynesianism Across Nations*, Princeton, NJ: Princeton University Press, p. 406.

Hall, P.A. and Soskice, D.W. 2001. *Varieties of Capitalism: The Institutional Foundations of Comparative Advantage*, Oxford, New York: Oxford University Press, p. 540.

Hartz, P. 1996. *The Company That Breathes: Every Job Has a Customer*, Berlin and New York: Springer, p. 230.

Harvey, D. 2005. *A Brief History of Neoliberalism*, Oxford: Oxford University Press, p. vii, 247 p.

Hassel, A. 2009. 'Policies and politics in social pacts in Europe'. *European Journal of Industrial Relations*, 15 (1): 7–26.

Hauptmeier, M. 2009. *Constructing Institutions: Collective Bargaining in the United States, Germany and Spain*, Cornell University.

Hay, C. 2006. 'Constructivist institutionalism'. In Rhodes, R.A.W. et al. (eds) *Oxford Handbooks of Political Science*, Oxford: Oxford University Press, pp. 56–74.

Hirschman, A.O. 1970. *Exit, Voice, and Loyalty; Responses to Decline in Firms, Organizations, and States*, Cambridge, Mass.: Harvard University Press, p. 162.

Hollingsworth, J.R., Streeck, W. and Schmitter, P. (eds). 1994. *Governing Capitalist Economies: Performance and Control of Economic Sectors*, New York: Oxford University Press, p. 316.

Jabko, N. 2006. Playing *the Market: A Political Strategy for Uniting Europe, 1985–2005*. Ithaca, N.Y.: Cornell University Press, p. 206.

Jacobides, M.G. 2005. 'Industry change through vertical disintegration: how and why markets emerged in mortgage banking'. *Academy of Management Journal*, 48 (3): 465–98.

Jacoby, S. (2004) *Employing Bureaucracy: Managers, Unions, and the Transformation of Work in the 20th Century*, revised edition, Mahwah NJ, Lawrence Elbaum Associates Publishers.

Jones, C., Parker, M. and ten Bos, R. 2005. *For Business Ethics*, London: Routledge, p. xi, 210 p.

Katz, H.C. and Darbishire, O. 2000. *Converging Divergences: Worldwide Changes in Employment Systems*, Ithaca, NY: Cornell University Press, p. 321.

Keltner, B. and Finegold, D. 1999. 'Market segmentation strategies and service sector productivity'. *California Management Review*, 41 (4): 84–102.

Kersley, B. 2006. *Inside the Workplace: Findings from the 2004 Workplace Employment Relations Survey*, London: Routledge, p. xvii, 388 p.

Keynes, J.M. 1936. *The General Theory of Employment, Interest and Money*, London: Macmillan and Co., p. 403.

Kurdelbusch, A. 2002. 'Multinationals and the rise of variable pay in Germany'. *European Journal of Industrial Relations*, 8(3): 325–49.

Lazonick, W. 1991. *Business Organization and the Myth of the Market Economy*, Cambridge: Cambridge University Press, p. 440.

Locke, R. 1992. 'The decline of the national union in italy: lessons from comparative industrial relations theory'. *Industrial and Labor Relations Review*, 45 (Journal Article): 289–303.

Locke, R. and Thelen, K. 1995. 'Apples and oranges compared: contextualised comparisons and the study of comparative politics'. *Politics and Society*, 23 (3): 337–67.

Locke, R.M. and Romis, M. 2007. Beyond corporate codes of conduct: Work organization and labour standards at Nike's suppliers. *International Labour Review*, 146 (1/2): 21–37.

Locke, R.M., Qin, F. and Brause, A. 2007. 'Does monitoring improve labor standards? Lessons from Nike'. *Industrial & Labor Relations Review*, 61 (1): 3–31.

Marchington, M. and Parker, P. 1990. *Changing Patterns of Employee Relations in Britain*, London: Harvester Wheatsheaf, p. ix, 283 p.

Marginson, P., Armstrong, P., Edwards, P.K. and Purcell, J. 1995. 'Extending beyond borders: multinational companies and the international management of labour'. *International Journal of Human Resource Management*, 6 (3): 702–19.

Moody, K. 1997. 'Workers in a lean world: unions in the international economy'. New York: Verso, p. 342.

Morgan, G., Kristensen, P.H. and Whitley, R. (eds). 2001. *The Multinational Firm: Organizing Across Institutional and National Divides*, Oxford and New York: Oxford University Press, pp. viii, 321 p.

Mueller, F. and Purcell, J. 1992. 'The Europeanization of manufacturing and the decentralization of bargaining: multinational management strategies in the European automobile industry'. *International Journal of Human Resource Management*, 3 (1): 15–34.

Pendleton, A., Whitfield, K. and Bryson, A. 2009. The changing use of contingent pay at the modern British workplace. In Brown, W. et al. (eds) *The Evolution of the Modern Workplace*, Cambridge: Cambridge University Press, pp. 256–83.

Pierson, P. 2001. *The New Politics of the Welfare State*, Oxford: Oxford University Press, pp. xiii, 514 p.

Pine, B.J. 1993. *Mass Customization: The New Frontier in Business Competition*, Boston, Mass.: Harvard Business School Press, p. xxi, 333 p.

Piore, M.J. and Safford, S. 2006. 'Changing regimes of workplace governance, shifting axes of social mobilization, and the challenge to industrial relations theory'. *Industrial Relations*, 45 (3): 299–325.

Polanyi, K. 1944. *The Great Transformation*, New York, Toronto: Farrar & Rinehart, inc., pp. 1, 305.

Ross, A. 1997. *No Sweat*, New York: Verso.

Ruggie, J.G. 1982. 'International regimes, transactions, and change: embedded liberalism in the postwar economic order'. *International Organization*, 36 (2): 379–415.

Sabel, C.F. 1984. *Work and Politics: The Division of Labor in Industry*, Cambridge, Cambridgeshire and New York: Cambridge University Press, p. 304.

Salverda, W., Van Klaveren, M. and van der Meer, M. (eds). 2008. *Low-Wage Work in the Netherlands*, New York: Russell Sage Foundation, pp. vi, 332 p.

Scharpf, F.W. 1999. *Governing in Europe: Effective and Democratic?* Oxford and New York: Oxford University Press, p. 243.

Scharpf, F.W. and Schmidt, V.A. 2000. *Welfare and Work in the Open Economy*, Oxford and New York: Oxford University Press.

Schuler, R.S. and Jackson, S.E. 1987. 'Organizational strategy and organization level as determinants of human resource management practices'. *Human Resource Planning*, 10 (3): 125–42.

Schumpeter, J.A. 1942. *Capitalism, Socialism, and Democracy*, New York and London: Harper & Brothers, pp. x, 381 p.

Sisson, K. 1987. *The Management of Collective Bargaining: An International Comparison*, Oxford, UK; New York, NY, USA: Blackwell, p. 230.

Sisson, K., Arrowsmith, J. and Marginson, P. 2003. 'All benchmarkers now? Benchmarking and the 'Europeanisation' of industrial relations'. *Industrial Relations Journal*, 34 (1): 15–31.

Stiglitz, J.E. 2002. *Globalization and Its Discontents*, New York and London: W.W. Norton & Co., p. 282.

Streeck, W. and Schmitter, P.C. 1985. 'Community, market, state – and associations? The prospective contribution of interest governance'. In Streeck, W. and Schmitter, P.C. (eds) *Private Interest Government: Beyond Market and State*, London and Beverly Hills: Sage Publications, pp. 1–29.

Tilly, C. 1995. 'Globalization threatens labor's rights'. *International Labor and Working-Class History*, 47 (1): 1–23.

Ulman, L. 1966. *The Rise of the National Trade Union: The Development and Significance of Its Structure, Governing Institutions, and Economic Policies.* Cambridge: Harvard University Press, p. 639.

Weber, M. 1948. *From Max Weber: Essays in Sociology*, London: Routledge & Kegan Paul.

Weber, M., Roth, G. and Wittich, C. 1978. *Economy and Society: An Outline of Interpretive Sociology*, Berkeley, CA: University of California Press, pp. 1469, lxiv.

White, H.C. 1981. 'Where do markets come from?' *The American Journal of Sociology*, 87 (3): 517–47.

Williamson, O.E. 1983. *Markets and Hierarchies: Analysis and Antitrust Implications; A Study in the Economics on Interna L Organization.* 1. paperback ed. New York u.a.: Free Press u.a., pp. XVII, 286 S.

Windolf, P. 1989. 'Productivity coalitions and the future of european corporatism'. *Industrial Relations*, 28 (1): 1.

World Trade Organization (WTO) 2008. *International Trade Statistics*, Geneva: WTO.

Can workers of the world unite? Globalization and the employment relationship

Jean Jenkins and Peter Turnbull

Introduction

The impact of competitive pressure originating in markets beyond the borders of the nation state is nothing new. In fact, such pressures are inherent to capitalism:

> The need of a constantly expanding market for its products chases the bourgeoisic[1] over the whole surface of the globe. It must nestle everywhere, settle everywhere, establish connections everywhere.
>
> (Marx and Engels, [1848] 1967: 83)

The geographic expansion of the market, which brings with it greater competition between firms, can in turn have detrimental effects on workers' terms and conditions of employment. As a result, trade unions have always 'followed the market' because it is only by organizing across the employers' product market, and including all potential competitors within the remit of collective labour agreements, that unions can hope to protect workers' interests in the corresponding labour market (Brown, 2008). Today, however, in the 'borderless world' of the global economy (Ohmae, 1990) it is often observed that capital is now capable of transcending space while labour is necessarily confined to place – 'a confinement which will encourage workers to be quiescent if they hope to secure their economic futures through drawing mobile capital to their community' (Herod et al, 2007: 250). But does this combination of capital mobility and labour quiescence necessarily lead to an international 'race-to-the-bottom' in respect of workers' terms and conditions of employment, as is often assumed? Alternatively, can workers of the world unite to ensure they retain a voice at work and decent standards of employment?

The contrast between capital mobility and labour immobility can be something of a caricature. In reality there are always limits to capital mobility. All capital, at some stage, must create particular 'spatial fixes' to allow accumulation to proceed (Harvey, 1982). Put differently, firms need to be embedded in local networks of suppliers, finance, education and training, labour supply, etc., if they hope to realize surplus value and turn a profit. At least initially, capital 'must spend some time as a cocoon before it can take off as a butterfly' (Marx, 1973: 548–9). But even after it takes off, 'the most flighty of capital must come to ground at some point, since for all of their innovative capacities capitalists have yet to find . . . an ethereal way of accumulating capital' (Herod et al., 2007: 253). As a result, the fixity of capital, even in a global economy, might be assumed to give organized labour at least some leverage in negotiations with capital. All too often, however, the *threat* of relocation cows workers to accept industrial restructuring. To be sure, employers have always used the threat of relocation to counteract collective organization at the workplace level, but today relocation more readily extends beyond the regulatory space and scope of most trade unions. Thus, globalization throws the dual logic of capitalist economic development – the intensification of exploitation through both industrial restructuring and technological upheaval (the vertical or temporal dimension) and worldwide expansion (the horizontal or geographical dimension) (Fourcade, 2006: 146) – into much sharper focus. The challenge of globalization for organized labour is not only how to contain foreign and domestic corporations within the regulatory frameworks of national industrial relations systems, but how to stop these companies vacating national industrial relations systems in search of lower wages, greater flexibility and more business friendly climes.

There is little doubt that industrial restructuring at home and the transfer of capital overseas plunged most of the Western working class 'into social and organisational disarray' (Moody, 1997: 180). Workers' rights are firmly wedded to the nation state and their collective organizations are typically centred on domestically based firms, industries and occupations. Consequently, the repertoire of power or 'inventory of available means' (Tilly, 1984: 308) that workers can draw upon is usually local, often national, but rarely international. Trans-national unity is therefore highly unlikely to be possible for all workers everywhere. While the rallying cry of yesteryear – 'Workers of the World, Unite!' – 'may historically have provided inspiration and perhaps helped generate a reality approximating to the ideal [it] probably can no longer do so ... collectivism, particularly of an encompassing character, is therefore a project demanding new forms of strategic intervention' (Hyman, 1999: 94). Put differently, 'If workers are to enjoy collective rights in the new world order, they will have to invent new strategies at the scale of international capital' (Tilly, 1995: 5). Of course, not all workers are equally affected by globalization and some will have more, or less, capacity to defend their terms and conditions of employment.

What, then, determines the impact of globalization on the employment relationship? First, much will depend on the regulation of product and labour markets. As markets are neither natural nor self-correcting, as the recent global economic crisis clearly demonstrates, we can state categorically that institutions matter. Globalization might well signal the emergence of new non-territorial spaces and management systems, which of course create a significant challenge for traditional territorially based rule-making, but at the same time this opens up a space for other social actors, such as orga-nized labour, to graft their pursuit of a broader social agenda onto the global reach and capacity of transnational corporations (TNCs). This is most evident within the European Union (EU) where the process of economic integration is played out between contending political philosophies in high-level regional institutions. Neither the institutional framework nor the political commit-ment to social democratic intervention is to be found in other free trade arrangements such as NAFTA (North American Free Trade Agreement), APEC (Asia Pacific Economic Cooperation) or MERCOSUR (Mercado Común del Sur).

Secondly, the impact of globalization on the employment relationship will depend on the relative mobility of capital and labour, since both factors of production can be essentially fixed (localized) or especially mobile (interna-tionalized) (Levi and Alhquist, 2004). For example, mining activities are tied to local natural resources whereas some manufacturing activities can now be located almost anywhere around the world. Local authority (public sec-tor) workers, by definition, are tied to a particular place whereas workers in the knowledge-based industries are often highly mobile. Factor mobility will endow social actors with more or less bargaining power *vis-à-vis* their coun-terparts in the employment relationship, which in turn will have an impact on labour market outcomes.

While some workers might use their personal mobility to side-step any race-to-the-bottom, for most workers the impact of globalization will depend, thirdly, on how, and to what extent, they can redefine and reinforce their interests in ways that will help them to overcome their collective action, coordination and coalition problems. As Tarrow (1999) notes, workers' interests are invariably embedded in their everyday working lives whereas the logic of globalization appears to call for a more detached identity that will travel across borders. In other words, labour must organize at the international as well as the national level. Thus, to the extent that labour 'can move across scales – that is, to the extent that they can take advantage of the resources at one scale to overcome the constraints encountered at different scales in the way that more powerful actors can do – they may have greater potential for pressing their claims' (Staeheli, 1994: 388).

These three factors – social institutions, the relative mobility of capital and labour, and the ways in which workers define and defend their collective interests in a both national and international context – are elaborated in more detail in the following section. We then discuss two polar cases, namely garment manufacture and port transport, where workers have respectively been the victims of, and the victors over, the forces of globalization. Dock workers have a long tradition of union organization and industrial militancy (Turnbull and Sapsford, 2001) as well as international solidarity action in the face of globalization (Turnbull, 2000, 2006). Garment workers have no such history of organization or capacity to engage in international solidarity action (Hurley and Miller, 2005: 16–35; Jones, 2006; Rosen, 2002: 240). While (male) dock workers in most developed countries enjoy relatively high wages and 'decent work' (Turnbull and Wass, 2007), (female) garment workers worldwide inhabit an industry characterized by 'insecure, unstable work [as part of] a marginalised workforce' (Hurley, 2005: 116).

Social institutions, factor mobility and communities of fate

In the global era of capitalist economic development, 'when the movement of goods, capital and labor across borders seems to escape the control of the nation state, *laissez-faire* arguments gain heft' (Fox Piven, 2006: 44). As Myconos (2005: 120) demonstrates, 'Confronting labour is what amounts to a network of interlocking regimes of governance committed to administering a global neo-liberal market-based system'. But free markets demand a very active, interventionist state, even if states now operate through supra-national institutions such as the EU or World Trade Organisation (WTO). For example, states might change the rules governing access to the market. Between 1991 and 2000, a total of 1185 regulatory changes were introduced to national rules and regulations governing foreign direct investment (FDI), of which

1121 (95 per cent) were in the direction of creating a more favourable environment for FDI. Over the same period, FDI inflows and outflows increased from US$437 bn to US$2421 bn (at 2000 prices) while employment at foreign affiliates increased from 24 million to 45 million workers worldwide (UNCTAD, 2001: 2, 12).[2] TNCs dominate international markets because states have opened access to their national markets and facilitated trade between different countries around the world, especially within regional trade blocs.

It is only in the theoretical world of perfect competition where markets are governed purely by the so-called invisible hand of supply and demand. In the real world, markets are also governed by rules and regulations determined in the public domain as well as social norms that will influence actors' behaviour. The latter is especially important in the labour market, which is governed by a combination of employment law, collective bargaining agreements, and a range of norms, beliefs and values. As a result, in all employment relationships there is a tension 'between market pressures towards the commodification of labour (power) and social and institutional norms which ensure its (relative) "decommodification"' (Hyman, 2001: 285). Industrial relations is therefore 'an arena in which the contest between the pursuit of a "market society" and the defence of principles of "moral economy" is played out' (ibid.). Globalization threatens the moral economy, and undermines democracy, because it creates new centres of authority beyond the nation state. What made democracy so compelling through the centuries was the idea that 'if people have influence on the state, they can use that influence to shape the conditions of their own well-being' (Fox Piven, 2006: 44). As the World Commission on the Social Dimensions of Globalization (2004: 2) recently concluded, 'the current path of globalization must change. Too few share in its benefits. *Too many have no voice in its design and no influence on its course*' (emphasis added).

Some workers, however, *do* have a say in the current path of globalization because the path leads to the creation of *regional* as opposed to a purely global economy (the so-called global triad of North America, Europe and South East Asia). In fact, if globalization is understood to be 'a process (or set of processes) which embodies a transformation in the spatial organisation of social relations and transactions ... *generating transcontinental or interregional flows and networks of activity, interaction, and the exercise of power*' (Held et al., 1999: 16, emphasis added) then questions can be raised about the real extent, or even the very existence, of *global*ization (e.g. Hirst and Thompson, 1999). For example, the foreign trade dependence of the United States, Japan and the EU is in each case less than 10 per cent of gross domestic product (GDP). Likewise, only 10–15 per cent of the world's labour force has a direct and easily observable linkage with the global political economy (Harrod and O'Brien,

2002: 13–14). As Dicken (2007) makes clear, globalization processes are predominantly *regional*, above the national but below the global. For example, 22 per cent of manufacturing exports from North America go to Asia, 18 per cent to Western Europe and 16 per cent to Latin America, but 40 per cent is internal trade. Just over a quarter of Asia's manufacturing exports go to North America, 17 per cent go to Western Europe, but half is internal trade. North America receives 11 per cent of all manufacturing exports from Western Europe while Asia takes 8 per cent, but two-thirds is internal trade. Not only do EU Member States trade predominantly with each other, but most FDI originating in EU Member States is destined for other EU Member States. In the light of such evidence, Hay (2006) poses the question: 'What's globalisation got to do with it?'

In answer, we may look to European integration – the creation of a single European market with freedom of movement for capital, labour, goods and services – as an example of 'a process of *economic liberalization by international means* . . . the opening up of national economies through an internationally negotiated expansion of markets beyond national borders' (Streeck, 1998: 429, original emphasis). The key point here is that the single market is *internationally negotiated*. What marks out the EU from other free trade zones is that there are supra-national institutions – the Council, the Commission and the European Parliament – that are open to representation and lobbying by social actors, including organized labour, and there are international enforcement mechanisms in place to ensure compliance with the European social agenda. To be sure, social (market correcting) policies are secondary and subservient to economic (market making) policies in the EU, giving rise to (labour cost) competition between Member States but social protection is now enshrined in the European Treaty, which aims to:

> promote employment, improved living and working conditions, so as to make possible their harmonisation while the improvement is being maintained, proper social protection, dialogue between management and labour, the development of human resources with a view to lasting employment and the combating of exclusion.
>
> (Amsterdam Treaty, 1997, Art. 136)

In the European workplace, workers typically enjoy better social protection, their terms and conditions of employment are usually the subject of a collective agreement, and they are granted rights to information and consultation that are often denied to other workers around the world. European works councils (EWCs), for example, can make the 'invisible hand' of the TNC more transparent to the company's workforce.[3] Deliberative institutions such as EWCs 'can provide actors in a political economy with strategic capacities they would not otherwise enjoy' (Hall and Soskice, 2001: 12), and these capacities have been used to significant effect by workers in various manufacturing industries as well as the transport sector. An important qualification, however, is that while social institutions within the EU guarantee labour a voice, workers must still organize and 'shift scale' from the local and national to the EU level if they want their voice to be heard and in particular if they are to divert policy makers from the neo-liberal agenda.

In other parts of the world, individual working units may be part of a complex supply chain or wider corporate structures, which are typically opaque, impenetrable and often unintelligible to those outside the senior management team. By these means trans-national capital is distanced from accountability for labour conditions in the context of regulatory systems that are either weak or simply weakly enforced. Consequently, many workers enjoy little social protection and all too often have few, if any, opportunities or organizations for collective voice. For example, while East Asia might well be in the midst of an 'economic miracle' in terms of its increasing industrialization, its political regimes have generally 'exhibited strong authoritarian tendencies in relation to various social forces, including labour' (Hutchinson and Brown, 2001: 10). With a few exceptions, organized labour has been politically excluded (ibid.) and where regulation exists it may not be within reach of the individual worker. Where workers have no form of representation, violation of their (employment) rights will often go unchallenged. International benchmarks for 'decent work' are set by the International Labour Organisation (ILO), and these minimum labour standards are ratified by virtually all the nations of the world. Unfortunately, international labour standards are particularly difficult to enforce in the flexible labour market of a global era, especially as ILO Conventions are based on a conventional model of the employment relationship (i.e. full-time, 'male bread-winner' jobs). Attempts to introduce new Conventions that might address the contemporary world of work have either failed (e.g. a proposed Convention on Contract Labour)[4] or have been ratified by only a handful of states (e.g. the Home-working Convention, No. 177, passed in 1996 but only ratified by four European countries). According to Standing (2008: 381), 'the ILO has moved into the shadows of global rule-making', because while ILO Conventions might potentially limit labour cost competition between countries, both the world of work and ILO Conventions are now characterized by greater complexity, the ILO has less capacity to monitor the growing number of Conventions, fewer countries have ratified more recent Conventions, and there is simply less respect for international labour standards in the global economy (ibid.: 375–6). The ILO is certainly 'a testament to the past century of labourism trying to protect employees in the standard employment relationship', but 'like it or not, in the early twenty-first century labour *is* a commodity. And the ILO cannot do much about it' (ibid.: 382).

The upshot is that millions of workers, particularly but not exclusively those in the newly industrialized economies, work in conditions that are morally indefensible (Bhatt, 2006; Hearson and Eagleton, 2007). In simple terms, 'Seen through the eyes of the vast majority of women and men, globalization has not yet met their simple and legitimate aspirations for decent jobs and a better future for their children' (World Commission on the Social Dimensions of Globalization, 2004: x). While some observers might hold out hope for a new era of corporate social responsibility, and in particular codes of conduct that (supposedly) govern employment relationships in the subsidiaries and supplier networks of TNCs, these codes are no more than a speed bump for the juggernaut of globalization. Likewise, non-governmental organizations (NGOs) may make a useful contribution to the debate on international labour standards through various campaigns, supporting other social actors and pricking the conscience of Western consumers, but they do not have the resources to effectively monitor corporate codes of conduct or labour standards in every workplace.

While the activities of social institutions, or conversely their absence or underdevelopment, clearly matters, so too does the labour market situation of specific workers. In general, capital, both physical and financial, is more mobile than labour. Workers' mobility will be constrained by their assessment of projected gains balanced against possible risk factors such as the social dislocation caused by uprooting from their community and familial ties, the perceived risks of job insecurity, the lack of perfect knowledge of the (external) labour market and the fear of any further erosion of working conditions or future workplace relocation and the economic consequences of job loss (Levi and Ahlquist, 2004). In contrast, multi- and trans-national corporate structures allow the firm far greater access to information and facilitate longer term corporate strategies. For example, a firm's exit from a particular location may be planned well in advance and executed at the corporation's convenience, while publicly being attributed to more immediate factors associated with a (real or supposed) lack of competitiveness, workers' resistance to change or the threat or actual incidence of industrial action (Jenkins, 2008).

Levi and Ahlquist (2004) identify different combinations of capital and labour mobility that will significantly influence the bargaining power of each party. For example, workers' bargaining power is likely to be greater in localized selling markets where labour is tightly linked to a highly specific asset or market. Employers owning these geographically circumstantial assets or selling products that are location specific face localized labour markets that trade unions can more easily organize. In contrast, firms in industries where capital is easily moved and product transportation costs are low enjoy expansive labour markets where they can search for workers across institutional contexts that offer the lowest labour costs. In these markets, employers enjoy much greater bargaining power arising from the very real threat of relocation. It should also be acknowledged, however, that some workers might also face an expansive market in which to sell their labour if they possess relatively rare skills and are willing and able to relocate. Conversely, even workers in a relatively 'fixed' local labour market – for example, skilled workers in a local hospital, such as nurses, or unskilled agricultural workers – may face competition from workers relocating to enter their labour selling markets, including immigrant labour, which reduces their bargaining power.

Where the markets facing capital and labour are localized, such as government services, workers might hardly be touched by globalization. In contrast, where labour is localized but firms are increasingly mobile as a result of falling transport costs and new production strategies, employers enjoy a significant increase in their labour purchasing options relative to workers selling opportunities. Textile, garment and footwear workers fall into this category. In the 1970s, the expanding product market was regulated by the Multi-Fibre Agreement (MFA), a worldwide trade agreement that exempted the garment industry from the free trade provisions of the General Agreement on Tariffs and Trade (GATT). The MFA (1974) placed quotas on apparel imports to the United States and Europe from developing countries for the next 30 years, but this did not prevent, nor was it ever designed to prevent the rise of sweatshops in the newly industrialized countries or their widespread return to developed economies like the United States (Rosen, 2002: 2). The result has been a global 'race to the bottom' in terms of wage rates and working conditions (ibid.). Consequently, workers in industries such as textiles and garments, above all others, may be in need of a broad trans-national labour movement, but as Levi and Ahlquist (2004) point out they are also the least likely to achieve it. Instead, they focus on concession bargaining to save jobs and their defence of (local) place often blinds these workers to their wider (international) class interests, although the significance of local struggles should not be underestimated, both in terms of the potential impact on the global activities of the organization (Herod, 2002) and the personal costs for those involved in organized resistance.[5]

Confrontation between capital and labour, rather than quiescence, is more often found in industries where capital is highly localized, in the sense of being geographically dependent, even though the industry is thoroughly entangled with the international economy (Cronin, 1979). In the transport sector, for example, services are tied to expensive infrastructure (e.g. seaports and airports) and these are some of the industries with the highest (cross-national) labour militancy (Silver, 2003: 97–103; see also Turnbull, 2000; Turnbull and Sapsford, 2001). However, while the market might confer greater bargaining power on these workers, it is only through collective organization that they can realize this potential advantage. Transport unions differ markedly in their approach to internationalism (Levi and Ahlquist, 2004), even within regional markets such as the EU (Turnbull, 2010), which can have a significant impact on how globalization is mediated in different transport sectors.

Collective action, whether local, national or international, begins with the identification of common interests between workers but always depends on much more (Kelly, 1998). Unless workers share a community of fate they are unlikely to join forces to redress the inherent imbalance of power that characterizes all employment relationships. In the early years of the last century, for example, it was no small task to transform a 'collection of often strictly self-contained little worlds' of workers around Britain into a national working class movement. Only then could Hobsbawm (1999: 93) talk of 'a growing sense of a single working class, bound together in a community of fate irrespective of its internal differences'. If we fast forward to the present century, we find that even where the worker's job is part of a highly integrated global supply chain, the worker's world is invariably the immediate workplace and they rarely look beyond that world. The contemporary call for 'workers of the world to unite' faces a familiar dilemma: international solidarity is highly unlikely in the face of unemployment, poverty and the need to work at any cost (wage), but it is also a potentially transformative evocation of the effects of solidarity that might bring slight but crucial improvements to workers' daily lives.

Against all the odds, workers around the world continue to resist the forces of capital. Workers confront their employers in myriad workplaces around the globe, even in industries such as textiles and garments, but can these domestic activists 'find one another, gain legitimacy, form collective identities, and go back to their countries empowered with alliances, common programs, and new repertoires of collective action' (Tarrow, 2001: 15)? An institutional approach to trans-national contention suggests several mechanisms through which this might be possible:

Brokerage – making connections between otherwise unconnected domestic
   actors in a way that produces at least a temporary political identity that
   did not exist before
Certification – the recognition of the identities and legitimate public activity
   of either new actors or actors new to a particular site of activity

Modelling – the adoption of norms, forms of collective action or organization in one venue that have been demonstrated in another

Institutional appropriation – the use of an institution's resources or reputation to serve the purposes of affiliated groups (ibid.)

Tarrow's assessment of whether any *single* international institution is able
to provide the mechanisms to facilitate all of these steps is somewhat pessimistic – 'most fall well short of that threshold' (ibid.). Most trade union
organizations would certainly fall short, as the experience of the garment
industry would appear to testify. However, there is emerging evidence of coalition building between unions, civil society organizations (CSOs) and other
social movements in pursuit of social justice for some of the world's most vulnerable textile and garment workers (Merk, 2009). Elsewhere there is stronger
evidence of 'a multi-faceted form of trade unionism ... a layered form of organization, with different levels working to achieve recognition and an impact
in international sectors and regions' (Fairbrother and Hammer, 2005: 418).
Moreover, the activities of many global union federations (GUFs) 'are rooted
in the day-to-day realities of members, and not the musings of remote international leaders' (ibid.: 422). The campaigns of international action organized
by European dockworkers to halt the march of neo-liberalism in the EU's port
transport industry are remarkable cases in point.

The international clothing industry

Perhaps more than any other industrial sector, textile and garment[6]
manufacture has come to epitomize some of the ills of the globalized economy
of the twenty-first century, with its combination of buyer-driven (as opposed
to producer-driven) supply chains (Gereffi, 1999), highly mobile capital and
sweated labour (ILO, 2000).[7] In many respects, the conditions experienced
by workers employed in the garment industry at the end of the nineteenth
century (Phizacklea, 1990: 225–6) are being replicated in twenty-first century workshops. Yet the workers of the past century, by dint of regulation,
organization and collective bargaining, had managed to improve their working conditions. By the 1950s and 1960s, when 92 per cent of global garment
production was concentrated in mature developed economies (Phizacklea,
1990: 38), the sweatshop came to be something regarded as an historical relic,
never expected to return (Rosen, 2002: 1–4). Like many other workers, textile
and garment workers benefited from the relative prosperity of the post-1945
era, but as the twentieth century progressed, the dominance of neo-liberal

ideals and the supremacy of the market provided a very different context for the onward march of globalization and the restructuring of the international garment sector. As an industry that is typically in the vanguard of industrialization (Dicken, 2007) garment manufacture has also been at the forefront of the struggle for decent work.

Historically, unionization in the textile and garment industries acted more as a barrier against management's worst excesses rather than a significant threat to managerial prerogative (Edwards and Scullion, 1982: 259). Even when union membership was high, union influence was generally low (Winterton and Taplin, 1997: 14). Having said that, there were exceptions, most notably the United States where garment workers became the country's second highest paid production workers by the early 1950s (Quan, 2008: 194, 198). The International Ladies' Garment Workers' Union (ILGWU) was able to follow and organize the industry across the United States and even into Puerto Rico, with union density reaching 70 per cent compared to only 35 per cent for all workers nationally (ibid.: 198). The influence of the ILGWU was closely linked to a unique triangular relationship established within US territorial borders, whereby the Union was a party to tripartite negotiations with 'jobbers' who designed and sold clothing (in much the same way as global brands such as Nike and The Gap do today) and 'contractors' (whose contemporary equivalents would be the factory owners and manufacturers) who actually produced the clothes. The key to safeguarding labour conditions in this triangular relationship was the 'pass through' provision, whereby the union negotiators were able to ensure that increases in the prices negotiated between jobbers and contractors were 'passed through' to workers in their wages and conditions. In this way, value was distributed from the jobbers through the contractors to the workers (ibid.: 197). By the 1960s, however, markets were expanding and jobbers were sourcing clothing in Latin America and Asia, well beyond the organizational reach of the ILGWU, presaging today's buyer-driven commodity chains where prices for the supply of garments are agreed between brands, retailers and the factory owners, and labour costs are then settled (generally driven downward) accordingly. The sweatshop has returned and union organization will have to begin again, from the bottom up (i.e. from the local to the national and international levels).

By the end of the twentieth century the largest exporters of clothing to world markets were those with the lowest labour costs (ILO, 2000: 41) and the prevalence of sweatshop conditions is a function of capital's mobility, corporate strategy, international policy on tariffs and trade, and labour's own (in)capacity to organize. In this scenario, the role of national and supra-national state policies, most notably the MFA (Winterton and Winterton, 1997: 21), has been of crucial importance. It was widely predicted, and subsequently observed, that the end of protectionism associated with the phased demise of the MFA – a process begun in 1994 and finally ended in 2004 – would signal devastation for garment manufacture in mature economies (Phizacklea, 1990: 38). But relocation of production had begun long before the MFA was abandoned. Some western countries (e.g. Italy) sought to preserve the industry within their borders (Belussi, 1997; Jones, 2006: 168) but elsewhere in Europe the survival of textile and clothing production was not afforded any political priority and 'outward processing'[8] and relocation were positively promoted by national governments and the supra-national (EU) state. There were substantial financial grants and assistance for firms who restructured to become competitive internationally (Jones, 2006: 194; Phizacklea, 1990: 39–42; Winterton and Winterton, 1997: 21). Today even the high end of the retail market increasingly sources garments overseas (Blyton and Jenkins, 2010), and the restructured international garment industry is now characterized by complex, opaque, globally dispersed supply chains that have not only 'increased the power and profits of lead firms' (Gereffi, 1999; Hurley and Miller, 2005: 21) but also distanced international brands and producers from direct employment relationships and complicated the auditing of employer practice.

In this context, as triangular and other collective bargaining strategies broke down[9] textile and garment unions faced an uphill battle to defend their members' terms and conditions and retain employment in mature locations. To be sure, trade unions opposed the employers' strategy of labour cost minimization from the earliest days of outward processing (Phizacklea, 1990: 41), but as labour became increasingly replaceable on the international stage, unions found their bargaining leverage weakened incrementally and irrevocably. There is overwhelming evidence that 'comparative labour costs are a significant variable in location decisions' (Hale and Burns, 2005: 217; see also Hurley and Miller, 2005: 18; Rosen, 2002: 202–3; and Winterton and Taplin, 1997: 11). Under the credible threat of workplace relocation – for example, many of the larger UK manufacturers also owned or controlled factories in overseas locations and 'sister' plants were direct competitors for work – garment workers were ever more willing to entertain new forms of work organization in attempts to increase productivity and retain domestic production. The introduction of increased automation and intensified working systems was evident in a range of mature industrialized locations, and with labour substitution characterized by enormous wage disparity between workers (Hutchinson and Brown, 2001: 15) there was also scope for employers to deploy 'wage-depression' tactics (Winterton and Taplin, 1997: 14). If we take Britain's garment sector as an example, real net output per head increased by a staggering 285 per cent between 1973 and 1993 while employment declined by 53 per cent over the same period (Winterton and Winterton, 1997: 27), and yet the industry still moved offshore.

Faced with a combination of poor organizational capacity and ever weaker institutional protection to buttress their collective bargaining strategies, it is difficult to claim that textile unions in Europe and North America have been able to influence corporate strategy to any significant – or even noticeable – degree. While this sector is one that might conceivably benefit from a strong trans-national labour movement, the odds against any identification of any 'community of fate' between garment workers *across* geo-political borders are enormous, particularly since robust collective organization, solidarity and militancy *within* national boundaries, or even within firms and plants, has not been a feature of its industrial relations.

By way of example, consider the recent campaign by Burberry workers in south Wales against the relocation of their work to China (Blyton and Jenkins, 2010; Jenkins and Blyton, 2009). Initially, several factors appeared to work in labour's favour, not least the fact that Burberry was exceptional in retaining a vertically integrated structure, which meant that unions could protest against much more than just a brand or a label. The union's ability to expose a vertically integrated supply chain is a privilege rarely afforded to the majority of the world's garment workers, as most firms are characterized by vertical segmentation of production and a distinct lack of transparency (Winterton and Winterton, 1997: 30). The Burberry dispute attracted remarkable public attention as workers, under their union banner, mounted a fierce campaign that encompassed skilful use of the media, direct protest, political lobbying and legal action. There was also an international dimension in the form of protests by affiliated unions in France and the United States. Yet this support was largely symbolic as it did not involve other workers employed by Burberry, either at home or abroad. In fact, unionized Burberry plants in the north east of England refused requests for solidarity from the south Wales plant, fearing 'they would be next' in the relocation stakes if they did not work normally. Ironically then, although workers in a small south Wales community *were* able to mount an international campaign, they could not garner support from fellow workers and union members in the United Kingdom. Relocation was delayed and made more costly for the corporation, but the south Wales plant closed in 2007 and substantial redundancies were announced at the surviving plants in 2009.

In newly industrializing countries of the global South and East, garment assembly is generally feminized, unions are rarely recognized, health and safety and other forms of regulation is generally poor, hours are long, rest days are infrequent, holidays are a luxury and even statutory minimum pay rates are evaded (Esbenshade, 2004: 124; see also Hurley, 2005: 116; Hurley and Miller, 2005: 35; Jones, 2006; Pangsapa, 2007: 23; Rock, 2001; Rosen, 2002: 240; Winterton and Taplin, 1997: 10). There is also widespread evidence of forced labour, child labour, debt-bondage and human trafficking within the global supply chains that extend all the way from respectable high street outlets in the west to the urban slums of developing countries (ILO, 2000). The state may repress unionization (Hutchinson and Brown, 2001: 8–14), but even where freedom of association is enshrined in law the fact that the labour force is feminized – typically young, first or second generation rural migrants, unmarried and childless when they first enter the factory – offers management social and cultural opportunities for control, in addition to the obvious economic power that capital wields over labour under such circumstances. To say these workers represent a challenge for trade union organization would be an understatement of the highest order. But to suggest that these workers cannot be organized, that they do not want to fight for their employment rights and decent work would be equally facile.

Traditional methods of union organization and representation, on their own, have rarely succeeded when it comes to organizing garment workers in the new sweatshops of the global economy (Wills and Hale, 2005: 11). Established industrial unions, such as those in India for example, have found themselves ill-equipped for the task, claiming that garment workers are simply not 'amenable' to ideas of unity and are 'resistant' to unionization (Jenkins, 2010). There is undoubtedly some truth in this, and for very good reason. Female garment workers, in particular, find it difficult to participate in union activities due to the simple, practical constraints of household labour which circumscribe their days and nights and allow little spare energy or time for organization around class interests; the battle for individual survival fills every waking moment (Wills and Hale, 2005: 11). Furthermore, employers in the sector routinely and very deliberately repress attempts at organization. For socially and economically impoverished workers, employment laws invariably prove to be ineffective and rather distant instruments of redress. Moreover, no matter what corporate codes of conduct say about upholding freedom of association, workers and activists routinely face the full gamut of anti-union tactics and personal intimidation if they attempt to organize, and they are likely to lose their jobs if discovered (Hearson and Eagleton, 2007). Even on a local scale, therefore, brokerage is unlikely and unions struggle to secure certification.

Organizing such workers requires innovative methods aimed at the cultivation of long-term relationships based on trust and the framing of issues of direct relevance to workers' daily lives. On this basis organization *is* taking place where capital settles and clusters in new localities (Gereffi, 1999: 64), usually as a result of innovative organizational techniques driven by a range of civil society organizations and unions. In their daily work, activists focus on small gains for local workers using the wider international context for leverage, rather than conceiving their activities as a full frontal assault on international capital. This is painstaking work but it can deliver real, if only marginal, improvements in workers' conditions of employment. Unfortunately, traditional unions have shied away from engaging in this sort of laborious effort, preferring to retreat to the glory of 'grand campaigns' (Sherlock, 2001: 149). This is perhaps the crux of the matter in terms of any interpretation of what 'unity' means in this context. The tendency to portray garment workers as disempowered victims in a way that infantilizes them ignores the rights and aspirations of arguably some of the most vulnerable workers in developing countries. In particular, unions that overlook the efforts of workers who do organize and resist the might of capital undermine any bargaining power that they may wrest from their employers, and this turns the claim that garment workers 'cannot be organised' into a self-fulfilling prophesy (Pangsapa, 2007: 4).

Despite a catalogue of difficulties, there are still opportunities for modelling and institutional appropriation in this sector. For example, NGOs can fill an 'institutional gap' by campaigning for social equality and empowerment (Hutchinson and Brown, 2001: 12) as well as providing assistance to community groups who help workers to organize at the local level. While these groupings may not begin as independent trade unions they frequently evolve and grow through novel forms of brokerage, such as community projects, microfinance projects and self-help groups, and in this way some of the world's most vulnerable garment workers have come together and drawn support (institutional appropriation) from a trans-national network of civil society organizations and NGOs (e.g. the Clean Clothes Campaign, Oxfam, Amnesty International and Action Aid). This is how the Garment and Textile Workers' Union (GATWU) based in Bangalore, India developed. The Bangladesh Independent Garment Workers' Union (BIGU) offers another example of how work organization and workers' experience of harsh working conditions can promote activism among women stereotypically labelled as quiescent by their cultural setting and subservient position in the production process (Rock, 2001: 27). BIGU and GATWU are unions formed out of workers' own drive for organization, with the support of NGOs but independent of political affiliation. They are both examples of the rise of workers' voice in the global south.

With the support of NGOs such as the Clean Clothes Campaign and its British arm, Labour Behind the Label, the International Textile Garment and Leather Workers' Federation (ITGLWF), which currently brings together 217 affiliated trade union organizations across 110 countries, has been able to negotiate the first International Framework Agreement on conditions in the international garment sector, with the Spanish giant Inditex (the corporation behind the Zara chain). This Agreement, built on the foundations of institutional appropriation, represents a new form of certification for the labour movement. The impact of the Framework Agreement on the ground is, as ever, only as good as its enforcement, and the global union recognizes that in most locations there is a long way to go before mature systems of industrial relations are established. Nevertheless, without a trans-national dimension, local activists would have far less leverage in negotiations in their domestic space. Somewhat paradoxically it is the very nature of the international brand and its accountability to its market/customers which affords opportunity to activists. On the ground, although it is well recognized that the auditing of employer practice is subject to corruption and collusion and is often poorly enacted (Esbenshade, 2004), codes of conduct nevertheless afford workers some extra leverage with which to take local disputes to the international stage, either through single issue campaigning organizations or the ITGLWF. The demands of export-led production can crystallize conflicts over work intensification and be the catalyst for trade union formation (Hutchinson, 2001: 72), and once organized, activists can use corporate codes of social responsibility as well as legal compliance as bargaining leverage as they seek to hold international brands to account.

Does such organization and action make a difference? Hard evidence on the general relationship between ethical concerns about labour conditions and the effect of consumer behaviour on sales is limited (Jones, 2006: 190), but modelling subsequent campaigns on previous successes is bearing fruit. For example, a recent boycott of Fruit of the Loom and Russell Athletic garments, led in the United Kingdom by Labour Behind the Label (LBL), asked universities and student unions to join the boycott over alleged union busting tactics associated with the closure of a factory making products for both brands in Honduras. The campaign was supported by nine universities in the United Kingdom as well as United Students Against Sweatshops (USAS) in the United States and over 100 universities worldwide. LBL announced on 23 November 2009 that as a result of the campaign, an agreement had been signed between the factory and the local union and the factory had re-opened. In another new development, an international coalition between civil society and unions across Europe and Asia has resulted in the Asia Floor Wage Alliance, a campaign based around the first mathematical formula for the calculation of a 'living wage' which may be applied across geo-political-economic boundaries (Merk, 2009). This is a tangible development in trans-national communication and co-ordinated campaigning, and its proponents hope it will bear fruit in terms of organizing structures for the future. In this labour movement for the twenty-first century, victories may be small and they are always hard won (Wills and Hale, 2005: 11). But small victories can build the foundations for workers' awareness, which is the first step on the road to finding other workers who face similar struggles, forming collective identities, and developing new repertories of collective action.

The European port transport industry

Like textiles and garment manufacture, dock work was once a sweated trade (Beveridge, 1909; Lascelles and Bullock, 1924; Phizacklea, 1990: 225–6). Today, however, across Europe, port workers are well organized and the dockland labour market, with some notable exceptions (e.g. Ireland and the United Kingdom) is highly regulated. For example, dockworkers are now covered by mandatory and intensive training programmes in most EU Member States and are generally afforded professional status. Moreover, labour supply is often governed by state regulations for all dock workers (e.g. Belgium) or at least for any additional labour that employers may wish to hire beyond their 'core' labour force (e.g. Germany, Italy and Spain).[10] European port unions have been adept at exploiting these national institutional arrangements to defend their members' interests, and union organization has proven highly resilient in the face of concerted attempts by the state and port employers to reform the dockland labour market (again with some notable exceptions such as the United Kingdom) (Turnbull and Wass, 2007). To be sure, port unions in several Member States (e.g. Belgium, Germany, Ireland, Italy, the Netherlands and Portugal) have worked in concert with employers and the nation state to reform work practices and improve productivity. But in other countries, port unions have mobilized their national institutional resources to defend workers' interests and resist more extensive labour market reforms (ibid.: 607–9). In a comparative international context, this enabled European port workers to fare much better than dockworkers elsewhere during the latter part of the last century (ibid.: 598–609). With the onset of globalization and the conflicts that lay ahead in the twenty-first century, the existence of supranational governance institutions, with jurisdiction coterminous with the scope of the capital–labour struggle in question, provided a focal point for

European dockworkers to successfully press their claims at the international level.

Given the sheer size of the European market, trade is unlikely to go elsewhere. Given the value to weight ratio of most traded goods, cargo is unlikely to switch from shipping to other modes of transport. The maritime regions of the EU account for over 40 per cent of its GDP and ports handle over 40 per cent of intra-EU traffic and over 90 per cent of Europe's external trade (CEC, 2006: 3). While there is certainly competition between EU ports, and indeed some scope to build new port facilities to serve the European market and beyond (e.g. Wilhelmshaven in Germany, Giaio Tauro in Italy, Marsaxlokk in Malta and Algeciras in Spain), this does not mean that capital can 'run away' from trade unions, national industrial relations systems or EU regulation. In fact, by virtue of being located within the borders of the EU, even green-field ports are quickly organized and subject to comparable regulatory conditions. International capital is therefore highly dependent on location-specific assets (seaports). For their part, dock workers have strong ties to their local communities, although they all interact on a daily basis with workers from around the globe as vessels come and go.

Faced with such regulation and a well-organized workforce, TNCs demanded greater 'market access' (i.e. liberalization) in order to reduce operating costs. In the port services market, for example, some international shipping lines would prefer to handle their own vessels instead of contracting with local cargo handling companies, which in some EU Member States are still under the direct financial or even operational control of the state. In the labour market, service providers might demand access to alternative (cheaper) labour, such as agency workers, sub-contractors, temporary staff or immigrants. At the behest of international shipping lines and shippers, and without any proper consultation with the European Transport Workers' Federation (ETF),[11] this is exactly what the Commission proposed when it published a draft Directive *On Access to the Port Services Market* in February 2001 (CEC, 2001).

The Directive stipulated a minimum of two service providers for each category of cargo handling and other port services such as pilotage, stowage, mooring and passenger services, thereby opening access and ensuring competition in the product market. Indirectly, this would create more competition in the labour market as firms seek to cut costs and win business from their rivals. More directly, the labour market would be liberalized through provisions for 'self-handling', defined as 'a situation in which a port user provides for itself one or more categories of port services' (CEC, 2001: 28) which implied 'the right to employ personnel *of his own choice* to carry out the service' (ibid.: 29, emphasis added). This would allow shipping lines, for example, to employ seafarers on cargo handling activities while the ship is in port (e.g. to un/lash containers on deep-sea services or un/lash roll-on/roll-off vehicles on short-sea services) or allow shipping lines and terminal operators to hire non-recognized dockworkers from employment agencies or other sources of labour supply. In some EU Member States there is already competition in the product market, most notably in Northern Europe, and in others there is already competition and casual employment in the labour market, most notably the United Kingdom. But in the Mediterranean in particular there is still limited or no competition in either market. International shipping lines were especially keen to see more open access to ports in the Mediterranean, where the state plays a much larger role than in the north European ports, as this would allow them to develop inter-modal transport services to Central and Eastern Europe (instead of calling at North European ports) when plying the dominant east↔west trade routes via the Suez Canal.

In response to the proposed Directive, dock workers 'declared war' on the supra-national state, or to be more precise the International Transport Workers' Federation (ITF) declared war on their behalf (Turnbull, 2006). Most European transport unions are affiliated to the ITF but there are some notable omissions, including major port unions in France, Spain and Sweden. There is also an uneasy relationship between the ITF and the ETF which dates back to jurisdictional disputes between the ITF and the Federation of Transport Workers' Unions in the European Union (FST), the forerunner of the ETF,[12] which was only partially resolved by an agreement reached in 1994 recognizing the ITF's responsibility for the coordination of international solidarity and relations with non-EU institutions and the primary role of the FST with respect to the institutions of the EU. The emergence of a rival international organization in the late 1990s, the International Dockworkers' Council (IDC), created an additional fissure at both the international and national levels of union organization.[13] The first task of the ITF was therefore to establish stronger connections, and in some cases *rapprochement*, between these different actors in a way that would produce at least a temporary political alliance (i.e. brokerage).

At the local and national levels, unions needed the resources of the ITF to press their claims (i.e. institutional appropriation).[14] In the absence of any prior consultation with the European Commission, or any social dialogue with employers, organized labour was ill-prepared when the Directive *On Market Access* was first published. The initial task of union leaders was therefore to convince rank-and-file dockworkers of the threat posed by the Directive. Within the ETF, several prominent unions, most notably Ver.di

(Germany), were confident that various Articles in the proposed Directive on authorizations (Article 11), safety (Article 14) and social protection (Article 15), if suitably amended, would be sufficient to protect established terms and conditions of employment. The ITF disagreed, likening the potential impact of the Directive to 'flags of convenience' (FOC) shipping that have driven down the wages of seafarers employed as a 'crew of convenience' (Lillie, 2004). By raising the prospect of European 'ports of convenience', where pay and conditions would be driven down to the lowest common denominator, the ITF struck a chord with European dockers, establishing a role for itself (alongside the ETF) in a new site of activity (i.e. certification). For example, at the local level the ITF organized a coordinated programme of 'educational stop-work meetings' across the EU to explain both the contents and the purpose of the Directive to rank-and-file dockers. These meetings took place during the ITF's Week of Action on FOC Shipping, just to reinforce the point, and involved ITF Inspectors who constitute a network of workplace representatives that is unique among the global union federations.[15] At the regional (European) level, the ITF/ETF coordinated action against international shipping lines and more importantly the supra-national state. In particular, whenever the Directive was being debated in specialist committees or the European Parliament, dock workers took to the streets of Brussels, Strasbourg and major European city-ports to demonstrate their opposition to liberalization.

Through these activities, port workers came to appreciate that they shared a 'community of fate' as *European* dockers, whereby any local or national employment protection they enjoyed was now dependent on collective action at the international level. Their domestic union organization and participation in previous international solidarity campaigns (i.e. modelling) gave them the confidence to 'shift scale' to the regional level, as did the emergence of new union networks. The latter were both 'relational' – based on strong bonds of kinship, trust and cultural identity within specific port ranges such as the Baltic, northern Europe and the Mediterranean – and non-relational (e.g. electronic networks created by union activists).[16] Significant broadsides were fired across the bows of global capital and the supra-national state when dockers staged the first ever pan-European dock strike in January 2003, involving 20,000 dockworkers, and mass demonstrations in Rotterdam and Barcelona, involving 9000 and 6000 dockers, respectively, to coincide with the final debate on the Directive in the European Parliament. Bill Milligan, Chief Executive of the Strike Club (the mutual insurer of ship owners, charterers and vessel operators against strikes and other causes of delay), acknowledged that the pan-European dock strikes and mass demonstrations that marked the 'war on

Europe's waterfront' had 'opened a new chapter in labour activism' (*Lloyd's List*, 24 October 2004).

The Directive was narrowly, and surprisingly, rejected by the European Parliament in November 2003. Surprising, because only the dockworkers opposed the final draft. However, although they had won this particular battle, the war was by no means over. It was precisely because the proposed Directive had the trenchant support of global capital, and the acceptance of most national port employers and Member States, that the Commission published a second proposed Directive *On Market Access to Port Services* in October 2004 (CEC, 2004). But with the second proposed Directive, the Commission seriously miscalculated the interests and intentions of the industry's principal stakeholders. For organized labour, this created an organizing space for new coalitions with other stakeholders (Turnbull, 2007).

The basic principles, underlying doctrine and key objectives of the second ports package were the same as the first (CEC, 2004: 2), but the devil really was in the detail as there were important differences that raised the ire of virtually all stakeholders (e.g. on concessions or lease periods for new service providers and compensation for outgoing service providers). This facilitated a new phase of brokerage and institutional appropriation as a previously unthinkable 'alliance' was formed between the ETF and their European counterparts representing public port authorities (the European Sea Ports Organisation, ESPO) and private operators (the Federation of European Private Port Operators, FEPORT). In a significant shift in policy, both ESPO and FEPORT no longer insisted on the inclusion of self-handling in the proposed Directive, and both organizations, for 'reasons of proportionality and subsidiarity', determined that these issues were best set out at local or national level (ESPO, 2005a, 2005b: 5; FEPORT, 2005: 8–9). More telling, both organizations expressed their desire 'to avoid unnecessary social unrest' (FEPORT, 2005: 9), which 'could create an unstable climate for potential investors' (ESPO, 2004: 2) and impose direct costs on service providers and users that 'seem to go unnoticed by the European legislative authorities' (FEPORT, 2005: 9). Even the European Community Shipowners' Association (ECSA, 2005: 6) was prepared to see self-handling excluded from the second ports package, despite previously championing this issue (Turnbull, 2007: 133). Having exercised the argument of force, it seemed that other stakeholders, and crucially important EU institutions (e.g. CoR, 2005: para. 1.22; EESC, 2005: para. 3.15), were now prepared to accept the force of labour's argument (i.e. the liberalization of the labour market *would* lead to a deterioration in safety standards and social conditions, contrary to the European Treaty).

At the initiative of ESPO, the major stakeholders held what they called a 'non-meeting' in Antwerp in late December 2005.[17] While the employers were principally motivated by a desire to develop contingency plans for the disruption they knew would accompany the final debate and vote on the Directive in the European Parliament the following month, there was also a genuine desire to move away from social conflict towards social dialogue and establish a more united position towards the Commission. Unlikely coalitions often form in the face of a common threat, and this was certainly how the Commission was increasingly perceived by a growing number of European port interests. As a result, with a much broader alignment of opposition against the Directive, in January 2006 the European Parliament voted by 532 to 120 (with 25 abstentions) to reject the liberalization of the port services market. In March 2006, the Commission officially withdrew its proposals for a port services Directive. Only three of more than 1000 Directives considered by the European Parliament between 1999 and 2004 were rejected. The *Port Services* Directive now bears the ignominious distinction of being the only Directive to have been rejected twice.

Further non-meetings were held throughout 2006, at first to ensure that port services were excluded from the controversial Bolkestein Directive on services in the EU internal market and then to formulate a 'common response' to a series of port policy workshops organized by the Commission in late 2006 and throughout 2007. During this period of consultation, FEPORT finally agreed to establish a European Sector Social Dialogue Committee with the trade unions (see endnote 11), which ESPO subsequently decided to join. Once certified, this Committee potentially removes many areas of port employment policy from the remit of the Commission. More importantly, it was the industry itself that was now steering the future course of EU ports policy, not the supra-national state. As the Transport Commissioner at the time was forced to concede, the industry has 'take[n] its own future in hand' (Barrot, 2007: 2).

In late 2000, when the ITF/ETF first heard rumours in the corridors of Brussels that the Commission was planning a Directive *On Access to the Port Services Market*, their requests for information and consultation were largely ignored. In late 2007 when the ETF learnt that the Commission was planning a legal review of port labour pools, no doubt with a view to launching a legal challenge against these 'labour monopolies' (CEC, 1997: 19), the ETF demanded an immediate meeting and the legal review was scrapped forthwith. When a 'non-meeting' was held between all the stakeholders in December 2002 during the war on Europe's waterfront, port authorities and private port operators refused to sign a joint declaration against self-handling. During the campaign against the second *Port Services* Directive they called on the Commission to remove the Articles on self-handling. During the subsequent port policy workshops organized by the Commission (2006–07) even the European Community Shipowners' Association declared that 'the words "self-handling" have been deleted from our word processors' (Meeting Notes, 2007). At every stage, organized labour prevailed. European port unions openly acknowledge that it would be foolhardy to assume that the jobs of European dock workers are now secure, but they have demonstrated the political will and capacity to defend their interests and build a dam to prevent the tsunami of liberalization and globalization flooding their industry. Behind this dam, dockworkers continue to enjoy 'decent work' and they are still among the highest paid manual workers in the EU.

Conclusions

When we ask an age-old question in a contemporary context – 'Can workers of the world unite?' – the answer is equivocal. Independent collective organization is one of the few bulwarks that provide shelter for workers in the global economy, but there are immense barriers to unity where frameworks of social protection and effective mechanisms for the enforcement of law are weak or non-existent. In some of the newly industrializing regions of the world freedom of association is not enshrined in law, and even where such rights are on the statute book, organization may be hazardous and leave workers exposed and unable to access their human rights to decent work. In a truly global industry such as garment manufacture, where capital is highly mobile, social institutions are weak, and workers' freedom to associate is everywhere under threat, workers endure harsh working conditions and pitiful rates of pay. Yet in more geographically confined markets, such as the EU, where capital must embed itself if it wants access to the market, where social institutions are more robust, and trade unions firmly entrenched, then many workers continue to enjoy decent work and fair remuneration.

Our cases clearly demonstrate that institutions matter in providing leverage for workers within the globalized employment relationship. In the textile and garment sectors, new forms of collective organization have emerged and resistance is found in all corners of the globe, but success is limited. The women who toil in the buyer-driven supply chains that now extend across the globe are not well organized and all too often are neglected by established trade unions. Consequently, without effective regulation of employers and their product markets, alongside national enforcement of employment laws and some form of supra-national legal intervention to promote workers' rights and collective bargaining, it is difficult to imagine any material gains for textile and garment workers extending beyond the immediate and the local. In contrast, the almost exclusively male workforce employed in European ports have a long history of union organization and industrial militancy, they are well versed in national politics and the defence of their statutory rights, and they have demonstrated a capacity to extend their repertoire of contention to the supra-national level. Very few workers in the global economy enjoy such protection or possess the capacity to develop such protection. These contrasting cases demonstrate why it is that very few workers of world can truly unite, but also why unity is essential for workers to create a better world in which to work.

Notes

1. Marx and Engels (1967: 79) defined the bourgeoisie as 'the class of modern capitalists, owners of the means of production and employers of wage labour'.
2. In 2006, there were 77,000 TNCs that had ownership in over 770,000 foreign affiliates, compared to 11,000 and 82,600, respectively, in 1976. These affiliates now employ well over 60 million workers worldwide.
3. If an EU-based corporation employs a thousand workers in total and more than 150 employees in two or more Member States, then it falls under the provisions of the Works Council Directive (94/45/EC). There are almost 900 active EWCs with around 20,000 representatives. Approximately 16 million workers across the EU have the right to information and consultation on company decisions at European level through their EWCs.
4. This Convention was intended to address situations where employment contracts are replaced by commercial contracts but employers vehemently resisted the proposal and killed the draft Convention. This was the first time in 80 years when the standard-setting machinery failed.
5. These costs are not simply economic. In many countries, union activists face verbal intimidation, harassment and physical violence. Worldwide, at least 76 labour activists were killed as a result of their actions for workers' rights in 2008 (go to: http://survey09.ituc-csi.org/survey.php?IDContinent=0&Lang=EN).
6. The textile industry refers to the production of cloth and fibres whereas garment or apparel manufacture refers to the manufacture of clothing, specifically garment assembly which is the focus here.
7. Sweated trades are defined in terms of long hours, poor conditions, unsanitary workplaces, and low pay, as well as non-compliance with statutory minimum labour standards (Merk, 2009; Rosen, 2002: 2).
8. Originally conceived as a means of negotiating ways around import controls and tariffs, outward processing involved relocating the low-skilled and rather labour intensive garment assembly stage of production from the EU to low cost-wage locations, while retaining the more skilled, capital intensive research and development stages of garment design in the producer's country of origin.
9. For example, Trade Boards and Wages Councils in the United Kingdom provided a 'floor' for union negotiations with the British Clothing Industry Association and individual employers, prior to the abolition of Wages Councils by the Thatcher government.

10. As the demand for labour fluctuates widely over the trade cycle, with seasonal cargoes, as a result of the weather, or simply the arrival and departure of shipping, employers often need additional labour which they can only hire from these state-mandated companies or 'labour pools' (i.e. they are denied access to the external labour market).

11. The ETF is a European industry federation affiliated to the European Trade Union Confederation (ETUC). It represents European workers in all the transport modes and is the officially recognized 'social partner' on European Sector Social Dialogue Committees for road, rail, civil aviation, inland waterways and maritime (sea) transport. Port transport is the only transport sector without a European Sector Social Dialogue Committee.

12. In 1999, the FST was dissolved and its members joined with the ITF's European affiliates to create the ETF.

13. In several Member States (e.g. Spain and Sweden) rival national port unions are affiliated to different international federations (ITF/ETF or IDC), which has exacerbated domestic union rivalries and transposed these differences to the international arena.

14. At the most elementary level, the ITF provided expert advice on the proposed Directive to affiliated unions, produced campaign materials, and even drafted and translated letters of opposition for unions in different EU Member States to send to their national members of parliament and members of the European Parliament.

15. ITF Inspectors are seconded from, and paid by, local (trans)port unions. They are employed by the ITF to inspect FOC vessels when they call in port and organize action against these vessels if they fail to comply with ITF standards.

16. See http://www.havenarbeiders.be and http://www.havenforum.nl. These (horizontal) labour networks cut across, and interconnected, the various levels of the (vertical) union hierarchy. They not only promoted 'internal debate' but also helped to ensure more effective 'union articulation' (i.e. stronger inter-relationships between the workplace, national and international levels of organization).

17. This was an informal meeting with no minutes.

References

Amsterdam Treaty (1997) *The Treaty of Amsterdam Amending the Treaty on European Union, the Treaties Establishing the European Communities and Certain Related Acts*, 2 October, Amsterdam: European Union.

Barrot, J. (2007) 'Keynote Speech: "European Port Policy" '. Presented at the ESPO Annual Conference, Algeciras, Spain, 1 June.

Belussi, F. (1997) 'Dwarfs and Giants Maintaining Competitive Edge: The Italian Textile Clothing Industry in the 1990s', in I.M. Taplin and J. Winterton (eds.) *Rethinking Global Production – A Comparative Analysis of Restructuring in the Clothing Industry*, Aldershot: Ashgate, pp. 77–130.

Beveridge, W. (1909) *Unemployment: A Problem of Industry*, London: Longmans.

Bhatt, E.R. (2006) *We Are Poor But So Many: The Story of Self-Employed Women in India*, New York: Oxford University Press.

Brown, W. (2008) 'The Influence of Product Markets on Industrial Relations', in P. Blyton, N. Bacon, J. Fiorito and E. Heery (eds) *The Sage Handbook of Industrial Relations*, London: Sage, pp. 113–28.

Blyton, P. and Jenkins, J. (2010) 'Ways of Life After Redundancy: Anatomy of a Community Following Factory Closure', in P. Blyton, B. Blunsdon and A. Dastmalchian (eds) *Ways of Living*, pp. 202–19.

CEC (1997) *Green Paper on Sea Ports and Maritime Infrastructure*, COM(97)678, Brussels: Commission of the European Communities.

CEC (2001) Proposal for a Directive of the European Parliament and of the Council On Market Access to Port Services, COM(2001)35, Brussels: Commission of the European Communities.

CEC (2004) Proposal for a Directive of the European Parliament and of the Council On Market Access to Port Services, COM(2004)654, Brussels: Commission of the European Communities.

CEC (2006) Green Paper – Towards a Future Maritime Policy for the Union: European Vision for the Oceans and Seas, COM(2006)275 final, Brussels: Commission of the European Communities.

CoR (2005) 'Opinion of the Committee of the Regions on the Proposal for a Directive of the European Parliament and Council *On Market Access to Port Services*', Brussels: Committee of the Regions.

Cronin, J.E. (1979) *Industrial Conflict in Modern Britain*, London: Croom Helm.

Dicken, P. (2007) Global Shift: Mapping the Changing Contours of the World Economy, 5th Edition, New York: Guilford Press.

Edwards, P. and Scullion, H. (1982) *The Social Organisation of Industrial Conflict*, Oxford: Blackwell.

ECSA (2005) 'European Parliament Working Document on *Market Access to Port Services*', Brussels: European Community Shipowners' Association.

EESC (2005) 'Opinion of the European Economic and Social Committee on the Proposal for a Directive of the European Parliament and Council *On Market Access to Port Services*', Brussels: European Economic and Social Committee.

Esbenshade, J. (2004) *Monitoring Sweatshops: Workers, Consumers and the Global Apparel Industry*, Philadelphia: Temple University Press.

ESPO (2004) '*Directive Proposal on Market Access to Port Services* – Initial Response of ESPO', Brussels: European Sea Ports Organisation.

ESPO (2005a) 'Market Access to Port Services: European Parliament – TRAN Committee – Public Hearing 14 June', Statement by Giuliano Gallanti, Chairman of ESPO, Brussels: European Sea Ports Organisation.

ESPO (2005b) 'Market Access to Port Services: Paper adopted by ESPO General Assembly', Brussels: European Sea Ports Organisation.

Fairbrother, P. and Hammer, N. (2005) 'Global Unions: Past Efforts and Future Prospects', *Relations Industrielles*, 60(3): 405–31.

FEPORT (2005) 'Position Paper on the Proposed Directive *On Market Access to Port Services*', Brussels: Federation of European Private Port Operators.

Fourcade, M. (2006) 'The Construction of a Global Profession: The Transnationalization of Economics', *American Journal of Sociology*, 112(1): 145–94.

Fox Piven, F. (2006) 'Response to the "American Democracy in an Age of Inequality"', *Political Science & Politics*, January: 43–6.

Gereffi, G. (1999) 'International Trade and Industrial Upgrading in the Apparel Commodity Chain', *Journal of International Economics*, 48: 37–70.

Hale, A. and Burns, M. (2005) 'The Phase-Out of the Multi-Fibre Arrangement from the Perspective of Workers' in A. Hale and J. Wills (eds) *Threads of Labour: Garment Industry Supply Chains from the Workers' Perspective*, Oxford: Blackwell, pp. 210–39.

Hall, P.A. and Soskice, D. (2001) 'An Introduction to Varieties of Capitalism', in P.A. Hall and D. Soskice (eds) *Varieties of Capitalism: The Institutional Foundations of Comparative Advantage*, Oxford: Oxford University Press, pp. 1–68.

Harrod, J. and O'Brien, R. (2002) 'Organized Labour and the Global Political Economy', in J. Harrod and R. O'Brien (eds) *Global Unions? Theory and Strategies of Organized Labour in the Global Political Economy*, London: Routledge, pp. 3–28.

Harvey, D. (1982) *The Limits to Capital*, Oxford: Basil Blackwell.

Hay, C. (2006) 'What's Globalization go to do with it? Economic Interdependence and the Future of European Welfare States', *Government & Opposition*, 41(1): 1–22.

Hearson, M. and Eagleton, D. (2007) *Who Pays? How British Supermarkets Are Keeping Women Workers in Poverty*, Action Aid International UK.

Held, D., McGrew, A. Goldblatt, D. and Perraton, J. (1999) *Global Transformations: Politics, Economics and Culture*, Cambridge: Polity Press.

Herod, A. (2002) 'Organizing Globally, Organizing Locally: Union Spatial Strategy in a Global Economy', in J. Harrod and R. O'Brien (eds) *Global Unions? Theory and Strategies of Organized Labour in the Global Political Economy*, London: Routledge, pp. 83–99.

Herod, A., Rainnie, A. and McGrath-Champ, S. (2007) 'Working Space: Why Incorporating the Geographical Is Central to Theorizing Work and Employment Practices', *Work, Employment & Society*, 21(2): 247–64.

Hirst, P. and Thompson, G. (1999) Globalization in Question: The International Economy and the Possibilities of Governance, Cambridge: Polity.

Hobsbawm, E. (1999) 'The Making of the Working Class – Ford Lecture, Oxford University, 1981,' in E. Hobsbawm, *Uncommon People: Resistance, Rebellion and Jazz*, London: Abacus, pp. 76–99.

Hurley, J. (2005) 'Unravelling the Web: Supply Chains and Workers' Lives in the Garment Industry', in A. Hale and J. Wills (eds) *Threads of Labour: Garment Industry Supply Chains from the Workers' Perspective*, Oxford: Blackwell, pp. 95–132.

Hurley J. and Miller, D. (2005) 'The Changing Face of the Global Garment Industry', in A. Hale and J. Wills (eds) *Threads of Labour: Garment Industry Supply Chains from the Workers' Perspective*, Oxford: Blackwell, pp. 16–39.

Hutchinson, J. (2001) 'Export Opportunities: Unions in the Philippine Garments Industry', in J. Hutchinson and A. Brown (eds.) *Organising Labour in Globalising Asia*, London: Routledge, pp. 71–89.

Hutchinson, J. and Brown, A. (2001) 'Organising Labour in Globalising Asia: An Introduction', in J. Hutchinson and A. Brown (eds) *Organising Labour in Globalising Asia*, London: Routledge, pp. 1–26.

Hyman, R. (1999) 'Imagined Solidarities: Can Trade Unions Resist Globalization?' in Leisink, P. (ed.) *Globalization and Labour Relations*, Cheltenham: Edward Elgar, pp. 94–115.

Hyman, R. (2001) 'The Europeanisation – or the Erosion – of Industrial Relations', *Industrial Relations Journal*, 32(4): 280–94.

ILO (2000) Labour Practices in the Footwear, Leather, Textiles and Clothing Industries, Geneva: International Labour Office.

Jenkins, J. (2008) 'Pressurised Partnership: A Case of Perishable Compromise in Contested Terrain', *New Technology, Work and Employment*, 23(3): 167–80.

Jenkins J. (2010) 'Courage, Knowledge and the Power of Organisation', Paper to the Annual International Labour Process Conference, 15–17 March, Rutgers University, New Jersey.

Jenkins, J. and Blyton, P. (2009) 'The End of the Campaign', Paper to the Annual Conference of the British Universities Industrial Relations Association, Cardiff, 2009.

Jones, R.M. (2006) *The Apparel Industry, Second Edition*, Oxford: Blackwell.

Kelly, J. (1998) *Rethinking Industrial Relations: Mobilization, Collectivism and Long Waves*, London: Routledge.

Lascelles, E.C.P. and Bullock, S.S. (1924) *Dock Labour and Decasualisation*, London: P.S. King & Sons.

Levi, M. and Ahlquist, J.S. (2004) 'Labor Power and Mobile Capital: The Market Geography of Solidarity', mimeo, University of Washington.

Lillie, N. (2004) 'Global Collective Bargaining on Flag of Convenience Shipping', *British Journal of Industrial Relations*, 42(1): 47–67.

Marx, K. (1973) *Grundrisse: Foundations of the Critique of Political Economy*, London: Penguin.

Marx, K. and Engels, F. (1967) *The Communist Manifesto*, with an Introduction by A.J.P. Taylor, Harmondsworth: Penguin.

Meeting Notes (2007) 'European Commission Port Policy Workshops, Workshop No. 4 – Labour Issues, Cargo-handling, Technical-nautical Services', Valencia, 8–9 March (author's transcript).

Merk, J. (2009) Stitching a Decent Wage Across Borders: The Asia Floor Wage Proposal, Clean Clothes Campaign/Asia Floor Wage Alliance.

Moody, K. (1997), *Workers in a Lean World*, London: Verso.

Myconos, G. (2005) *The Globalization of Labour 1945–2005*, Houndmills: Palgrave Macmillan.

Ohmae, K. (1990) *The Borderless World: Power and Strategy in the Interlinked Economy*, New York: Harper Business.

Pangsapa, P. (2007) *Textures of Struggle: The Emergence of Resistance Among Garment Workers in Thailand*, Cornell: Cornell University Press.

Phizacklea, A. (1990), Unpacking the Fashion Industry: Gender, Racism and Class in Production, London: Routledge.

Quan, K. (2008) 'Evolving Labor Regulations in the Women's Apparel Industry', in C.J. Whalen (ed.) *New Directions in the Study of Work and Employment: Revitalizing Industrial Relations as an Academic Enterprise*, Cheltenham: Edward Elgar, pp. 194–210.

Rock, M. (2001) 'The Rise of the Bangladesh Independent Garment Workers' Union (BIGU)', in J. Hutchinson and A. Brown (eds) *Organising Labour in Globalising Asia*, London: Routledge, pp. 27–47.

Rosen, E.R. (2002) *Making Sweatshops: The Globalization of the U.S. Apparel Industry*, Berkeley: University of California Press.

Sherlock, S. (2001) 'Labour and the Remaking of Bombay', in J. Hutchinson and A. Brown (eds) *Organising Labour in Globalising Asia*, London: Routledge, pp. 147–67.

Silver, B.J. (2003) *Forces of Labor: Workers' Movements and Globalization Since 1870*, New York: Cambridge University Press.

Staeheli, L.A. (1994) 'Empowering Political Struggle: Spaces and Scales of Resistance', *Political Geography*, 13: 387–92.

Standing, G. (2008) 'The ILO: An Agency for Globalization?' *Development & Change*, 39(3): 355–84.

Streeck, W. (1998) 'The Internationalization of Industrial Relations in Europe: Prospects and Problems', *Politics & Society*, 26(4): 429–59.

Tarrow, S. (1999) 'International Institutions and Contentious Politics: Does Internationalization Make Agents Freer – or Weaker?' Paper presented to the American Sociological Association, Chicago, IL.

Tarrow, S. (2001) 'Transnational Politics: Contention and Institutions in International Politics', *Annual Review of Political Science*, 4(1): 1–20.

Tilly, C. (1984) 'Social Movements and National Politics', in C. Bright and S. Harding (eds) *Statemaking and Social Movements*, Ann Arbor: University of Michigan Press, pp. 297–317.

Tilly, C. (1995) 'Globalization Threatens Labor's Rights', *International Labor and Working Class History*, 47 (Spring): 1–23.

Turnbull, P. (2000) 'Contesting Globalization on the Waterfront', *Politics & Society*, 28(3): 273–97.

Turnbull, P. (2006) 'The War on Europe's Waterfront – Repertoires of Power in the Port Transport Industry', *British Journal of Industrial Relations*, 44(2), 305–26.

Turnbull, P. (2007) 'Dockers *versus* the Directives – Battling Port Policy on the European Waterfront', in K. Bronfenbrenner (ed.) *Global Unions and Global Companies*, Ithaca, NY: Cornell University Press, pp. 120–49.

Turnbull, P. (2010) 'Creating Markets, Contesting Markets: Labour Internationalism and the European Common Transport Policy', in S. McGrath-Champ, A. Herod and A. Rainnie (eds) *Handbook of Employment and Society: Working Space*, Cheltenham: Edward Elgar, pp. 35–52.

Turnbull, P. and Sapsford, D. (2001) 'Hitting the Bricks: An International Comparative Study of Conflict on the Waterfront', *Industrial Relations*, 40(2): 231–57.

Turnbull, P. and Wass, V. (2007) 'Defending Dock Workers – Globalization and Industrial Relations in the World's Ports', *Industrial Relations*, 46(3): 582–612.

UNCTAD (2001) *World Investment Report: Promoting Linkages*, United Nation Conference on Trade & Development, New York and Geneva: United Nations.

World Commission on the Social Dimensions of Globalization (2004) *A Fair Globalization: Creating Opportunities for All*, Geneva: International Labour Organisation.

Wills, A. and Hale, A. (2005) 'Threads of Labour in the Global Garment Industry', in A. Hale and J. Wills (eds) *Threads of Labour: Garment Industry Supply Chains from the Workers' Perspective*, Oxford: Blackwell, pp. 1–15.

Winterton, J. and Taplin, I.M. (1997) 'Restructuring Clothing', in I.M. Taplin and J. Winterton (eds) *Rethinking Global Production – A comparative Analysis of Restructuring in the Clothing Industry*, Aldershot: Ashgate, pp. 1–18.

Winterton, J. and Winterton, R. (1997) 'Deregulation, Division and Decline: The UK Clothing Industry in Transition', in I.M. Taplin and J. Winterton (eds) *Rethinking Global Production – A Comparative Analysis of Restructuring in the Clothing Industry*, Aldershot: Ashgate, pp. 18–40.

10

Institutions, investors and managers: the impact of governance on the employment relationship

David Nash

Introduction

There has been widespread and growing public interest in how companies are run in the wake of the global financial crisis. Increasingly questions have been asked about the accountability of executives, excessive risk-taking and who should bear the cost of failing firms. These questions lie at the heart of the debate around the governance of firms, that is to say how firms are owned, financed and managed. The aim of this chapter is to examine the links between governance, sources of finance and patterns of employment relations.

The study of corporate governance was traditionally confined to a range of narrow issues such as the composition of boards and the fiduciary duties of directors. The primary focus of this work has been how the relationship between shareholders, management and the board of directors determines the direction and performance of corporations (Monks and Minow, 2001). A second, and important strand in the governance literature has concentrated on case studies of non-conventional enterprises such as mutuals, co-operatives and partnerships. Examples of this literature are the studies of the Spanish Mondragon cooperative and Britain's John Lewis Partnership (Bradley and Estrin, 1992; Whyte, 1988). The purpose of this chapter is not to add to these literatures but to analyse how the governance of firms impacts more generally upon the management of labour. Until relatively recently, governance has been absent from the study of Industrial Relations. Accounts of both continuity and change in employment patterns have tended to concentrate on other causal factors. These include the changing role of the state (Hyman, 2008) and how increased competition in product markets has dramatically reduced the efficacy of trade unions (Brown, 2008; see also Hauptmeier, this volume). The purpose of this book is to reanalyse the employment relationship in the context of competing narratives and substantive change. This chapter aims to contribute to this analysis by examining how governance structures may have an important role to play in shaping employment outcomes.

The chapter will begin by outlining the importance of understanding the institutional context within which labour management takes place. That there are different configurations of labour institutions and actors that combine to produce different labour market outcomes is not new. However, over the last decade there has been renewed interest in this topic, thanks in large part to Hall and Soskice's (2001) varieties of capitalism (VoC) model. This model will be evaluated and the implications for employment relations explored. The analysis will then move on to examine new developments in governance, such as shareholder activism and private equity that are at odds with how the VoC model depicts the British economy. The chapter will argue that governance has a significant impact upon employment outcomes. The emergence of shareholder value maximization as a management credo has had negative consequences for labour. When compared to many of their European counterparts British workers endure short-term management regimes, are excluded from meaningful workplace participation and bear the costs of adjustment in any corporate restructuring. The chapter concludes that these negative tendencies of the British governance system are increasingly being mitigated by new institutional arrangements and raises the question of whether this trend will continue in the wake of the global financial crisis.

Varieties of capitalism and the management of labour

The last decade has seen increasing interest in the study of the institutional framework within which firms operate. It has been argued that certain configurations of institutions lead to different capabilities and opportunities for firms and their stakeholders. The work of Hall and Soskice (2001) built on previous analysis of comparative capitalism. They argue that institutions can be conceptualized in a number of ways that help to explain their significance.

The first conception is of institutions as socializing agencies that imbue certain values into employees or other stakeholders. An alternative perspective sees institutions exhibiting power through formal sanctions in the way that trade unions or policy makers have the ability to do. Finally, institutions can be modelled as a matrix of sanctions and incentives from which it is possible to predict the behaviour of organizations.

From this starting point Hall and Soskice devote much attention to the strategic interaction between institutions to explain the behaviour of economic actors. Their conception of the VoC approach is of an actor-centred model with firms as the agents of adjustment. The firm is seen as relational both internally with its own employees but also externally with a range of agents such as suppliers, clients, collaborators, trade unions, business associations and governments. The problem facing firms is that these relationships are subject to opportunistic behaviour stemming from asymmetric information. The problem of moral hazard occurs if the managers of firms cannot be sure that the actions of its stakeholders are sufficiently aligned with their own interests (Arrow, 1963). A related problem is that of adverse selection, where managers may make sub-optimal choices due to a lack of appropriate information (Akerlof, 1970). Asymmetric information presents managers with the more immediate problem of ensuring that their employees are working at the required level and not taking advantage of the lack of perfect monitoring in the workplace by avoiding work or 'shirking' (Stiglitz, 1974). Therefore, in the face of this uncertainty, the success of a firm will largely depend upon its ability to forge effective relationships with a range of actors.

These relationships are divided into five areas by Hall and Soskice, three of which relate to the management of labour – industrial relations, vocational education and the employment relationship. Industrial relations are seen as important in determining productivity and wage levels for the individual firm as well as determining macroeconomic outcomes such as inflation and unemployment. Vocational education and training has obvious micro- and macro-level implications, such as of workers' productivity and the employability of labour. The final labour-related area that Hall and Soskice identify as contentious is the employment relationship itself; firms need to resolve the inherent asymmetry of information. A principal–agent problem exists where there is imperfect information on the part of the management (principal) as to the motivations and actions of its employees (agents) (Stiglitz, 1974). Managers must also be mindful of the possibility that employees who have firm-specific human capital may be able to use this as a bargaining lever in wage negotiations and extract economic rents or 'hold-up' the firm (Malcomson, 1997). In addition to these internal relationships there are inter-firm relations made with suppliers and clients that are important for ensuring stable demand and appropriate inputs, as well as access to technology. These relations may take the form of technology transfer or business associations but can be difficult to achieve because of concerns about proprietary information. Lastly, corporate governance regimes are important in that they determine the availability of finance and the terms under which it is offered.

The VoC model proposes that these relationships may be mediated by competitive markets, relational contracting or some combination of the two. Indeed, the model proposes there is a continuum along which states can be placed according to the extent to which market mechanisms are used in favour of more collaborative ones. Hall and Soskice's analysis goes further and proposes that there are two ideal types at the extremes of this continuum, which are labelled liberal and coordinated market economies. Liberal market economies (LMEs) are characterized by market arrangements, which mediate the exchange of goods and services. In accordance with neoclassical economic theory, actors' willingness to buy and sell responds to price signals. Coordinated market economies (CMEs) rely more on relational contracting, and network monitoring based on the exchange of private information. Thus, it is not the interaction of supply and demand that determines outcomes in this model, but rather the strategic interactions between actors.

Institutions play a central role in Hall and Soskice's analysis and are defined as a 'set of rules, formal or informal, that actors generally follow, whether for normative, cognitive or material reasons' (Hall and Soskice, 2001: 9). Markets are an example of institutions that support certain types of relationship; namely arms length and highly competitive. They do not exist in a vacuum, however, and require a legal system that supports formal contracting and encourages complete contracts. In CMEs markets and hierarchies exist alongside other institutions that reduce uncertainty and allow credible commitments to be made to each other. Examples of such institutions include business associations, strong trade unions, extensive networks of cross shareholding and a strong regulatory system. These institutions all serve to facilitate the exchange of information, the monitoring of behaviour and the sanctioning of non-compliance. It is the existence of these institutional arrangements that lead to the general conclusion that firms in CMEs are more willing to invest in co-specific assets, those which cannot easily be used for another purpose and depend on the cooperation of others. This contrasts with firms in LMEs, which tend to invest in switchable assets that can be used for a variety of purposes such as general skills.

According to this analysis, differences in institutional structure across LMEs and CMEs produce systematic differences in corporate structure. Evidence comes from Knetter (1989) when looking at the response to an exchange rate shock in the United Kingdom and Germany. British firms tend to pass on the price increase to consumers to maintain profitability, while German firms maintain price in order to preserve market share. This is due to the fact that in the United Kingdom access to financial resources depends on preserving profitability, as does the ability to stave off take-over threats. In the German system, however, access to capital is not dependent on current profit levels. Maximizing market share is also important to preserve employment levels as this is central to the labour strategies agreed between firms and unions. Thus the institutional arrangements of a particular state can have profound implications for the management of labour.

Finally, Hall and Soskice use the notion of complementarities to explain how institutional arrangements of a certain type may not be randomly distributed across countries but clustered together. Heery (2008) claims that the VoC model is the latest manifestation of systems thinking in industrial relations. The argument is that institutions in one sphere may be mutually reinforced by the institutional configuration in another. Hence, Aoki (1994) argues that long-term employment may be more feasible when the sources of finance are divorced from current levels of profitability. Similarly, cooperative industry-wide vocational training systems may encourage industrial standard setting. Thus, Hall and Soskice chart developed countries according to the degree of stock market capitalization and employment protection and find two broad clusters of nations with the United Kingdom, United States, Australia and Canada as the LMEs and the remaining developed countries being classed as CMEs. Although the possibility of a sub-cluster of Mediterranean countries is raised, it is not discussed in any detail.

While hugely significant, Hall and Soskice's analysis is not without its critics. One area that has been particularly challenged is the perceived over-simplistic categorization of types of capitalist economy. Hamann and Kelly (2008) present empirical data to determine the usefulness of the VoC approach in explaining international differences in industrial relations outcomes. They find that in terms of bargaining coverage, there is a clear difference between LME and non-LME countries, whereas there is a divide between the central European CMEs and the rest when looking at industrial conflict. When the comparative analysis is extended beyond these two variables, Hamann and Kelly (2008: 142) argue that the binary distinction between LMEs and CMEs is of limited use; the data suggest that the Mediterranean and Scandinavian economies are distinct and coherent types. Crouch (2005: 44) also argues that the dualistic typology of the VoC approach masks important explanatory detail. He goes on to claim that the account of these two ideal types has been too closely associated with the polemic debate between neo-liberalism and social democracy. Consequently, the original VoC approach has been adapted in the face of these criticisms. For example, Hancké et al. (2007) extend the basic typology used by Hall and Soskice to include two new categories, mixed market economies (MMEs) and emerging market economies (EMEs) that mix market regulation with a degree of coordinated, relational arrangements.

A further criticism of the approach taken by Hall and Soskice is that despite claiming to be firm-centred, in reality much of the analysis concentrates on the macro behaviour of the nation-state. Crouch argues that the neo-institutionalist approach taken by Hall and Soskice mirrors that of neo-classical economics; firms are portrayed as passive 'institution takers', in much the same way as firms are price-takers in competitive markets (Crouch, 2005: 67). This notion of 'disconnected capitalism' is picked up by Thompson (2003) who claims that in the decentralized and uncoordinated British economy, managers have less control of events and fewer levers to pull. Thompson uses the term 'disconnected' to highlight the fact that managerial objectives in the area of labour management may be frustrated by the various impacts of forces such as globalization and the shift to shareholder value in capital markets (ibid.: 371).

The centrality of the nation state in Hall and Soskice's analysis and their rebuttal of the claim that globalization will erode this importance has led to the criticism that their approach is static in nature and ill equipped to deal with the dynamics of convergence or divergence of national systems (Streeck and Thelen, 2005). Hamann and Kelly (2008) argue that the VoC model does have the potential to incorporate mechanisms of institutional change. This could be the outcome of incremental change; the result of ongoing and repeated negotiation between the various parties. Alternatively, this change may be the result of government action, both directly through changes to the institutional configuration of the economy, or indirectly through economic management and the consequent effects that follow (Hamann and Kelly, 2008: 143). It remains to be seen whether the recent global financial crisis will prove to be a disjuncture in the trajectories of those affected economies.

Governance and the employment relationship

So far the analysis of governance has centred on how different configurations of macro level institutions can impact upon the capabilities of organizations. The analysis will now turn to examine how governance may directly interact with the conduct of labour management. In some cases the links between governance is more obvious than in others. For example in countries like Germany, with its strongly embedded norm of employee voice through worker directors and works councils, the mechanisms that link governance and labour are comparatively transparent. Gospel and Pendleton (2005) argue that the presence of codetermination rights may be partially responsible for the relative lack of hostile takeovers in Germany. In systems where such visible codetermination rights do not exist, the analysis turns to how governance and finance in particular impact upon management's approach to managing labour.

Finance creates direct constraints upon management action and priorities. In recent years it has been argued that equity owners have promoted their interests as being primary, and maximizing shareholder value as the main priority, if not duty, of managers (Lazonick and O'Sullivan, 2000). The market for corporate control can act as a powerful disciplining device to achieve this shareholder primacy. Thus it can be argued that in economies such as the United States and United Kingdom where equity markets are used as a primary means of raising capital, this requirement to satisfy shareholder interests will have negative effects for labour. This may be because the ability of firms to generate rents that can be shared with the workforce is of secondary importance to that of maintaining equity values and dividends. It may also be that as firms seek to cut costs to maximize shareholder value, downsizing results, further weakening labour's position. The VoC framework explains this shift in the balance of managerial decision making by pointing out the weaker statutory protection for labour in LMEs. As Hall and Soskice point out, CMEs such as Germany with its direct representation of both capital and labour are more likely to achieve a balance between these two interests. The same can also be said of Japan where pervasive cultural norms prevent managers from acting against the interests of labour (Jacoby, 2005).

Corporate governance can significantly impact upon labour management through time-horizons. Hutton (1996) argues that in marketized systems like the United Kingdom, where there are much stronger incentives created by the financial system, managers are encouraged into short-term thinking. This is due to the owners of equity, often large pension or mutual funds, wanting to see short-term returns on their investment. Thus, managers are heavily incentivized to run the firm in such a way as to maximize profits and share prices. This pressure, together with the concomitant high cost of capital means that investment projects like training and other forms of human resource development, which have a longer and less tangible effect on profitability, are less attractive. By contrast, in insider or relational economic systems, characterized by Hall and Soskice's CMEs, managers are able to take a longer-term approach.

Cross-shareholdings and long-term debt from banks, together with a closer relationship between firms and financiers feeds through into longer-term strategic policies being undertaken by managers.

Governance and finance regimes can also affect labour through the business strategies that firms employ. Hall and Soskice argue that CMEs, for example, are more likely to pursue a strategy of maximizing market share as opposed to simple profit maximization. German manufacturing is a good example of where market share is maintained by producing complex goods that require both a complex production process and a highly skilled workforce. In these firms, competitive advantage is achieved by incremental and continuous innovations in production (Streeck, 1992). In LMEs, by contrast, the pressure to achieve short-term results tends to discourage incremental product development. Instead, the more flexible labour markets and fluid capital markets are conducive to more radical product innovation. This may take the form of flotations or spin-offs of innovative, high growth firms as characterized by the biosciences or information technology sectors. These differences in product market strategy will have important effects on how labour is managed within these firms, both in terms of training and also employment patterns. In CMEs, longer-term employment with high levels of firm-specific training will be favoured, while LMEs are likely to be characterized by more generic training and flexible employment patterns.

A fourth link between governance and labour management that Gospel and Pendleton identify is the presence of financial market-based pressures within an organization. The argument is that firms in LMEs tend to focus on internal measures of performance that are financial in nature. This has the twin effects of transmitting financial imperatives throughout the organization and prompting managers to direct their attention on outcomes that are financially quantifiable. In this environment, it is possible that activities that are less tangible, such as human capital formation may be overlooked.

A related issue is that of payment systems. In LMEs where market-based relationships predominate, firms are more likely to use financial means to secure the motivation and commitment of staff. Due to the model of financing in these firms there exists a separation of control between the shareholders and the managers who run the firm on their behalf. As principal–agent theory describes there emerges a problem of incentives, where the interests of the two parties may be divergent (Stiglitz, 1974). In order to realign these interests remuneration schemes are devised to try and motivate management into appropriate types of behaviour. These schemes can take the form of share-based payments or some form of performance-related pay. These variable pay schemes are also likely to be found at lower levels in the organization.

Managers will favour ways of eliciting commitment that are tied to measurable performance targets. Such schemes also have the advantage of allowing firms to be flexible in their pursuit of profits. The picture in CMEs is very different, where there is no such separation of ownership and control. The interests of managers and owners are more likely to be congruent, thus obviating the need for such highly geared incentive schemes. Similarly, employee commitment throughout the organization will tend to revolve around employee voice as opposed to market-based financial instruments.

The final argument regarding the link between governance and the employment relationship concerns the pattern of interlocking ownership that is seen in CMEs. Gospel and Pendleton point out that where this exists there may be greater cooperation between firms, which will, in turn, have implications for the management of labour. One obvious example is the system of vocational training in Germany, which is designed and administered on a sectoral or occupational basis by coalitions of firms and business associations (Jackson et al., 2005). Another practice that is seen as compatible with cross-ownership and employer cooperation is multi-employer collective bargaining. While there has been a decentralization of bargaining to enterprise level in many LMEs such as Britain, industry level agreements have remained more robust in countries like Germany. This is illustrated by the data in Table 10.1,

Table 10.1 Union density and collective bargaining in selected European Union countries 2006

Country	Union density (%)	Collective bargaining coverage (%)
Belgium	49	96
Estonia	14	22
France	8	90
Germany	8	65
Greece	20	65
Italy	34	70
Latvia	16	20
The Netherlands	25	81
Poland	17	35
Spain	16	81
Sweden	77	92
The United Kingdom	29	35
EU Average	25	66

Source: Data taken from European Foundation for the Improvement of Living and Working Conditions (2006).

which show that the United Kingdom has one of the lowest rates of collective bargaining coverage within the European Union.

Governance and labour management

It is undeniable that equity markets play a central role in the economic system in Britain. The London Stock Exchange lists over twice as many companies as its German equivalent and the market capitalization of those firms listed is also twice that of the Deutsche Borse. The World Federation of Exchanges reports that London is the fifth most important stock exchange in terms of both number of firms and market capitalization behind the New York, Tokyo, NASDAQ and Euronext (the combined Belgian, Dutch, French and Portuguese) exchanges (World Federation of Exchanges, 2009). The pattern of equity ownership in the United Kingdom is also distinctive. Franks and Meyer (1997) found that shares are more widely dispersed than in North America or continental Europe. Despite this dispersion in ownership, large institutional investors such as pension funds, investment trusts and other non-bank financial institutions dominate the UK equity market. Cross-holdings of shares between companies are rare in the United Kingdom, as is equity being held by commercial banks. This contrasts with CMEs in Europe, where such practices are more common.

Due to the separation of ownership and control that is characteristic of firms in LMEs shareholder influence is exercised through the selling of shares (a strategy known as 'exit') rather than actively trying to influence management action (the 'voice' approach). The market for corporate control acts to discipline managers who fear that shareholders might exit and be replaced with owners with their own management agenda. Such an approach is characterized as an 'outsider' system of control and contrasts sharply with what happens in much of continental Europe where the higher concentration in ownership leads to more direct owner-control (Franks and Meyer, 1997). The German case is a good example of where bank and corporate cross-ownership lead to a more relational or 'insider' system. The United Kingdom's preference for exercising control through exit rather than voice is reinforced by the predominance of institutional investors in the equity market. The funds themselves tend to devolve management responsibility to specialist fund managers who have little incentive to intervene in the running of the company since they will not reap the benefit from doing so. A further explanation for exit being preferred to voice is the striking increase in foreign ownership of UK firms. Under these circumstances overseas owners may be deterred from investing due to the increased information costs.

The evidence surrounding whether the differing governance structures found in the United Kingdom leads to material differences in management practice is certainly suggestive. In their international study of management attitudes Allen and Gale (2000) find that 70 per cent of managers in the United Kingdom prioritize shareholder interests above all others. This compares to 17 and 22 per cent in Germany and France respectively. Even more telling is the finding that 89 per cent of British managers stated that firms should maintain dividend payments to shareholders even if it meant reducing employment levels. This is more than double the figure reported in France and Germany. According to research by Carr and Tomkins this shareholder orientation translates into management practices (Carr and Tomkins, 1998). Their study of managerial decision making in the United Kingdom, United States, Germany and Japan found that British and American firms place three times as much emphasis on financial issues than their German and Japanese counterparts. The study also found that the payback period on investment was shorter and the required internal rate of return on investments was higher in the Anglo-Saxon countries. Thus, differences in governance and finance structures seem to have a discernible effect on managerial decision-making.

The effect of changing governance structures can be observed at a macroeconomic level. Ryan (1996) notes that the share in national income accruing to labour started to fall from around 1980, while investment-related income started to rise. At the same time the distribution of corporate income shifted decisively in favour of shareholders, with the proportion of profits paid in dividends increasing from 6.7 per cent in 1978 to 27.7 per cent 18 years later in 1996 (Pendleton and Gospel, 2005: 66). The timing of this shift in income shares is significant in that it roughly coincides with the rise of shareholder primacy in the United Kingdom. The election of the first Thatcher government, with its anti-union agenda, no doubt accelerated this process. Mayer and Alexander's (1990) research highlighted that shareholders of UK firms enjoyed a far higher share of company profits than their German counterparts. The overall picture appears to be that shareholder interests have been afforded greater priority over the last 30 years, and this has been at the expense of labour.

A central critique of the outsider or market-based system that characterizes the US and British economies is that there are strong incentives to maximize share prices to deter potential take-overs, and this in turn incentivizes managers to cut jobs or outsource employment to control labour costs. Whereas there is evidence to support this phenomenon in the United States (Abowd et al., 1990), there has been little empirical investigation of this in the United Kingdom. The evidence that supports this shareholder critique of equity prices rising after an announcement of job losses has to be placed in the context of shares having been marked-down prior to the announcement because of the market's underlying perception of the state of the business (Edwards, 2004).

A further implication of the outsider model is that merger and acquisition activity has negative repercussions for labour. Even if the merger is only threatened it is probable that these events will constitute a violation of the psychological contract between management and workers. This is the implicit and reciprocal agreement between an employer and employee, in which fairness of treatment by the employer is exchanged for increased employee motivation (Guest and Conway, 2002). In the event of a change in ownership, Shleifer and Summers (1988) find that there are often adverse effects on employment and wage levels. This is even more likely where there is weak regulation of labour and an absence of trade unions. The reasons that lie behind this finding are multifarious. Perhaps most importantly the rationale of undertaking merger or take-over is to enhance shareholder value and this is often achieved with rationalization of operations and consequent job losses. This predilection for downsizing is in part facilitated by the relative weakness of statutory employment protection in the United Kingdom, which allows managers to change the terms of employment contracts post-merger.

It would be misleading to suggest that there is a total absence of employment protection in the United Kingdom. British employees have enjoyed limited consultation rights since the 1970s, over issues such as redundancies and restructuring resulting from business transfers (Hall, 2005). Indeed, following British adoption of the European Works Council Directive and incorporation of the Information and Consultation of Employees (ICE) Regulations, it can be argued that the obligations facing British employers to consult with their staff over issues that directly affect them have never been higher. The TUC stated that the adoption of the ICE regulations 'could lead to the biggest change in workplace relations for a generation' (Hall, 2005: 103). Despite these developments, UK employees do not enjoy the same depth of representation as many of their continental European counterparts; the incidence of worker representation at board level via worker-directors is extremely rare, for example (Eironline, 1998). There is also some doubt as to whether the consultation rights outlined above will protect workers in the case of a takeover. Deakin et al. (2003) state that the requirement to consult employees in the case of a business transfer do not apply in the case of a takeover. This has the implication that labour finds itself in a highly vulnerable position when mergers or takeovers are threatened.

A prediction of the VoC model is that firms will favour market-based reward strategies. A consequence of this has been the growing inequality of pay within organizations. Survey data that show the ratio of chief executive pay to that of manufacturing workers is 25:1 in the United Kingdom, compared to 16:1 and 13:1 in France and Germany respectively (Pendleton and Gospel, 2005: 68). Not only is inequality greater in the market-based governance system of the United Kingdom, it has also grown faster. By analysing OECD data Machin (2008) finds that wage inequality is both highest and grew fastest in the LME economies of the United States, United Kingdom and Australia. The data also show that the 1980s saw faster inequality growth than the subsequent decades (Machin, 2008: 21). This is perhaps unsurprising given that was the decade when the neo-liberal policies of the Thatcher and Reagan administrations were in full force.

Part of the explanation for this is the growth in management remuneration, which may be attributable to multiple causes. First, the market for management talent has become increasingly competitive since the 1970s, which may partly reflect the increasing importance placed on maximizing shareholder value over the same period and hence the importance in attracting an effective management cadre. The emergence of an active managerial labour market has the additional consequence that pay levels have been 'ratcheted-up' in the face of open competition between employers. Another obvious link between governance structures and managerial pay is the rise of stock-based remuneration plans. The rapid growth in share and share-option pay systems since the mid-1980s has seen managerial wealth increasingly tied up with the company's share price (Deakin, 2005). The governance system in market-based economies also influences wage inequality at the bottom of the income distribution through its effect on the pay of shop-floor workers. Abowd and Bognanno (1995) find that the wages of manufacturing workers are lower in the United Kingdom than in other Western European countries. Thus the impulse to maximize shareholder value has been a prime driver in widening wage inequality by both pulling up the pay of senior executives through equity-based remuneration, while at the same time suppressing the pay of ordinary workers as firms embark on cost-minimizing business strategies (see also Turnbull and Wass, this volume).

Hall and Soskice's analysis stressed the importance of inter-firm cooperation and raised the possibility that via institutional complementarities it may be associated with factors such as vocational training and coordinated wage bargaining. The role of training is seen of vital importance in the VoC model, indeed it is seen as a central pillar of the success of the CME model. It might be expected, therefore, that in the United Kingdom with its market-based governance system that training systems and quality are not well developed. The United Kingdom does have a weak formalized system of training, with only about a third the number of trainees as Germany (Estevez-Abe et al., 2001). The VoC model argues that this is due to the lack of inter-firm cooperation that encourages industry-wide apprenticeships in countries like Germany. However, the incidence of continuing vocational training by larger British firms compares favourably with the rest of Europe. According to OECD data, the amount that employers spend on formal training is higher in the United Kingdom than anywhere else in the EU (OECD, 1998). Thus the link between governance and training is more complex than the VoC model predicts.

The characteristics of wage determination in the United Kingdom also points to the fact that employer coordination is lower than elsewhere in Europe. Britain is certainly an outlier when it comes to bargaining patterns, with a strong predominance of single-employer agreements. Data from the most recent Workplace Employment Relations Survey show that collective bargaining only applies to about a third of employees in the United Kingdom. If the more unionized public sector is excluded, then this figure falls to just over a quarter (Brown and Nash, 2008). The figures also indicate that multi-employer bargaining covers only five per cent of private-sector employees. It is difficult to attribute causality for this phenomenon to the United Kingdom's governance structures since there are numerous other plausible explanations such as the more hostile regulatory framework that has existed since 1979. However, Hall and Soskice's concept of institutional complementarities is relevant here given that the move towards a more decentralized system of wage determination has coincided with the rise in shareholder value as a managerial objective. Another feature of remuneration systems in the United Kingdom is the extensive use of share-ownership plans. Equity-based pay is not just the preserve of senior management, and the United Kingdom has the highest incidence of all-employee share plans in Europe (Pendleton et al., 2001). One explanation for this is that firms seek to enhance employee motivation by tying pay to company performance. A beneficial consequence of this may be that the notion of 'shareholder value' becomes more widely accepted by employees and is seen as a legitimate target for management to pursue.

The evolving nature of governance

Having outlined the links between corporate governance and labour management it is important to point out some caveats. While it is analytically attractive to see governance and finance impacting upon employment relations, causality could run the other way (Black et al., 2007). This is especially true in non-Anglo Saxon countries where labour may be able to exercise a degree of influence over governance. Germany is an example where the institutions of worker directors and works councils with powers of codetermination mean that labour has the potential to determine decisions of finance and ownership. Japan is another example where, despite the absence of formal mechanisms of worker participation that are found in Germany, there are strong cultural norms that provide direct and indirect labour voice. This is partially due to the system of enterprise unionism that is a central pillar of the Japanese employment system (Araki, 2005). Indeed, it can be argued that organized labour can be effective at influencing governance both directly in their relationships with management but also indirectly through involvement in policy making via corporatist arrangements (Roe, 2003).

An important feature of the outsider model, that of dispersed share ownership, has been declining in the United Kingdom for a number of years. Research by Mayer (2000) finds that the median British shareholder holds 9.9 per cent of equity; almost double that of the American counterpart. The next two largest block-holders hold 7.3 and 5.2 per cent, respectively. The data also show that these large blocks of shares are not exclusively held by institutional investors; individuals such as family owners and directors were also found to have significant shareholdings. Franks and Mayer (2000) note that despite the United Kingdom being characterized by 'exceptionally dispersed ownership', there are examples of companies where small coalitions of shareholders control 30 per cent of equity. Golding (2001) attributes this increasing concentration of institutional ownership to, among other things, herding by investors and a growing aversion to holding the stocks of small companies.

The fact that United Kingdom share ownership may be more concentrated than predicted by the VoC model has important implications for the relationship between investors and firms. It suggests that the investors may engage in forms of governance other than the market discipline of exit. Higher levels of concentration increase the incentive for investors to engage in monitoring and engage in shareholder activism. Similarly, as Golding (2001) observes, as the number of shareholders declines, the cost of cooperation between them also falls. Larger shareholdings will also tend to lock-in investors due to the difficulty in divesting large block-holdings. This is due to the negative market signals associated with selling a large tranche of shares. A related argument is presented by Deakin (2005) who claims that the institutionalization of share ownership in the United States and United Kingdom has created a new category of 'universal owners'. It is argued that due to the need to diversify investment portfolios, these owners will have broad shareholdings across all sectors of the market. As a consequence of this, investors will have an interest in how the economy as a whole performs and develop longer time-horizons over which to assess corporate performance. As Deakin states 'being subject to lock-in makes [investors] more likely to engage with management on a long-term basis to improve performance, and less likely to respond to managerial failure by selling their stakes in the companies concerned' (ibid.: 16).

Further doubts can be cast on the role of other forms of market-based regulation on management behaviour. Research undertaken by Corbett and Jenkinson (1996) found that managers were not as reliant on the market for new equity capital as had previously been supposed. Their analysis showed that 97 per cent of physical investment over the period 1970–89 had been internally financed, compared to 91 per cent in the United States, 81 per cent in Germany and 69 per cent in Japan (1996: 77). Indeed, more recent data suggest that issuing new equity accounts for less than 12 per cent of investment finance in the United Kingdom (Beck et al., 2008: 471). These findings paint a picture of UK firms that are not constrained by the demands of equity markets in order to secure investment but, instead, choose internal sources of finance.

A further argument undermining the stereotypical view of the United Kingdom's governance system surrounds the efficacy of the market for corporate control as a disciplining device for managers. The supposed threat of takeover acting as a sword of Damocles over management is undermined by the observation that the overwhelming majority of takeovers in Britain are friendly rather than hostile (Deakin and Slinger, 1997). Takeovers are more likely to be motivated by a desire to expand the firm through increased market share or realizing economies of scale than by investors' attempts to change the management team. Indeed, the United Kingdom has a long tradition of firms growing by merger and acquisition rather than by relying on internal or organic growth (Chandler, 1990). Nor is the threat of takeover a prominent one; mergers and acquisitions tend to be concentrated in waves, interspersed with periods of inactivity (Martynova and Renneboog, 2008). Thus the market for corporate control may impinge upon managerial decision-making less frequently than predicted by the outsider model of governance.

When viewed in the round these developments appear to suggest that the governance regime in the United Kingdom cannot be simply viewed as a purely market driven, outsider model. Indeed it can be argued that there have been developments in the British system that more closely resemble the institutional arrangements found in coordinated market economies. One such development is the rise in shareholder activism. A recent review of the field found that 'activism used to be the preserve of a small minority, but most large investors are now prepared to question companies' corporate governance policies and practices, engage with them on questions of strategy and performance, vote against management resolutions and in many cases take their criticisms to the press' (Hendry et al., 2007: 224). New administrative structures and communication channels have been established in order to deal with this new, broader form of investor monitoring. While Hendry et al. (2007) question the motives for this new wave of shareholder activism, claiming it is as likely to be the pursuit of shareholder returns as a new moral and political commitment to responsible ownership, the fact remains that the relationship between investors and management is becoming longer-term and more relational.

Evidence that the United Kingdom is a less than pure outsider system is presented by Armour et al. (2003). They acknowledge that at its core the UK system of governance places shareholder interests above all else. Evidence for this can be found in the regulations governing mergers and takeovers, corporate governance codes and the law relating to directors' fiduciary duties (ibid.: 531). Their analysis draws attention to a number of contrary facets in the British governance system, however. The first surrounds the rights of other stakeholders beyond the core governance institutions. In particular, during the process of corporate restructuring the twin forces of the EU Acquired Rights Directive and Collective Redundancies Directive contrived to grant employee representatives considerable information and consultation rights (ibid.). Thus, even though the interests of stakeholders do not occupy as central a position in the minds of managers as shareholder value, it would be inaccurate to argue that they are totally absent.

There is growing evidence that some institutional investors are using their influence to actively monitor company performance, as opposed to exercising their control simply by exit (Armour et al., 2003). The issues that are being monitored by investors do not solely impinge upon economic performance, but also on a range of social and environmental factors that affect a wide range of stakeholders. The motives behind this new intervention may still be rooted in a desire to maximize shareholder value, but this desire is tempered by a recognition that companies, which ignore wider stakeholder concerns, may be endangering shareholders' interests. This firm-level shareholder activism takes three principal forms: through voting at company AGMs; through ongoing dialogue and discussion between investors and managers; and, finally, through attaching conditions to any future investment (ibid.: 546).

The fact that the market plays less of a disciplining role on managers in British firms than suggested by the market/outsider model has important implications for labour management. One consequence may be that employers have more autonomy to choose employment relations strategies than previously thought. Aguilera and Jackson (2003) state that the extent to which managers enjoy this autonomy will depend on the social norms and interests of both management and investors. Hendry et al. (2007) argue that a powerful norm in the British context is that investors do not micro-manage the firms they have invested in. With the possible exception of corporate governance issues, most issues of operational management within a firm are seen as the prerogative of the firm's managers.

The notion that some managers enjoy considerable independence in choosing their preferred business strategy is supported by research evidence. In a study of governance and partnership approaches to labour management, Deakin et al. (2002: 351) claim that 'corporate managers can feasibly aim to reconcile the interests of stakeholder groups with the goal of enlightened shareholder value.' This suggests that management have the ability to influence investors' way of thinking and convince them to support the policies and strategies that they want to enact. More than this even, managers who have long-term employment strategies and employ high-road human resource management techniques may be able to attract investors who are supportive of such techniques (ibid.). This notion that management has the ability to be selective in equity markets is totally at odds with the image that firms are institution-takers that is implied in the VoC model.

The debate about the degree of autonomy in the investor–manager relationship is further complicated by the rise to prominence of a new form of ownership in the United Kingdom. Private equity is defined as any investment in the equity of an asset that cannot be freely traded on a stock market (Clark et al., 2008). This umbrella term covers a wide variety of arrangements from investing start-up capital in unquoted companies, buying shares from an existing shareholder (a 'buy-out') or an investment in new shares providing investment capital for the company in question (Wright et al., 2009). Investment can also be internally driven in the form of a management or employee buy-out, or externally driven in the case of management buy-ins or investor led buy-outs. Clark et al. (2008: 21) estimate that ten per cent of the British workforce is employed in private-equity owned businesses, while 19 per cent of employees work in firms that have been owned by private equity at some point in their history.

The impact of private equity ownership on labour management is ambiguous. Critics such as Clark maintain that private equity reinforces the primacy of shareholders at the expense of other stakeholders, most notably labour (Clark, 2007; Clark et al., 2008). This is, in part, due to the fact that the Transfer of Undertakings (Protection of Employment) (TUPE) regulations do not apply to workers in firms that are controlled by private equity. This is due to the regulations not covering changes of ownership that have been achieved by a sale of shares in the target company. Clark (2007: 225) argues that 'private equity brings with it a clear value-creation strategy that incentivizes senior managers in an acquired firm to act like owners, not managers'. The interests of owners in this case are taken to include cost-effectiveness, flexibility and short-termism. Clark argues that many private equity owners will be 'more concerned with the long-term health of their parent investment fund than the latest business they've added to their portfolio' (Clark et al., 2008: 20).

Evidence of the effects of private equity buy-outs for workers is mixed. Research by Wright et al. (2009) suggests that the employment effects of private equity are contingent on a number of factors, including the prevailing economic conditions of the time. Employment levels were observed to fall where the change of ownership was preceded by hostile trading conditions, with some subsequent increases. There is a similar pattern when it comes to wage levels; firms with private equity backed buy-outs paid lower wages than comparable non buy-out firms. There was, however, evidence of a higher incidence of non-managerial share ownership among buy-out firms (Wright et al., 2009: 508). Care should be taken not to interpret the evidence regarding employment and wage levels too negatively. As Wright et al. point out, in many cases where a firm had been struggling prior to being taken over with private equity, the alternative was bankruptcy. In this context, any continuation of the business, albeit with a reduced workforce and lower wages may be desirable. The same research found that private equity is associated with increased use of high commitment management practices, and a general upgrading of employment practices. Finally, the effect of private equity on unionization was found to be broadly neutral, with instances of post buy-out derecognition being rare (ibid.: 509).

The implications of the rise of private equity as a business model for labour are, thus, ambiguous. It is certainly true that at a theoretical level, this emerging form of ownership would appear to reassert the principle of shareholder primacy and contribute to Thompson's (2003) notion of 'disconnected capitalism'. In their analysis of the effects of private equity, however, Wright et al. (2009) urge caution. They stress the importance of taking contextual factors such as the prevailing economic conditions, and the type of buy-out into account. In many cases where the evidence seems to point to post buy-out firms creating shareholder value at the expense of other stakeholders, a more accurate description might be that private equity facilitated the restructuring of firms that were being run in an unsustainable manner.

Concluding remarks

This chapter has shown that the institutional context within which firms operate can have a profound impact on the management of labour. The VoC model, despite its imperfections, provides a starting point from which to contrast the institutional arrangements in different economic systems. Using this framework, the chapter has outlined how the choices facing managers in the United Kingdom is predicted to be different to those in more coordinated economies such as Germany. By discussing how these linkages between institutional frameworks and labour management operate, it becomes clear that the structure of finance and ownership is of paramount importance. The role of external investors and the pre-eminence of maximizing shareholder value as a business strategy have profound, and potentially negative, implications for employees in British firms.

In practice, the relationship between a firm's managers and shareholders appears more complex than the VoC model suggests. On the one hand there is increasing evidence that investors are not content to exercise control through 'exit' but are choosing to monitor and influence managerial decision-making through a variety of relational forms that seem at odds with the characterization of the United Kingdom as an outsider, market driven model. Running contrary to this argument, however, is research that suggests that managers have more, rather than less, autonomy to determine their chosen strategy. The relationship between management and shareholders may be such that the former are able to win investor support for an unconventional business approach. There is even the possibility that matching takes place in equity markets, with investors being chosen according to their willingness to support management's chosen strategy.

The degree to which firms exercise agency is at the centre of the debate surrounding governance and the employment relationship. Portraying firms as passive 'institution takers' that are constrained by national institutional configurations is too narrow a view and ignores the observed heterogeneity of management approaches within a particular national system. The emergence of shareholder activism and new forms of ownership such as private equity have blurred the neat distinction between pure market-based forms of governance and the more relational insider systems that were seen as more typical of continental European economies. More research is needed to analyse the evolving nature of governance, and how the interests of the various stakeholders are mediated. The recent global financial crisis provides an apposite time for such research. It is probably too early to tell whether the crisis represents a turning point in the trajectory of capitalism. Early indications are that there has been little change in the governance practices in the developed world. However, the state is now a much larger direct stakeholder in many firms as a result of government bailouts and it will be interesting to see how this impacts upon the management of such firms. The debates surrounding governance and management are likely to achieve greater prominence in the years to come.

References

Abowd, J., Milkovich, G., and Hannon, J. (1990) 'The effects of human resource management decisions on shareholder value', *Industrial and Labor Relations Review*, 43(3), pp. 203S–36S.

Abowd, J., and Bognanno, M. (1995) 'International differences in executive and managerial compensation', in R. Freeman and L. Katz (eds) *Differences and Changes in Wage Structures*, Chicago, University of Chicago Press.

Aguilera, R., and Jackson, G. (2003) 'The cross-national diversity of corporate governance: dimensions and determinants', *Academy of Management Review*, 28, pp. 447–65.

Akerlof, G. (1970) 'The market for "lemons": quality uncertainty and the market mechanism', *The Quarterly Journal of Economics*, 84(3), pp. 488–500.

Allen, F., and Gale, D. (2000) *Comparing Financial Systems*, Cambridge, MA., MIT Press.

Aoki (1994) 'The Japanese firm as a system of attributes: a survey and research agenda', in M. Aoki and R. Dore (eds) *The Japanese Firm: The Sources of Competitive Strength*, Oxford, Oxford University Press.

Araki, T. (2005) 'Corporate governance, labour, and employment relations in Japan: the future of the stakeholder model?', in Gospel, H., and Pendleton, A. (eds) *Corporate Governance and Labour Management: an International Comparison*, Oxford, Oxford University Press.

Armour, J., Deakin, S., and Konzelmann, S. (2003) 'Shareholder primacy and the trajectory of UK corporate governance', *British Journal of Industrial Relations*, 41(3), pp. 531–55.

Arrow, K., (1963) 'Uncertainty and the welfare economics of medical care', *American Economic Review*, 53, pp. 941–73.

Beck, T., Demirgüç-Kunt, A., and Maksimovic, V. (2008) 'Financing patterns around the world: are small firms different?', *Journal of Financial Economics*, 89, pp. 467–87.

Black, B., Gospel, H., and Pendleton, A. (2007) 'Finance, corporate governance and the employment relationship' *Industrial Relations*, 46(3), pp. 643–50.

Bradley, K., and Estrin, S. (1992) 'Profit sharing in the British retail trade sector: the relative performance of the John Lewis Partnership', *The Journal of Industrial Economics*, 40(3), pp. 291–304.

Brown, W. (2008) 'The influence of product markets on Industrial Relations', in P. Blyton, N. Bacon, J. Fiorito and E. Heery (eds) *The Sage Handbook of Industrial Relations*, London, Sage.

Brown, W., and Nash, D. (2008) 'What has been happening to collective bargaining under New Labour? Interpreting WERS 2004', *Industrial Relations Journal*, 39(2), pp. 91–103.

Carr, C., and Tomkins, C. (1998) 'Context, culture and the role of the finance function in strategic decisions: a comparative analysis of Britain, Germany, the USA and Japan', *Management Accounting Research*, 9, pp. 213–39.

Chandler, A. (1990) *Scale and Scope: The Dynamics of Industrial Capitalism*, Cambridge, MA, Harvard University Press.

Clark, I. (2007) 'Private equity and HRM in the British business system', *Human Resource Management Journal*, 17(3), pp. 218–26.

Clark, I., Bacon, N., and Wright, M. (2008) 'Private equity', *People Management*, 14(17), pp. 18–22.

Corbett, J., and Jenkinson, T. (1996) 'The financing of industry 1970–1989: an international comparison', *Journal of the Japanese and International Economies*, 10, pp. 71–96.

Crouch, C. (2005) *Capitalist Diversity and Change: Recombinant Governance and Institutional Entrepreneurs*, Oxford, Oxford University Press.

Deakin, S. (2005) 'The coming transformation of shareholder value', *corporate governance*, 13(1), pp. 11–18.

Deakin, S., Hobbs, R., Konzelmann, S., and Wilkinson, F. (2002) 'Partnership, ownership and control: the impact of corporate governance on employment relations', *Employee Relations*, 24(3), pp. 335–52.

Deakin, S., Hobbs R., R., Nash, D., Slinger, G. (2003) 'Implicit Contracts, Takeovers and corporate governance: In the Shadow of the City Code', in D Cambell, H Collins and J Wightman (eds) *Implicit Dimensions of Contract*, Oxford, Hart Publishing.

Deakin, S., and Slinger, G. (1997) 'Hostile takeovers, corporate law, and the theory of the firm', *Journal of Law and Society*, 24, pp. 124–51.

Edwards, T. (2004) 'Corporate governance, industrial relations and trends in company-level restructuring in Europe: convergence towards the Anglo-American model?', *Industrial Relations Journal*, 35(6), pp. 518–35.

Eironline (1998) 'Board-level employee representation in Europe', www.eurofound.europa.eu/eiro/1998/09/study/tn9809201s.htm.

European Foundation for the Improvement of Living and Working Conditions (2006) *Industrial Relations Developments in Europe 2006*, Luxembourg, Office for Official Publications of the European Communities.

Estevez-Abe, M., Iversen, T., and Soskice, D. (2001) 'Social protection and the formation of skills: a reinterpretation of the welfare state', in Hall, P., and Soskice, D. (eds) *Varieties of Capitalism: The Institutional Foundations of Comparative Advantage*, Oxford, Oxford University Press.

Franks, J., and Mayer, C. (1997) 'Corporate ownership and control in the UK, Germany, and the US', in Chew, D. (ed.) *Studies in International Corporate Finance and Governance Systems*, New York, Oxford University Press.

Franks, J., and Mayer, C. (2000) 'Governance as a source of managerial discipline', *Company Law Review, Committee on Corporate Governance*, London, Department of Trade and Industry.

Golding, T. (2001) *The City: Inside the Great Expectation Machine*, London, Financial Times.

Gospel, H., and Pendleton, A. (eds) (2005) *Corporate Governance and Labour Management: An International Comparison*, Oxford, Oxford University Press.

Guest, D., and Conway, N. (2002) *Pressure at Work and the Psychological Contract*. London, CIPD.

Hall, M. (2005) 'Assessing the Information and Consultation of Employees Regulations', *Industrial Law Journal*, 34(2), pp. 103–26.

Hall, P., and Soskice, D. (eds) (2001) *Varieties of Capitalism: The Institutional Foundations of Comparative Advantage*, Oxford, Oxford University Press.

Hamann, K., and Kelly, J. (2008) 'Varieties of capitalism and Industrial Relations', in P. Blyton, N. Bacon, J. Fiorito and E. Heery (eds) *The Sage handbook of Industrial Relations*, London, Sage.

Hancké, B., Rhodes, M., and Thatcher, M. (2007) *Beyond Varieties of Capitalism: Conflict, Contradictions and Complementarities in the European Economy*, Oxford, Oxford University Press.

Heery, E. (2008) 'System and change in Industrial Relations analysis', in Blyton, P., Bacon, N., Fiorito, J. and Heery, E. (eds) *The Sage handbook of Industrial Relations*, London, Sage.

Hendry, J., Sanderson, P., Barker, R., and Roberts, J. (2007) 'Responsible ownership, shareholder value and the new shareholder activism', *Competition and Change*, 11(3), pp. 223–40.

Hutton, W. (1996) *The State We're In*, London, Vintage.

Hyman, R. (2008) 'The state in Industrial Relations', in Blyton, P., Bacon, N., Fiorito, J. and Heery, E. (eds) *The Sage Handbook of Industrial Relations*, London, Sage.

Jacoby, S. (2005) *The Embedded Corporation: Corporate Governance and Employment Relations in Japan and the United States*, Princeton, NJ, Princeton University Press.

Jackson, G., Höper, M., and Kurdelbusch, A. (2005) 'Corporate governance and employees in Germany; changing linkages, complementarities, and tensions', in Gospel, H., and Pendleton, A. (eds) *Corporate Governance and Labour Management: An International Comparison*, Oxford, Oxford University Press.

Knetter, M. (1989) 'Price discrimination by US and German importers', *American Economic Review*, 79(1), pp. 198–210.

Lazonick, W., and O'Sullivan, M. (2000) 'Maximising shareholder value: a new ideology for corporate governance', *Economy and Society*, 29, pp. 13–35.

Machin, S. (2008) 'An appraisal of economic research on changes in wage inequality', *Labour*, 7, pp. 7–26.

Malcomson, J.M. (1997) 'Contracts, hold-up, and labor markets.' *Journal of Economic Literature*, 35(4): 1916–57.

Martynova, M., and Renneboog, L. (2008) 'A century of corporate takeovers: what have we learned and where do we stand?', *Journal of Banking and Finance*, 32, pp. 2148–77.

Mayer, C. (2000) 'Financial systems, corporate finance, and economic development', in Hubbard, R. (ed.) *Asymmetric Information, Corporate Finance and Investment*, Chicago, University of Chicago Press.

Mayer, C., and Alexander, I. (1990) 'Banks and securities markets: corporate financing in Germany and the United Kingdom', *Journal of Japanese and International Economies*, 4, pp. 450–75.

Monks, R., and Minow, N. (2001) *Corporate Governance*, 2nd ed., Oxford, Blackwell.

OECD (1998) 'Training of adult workers in OECD countries: measurement and analysis', *Employment Outlook*, Paris, OECD.

Pendleton, A., Poutsma, E., van Ommeren, J., and Brewster, C. (2001) *Employee Share Ownership and Profit Sharing in the European Union*, Luxembourg, Office for Official Publications of the European Union.

Pendleton, A., and Gospel, H. (2005) 'Markets and relationships: finance, governance, and labour in the United Kingdom', in Gospel, H., and Pendleton, A. (eds) *Corporate Governance and Labour Management: An International Comparison*, Oxford, Oxford University Press.

Roe, M. (2003) *Political Determinants of Corporate Governance*, Oxford, Oxford University Press.

Ryan, P. (1996) 'Factor shares and inequality in the UK', *Oxford Review of Economic Policy*, 12, pp. 106–26.

Shleifer, A., and Summers, L. (1988) 'Breach of trust in hostile takeovers', in A. Auerbach (ed.) *Corporate Takeovers: Causes and Consequences*, Chicago, University of Chicago Press.

Stiglitz, J.E. (1974) 'Incentives and risk sharing in sharecropping.' *Review of Economic Studies*, 41(2): 219–55.

Streeck, W. (ed.) (1992) *Social Institutions and the Economic Performance*, London, Sage.

Streeck, W., and Thelen, K. (eds) (2005) *Beyond Continuity: Institutional Change in Advanced Political Economies*, Oxford, Oxford University Press.

Thompson, P. (2003) 'Disconnected capitalism: or why employers can't keep their side of the bargain', *Work, Employment and Society*, 17(2), pp. 359–78.

Wright, M., Bacon, N., and Amess, K. (2009) 'The impact of private equity and buyouts on employment, remuneration and other HRM practices', *Journal of Industrial Relations*, 51(4), pp. 501–15.

Whyte, W. (1988) *Making Mondragon: The Growth and Dynamics of the Worker Cooperative Complex*, Ithaca, NY, ILR Press.

World Federation of Exchanges (2009) *2009 Market Highlights*, Paris, World Federation of Exchanges.

11

Governing employability: business school accreditation as 'soft' regulation

Hugh Willmott

Introduction

Accreditation gives reassurance of your degree's value and relevance at a time when the market risks saturation. Your qualification will be recognised by employers as carrying a stamp of quality assurance.

> Association of MBAs (http://accreditation.mbaworld.com/content/newaccredit1/index.html Accessed 6 March 2009)

The bargain struck between an employer and employee, including an agreed wage for the labour provided, is, in neo-classical thinking, an outcome of the operation of market forces.[1] The agreed contract is set by the availability of labour supply and the strength of demand, and ultimately by employers' calculations of the marginal utility yielded by the purchase of an additional unit of labour. In principle, the optimum allocation of resources (e.g. the productive capability of labour) is attained when market forces operate without regulatory hindrance. This orthodox, neo-classical conception of the exchange between buyers and sellers of labour focuses upon the moment of the transaction. It disregards the institutional processes through which the supply of, and demand for, labour are established and maintained. In heterodox analysis (e.g. Hodgson, 2004), in contrast, labour markets and employment relationships are conceived to be embedded in institutional media which enable and constrain their operation. Included in these media are international and national legislation, government policies, established pay differentials,

249

employers associations and trade unions, corporate HRM policies covering recruitment, selection, appraisal and so on (see Marsden, 1986). These media also include forms of licensing, certification and accreditation. Instead of treating transactions as if they were products of ostensibly impersonal laws of supply and demand,[2] heterodox analysis understands them to be conditioned by calculations of political advantage, on going struggles and precarious bargains. In short, a dynamic and extensive apparatus of institutions is seen to constitute and govern the transactions that comprise and maintain labour markets and employment relationships.

There are 'soft' as well as 'hard' forms of regulation within the institutional apparatus that intermediates the formation, sale and allocation of labour. The 'harder', more visible elements are provided by legislation and are enforceable by the state (see Heery, in this volume). Less visible but not insignificant are 'soft' means of regulation, including accreditation, that rely upon 'open-ended processes such as bench marking and peer group audit, with "moral-suasion" for enforcement' (Sisson and Marginson (2001: 4). Many of these 'soft' forms of governance are initiated and regulated by bodies and agencies that lack public accountability (see Streeck and Schmitter, 1985). In financial markets, rating agencies (e.g. Standard and Poor) are key intermediaries. In labour markets, NGOs have emerged to issue standards, codes and awards to employers with policies that are, for example, supportive of gays, lesbians and bisexuals. Agencies that provide peer-based accreditation, the focus of this chapter, have also formed and expanded as intermediaries alongside other media of labour market and employment relationship regulation. More specifically, this chapter considers the market for executive labour where the kite mark of accreditation, together with other forms of publicly available information[3] intermediates the employer–employee relationship as an element in the governance of employability.

Accreditation processes and outcomes are examined as part of a wider framework of governance of labour markets and employment relationships in which, as Sisson (2006a: 14) puts it, there are multiple 'rules of the game' with different 'sources and levels'. Much discussion of this 'game' has addressed the rules of corporate governance and/or concepts of citizenship. In this chapter, the scope of governance is conceived to extend to 'relational contracting, "organized markets" in group enterprises, clans, networks, trade associations and strategic alliances' (Jessop, 1995: 310). Players in a particular field – such as those participating in the 'game' of awarding business degrees – may, for example, engage in intermediary innovations by devising additional rules, incentives and sanctions that differentiate accredited institutions or degree programmes from those lacking such accreditation. The formation of accreditation agencies by, and for, business schools contributes to the 'soft' governance of employability.

Despite contributing substantially to regulation of labour markets and employment relationships, the growth and significance of accreditation has been lamentably under-researched.[4] Kleiner (2000: 199) has suggested that is perhaps because 'soft' regulation 'lies at the intersection of labour economics, law and industrial organization' so that it falls into the cracks between these scholarly silos. In the field of employment relations, the neglect may also be attributable to a practitioner-oriented tendency to conceive of, the employment relationship as being *within the firm* (e.g. Emmott, nd.) in a way that disembeds this relationship from the conditions of its formation and reproduction, including its constitution by institutional media of labour supply and assessment. As an element of increasing significance within these media, accreditation is seen to form part of an extensive, 'professionalizing' technology of division and exclusion that operates to pave (and narrow) access to many of the more prestigious and well-remunerated employment opportunities.

The remainder of this chapter comprises two major sections. The first sets accreditation in the broader context of the regulation of labour markets and employment relationships. The second section attends more directly to the role of accreditation in intermediating relationships between employees and employers, making specific reference to the accreditation of business schools and their programmes. Overall, the aim of the chapter is to appreciate the role of accreditation as a form of 'soft' regulation of employability in a way that demonstrates the distinctiveness and relevance of heterodox analysis. So doing, it is hoped that further examination of accreditation in the regulation of labour markets and employment relationships will be stimulated.

Markets and the lawful institutionalization of their discontents

To appreciate how employment relationships are irreducible to market transactions, it is relevant to explore how uncertainty and risk, but also trust and coercion, are endemic to their organization. On the one side, employers seeking to extract value from labour face the conundrum of how to ascertain what skills and potential are contained within the labour power that presents itself for hire. How tractable is it? How much value will it create when mixed with other factors of production? For the sellers of labour power, on the other side, there is the issue of how to detect and secure satisfactory terms and conditions of employment. What reputation does this employer have, and will promises be honoured? Given these uncertainties, there is an incentive for each party to preserve, construct, impose and/or support a number of institutions, independently or jointly, that mitigate uncertainties and vulnerabilities, or capitalize upon them. These uncertainties also present opportunities for third parties – both public and private – to develop regulatory media that can reduce and manage risks associated with the operation of labour markets and employment relationships.

> There are institutions that deal with the organization of work, i.e. job design, the grouping of jobs into activities and the structures used to co-ordinate these activities. There are institutions that deal with recruitment and selection and training and development. There are institutions that deal with 'performance management', i.e. the type of payment system and the level of wages, the working time arrangements, the disciplinary arrangements and so on.
>
> (Sisson, 2007: 8)

The regulatory institutions bring a measure of predictability to politico-economic relations in which primacy is given to the inherently hazardous exchange of labour power for a wage – that is, within the 'cash nexus'.[5] Regulatory intervention implicitly recognizes the secondary or epiphenomenal status of markets that cannot exist or operate without a minimum of 'social capital' in the form of institutionalized trust. Nonetheless and despite the primacy of the social, or political, over the economic, the architects of regulatory institutions routinely give priority to supporting and sustaining the operation of the cash nexus, albeit in ways that are calculated to be to their material advantage.[6] With these considerations in mind, it is relevant to explore further the relationship between the cash nexus and regulatory institutions.

Serving the cash nexus

> The bourgeoisie ... has pitilessly torn asunder the motley feudal ties that bound man to his "natural superiors", and has left no other nexus between man and man than naked self-interest, than callous "cash payment". It has drowned out the most heavenly ecstasies of religious fervor, of chivalrous enthusiasm, of philistine sentimentalism, in the icy water of egotistical calculation.
>
> (Marx and Engels: 1998: 37)

Tearing down pre-capitalist regulatory institutions to leave only the 'egoistic calculation(s)' of the cash nexus is a necessary yet unstable basis for capitalist development. The very iciness and indifference of purely egoistic calculation tends to stifle goodwill and foster resentment. In turn, the disaffecting (e.g.

demotivating) effects upon labour when treated as a commodity inhibits and restrains continuity and loyalty of employment (e.g. in the collective organization of labour found in factories) which is an important precondition of the stability required for capital investment. In the absence of an institutional complex capable of minimizing or overcoming the socially dislocating and divisive effects of 'egotistical calculation', the yield from hiring labour is sub-optimal. Nonetheless, in capitalist economies, employment relationships increasingly take the form of contracts (oral and/or implied as well as written[7]) between providers and purchasers of labour power which are based upon the idea that labour is a *freely* and *fairly* traded commodity that self-interestedly pursues its highest price. According to neo-classical thinking, possessors of labour are free to offer their capacities (e.g. strength, skill) for hire to prospective purchasers; and employers are *free* to mix such capacities with other factors of production. When the revenues derived from productive activity comfortably exceeds its costs, a return is generated sufficient to attract and compensate investors for the risks they take.[8] The trade between seller and buyer is conceived to be *fair* when the price received reflects the unfettered operation of impersonal forces of supply and demand. Fairness results when the economic freedom of each party to trade their resources is unimpeded. 'Freedom' and 'fairness' are, in this formulation, conceived as narrowly economic categories, even if they are repeatedly pressed into service as moral or political ones when defending capitalism against its critics.

Fairness at work?

This understanding of how ideas of fairness and freedom are invoked in defence of regulatory intervention can be illustrated by reference to reforms of employment law contained in the UK Employment Relations Act of 1999. In *Fairness at Work,* the White Paper which preceded this Act, Prime Minister Blair wrote in the Preface that it was intended to 'replace the notion of conflict between employers and employees with the promotion of partnership' (Smith and Morton, 2001: 122 citing DTI 1998: 2). Despite an avowed concern with 'fairness', critics of *Fairness at Work* have argued that it conveys 'no sense of the partnership between employers and employees as an undertaking between equals or as a shared project embodied in institutional arrangements'. Smith and Morton conclude that,

> The devil in Labour's employment law programme is its commitment to a particular form of *employer domination* of the employment relationship. From this flows its support for a minimalist regulation of the employment relationship and hostility

to the politics and practice of trade unionism conceived as the mobilization of workers' collective power (2001: 135, emphasis added).

(Smith and Morton, 2001: 122)

Reforms introduced in the name of partnership are seen to hold out scant prospect of being 'fair' in practice as they assume and naturalize the fairness of markets[9] and employers' entrenched 'domination of the employment relationship'. There is an echo here of how Marx (1976: 280), in darkly ironic mood, characterizes employment relations under capitalism as inhabiting 'the exclusive realm of Freedom, Equality, Property and Bentham'. Why Bentham? Because buyer and seller, employee and employer, 'looks only to his (sic) own advantage.... And precisely for that reason, either in accordance with the pre-established harmony of things, or under the auspices of an omniscient providence, they all work together to their mutual advantage, for the common weal, and in the common interest' (ibid.). Marx is highly sceptical of this unitarist vision because it disregards the asymmetries inherent within the relationship between suppliers and hirers of labour. Far from being distinguished by 'harmony', the employment relationship is seen to be marked and conditioned above all by forms of material and moral coercion.

From this perspective, the 'freedom(s)' and 'fairness' provided by the 'cash nexus' is constrained by the exclusion of employees from ownership over, and control of, the institutions that condition the meaning of these terms. The employment relationship is regarded as one of *domination* where control over labour time and its application is ceded to, and governed by others – in the form of supervisors and managers who act primarily as comparatively well rewarded and autonomous agents of the owners. It is also a relationship of *exploitation* wherein employees are systematically organized in a way that secures the private appropriation of their productive activity by the owners of capitalist enterprise. Each party is formally 'free' to participate in, or withdraw from the transaction; but the relationship is itself systemically weighted in favour of employers who command, or have better access, to relevant resources which include, most critically, the means of earning a wage. In his Forward to *Fairness at Work*, Tony Blair is perhaps unintentionally, and certainly uncharacteristically, candid when he writes that 'These proposals, together with the introduction of a minimum wage – set sensibly, implemented sensibly – put a very minimum infrastructure of decency and fairness around people in the workplace.' (DTI, 1998: 2, emphasis added).

Fairness at Work can be read as the most recent chapter in a history of the regulation of the employment relationship that, in general, is sought by employees and resisted by employers.[10] According to *Fairness at Work*, the aim is to chart a 'way between the absence of minimum standards of protection at the workplace, and a return to the laws of the past. It is based on the rights of the individual, whether exercised on their own or with others, as a matter of their choice. It matches rights and responsibilities. It seeks to draw a line under the issue of industrial relations law.' (ibid.: 2). It is notable that the emphasis is upon individuals abstracted from the wider institutional context in which employers deploy resources (e.g. connections to the media, the best legal advisors) to threaten the loss of employment or to downgrade terms and conditions of employment in preference to reducing the remuneration of senior executives or the reduction of dividends.

Representations of the employment relationship that emphasize individual freedom and fairness promote an appealing fiction whose 'utility' resides in ignoring the *systematic* domination and exploitation of labour within capitalist employment relations. That 'ignorance' extends to the introduction of a minimum wage as adequate or 'fair' compensation for those who would otherwise be even more flagrantly exploited by the unrestrained operation of market forces. Instead of highlighting how 'free' markets are socially divisive in depressing wages to poverty levels while simultaneously awarding huge salaries, share options and bonuses to senior executives, the fig leaf of the minimum wage is introduced to mitigate the most revealing and de-legitimizing consequences of a minimally regulated labour market. In *Fairness at Work*, no consideration is given to how the purchase and mobilization of labour involve a *social relationship* that is *before* as well as 'beyond contract' (Fox, 1974). This relationship is governed through 'hard' and 'soft' media of regulation.

'Hard' regulation

Legislation provides the 'hardest' form of regulation as it is underwritten by the violence of the state applied through courts of law. Employment legislation defines and institutionalizes obligations and rights between employers and employees[11] (see Edelman and Suchman, 1997). Consider, for example, the International Labour Office (ILO) which was established to set out, promote and protect the rights of labour (see Rubery and Grimshaw, 2003, Ch. 10):

> It is through the employment relationship, however defined, that reciprocal rights and obligations are created between the employee and the employer. *The employment relationship has been, and continues to be, the main vehicle through which workers gain access to the rights and benefits associated with employment in the areas of labour law and social security. It is the key point of reference for determining the nature and extent of employers' rights and obligations towards their workers.*
>
> (ILO, 2005: 3, emphasis added)

By characterizing the employment relationship as a *'legal notion'* and by underscoring the importance of 'labour law' in providing benefits within and beyond the workplace, the ILO implicitly challenges the neo-classical view that this relationship is essentially a *market* transaction between the buyer and seller of a commodity. But the ILO's exclusive emphasis upon the legal dimension of the employment relationship simultaneously distracts attention from the wider institutional – social and political – organization of labour markets and workplace relations.[12] Minimal account is taken of other institutional media that govern employment relationships, including those through which employment legislation develops, is interpreted and applied.[13] Among these media are 'softer' forms of regulation, including accreditation.

Beyond 'hard' regulation: The case of the accreditation

In a situation where labour is treated as a tradable commodity, providers of labour are attentive to the attractiveness of their productive power to potential purchasers; and purchasers are attentive to the capabilities of the labour they are hiring. For each party, a reliable, impersonal indicator of the value of the exchanged commodity – in the form of a qualification, for example – is of potential benefit when making the transaction. A recent study of the labour market effects of nationally recognized qualifications reached the following conclusions:

- **Qualifications pay.** Additional qualifications increase the earning potential of workers. For instance, workers with degrees or HNCs/HNDs earn around 75 per cent more on average than similar workers with no qualifications;
- **Having a qualification also helps in finding and sustaining work.** Three-quarters of working-age Scots with 5 Standard Grades are in work, compared to half of working age Scots with no qualifications;
- **Graduates continue to earn more than non-graduates.** The wage premium associated with a degree has been maintained in recent years; and
- **Education and training makes the difference.** The employment and wage benefits associated with qualifications reflect the knowledge gained and its value in the labour market. (Walker and Zhu, 2007: 5)

Qualifications, operating as proxies for skills and/or knowledge, are central elements within an institutional complex of employment regulation. But can the purchaser – whether s/he is a student seeking a qualification or an employer hiring the qualified student – have confidence in (exchange value of) the qualification? Part of the response to such uncertainty has been a rapid expansion of forms of intermediation, including processes of accreditation, that offer an assurance concerning the standard obtained by those presenting a given qualification, such as an MBA.

Accreditation, licensing and certification

Accreditation can be differentiated from licensing and certification as related forms of regulation. *Licensing* is generally overseen by statutory authorities and restricts employment to those who have successfully passed a series of tests.[14] Licensing is, in this respect, a comparatively 'hard' form of regulation. *Certification* is not restrictive but it may nonetheless provide employers with a degree of assurance concerning a person's competence to complete a job or task so that they prefer to hire labour that has the relevant certificates.[15] *Accreditation* is broadly similar to certification but it is applied to institutions, including educational programmes, rather than to their alumni. Unlike sellers of labour who are licensed or certificated, those gaining a qualification from an accredited institution do not offer prospective employers any direct assurance of their competence; and employment requiring those competences is not reserved for prospective recruits who have gained an accredited qualification. The award of an accredited MBA degree, for example, does not certify or license the recipient to practice as a manager. In practice, however, there is a strong belief, and supportive evidence (e.g. Baruch and Peiperl, 2000), that possession of an MBA can be critical for gaining admission to particular employment opportunities.

Licensing, certification and accreditation have been proliferating as media that contribute to the governance of employability. In the case of bodies that accredit business qualifications, their development and expansion has been prompted by uncertainties about the value and contribution of such qualifications. Sellers of labour are concerned with the question of how to enhance their employability: will prospective employers place a premium on their qualifications? Employers are concerned with the calibre and contribution of prospective employees. Uncertainties reside at the centre of impersonal market transactions; and the desire to mitigate such uncertainties generates a demand for information to which the formation of accreditation agencies has been a response.

Illustrative of uncertainties about the reliability of qualifications and the value attributed to their accreditation, a recent OECD study[16] concludes that,

...there do appear to be problems with graduates not always having the skills required by employers. This is evident in employer surveys and in some data analysis which shows a negative wage premium associated with 'skill mismatch'. One response to this is to make sure that vocational courses meet the requirements of employers *and to ensure that the accreditation system is appropriate.*

(Machin and McNally, 2007: 30, emphasis added)

'Negative wage premiums' identified in this report are likely to be of considerable concern to those who expend time, and may incur significant debt, in efforts to increase their 'human capital'. Prospective employers are likely to be concerned about those with qualifications who present themselves for employment without the expected 'skill set'. Diverse forms of intermediation – such as Work Trials and Job Introduction schemes in the United Kingdom[17] – have been developed to address such concerns. And these concerns extend to governments and citizens wishing to minimize public expenditures on the creation of unproductive labour capacity and economically irrelevant educational provision.

Accreditation as institutional intermediation

To address the instability and associated hazards of marketized relations in which 'egotistical calculation' prevails – as demonstrated most dramatically by the repeated failures and scams in financial markets (Kindleberger and Aliber, 2005) – numerous intermediating institutions have been accommodated or introduced to mitigate the full destructive force of the cash nexus. Instead of drowning in its 'icy water', 'soft' regulatory media have been preserved, revived, refined, devised and elaborated to facilitate the smoother operation of employment relationships. These media include, but are by no means restricted to family, friendship and occupational networks (Granovetter, 1985: 498 *et seq*) which are trusted to provide comparatively unvarnished commendations of employers or of employees. These commendations can carry considerable weight when assessing prospective recruits, promotion hopefuls and reputable employers. In short, elements of 'social capital' play their part in the formation and distribution of 'human capital' as these compensate for, or circumvent, pressures to reduce economic exchange to a cash nexus in which 'soft' media play no legitimate role.

When commenting upon the ILO's conception of the employment relation as a 'legal notion', it was noted that a contract of employment contains whatever legally permissible terms and conditions have been agreed between the two parties.[18] Surrounding and underpinning the contact, however, is a dense institutional web that bestows a measure of legitimacy upon employment law, and without which there is a resort to force. This web supports and binds relationships of employment that otherwise would be prone to more breakdown and renegotiation. Within this web are to be found processes of accreditation. With regard to (business) schools and their programmes, accreditation agencies provide evaluations of the institutions and qualifications in which students (and taxpayers) invest; and for which employers, as recruiters, have demonstrated a willingness to pay a premium.

Accrediting elite business qualifications

In the United Kingdom, higher education institutions must be accredited by a Royal Charter or Act of Parliament in order to award degrees.[19] Such publicly accountable forms of accreditation are then supplemented by privately organized forms accreditation, such as those offered by agencies that accredit business schools and/or their programmes. The endorsement of an institution or a degree by a private accreditation agency has no direct bearing upon the *award* of degrees *per se*. But accreditation can differentiate programmes from those that lack this *imprimatur*. As business education has expanded, competition between business schools has intensified – internationally, nationally and regionally – especially in the Masters of Business Administration (MBA) market. Phelps and Aggarwal (2006: 61) observe that business education is 'a highly competitive industry characterized by significant excess capacity' which, arguably, increases the importance of accreditation as a means of 'product differentiation'.[20] For schools, accreditation provides a means of *warranting the value of their offer* to prospective students and the hirers of their labour (see Baruch and Peiperl, 2000). An upbeat assessment of the value of an MBA is provided by Sturgess et al. (2003) who conclude that

> Not only can an MBA contribute to increased pay, status and promotion, it can also enhance career opportunities in a broader sense through giving individuals greater career clarity, increased confidence and higher perceived credibility . . . such courses cultivate a broader range of skills than potentially might have been expected . . . .
> (ibid.: 64–65)

It is assessments of this kind that support the calculation that the cost of obtaining a business qualification – including loss of earnings, increased indebtedness and additional pressures (see Blundell et al., 1999) – is more than compensated when it facilitates entry into a well-paid job with good prospects or enables a change of career. Surveys have reported that the most-cited reason for undertaking an MBA is the aspiration to improve job opportunities (e.g. Hawksley, 1996); and that promotions and salary increases tend to follow the acquisition of an MBA (Forrester, 1986; MacErlean, 1993; Schofield, 1996). In response to competitive pressures that are aggravated by 'significant excess capacity' (Phelps and Aggarwal, 2006: 61) and an associated shortage of well-qualified candidates, business schools have reduced the temporal and financial demands upon the purchasers of degrees – notably, by shortening the duration of the MBA or by reducing the number of courses, contact hours and/or assignments. This stratagem may, however, be assessed to damage credibility, to drain cash flow or to be necessary yet insufficient to maintain competitiveness. Accreditation of 'the quality of education on offer, the facilities... and the faculty' (ibid.: 62) may then offer a further means of responding to competitive pressure.

The three principal accreditation agencies for business school programmes – notably, AACSB,[21] EQUIS[22] and AMBA[23] – differ with regards to their origins, size and form of accreditation but they are all self-regulating bodies. The US-based AACSB was founded in 1919 by a small number of elite business schools and has expanded to become the biggest accreditor of undergraduate and postgraduate business programmes. By 2007, AACSB had accredited 540 schools of which 90 were outside the United States.[24] EQUIS was established in 1997 by the European Foundation for Management Development. Based in Brussels, EQUIS had accredited over 100 schools in 31 countries by April 2007. AMBA was founded in 1967 by eight UK graduates from Harvard. It started life as the Business Graduates Association (BGA) and subsequently developed into the Association of MBAs which began to accredit MBA programmes in the 1970s. By April 2007, it had accredited 115 BA and Masters courses worldwide. In contrast to AACSB and EQUIS, AMBA is a consumer organization, with membership open to any individual who attended or is currently studying at, an AMBA-accredited business school. AMBA accredits programmes but not schools. AACSB accreditation is distinctive in being mission-based rather than reliant upon more universal or standardized requirements. Despite these differences, the agencies articulate their aims in broadly similar terms.

Pitching for accreditation

The mission of the accreditation agencies is generally represented in ways that stress their contribution to advancing the aims of business schools. Included in these aims are: developing their knowledge base, improving teaching, enriching students' learning experience and producing graduates with enhanced skill sets. For example, the AACSB assures stakeholders that its accredited schools:

'Manage resources to achieve a vibrant and relevant mission.

Advance business and management knowledge through faculty scholarship. Provide high-caliber teaching of quality and current curricula. Cultivate meaningful interaction between students and a qualified faculty. Produce graduates who have achieved specified learning goals.' (http://www.aacsb.edu/accreditation/Accessed 1 December 2008; cf EQUIS at http://www.efmd.org/index.php/component/efmd/? cmsid=041004geyi)

During the past decade and more, accreditation agencies have become increasingly significant in constituting the standing, and the related 'pulling power', of business schools and their courses. This is especially so for Masters programmes which are, in substantial part, self-funded. The growth and influence of the agencies has coincided with a neo-liberal turn in education policy where the acquisition of a degree is unblushingly marketed as an investment for career, and participation is conditional upon taking out substantial loans to support study. In this context, concerns about the reputation and market value of the 'product' being purchased – whether by the student embarking upon a degree or the employer assessing the credentials of job applicants – are heightened. Accreditation is intended to provide some reassurance about the soundness of the investment. At least, that is the pitch of the accreditation bodies, as exemplified by Jeanette Purcell, chief executive of AMBA:

what accreditation shows is that a school has reached set minimum standards; that it has a quality team of academics behind it and offers a set range of core subjects.
(Quoted in Paton, 2007)

On the AMBA website, potential hirers of graduates from accredited institutions are assured that

our accredited programmes have rigorous selection criteria for their student cohorts, and these students are ... taught by high quality faculty and they learn alongside other high-achievers from diverse business backgrounds. *To recruit a graduate from an accredited programme is to recruit top talent.* (http:// accreditation.mbaworld.com/content/newaccredit1/index.html, emphasis added. Accessed 1 December 2008)

In the accreditation literature, the purpose of accrediting business schools or their programmes is represented as the improvement of the quality of education (Hedmo et al., nd.: 8; Vaughn, 2002). What has been argued here, in contrast, is that the principal purpose of accreditation is to offer a measure of assurance about 'product' quality for those investing time and resources in the acquisition of degrees as well as those who recruit business school graduates. For the schools that seek, and pay handsomely for, the *soubriquet* of accreditation, its appeal resides primarily in securing and raising the value of a programme or a school in the face of competition from other suppliers who threaten to undercut the price and/or debase the MBA currency and ultimately threaten the employment security of those who deliver the programmes.

The opportunity to improve their employment prospects by obtaining a comparatively scarce qualification, in the form of an accredited degree is, for many students, the most important motivation for studying for a business degree. The accreditation kite mark is valued not only, or even primarily, as an indicator of educational 'quality' or 'excellence' but also, and perhaps most importantly, as a passport for competing more effectively as sellers of labour power. As suppliers to this group, schools are generally less interested in improving *educational* 'quality' *per se*, despite their public protestations to the contrary, than in acquiring a badge of product differentiation which, they anticipate, will make their degrees more attractive to students and recruiters who regard accreditation as a credible indicator of *labour* quality.[25] Whether either party fully believes this pitch is irrelevant so long as they are persuaded that an accredited qualification may help reduce the risk and/or enhance the return of their respective investments, or at least provide them with a reassuring rationale for their choices.[26]

A flavour of what business schools seek to gain by their investment in accreditation is conveyed in the following excerpt taken from MBA pages of the University of Strathclyde website. Placing great emphasis upon its 'triple accreditation' by AMBA, EQUIS and AACSB, the writer of this copy declares that

> Less than 1% of business schools in the world hold "triple accreditation" – Strathclyde is one of them. Currently, only 27 business schools out of around 3500 worldwide have been fully accredited.... These accreditations are rigorous processes that involve assessment of numerous aspects of the school and its programmes.... Once you've thought about your budget, preferred location and/or how you want to study, you can start to narrow things down a little, but thereafter how can you make the best choice? Accreditation of business schools and their programmes can help, *as these official seals of approval offer a very objective way of measuring a school's credentials.* For example, the quality of education on offer, the facilities, the student body and the faculty are all reviewed. (http://www.gsb.strath.ac.uk/mba/accreditation/emphasis added. Accessed 1 December 2008)

The claim that accreditation offers 'a very objective way of measuring a school's credentials', implies that lack of accreditation indicates quality insufficient to obtain the desired *imprimatur*. By stabilizing, if not increasing the supply of 'higher flying' students, accreditation may also provide some reassurance for staff in those institutions about the market viability and durability of the programmes, and thereby contribute to enhancing their security as well as assisting with faculty recruitment. According to Paul Bates, the Dean of the DeGroote School, McMaster University, accreditation

> ... puts a seal of approval, so to speak, on what we do as a School. When it comes to recruiting of students and recruiting of faculty, it's a critical additional affirmation that we're a place worth coming to. (See http://www.degroote.mcmaster.ca/News/ pdfs/2006-04-18AACSB.pdf Accessed 6 April 2008)

It is not necessary to accept the hyperbole of the claims of accreditation agencies or accredited institutions to acknowledge that accreditation offers a prized, as well as a demanding and costly, badge of differentiation. Accreditation is undertaken, often reluctantly, in the belief that its absence will be damaging for recruitment (of students but also of staff) even if its receipt does not significantly enhance the reputation or appeal of an institution, or a specific programme, to prospective students and employers.[27] The accreditation bodies feed off the uncertainties associated with the impersonality of market relations as they operate, in effect, as 'protection agencies' for their members (Lowrie and Willmott, 2009). Business schools are willing to submit themselves to accreditation processes as a means of differentiating and shielding themselves from competitors who lack the distinguishing kite mark. The cost is born initially by the schools but is passed on to students, taxpayers, their employers and ultimately to the consumers of the products and services in which the (more costly) accredited labour is embodied. Although all the parties who participate in the game – business schools, agencies, students, employers – anticipate that they will derive some advantage (or, at least, hedge against some potential disadvantage), it is perhaps not unduly cynical to suggest that the principal beneficiaries of accreditation are the staff of the accreditation agencies and those who act as paid advisors to them (see Lowrie and Willmott, 2009).

Conclusion

The involvement of institutions in the organization and regulation of economic transactions has been illustrated through the example of accreditation in the governance of employment relationships. The presence of these regulatory media is an unwelcome irritant or embarrassment to neo-classical thinking where market forces alone are conceived to produce an optimum outcome. In principle, *'caveat emptor'* (buyer beware) is considered sufficient to ensure efficient market transactions. From a heterodox perspective, in contrast, forms of regulation, 'soft' as well as 'hard', provide a framework within which market transactions are accomplished, and without which markets freeze up from lack of trust and/or stability. Efforts to dismantle and/or elaborate this regulatory framework – for example, by reducing 'hard' regulation while encouraging the development of 'soft' forms of regulation, such as accreditation – is regarded as the outcome of on going struggles to secure material and symbolic advantage, or at least to limit disadvantage, and not as a step towards more perfectly functioning markets.

Accreditation, as a 'soft' form of regulation, contributes to mitigating uncertainties not only for the providers and hirers of labour power but also for its developers. The presence of uncertainties means that benefits can be derived from the 'soft' regulatory activities of agencies that intermediate aspects of the employment relationship. For prospective employees, an accredited qualification can instil confidence in making a substantial investment of time and money to obtain a qualification which promises to augment their 'human capital' and thereby improve their prospects of negotiating more favourable terms and conditions. For prospective employers, accreditation of a qualification can offer a measure of assurance about the competencies and capabilities of job applicants and promotion hopefuls. At the very least, an accreditation kite mark can provide a formally rational justification for a decision to select a particular qualification provider or for making a specific hiring or promotion decision.[28] But, of course, the initial target of the agencies is not those wishing to gain a qualification or the hirers of their labour but, rather, the organizations, including business schools, that deliver the programmes which enable students to acquire (accredited) qualifications.

Accreditation of qualifications forms part of an extended web of regulation in which providers and hirers of labour are engaged in struggles to establish, deploy, defend or reform institutions, including the institutions of accreditation that exploit and/or mitigate their respective vulnerabilities. In the case of accreditation, the regulation is 'private' and 'soft': it is organized on a voluntary basis rather than imposed by the state. Forms of 'soft' regulation have prospered in the post-1970s climate of neo-liberalism. In higher education, there has been a rapid expansion of business schools, with related uncertainties about the quality of their offerings and the esteem in which they are held by prospective employers of their graduates. Accreditation agencies have emerged and/or expanded in response to opportunities presented by this growth, competitiveness and uncertainty. During a period when neo-liberal hegemony devalued more 'public' or collective forms of regulation have, regulations intended to correct and tame the divisive effects of markets have been supplanted by softer measures – notably, in forms of 'deregulation' and 're-regulation' – intended to liberate them with minimal regard for the their limited effectiveness.

A focus upon accreditation as a form of 'soft' regulation draws attention to the integral part played by intermediating agencies in the governance of employability. Studying these agencies helps to highlight the neglect of their role in facilitating and legitimizing the credentializing of labour power. This focus raises or reinforces awareness of the irreducibility of market relations to the cash nexus even when the latter is held up as an ideal by participants in these relations. For the agencies are seen simultaneously to exploit, and offer a degree of protection from, the risks of investing in educational provision when the design and delivery of courses is left largely to the operation of market forces. The promise of accreditation is to protect and enhance the market value of degrees by differentiating accredited from non-accredited institutions and programmes from those that are unaccredited. Nonetheless, the very demand for accreditation places in question the intellectual coherence, in addition to the moral defensibility, of treating labour as a commodity. In turn, such reflection may fuel critical reflection upon power relations that favour, or at least more willingly accommodate, regulation that is privately arranged rather than publicly accountable and enforceable.

Notes

1. I would like to thank Ed Heery, Peter Turnbull and Anthony Lowrie for their detailed and incisive comments on earlier drafts of this chapter.
2. It is relevant to note the neo-classical rebuttal to such critiques. Its defenders contend that the neo-classical model offers a useful approximation, not a perfect representation, of transactions. Criticism of its empirical emptiness is parried by denials that the model is intended to be empirically exact. And challenges to its ontology are met by the rejoinder that 'it is merely a practical instrument for anyone who happens to want to maximize his or her utility' (Streeck, 2003: 126).
3. Notably, the rankings of business schools generated by commercial organizations such as *Business Week* and the *Financial Times* as well as the results of research and teaching assessments.
4. It receives no attention in Rubery and Grimshaw (2003), for example. Even those who have questioned the narrowness and managerialism of a focus on practices internal to the employing organization, and stress how employee relations are organized through ' "the rules of the game" [which] give markets shape and direction' (Sisson, 2006a: 8), have little to say about the involvement of forms of licensing, etc. in multiplying and cementing these 'rules'. Discussion tends to be confined to collective agreements, internal workplace governance arrangements and individual employment legislation. With

specific regard to the role of accreditation in the governance of executive labour, there is a tension between its neglect and the contention that 'most in need of change ... will be changes in the recruitment and training of managers' (Sisson, 2006b: 15) where, arguably, the kite mark of accreditation is relevant to hiring and promotion decisions. Considering the investment of time and effort made by 'employment relations' academics in securing course accreditation – notably, in the United Kingdom, for courses accredited by Chartered Institute of Personnel and Development (CIPD) – the oversight is surprising. Could it be that critical scrutiny of this area is assessed to be too sensitive or risky for maintaining cooperative relationships with accreditation bodies?

5. The 'cash nexus' refers to the reduction of human relationships, and especially relations of production and consumption, to monetary exchange.

6. There is also common ground when, for example, a fraction of influential employers makes the calculation that legislation is necessary to secure stability and/or legitimacy or gains some competitive advantage. Awareness of the risks of failing to introduce factory legislation, for example, permitted pragmatic employers to compromise their neo-classical principles by reluctantly accepting factory legislation (Gray, 1996). In the case of factory legislation, it was enabled by stirrings of patrician benevolence which were subsequently moderated in circumstances where it has proved easier and permissible to cut costs by reducing, intensifying, outsourcing or offshoring the inputs of labour than by trimming the costs of other factors of production.

7. In the United Kingdom at least, an oral contract is as binding as a written one, although its terms may be more difficult to prove. The Employment Rights Act of 1996 requires employers to provide the employee with written particulars relating to the oral contract within 2 months of the commencement of employment.

8. Employees' investment of 'human capital' in capitalist enterprise is also placed at risk but this is overlooked so that labour generally receives no compensation for this risk. That is because labour is treated as a factor of production equivalent to machinery or raw materials. In the case of non-capitalist work organizations, including state employment, the employment relationship is based upon an alternative logic of redistribution or reinvestment in which the capacity to generate taxation revenues that fund public sector employment in combination with political decisions about their allocation, rather than the profitability of the enterprise, is key to shaping the risks faced by public sector employees.

9. The second paragraph of *Fairness at Work* asserts the importance of preserving 'open markets' as it underscores the Government's commitment 'to economic stability, based on low inflation, sound public finances and open markets.' This is followed immediately by a phrase that has returned to haunt an administration committed to making Britain 'the most lightly regulated labour market of any leading economy in the world' (DTI, 1998: 2): 'We are determined there will be no return to economic boom and bust.' (ibid.: 4)

10. The principal exception concerns legislation introduced to restrict or undermine the capacity of employees to organize collectively in pursuit of improvements in their terms and conditions of employment.

11. According to the ILO (2005: 3), 'The employment relationship is a legal notion widely used in countries around the world to refer to the relationship between a person called an employee (frequently referred to as a worker) and an employer for whom the employee performs work under certain conditions in return for remuneration.

12. It also has the perverse effect of excluding growing areas of employment, such as self-employment, from 'the employment relationship'. Later in the ILO document, reference is made to 'civil or commercial contractual relationships under which the services of self-employed workers may be procured, but on terms and conditions which differ from those within an employment relationship'. It continues: 'Frequent recourse to such contractual arrangements has become increasingly widespread in

recent years. From a legal standpoint, these arrangements lie *outside* the framework of the employment relationship' (ILO, 2005: 7, emphasis added).

13. The disinclination to situate employment law within the context of an evolving social relationship is perverse since, according to the ILO's own account of its history, its creation was motivated by a concern for the 'condition of workers, more and more numerous and exploited with no consideration for their health, their family lives and their advancement, that was less and less acceptable'; and the Preamble to its Constitution refers to 'conditions of labour exist involving... injustice, hardship and privation to large numbers of people' (ILO, nd.). There is little doubt that the establishment of the ILO in 1919 was intended as an intervention in the social organization of employment relationships by creating a body capable of pressurizing governments of industrializing countries to introduce legislation that would change/improve the terms of employment relationships and *inter alia* reduce 'injustice, hardship and privation'. It would seem that this understanding of the ILO has been forgotten or suppressed in its naturalization of employment law and its preoccupation with standard setting (that it lacks the power to enforce). For a wide-ranging critique of the ILO, see Standing (2008) who notes how 'when referring to employment objectives, [the ILO] has failed to forge an agenda on occupational regulation, which may prove a crucial omission.' (ibid.: 381). This omission is a common characteristic of bodies, initiatives and legislation – regional and national as well as international, bodies – that is intended to address the vulnerability of labour, including the EU's guidelines on employment contained in the European Employment Strategy (See http://ec.europa.eu/social/main.jsp?catId=108&langId=en, accessed 6 July 2009). In the ILO's case, a possible explanation for this absence is the tripartite organization (comprising representatives of employees, employers and governments) of the ILO which makes it difficult, and perhaps impossible, to acknowledge that this struggle occurs between parties with different mobilities and differential access to resources, including access to political and regulatory elites.

14. Auditors of the accounts of public companies are an example of a licensed occupation.

15. In the United Kingdom, the Confederation for the Registration of Gas Installers' (Corgi) is an example of a certifying body. It was formed in 1970, 2 years after a 22 storey apartment block in London was devastated by a massive gas blast that claimed five lives.

16. This study was commissioned to examine how the organization, financing and management of higher education can help countries achieve their economic and social objectives.

17. According to the Department of Work and Pensions (2009), a *Work Trial* enables an employer to 'try out a potential employee for up to 30 days, at no cost to your business, before you decide whether to make them a job offer. It is, in effect, a test period in a real job, and an ideal opportunity to fill a vacancy with minimum risk'. Work Trials that can last up to 30 days and the candidate receives an allowance for travel up and up to £3 for food (see also http://www.jobcentreplus.gov.uk/JCP/Employers/advisoryservices/diversity/Dev_015794.xml.html). According to Bates (2006), 'They are really extended interviews – a chance for the potential employee to find out about the job and show the employer what they can do.' The *Job Introduction* scheme is for candidates with a disability and lasts for 6 weeks. The employer is paid £75 per week for 6 weeks and the person on the scheme is paid the going rate for the job. The benefits for the employer are said to be that 'they get the chance to assess a potential employee' and also that the scheme 'offers a way to exercise corporate responsibility and reap its many benefits, including reputation and risk management, employee satisfaction, innovation and learning, access to capital and improved financial performance' (Bates, 2006). For the employee, it is said to 'give them an opportunity to learn technical and social skills; make friends, grow in confidence and independence; gain a

clearer vision of what they like and dislike; establish a routine of timekeeping and attendance; and find out about this workplace in particular and also the general impact of work on their life' (ibid.). See also http://www.jobcentreplus.gov.uk/JCP/Employers/advisoryservices/diversity/Dev_015794.xml.html

18. To be legally enforceable, these terms must be sufficiently explicit to enable a court to reach a judgment in the event of a dispute over any alleged breach of the contract.

19. In the United Kingdom, an external assessment of institutions seeking to award degrees is undertaken by a government body, the Quality Assurance Agency for Higher Education (QAA). The QAA makes recommendations to the government minister with relevant territorial responsibilities (e.g. for Wales). The Minister then submits advice to the Privy Council which, under an Act of Parliament (1992), is charged with authorizing applications. Elsewhere, significantly different procedures for such accreditation have developed. In the United States, for example, the accreditation of higher education institutions is a state, not a federal, responsibility. The US Department of Education authorizes private agencies to undertake the work of accreditation. Additional complexities arise in circumstances where franchises are in operation or where higher education provision is delivered virtually and/or by virtual institutions (see Farrington, 2001 for an extended discussion).

20. Phelps and Aggarwal (2006) base these observations on the US scene where accreditation of management and business programmes is longest established, but the picture is familiar elsewhere.

21. The Association to Advance Collegiate Schools of Business.

22. The European Quality Improvement System.

23. The Association of MBAs.

24. The following figures are taken from Paton (2007).

25. 'Educational quality' and 'labour quality' may overlap but they are by no means synonymous as the former has wide relevance and application whereas the latter is evaluated more narrowly in relation to gainful employment.

26. Of course, to argue that accreditation is not sought primarily for educational reasons does not imply that accreditation exerts an inherently negative influence upon the educational experience. See, for example, Stella and Spooner (2007).

27. It is relevant to recall that, being voluntary, the absence of accredited status does not mean that a particular school or programme is sub-standard or deficient. It may be that accreditation has not been sought because it is deemed irrelevant to a specialist programme, to the targeting of a local market, or because the anticipated benefit is assessed to be insufficient to warrant the investment of time and resources required to acquire and retain the *imprimatur*. Whether such considerations are taken into account by prospective applicants to non-accredited programmes, or by employers recruiting their alumni, is a moot point. That so many schools have sought accreditation from at least one agency, or are seeking to do so, suggests that the lack of a kite mark is assessed to send a weak or negative signal to applicants as well as prospective hirers of their labour.

28. Formally rational in the sense that the person who is hired or promoted may not be substantively the most competent or capable of the applicants but the possession of a accredited qualification may provide a formal basis for justifying the appointment.

References

Bates, P. (2006) *Unpaid Work Experience – Getting it Right*, Bath: National Development Team for Inclusion.

Baruch, Y. and Peiperl, M. (2000), 'The Impact of an MBA on Graduate Careers', *Human Resource Management*, 10, 2: 69–90.

Blundell, R., Dearden, L., Meghir, C. and Sianesi, B. (1999), 'Human Capital Investment: The Returns from Education and Training to the Individual, the Firm and the Economy', *Fiscal Studies*, 20, 1: 1–23.

Department of Trade and Industry (DTI) (1998), *Fairness at Work*, Command 3968. London: Stationery Office, available at http://www.berr.gov.uk/files/file24436.pdf, accessed 3 February 2009.

Department of Work and Pensions (2009), 'Work Trial', available at http://www.jobcentreplus.gov.uk/JCP/Employers/advisoryservices/recruitment/Dev_015800.xml.html, accessed 4 February 2009.

Edelman, L.B. and Suchman, M.C. (1997), 'The Legal Environments of Organizations', *Annual Review of Sociology*, 23: 479–515.

Emmott, M. (nd.), 'What is Employee Relations?', London: Chartered Institute of Personnel and Development, available at http://buira.org.uk/index.php?option=com_docman&task=doc_view&gid=102, accessed 26 January 2009.

Farrington, D.J. (2001), 'Borderless Higher Education: Challenges to Regulation, Accreditation and Intellectual Property Rights', *Minerva*, 39: 63–84.

Forrester, P. (1986), *The British MBA*, Cranfield: Cranfield Press.

Fox, A. (1974), *Beyond Contract*, London: Faber.

Granovetter, M. (1985), 'Economic Action and Social Structure: The Problem of Embeddedness', *American Journal of Sociology*, 91, 3: 481–510.

Gray, R. (1996), *The Factory Question and Industrial England, 1830–1860*, Cambridge: Cambridge University Press.

Hawksley, F. (1996) 'In the Right Place at the Right Time', *Accountancy*, 117, 1233: 40–2.

Hedmo, T. Sahlin-Andersson, K. and Wedlin, L. (nd.), 'The Emergence of a European Regulatory Field of Management Education – Standardizing Through Accreditation, Ranking and Guidelines', SCORE (Stockholm Center for Organizational Research) Working Paper, available at http://www.score.su.se/pdfs/2001-7.pdf, accessed 30 January 2009.

Hodgson, Geoffrey M. (2004), *The Evolution of Institutional Economics: Agency, Structure and Darwinism in American Institutionalism*, London: Routledge.

International Labour Office (nd.), ILO History, available at http://www.ilo.org/public/english/about/history.htm, accessed 30 January 2009.

International Labour Office (2005), The Employment Relationship Report V(1), Geneva: International Labour Office, available at http://www.ilo.org/public/english/standards/relm/ilc/ilc95/pdf/rep-v-1.pdf, accessed 25 January 2009.

Jessop, B. (1995), 'The Regulation Approach, Governance and Post-Fordism', *Economy and Society*, 24: 307–333.

Kindleberger, C.P. and Aliber, R. (2005), *Manias, Panics and Crashes: A History of Financial Crises*, 5th edition, Hoboken, New Jersey: John Wiley.

Kleiner, M.M. (2000), 'Occupational Licensing', *Journal of Economic Perspectives*, 14, 4: 189–202.

Lowrie, A. and Willmott, H.C. (2009), 'Accreditation Sickness in the Consumption of Business Education: The Vacuum in AACSB Standard Setting', *Management Learning*, 40, 4: 411–420.

MacErlean, N. (1993), 'Master Classes', *Accountancy*, 111: 29–34.

Machin, S. and McNally, S. (2007), 'Tertiary Education Systems and Labour Markets' Education and Training Policy Division, OECD, available at http://www.oecd.org/dataoecd/55/31/38006954.pdf, accessed 23 January 2009.

Marsden, D. (1986), *The End of Economic Man? Custom and Competition in Labour Markets*, Brighton: Wheatsheaf Books.

Marx, K. (1976), *Capital*, Vol. 1, Harmondsworth: Penguin.

Marx, K. and Engels, F. (1998), *The Communist Manifesto: A Modern Edition*, London: Verso.

Paton, N. (2007), 'Why MBA Accreditation is a "Must Have"', The Independent, available at http://www.independent.co.uk/student/postgraduate/mbas-guide/why-mba-accreditation-is-a-must-have-445225.html, accessed 3 March 2009.

Phelps, R.A. and Aggarwal, A.K. (2006), 'Looking for Niches in All the Right Places: Designing an MBA Program for the Next Decade', Journal of College Teaching and Learning, 3, 9: 61–70.

Quality Assurance Agency for Higher Education (nd) 'A brief guide to QAA's involvement in degree-awarding powers and university title' http://www.qaa.ac.uk/reviews/dap/briefGuideDAP.asp, accessed 1 December 2008.

Rubery, J. and Grimshaw, D. (2003), The Organization of Employment: An International Perspective, London: Macmillan.

Schofield, P. (1996), 'The MBA: Managers Only, Please', Accountancy, 117, 1233: 40–42.

Sisson, K. (2006a), 'Responding to Mike Emmott: What "Industrial Relations" suggests should be at the heart of "employee relations"', available at http://buira.org.uk/index.php?option=com_docman&task=doc_view&gid=103, accessed 13 December 2008.

Sisson, K. (2006b), 'Industrial Relations in outline: Annex to "Responding to Mike Emmott"', http://buira.org.uk/index.php?option=com_docman&task=doc_view&gid=104, accessed 13 December 2008.

Sisson, K. (2007), Revitalising industrial relations: making the most of the "institutional turn", Warwick Papers in Industrial Relations, Number 85, http://www2.warwick.ac.uk/fac/soc/wbs/research/irru/wpir/wpir_85.pdf, accessed 30 January 2009.

Sisson, K. and Marginson, P. (2001), ' "Soft Regulation" – Travesty of the Real Thing or New Dimension?' http://www.one-europe.ac.uk/pdf/w32marginson.pdf, accessed 30 November 2008.

Smith, P. and Morton, G. (2001), 'New Labour s Reform of Britain's Employment Law: The Devil is not only in the Detail but in the Values and Policy Too', British Journal of Industrial Relations, 39, 1: 119–138.

Standing, G. (2008), 'The ILO: An Agency for Globalization?', Development and Change, 39, 3: 355–384.

Stella, N.G. and Spooner K. (2007) 'From IR to HRM: Thank God for AACSB!', New Zealand Journal of Employment Relations (Online) 32, 2: 69–86.

Streeck, W. (2003), 'Social Science and Moral Dialogue', Socio-Economic Review, 1 (1): 126–129.

Streeck, W. and Schmitter, P.C. (1985), eds, Private Interest Government: Beyond Market and State, London: Sage.

Sturgess, J., Simpson, R. and Altman, Y. (2003), 'Capitalizing on Learning: An Exploration of the MBA as a Vehicle for Developing Career Competencies', International Journal of Training and Development, 7, 1: 53–66.

Vaughn, J. (2002), 'Accreditation, Commercial Rankings, and New Approaches to Assessing the Quality of University Research and Education Programmes in the United States', Higher Education in Europe, 27, 4: 433–441.

Walker, I. and Zhu, Y. (2007), 'The Labour Market Effects of Qualifications: A Summary of Research Produced for Futureskills Scotland', available at http://www.scotland.gov.uk/Resource/Doc/919/0065443.pdf, accessed 22 January 2009.

part 3

Substantive developments in the employment relationship

12

Earnings inequality and employment

Peter Turnbull and Victoria Wass

National income per person has more than doubled in Britain since the 1950s. But despite our growing wealth, Britain is not a happy society. To be sure, as *individuals* our happiness increases with wealth, but as western *societies* have become richer over the past 50 years they have not become any happier. According to Richard Layard (2005: 3), this is the paradox at the heart of our lives. If people work longer hours, sacrifice their leisure time and family life, or simply work harder, then they raise their own relative income (which they like), but they lower the relative income of other people (which those people dislike). In this way, the aspiration to better one's own position imposes an 'external dis-benefit' on others (ibid.: 153). As a result, for society as whole, the struggle for relative income can be totally self-defeating (Blanchflower and Oswald, 2004). Inequality, it seems, has an adverse effect on us all, whether rich or poor.

According to Wilkinson and Pickett (2009: 29), we have come to the end of what higher material living standards can offer us. In fact, as we strive for greater material wealth in liberal market economies (LMEs), we find ourselves anxiety-ridden, prone to depression, worried about how others see us, unsure of our friendships, driven to consume and with little or no community life. Lacking the relaxed social contact and emotional satisfaction we all need, we seek comfort in over eating, obsessive shopping and spending, or become prey to excessive alcohol, psychoactive medicines and illegal drugs (ibid.: 3).

These are the principal manifestations of what the Conservative Party has labelled our 'broken society' (Social Justice Policy Group, 2006, 2007). To mend our 'broken society', the Conservative Party has proposed no less than 190 policy measures. But nowhere in their Report on *Ending the Costs of Social Breakdown* is there any extended discussion of inequality, despite the fact that inequality seems to make people so unhappy (Layard, 2005) and societies so dysfunctional across a wide range of outcomes (Wilkinson and Pickett, 2009).

Britain used to be one of the most equal of developed nations. Today it is one of the most unequal (Brewer et al., 2009: 24; Lansley, 2009: 5; Wilkinson and Pickett, 2009: 17). In the immediate post–World War II period, British society resembled a 'pyramid' with a small and privileged elite at the top, a larger but still relatively small and comfortable middle class, and a large working class at the bottom. By the end of the 1970s, with increasing affluence and the long-term decline of the manual working class, Britain had moved closer to a 'diamond' shape with a relatively small group of rich and poor at the top and the bottom and a much fatter middle. Since then, the economy has witnessed a meteoric rise in the 'super rich' and a much greater concentration of the population by income in the bottom half of the distribution. Britain is now more unequal than at any time since modern records began. Inequality in Britain today is pervasive (evident across all important sub-groups), cumulative (over the course of a life time) and hereditary (across generations) (National Equality Panel, 2010).

Statistically, growing inequality is primarily the result of those at the top of the earnings distribution doing better than all the rest. As we demonstrate in the following section, as the rich became progressively richer over the past 30 years, those at the bottom were left behind. But why are those at the top doing so (relatively) well and those at the bottom so (relatively) badly? As Goos and Manning (2007) and others (e.g. Lansley, 2008) have asked, why has there been an increase in 'lousy jobs' (mainly in low-paying service occupations) together with a larger increase in 'lovely jobs' (mainly in professional and managerial occupations in finance and business services) and a decline in the number of middling jobs (mainly clerical jobs and skilled manual jobs in manufacturing)? Conventional economic wisdom focuses on a decline in demand for unskilled labour as jobs in sectors such as clothing and textiles are relocated overseas (see Jenkins and Turnbull in this volume) but more importantly as a result of skill-biased technological change and compositional shifts in the labour market towards sectors using information technology (Berman et al., 1998; Machin and Van Reenen, 1998; Nickell and Van Reenen, 2001). However, while the returns to skill and education have certainly increased in recent years, which explains much of the rise in 'upper tail' inequality, it cannot fully explain the changing pattern of inequality in the 'lower tail' of the income distribution. Nor can it fully explain increasing inequality within clearly defined occupational groups.

Skill-biased technological change is not only at odds with the type of inequality observed in the labour market but also its timing (i.e. inequality accelerated before the widespread introduction of information and communication technologies) (see Card and DiNardo, 2002). Changes in the role of labour market institutions also matter, most notably the decline of trade union membership, the shrinking coverage of collective agreements and the decentralization of collective bargaining, as well as the weakening (1980s) and abolition (1993) of the wages councils and the later (1999) introduction of a National Minimum Wage (NMW). Unions act to compress wage differentials, both within and between occupations (Metcalf, 2005; Turnbull, 2003), while the NMW has provided sizeable relative wage gains for lower paid workers in recent years (Dickens and Manning, 2004). The impact of labour market institutions is consistent across developed countries, at least in respect on income inequality. As Freeman (2008: 651) demonstrates, 'For all the difficulties in pining down the impact of institutions on aggregate economic performance across countries, analyses have found that institutions have a major impact on one important outcome: the distribution of income'.

The statistical analysis presented in the following section explores all these changes in earnings and employment both between and within occupational groups over the period 1975–2008. However, exploring inequality *within* society – across individuals and jobs/occupations – overlooks a potentially more telling question: why do some developed countries manage to achieve far greater equality? The answer to this questions lies with politics, not economics. In the 1980s, Mrs Thatcher implored us all to 'glory in inequality' as the neo-liberal mantra dictates that 'there needs to be fear and greed in the system to make it tick' (Hutton, 1996: 173), the former to prevent dependency and the latter to encourage enterprise and efficiency. However, contrary to neo-liberal economic theory, the benefits failed to 'trickle down' – a rising tide does not lift all boats equally – and a New Labour government was elected in 1997 on the promise of 'fairness' and 'governing for the many, not the few'. Initially, equity-oriented policies were the order of the day (e.g. a 10 per cent tax band, tax credits for working families and a National Minimum Wage) and Mr Blair's government presided over a reduction in the growth of inequality, especially during Labour's second term in office. But since 2004–05 inequality has increased, such that the level of inequality in 2008 was higher than when Labour came to power (Brewer et al., 2009). In the words of Peter Mandelson, New Labour was 'intensely relaxed about people getting filthy rich'. Greed, it seems, 'has become acceptable, indeed imperative' (Lansley, 2009: 12).

Following our review of the statistical evidence on earnings inequality, we therefore turn to the role of labour market institutions and the political abandonment of equality in Britain over the past 30 years. During what Standing (1999) describes as the 'egalitarian age' of the immediate post–World War II period, the employment relationship was built on the foundations of efficiency, equity and voice: 'A productive workforce provides the economic resources for equitable working conditions that include employee voice in decision making. And equitable treatment and employee participation can provide the avenues for reducing turnover, increasing employee commitment, and harnessing workers' ideas for improving productivity and quality' (Budd, 2004: 1). The impact of favouring efficiency *at the expense of* equality and employee voice is clear for all to see: an unprecedented rise in earnings inequality and the emergence of a 'representation gap' at work (Heery, this volume; Towers, 1997). The result is our 'broken society' (Wilkinson and Pickett, 2009), which now resembles a caravan crossing the desert, with the sheikhs and their entourage at the front and the 'working poor' at the back: 'When the front and the back are stretched so far apart, at what point can they no longer be said to be travelling together at all, breaking the community between them?' (Toynbee, 2003: 3–4).

Inequality in the labour market

Our first task is to describe the surge in earnings inequality that occurred over the last 30 years. If we measure the rise in living standards by the growth in real earnings,[1] that is the growth in earnings (Average Earnings Index) above the growth in prices (Retail Prices Index), then living standards have increased by an average of 1.40 per cent in each year between 1975 and 2008. This growth has not, however, been equally spread across the workforce. Earnings growth for the lowest wage earners (as defined by the threshold level of earnings under which the lowest 10 per cent of earnings lie) were on average 1.20 per cent per annum compared to 1.72 per cent per annum for those on the threshold of the highest 10 per cent of earners. Growth is a cumulative process which, rather like compound interest, builds on itself over successive years. An average difference in growth rates of 0.52 percentage points in each year over a period of 33 years means that the earnings distribution at the end of the period was far more unequal than it had been at the beginning. Table 12.1 reports earnings growth across the distribution of gross weekly earnings at the decile and quartile percentile points to illustrate how different earnings groups have fared in recent years. Earnings growth is measured as aggregate averages annualized

Table 12.1 Annual average growth rates (%) for nominal and real gross weekly earnings across the earnings distribution, UK 1975–2008

Percentile	10	20	25	30	40	50	60	70	75	80	90	RPI
1975–2008												
Nominal	7.12	7.01	7.00	6.99	7.02	7.10	7.19	7.30	7.36	7.42	7.68	5.54
Real	1.20	1.09	1.08	1.07	1.10	1.17	1.26	1.36	1.42	1.48	1.72	
1975–1979												
Nominal	13.81	13.71	13.54	13.33	13.32	13.44	13.55	13.52	13.48	13.54	13.69	13.50
Real	0.27	0.18	0.03	−0.15	−0.16	−0.05	0.04	0.02	−0.01	0.04	0.17	
1980–1989												
Nominal	7.82	8.02	8.06	8.18	8.38	8.62	8.83	9.05	9.21	9.25	9.68	6.27
Real	1.46	1.64	1.69	1.80	1.98	2.21	2.41	2.61	2.76	2.80	3.21	
1990–1999												
Nominal	4.52	4.53	4,51	4.50	4.46	4.45	4.52	4.64	4.69	4.74	4.87	3.14
Real	1.34	1.35	1.33	1.32	1.28	1.27	1.34	1.45	1.50	1.55	1.68	
2000–2008												
Nominal	3.51	3.29	3.32	3.29	3.33	3.43	3.49	3.60	3.69	3.77	4.09	2.91
Real	0.58	0.37	0.40	0.36	0.40	0.50	0.56	0.67	0.76	0.83	1.14	

Source: New Earnings Survey (NES) Microdata at the Virtual Micro Laboratory (VML), Office for National Statistics; Retail Prices Index (RPI) at www.statistics.gov.uk.

over the specified period, reported in both nominal and real terms for each decade and for the entire period 1975–2008. Full detail of the data sources and methods is provided in Appendix I.

The top two rows of Table 12.1 summarize aggregate average annualized earnings growth (nominal and real) across the distribution over the entire 33 year period and thus include the effects of methodological changes (as detailed in Appendix I). The annual average rate of growth of real earnings at the median level of earnings was 1.17 per cent. It was generally lower than this at earnings levels below the median and higher above. There is clear evidence of the effects of market interventions in low wage labour markets. Earnings growth for employees within the bottom decile was bolstered by the Wages Councils during the 1970s and the National Minimum Wage during the new millennium. Above the median, the annual average growth rate increases as the level of earnings increases. For example, at the 60th percentile the annualized average rate of growth is 0.09 percentage points above that at the median level of earnings, rising progressively to 0.55 percentage points above growth at the median at the 90th percentile.

The division of the data into four decades is largely dictated by changes to the definition and collection of data (see Appendix I) but these periods broadly correspond to Labour (1974–79), Conservative (1979–97) and New Labour governments (1997 to date). During the last half of the 1970s price and wage inflation were both high by historical standards. Real earnings growth was low and was negative for those employees earning between the 30th and 50th percentiles. Importantly, given later events, earnings growth was slightly higher at low levels of earnings than it was at high levels of earnings. This compression in the earnings distribution, albeit limited, has been attributed to the effects of the flat rate incomes policies implemented by the Labour government of 1974–78 (see Blackaby, 1978; Peden, 1985).

The decade of the 1980s witnessed a complete reversal of these earlier trends. Inflation was brought under control through a policy of aggressive deflation, with a reduction from 12 per cent between 1980 and 1981 to 4 per cent between 1987 and 1988. Real wage growth was very high, measuring 2.21 per cent per annum at the median (middle) level of earnings. Contrary to previous cyclical behaviour, real earnings growth, measured in absolute and relative terms, was high at the beginning of the 1980s despite the recession and record levels of unemployment. In comparison to annualized average growth at the median level of earnings, earnings growth was on average 0.75 percentage points lower at the 10th percentile and a full 1 percentage point higher at the 90th percentile. Across the earnings range, it was more than twice as high for those earning at the 90th percentile of the earnings distribution (3.21 per cent) than it was for those at the 10th percentile (1.46 per cent). As the data in Table 12.1 reveal, above median earnings begin to accelerate away from the centre and, in contrast to later years, the bottom of the distribution is allowed to fall away. It is no coincidence that during this decade of growing inequality, the regulatory framework that had previously governed wage setting was systematically dismantled.[2]

Average annual inflation rates during the 1990s were half those recorded over the 1980s and real wage growth, measured at the median level of earnings, reduced from 2.21 per cent per annum to 1.27 per cent per annum. During the 1990s, high earnings were still growing faster than were low earnings but the growth differential was much lower than in the previous decade (1.34 per cent per annum at the 10th percentile compared to 1.68 per cent per annum at the 90th percentile). Moreover, above-average growth was confined to those in the top third of the earnings distribution. Those in the bottom two-thirds experienced similar earnings growth across the distribution with those in the middle doing slightly worse than those at the bottom. By 1997, and the change of government, the pace of increasing inequality had already slowed. With the differential in the growth of earnings between the working rich and the working poor now at a much less alarming level, the focus of policy makers shifted from inequality to exclusion (i.e. to those 'left behind'). The incoming Labour government sought to fulfil its election promises for a fairer society with rather modest social policies directed exclusively to the poorest working families. The impact of government policy, as observed in the dispersion of earnings, has been correspondingly modest and has been limited to the bottom decile of earnings.

In the first 9 years of the new millennium, price and wage inflation continued to fall, but at a slower rate. Real wage inflation more than halved again from its average across the previous decade to 0.50 per cent per annum at the median. In a pattern similar to that of the 1990s, earnings between the 60–70th percentile marks a dividing point from which earnings growth accelerates away for the upper third of the distribution. The annual average growth rate at the 90th percentile is three times that at the 20th and 30th percentiles. At the start of the millennium, minimum wages were given a boost by the Low Pay Commission and this is reflected in above-average earnings growth for those below the 10th percentile, although it remained lower than for those at and above the 70th percentile.

With higher earnings growing more than lower earnings, the gap between the tails of the distribution increased over time and the tails themselves became thicker. The widening gap is depicted in Figure 12.1 which illustrates the distribution of real gross weekly wages in each year between 1975 and 2008. The 25th and 75th percentile points define the 25 per cent tails of the distribution

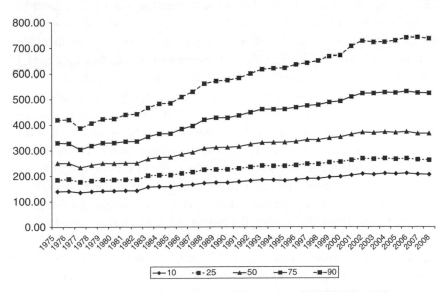

Figure 12.1 Quantile real gross weekly earnings (£), UK 1975–2008
Source: NES at the VML.

and the 10th and the 90th points define the thresholds of the 10 per cent tails. The area between the 25th and the 75th percentiles marks out the middle 50 per cent of the earnings distribution. There is a positive skew evident in the distribution of earnings as early as 1975 which is demonstrated by the relatively larger gap between the median and the 75th and the 90th percentiles as compared to the median and the 25th and the 10th percentiles. As a result of differential growth rates at different points in the distribution this gap increases progressively over time, most especially in the top quarter and top tenth of the distribution. There is a positive relationship between earnings levels and earnings growth which is apparent from the early 1980s and which is responsible for what Atkinson (2000a: 379) describes as a 'fanning out' at the top of the distribution.

An alternative way of representing the data is to look at summary measures of inequality using percentile ratios. Three ratios are reported in Table 12.2 to illustrate the widening distribution of earnings: the 90th/10th measures widening across the whole distribution, the 90th/50th measures widening in the top half of the distribution and the 50th/10th measures widening in the bottom half of the distribution. Table 12.2 also reports the standard deviation as a single summary measure of dispersion, having first transformed real weekly earnings to natural logarithms. Once again, the data (all measures) reveal a small reduction in earnings inequality between 1975 and 1979. From 1980 to 2008, the standard deviation of log earnings increases from 0.41 to 0.52, an increase of 27 per cent. The same percentage increase is recorded in the ratio between the 90th and the 10th percentiles. However, when we divide the distribution at the median level of earnings, the increase in inequality is seen to be considerably higher in the upper half of the distribution (a 19 per cent increase) compared to the lower half (a 6 per cent increase).

While the bottom fell away from the middle during the 1980s, subsequent efforts to shore up the earnings of the low paid have been successful, at least in keeping them attached to the middle. However, it is the behaviour of above-median earnings that has been driving inequality since the mid 1990s. The rise of the 'super-rich' has attracted considerable media interest in recent years – leading to the inevitable contrast between the 'haves' and the 'have yachts' – but there has been far less public policy debate on the impact of this group on society as a whole. To be sure, the pay of executives has attracted considerable attention and the 'credit crunch' has certainly focused the spotlight on the salaries and bonuses of the super-rich, most notably those in the City of London where salaries are more than double the UK average and 60 per cent more than the London average (Lansley, 2009: 20). But politicians are now far more relaxed about the super-rich – we might no longer be implored to

Table 12.2 Inequality measures based on real weekly earnings, 1975–2008

Year	Percentile ratio 90/10	Percentile ratio 90/50	Percentile ratio 50/10	sd log wage
1975*	3.00	1.68	1.79	0.44
1976*	2.98	1.68	1.77	0.43
1977*	2.86	1.66	1.72	0.42
1978*	2.92	1.67	1.74	0.43
1979*	2.99	1.69	1.77	0.44
1980	2.81	1.68	1.67	0.41
1981*	3.07	1.76	1.75	0.45
1982*	3.10	1.77	1.76	0.45
1983	2.97	1.75	1.70	0.43
1984	3.04	1.77	1.72	0.44
1985	3.06	1.77	1.73	0.44
1986	3.10	1.78	1.74	0.45
1987	3.17	1.81	1.76	0.46
1988	3.25	1.82	1.79	0.47
1989	3.27	1.83	1.79	0.48
1990	3.30	1.84	1.79	0.48
1991	3.28	1.85	1.78	0.48
1992	3.30	1.85	1.79	0.48
1993	3.33	1.86	1.79	0.49
1994	3.37	1.87	1.80	0.49
1995	3.41	1.87	1.82	0.50
1996	3.42	1.89	1.80	0.50
1997	3.37	1.87	1.80	0.50
1998	3.41	1.90	1.80	0.50
1999	3.40	1.91	1.78	0.50
2000	3.38	1.90	1.78	0.50
2001	3.47	1.94	1.79	0.51
2002	3.48	1.96	1.78	0.51
2003	3.49	1.95	1.79	0.51
2004**	3.43	1.94	1.77	0.50
2005**	3.48	1.96	1.77	0.51
2006**	3.49	1.98	1.77	0.51
2007**	3.56	2.02	1.76	0.51
2008**	3.56	2.00	1.77	0.52

Source: New Earnings Survey (NES) Microdata at the Virtual Micro Laboratory (VML), Office for National Statistics.
Note: * Includes youth rates.
** Annual Survey of Hours and Earning (ASHE) methodology includes new questionnaire and imputation of missing values.

'glory in inequality', as Mrs Thatcher entreated us all to do, but we are certainly cautioned against the 'politics of envy'.

The fact that the growth in earnings inequality is concentrated at the top of the earnings distribution is clearly consistent with explanations which focus on an increasing demand and supply of knowledge-based and technical skills, but is this sufficient to explain rising inequality? One way to explore the impact of knowledge-based technological change is to focus on occupational groups. Occupation combines qualitative and quantitative aspects of skill and disaggregating the growth in earnings dispersion by occupation allows us to examine the various mechanisms by which a changing skills mix and changing rewards to different skills can influence the spread of earnings at the aggregate level. Empirically, the growth in the dispersion of aggregate earnings can be decomposed initially into that part which is driven by an increase in the earnings gap between defined groups, what we call 'between group' differentials. It is this increasing gap, between high paying occupations, such as senior managers, and low-paid occupations, such as teaching assistants and cleaning staff that we generally think of as causing greater earnings dispersion. Formally, occupational earnings differentials can be measured by the difference between the mean of a particular occupational group (j) and the aggregate mean for all workers ($\overline{W}j - \overline{W}$). There is also the distribution of wages *within* a defined group to consider. This arises because membership of a particular occupational group does not fully determine an individual's earnings or the wage attached to a particular job.[3] Statistically, the 'within group' variance is that part of the distribution of earnings which is not explained by occupational earnings differentials, but rather by other characteristics which are not measured, or at least not accounted for, in the published occupational wage data. A change in the rewards to these unmeasured characteristics can increase the dispersion of wages within an occupational group and in turn increase the dispersion of earnings measured at the aggregate level.

In order to establish the relative importance of occupational differentials *between* Standard Occupational Classifications (SOCs) and earnings variance *within* occupational groups in generating an earnings distribution, the total variance in earnings in each year can be decomposed into its separate 'between' and 'within' components as follows:

$$\sigma_t^2 = \sum_t o_{jt}\sigma_{jt}^2 + \sum_j o_{jt}(\bar{w}_{jt} - \bar{w}_t)^2 \qquad (1)$$

Where: σ_t^2 is the cross-section variance of aggregate log earnings in year t, o_{jt} the employment share of occupation j (where j $1 = 9$) in year t, σ_{jt}^2 the intra-occupational variance of log earnings within occupation j in year t, $\bar{w}_{jt}$ the mean level of log earnings in occupation j in year t, and $\bar{w}_t$ the mean aggregate level of log earnings in year t.

The first term is the 'within' occupational earnings variance, σ_{jt}^2, weighted by the employment share of that occupational group, o_{jt}. The second term is the earnings gap between the occupational mean and the aggregate mean $(\bar{w}_{jt} - \bar{w}_t)$ again weighted by the employment share of that wage gap, o_{jt}.

Table 12.3 compares inter-occupational wage differentials and intra-occupational wage dispersion between nine broadly defined occupational groups between 1975 and 2005 at 5-year intervals. Occupational groups are defined at the one-digit level with descriptions under the SOC 90 and SOC 2000 reported in Appendix II. Aggregate average earnings for all occupations and the variance in earnings (in italics) are reported in the first column. The

Table 12.3 Occupational log wage differentials and intra-occupational log wage dispersion, UK 1975–2005

SOC	All occupations	1	2	3	4	5	6	7	8	9
1975*	5.51	0.28	0.36	0.12	−0.27	0.05	−0.11	−0.24	0.01	−0.11
	0.20	*0.22*	*0.14*	*0.18*	*0.12*	*0.15*	*0.18*	*0.41*	*0.13*	*0.14*
1980*	5.55	0.28	0.28	0.14	−0.26	0.05	−0.11	−0.18	−0.01	−0.16
	0.17	*0.18*	*0.13*	*0.16*	*0.37*	*0.12*	*0.19*	*0.21*	*0.16*	*0.14*
1985*	5.62	0.32	0.32	0.13	−0.24	0.02	−0.10	−0.16	−0.12	−0.21
	0.19	*0.46*	*0.13*	*0.18*	*0.10*	*0.14*	*0.23*	*0.23*	*0.13*	*0.14*
1990*	5.76	0.34	0.36	0.20	−0.26	−0.01	−0.16	−0.19	−0.11	−0.26
	0.24	*0.28*	*0.13*	*0.21*	*0.11*	*0.15*	*0.21*	*0.25*	*0.14*	*0.16*
1991	5.77	0.35	0.38	0.18	−0.24	−0.03	−0.19	−0.21	−0.12	−0.28
	0.23	*0.28*	*0.13*	*0.18*	*0.11*	*0.15*	*0.22*	*0.24*	*0.14*	*0.15*
1995	5.82	0.37	0.38	0.18	−0.25	−0.04	−0.26	−0.24	−0.14	−0.31
	0.25	*0.28*	*0.14*	*0.19*	*0.11*	*0.16*	*0.22*	*0.24*	*0.15*	*0.18*
2000	5.90	0.39	0.36	0.17	−0.30	−0.06	−0.27	−0.29	−0.16	−0.33
	0.25	*0.52*	*0.14*	*0.17*	*0.08*	*0.14*	*0.19*	*0.21*	*0.13*	*0.13*
2005**	5.96	0.43	0.40	0.14	−0.26	−0.06	−0.41	−0.47	−0.15	−0.36
	0.27	*0.56*	*0.17*	*0.15*	*0.10*	*0.14*	*0.10*	*0.11*	*0.12*	*0.13*

Source: New Earnings Survey (NES) Microdata at the Virtual Micro Laboratory (VML), Office for National Statistics.
Note:
* Includes youth rates.
** Annual Survey of Hours and Earning (ASHE) methodology includes new questionnaire and imputation of missing values.
Wage gap measured by $\bar{W}_j - \bar{W}$ where j is one-digit occupational group and wages are in logs.
Wage dispersion measured by σ^2 (variance) of the log wage.

differences between the aggregate average level of earnings and that for each of the nine occupational groups are reported across each row. Earnings are measured in natural logarithms. The variance in earnings by occupational group is reported in italics.

Reading down the first column of Table 12.3, we observe a large increase in overall earnings inequality which is concentrated during the 1980s. At the intra-occupational level (subsequent columns), there is a notably large increase in earnings variance for SOC 1 (Managers and Senior Officials) but not for the other broadly defined groups. In fact the dispersion of earnings within clerical and retail occupations falls (SOC 4 & 7). Turning to the inter-occupational level, we observe that in the occupational hierarchy in 1975, managers and senior officials and professionals (SOC 1 & 2) earn a large earnings premium while administrative, clerical and retail workers (SOC 4 & 7) suffer a large pay penalty (row 1). Combining rows and columns to consider changes in the pay gap over time and across occupational groups, we observe that earnings for managers and engineers increase relative to the mean while there is a large decline in relative earnings for all manual workers (craft, semi- and unskilled) (SOC 5 & 8) and for employees in personal services (SOC 6). The pay hierarchy in 2005 is still topped by managers and professionals but they are further away from the middle. Personal services (SOC 6) and semi-skilled manual workers (SOC 8) have joined clerical and administrative employees (SOC 4) and retail staff (SOC 7) at the bottom with a big pay penalty. In 1990, for the first time, the craft premium turns into a penalty when craft wages (SOC 5) dip below the average wage.

The evidence in Table 12.3 is basically consistent with an increased role for skill in pay determination, most especially knowledge-based skills and technical skills. Overall, skilled white collar employees have become better paid over time than manual workers at all skill levels and workers in personal services have become worse paid relative to the mean. Furthermore, it is increases in between group pay gaps, rather than any increase in intra-occupational earnings variance, which appear to account for most of the increase in variance measured at the aggregate level, with the exception of a large increase in the earnings dispersion for the skilled non-manual employees in SOC 1. To explore this further, an alternative approach is to identify that part of the wage distribution which can be explained by occupational earnings differentials and that part which is due to differential returns to other factors. Formally, this is achieved by regressing individual log earnings on nine occupational dummy variables and then comparing the proportion of the earnings variance explained by occupation (based upon the R^2 statistic) with the residual, or unexplained, proportion. The former represents the contribution to

Table 12.4 The proportion of earnings variance 'explained' by occupation, 1975–2008

	Total variance	Percentage 'explained' by occupation	Percentage 'unexplained' by occupation
1975	0.192	0.202	0.798
1979	0.192	0.187	0.813
1980	0.170	0.204	0.796
1990	0.231	0.249	0.751
1991	0.233	0.264	0.736
2001	0.255	0.335	0.665
2002	0.258	0.368	0.632
2008	0.266	0.371	0.629

Source: New Earnings Survey (NES) Microdata at the Virtual Micro Laboratory (VML), Office for National Statistics.

overall earnings inequality of the 'between' group earnings gap and the latter represents the contribution of 'within' group inequality. Annual regression results are reported in Table 12.4, indicating that occupation accounts for a relatively small proportion of the dispersion of earnings before the election of Mrs Thatcher's government (19 per cent in 1979) but this proportion has increased very considerably over the past 30 years (to 37 per cent in 2008). Some caution is required when interpreting this result over the full period because part of the measured increased contribution from occupation is likely to have arisen from the two occupational reclassifications in 1991 and in 2001 (see Appendix II). As reported in Table 12.4, there is a step jump in the 'explained' variance cither side of the occupational reclassification between 1990–91 and 2001–02. Repeating these calculations for every year in the data period reveals that the proportion of the increasing earnings variance which is accounted for by inter-occupational earnings differentials increases until 2004, after which it levels off.

A further consideration for any analysis of inequality is the impact of the shifts in the composition of employment (e.g. the decline of skilled manual work in the manufacturing sector and the growth of low skilled, low paid work in the service sector) (see Newell, 2007). A shift in the composition of employment at the occupational level could generate an increase in measured earnings inequality even if there were no change in the underlying earnings structure. This can occur through two channels in equation (1). There is a potential 'between' group effect where the earnings gap between the occupational mean and the aggregate mean is different and there is an employment shift into the group in which earnings are further from the mean (either higher or lower). There is a second potential 'within' group effect, because if within group earnings dispersion varies across occupations and there is a shift in employment towards an occupational group where earnings are more unequal, then the variance of wages measured at the aggregate level would increase. In order to measure the relative magnitude of these employment effects, relative to earnings effects, the following analysis uses a further decomposition of equation (1). A first difference of equation (1) generates equation (2) in which the four components we wish to distinguish are identified.

$$\Delta\sigma^2 = \sum_j o_{jt}\Delta\sigma_j^2 + \sum_j \sigma_{jt}^2\Delta o_j - \sum_j (\bar{w}_j - \bar{w})_t \Delta o_j - \sum_j o_{jt}\Delta(\bar{w}_j - \bar{w})$$
$$\text{(i)} \qquad\qquad \text{(ii)} \qquad\qquad \text{(iii)} \qquad\qquad\qquad \text{(iv)}$$
$$(2)$$

Where: (i) is the change in earnings variance within occupational groups, (ii) the employment shift between occupational groups of differing within group variance, (iii) the employment shift between occupational groups of different earnings gap, (iv) the change in earnings gap between occupational groups.

The results of this decomposition are reported in Table 12.5 for the same time periods used in Table 12.4.

Table 12.5 reinforces the earlier observation that most of the expansion in the earnings distribution occurred during the 1980s. This was primarily driven by an increase in 'within group' earnings dispersion but also by the earnings gap between occupational groups. As trade unions declined and collective bargaining was decentralized (from industry-wide to company-based agreements) and new forms of individualism entered the workplace (e.g. personal contracts and individual performance-based pay), earnings dispersion increased in all occupational groups, with the exception of professionals and personal services, both of which have a relatively large proportion of public sector employment (where unions remain strong and collective bargaining still dominates wage setting). There was also a sizable increase in employment in managerial (SOC 1) and associated professional and technical

Table 12.5 Double decomposition of growth in variance of earnings, 1975–2008

	Change in total variance	(i)	(ii)	(iii)	(iv)
1975–1979	0.04	0.16	0.14	0.10	−0.37
1980–1990	5.65	3.26	0.29	0.39	1.70
1991–2001	2.14	−0.90	0.62	0.51	1.91
2002–2008	0.55	0.24	0.32	0.60	−0.62

Source: New Earnings Survey (NES) Microdata at the Virtual Micro Laboratory (VML), Office for National Statistics.

(SOC 3) occupational groups, both of which are characterized by above average earnings and the former by a particularly large and rising earnings gap over other occupational groups. In the decade that followed, the growth in overall variance is half the rate recorded during the 1980s. The increase in earnings variance is driven primarily by the change in earnings gap between occupational groups and relative growth in employment in occupations characterized by a high earnings differential, the top three one digit SOC groups. From 2002, the increase in earnings inequality is relatively modest. At the inter-occupational level of analysis, the effect of rising occupational pay differentials is offset by a movement in jobs from high to low wage gap occupations. At the intra-occupational level, increasing within group variance and an employment shift towards high variance occupations both contribute to the increase in aggregate earnings inequality.

The pattern of growth of earnings dispersion within as well as between occupational groups does not sit well with conventional wisdom on inequality, which as Atkinson (2000b) demonstrates relies far too heavily on a presumed shift in demand away from unskilled workers. The picture presented in this section is more complex. To be sure, upper tail inequality can in large part be attributed to skill-biased technological change, but not the rise in lower tail inequality in the 1980s (or its subsequent 'bounce back' in the 2000s) (Machin, 2008). The latter requires attention to labour supply as well as labour demand, because LMEs typically have a more flexible labour market with a large low wage sector, invariably populated by women, ethnic minorities, immigrants, part-timers, temporary workers, agency staff and the like. With much lower social protection in these economies, labour supply is 'inflated', which, in turn, lowers wages as there is more competition for jobs (Esping-Andersen, 1990: 150). Nor can changes between and within occupations be explained simply by changing patterns of labour market demand, as the decomposition presented in Table 12.5 clearly demonstrates. To go beyond the 'Transatlantic consensus' that locates increasing inequality almost exclusively in the demand for labour (Atkinson, 2000b) we need to look beyond the shores of liberal market (Anglo-Saxon) economies to the political choices made by European policymakers and the impact of labour market institutions such as trade unions and collective bargaining.

Markets, institutions and inequality

If rising earnings inequality can be attributed solely to skill-biased technological change and the impact of globalization, which both reduce the demand for unskilled labour in developed economies, then why do labour market outcomes differ so dramatically across countries? For example, the pace at which inequality increased in the United Kingdom in the 1980s was faster than any other developed country, with the exception of New Zealand (another liberal market economy) while the incidence of low pay in the United Kingdom (at almost 22 per cent of the workforce in 2003–05) is double that of France (11 per cent) and approaching three times that of Denmark (8 per cent).[4] When labour market institutions break down or when their ability to coordinate economic activities is reduced, or conversely when market forces are given freer reign, then income inequality increases. As Freeman (2008: 652) and others have demonstrated, 'Movement toward market-determined pay widens earnings distribution. Movement toward more institutional wage determination narrows earnings inequality'.

As a member of the European Union (EU), under Article 136 of the Amsterdam Treaty (1997), the UK government is formally committed to 'the promotion of employment, improved living and working conditions, so as to make possible their harmonization while the improvement is being maintained, proper social protection, dialogue between management and labour, the development of human resources with a view to lasting employment and the combating of exclusion'. In its simplest expression, the European social model represents a commitment to provide all European citizens with a right to work, the right to social protection and the right to civilized standards in the workplace, including a living wage, access to education and training, equality and opportunity and rights to representation and voice at work. To what extent does the United Kingdom meet these expectations, and to what extent does growing inequality make the attainment of such rights more elusive?

The UK and other liberal market economies appear to be relatively successful when it comes to creating jobs (the right to work) as they display much higher employment rates (around 69 per cent) than coordinated (Continental European) or Mediterranean economies (around 62–3 per cent) (Sapir, 2006: 318), although many of the jobs created in the United Kingdom in recent years have been part-time, temporary and low-skilled ('lousy') jobs rather than high-skilled/knowledge-based ('lovely') jobs (Goos and Manning, 2007).[5] More telling is the fact that employment rates in Nordic countries (over 70 per cent) are even higher than the United Kingdom and workers in these countries enjoy much stronger employment protection (via the law) and social protection (via expansive and more generous social benefits) (Freeman, 2008: Hamann and Kelly, 2008; Sapir, 2006). Workers in Nordic countries are also much more likely to be in a position to take advantage of skill-biased technological change as they are far more likely than UK workers to leave secondary education with meaningful qualifications. In general, more unequal societies have worse educational attainment (Wilkinson and Pickett, 2009: 105).

Across a range of equity measures, not just income but also gender, ethnicity, poverty and the like, Nordic and Continental European countries outperform the United Kingdom. The ideal situation, as illustrated in Figure 12.2, is the Nordic combination of equality and efficiency (see also Fellman et al., 2008), which is testament to the observation that 'an economy can only perform well to the extent that it is embedded in a well-integrated society . . . a society exists only to the extent that it is capable of imposing normative constraints, or social obligations, on the pursuit of individual interest' (Streeck, 1997: 199). Across a broad spectrum of countries there is a positive association between balanced income distribution and aggregate economic performance (e.g. Alesina and Rodrik, 1994; Persson and Tabellini, 1994) as well as a host of social outcomes that we all value (Wilkinson and Picket, 2009).

Of particular importance in explaining inequality across countries is the role of labour market institutions, most notably trade unions and collective bargaining. We have already noted that the explosion of inequality in the United Kingdom in the 1980s coincided with the decline of trade unions and collective bargaining. Our dominant method of wage determination is now unilateral pay setting by management (Kersley et al., 2006: 179, 184; Rubery, 1997) whereby CEOs and senior managers deny many workers a living wage while paying themselves huge salaries. In the 1960s, the main basis of pay determination was industrial (multi-employer) collective bargaining. By 2004, industrial agreements covered only 4 per cent of private sector workers (in workplaces with ten or more employees) (Kersley et al., 2006: 186). Almost two-thirds of all workplaces have no trade union members (ibid.: 111) and

EFFICIENCY			
E		Low	High
Q			
U	Low	Mediterranean	Anglo-Saxon
I			
T	High	Continental	Nordic
Y			

Figure 12.2 The efficiency and equity of four European social models
Source: Adapted from Sapir (2006: 380).

aggregate union density in the United Kingdom is now below 30 per cent. Union membership is actually much lower in many other EU Member States, including Germany, France and the Netherlands, but in all these countries the coverage of collective agreements is much higher (typically around 70–90 per cent) because multi-employer bargaining still prevails. Union density and collective bargaining have been found to be the single most important factors influencing wage inequality across institutional contexts, inasmuch as unions consistently produce more egalitarian outcomes (Metcalf, 1982; Rueda and Pontusson, 2000) and more centralized collective bargaining leads to lower degrees of wage dispersion (Wallerstein, 1999; see also European Commission, 2009: 89; Freeman, 2008: 651; Hamann and Kelly, 2008: 139; OECD, 2004: 160–1; Weeks, 2005).

Given the continuities of industrial relations policy from Thatcherism to New Labour (Howell, 2005: 215), famously expressed by Tony Blair in the foreword to *Fairness at Work* where he stated in no uncertain terms that even after his government's Employment Relations Act (1999) 'Britain [will] still have the most lightly regulated labour market of any leading economy in the world' (Department of Trade & Industry, 1998), is it any surprise that our society is broken by inequality? There is now a democratic deficit in the United Kingdom's socio-economic institutions that protects inequality, (re)enforces hierarchy and damages our experience of work. Socio-economic policies have systematically undermined the foundations of labour market equality over the past 30 years (e.g. restrictive trade union laws, a decline in the 'progressivity' of national tax structures, a reduction in expenditure on universal social programmes, and a concentration of power in the boardrooms of leading corporations) but as yet there is no clearly articulated radical critique to provide the language, or the resources, to oppose growing inequality. During the mid- to late-1980s and the early 1990s when inequality was growing fastest, British social attitudes were increasingly in favour of redistribution from the better off to those who were less well off, but since the election of New Labour support for redistribution has plummeted to a new low (Georgiadis and Manning, 2007). Fewer people, it seems, now believe in the 'class war' – the idea that there is one law for the poor and one for the rich, or that big business benefits owners at the expense of workers (ibid.) – despite the steady fall in the share of wages in GDP and the corresponding rise in the share of profits. As a result, inequality is increasingly viewed as both socially and politically acceptable by the electorate (Pahl et al., 2007). According to André Sapir, Chair of the Independent High-Level Study Group established on the initiative of the President of the European Union to establish 'An Agenda for a Growing Europe' (Sapir et al., 2003), the United Kingdom's social model is sustainable not simply because it is 'efficient' – in terms of its ability to generate jobs, regardless of whether they are lovely or lousy – but because inequality is now politically acceptable:

> Models that are not efficient are simply not sustainable in the face of growing strains on public finances coming from globalization, technological change and population ageing ... On the other hand, models that are not equitable can be perfectly sustainable, provided they are efficient. The reason is that, at least in Europe (but also obviously in America), the degree of equity of a social model reflects a viable political choice.
>
> (Sapir, 2006: 380–1)

In a comparative international context, the political persuasion of the government (left or right) is found to matter for wage inequality, especially in LMEs (Rueda and Pontusson, 2000: 380), which makes the failure of New Labour to reverse inequality all the more alarming.[6] As Brady (2009) demonstrates in his recent study of 18 rich nations over the period 1969–2002, the fundamental cause of those at the bottom being left behind is politics, or more precisely institutionalized political perspectives about the poor, the uneducated, the low skilled, *inter alia*, that in turn determines the nature, scope and generosity of state welfare programmes, active labour market policies, the national minimum wage, etc. If the national minimum wage is compared to average earnings, for example, then the United Kingdom has a much lower (relative) minimum wage than other EU-15 countries (Schulten, 2007).[7]

Politicians are hardly troubled by our apparent indifference to the plight of the low paid, but public outrage over 'fat cat' salaries and bankers' bonuses might well be sufficient to push inequality back onto the political agenda. The vast majority of people in the United Kingdom currently regard income differences as too big, even though most underestimate how large income differences actually are (Orton and Rowlingson, 2007). Those on 'middle incomes' are especially likely to agree that 'ordinary working people do not get their fair share of the nation's wealth' (Lansley, 2009: 39). As yet, however, there is still no significant political support for redistribution or even recognized forms of representation at work, such as trade unionism, that might redress some of the inequalities that now blight British society.

Conclusions

Inequality 'gets under our skin' (Wilkinson and Pickett, 2009: 31–45) because we try to defend our 'social self' from any 'social evaluative threat' (Dickerson and Kemeny, 2004). In a liberal market economy characterized by the rampant growth of individualism, income is a primary measure of how we are valued, and how we value others. Simply put, our income is a 'badge of status'. As a result, our interpretation of a 'fair day's pay for a fair day's work' extends beyond our assessment of inputs (e.g. time, effort, skill, loyalty, commitment, adaptability, flexibility, tolerance, enthusiasm and personal sacrifice) versus outputs (e.g. salary, job security, esteem, recognition, reputation, sense of achievement and simple thanks) to also include comparisons with 'referent others'. As Adams (1965) pointed out, equity does not depend simply on our input-to-output ratio alone, it also depends on the comparisons between our ratio and the ratio of others. This is why our own promotion or pay rise can have a de-motivating effect on others and this is why the growth and conspicuous consumption of the 'super-rich' really do matter (Lansley, 2008).

Sadly, in today's society there is a tendency to denigrate those below us, especially those at the bottom of the pile such as people on benefits, refugees, immigrants and asylum-seekers, while we aspire to live the lifestyle of the rich and famous, a condition, or rather an affliction that is variously described as 'luxury fever' (Frank, 1999) or 'affluenza' (James, 2007). As the quality of social relationships deteriorate in 'broken Britain', and as we increasingly use income as a measure of status differences, we all become more dissatisfied with what we have, while working ever harder in a forlorn attempt to realize our aspirations. Many years ago, Thorsten Veblen (1934) argued that consumption is driven by a desire for social standing as well as for the enjoyment of goods and services *per se*. Our desire to live up to the 'conventional standard', which is perpetually raised by the lifestyles of the rich and famous, induces us all to work longer hours, neglect our health, and sacrifice our family-life and leisure time (Bowles and Park, 2005; Wilkinson and Pickett, 2009: 223–4). Inequality has not simply broken British society but made it increasingly difficult to mend.

Disclaimer

This chapter contains statistical data from the Office for National Statistics (ONS) which is Crown copyright and reproduced with the permission of the controller of HMSO and Queen's Printer for Scotland. The use of the ONS statistical data in this work does not imply the endorsement of the ONS in relation to the interpretation or analysis of the statistical data. The chapter uses research data sets which may not exactly reproduce National Statistics aggregates.

Acknowledgements

We would like to thank the Office for National Statistics (ONS) for permission to use individual New Earnings Survey (NES) Panel Data which was accessed through the Virtual Micro Laboratory (VML). The empirical research was undertaken with financial assistance from the Leverhulme Trust (Grant Ref/7/rfg/2007/0268). Neither organization is responsible for the opinions expressed.

Appendix I: Data sources and measures

The information source on earnings is the New Earnings Survey (NES) 1975–2004 and its successor the Annual Survey of Hours and Earnings (ASHE) 2004–2008. The focus of these surveys is the structure of earnings and each provides data for a large sample of employees over a long period of time. The surveys are undertaken annually with a reference point of the first full week in April. The sample is a 1 per cent random sample of employees registered for PAYE where selection is based on National Insurance numbers. The number of observations in each year is around 130,000. The questionnaires are distributed for completion by employers during the summer. Summary statistics are published as a first release in the autumn of the same year. Final statistics are published some 18 months after the survey date. This chapter uses micro (individual) data which are available to approved users for analysis in the Virtual Micro Laboratory (VML) at the Office for National Statistics (ONS).

Earnings are measured as gross weekly pay and the sample is restricted to full-time employees on adult rates of pay whose pay was not affected by absence. The data are collected as weekly earnings and it is this, as opposed to a derived hourly earnings variable, which we use in this chapter. Because we are using weekly earnings, part-time workers are excluded. Self-employed earnings are also excluded because they are not collected. Our interest is in real wage growth and the issue of price inflation is managed by deflating nominal wages to real wages at constant 2000 prices using the monthly RPI measured each April. Earnings-related characteristics are collected in the same survey and include sex, age group, industry, region and occupation.

While the series of surveys provide 33 years of data, each annual survey is intended as a cross-section survey. Changes in methodology and classifications introduce data discontinuities which present difficulties in the context of a long-time series analysis. The first major discontinuity arises in 1980 when employees on youth rates of pay were recorded separately for the first time.

The two subsequent discontinuities affect the analysis by occupation because occupational groups were reclassified in 1991 (to Standard Occupational Classification 1990) and again in 2001 (to Standard Occupational Classification 2000) (see Appendix II). A new and improved survey was launched in 2004 as ASHE and includes changes to the questionnaire, the use of employment weights in the published estimates and data imputation for certain missing values. The choice of periods over which the growth in earnings dispersion is measured is to a large degree governed by the occurrence of these discontinuities.

The aggregate earnings distribution has a strong positive skew reflecting a small number of employees with high levels of earnings, including exceptionally high earnings. It is sufficiently non-symmetrical to preclude the use of parametric techniques (those based on the mean and the standard deviation such as regression analysis) which assume an approximately normal distribution. Empirical studies of earnings which use parametric statistics usually transform earnings data in to their natural logarithm form. The distribution of log earnings is a sufficiently close approximation to the normal to allow the use of parametric statistics. Since our interest is in earnings growth, the log transformation allows us to readily measure proportionate growth.

Appendix II: Standard Occupational Classifications

Prior to 1991, the New Earnings Survey (NES) used a set of occupational codes based on the CODOT classification but specific to the NES. The codes were simply a list of job titles in no particular order and with no hierarchy. The Standard Occupational Classification (SOC) marks a major event in occupational classification with the introduction of an ordered taxonomy of jobs in which narrowly defined jobs at the three-digit level are included within a wider definition at the two-digit level and these are included within a still wider category at the one-digit level. The classification was expanded in SOC 2000 to include a further level, a four digit classification.

For example, Care Assistants and Home Carers (6115) are included within the three-digit group Healthcare and Related Personal Services (611), at the two-digit level within Caring Personal Service Occupations (61) and at the one-digit level within Personal Service Occupations (6). Although SOC 90 and SOC 2000 share the same one-digit labels, as listed below, they have different constituent lower level groups.

SOC 1	Managers and Senior Officials
SOC 2	Professional Occupations
SOC 3	Associate Professionals & Technical Occupations
SOC 4	Administrative & Secretarial Occupations
SOC 5	Skilled trades Occupations
SOC 6	Personal Service Occupations
SOC 7	Sales & Customer Service Occupations
SOC 8	Process Plant and Machine Operatives
SOC 9	Elementary Occupations

The NES adopted SOC 90 in 1991 and SOC 2000 in 2002. For the purpose of data analysis, the occupational codes between 1975 and 1990 are mapped on to the SOC 90 at the two-digit level using a programme developed by Elias and Gregory (1994) and are then aggregated up to the one-digit level. However, the consistency in occupational codes between 1975 and 1991 may be more apparent than real and it is for this reason that any time series analysis that uses occupation is broken down into periods which are not affected by a change in classification. No attempt has been made in this chapter to map SOC 90 on to SOC 2000.

Notes

1. The focus is on earnings rather than income as our primary concern is the labour market and employment relationships. Since household income largely comprises earnings, patterns of inequality are not dissimilar (NEP, 2010).
2. It is worth remembering that pre-1979, the United Kingdom displayed many characteristics of a co-ordinated market economy (CME) rather than a liberal market economy (LME) (e.g. industry-wide collective bargaining, a high proportion of the workforce were covered by collective agreements, the coordination of training at the industry level, and strong internal labour markets that helped firms retain jobs). As Hamman and Kelly (2008: 144) point out, 'Only when Margaret Thatcher ... legislated a series of sweeping reforms in the political economy did Britain metamorphose into a paradigmatic example of an LME'.
3. Nearly two-thirds of all workplaces now conduct regular performance appraisal for most (more than 60 per cent) of all non-managerial employees (compared to less than half in 1998) (Kersley et al., 2006: 87) and there has been a substantial increase in performance-related pay schemes (from 20 per cent of workplaces in 1998 to almost a third in 2004) (ibid.: 101).
4. Low pay is defined as two-thirds of the median (full-time) wage.
5. Rapidly growing 'lousy' jobs (defined principally in terms of pay rather than job content) include care assistants and attendants, educational assistants, hospital ward assistants, hotel porters, window dressers and travel and flight attendants (Goos and Manning, 2007: 124–5).
6. Unless, of course, one accepts that New Labour is no longer a socialist political party.
7. New Member States are the only distinctive group with a lower minimum wage than the United Kingdom. Where there is no national statutory minimum wage (e.g. Austria, Denmark, Finland, Germany, Italy and Sweden), the high coverage of collective agreements ensures a functioning system of agreed minimum wage protection.

References

Adams, J.S. (1965) 'Inequity in Social Exchange', in L. Berkowitz (ed.) *Advances in Experimental Social Psychology*, vol. 2, New York: Academic Press, pp. 267–99.

Alesina, A. and Rodrik, D. (1994) 'Distributive Politics and Economic Growth', *Quarterly Journal of Economics*, 109(May): 465–90.

Atkinson, A.B. (2000a) *The Changing Distribution of Earnings in OEDC Countries*, Oxford: Oxford University Press.

Atkinson, A.B. (2000b) 'The Changing Distribution of Income: Evidence and Explanations', *German Economic Review*, 1(1): 3–18.

Berman, E., Bound, J. and Machin, S. (1998) 'Implications of Skill-Biased Technological Change: International Evidence', *Quarterly Journal of Economics*, 113(4): 1245–80.

Blackaby, F. (1978) 'Incomes Policy', in F. Blackaby (ed.) *British Economic Policy 1960–74*, Cambridge: Cambridge University Press, pp. 360–401.

Blanchflower, D.G. and Oswald, A.J. (2004) 'Well-Being Over Time in Britain and the USA', *Journal of Public Economics*, 88(7–8): 1359–86.

Bowles, S. and Park, Y. (2005) 'Emulation, Inequality, and Work Hours: Was Thorsten Veblen Right?' *Economic Journal*, 115(507): F397–412.

Brady, D. (2009) *Rich Democracies, Poor People: How Politics Explain Poverty*, New York: Oxford University Press.

Brewer, M., Muriel, A., Phillips, D. and Sibieta, L. (2009) *Poverty and Inequality in the UK: 2009*, London: Institute for Fiscal Studies.

Budd, J.W. (2004) *Employment with a Human Face: Balancing Efficiency, Equity and Voice*, Ithaca, NY: Cornell University Press.

Card, D. and DiNardo, J.E (2002) 'Skill Biased Technical Change and Rising Wage Inequality: Some Problems and Puzzles', *Journal of Labor Economics*, 20(4): 733–83.

Department of Trade & Industry (1998) *Fairness at Work*, London: HMSO.

Dickens, R. and Manning, A. (2004) 'The National Minimum Wage and Wage Inequality', *Journal of the Royal Statistical Society Series A*, 167(4): 613–26.

Dickerson, S.S. and Kemeny, M.E. (2004) 'Acute Stressors and Cortisol Responses: A Theoretical Integration and Synthesis of Laboratory Research', *Psychological Bulletin*, 130(3): 355–91.

Elias, P. and M. Gregory (1994) *The Changing Structure of Occupations and Earnings in Great Britain, 1975–1990. An Analysis Based upon the New Earnings Survey Panel Dataset*, Sheffield: Employment Department.

Esping-Andersen, G. (1990) *The Three Worlds of Welfare Capitalism*, Princeton NJ: Princeton University Press.

European Commission (2009) *Industrial Relations in Europe 2008*, Luxembourg: Office for Official Publications of the European Communities.

Fellman, S., Iversen, M.J., Sjögren, H. and Thue, L. (eds) (2008) *Creating Nordic Capitalism: The Business History of a Competitive Periphery*, Houndmills: Palgrave Macmillan.

Frank, R. (1999) *Luxury Fever*, New York: Free Press.

Freeman, R. (2008) 'Labor Market Institutions Around the World', in P. Blyton, N. Bacon, J. Fiorito and E. Heery (eds) *The Sage Handbook of Industrial Relations*, London: Sage, pp. 640–58.

Georgiadis, A. and Manning, A (2007) 'Spend it like Beckham? Inequality and Redistribution in the UK, 1983–2004', Centre for Economic Performance DP 816, London School of Economics and Political Science.

Goos, M. and Manning, A. (2007) 'Lousy and Lovely Jobs: The Rising Polarization of Work in Britain', *Review of Economics and Statistics*, 89(1): 118–33.

Hamann, K. and Kelly, J. (2008) 'Varieties of Capitalism and Industrial Relations', in P. Blyton, N. Bacon, J. Fiorito and E. Heery (eds) *The Sage Handbook of Industrial Relations*, London: Sage, pp. 129–48.

Howell, C. (2005) *Trade Unions and the State: The Construction of Industrial Relations Institutions in Britain, 1890–2000*, Princeton, NJ: Princeton University Press.

Hutton, W. (1996) *The State We're In*, London: Vintage.

James, O. (2007) *Affluenza: How to be Successful and Stay Sane*, London: Vermilion.

Kersley, B., Alpin, C., Forth, J., Bryson, A., Bewley, H., Dix, G. and Oxenbridge, S. (2006) *Inside the Workplace: Findings from the 2004 Workplace Employment Relations Survey*, London: Routledge.

Lansley, S. (2008) *Do the Super-Rich Matter?* Touchstone Pamphlet 4, London: Trades Union Congress.

Lansley, S. (2009) *Life in the Middle: The Untold Story of Britain's Average Earners*, Touchstone Pamphlet 6, London: Trades Union Congress.

Layard, R. (2005) *Happiness: Lessons from a New Science*, London: Allen Lane.

Machin, S. (2008) 'Rising Wage Inequality', *CentrePiece*, Autumn: 8–10.

Machin, S. and Van Reenen, J. (1998) 'Technology and Changes in Skill Structure: Evidence from Seven OECD Countries', *Quarterly Journal of Economics*, 113(3): 1215–44.

Metcalf, D. (1982) 'Unions and the Dispersion of Earnings', *British Journal of Industrial Relations*, 20(2): 170–85.

Metcalf, D. (2005) 'Trade Unions: Resurgence or Perdition? An Economic Analysis', in S. Fernie and D. Metcalf (eds) *Trade Unions: Resurgence or Demise?* London: Routledge, pp. 83–117.

National Equality Panel (2010) *An Anatomy of Economic Inequality in the UK: Report of the National Equality Panel*, London: Government Equalities Office.

Newell, A. (2007) 'Structural Change', in N. Crafts, I. Gazeley and A. Newell (eds) *Work and Pay in 20th Century Britain*, Oxford: Oxford Univesity Press, pp. 35–54.

Nickell, S. and Van Reenan, J. (2001) 'Technological Innovation and Economic Performance in the United Kingdom', in B. Steil, A. Victor and R. Nelson (eds) *Technological Innovation and Economic Performance*, Princeton, NJ: Princeton University Press, pp. 167–99.

Organisation for Economic Cooperation and Development (OECD) (2004) 'Wage Setting Institutions and Economic Performance', in *OECD Employment Outlook 2004*, Paris: Organisation for Economic Cooperation and Development.

Orton, M. and Rowlingson, K. (2007) *Public Attitudes to Economic Inequality*, York: Joseph Rowntree Foundation.

Pahl, R., Rose, D. and Spencer, L. (2007) 'Inequality and Quiescence: A Continuing Conundrum', Institute for Social and Economic Research WP22, University of Essex.

Peden, G. (1985) *British Economic and Social Policy: Lloyd George to Margaret Thatcher*, Oxford: Philip Allen.

Persson, T. and Tabellini, G. (1994) 'Is Inequality Harmful for Growth?' *American Economic Review*, 84(June): 600–22.

Rubery J. (1997) 'Wages and the Labour Market', *British Journal of Industrial Relations*, 35(3): 337–66.

Rueda, D. and Pontusson, J. (2000) 'Wage Inequality and Varieties of Capitalism', *World Politics*, 52(3): 350–83.

Sapir, A., Aghion, P., Bertola, G., Hellwig, M., Pisani-Ferry, J., Rosati, D., Viñals, J. and Wallace, H. (2003) *A Agenda for a for a Growing Europe: Making the EU Economic System Deliver. Report of an Independent High-Level Study Group Established on the Initiative of the President of the European Commission*, Brussels: European Commission.

Sapir, A. (2006) 'Globalization and the Reform of European Social Models', *Journal of Common Market Studies*, 44(2): 369–90.

Schulten, T. (2007) 'Towards a European Minimum Wage Policy? Fair Wages and the European Social Model', paper presented at the 8th European Congress of the International Industrial Relations Association (IIRA), Manchester.

Social Justice Policy Group (2006) *Breakdown Britain: Interim Report on the State of the Nation*, London: Social Justice Policy Group.

Social Justice Policy Group (2007) *Breakthrough Britain: Ending the Costs of Social Breakdown*, London: Social Justice Policy Group.

Standing, G. (1999) *Global Labour Flexibility: Seeking Distributive Justice*, Basingstoke: Macmillan.

Streeck, W. (1997) 'Beneficial Constraints: On the Economic Limits of Rational Voluntarism', in J.R. Hollingsworth and R. Boyer (eds) *Contemporary Capitalism: The Embeddedness of Institutions*, Cambridge: CUP, pp. 197–219.

Towers, B. (1997) *The Representation Gap: Change and Reform in the British and American Workplace*, Oxford: Oxford University Press.

Toynbee, P. (2003) *Hard Work: Life in Low-Pay Britain*, London: Bloomsbury.

Turnbull, P. (2003) 'What Do Unions Do Now?' *Journal of Labor Research*, 24(3): 491–527.

Veblen, T. (1934) *The Theory of the Leisure Class*, New York: Modern Library.

Wallerstein, M. (1999) 'Wage Setting Institutions and Pay Inequality in Advanced Industrial Societies', *American Journal of Political Science*, 43(3): 649–80.

Weeks, J. (2005) 'Inequality Trends in Some Developed OECD Countries', DESA Working Paper 6, School of Oriental and African Studies, University of London.

Wilkinson, R. and Pickett, K. (2009) *The Spirit Level: Why More Equal Societies Almost Always Do Better*, London: Allen Lane.

13

Working time, work–life balance and inequality

Paul Blyton

Introduction

In a recent study, my colleague Jean Jenkins and I followed the fortunes of a group of 80 workers in South Wales made redundant from a multinational clothing manufacturer (Blyton and Jenkins, 2009, 2010). Until the factory closed, the workers, most of whom were women, had been employed full-time, mainly as sewing machinists. When we renewed our contact with them a year on from the closure, three-quarters had found alternative employment. However, two things were striking about the jobs many had secured. First, for over half of those in paid work, the jobs they now held were part-time, not through choice but because these were the only jobs they had been able to find. Second, a majority of the part-time contracts (for example, as care assistants or supermarket staff) involved working time patterns that not only varied from week to week but were highly unpredictable, in terms of both timing and duration. Typically, both the care and retail contracts specified a minimum number of hours (16 hours was the most common, though this could be as low as 4 or 5) with employees agreeing to work additional hours (up to 30 or 35 hours) in any week. For the majority of workers holding such contracts, these hours could be scheduled during the daytime, evening or weekends, and for many their forthcoming weekly schedule was known only at the latter end of the previous week. Some of the men who had been employed at the clothing factory were subject to a similar work pattern. One, for example, now employed on maintenance work at an amusement park, worked a variable number of hours and shifts, with his schedule only available the day before the following work week, and even this was subject to change on a daily basis.

Jobs with such variable and unpredictable hours have become relatively common in sectors such as retailing (Backett-Milburn et al., 2008; Henly et al., 2006; Lambert, 2008; Zeytinoglu et al., 2004) and care (Henninger and Papouschet, 2008; Rubery et al., 2005). It is also clear that further variability occurs in 'real time' as employees are requested at short notice to stay on, or leave early, to reflect particular work circumstances. For management, this access to variable hours offers a means of deploying labour to shadow fluctuations both in demand and available staff. But for the people we were interviewing, this variability and unpredictability had many drawbacks, in particular: a general uncertainty over their work schedule, making it difficult to plan activities outside work; for some, increased problems of organizing childcare and maintaining a consistent care arrangement; a disruption to domestic routines such as meal times; and a lack of stable income as earnings fluctuated with the actual hours worked.

What the situation of these part-time workers also highlights is an experience quite at odds with how current working time developments are frequently portrayed. For example, there has been much reporting in the UK and elsewhere of employees enjoying greater access to working time flexibility as a result of, for instance, the extension of parental leave and the gradual spread of flexitime and other temporal arrangements to a larger proportion of the workforce (see Kersley et al., 2006; Whitehouse et al., 2007). It is clear that significant change has occurred in these areas, and we examine the developments in more detail below. But as some commentators have pointed out, a number of the developments in working time flexibility, such as the use of zero and annual hours contracts, as well as the variable hours arrangements noted above, have provided temporal flexibility for employers to a far greater extent than for employees – increasing employers' ability to adjust working time patterns but at a cost of greater irregularity and unpredictability for employees (Fleetwood, 2007; Golden, 2001; Houseman, 2001; Zeytinoglu et al., 2004).

Further, in parallel discussions of working time and work–life balance, part-time working has been highlighted as a widespread work–life balance arrangement increasingly offered by employers and utilized by dual-earner couples: one of the couple (most usually the female) working part-time in order to retain more time for non-work activities (Bonney, 2005: 396; Kersley et al., 2005: 30; see also Hakim, 2000). And clearly for many couples this 'modified breadwinner' arrangement represents an effective way of both engaging in paid work while maintaining other responsibilities and activities. But as some critics have also pointed out, while for dual earners in certain circumstances (those with access to better paid, secure jobs) part-time work may be a route to a more successful work–life balance, for others the outcome of part-time work is low pay, poor prospects and unsatisfactory work patterns (Heery, 2006: 45; Lausch and Scully, 2007; Walsh, 2007; Warren, 2004). Among many of our former sewing machinists, the drop in income resulting from moving from full-time to part-time work, coupled with the variable and often unsociable work hours, meant that working part-time was anything but a source of work–life balance – an outcome reinforced by the significantly greater number who commented that both their social activities and their involvement in the community had deteriorated, rather than improved, since leaving full-time employment (Blyton and Jenkins, 2009).

Too often, what many analyses of working time and work–life balance have tended to do is preference certain groups, trends and developments over others. We will examine this further in relation to discussions over long hours working, patterns of actual and preferred work hours and employers' work–life balance provisions. What these examples underline is the need for greater acknowledgement of the *differentiated* experience of working time and access to work–life balance arrangements. For closer inspection indicates how many of the recent developments in employee behaviour and attitudes are acting, in important ways, to deepen existing disparities within occupational hierarchies. Those groups already enjoying various advantages, by virtue of their position within upper levels of employment hierarchies, are also benefiting from access to work time choices and work–life balance provisions to a much greater degree than their counterparts at lower levels in those hierarchies. Thus, despite recent legislation in the UK and elsewhere designed to extend work–life balance provisions to broad employee categories (such as working parents with young children) across all occupational groups, in practice, as we shall see, they are benefiting some groups much more than others.

Recent analyses of the labour market such as McGovern et al. (2007) have utilized a class-based analysis to explore the disparities in employment hierarchies which include not only earnings disparities but also differences in the power and privilege of the groups or social classes that occupy different positions in that hierarchy. McGovern and colleagues follow Goldthorpe (1982, 2000) in this analysis, identifying those occupying managerial and professional positions as enjoying particular work characteristics that involve a more diffuse exchange of effort and reward between employer and employee, greater employee autonomy and discretion and with a longer-term orientation (reflected in the expectation of salary increments, security and career opportunities) than those holding waged labour contracts (Goldthorpe, 1982; McGovern et al., 2007: 23). In turn, these favourable job attributes typically reflect those at the senior levels holding knowledge and skills that are particularly valuable to the employer and more difficult to replace from the external labour market than those skills held at lower levels.

In a similar way, it is argued here that because of this position of relative power held by senior level employees, compared to their counterparts at lower levels, coupled with the reliance of employers on the former to perform their work without close monitoring (reflecting the greater difficulty of closely monitoring the quality and quantity of their output, compared to many undertaking more routine tasks) employees at higher levels in employment hierarchies are generally able to secure much greater discretion over their work time. This analysis, based on the relative power of groups at different hierarchical levels, seems to explain access to discretion and work time flexibility more satisfactorily than possible competing arguments such as the role of gender. It is the case that a disproportionate number of those experiencing greatest unpredictability of work time and least control over hours are women. But it is argued here that this is a reflection of the experience of those in the lowest levels of employment hierarchies – levels that for a number of reasons are disproportionately populated by female workers – than a reflection of gender inequality *per se*.

To consider these issues in more detail, the remainder of the chapter proceeds as follows. First, we examine briefly the nature of regulation of working time and work–life balance, identifying the changing significance of the state, management, trade unions and employees in the regulation of working time patterns. Second, we note the significance of several key developments occurring in the working time area, particularly the retreat from standard work hours, the growing flexibilization of working time and the different consequences of that flexibility: not least that while for some, flexibility leads to greater and much valued discretion over work time arrangements, for others it acts a source of irregularity and undesired variability. Third, as a bridge between the working hours and work–life balance parts of our discussion, we review the evidence on employees' actual and preferred work hours. While frequently the results of these studies have been reported as evidence of a widespread preference for shorter hours, in practice the findings are far more diffuse, and again highlight the different experiences and outlooks of those at higher and lower levels within employment hierarchies.

Fourth, turning to work–life balance more directly, we examine the nature of work–life provisions and the behaviour and attitudes towards those provisions among different groups. This includes, for example, access to different work time options (such as the ability to work partly from home), and employees' perceptions of whether they have access to flexibility should their personal circumstances require it. Finally, a brief concluding discussion summarizes the need for analysing temporal aspects of the employment relationship within the broader context of the inequalities and contrasting experiences of work in contemporary society.

The regulation of working time

Working time is a key feature of the employment relationship in general, and the employment contract in particular. For the majority of employees, their usual working hours, together with the amount of holiday they are entitled to, are among the most clearly-defined elements of the employment contract. Given the difficulties of specifying in such contracts precisely *how much* work an individual is required to perform, *how long* he or she is required to work, is widely used as a proxy for the amount of work expected. The majority of employment contracts, particularly for manual and (non-managerial) white-collar jobs, specify a level of reward in return for the supply of an agreed amount of labour time.

All the major direct and indirect parties to the employment relationship – employees and employers, the state and trade unions – exert some regulatory influence over the pattern of working time. The shifting degree of influence of each of these parties in recent years, however, has created a working time landscape far different from that prevailing a generation ago.

Statutory regulation

Laws on working time exist in all industrial countries, designed partly to offer some protection against the health consequences of long or unbroken work periods, and in some jurisdictions (such as in the USA under the Fair Labor Standards Act) to establish standard weekly hours beyond which overtime premia are payable (McCann, 2005). The significance of working time legislation, however, varies from country to country, reflecting such factors as the range of laws promulgated, the number of exemptions allowed for different work groups and the extent to which the laws are adequately enforced (ibid.). What is generally evident, however, is that since the late 1990s, there have been a number of legislative changes, both in Europe and elsewhere, that have extended the range of statutory regulation of working time. In the EU, where such developments have been most in evidence, statutory changes have stemmed primarily from Directives on time-related issues, such as parental leave and part-time working, and most notably from the earlier Working Time Directive that required Member States to set limits on the length of the working day and working week, and to establish a minimum amount of annual paid leave. In practice, in several EU states the provisions of these Directives have been equivalent to, or less than, extant national legislation, and thus have had only limited impact. Their relevance has been greater in countries such as the UK, where previously for example, most workers were not covered by any maximum hours regulation or minimum paid holiday provision. Yet, by allowing exemptions, opt-outs and lengthy adjustment periods, the Working Time Directive has overall been more limited in its impact on weekly hours than many initially supposed, though its influence on paid holiday provision, particularly for lower-paid workers, has been more evident (Green, 2003).

A second example from Europe relates to the introduction of a statutory obligation on employers to accommodate, or consider, requests from employees with young or disabled children or adult caring responsibilities, to alter their pattern of working hours. Assessments show that, in the UK for example (where the legislation requires employers to 'consider' requests from relevant employees) the large majority of requests are accommodated by employers (Holt and Grainger, 2005). In practice, however, these requests, together with a knowledge of the legislation, are far from equally distributed across all occupational groups, an issue we return to below.

A range of other statutory interventions are evident at national level, ranging from the legislation in France which established a 35-hour work week (Durand and Martin, 2004) to significant extensions to statutory parental leave provisions, most notably in the Nordic countries (Moss and O'Brien, 2006). Together, these developments reflect an enhanced statutory role in recent years in the regulation of working time. However, as we move on to discuss, this greater state involvement has *not* been sufficient to offset fully the decline in the joint regulation of work time by management and trade unions, the result of which has been a net increase in the managerial control of working time patterns.

Union–management relations

Given the centrality of time in the employment contract and workers' overall experience of work, it is not surprising that temporal issues of one form or another have figured prominently throughout the development of union–management relations. Campaigns for reductions in work hours were a key early focus for trade union organization in Britain and elsewhere (Arrowsmith, 2002) and in more recent times, campaigns for shorter hours were prominent in Germany in the 1980s and early 1990s. More recently, long hours working has again become a focus of concern for the TUC in the UK (Heery, 2006).

The prominence of temporal issues within collective union–management relations continues to be evident. In the UK in the latest WERS survey for example, working hours represented the second most frequent topic (after pay) that managers negotiated with trade unions, with holidays the third most frequent (Kersley et al., 2006: 194). What *has* changed however, is the overall coverage and scope of those collective relations, both in the UK and elsewhere, reflecting the shrinking of trade union presence and influence over the past three decades (Blyton and Turnbull, 2004; Kersley et al., 2006) And even where those collective relations have remained in place, many working time issues have come increasingly to be dealt with at a more local level than hitherto – a decentralization particularly evident in Australia, France, Germany and the UK (Blyton, 2008: 520–1). As a result of a weaker union voice, a concomitant strengthening in management's position, and the decentralization of collective relations to local level, working time agendas have broadened and become more closely associated with the particular temporal requirements of individual organizations – requirements covering the arrangement and utilization of work hours as well as their overall duration.

Management and employees

The decline in the centralized regulation of weekly work hours and holidays, and more generally the growing absence of collective bargaining machinery from the majority of UK workplaces, has further strengthened managers' ability to regulate unilaterally many aspects of working time and move away from standardized patterns. This is true not only in the UK but elsewhere, including the US where 'control over working time rest[s] largely with employers' (Berg et al., 2004: 31). Management secure this control formally through the specification of work hours' duration, holidays and work periods (shift patterns, start and stop times and so on) within employment contracts and job descriptions and monitor these in various ways in relation to employee attendance and punctuality. In addition, managers regulate working time patterns through various informal mechanisms, including *ad hoc* arrangements with employees to complete particular work assignments (see for example, Marsh, 1991). More generally, management crucially shape the nature of working time cultures within organizations, which influence for example, whether employees feel under pressure to work long hours, or whether they perceive the organization as supportive towards requests for a change in work arrangements (BRMB Social Research, 2004; Perlow, 1999).

This portrait of managerial dominance over working time patterns, strengthened by the gaps left by partial (though slowly growing) statutory regulation and weakening collective regulation, needs tempering however, by recognizing the important influence that employees exert over their own working time. As well as the provisions available to employees to adjust their normal work pattern – for example, through statutory rights to parental leave, or for parents to seek changes to their work pattern – there are various informal practices by which employees secure a measure of discretion over their working time. These range from arrangements with co-workers to alter the given shift allocation (shift swapping) to reducing their work time via voluntary absence or unofficial breaks (for a fuller discussion, see Noon and Blyton, 2007: 90–6). The upshot is a continuing contested terrain between management and workforce over the duration, arrangement and utilization of working time, with workers demonstrating a sustained ability to modify formal work time and monitoring arrangements and thereby gain some control over their working period.

But to return to our earlier point, this ability of workers to exercise discretion and to a degree shape their working pattern is not equally distributed across organizational hierarchies and occupational groups. Those in the least skilled and lowest level jobs, particularly those involved in short-cycle, repetitive operations, and where work operations are subject to direct monitoring and supervision, generally have less scope for gaining control over their work time (Mars, 1982). In contrast, those employees occupying higher positions within employment hierarchies frequently enjoy a greater level of temporal autonomy – for example, over their start and stop times, or choice over whether to work partly from home. We return to this issue later.

The changing nature of working time

Patterns of working time have been characterized in recent years not only by changes in the processes of regulating working time (as outlined in the previous section) but also in substantive aspects of work time patterns. In particular, and partly as a result of the reduction in more centralized, collective regulation of work hours, there has been a shift to more heterogeneous and individualized patterns, both in terms of the duration of time that people work and the periods when they perform that work (Anxo et al., 2004). The UK is an exemplar of this heterogeneity with, for example, above average proportions (compared with other EU countries) of the workforce regularly working very long (48 hours +) or very short (8 hours or less) schedules (Noon and Blyton, 2007). Extensions in opening and operating hours, including the growth of 24-hour trading, have led to a growth of work schedules that cover this expansion in evening, night and weekend operations (see for example, Presser and Gornick, 2005). The increase in part-time working, as well as the more diverse scheduling of full-time hours, has resulted in a progressively smaller proportion of the workforce working what was formerly considered to be a 'standard' work day or work week (Hill, 2000). A parallel development (and one reflecting the shift in power away from trade unions) has been a widespread re-definition, and extension of 'standard' hours, that is those hours paid at a non-premium (overtime) rate (Blyton, 2008: 517). As a result, work schedules covering trading hours that extend into evenings or weekends are now far more likely to be paid at a standard rate than was the case when operating/opening hours were more restricted and collectively regulated.

Actual and preferred hours

One reason widely adduced for the increased attention being paid to work–life issues is a concern with long and/or increasing working hours. The general assumption is that working long hours will have a negative spillover into non-work life by restricting the time available for activities outside paid work. The UK has frequently been reported as having the longest average work hours in western Europe, with a significant proportion of its workforce regularly working over 48 hours each week (Bunting, 2004; Noon and Blyton, 2007: 101; ONS, 2009). As Bonney (2005: 391) notes, 'campaigns, research by foundations and government policies under the banner of balancing work and family life have all emphasised the alleged prevalence of a long working hours culture and the need to bring about a reduction in the hours of paid work'.

However, there are assumptions underlying this link between long hours and work–life balance that need further examination. Two issues in particular need exploring: whether the long hours picture is accurate; and whether a clear preference exists for shorter working hours. On the first, as Bonney (2005) points out, in practice the picture of long hours working in the UK primarily reflects the situation of *one particular group* within the workforce: men working full-time, or more accurately, a proportion of those workers. Long work hours are much less pronounced (though increasing somewhat) among women full-time workers (Noon and Blyton, 2007: 101) and the long hours 'headline' takes no account either of the widespread fall in work hours that has characterized many occupations over the past generation (MacInnes, 2008) or that proportion of the UK workforce who work part-time. Indeed, not only is the level of part-time working comparatively high in the UK (OECD, 2005), but also a substantial proportion of those part-time contracts comprise short, or very short, weekly schedules. Almost half of part-time male workers in the UK and approaching two in five female part-time workers work sixteen hours or fewer each week, and around one in five of those men and one in eight of the women have part-time jobs involving eight hours a week or fewer (Noon and Blyton, 2007: 103). Thus, while it is the case that full-time male workers work a high average number of hours in the UK, this section of the working population does not accurately characterize the workforce as a whole.

Even among this latter category, those working long weekly hours are not spread evenly across the male full-time workforce but are concentrated particularly within two distinct groups: those in higher levels of the employment hierarchy (managers and professionals) and those much lower in that hierarchy in semi-skilled machine operative and process work activities (ONS, 2009: 54). These are frequently portrayed and discussed as a single group ('those working long hours') but it is problematic to do so: the motivations for, and incentives accruing to, those working additional hours, not to mention the nature of the work that the different groups are undertaking, are quite distinct. Among semi-skilled operatives, the extra hours are more likely to be worked as paid overtime, thus representing a means of increasing earnings by supplementing basic weekly pay levels. Among managers and professionals, however, the additional hours worked are much less likely to be compensated by overtime payments (employment contracts for such groups normally defining an annual salary for the position, rather than an hourly rate). Yet, as Echtelt et al. (2007) rightly point out, to view these hours worked by the latter group as 'unpaid' can also be misleading, for it may be more a question of the timing of the reward, rather than its presence or absence. For while paid overtime represents a direct and short-term reward (in the form of the overtime payment), managers and professionals are more likely to be rewarded for working additional hours via more indirect, longer-term incentives – such as career advancement – as a consequence of the additional work they do. This long hours working may not be an entirely (or even partly) voluntary decision on the latter's part – there are many studies that demonstrate the requirement for employees, particularly in career-aspiring positions, to show their commitment and motivation by working long hours (see for example, Perlow, 1999). Nor does this minimize the work pressures that exist for many in managerial and professional positions to 'see the job through', pressures that are particularly evident in organizations adopting 'high performance' human resource management practices (McGovern et al., 2007; Echtelt et al., 2007). But it does indicate a different set of calculations, and nature of the compensation for working additional hours among those groups reporting regularly working long hours. As a result, treating them as a single category of those working long hours could be more misleading than enlightening, and obscure important differences in orientation and opportunity existing at different levels in the employment hierarchy.

Examination of studies of working time preferences similarly indicates that headlined findings have tended to provide a partial and oversimplified picture. There are two main ways of investigating employee preferences or desires over their working hours. The first (and the most common in terms of number of studies undertaken) is to ask people about their actual and desired work hours. A second method is to examine behaviour: for example, do those expressing preferences for different work hours move, over time, to positions reflecting those preferences? We will examine each of these approaches briefly in turn.

Attitudes to preferred work hours

Attitudes towards working hours have been studied in many countries, though direct comparisons are hampered by variations in question phrasing used in the investigations (Golden and Gebresalassie, 2007: 20). Typical forms of question, however, ask the respondent whether, given the choice, would he/she prefer to work: fewer hours but earn less money; the same number of hours for the same money; or work more hours for more money? Several studies have reported a substantial minority (around two in five) indicating a preference for shorter hours; see for example Pocock et al. (2008) reporting on an Australian sample, Reynolds (2003) using data from the United States, Tijdens (2007) reporting a large-scale Dutch study and Böheim and Taylor (2004) drawing on British Household Panel Survey (BHPS) data. Studies of specific occupations have also reported findings broadly in line with this pattern – for example, Preston's (2005) study of registered nurses in Australia.

However, two factors complicate this picture and raise important questions for the work–life balance debate. First, notwithstanding the pattern of results in the aforementioned studies, overall there is a marked lack of consistency between many of the national and international surveys conducted. In the US, for example, two large-scale studies drawing on different nationwide samples have reported substantially different proportions indicating a preference for shorter work hours (see Golden and Gebresalassie, 2007; Reynolds, 2003). Tijdens (2007: 110) similarly identifies considerable variation between Dutch studies depending on the precise wording of the questions concerning actual and desired hours. In practice, variation may be the result of several factors (including question wording and prevailing economic and employment conditions), but overall the lack of consistency across many studies of this type raises concern about the true extent to which there exists an untapped demand for reduced working time.

The picture is further complicated when we take account of findings – often less prominently reported in these studies – relating to the proportion of respondents desiring to work not fewer but *more* hours. For it is the case that far from there being common agreement over a preference for shorter hours, for a significant proportion – and in certain studies a *higher* proportion than those preferring fewer hours – the preference is to increase their existing work hours. Further, it is not only those on comparatively short work time schedules who express a desire for more work hours. Indeed, Golden and Gebreselassie (2007: 24) report that even among those working very long schedules (60+ hours) in the US in 2001, over 1 in 5 expressed a desire to extend their work hours yet further. Several other studies (for example, McGovern et al., 2007; Pocock et al., 2008; Reynolds, 2003) also identify significant minorities preferring longer hours, while Stier and Lewin-Epstein (2003) report this to be a prominent finding in some countries, though less so in others. As with preferences towards shorter hours, however, findings also vary considerably over preferences for longer work hours, further underlining the variability of the evidence on working time preferences across different samples.

Behaviour studies

Given this variability concerning attitudes to preferred work hours, studies reporting behaviour in regard to working time are potentially very useful. Such studies are few in number, but three in particular, are insightful. First, Böheim and Taylor (2004) used longitudinal data from the BHPS to examine whether a preference for reduced hours leads over time to a reduction in hours worked. Over the 1990s, they found a trend in this direction: those working more hours than they desired were more likely to reduce their hours over time (and *vice versa* for those desiring more hours).

Two Dutch studies, however, suggest that when faced with a choice between reduced hours *or* increased earnings, the desire for the latter could well outweigh the former. In a study of university workers in the Netherlands, Delsen and his colleagues (2006) found that when employees were offered various choices such as buying extra leave days or selling leave days for extra salary, the latter proved far more popular than the former. A very similar finding was obtained in a study of Dutch civil servants by Hillebrink et al. (2007). While the trading of time and money under the organization's flexible benefit plan was popular, for over nine out of ten of those participating in the scheme, their preference was to choose additional financial benefit (by trading in leave or by working more hours per week) rather than buying additional time off.

In combination, these attitudinal and behavioural studies signal the dangers of over-generalizing from part of the results. While it is clear that sections of the workforce indicate a preference to work fewer hours, even if this entailed a cut in their income, this is not a work–life recipe favoured by all, or even a majority. Indeed for some, an improved work–life balance would more likely result from an increase in work hours to secure a higher income.

Work–life balance

At the head of the chapter we discussed how part-time working could act favourably or unfavourably on non-work outcomes: while for some part-time work could be a means of successfully engaging in work and non-work activities, for others it represents a form of low-wage and unpredictable work that hinders successful participation in non-work life.

The fulfilment of both work and non-work goals is an objective relevant across the working population. This is recognized in the applicability of various statutory work–life provisions – from regulations over minimum rest periods and paid holiday rights to parents requesting flexible working – across all occupational categories. Yet in practice, the evidence suggests that rather than blunt differences within the employment hierarchy evident in respect to other aspects of the employment relationship (earnings, job quality and prestige, for example) key aspects of work–life balance provision act to attenuate those differences. Indeed, just as those on higher incomes enjoy an advantageous position outside the workplace to secure work–life balance by outsourcing various tasks – their income enabling choices over whether to purchase childcare, cleaning or gardening services, for example – so too it is evident how inside the workplace too, access to work–life balance currently favours those at more senior organizational levels.

Some brief examples will establish this point more clearly. First, in terms of those identifying a preference for shorter hours, a number of studies have shown that these are more likely to be where household incomes are higher, and (relatedly) where respondents hold senior positions within organizations (see for example, Hooker et al., 2007: 172). While for some this may reflect the relatively long hours they are currently working, for others it is likely to indicate a financial ability to contemplate exchanging income for more non-work time.

In addition, while statutory regulation may be designed to allow widespread access to particular provisions, this takes no account of other factors influencing the take up of those provisions. For example, it is evident that those at higher income levels have a greater knowledge of their statutory rights. In the Third Work–Life Balance Employee Survey in the UK, for example (Hooker et al., 2007), when asked about their awareness of parents with young children having the right to request flexible working, that awareness was highest among those with a higher household income (>£40 k) and particularly low among the lowest household income group (< £15 k) (ibid.: 54). In the same survey, similar variations in perceived access to work–life balance provisions were also evident. When asked, for example, what arrangements they thought would be available if needed, those in managerial and/or professional positions were more likely (compared to those at lower levels) to believe that they would have access to flexible working time, to working reduced hours for a limited period, working a compressed week and working partly from home (Hooker et al., 2007: 37–40). Likewise this survey and others have shown that those at lower levels in the employment hierarchy have less access overall to provisions such as working time flexibility (ibid.: 41; Whitehouse et al., 2007: 33–4).

This differentiated access to work time flexibility is not a phenomenon peculiar to the UK. In the US, Lambert and Haley-Lock (2004: 180) for example, have drawn attention to the 'inequality and inequity in the distribution of supports for work-life balance', an unequal distribution that reflects 'the significant discretionary role employers play in structuring access to opportunities for work-life balance', the effect of which is to 'only widen existing inequalities' (ibid.: 191). Golden (2009) draws on a very large nationwide sample similarly to highlight the much greater access to work time flexibility (both formally and informally arranged) among managers, sales personnel and professionals in the US compared to most semi- and unskilled occupations. Golden concludes that 'flexible scheduling . . . is accessed more by workers . . . that already enjoy an advantage in the workplace and labor market' (2009: 50). This echoes a similar pattern evidenced in Australia by Gray and Tudball (2003) regarding employees' degree of autonomy over their start and finish times.

Taking one of these examples – the ability to work partly from home – a little further, the study quoted above by Hooker et al. (2007) found that while overall, less than a quarter of employees thought that working partly from home would be available to them if needed, among managers and professionals this proportion was over one-third. A similar finding is reflected in other surveys and case studies. The latest UK Workplace Employment Relations Survey (Kersley et al., 2006: 253), for example, found that the proportion of managers indicating that they would be allowed to work partly from home was three times that of non-managerial employees. Tietze et al. (2006) in a local authority study also found that working from home was disproportionately available to those in more senior positions – a differential access which not only advantaged the senior employees in terms of their ability to adjust work and non-work responsibilities, but also disadvantaged their lower-level, office-bound colleagues who expressed some injustice at their lack of access to working from home. Similarly, in the Netherlands, Peters and van der Lippe (2007) report that occupations such as policy makers, managers and professionals are most likely to have access to home-based telework in their jobs. In their study of over a thousand employees in 30 Dutch organizations (over one in four of whom had access to home-based telework), those employees who had more control over their work time – disproportionately the more highly educated employees whose work was more likely to be judged on their output than their time at work – were more likely to have access to working from home.

Conclusion

It is arguable that the people who need access to working time flexibility and work–life balance provisions the most are those occupying lower-level, lower-paid jobs. For it is this group that lacks the financial resources to fulfil their various work and non-work responsibilities by means other than by self-provisioning. While those in higher paying jobs can exercise choice over whether or not to purchase assistance to help them maintain their non-work lives, those who lack discretionary income have only themselves, and their family and friends, to call on.

Yet, as we have seen, in many important respects, access to working time flexibility and work–life balance provisions is uneven, favouring those already benefiting from a more advantageous employment relationship. Those in higher level, better paid jobs also tend to be those with greater time sovereignty, in terms of their discretion over when to start and finish work, for example, or work partly from home, and are the people more likely to be informed about work–life provisions.

In part, as Golden (2009: 49) has argued, this situation may reflect an (implicit) reciprocity between employers and senior level employees. Many of the latter work relatively long hours, and in this situation flexibility over time may be the *quid pro quo* for this additional working (the *quid pro quo* for lower levels working additional hours being overtime payments). But in part too, the uneven distribution of flexibility and time autonomy reflects the greater organizational power held by managers and professionals, and a broader reciprocation that involves the granting of autonomy over time in exchange for a commitment to perform a work role, that by its diffuse nature cannot be subject to more direct controls by the employer (McGovern et al., 2007). In this respect, access to flexible working is a further manifestation of the hierarchical or social class differentiation that exists in workplaces that favours those with scarcer skills and stronger labour market power, and job roles that cannot successfully be subjected to rigid time-based controls. Such class differences tend to be underrepresented in analyses which portray working time primarily in terms of individual choice or preference (Hakim, 2000). Individual choice does indeed have a part to play, but the location of individuals within particular employment hierarchies exerts a critical influence over access to working time discretion and flexibility.

The differential access to flexibility also reflects the employer's power to distribute work–life balance provisions selectively, where these are not subject to statutory requirement. What this underlines is the importance of continued statutory provision in the work–life area, to ensure a greater coverage and increased equity within organizations. In so doing, state action can mitigate work–life provision and working time flexibility being further differentiators in employment relationships experienced by those at higher or lower levels within employment hierarchies.

Acknowledgement

I am grateful for the very useful comments made by Ed Heery and Pete Turnbull on an earlier draft of this chapter.

References

Anxo, D., Fagan, C., McCann, D., Lee, S. and Messenger, J.C. (2004) 'Introduction: working time in industrialized countries', in J.C. Messenger (Ed.) *Working Time and Workers' Preferences in Industrialized Countries: Finding the Balance*, London: Routledge, pp. 1–9.

Arrowsmith, J. (2002) 'The struggle over working time in nineteenth and twentieth century Britain', *Historical Studies in Industrial Relations*, 13: 83–117.

Backett-Milburn, K., Airey, L., McKie, L. and Hogg, G. (2008) 'Family comes first or open all hours?: how low paid women working in food retailing manage webs of obligation at home and work', *The Sociological Review*, 56 (3): 474–96.

Berg, P., Appelbaum, E. Bailey, T. and Kalleberg, A.L. (2004) 'Contesting time: international comparisons of employee control of working time', *Industrial and Labor Relations Review*, 57 (3): 331–49.

Blyton, P. (2008) 'Working time and work-life balance', in P. Blyton, N. Bacon, J. Fiorito, and E. Heery (Eds) *The Sage Handbook of Industrial Relations*, London: Sage, pp. 513–28.

Blyton, P. and Jenkins, J. (2009) 'Changed work, changed lives? Workers' experience of redundancy within their community'. Paper presented at the 15th International Industrial Relations Association World Congress, Sydney.

Blyton, P. and Jenkins, J. (2010) 'Ways of life after redundancy: anatomy of a community following factory closure', in P. Blyton, B. Blunsdon, K. Reed and A. Dastmalchian (Eds) *Ways of Living: Work, Community and Lifestyle Choice*, Basingstoke: Palgrave Macmillan, pp. 202–19.

Blyton, P. and Turnbull, P. (2004) *The Dynamics of Employee Relations*, 3rd Edition, Basingstoke: Macmillan.

Böheim, R. and Taylor, M.P. (2004) 'Actual and preferred working hours', *British Journal of Industrial Relations*, 42 (1): 149–66.

Bonney, N. (2005) 'Overworked Britons?: part-time work and work-life balance', *Work, Employment and Society*, 19 (2): 391–401.

BRMB Social Research (2004) *A Survey of Workers' Experience of the Working Time Regulations*, Employment Relations Research Series No. 31, London: Department of Trade and Industry.

Bunting, M. (2004) *Willing Slaves*, London: Harper Collins.

Delsen, L., Benders, J. and Smits, J. (2006) 'Choices within collective labour agreements "à la Carte" in the Netherlands', *British Journal of Industrial Relations*, 44 (1): 51–72.

Durand, M. and Martin, J. (2004) 'The 35-hour week: portrait of a French exception', *OECD Observer*, 24: 10–12.

Echtelt, P. van, Glebbeek, A.C., Wielers, R. and Lindenberg, S. (2007) 'The puzzle of unpaid overtime: can the greediness of post-fordist work be explained?', in T. van der Lippe and P. Peters (Eds) *Competing Claims in Work and Family Life*, Cheltenham: Edward Elgar, pp. 125–42.

Fleetwood, S. (2007) 'Why work-life balance now?', *International Journal of Human Resource Management*, 18 (3): 387–400.

Goldthorpe, J.H. (1982) 'On the service class, its formation and future', in A. Giddens and G. McKenzie (Eds) *Social Class and the Division of Labour*, Cambridge: Cambridge University Press, 162–185.

———(2000) *On Sociology: Numbers, Narratives and the Integration of Research and Theory*, Oxford: Oxford University Press.

Golden, L. (2001) 'Flexible work schedules: what are we trading off to get them?' *Monthly Labor Review*, March: 50–67.

———(2009) 'Flexile daily work schedules in US jobs: formal introductions needed?', *Industrial Relations*, 48 (1): 27–54.

Golden, L., and Gebreselassie, T. (2007) 'Overemployment mismatches: the preference for fewer work hours', *Monthly Labor Review*, April: 18–37.

Gray, M. and Tudball, J. (2003) 'Family-friendly work practices: differences within and between workplaces', *Journal of Industrial Relations*, 45 (3): 269–91.

Green, F. (2003) 'The demands of work', in R. Dickens, P. Gregg and J. Wadsworth (Eds) *The Labour Market under New Labour: The State of Working Britain 2003*, Basingstoke: Palgrave Macmillan, 137–49.

Hakim, C. (2000) *Work-Lifestyle Choices in the 21st Century: Preference Theory*, Oxford: Oxford University Press.

Heery, E. (2006) 'Bargaining for balance: union policy on work-life issues in the United Kingdom', in P. Blyton, B. Blunsdon, K. Reed and A. Dastmalchian (Eds) *Work-Life Integration: International Perspectives on the Balancing of Multiple Roles*, Basingstoke: Palgrave Macmillan, pp. 42–62.

Henly, J.R., Shaefer, H.L. and Waxman, E. (2006) 'Nonstandard work schedules: employer- and employee-driven flexibility in retail jobs', *Social Service Review*, 80: 609–34.

Henninger, A. and Papouschek, U. (2008) 'Occupation matters – blurring workforce boundaries in mobile care and the media industry', in C. Warhurst, D.R. Eikhof and

A Haunschild (Eds) *Work Less, Live More? Critical Analysis of the Work-Life Boundary*, Basingstoke: Palgrave Macmillan, pp. 153–72.

Hillebrink, C., Schippers, J., Peters, P., Doorne-Huiskes, A. van (2007) 'Trading time and money: explaining employee participation and leave choices in a flexible benefit plan', in T. van der Lippe and P. Peters (Eds) *Competing Claims in Work and Family Life*, Cheltenham: Edward Elgar, pp. 179–94.

Hill, R. (2000) 'New Labour Force Survey questions on working hours', *Labour Market Trends*, January: 39–47.

Holt, H. and Grainger, H. (2005) *Results of the Second Flexible Working Employee Survey*, Employment Relations Research Series No. 39, London: Department of Trade and Industry.

Hooker, H., Neathey, F., Casebourne, J. and Munro, M. (2007) *The Third Work-Life Balance Employee Survey: Main Findings*, Employment Relations Research Series No. 58, London: Department for Trade and Industry.

Houseman, S.N. (2001) 'Why employers use flexible staffing: evidence from an establishment survey', *Industrial and Labor Relations Review*, 55 (1): 149–70.

Kersley, B., Alpin, C., Forth, J., Bryson, A., Bewley, H., Dix, G. and Oxenbridge, S. (2006) *Inside the Workplace: Findings from the 2004 Workplace Employment Relations Survey*, London: Routledge.

Lambert, S. (2008) 'Passing the buck: labor flexibility practices that transfer risk onto hourly workers', *Human Relations*, 61 (9): 1203–27.

Lambert, S.J. and Haley-Lock, A. (2004) 'The organizational stratification of opportunities for work-life balance', *Community, Work & Family*, 7 (2): 179–95.

Lausch, B.A. and Scully, M.A. (2007) 'Restructuring time: implications of work-hours reduction for the working class', *Human Relations*, 60 (5): 719–43.

MacInnes, J. (2008) 'Work-life balance: three terms in search of a definition', in C. Warhurst, D.R. Eikhof and A. Haunschild (Eds) *Work Less, Live More? Critical Analysis of the Work-Life Boundary*, Basingstoke: Palgrave Macmillan, pp. 44–61.

Marsh, C. (1991) *Hours of Work of Women and Men in Britain*, London: HMSO.

Mars, G. (1982) *Cheats at Work: An Anthropology of Workplace Crime*, London: Allen and Unwin.

McCann, D. (2005) *Working Time Laws: A Global Perspective*, Geneva: International Labour Organisation.

McGovern, P., Hill, S., Mills, C. and White, M. (2007) *Market, Class and Employment*, Oxford: Oxford University Press.

Moss, P. and O'Brien, M. (2006) *International Review of Leave Policies and Related Research*, Employment Relations Research Series No. 57, London: Department of Trade and Industry.

Noon, M. and Blyton, P. (2007) *The Realities of Work: Experiencing Work and Employment in Contemporary Society*, 3rd Edition, Basingstoke: Palgrave Macmillan.

OECD (2005) *Employment Outlook*, Paris: Organisation for Economic Cooperation and Development.

ONS (2009) *Social Trends 39*, London: Office for National Statistics.

Perlow, L.A. (1999) 'The time famine: toward a sociology of work time', *Administrative Science Quarterly*, 44: 57–81.

Peters, P. and van der Lippe, T. (2007) 'Access to home-based telework: a multi-level and multi-actor perspective', in T. van der Lippe and P. Peters (Eds) *Competing Claims in Work and Family Life*, Cheltenham: Edward Elgar, pp. 233–48.

Pocock, B., Skinner, N. and Williams, P. (2008) 'Measuring work-life interaction: the Australian Work and Life Index (AWALI) 2007', *Labour and Industry*, 18 (3): 19–43.

Presser, H.B. and Gornick, J.C. (2005) 'The female share of weekend employment: a study of 16 countries', *Monthly Labor Review*, August: 41–53.

Preston, A. (2005) 'Registered nurses: who are they and what do they want?', *Australian Bulletin of Labour*, 31 (4): 321–49.

Reynolds, J. (2003) 'You can't always get the hours you want: mismatches between actual and preferred work hours in the US', *Social Forces*, 81 (4): 1171–99.

Rubery, J., Ward, K., Grimshaw, D. and Beynon, H. (2005) 'Working time, industrial relations and the employment relationship', *Time and Society*, 14 (1): 89–111.

Stier, H. and Lewin-Epstein, N. (2003) 'Time to work: a comparative analysis of preferences for working hours', *Work and Occupations*, 30 (3): 302–26.

Tietze, S., Musson, G and Scurry, T. (2006) 'Improving services, balancing lives? A multiple stakeholder perspective on the work-life balance discourse' in P. Blyton, B. Blunsdon, K. Reed and A. Dastmalchian (Eds) *Work-Life Integration: International Perspectives on the Balancing of Multiple Roles*, Basingstoke: Palgrave Macmillan, pp. 180–95.

Tijdens, K.G. (2007) 'Employees' preferences for longer and shorter working hours', in T. van der Lippe and P. Peters (Eds) *Competing Claims in Work and Family Life*, Cheltenham: Edward Elgar, pp. 109–24.

Walsh, J. (2007) 'Experiencing part-time work: temporal tensions, social relations and the work-family interface', *British Journal of Industrial Relations*, 45 (1): 155–77.

Warren, T. (2004) 'Working part-time: achieving a successful "work-life" balance?', *British Journal of Sociology*, 55 (1): 99–122.

Whitehouse, G., Haynes, M., Macdonald, F. and Arts, D. (2007) *Reassessing the 'Family-Friendly Workplace': Trends and Influences in Britain, 1998–2004*, Employment Relations Research Series No. 76, London: Department for Business, Enterprise & Regulatory Reform.

Zeytinoglu, I.U., Lillevik, W., Seaton, I.M.B. and Moruz, J. (2004) 'Part-time and casual work in retail trade: stress and other factors affecting the workplace', *Relations Industrielles*, 59 (3): 516–43.

14

The past, present and future of workplace equality agendas: problems of intersectionality in theory and practice

Deborah Foster with Laura Williams

Introduction

The purpose of this chapter is to examine influences on British law and employment policy and practice in the area of equality and diversity and to provide a 'map' to negotiate what has become an increasingly complex landscape. In doing so, we focus on four key areas of interest. We begin by tracing the historical context in which equality law has evolved. The role played by social movements is explored, which we illustrate by drawing on experiences from the women's and disability movements in Britain and America. We then examine the influence of national and European approaches to politics and labour markets and demonstrate how contemporary developments, such as the European Union (EU) Amsterdam Treaty of 2000, have significantly extended the scope of British anti-discrimination law and facilitated the establishment of a new Equalities and Human Rights Commission (EHRC). Secondly, we consider central concepts and theories that have underpinned different approaches to equality law and policy. We note how in the past, British law was founded on a liberal approach to equal opportunities that sought to achieve formal equality and focused on equality of access to employment rather than outcomes. The character of recent Government initiatives, including the Public Sector Equality Duties and proposals contained in the

Single Equality Bill (2010), are then evaluated in terms of the extent to which they incorporate more radical concepts of substantive equality and recognize that multiple, 'intersecting' interests can exist in and between different groups in society. Our third area of interest focuses on how equalities agendas are pursued at the level of the workplace and the different roles of workplace actors. A decline in trade union recognition and membership means fewer British employees are covered by collective bargaining arrangements, a route through which equality agendas have traditionally been pursued. We examine the implications of increasingly relying on statutory equality provisions and how the TUC has interpreted and sought to influence future equality legislation. Finally, in our conclusion we consider potential practical, policy-related problems that might arise from the integration of the theory of 'intersectionality' into proposed legislation and whether the Labour Party's continued attachment to a 'utility model' of equalities will mean the potential opportunity for radical transformation in this sphere will not be realized.

Influences on British anti-discrimination employment law

The role of social and labour movements

An exploration of the historical development of equal opportunities legislation in any country provides us with access, not only to the ways in which social policy and legal provisions have evolved, but also to the struggles of those individuals and groups that fought for new rights in that society. Such groups include political parties, labour and social movement organizations and pressure groups. We begin by examining the significance of relationships between such organizations by reference first, to the campaigns of the early women's movement in America and Britain and then, to the more contemporary disability movements in these two countries, which drew inspiration from earlier struggles. We illustrate how the national political context in which these struggles occurred was important, but also show how campaigns for equality and social justice can take their inspiration from transnational events. Discussion in the next section is then brought up to date by examining the role that the EU has played on contemporary developments in British equalities policy and law.

The impact of labour movement institutions on equalities policy and law has been significant, but has varied from country to country. For example, in Britain during the late nineteenth and early twentieth centuries trade unions and employers defended the idea of superior male wages on the basis that men, irrespective of marital status, needed to earn a 'family' wage. Support among male-dominated unions for equal pay between men and women, however, developed when wartime labour markets demanded women perform what had previously been regarded as exclusively male jobs (Boston, 1987; Meehan, 1985). Male trade unionists, anxious to protect their rates of pay and counter cheap female labour, whether inspired by self-interest or not, facilitated important relationships between the trade union, labour and women's movements. Relationships which Meehan (1985: 57–71), in her account of the history of women's rights at work, cites there relationships as particularly significant when comparing the histories and development of equality law in the UK and the US.

Support for the principle of equal pay had existed within the British Trades Union Congress (TUC) since 1888. Campaigns for equal pay among public sector unions, moreover, date back as far as the 1940s (Walby, 1991). In 1961, the TUC requested the British Government comply with the 1951 International Labour Organisation's Convention 110 on equal pay for work of equal value (Meehan, 1985). It also drew attention to the fact that if Britain were to join the European Community, the principle of equal pay between men and women was enshrined in Article 119 of the Treaty of Rome. The Government's response was interesting. It claimed that equal pay was a matter for industrial negotiation not state intervention (Meehan, 1985: 64–5), thus upholding the British tradition of voluntarism in industrial relations. Nevertheless, the incoming Labour government of 1964 included a commitment to equal pay in the Party's manifesto, only to later disassociate itself from this objective when a tripartite study group in 1966 suggested the costs of realizing it might be too high (Meehan, 1985: 65). The appointment in 1968 of Barbara Castle as Minister of Labour marked the resumption of talks, though these were soon to be overshadowed by events at Ford's Dagenham plant, where women sewing machinists had gone on strike. What had begun as a grading dispute between two groups of women machinists following a job evaluation exercise, developed into an equal pay dispute between men and women working in the factory (Conley, 2008: 3), which did not end until the Labour government agreed to table legislation on equal pay (Friedman and Meredeen, 1980). The fact that this was a strike by women over work that was clearly defined as 'women's work' was, argues Boston (1987), important. The Equal Pay Act of 1970 was passed, though as Conley (2008) points out it failed to address the problem of gendered job segregation, which was at the heart of the dispute at Ford. In 1975, the Sex Discrimination Act was passed, but it was not until 1984 when the Equal Value Amendment Regulations came into force and recognized equal pay for work of equal value that the Ford women's grievances were addressed. The role of the EU was important in securing the latter rights, after the European Commission took enforcement procedures against the UK Government through the European Court of Justice (Walby, 1991).

Boston (1987: 279) argues that mutual influence and understanding grew between the women's liberation movement and trade union movements in Britain as a consequence of the Ford dispute. However, in the US, women trade unionists tried but failed to mobilize support for equal pay within the union movement and instead forged alliances with the broader civil rights movement. Meehan (1985) observes that while in Britain gender equality was often viewed by labour and trade union movements as a diversion from the primary goal of achieving class equality, in the US, the proximity of the women's movement to the civil rights movement meant gender issues were regarded as secondary to the goal of achieving race equality. During the hearings of the US Civil Rights Bill in 1963, female employment and sex discrimination were not even considered (Randall, 1982). Moreover, it was only after fierce independent lobbying by the US women's movement that women were included in Title VII of the US Civil Rights Act 1964 at all and even then, little consideration was given to how the Act would actually work for women. Some of the wider victories of the civil rights movement did, however, have a positive impact on the women's movement. The concept of 'affirmative action', coined by President Kennedy in 1961 in relation to racial minorities, recognized the existence of deeply embedded discriminatory practices in society and was later extended to women in the labour market by his successor President Johnson. Contractors receiving public funds, moreover, had to show they had an affirmative action programme to address labour market inequalities (Meehan, 1985). The first US Equal Pay Act was introduced in 1963, though interestingly, by the time it had been implemented 22 States already had their own laws. The 1963 Act was extended in 1972 and 1974 to protect most workers in private and public employment, and US case law established the principle that work did not have to be identical to bring an equal pay claim early on. Judges in the US were much bolder in their rulings relating to indirect discrimination than in Britain and overall, sanctions for non-compliance with statutory equality provisions have generally been higher and more effective (Meehan, 1985: 68–75).

The experiences of the women's and civil rights movements in the UK and the US and the tactics they used in their campaigns served as an inspiration for other groups seeking protection from workplace discrimination. A more recent example can be found in the activities of the disability movement. British disability activists (c.f. Oliver 1996; Pagel, 1988; Shakespeare,

2006; Thomas, 2007) believe the absence of an organized civil rights movement, through which different social movements could coalesce and channel their collective political demands in Britain, was significant. The emerging political disability movement of the late 1960s and early 1970s, unlike its US counterpart, was inward looking and internally divided (Pagel, 1988). Campaigning focused on single issues, for example, the establishment of a state wage for disabled people; an objective regarded as patronizing by some activists who wanted civil rights not charity and state dependency (cf. Oliver, 1996). Thus, while US disability activists argued for and won the right to be consulted on new anti-discrimination employment legislation in the late 1980s, British activists were making little impact on mainstream public and political opinion. The US campaigners successfully argued that the Americans with Disabilities Act (ADA) 1990 should recognize that discrimination and prejudice arises from *social* misconceptions about disabled people (Goss et al., 2000). Meanwhile, their British counterparts were battling against a patronizing 'personal tragedy' model of disability. This approach shaped British public policy and, instead of giving new rights to disabled people themselves, emphasis was put on 'experts' or medical professionals being empowered to act on their behalf (Foster and Fosh, 2009; Pagel, 1988). Interestingly, only when the British disability movement began to organize acts of civil disobedience and demonstrations against what Shakespeare (2006) refers to as patronizing 'charity spectacles' (including television fundraising for disability groups) did political opinion begin to change. However, as Foster and Fosh (2009) observe, even when legislation was secured in the form of the UK Disability Discrimination Act (DDA) in 1995, its premises were founded on an individual model of disability and employment rights, rather than the more radical, social model of disability that underpinned the US ADA.

As we have seen, acts of civil disobedience and workplace disruption adopted by the disability movement, by the women at Ford and campaigners in the US civil rights movement provided the catalyst for change and anti-discrimination legislation. This connection conforms to a broader pattern of research which has established a link between the willingness of social movements to use disruptive tactics and their success in bringing about political change (Guigni, 1998: 376).

The influence of national and European approaches to politics and labour markets

The character of a country's politics, labour markets and industrial relations can influence approaches to equal opportunities. For example, the reluctance of US unions to engage with civil rights issues has been attributed to their attachment to a form of voluntarism that favoured white, male trade unionists (Conley, 2008; Robertson, 1999). Voluntarism as opposed to labour market regulation has also tended to be favoured by British unions, though more recently some have suggested they may be moving into a post-voluntarist phase (c.f. Clough, 2007; Heery et al., 2004). Conley (2008), for example, cites a number of landmark equality and equal pay victories in Britain that were won through legal channels with union support. A gradual acceptance of some forms of employment regulation may also have been influenced by union experiences of labour exclusion during the 1980s and 1990s. An attachment to *laissez faire* solutions, including deregulation and privatization, has certainly marked Britain out from its more regulationist EU counterparts (cf. Foster and Scott, 1998, 2003). It was, therefore, within this political and economic climate that the 'business case' for equality emerged as a favoured approach within Government and business circles in Britain.

Regarded as a new approach to workplace equality the 'business case' marked a shift away from the social or moral rationale for equality, towards one based on the self-interested company (Dickens, 1999). It focused on how organizations could best manage scarce resources (Gilbert and Stead, 1999) and was promoted as a strategic option for firms wanting to keep ahead of the competition (Liff, 1999). Diverse employees, would, it was argued, allow organizations to interact sensitively with diverse customers who shared similar contextual references: helping to increase organizational competitiveness (Liff, 1999). Subsequently the 'business case' and associated 'managing diversity' rhetoric has, nonetheless, come under attack. In particular, the approach has been accused of de-politicizing organizational equality agendas by focusing on individuals and by marginalizing social disadvantage (Greene and Kirton, 2004; Liff and Wajcman, 1996; Noon, 2007; Noon and Ogbonna, 2000). Unable to confront 'power relations, dominant ideologies or organizational goals', diversity discourses, argues Noon (2007: 775), leave deeply embedded structural problems within organizations untouched. Regarded by many as dependant upon good economic conditions and changes in language, neither of which necessarily change behaviour or organizational practices, the 'business case' concentrates primarily on the needs of employers rather than employees. Thus, many believe, it fails to address problems associated with the structures that created inequalities in the first place, many of which exist beyond the organization in the wider economy, society and labour market (Dickens, 1994; Noon, 2007; Squires, 2008).

The election of New Labour in 1997 raised hopes that the British Government would be more willing to intervene in the labour market to address persistent inequalities than previous neoliberal Conservative administrations (Dickens and Hall, 2006). Indeed, one of Tony Blair's first actions as prime minister was to sign the EU Social Chapter previously rejected by the Conservatives and, the prospect of a closer relationship with the EU, which had advanced important employment rights for women in areas such as pay, pensions and maternity leave (Walby, 1991), appeared positive. Despite this optimism, it is important, nonetheless, not to overstate the historic role of the EU in addressing labour market inequalities. Until relatively recently for example, Bell (2008) argues, EU equalities policies have concentrated on 'market integration' rather than social justice or 'social citizenship' objectives. The much-cited Article 119 of the Treaty of Rome which committed the EU to promoting equal pay between men and women originated not from a desire to promote social justice but from the economic concerns of the French who feared they would be competitively disadvantaged because equal pay was enshrined in their constitution (Adnett and Hardy, 2007). In 2000, however, two developments signalled a significant shift in EU equalities policy. The first was the inclusion in the Lisbon Strategy (the EU's 10-year plan for employment and growth) of the need to address a broad range of labour market inequalities: though some have argued this was primarily inspired by demographic changes and skill shortages in Europe (Adnett and Hardy, 2007; Bell, 2008). The second was the Amsterdam Treaty, which introduced two key Directives that for the first time sought to address a wide range of discriminatory practices in the European labour market beyond gender and nationality.

Article 13 of the Amsterdam Treaty 2000 extended the scope of EU anti-discrimination initiatives to include action in the areas of racial or ethnic origin, age, religion or belief, sexuality and disability by means of the Racial Equality Directive (RED) and Employment Equality Directive (EED). The RED addressed discrimination on grounds of race or ethnic origin in and beyond the labour market, to include housing, health care and education. The scope of the EED was in contrast limited to discrimination in employment and vocational training, though trade unions in Europe are currently lobbying for its extension to all areas cited in the RED. The impact of both Directives on existing British law has meant the grounds on which discrimination in employment can be claimed have been significantly extended. The Directives also make explicit reference to the human rights basis of non-discrimination and focus on the need to ensure equal treatment (Bell, 2008). They incorporate the principles of 'harassment' and of 'discrimination by association' (Howard, 2005). Moreover, in most instances, they reverse the burden of proof in discrimination cases so that it now rests with the defendant (usually the employer).

During the drafting of these two new EU Directives, interestingly, it became apparent that attempts to regulate inequalities in the labour market transnationally had to take account of different social and cultural meanings attached to 'protected' groups. For example, a number of EU states objected to the way the term 'race' was initially used in the RED, forcing the EU to insert a preamble into the Directive that made clear that it rejected all theories that 'attempt to determine the existence of separate human races' (Recital 6, quoted in Bell, 2008: 37). This did not, however, address problems arising from the absence in the RED of a definition of ethnic origin. Ethnic discrimination was largely presented as a matter affecting immigrants, yet most member states that had joined the EU since 2004 had little history of immigration. For these countries, ethnic discrimination, therefore, held a very different meaning and usually referred to national minorities (Bell, 2008: 37–8). The absence of a definition of 'disability' in the EED created further ambiguity (Waddington, 2005). Our earlier review of differences between US and UK disability legislation helps illustrate this. The more political, 'social model' of disability that guided the US ADA was not used in the Directive and as a consequence a majority (though not all) EU countries have adopted the individualistic medical model, which underpins British law (Bell, 2008; Foster and Fosh, 2009). Contrasts between US and EU law have also been drawn in the sphere of age discrimination. O'Cinneide (2005) notes that while US law provides clear guidelines, EU legislation fails to define what it means by 'age'. Indeed, Adnett and Hardy (2007: 32) argue, the EED appears to spend more time defining which ageist policies *are* justifiable in certain employment contexts, than which are not.

A significant, though often under-reported, requirement of the RED was an obligation on member states to set up national bodies to promote equal treatment of persons irrespective of racial or ethnic origin. Such bodies are charged with providing assistance to victims of discrimination and researching and publishing data that would support measures to address future discrimination in the labour market or in the provision of goods and services (Rorive, 2009). Belgium, Britain, Sweden and Denmark all had pre-existing anti-racism bodies and the Netherlands and Ireland addressed racism through general anti-discrimination organizations. Similar EU provisions had existed to promote gender equality; however, an unintentional consequence of the RED was that it stimulated the birth of a new generation of national anti-discrimination umbrella organizations across Europe, many of which are responsible for areas of discrimination covered by the EED, not just race. This has been the case in Britain where despite the existence of a 'Commission for Racial Equality' the EHRC was established to address a broader equalities remit. Interestingly, Rorive (2009: 144–5) observes how the Directive has given rise to a wide variety of equality bodies, which accommodate different national, political, historical and legal differences. Problems with co-ordinating equality policy across member states are, however, to some extent addressed by the European Network of Equality, 'Equinet', which has formally facilitated benchmarking and the exchange of information and best practice across the EU since 2003.

Concepts and theories of equality: past, present and future influences on law and policy

Concepts and theories of equality

The aim of legislation is to prohibit discrimination and promote equality, though as Howard (2008: 169) notes, the term 'equality' does have a number of different meanings: 'it can denote formal equality or equality of treatment; substantive equality, which encompasses equality of opportunity and equality of results'. The concept of 'formal equality', or 'equal treatment' underpinned the British Sex Discrimination Act 1975 and Race Relations Act 1976 and is generally understood as the right to be treated the same as any other person in the same situation. It is also to be found in the EU RED and refers to less favourable treatment in a comparable situation on grounds of racial or ethnic origin (Howard, 2008: 170). Equal treatment as a principle demands *consistency*, as such, it tends to appeal to people's sense of fairness and justice (Friedman, 2002). Nevertheless, critics of 'formal equality' believe it provides an inadequate basis on which to formulate law. It ignores 'difference' and, argue some, fails to acknowledge the role that historical or social disadvantages have played in the perpetuation of inequalities and why positive action may be necessary to address these (Howard, 2008: 170). The concept of 'substantive equality' was, therefore, developed in response to the perceived shortcomings of 'formal equality'.

'Substantive equality' acknowledges that some groups may have suffered from past and ongoing discrimination and tries to compensate for any social disadvantages experienced. It incorporates a belief that it is important to acknowledge *difference* and that equality can only be created if people are treated according to their needs (Bacik, 1997). The introduction in Britain of the Disability Discrimination Act (DDA) in 1995 was significant because it allowed for 'different', unequal and, importantly, the 'more favourable treatment' of disabled people (Dickens, 2007; Foster, 2007). The DDA differed from previous *symmetrical* sex and race equalities legislation because it was *asymmetrical* – that is, it only afforded protection against discrimination to disabled people (Waddington, 2005). Nonetheless, in practice, more favourable treatment or positive discrimination can be problematic. Unlike 'equal treatment' it can go against some people's instinctive feelings about what constitutes 'equality' and 'fairness'. For example, research on disability (Foster, 2007; Foster and Fosh, 2009) suggests that some disabled people experience problems in employment because, while the law gives them the right to request adjustments to their work and allows managers to treat them 'differently', some managers, used to equal treatment requirements that outlaw positive discrimination, do not understand this. *Indirect discrimination*, which is also associated with 'substantive' rather than 'formal' equality, can similarly be misunderstood. Indirect discrimination takes account of 'differences and of the disparate impact equal treatment can have' (Howard, 2008: 171). It, thus, refers to those provisions, criteria or practices that might appear neutral, but would put a person from one group at a disadvantage compared with a person from another group (cf. Howard, 2008: 171).

Formal equality relies on formal procedures and processes to achieve equality of opportunity and presupposes that all individuals entering the labour market compete within it as equals (Dickens, 1994; Friedman, 2001). Primarily concerned with equality of *access* not equality of *outcomes* (Dickens, 1994) this liberal approach puts its faith in perceived 'neutral' bureaucratic solutions, such as top-down organizational procedures to rectify perceived 'anomalies' in the labour market believed to be the source of discrimination (Rubin, 1997). Substantive equality, by contrast, is concerned to utilize measures that both aim to achieve equality of opportunity, which concentrate on equalizing *starting points*, and to measure that focus on equality of *outcomes*. An example of attempts to equalize starting points might include the provision of separate training for women, or female-only mentoring schemes: initiatives that acknowledge historic disadvantage. A concern for equality of *outcomes* also acknowledges past discrimination, and recognizes that this may have resulted in an unequal distribution of economic resources and representation: it is, therefore, concerned with the creation of a fairer society (Howard, 2008; Townshend-Smith, 1998). Both approaches allow for 'positive action', but some have argued that because 'equality of outcomes' is also concerned with economic and re-distributive objectives, it makes value judgements about the worth of some groups over others (Townshend-Smith, 1998). Friedman (2001), for example, questions this focus on re-distribution and outcomes, arguing that it does little to address the structures that perpetuate discrimination and pays too little attention to 'equality of diversity'.

Recent and proposed changes in equalities law, policy and governance in Britain

The recent introduction of Equality Duties in the UK public sector signalled a move away from the concepts of 'equal treatment', 'non-discrimination' and 'equality of opportunity' that have dominated domestic legislation, to allow for 'positive action'. These Duties look beyond symmetry and, as O'Brien (2008: 28) notes, are concerned with *preventing* discrimination rather than individual *retrospective* rights. Since 2001, there has been a duty to positively promote race equality in the public sector. This took the form of an amendment to the Race Relations Act following the McPherson Inquiry, which reported on institutional racism in the London Metropolitan Police Force. In 2006, a Disability Equality Duty (DED) and in 2007, a Gender Equality Duty (GED) were also introduced in the public sector, as part of the Equality Act 2006. The significance of Equality Duties is that they are concerned with existing unlawful discrimination *and* the promotion of equality of treatment in the future. They are about 'fair outcomes and civic participation, their target is not so much the irrational prejudices of individual "bad apples", but the systematic barriers to equal participation that carry the label of institutional discrimination' (O'Brien, 2008: 28). Significantly, the Duties also promote a concept of 'different treatment', which previously only existed in the UK DDA and which O'Brien (2008: 30) argues signals a 'more value-driven and intellectually compelling account of purpose than can be yielded from the bare bones of equal treatment'. We will explore Public Sector Equality Duties further in the next section when we focus on workplace equality agendas.

The concepts of equality discussed thus far primarily take the needs of *groups* as their reference point. This approach has dominated UK legislation and has meant that the goals of sex, race and disability equality have traditionally been pursued separately. The Equality Act 2006, which created the EHRC in 2007, was intended to replace and integrate the three previously separate – Equal Opportunities, Racial Equality and Disability Rights Commissions (DRC). Although not fully operational until 2009, Squires (2008) believes two recent developments rendered the 'single strands' approach in Britain untenable. The first was the aforementioned introduction of EU equalities Directives in 2000, which widened the scope of equality legislation and provided the government with the political opportunity to open a debate about replacing existing agencies with a single body. The second was the devolution of responsibility for equality to new administrations in Scotland and Wales (c.f. Chaney, 2009; Chaney and Fevre, 2002), which along with Northern Ireland, offered alternative approaches to equalities and different levels of provision for different peoples within different territories.

Optimists believe the EHRC will facilitate an 'integrated mandate' and a 'unified "equalities" agenda' (Niven, 2008: 17) that might better address multiple forms of inequality and issues of 'intersectionality' (Squires, 2008: 53). It is claimed that the EHRC should be better placed to address diversity within and between groups (Simon, 2004) and will invite 'a fresh reflection on the relationship between equality and human rights and, on the extent to which they coalesce' (O'Brien, 2008: 27). The abandonment of the old Commissions and rejection of a group-discrimination discourse has, nonetheless, raised concerns (Squires, 2008: 55). Some fear that valuable group-based expertise and resources that have been built up over many years may be lost. Others have expressed concern that some groups might become marginalized within the new Commission and a hierarchy of discrimination could emerge. This latter point was raised by the DRC prior to the launch of the Commission and the appointment of specialist Commissioners was intended to address this, yet recently, Sir Bert Massie (2009: 1) former Chair of the DRC has criticized the EHRC for being 'intoxicated by the idea of cross-strand work at the expense of the important issues that affect only one minority'. This criticism reinforces warnings from other countries, including Australia, where the single equalities Commission route was pursued and disability issues were marginalized (Mabbett, 2008).

The recognition that existing legislation fails to appreciate that people may have complex, multiple identities and interests that cut across established group-based legislation should be welcomed. The concept of 'intersectionality' recognizes the interaction of different forms of oppression, by acknowledging that 'discrete forms of oppression shape, and are shaped by, one another' (Squires, 2008: 55). Intersectionality, does, however, raise a number of new problems. Squires (2008), for example, argues that too much of a focus on individual differences or diversity may mean that knowledge about the historic and social character of discrimination, which is group based, will be lost; a point also made by a government-sponsored Equalities Review in 2007, chaired by Trevor Phillips of the EHRC. This reaffirmed the significance of deep-seated persistent group-specific inequalities, such as unequal pay between men and women; unequal educational and employment opportunities within certain Black Minority Ethnic communities; and poverty among disabled people. It cautioned against the abandonment of group-based analyses (Niven, 2008: 19). Some have consequently argued that the retention of a group focus alongside an acknowledgement that there are 'contradictions and antagonisms within as well as between groups' (Squires, 2008: 55), is, therefore, essential. This 'additive' approach has some obvious advantages, though there is a danger that the promotion of one equality strand may erode or conflict with another. For example, the goal of gender equality may conflict with religious identity. An alternative would, as Squires (2008) suggests, be to focus on individuals as core equality 'subjects' and abandon the 'group' approach altogether. However, she also cautions that such an individualistic approach has much in common with the 'diversity management' literature, we discussed earlier.

Interestingly, a range of evidence from speeches by Labour Ministers and circulars issued by the then Department of Trade and Industry (DTI) is presented by Squires (2008: 57–8), which suggest that the formation of the EHRC was framed within a 'business case' model. The use of what she terms a 'utility-based argument' (Squires, 2008: 58) to justify giving attention to multiple equality strands would seem to indicate that like the Conservatives, Labour has replaced the principle of social justice with the language of competitiveness and productivity. In 2004, the DTI produced a leaflet entitled 'The Business Case for Diversity and Equality' in which promoting equality was couched in terms of the benefits for business: of retaining skilled employees and employing a range of people who can identify with diverse customers. 'Fairness at Work', as Dickens (2007) observes, has also been concerned to not overburden employers. The influence of the corporate discourse of 'diversity management' on Labour thinking may also indicate that academic theories of intersectionality that 'value' rather than 'manage' diversity have been displaced (Squires, 2008). If so, this would be worrying and might suggest that wider social justice concerns have been subsumed (Wrench, 2005). Squires (2008: 60) thus concludes that 'if the EHRC chooses to use this corporate diversity rhetoric to frame its own equality agenda as a way of resolving the difficulties of the group-based approach to intersectionality ... it will reduce the pursuit of equality to a utility-based exercise.'

The Labour Party manifesto of 2005 announced proposals for a Single Equality Bill (SEB), and it is anticipated that it will be granted royal assent by spring 2010. The Bill has two main objectives: to address the piecemeal way in which UK equalities legislation has evolved by harmonizing discrimination law and to strengthen the law to support progress on equality (see House of Lords, 2010). In 2005, Labour set up a Discrimination Law Review to address long-term concerns about inconsistencies in equality law, though this was criticized for merely consolidating existing equalities legislation when it reported in 2007 (EHRC, 2009b; TUC, 2009a). Further periods of consultation with 'stakeholders' followed, culminating in the presentation to Parliament of the SEB in April 2009. When or if, it takes effect, the Single Equality Act will repeal or revoke all previous legislation, though where it is appropriate to retain a distinctive approach to some forms of discrimination such as disability, this will continue (TUC, 2009a). Media attention has focused on measures in the Bill to improve pay transparency through pay audits and the abolition of pay 'gagging' clauses. Proposals that private sector employers with more than 250 employees will be required to publish information on male and female pay after 2013 to allow time for voluntary arrangements to emerge, however, appear limited when one considers that most of the private sector is comprised of small- and medium-size enterprises.

In June 2009, the Government published its proposals for a set of specific duties in the public sector, which would combine the previously separate equality duties on race, disability and gender and would incorporate new duties relating to age, gender reassignment, pregnancy and maternity, religion and belief and sexual orientation. In its policy statement on the specific duties, the Government states 'equality should be at the heart of what the public sector does – not an "add on" or after thought' (GEO, 2009b: 5), thus emphasizing both the proactive and ongoing character of the proposed duties, with an obligation to review, consult with stakeholders and up-date equality schemes every 3 years. 'A Fairer Future' (GEO, 2009a) the Equalities Office publication that accompanied the SEB, anticipated that the new Public Sector Equality Duty will require public bodies with over 150 employees to report on their gender pay and ethnic minority and disability employment rates. The Bill also extends equality duties to public procurement activities and the EHRC have been made responsible for revising the Pre-Qualification Questionnaire issued to contractors (EHRC, 2009a: 8).

In the context of earlier debate about 'substantive equality', the SEB contains significant positive action proposals and there is support for a shift from what is termed a 'process-based' to an 'outcome focused approach' (GEO, 2010: 10). The Bill permits action that is targeted at overcoming group disadvantage or tackling under-representation. It allows employers, for example, faced with two equally qualified candidates in a recruitment process, to select, if they wish, the successful candidate from an under-represented or disadvantaged group (EHRC, 2009a: 11). One aspect of the Bill that caused controversy on the Conservative opposition benches, however, is the inclusion of a new public sector duty to have regard for socio-economic disadvantage. This applies to public authorities and their strategic decision-making however, unlike other public sector duties that are policed by the EHRC, there is no obvious enforcement mechanism in this area.

The SEB also contains important new definitions and clauses relating to indirect discrimination, discrimination by association, victimization, harassment, perceived discrimination and multiple discrimination. Indirect discrimination had already applied to cases of sex and race discrimination but will now be extended. Because of EU legislation and a number of high-profile legal cases it was also necessary to strengthen clauses relating to discrimination by association and victimization. The case of Coleman v. Attridge Law (case c-303/06) [2008] I.R.L.R. 722 ECJ) is perhaps the best-known ruling and involved a mother who worked for a legal practice and was discriminated against because her child had a disability. ' "Association discrimination" occurs where a person is harassed or discriminated against for their association with a person from a protected group' (Connolly, 2009: 2). Perceived discrimination, by contrast, occurs when an employee is harassed or discriminated against because it is assumed incorrectly, that the person belongs to a protected group. A recent case highlighted by Connolly (2009: 2–5) of homophobic harassment where co-workers harassed an employee with sexual innuendo illustrates the complexities of this basis for discrimination. In this case both harassers and the harassed admitting that no one actually thought Mr English, the recipient of the harassment was actually gay, yet he won his case of unlawful harassment (on appeal) on grounds of sexual orientation because of the mockery he had experienced. Following further consultations clauses relating to multiple, or more accurately, 'dual discrimination' were also added to the SEB in July and December 2009. The Bill now offers 'protection if individuals experience discrimination because of a combination of two relevant protected characteristics' (House of Lords, 2010) however, the Government considered it too burdensome on business to extend to combinations beyond this (GEO, 2009b: 2). A number of other provisions within the Bill will influence the future of workplace representation and are of particular interest to trade unions; these will be explored further below when discussing the future of workplace equality agendas.

The future of workplace equality agendas

We have so far focused on the legal and policy contexts associated with employment equality initiatives: the concepts, theories and ideologies that have shaped these, and the groups, individuals and organizations (national and international) that have influenced them. In this final section, we examine the impact and mediation of equality initiatives at the level of the workplace. Traditionally, there have been three main routes through which workplace equality objectives have been pursued. Statutory determined rights are the most obvious and include legislation aimed at extending the employment rights of specific groups (e.g. women, disabled people); extensions or amendments to existing rights or legislation; and provisions not specifically introduced as equalities initiatives, but that impact on workplace equality such as maternity leave, family-friendly policies and work–life balance initiatives (cf. Dickens, 2007: 464–5). Collective bargaining is another route through which equality objectives are pursued and strategies have included workplace or sector equality bargaining (for example, on equal pay) or, in the public sector, bargaining related to sub-contracting and public procurement. A third route is the pursuit of individual litigation. The establishment of 'case law' has always been an important feature of the British equalities landscape and although this is a highly individualized route, it can involve workplace actors such as trade unions and non-governmental organizations as representatives. Precedents established through individual litigation, furthermore, often have wider collective implications and can be used as bargaining tools by workplace actors, such as trade unions (cf. Heery and Conley, 2007).

A decline in union membership in Britain, whereby fewer than 30 per cent of employees now belong to a trade union, has also been accompanied by a decline in those collective institutions that previously regulated employment for many (Heery et al., 2004). Traditional collective bargaining as a route to advance equality objectives, therefore, appears increasingly vulnerable. Evidence does, nevertheless, support the view that a union presence in the workplace is positively correlated with the existence of equal opportunities policies and practices, though as some have noted these can be 'empty shells' (Hoque and Noon, 2004). The main alternative to collective bargaining is to increasingly rely on statutory provisions, though an historic attachment to voluntarism means legal remedies have been least favoured by British trade unions. Heery, in Chapter 4 refers to what he terms the 'empirical puzzle' that surrounds the objective of achieving equal pay between men and women in Britain. Arguing that despite long-standing statutory provisions and the existence of a consensus among politicians, managers and unions that unequal pay needs to be addressed, a radical transformation in the gender pay gap in Britain has failed to occur. This suggests that there is no one easy solution to the problem of persistent inequalities in the labour market. Should the equalities agenda increasingly rely on statutory provisions and individual litigation, however, it might be possible to argue that membership of a trade union may become more, rather than less important, given that the absence of alternative financial support puts justice beyond the reach of all but a few. This has become increasingly important since the old single equality commissions have been replaced by the EHRC, because the latter abandoned the important single-strand legal case work previously championed by the former.

The value of the equalities work that trade unions undertake should not be overlooked and has become increasingly important as their memberships have diversified (Greene and Kirton, 2004; Munro, 2001). The plurality of interests that exist within the British trade union movement has, moreover, prompted the development of collectivist strategies to counter what can often be individual and isolating experiences of discrimination. Greene and Kirton (2004) argue that by acknowledging 'diversity' within a framework that retains the importance of group identity, unions have engaged in 'diversity management'. Significantly, they distinguish this from the unitary 'managing diversity' approach advocated by those who support the 'business case'. 'Diversity management' recognizes the value of both 'sameness and 'difference', which argue Greene and Kirton (2004: 5), can constructively co-exist within a pluralist, collectivist model motivated by social justice rather than business interests. Since the 1980s, most unions have also been concerned to reflect the increasing diversity of the labour market in the governance of their internal structures and to give voice to previously under-represented groups (Walby, 1991). A number of studies, largely focusing on gender and race, have detailed the effects of this process (cf. Colgan and Ledwith, 2000; Greene and Kirton, 2004; Healy et al. 2004; McBride, 2001Munro, 2001). Initiatives aimed at increasing representativeness inside UK unions have, nonetheless, followed the familiar path of encouraging the development of self-organizing separatist organizations based on group identities. Evidence of coalition building between and across different groups, however, is available from examples of union organizing in other countries such as Canada. Briskin's (2008) study of three Canadian unions highlights how constitutional, organizational and representational intersectionality can facilitate good intersectional political practices. She refers to 'cross-constituency organizing' (Briskin, 2008: 224) within these unions, which entails separate self-organizing groups being brought together under umbrella bodies inside unions such as equality steering, social justice or human rights committees. Dual, parallel and integrated structures, Briskin (2008: 242) argues, help to bring people out of their silos and address both the specific constituency-based interests of equality seeking groups and the interrelationship of equity issues, demonstrating that 'solidarity can be built on a foundation of diversity'. While admitting that it is too early to draw definitive conclusions from this emergent form of organizing, Briskin is optimistic that such coalition building inside unions will help build solidarities across identities and revitalize the union equity project. It will, therefore, be interesting to see whether unions will respond similarly to the intersectionality agenda in theory and practice in Britain.

During the consultation process that preceded the SEB the TUC raised a number of important concerns about Government proposals to amend equality legislation. It sought (TUC, 2009a: 12), but failed, to secure statutory recognition rights for trade union equality representatives, so that they would gain protection under law and access to paid time off work to undertake duties associated with their role. The Equalities Office did, however, agree to fund the TUC to undertake an evaluation of workplace equality representation to report by the end of 2009 (see TUC, 2010). The TUC continues to press for statutory rights for workplace equality representatives, many of whom have received education and training under schemes funded by the Government's Union Modernisation Fund. The omission of representative (or so-called class) actions from the proposed legislation, which would have facilitated the representation of groups of claimants as is common in the US, was also criticized by the TUC. So too were proposals that multiple discrimination provisions would only apply to instances of direct discrimination (TUC, 2009b: 1). The TUC points to differences between the Government's proposals and existing provisions in Northern Ireland, where multiple discrimination cases allow for indirect discrimination and harassment claims to be brought and there is 'no distinction between intersectional and additive multiple discrimination' (TUC, 2009b: 1).

The TUC has, nevertheless, welcomed provisions contained in the SEB aimed at strengthening the powers of British Employment Tribunals (ETs). Currently, ETs can only make a recommendation to an employer in a discrimination case if it will benefit the claimant, which ignores the fact that 70 per cent of employees that bring discrimination cases leave the organization that discriminated against them (GEO, 2009a: 23). To remedy this, the Bill proposes that in the future ETs will be allowed to make recommendations that would benefit the entire workforce, not just the person who brings a case. Failure to comply with such recommendations would, moreover, be used as evidence against an employer if future claims of a similar nature were to occur.

Many of the proposals contained within the SEB represent a significant shift in the UK approach to workplace equality. As noted earlier, the introduction of Public Sector Equality Duties utilized different concepts of 'equality' and, significantly, held *employers* accountable for their implementation as well as their *outcomes*. The SEB and proposed Single Equality Duties build on the perceived successes of the separate duties and, perhaps in the hope of restoring its 'model employer' image, propose that the public sector 'should lead the way' (GEO, 2010: 5). Provisions within the SEB also make it clear that employers must consult widely when reviewing business plans and formulating organizational equality objectives. This obligation is couched in terms of the need to present a viable evidence-base for codes of practice, which can only be done if employers engage with 'people with relevant protected characteristics, frontline staff, voluntary bodies and trade unions' (GEO, 2010: 7). In this regard legislation has tried to get away from the perception that equality concerns are the domain of organizational specialists and have attempted to 'mainstream' equalities (Conley, 2008). It also recognizes that equality objectives are not static and need to respond to change through regular reviews and analysis of new evidence. The participation of trade unions might prove important in formulating and collectivizing organizational equality agendas in the consultation and evidence gathering processes since many individual employees and service users lack the political, organizational and industrial relations experience to be effective. Unions could, therefore, play a valuable role in helping to police Duties alongside the EHRC who were given formal powers of investigation under the Equality Act 2006.

It is interesting, though perhaps not surprising, that 'New Labour' appears to have reserved its most radical proposals to reform the equality employment agenda in Britain for the public sector. Their reluctance to increase regulation in the private sector has, moreover, contributed to an ambiguity in the SEB around whether pay audits will ever be mandatory. The powers to conduct Formal Inquiries conferred on the EHRC under the Equality Act 2006 has perhaps been the exception to the general rule of non-intervention (ELB, February 2009). To date, three such inquiries into the meat processing, construction and financial services industries have taken place. Such inquiries require the industry to provide information, documentation or give oral evidence regarding a specified aspect of equalities. The recent Inquiry into the financial services sector (EHRC, 2009b), for example, demanded the industry provide statistics on pay and occupation by gender to explain the disproportionately high gender pay gap. It is thought the mere act of evidence gathering and associated requirement to defend practices in public, together with recommendations for change will help bring about reform in the private sector. Nevertheless, while employees in the public sector will enjoy much better protection with regard to both enhanced statutory equality rights and more developed unionization and workplace collective bargaining, employees in the private and voluntary sectors, though indirectly affected by proposals for equality regulations that govern public procurement, will have to rely more on 'naming and shaming' tactics. Given that two of the three routes we identified at the beginning of this section, through which equality objectives could be advanced are reduced in the private and voluntary sectors, we may be witnessing the emergence of a two-tier labour market in terms of equalities employment protection in Britain.

Conclusion: looking to the future – intersectionality in theory and practice

The purpose of this chapter has been to examine how equality law, policy and practice have evolved in Britain to identify key influences and the role of key actors and to review contemporary developments, which suggest a significant break with the past. Sustaining the concept of 'social justice' as the guiding principle of workplace equality and diversity initiatives will, we believe, be a central challenge for future campaigners. As Dickens (2007: 468) notes, while discrimination is a moral issue 'governmental concern is not only for justice and fairness but also competitiveness and efficiency'. In theory, at least, we have shown how the traditionally narrow objectives of British equality law have recently been addressed by New Labour policies and proposals, which have widened the scope of law and acknowledged that people have multiple, intersecting interests. We have, however, also highlighted criticisms that accuse Labour of political opportunism in setting up the EHRC; timidity in regulating the private sector; and missed opportunities in relation to 'class' actions and the role of workplace equality representatives. This has led some commentators (cf. Squires, 2008) to conclude that rather than a commitment to academic theories of intersectionality that 'value', rather than seek to 'manage' diversity, Labour still exhibits a political attachment to a 'utility model' of equalities, reminiscent of the bankrupt 'business case'.

The accommodation of multiple, intersecting interests and identities in approaches to workplace equality addresses some past shortcomings in UK legislation, but it also presents policy makers and workplace actors with a number of new dilemmas. Too much of a focus on differences between individuals could undermine the potential for collective action, effectively de-politicizing workplace equality agendas. Individuals that have multiple equality concerns may find that they conflict and policy that attempts to deal with such conflicts may be contradictory or inadequate. Fears that a hierarchy of equality might emerge in representative bodies such as the EHRC could also apply to trade unions and workplaces, with under-represented groups finding their concerns are further marginalized Evidence from the Government and EHRC, moreover, continues to suggest that deep-seated, group-based inequalities persist and need to be addressed by reference to the important social and historic characteristics of specific groups. A focus on difference at the expense of group-based experiences could, therefore, undermine valuable work that has already been done. If new equalities legislation does succeed in making it on to the statute books the UK employment provisions on equality will, hopefully, be more coherent. However, the jury is still out as to whether this will represent a radical transformation in the employment relationship.

Acknowledgements

We would like to thank Natasha Hirst of Wales TUC for her help and insights and the editors for constructive feedback on an earlier version of this chapter.

References

Adnett, N. and Hardy, S. (2007) The Peculiar Case of age discrimination: Americanising the European social model? *European Journal of Law and Economics*, 23, 29–41.

Bacik, I. (1997) Combating Discrimination: The Affirmative Action Approach, in R. Byrne and W. Duncun (eds) *Developments in Discrimination Law in Ireland and Europe*. Dublin: Irish Centre for European Law, pp. 119–30.

Bell, M. (2008) The Implementation of European Anti-discrimination Directives: Converging Towards a Common Model. *The Political Quarterly*, 79(1), 36–44.

Boston, S. (1987) *Women Workers and Trade Unions*. London: Lawrence and Wishart Ltd.

Briskin, L. (2008) Cross-constituency Organizing in Canadian Unions. *British Journal of Industrial Relations*, 46(2), 221–47.

Chaney, P. (2009) Equal Opportunities and Human Rights: The First Decade of Devolution in Wales. London: Equality and Human Rights Commission (EHRC).

Chaney, P. and Fevre, R. and (2002) *An Absolute Duty: A Report on the Welsh Assembly's Equality Policies and their Implementation July 1999 to January 2002*. Cardiff: Institute for Welsh Affairs.

Clough, B. (2007) From Voluntarism to Post-Voluntarism. The Emergence of Unions in the Vocatiohnal Education and Training System. Unionlearn, TUC.

Connolly, M. (2009) *Homophobic Harassment Where No One Is Seen to Be Gay – Opening Pandora's Attic?* Case comment: Employment Law Bulletin 89(February), 2–5. Westlaw, UK.

Colgan, F. and Ledwith, S. (2000) Diversities, Identities and Strategies of Women Trade Union Activists. *Gender, Work and Organisation*, 7, 242–57.

Conley, H. (2008) 'Trade Unions, Equality and the Law'. Paper Presented at Crafting Effective Interventions in Pursuit of Equality and Diversity Workshop, Queen Mary University of London, 12th September.

Dickens, L. (1994) The Business Case for Women's Equality. *Employee Relations*, 16(8), 5–18.

Dickens, L. (1999) Beyond the Business Case: a Three-Pronged Approach to Equality Action. *Human Resource Management Journal*, 9(1), 9–19.

Dickens, L. (2007) The Road is Long: Thirty Years of Equality Legislation in Britain. *British Journal of Industrial Relations*, 45(3), 463–94, September.

Dickens, L. and Hall, M. (2006) Fairness up to a Point, Assessing the Impact of New Labour's Employment Legislation. *Human Resource Management Journal*, 16(4), 338–356.

Department for Trade and Industry (DTI) (2004) *The Business Case for Diversity and Equality*, Stationary Office.

Equality and Human Rights Commission (EHRC) (2009a) Equality Bill: Parliamentary Briefing (House of Commons second reading), May.

Equality and Human Rights Commission (EHRC) (2009b) Financial Service Inquiry: sex discrimination and gender pay gap Report of the Equality and Human Rights Commission. EHRC.

Employment Law Bulletin (ELB) (2009) EHRC Inquiries 89 (February), 7–8. Westlaw, UK.

Foster, D. (2007) Legal Obligation or Personal Lottery? Employee Experiences of Disability and the Negotiation of Adjustments in the Public Sector Workplace. *Work, Employment and Society*, 21(1), 67–84.

Foster, D. and Fosh, P. (2009) 'Negotiating 'Difference': Representing Disabled Employees in the British Workplace', *British Journal of Industrial Relations* (DOI) 10.1111/j.1467-8543.2009.00748.x.

Foster, D. and Scott, P. (1998) Competitive Tendering of Public Services and Industrial Relations Policy: The Conservative Agenda under Thatcher and Major 1979–97. *Historical Studies in Industrial Relations*, Autumn(6), 101–32.

Foster, D. and Scott, P. (2003) Trade Unions, Public Services and the Euro, in Foster, D. and Scott, P. (eds) *Trade Unions in Europe: Meeting the Challenge*. Brussels: P.I.E-Peter Lang.

Friedman, S. (2001) Equality; A New Generation? *Industrial Law Journal*, 30(2), 145–68.

Friedman, S. (2002) *Discrimination Law*. Oxford: Clarendon Law Series.

Friedman, H. and Meredeen, S. (1980) *The Dynamics of Industrial Conflict: Lessons from Ford*. London: Croom Helm.

Gilbert, J. and Stead, B. (1999) Stigmatization Revisited. *Group and Organization Management*, 24(2), 239–56.

Guigni, M.G. (1998) Was it Worth the Effort? The Outcomes and Consequences of Social Movements. *Annual Review of Sociology*, 24, 371–93.

Greene, A.-M. and Kirton, G. (2004) Views from another Stakeholder: Trade Union Perspectives on the Rhetoric of Managing Diversity. Warwick Papers in Industrial Relations, no. 74, June.

Goss, D., Goss, F. and Adam-Smith, D. (2000) Disability and Employment: A Comparative Critique of UK Legislation. *The International Journal of Human Resource Management*, 11(4), 807–21.

Government Equalities Office (GEO) (2009a) *A Fairer Future: The Equality Bill and Other Action to Make Equality a Reality*. London: The Stationary Office Ltd.

Government Equalities Office (GEO) (2009b) *Equality Bill: Assessing the Impact of A Multiple Discrimination Provision: Summary of Responses*. London: The Stationery Office Ltd.

Government Equalities Office (GEO) (2010) *Equality Bill: Making It Work. Policy Proposals for Specific Duties (Policy Statement)*. London: The Stationary Office Ltd.

Healy, G., Bradley, H. and Mukherjee, N. (2004) Inspiring Activists: The Experiences of Minority Ethnic Women in Trade Unions, in Healy, G., Heery, E., Taylor, P. and Brown, W. (eds) *The Future of Worker Representation*. Basingstoke: Palgrave Macmillan.

Heery, E. and Conley, H. (2007) Frame Extension in a Mature Social Movement: British Trade Unions and Part-time Work, 1967–2002. *Journal of Industrial Relations*, 49(1), 5–29.

Heery, E., Healy, G. and Taylor, P. (2004) Representation at Work: Themes and Issues, in Healy, G., Heery, E., Taylor, P. and Brown, W. (eds), *The Future of Worker Representation*. Palgrave Macmillan.

Hoque, K. and Noon, M. (2004) Equal Opportunities Policy and Practice in Britain: Evaluating the 'Empty Shell' Hypothesis. *Work, Employment and Society*, 18(3), 481–506.

Howard, E. (2005) Anti Race Discrimination Measures in Europe: An Attack on Two Fronts. *European Law Journal*, 11(4), 468–86.

Howard, E. (2008) The European Year of Equal Opportunities for All – 2007: Is the EU Moving Away From a Formal Idea of Equality? *European Law Journal*, 14(2), 168–85, March.

House of Lords (2010) Equality Bill: Explanatory Notes, www.publications.parliament.uk/pa/ld200910/idbills/020/en/10020x–.htm.

Liff, S. (1999) Diversity and Equal Opportunities: Room for a Constructive Compromise? *Human Resource Management Journal*, 9(1), 65–75.

Liff, S. and Wajcman, J. (1996) 'Sameness' and 'Difference' Re-Visited: Which Way Forward for Equal Opportunities Initiatives? *Journal of Management Studies*, 33(1), 79–95.

Mabbett, D. (2008) Aspirational Legalism and the Role of the Equality and Human Rights Commission in Equality Policy. *The Political Quarterly*, 79(1), 45–52, January–March.

McBride, A. (2001) *Gender Democracy in Trade Unions*. Aldershot: Ashgate.

Massie, B. (2009) 'Equality body "failing disabled" ' BBC news UK, http://newsvote.bbc.co.uk 16 March 2009.

Meehan, E. (1985) *Women's Rights at Work: Campaigns and Policy in Britain and the United States*. Basingstoke: Palgrave Macmillan.

Munro, A. (2001) The Feminist Trade Union Agenda? The Continued Significance of Class, Race and Gender. *Gender, Work and Organization*, 8 (4), 454–71.

Niven, B. (2008) The EHRC: Transformational, Progressively Incremental or a Disappointment? *The Political Quarterly*, 79(1), 17–26.

Noon, M. (2007) The fatal flaws of diversity and the business case for ethnic minorities. *Work, Employment and Society*, 21(4), 773–84.

Noon, M. and Ogbonna, E. (2000) *Equality, Diversity and Disadvantage in Employment*. Basingstoke: Palgrave Macmillan.

O'Brien, N. (2008) Equality and Human Rights: Foundations of a Common Culture? *The Political Quarterly*, 79(1), 27–35, January–March.

O'Cinneide, C. (2005) *Age Discrimination and European Law*. Brussles: European Commission, Directorate General for Employment, Social Affairs and Equal Opportunities.

Pagel, M. (1988) *'On Our Own Behalf' – An Introduction to the Self-Organisation of Disabled People*. GMCDP, BEVC, Aked Close, Ardwick, Manchester (pages unpaginated).

Shakespeare, T. (2006) *Disability Rights and Wrongs*. London: Routledge.

Simon, H. (2004) Solving Problems vs Claiming Rights: The Pragmatist Challenge to Legal Liberalism. *William and Mary Law Review*, 41(1), 127–212.

Squires, J. (2008) Intersecting Inequalities: Reflecting on the Subjects and Objects of Equality. *The Political Quarterly*, 79(1), 53–61.

Randall, V. (1982) *Women and Politics*. London: Macmillan.

Rubin, J. (1997) Gender, Equality and the Culture of Organizational Assessment. *Gender, Work and Organization*, 4(1), 24–34.

Robertson, D.B. (1999) Voluntarism Against the Open Shop: Labour and Business Strategies in the Battle for American Labor Markets. *Studies in American Political Development (Spring)*, 12, 146–85.

Rorive, I. (2009) A Comparative and European Examination of National Institutions in the Field of Racism and Discrimination, in Boyle, K. (ed.) *New Institutions for Human Rights Protection*. Oxford: Oxford University Press.

Oliver, M. (1996) *Understanding Disability: from Theory to Practice*. Basingstoke: Palgrave Macmillan.

Trades Union Congress (2009a) Equality Bill (paper for the TUC Executive Committee). London: Trade Union Congress.

Trades Union Congress (2009b) Equality Bill: Assessing the Impact of Multiple Discrimination. TUC Consultation Response. London: Trades Union Congress.

Trades Union Congress (2010) TUC Equality Reps Project Extension Report (April 2009–December 2009).

Townshend-Smith, R. (1998), *Discrimination Law: Text, Cases and Materials.* London: Cavendish Publishing.

Waddington, J. (2005), Implementing the Disability Provisions of the Framework Employment Directive: Room for Exercising National Discretions, in Lawson, A. and Gooding, C. (eds) *Disability Rights in Europe: from Theory to Practice.* Oxford: Hart.

Wrench, J. (2005) Diversity Management Can Be Bad for You. *Race and Class*, 46(3), 73–84.

15

Assessing voice: the debate over worker representation

Edmund Heery

Introduction

Systems of representation that allow workers voice and enable them to participate in the governance and regulation of enterprise are a central aspect of the employment relationship in all developed economies. Until comparatively recently the pivotal institution within systems of representation was trade unionism. Trade unions organized workers and allowed the expression of voice through both their internal systems of government and through their hierarchies of paid and volunteer representatives. The latter monitored employer behaviour, raised grievances, negotiated collective agreements regulating the employment relationship and engaged in joint consultation and problem-solving with the employers of their members. For three decades, however, unions have been in retreat in most countries of the developed world and a more multiform system of worker representation has come to the fore. In the United Kingdom, according to the 2004 Workplace Employment Relations Survey, there are now roughly equal numbers of union and non-union representatives in UK workplaces, the latter largely appointed or supported by their employers (Charlwood and Forth, 2009: 94). In addition to employer-sponsored systems of worker involvement and participation, commentators have highlighted the significance of statutory systems of worker representation, such as works councils (Gumbrell-McCormick and Hyman, 2010; Jenkins and Blyton, 2008), and the increasingly active role of civil society organizations in campaigning for the interests of vulnerable workers and minority groups (Heery et al., 2010). There is a situation therefore in which the once predominant institution of worker representation has declined and a range of other institutions have either spread or assumed greater relative importance.

The purpose of this chapter is to review how the academic field of Industrial Relations (IR) has responded to the changing morphology of worker representation. It is concerned with the competing assessments and the often fierce debate that has circled around the empirical trends. In doing so, two main areas of debate are examined. The first is preoccupied with the labour movement and is concerned with the attempts to renew or revitalize trade unionism, which have been such a marked feature of trade union activity in recent years (Fairbrother and Yates, 2003; Frege and Kelly, 2004). Academic debate over union revitalization has been increasingly preoccupied with two issues, both of which are considered. One has examined the union response to the hegemony of neoliberalism and has addressed the international turn towards organizing (Daniels, 2009). The other deals with the union response to a more feminized and diverse workforce, composed of multiple ethnicities and a range of more assertive identity groups (Foley and Baker, 2009). Union attempts to represent diversity have become a major subject of academic inquiry and debate.

The other main focus of attention has been non-union institutions of worker representation, three of which have attracted most interest, statutory works councils, employer-sponsored participation and single-issue and community organizations. In this area, again, debate has tended to follow two avenues. Along the first, commentators have adopted different positions with regard to the relationship between non-union institutions and trade unionism. For some, the former promise or threaten to replace the latter and there is an assumption of conflicting institutional interests (Piore and Safford, 2006). For others, in contrast, coalition is possible and unions and non-union institutions can form a mutually beneficial partnership (Turner, 2007). Along the second, debate has been concerned with the relative effectiveness of union and non-union forms in representing workers (Freeman et al., 2007). Is it the case that non-union institutions perform similar functions for workers to those previously undertaken by unions and are they as equally or more successful in doing so? As we will see, there are not only sharply divergent answers to these critical questions but they can be posed in different ways.

Union revitalization: power and diversity

As has been pointed out, the recent literature on trade union revitalization has followed two broad lines of inquiry (see Table 15.1). On the one hand,

Table 15.1 Power and diversity in union revitalization

	Power	Diversity
Pressure for change	Loss of union power in era of neoliberalism due to reduced scope for accommodation with militant employers and hostile states	Increasing workforce diversity and more assertive identity groups
Prescription	Re-build union power to provide a counter to employers and states via 1) organizing campaigns that build membership and collective organization 2) union–community coalitions that bring additional resources and mobilizing capacity	Represent diversity via 1) internal strategies that both confer autonomy and integrate equity-seeking groups within union government 2) external strategies that use bargaining and law to eliminate discrimination and match job regulation to diverse interests
Internal debate	Debate over the conditions for effective organizing with opposed positions taken by those advocating 'strategic' and 'rank-and-file' organizing	Debate over the success of attempts to represent diversity with opposed positions taken by those who deem gender democracy effective and ineffective
External critique	Unions can make an effective accommodation with neoliberalism via labour–management partnership or participation in the re-regulation of labour markets	A diverse union constituency does not imply more differentiated representation as most categories express a common preference with regard to union representation

there is a current that focuses on the question of union power. The diagnosis in this case is that unions have declined because they lack power. Capacities that enabled influence in economy and politics and attracted workers into membership have been eroded and unions can only renew themselves, the argument goes, if they re-build these capacities or access fresh sources of power. On the other hand, there is a current that stresses diversity and the need for unions to recognize and effectively represent newly assertive identities among a changing, more diverse workforce. The diagnosis in this case is that unions have failed to respond to the identities and associated interests of a workforce in transition and that they must perforce adjust if they are to survive (Hyman, 1999). While the first current emphasizes union relationships with employers and state and the need to shift the balance of power in these relationships, the second emphasizes the relationship between unions and workers and the need for unions better to represent diversity.[1]

Power

The starting point for many of those making the power-centred argument is a claim that unions confront a neoliberal political and economic order that is global in scope (e.g. Fletcher and Gapasin, 2008; McIlroy and Daniels, 2009). Defining features of this order include the commitment of states (and supra-state institutions) to market creation, which *inter alia* encompasses the pushing back of union and associated forms of regulation, and increased pressure on employers to eliminate cost and drive up performance, emanating both from intensified competition and the financialization of the business system. It is also argued that neoliberalism is characterized by a fusion of state and business interests that squeezes out the interests of other social actors within government policy (Juravich, 2007). The main consequence for unions is that neoliberalism affords little space for the accommodation with state and employers based on mutual gains that was the hallmark of an earlier stage of capitalist development. Power resources that previously sustained trade unionism, such as legal support and acceptance as a social partner by the state, and willing recognition by employers have been eroded or collapsed altogether. In their stead, governments, including those of the centre-left, have followed policies of 'labour exclusion' (Crouch, 1986; Smith, 2009), while employer militancy has grown, fostering an industry of union-breaking and avoidance in its wake (Logan, 2006).

Within the power-centred account, it is argued that the logic of this situation requires unions to discover or rediscover fresh sources of power to replace those now denied them. Two main sources have been identified: the collective organization of workers, re-built through sustained organizing activity, and coalition with other civil society organizations to mobilize popular protest against neoliberal hegemony.

The turn towards organizing that has been such a marked feature of the international trade union movement in recent years (Gall, 2009) has been a major stimulus to the argument for power-centred revitalization. Investment in organizing has been seen as the main way in which unions can restore their failing capacities. For writers like Bronfenbrenner and Hickey (2004), effective organizing encompasses a 'union-building' project in which planned organizing campaigns not only attract workers into membership but create workplace organization and a capacity to mobilize workers in action against the employer. If an appropriate organizing strategy is pursued, they argue, then unions can rebuild their most fundamental resource, the collective organization of working people at the point of production.

Developing such a strategy is itself seen as dependent on unions creating a set of prior or supporting capacities. One such capacity is the development of a skilled organizing cadre, comprising paid organizers and lay activists who are equipped to lead organizing campaigns and trained through programmes such as the Organizing Institute in the USA, Organizing Works in Australia or the Organizing Academy in Britain (Phelan, 2007: 25). A second is a repertoire of organizing methods, such as workplace mapping, person-to-person recruitment, creation of an organizing committee and workplace actions that can draw workers into membership and activism (Bronfenbrenner and Hickey, 2004). A third element is a discursive resource, a language of justice, respect and rights that legitimates trade unionism and casts organizing as a moral imperative (Heery et al., 1999). Finally, unions may look beyond the workplace and seek backing from community and other civil society organizations, employing the method of coalition to attract workers into membership and pressure employers to concede recognition (Holgate and Wills, 2007).

In addition to organizing, coalition may be used by unions to advance other objectives and is regarded widely in the power-centred literature as another key strategy to promote union revitalization (McBride and Greenwood, 2009; Turner and Cornfield, 2007). Union–community coalitions can be used to augment union bargaining power, bolster the resolve of workers involved in disputes, oppose restructuring of public services and promote progressive reform and develop human rights campaigns and action on global labour standards. Coalition partners may also be highly variable and include faith organizations, community groups, environmental, human rights and identity organizations, bodies that provide advocacy to working people and issue-based campaigns, such as those for a living wage.[2] Coalitions themselves can assume a number of forms, ranging from short-term alliance to sustained cooperation (Tattersall, 2005), and are often difficult to forge and sustain, accompanied by tensions that arise from the competing objectives and divergent cultures of trade unions and their coalition partners (Fine, 2007; Holgate, 2009).

The overriding purpose of coalition is to help unions 'respond to crisis' characterized by declining membership and failing 'institutional support' (Tattersall, 2009: 161). Like organizing, it is a means to restore union power when other resources are ceasing to be available. Also like organizing, coalition can bring to unions a range of different capacities. According to Frege et al. (2004: 139–41), there are five distinct resources that coalition partners can mobilize for unions (see also Tattersall, 2005). Coalitions can provide unions with access to financial, material and human resources, including grants, premises and perhaps critically networks of activists and paid staff. Secondly, coalition partners may serve as channels of communication allowing unions to make contact with minority groups, immigrants or others whom unions seek to organize and represent but who are difficult to contact. Thirdly, many coalition partners possess specialist expertise upon which unions can draw. For unions seeking to organize or represent members of identity groups or to develop policy on work–life integration, the environment, economic development or human rights, NGOs and other coalition partners may serve as sources of knowledge and advice. Fourthly, coalition partners may confer legitimacy on union activity, bringing their own stamp of credibility and moral purpose to joint activity. Finally, coalition partners may have a mobilizing capacity and be able to generate protest, activism and political pressure on behalf of unions. In so doing, they may extend unions' own potential for collective action; the object of the other main strategy proposed by those who make the power-centred argument, union organizing.

Diversity

If the argument from power starts with a claim about neoliberal hegemony, then the argument from diversity starts from a claim about workforce change. This, in turn, has two main components. On the one hand, it is argued that unions must adapt to long-run changes in workforce composition, including feminization and the associated increase of workers in personal service roles (Cobble, 2007a), an increase in ethnic diversity driven by migration, the ageing of the workforce in developed economies and an increase in the proportion of workers engaged on non-standard contracts that depart from an earlier male norm of full-time continuous employment. On the other hand, there is an increased assertiveness of a range of identity groups, grounded in gender, ethnicity, faith, age, disability and sexuality, which demand that a range of institutions, including trade unions, respond more actively to their interests. Piore and Safford (2006) characterize this change as a shift in the 'axes of social mobilization' from class to identity and locate it against a broader transformation of economic and social organization, including the decline of the breadwinner family and the rise of a network economy. Others have also made this kind of argument, linking changes in workforce composition and associated worker interests to the emergence of a new form of capitalist economy (e.g. Cobble, 2007a; Wills, 2009).

The diversity argument in a nutshell therefore is that unions must respond to and accommodate newly assertive identities if they are to undergo revitalization (Briskin, 2008; Foley, 2009). Seen as central to this process is the feminization of trade unions and there is now a substantial and long-standing literature on women's trade unionism (Hunt, 1982), which continues to be elaborated today (Cobble, 2007b; Parker, 2009). Scholars have identified the failure of unions adequately to represent women, researched those pressing for change, particularly women activists, and evaluated the measures taken by unions to address the needs of working women (e.g. Briskin, 2006; Colling and Dickens, 1989; Ledwith et al., 1990; McBride, 2001b). Running alongside has been a less extensive though otherwise very similar literature dealing with unions and ethnic minorities (e.g. Edelson, 2009; Jefferys and Ouali, 2007).

In the last few years, however, these established themes in the identity-based literature have been supplemented by others. Researchers have examined the response of unions to older workers, gays and lesbians, the disabled and those with caring responsibilities (Colgan, 2000; Duncan et al., 2000; Firestein and Dones, 2007; Foster and Fosh, 2009; Gregory and Milner, 2009; Heery, 2006; Humphrey, 2002; Hunt and Bielski Boris, 2007). There is a burgeoning literature on unions and migrants (Cornfield and Canak, 2007; Fitzgerald, 2009; Milkman, 2000), and scholars have examined union representation of workers with non-standard contracts, such as part-timers and agency workers who are disproportionately female or likely to be drawn from minority groups (Heery, 2004; Heery and Conley, 2007; Wills, 2009). Once released, the identity genie has divided and multiplied, generating a broad range of research and commentary on union representation of particular sections of the workforce. Indeed, recent work has addressed the question of 'intersectionality', the degree to which unions accommodate those with complex identities, grounded in two or more 'equity-seeking groups', such as those of ethnic minority women (Briskin, 2008; Holgate et al., 2006).

If the first stage in the diversity argument is that unions must respond to multiple and overlapping identities, the second is that such a response must encompass both 'internal' and 'external' representation (Dickens and Bercusson, 1996: 7). The first comprises steps taken by unions in their internal systems of governance and management, which are designed to give a voice to women and other identity groups. The second covers attempts to ensure that the interests of such groups are expressed in systems of job regulation, developed by unions principally in interaction with government and employers. Both aspects of representation ideally should be reinforcing, with internal voice generating external job regulation, and can embrace a number of components. Their different features can best be illustrated by examining the most extensive body of diversity-based literature, that dealing with women and trade unions.

Systems of gender democracy and associated changes in trade union management encompass a wide range of measures. These include women's committees and conferences, reserved seats on union executives and delegations, appointment of women's officers, election of women's and equality representatives, women's self-organized groups and women-only training and networks. According to Briskin (2008: 237), these multiple elements can be grouped into two types of measure, both of which are deemed necessary if women's interests are adequately to be represented within unions. On the one hand, there must be 'autonomous' women's organization, exemplified by self-organized groups, which allow women trade unionists to develop a distinctive policy and foster activism. On the other hand, there must also be arrangements, such as reserved seats on executives that allow the voice of women members to be fed into wider union decision-making, to be integrated or mainstreamed. This combination of autonomy and integration, Briskin further argues, should also be used to promote 'cross-constituency organizing'. She means by this arrangements in which separate identity groups within unions, including women, all have their own autonomous organization but are brought together through an overarching human rights or equality committee. Cross-constituency organizing of this kind is intended to promote cooperation among 'equity-seeking groups' and inhibit the fragmentation of union purpose that might flow from separate and autonomous identity-based structures (Briskin, 2009; see also Foster and Williams this volume).

External representation can also include a wide range of activities though a particularly marked theme in the identity-based literature has been the need for unions to prioritize equality and diversity in their core method of job regulation, collective bargaining. Dickens and her collaborators (Colling and Dickens, 1989, 1998; Dickens and Bercusson, 1996) have examined the process of 'equality bargaining', in which gender equality is included formally on the bargaining agenda or existing collective agreements are audited to identify direct or indirect sex discrimination. Others have commented on unions' use of the method of legal regulation. Unions within the European Union and within member states, including the United Kingdom, have played an important part in campaigning and lobbying for stronger equality law and, at workplace level, are associated with compliance mechanisms, in the form of equal opportunities policy (Walsh, 2007: 307). They have helped positively mediate equality law. Unions have also articulated their use of legal regulation with collective bargaining, initiating strategic cases on equal pay and sex discrimination and then diffusing positive judgements from the courts through collective agreements with employers (Heery and Conley, 2007; Howell, 1996). Hybrid systems of job regulation have been developed in order to pursue identity-based interests, therefore, that combine joint regulation with use of law.

These methods of job regulation have been used to create different types of substantive employment rule. Here, there has also been a concern to balance opposing impulses, akin to that between autonomy and integration in the field of internal governance. On the one hand, unions seeking to eliminate discrimination and ensure equal treatment of women (and other identity groups) have sought to bureaucratize the employment relationship through formal rules, standard treatment and explicit procedures. This can be seen most clearly with regard to equal pay, where unions have negotiated job evaluation procedures based on the principle of equal value/comparable worth and have opposed discretionary or performance-based systems of payment that give managers scope to discriminate (Heery, 2009). On the other hand, unions seeking to respond to the particular interests of women workers and other groups have sought the flexibilization of employment rules, giving workers scope to choose an employment package that matches their specific needs. This impulse can be seen most clearly in the area of working time, where unions have negotiated flexible hours that allow work–life integration or flexible leave arrangements that accommodate the needs of carers or faith groups (Gregory and Milner, 2009; Heery, 2006). Responding to the pressure to represent diversity therefore has been seen to involve limiting the flexibility of employers, a source of unequal treatment, while developing 'positive flexibility' for workers.

Debate

There is now a very extensive body of IR literature making the argument for union revitalization on the basis of either power or diversity. In both strands there are different currents and writers who share the core assumptions of each argument nevertheless differ and engage in debate. It is not possible to identify all of these currents, but it is possible to trace the types of 'internal' debate that arise between scholars in both strands. One recurrent source of disagreement relates to the conditions within unions under which revitalization can occur and this can be illustrated by debate over union organizing. Another source of disagreement concerns the evaluation of attempts to revitalize unions: there are sharply divergent assessments of union strategy which can be illustrated by the literature on diversity.

Among those arguing that unions must organize to revive there have been increasingly sharp exchanges over the past decade. On one side are those who argue that organizing must be strategic. It must be directed at targets that have been researched and identified because of their significance to the future of the union, conducted through planned campaigns that make use of skilled personnel and specialist techniques and must attract sufficient investment to overcome anticipated resistance from employers (Milkman, 2006). A condition for strategic organizing of this kind is likely to be the centralization of organizing policy within unions and leadership commitment to organizing. It may also require preparedness to override opposition and transfer resources from existing members to workers who have been targeted for organizing activity (Heery et al., 1999). The contrary view is critical precisely on the grounds that strategic organizing implies centralization and legitimates the weakening of democratic processes within unions. Critical writers are also deeply sceptical about the commitment and ability of the 'official' union leadership to mount effective organizing and lean to a 'rank-and-filist' position, in which the effective renewal of unions is believed to stem from below (Carter, 2003; Fairbrother and Stewart, 2003). Thus, Cohen (2009: 41–2) after noting the 'cautious, institutionally structured perspectives of union leaderships formally embracing an "organizing perspective"', observes that, 'The key to union renewal would... appear to lie in a workplace-based process of self-activity and mobilization based on the concrete exploitation and intensification of labour'.

Those making the diversity argument have been less disputatious. Nevertheless, there are competing currents in this literature that offer different assessments of the degree to which unions have undergone change and the effectiveness of the reforms they have implemented. An issue where this can be seen is the degree of integration within unions of 'internal' and 'external' representation of gender interests. McBride's (2001a) study of gender democracy in the UK's main public services union, UNISON, adopts a rather sceptical position, suggesting that a major weakness of 'internal' structures, such as women's self-organized groups, is that they have only limited purchase over bargaining activity. The effect is that much of the union's ongoing collective bargaining and associated activity remains un-influenced by the creation of a system of gender democracy. A contrary argument is developed by Heery and Conley (2007) in their study of the development of union policy on part-timers across the UK trade union movement. Here, a key role for structures of gender democracy is identified in the development of bargaining and legal policy on behalf of women part-time workers, which itself is presented as non-trivial. Unlike the debate over strategic organizing, the difference in this case is mainly one of emphasis. The empirical work generated by interest of IR researchers in union revitalization has largely taken the form of policy evaluation, with scholars assessing the scale and significance of particular reforms and initiatives. Different assessments of the same set of changes have unsurprisingly been generated, and much 'internal' debate within the literature takes the form of an exchange between these competing empirical claims.

Critique

Like any other intellectual position, the arguments about union revitalization can also be subject to fundamental critique from external, opposed positions. The attack, in this case, is likely to be directed at the main causal propositions that lie at the heart of either the power or diversity version of the revitalization argument. In other words, the claim that attempts to build power are a necessary response to neoliberal hegemony or that more differentiated forms of trade union representation are essential if unions are to represent diversity.

The scope for critique of this kind can be illustrated by the case of the power-based argument.[3] As has been explained, a key element of this argument is that neoliberalism reduces the scope for unions to make an accommodation with states and employers and thereby pushes them to find alternative sources of strength and influence. The causal argument about the impact of neoliberalism on industrial relations is the peg on which the prescriptive argument about the need to organize or develop coalitions hangs. This causal argument can be questioned on two main grounds.

The first concerns the pervasiveness and universality of neoliberal hegemony. For those making the power-based argument, neoliberalism is a global system that is corrosive of all established national systems of industrial relations (Fletcher and Gapasin, 2008). But the latter may be more enduring and resistant to erosion than is suggested. The 'varieties of capitalism' literature, with its claim that national systems are path dependent, makes precisely this point and suggests that different patterns of employment relations with varying scope for accommodation between unions, state and employers will endure. In fact, even theorists of neoliberalism concede this point and have identified variants of the market-making project. Hall (2003: 19), for example, suggests that the United Kingdom under New Labour has witnessed experiment with a 'social democratic variant of neo-liberalism' that differs in important respects from that of the previous Conservative Government and which has allowed greater scope for union influence (see also McIlroy, 2009). In similar vein, Gamble (2009: 71–2) distinguishes between 'laissez faire neo-liberalism', committed to the release of market forces from state intervention, and a 'social market strand' that holds that markets need to be supported by an active, institution-building state.

The second potential challenge is that unions are endlessly adaptable and can reach a settlement with state and employers within a neoliberal order. The claim here is that, even if one accepts the pervasiveness of neoliberalism, there may still be room for accommodation and a union strategy other than that based on building new sources of power (though not necessarily precluding the latter). The argument that unions can form effective partnership arrangements with employers in free market systems would be one variant of this kind of claim (Kochan et al., 2009). In deregulated, competitive markets that are exposed to global competition, unions may lack the capacity to raise wages but may still be able to form a meaningful exchange with employers. The basis for this is likely to be a productivity coalition, in which unions facilitate change (flexible working) for the employer while securing institutional security for themselves and employment security for workers (Brown et al., 2001).

Another variant would be the argument that unions can exploit opportunities in the market-creating policies developed by states. A core aspect of the latter has been attempts to maximize the employment rate and, essentially, expand the scope of the formal labour market (Davies and Freedland, 2007). In Britain, this aim has been driven by not only a series of policies that include welfare reform (e.g. increasing the conditionality of benefits) but also labour market reforms to ensure that participation in paid work is attractive and that workers have skills that allow them to be employed. The result has been a series of policies on minimum wages, maternity and other leave, flexible hours and training that have been developed with union involvement. Thus, the UK's National Minimum Wage, designed to attract low-wage workers into employment, is recommended to Parliament by a tripartite Low Pay Commission upon which unions are represented, while under the union-learning scheme, unions are funded by the state to help facilitate skill acquisition among low productivity workers (McIlroy, 2009). The central state function within a neoliberal order, market creation, can involve deregulation and an assault on union influence, but it can also involve the creation of new labour market institutions and forms of intervention in which unions can take part.

Non-union representation

The second broad current of debate over worker representation has centred on non-union forms of worker representation. As the proportion of workers represented by unions has declined so the focus of attention has switched and there has been a growth of inquiry into alternative institutions. These include employer-sponsored forms of worker participation and involvement, statutory systems of worker participation, such as works councils and safety or other issue-specific committees, and civil society organizations (CSOs) that provide advocacy services to workers or campaign on particular issues or on behalf of particular identity groups (e.g. Abbott, 2004; Dundon and Rollinson, 2004; Fine, 2006; Jenkins and Blyton, 2008; Heery et al., 2010). In the real world of work, union decline is associated with the emergence of a more multiform system of worker representation and IR has responded to this development.

Work on non-union representative institutions has developed along a number of paths. These include the question of their origins, their impact on business performance and their place within the wider IR system. Across each of the three main forms (statutory, employer-supported and CSOs), however, two issues have been recurrent. These are the questions of the relationship between non-union forms and trade union representation and the relative effectiveness of non-union forms in representing workers when compared with trade unions. Both of these questions are explored below.

Relationship to unions

What is striking about the literature on the relationship between unions and statutory and employer-supported participation and civil society organizations is that the same themes reappear in work on each non-union form. Arguably two positions are dominant. On the one hand, writers have advanced a *replacement* thesis, claiming that each of the non-union forms poses a threat to trade unionism and may supplant it within the system of worker representation. On the other hand, a *reinforcement* thesis has been put forward, which holds that unions can forge coalitions or partnerships with each of the new forms that combine their strengths with that of trade unionism. These competing assessments rest on opposed understandings of the relative interests of trade unions and non-union institutions, conflicting in the first case and congruent or overlapping in the second.

With regard to statutory participation, the replacement thesis has been developed most fully in the case of Germany (Behrens, 2009). Works councils, it has been suggested, are increasingly independent of unions and express the sectional interests of workers in particular enterprises or workplaces against industrial or class interests articulated by trade unions. In so doing, they may actively conspire with employers to undermine industry-wide collective agreements negotiated by unions and generate a more fragmented system of worker representation. In Britain, where bargaining is itself decentralized, an alternative replacement thesis has been advanced. This emphasizes the fact that works councils are typically empowered only to receive information and engage in consultation with employers and are not bargaining agents like trade unions (Kelly, 1996). According to this militant critique, their spread has been promoted by states, seeking to reduce union influence over the employment relationship and displace more effective systems of worker representation with less effective forms that promote workplace cooperation.

A belief that non-union participation can displace unions by fostering commonality of interests and greater cooperation between workers and managers also features prominently in the replacement thesis for employer-sponsored representation. The focus here is on a range of forms of participation, including councils or forums established by employers and consisting of elected or appointed employee representatives, systems of communication and direct consultation based on briefing and staff surveys, small group participation through quality circles and kaizen programmes and, in some versions, financial participation through employee share ownership (Gollan, 2010; Kessler, 2010; Marchington, 2007). Techniques of this kind have often been introduced to forestall union organizing (Heery and Simms, 2010) and are prominent features of non-union firms (Jacoby, 1997). In some versions of the replacement thesis they reflect a long-term and deep-seated shift in the employment relationship from compliance to commitment. In more flexible and post-bureaucratic organizations, it is claimed, employer-sponsored participation is an integral feature of a 'high performance work system' that both rests upon and seeks to develop employee commitment (Kaufman and Taras, 2010). For at least some commentators there is little room for trade unions within organizations of this type.

The replacement thesis for civil society organizations rests largely on the arguments about changing workplace composition and patterns of mobilization that were outlined above with regard to change in trade unions. A key difference though is that unions tend to be viewed as irremediably flawed instruments or as simply too weak to adequately represent the interests of newly assertive identity groups or vulnerable workers (Crain and Matheny, 1999). Those whose interests have been neglected in the past or who lie beyond the margins of the union-organized workforce require their own institutions, single issue, identity and campaigning organizations to advance their interests (Fine, 2006). This argument is also often grounded in an account of long-run change in the employment relationship. Thus, Piore and Safford (2006) suggest that we have witnessed a transition from a collective bargaining regime, based on union representation, to an 'employment rights regime', in which single-issue organizations play a role in both pressing for employment law and ensuring managers comply with law at the workplace. As this example indicates, the replacement thesis is often (though not always) based upon 'epochalist' theories of social change (see Edwards, this volume), in which institutions of representation march in step with broader phases of social and economic transformation.

Rather more common than the replacement thesis in current IR literature is the reinforcement argument that non-union forms can work together with unions to develop more effective systems of representation. For example, it has been argued that German unions have often 'captured' works councils and, in return for the support that unions provide, they act as union recruiters and representatives within the firm (Behrens, 2009; Gumbrell-McCormick and Hyman, 2010). The rights to participation conferred on works councils in law, moreover, have provided unions with a degree of security in a period of retreat and employer dominance (Turner, 2003). A similar argument has been advanced for employer-sponsored forms of participation. Not only are the latter often found alongside unions but also, it has been claimed, substantive outcomes for workers are more positive where the two forms co-exist (Charlwood and Terry, 2007; see also Gollan, 2010). With regard to CSOs, the central reinforcement claims are that union–community coalitions can provide additional resources for unions and help them revive, while also providing union support for community movements and identity groups. In the USA, it has been argued that coalitions have been central to reviving both the labour movement and progressive politics in major cities like Los Angeles (Hauptmeier and Turner, 2007; Milkman, 2006). Unlike the 'epochalist' claims associated with the replacement thesis, arguments of this kind tend to assume that institutions like unions are adaptable to changing contexts and capable of hybridizing, working jointly with other institutions to form novel, complex systems of representation.

There are opposing interpretations of the relationship between unions and non-union forms within the literature, therefore, but which has greatest validity? One response to this question is that, in fact, neither of the rival interpretations is wholly valid because in combination they exclude a third possibility. This is that union and non-union forms of representation are *complementary*; that is, they perform separate and distinct functions and operate independently from one another. As a consequence, they may neither support nor threaten each other's position. Statutory worker participation, for instance, often forms part of a 'dual system' of representation, in which works councils deal with non-adversarial features of employer–employee interests, while unions express conflicting interests through the system of collective bargaining (Gumbrell-McCormick and Hyman, 2010: 307). Many elements of employer-sponsored participation also appear to operate within unionized firms without impinging greatly on the union's position. In Baddon et al.'s (1989: 44) study of profit-sharing for instance, the union response to schemes of this kind is described as one of 'bored hostility'; unions were not in favour of schemes that might not operate in the best interest of employees but they did not regard them as a major challenge. Finally, many CSOs provide advisory, advocacy and other labour market services to workers with minimal connection to unions, activities that at best complement the union role and do not undercut the union function.

Another response to the question is that both the replacement and reinforcement theses are valid, at least to a degree. There is certainly supportive evidence that non-union forms can reinforce union representation or pose a threat to unions, some of which has been described above. What this suggests is that the relationship between union and non-forms of worker representation is essentially contingent. In some situations the two may combine in a positive hybrid that works to the benefit of workers, while in others they may become rivals.

Seeking to identify the conditions that allow positive reinforcement to emerge has been a particularly notable theme in recent research on unions and civil society organizations. In Turner's (2007) study of union–community coalitions in American cities, for example, there is an emphasis on the structural conditions that encourage coalitions to emerge. Specifically, where the labour movement is weakly institutionalized and a relatively marginal actor in local politics, it is placed under pressure to seek coalition partners to accumulate influence. This is only part of the story, however, and Turner (2007: 4–5) also stresses 'the critical role of agency'. In cities, like Los Angeles and San Jose, where coalition-building emerged as a central union tactic this was because of a strategic choice by the local labour movement (and its partners), which in turn rested on leadership change, the renewal of activist cadres and the appointment of 'bridge-builders' to influential policy positions (see also Rose, 2000). The latter are labour movement activists with a background in other social movement organizations that allows them to draw coalition partners together. In this account reinforcement is a product of deliberate strategy, of unions seeking to work with other institutions and develop a reciprocal relationship based on mutual gains. The relationship between union and non-union institutions is actively constructed, rather than being an expression of a particular 'epoch' or stage of capitalist development.

Relative effectiveness

Another critical issue that has featured in the literature on non-union representation is the relative effectiveness of these alternative forms in protecting or advancing the interests of workers. Are these institutions equivalent, superior or inferior channels of worker representation when compared with trade unions, the default form for so many decades?

Once again, there are different positions in the literature. Commentators differ sharply in their assessments of the effectiveness as institutions of worker representation of works councils (Hyman, 1996; Kelly, 1996), employer-sponsored participation (Kaufman and Taras, 2000; Terry, 1999) and civil society movements, like the campaign for a living wage (Freeman, 2005; Luce, 2007).

However, as well as differences of this kind, over the substantive, empirical effects of forms of representation, there is another type of division, concerned with the standards that are used to compare and evaluate institutions. One option is to assess institutions of representation in terms of worker preferences, to pose the question: do forms of representation match the preferences or tastes of the workers who consume their services? This approach is exemplified by Freeman, Boxall and Haynes' book, *What Workers Say: Employee Voice in the Anglo-American Workplace* (2007). This presents survey findings, from several countries, of worker evaluations of different forms of representation and suggests that, while unions often suit the preferences of workers, especially moderate, cooperative unions, so do non-union systems, created by employers. The authors conclude that there should be a multiform system of representation, combining union and non-union forms, because this appears most closely to match the preferences of worker–consumers.

One problem with this criterion is that preferences may be malleable and so constitute an uncertain ground on which to evaluate institutions. As two contributors to the book acknowledge, trade unionism is an 'experience good' – assessments are sharply divergent among those who have and have not consumed it and tend to change following consumption (Bryson and Freeman, 2007: 90). The alternative is to use a conception of workers' interests as the evaluation standard; to pose the question which forms are most effective in advancing the interests of workers? Of course, there are also problems associated with this approach. We may attribute interests to workers that they do not in fact have and, when workers fail to act in accordance with the interests that we have imputed to them, explain this failure by resort to the concept of 'false consciousness'; the classic response to the failure of the working class to realize its imputed interest in overthrowing capitalism. These risks can be minimized, however, if it is accepted that workers have multiple and potentially contradictory interests that encompass both challenging and accepting the existing form of the employment relationship. If we are sensitive to the complexity implied by the concept, then it can still usefully guide the evaluation of institutions of worker representation.

In what follows, an 'interest framework' is put forward that can be used to evaluate institutions of worker representation, including unions and the three non-union forms described above. Reasons of space mean that application of the framework to the different institutions and the presentation of supporting evidence are not really possible. Sufficient material is presented, however, to suggest that across most elements of the framework trade unions remain the most effective institution for advancing workers' interests.

Framework for assessing forms of worker representation

What is presented below is essentially a checklist for evaluating institutions of worker representation. It has been designed to gauge the societal impact of institutions of this type and is based on the assumptions that workers have multiple and contradictory interests and also that workers are internally divided: they possess competing as well as shared interests. At its heart are claims that workers have an interest in social change and redistribution, improvements in work quality, in the representation of diversity and in the regulation of business activity through action directed above the employing enterprise. It also rests on the belief that workers' interests conflict with those of employers and that consequently there is a need for institutions that confer independent power resources on workers. Finally, it is suggested that desirable institutions of representation should balance their pursuit of the interests of workers with those of other stakeholders in the employment relationship, including consumers, communities, the physical environment and, indeed, employers (see Table 15.2).

Depth of interests: It can be said that workers have a hierarchy of interests of variable 'depth'. At the surface they have a quotidian interest in the incremental improvement in employment conditions within the prevailing social and economic structure. For many workers, though, everyday experience is one of subordination, exploitation, insecurity and high relative inequality. Accordingly, workers may also have an interest in challenging the prevailing order, in social change. If this is accepted, that workers have both immediate and more fundamental interests, then it follows that desirable institutions of representation will be those that encompass the full spectrum and are

Table 15.2 Criteria for assessing institutions of worker representation

Worker interests	Key requirements of institutions	Trade Unions	Non-union Institutions
Depth of interests	Redistribution of income, risk and power	Effective in redistributing income, promoting security and building countervailing power; though capacity reduced over time	Statutory institutions promote redistribution and confer power resources; many CSOs challenge inequality and contest power; employer-sponsored forms are non-redistributive
Range of interests	Improvements in quality of working life	Traditional neglect but growing concern with dignity, personal development and work–life integration	Employer-sponsored forms associated with some improvements in work quality
Diversity	Represent interests of women and minorities	Traditional neglect but more recent embrace of diversity agenda in both internal and external strategies of representation	Many CSOs represent equity-seeking groups and prioritize issues of equality and diversity at work
Levels of interest	Neither exclusion from nor confinement to workplace	Multi-level institutions of representation, active at all levels	Statutory and employer-sponsored forms largely confined to workplace; many CSOs excluded from workplace
Cooperation-conflict	Independence from employers and capacity to impose sanctions	Formally independent and able to sanction employers through strikes and other forms of industrial action	Statutory systems confer some independence and legal rights; reliance of CSOs on soft power; employer-sponsored forms are dependent and lack power
Balancing interests	Advance interests of workers without harming essential and legitimate interests of other stakeholders	Mixed impact on business performance; growing interest in working with end-user groups and other stakeholders	Statutory forms oblige balancing of worker–employer interests; employer-sponsored forms subordinated to employer interests; CSOs combine work and non-work interests for identity groups

oriented towards challenge and reform. At the very least, this implies that representative institutions must be *redistributive*. The task of redistribution, moreover, can be conceived of in different ways; as encompassing the redistribution of income, of economic risk and of power. In these regards trade unions have a good record. They are associated with higher relative wages and non-wage benefits, greater job security and lower exposure to the risks of dismissal, redundancy and contingent reward and the collective organization of workers, such that they accumulate power resources to balance those of employers (Heery, 2009; Metcalf, 2005). Works councils have also generated significant redistributive effects in countries, like Germany, where they are strongly institutionalized (Streeck, 1992), and many CSOs are clearly oriented towards radical change (Fine, 2006; Holgate and Wills, 2007). Of the four representative forms under consideration, it is employer-sponsored participation that seemingly has least transformative potential. This is an institution created and designed to function at the surface of capitalist societies, improving the functioning of business enterprises through employee involvement and engagement but, with few exceptions, free of any major redistributive intent.

Range of interests: Workers also have a range of interests, which in Hyman's terms (1997) encompass both 'quantitative' and 'qualitative' issues. Thus, workers have an interest in the improvement of terms and conditions of employment, including improvement in the social wage, provided through the welfare state. But they also have an interest in improving the quality of working life. This may embrace securing more satisfying work, protection from hazard, including bullying, harassment and overwork, a management style that preserves dignity and autonomy and a pattern of working life that permits work–life balance. A desirable institution of worker representation will cover both types of interest, enhancing reward while improving work. Trade unions traditionally have not advanced both types of interest to an equal degree, tending to focus much more on quantitative issues. In recent years, however, they have emphasized at least some aspects of a quality of work agenda and have pushed for dignity at work policies and for family-friendly practices (Heery, 2006). Unions of professional workers, in particular, have prioritized questions of workload, worker autonomy and opportunities for development (Bach and Kolins Givan, 2004). Non-union institutions have also advanced qualitative interests. This is perhaps the main strength of many employer-sponsored forms of participation, which grant workers more control over their immediate work environment and provide opportunities for influence and engagement. There is a critique of employee involvement as a form of work intensification, but in many cases programmes of this type are well-received by workers and seemingly enhance at least some features of the quality of working life (Bryson and Freeman, 2007; Cox et al., 2006).

Diversity of interests: Feminist IR scholars have repeatedly attacked the construct of the gender-neutral worker and have pointed out that workers of different gender have separate and competing interests (Holgate et al., 2006). The same is true for other forms of identity. If this critique is accepted, then it implies that institutions of worker representation should be judged on the degree to which they accommodate diversity and take action to address the interests of women and minorities. Unions have often been accused of failing in this regard and, indeed, of contributing to gender and racial oppression by privileging the interests of male or majority workers (e.g. Cockburn, 1983). Undoubtedly this is still a feature of trade union action. In the UK, and many other countries, however, one of the most striking long-term developments within trade unionism has been its acceptance of the need to represent diversity. As has been described above, unions have developed systems of internal and external representation to cater to the specific interests of working women and a range of other identity groups. Among non-union forms of representation this has also been a primary purpose of many CSOs, a large proportion of which have grown out of the new social movements and which define their constituencies in terms of gender, ethnicity and other diversity strands (Heery et al., 2010).

Levels of interest: The interests of workers are formed and can be advanced at different levels of the industrial relations system. These levels encompass the workplace and enterprise, industry, occupation and locality, the nation state and national economy and the regional and global (Heery et al., 2008: 6–9). Thus, at the workplace the interests of workers include securing improvements in work quality and enhancing reward, while at state level they may include securing changes in labour law or other policies that regulate the behaviour of employers. Desirable institutions of worker representation must be capable of operating across the levels and, in particular, should not be confined to the workplace or enterprise. Confinement of this kind is one of the weaknesses of both statutory participation and employer-supported systems. CSOs, in contrast, often suffer from exclusion from the workplace (Pollert and Charlwood, 2009), though they are typically very active at the level of the state and a significant force pressing for both state and civil regulation of employer behaviour (Freeman, 2005; Piore and Safford, 2006). Trade unions, however, are not confined in either of these ways but operate, albeit with varying emphasis and effectiveness, across the levels at which workers' interests require expression. In the UK, there continues to be a tradition of workplace trade union organization, though diminished compared to earlier times, and unions engage to considerable effect in the legal system, in the political system and within supra-state institutions (Heery and Conley, 2007). Uniquely, they are institutions of multi-level representation.

Cooperative–Conflicting interests: Workers share interests with their employers and there is a continual basis for cooperation within the employment relationship. Equally, though, workers have interests that conflict with those of employers and the employment relationship is also unavoidably adversarial. Given this dual nature to the employment relationship, it is important that institutions of worker representation do not privilege cooperation and neglect interests that are opposed to those of employers. Employer-sponsored systems suffer from precisely this problem and this might also be said of statutory systems, when these operate under a legal obligation to cooperate with the employer. Furthermore, if it is desirable that institutions represent opposed interests, then two other things are implied: that those institutions should be independent of the employer and be able to impose sanctions in order to overcome employer resistance. Trade unions historically have possessed both these attributes, in that they are formally independent of employers (though often in receipt of informal subsidy and support) and have developed a repertoire of sanctions, such as strikes and other forms of industrial action, to advance worker interests in the face of employer opposition. CSOs are also formally independent of employers, though much more likely than unions to receive employer subsidy (Heery et al., 2010). They also possess sanctions that can be used to counter employer resistance. What is notable about CSOs, however, is their reliance on relatively soft forms of power; shaping public opinion, demonstrations, consumer boycotts and acting through the political process (Fine, 2006; Freeman, 2005). These methods may be effective in securing changes in law and in pressing employers to introduce codes of conduct but they lack the direct purchase that unions may be able to exert through the collective organization of workers and their willingness to engage in strike activity.

Balancing interests: It is legitimate for workers to pursue their interests against those of other social actors, particularly those that are powerful or which seek to subordinate workers. Nevertheless, it is desirable that representative institutions balance the interests of working people against those of other stakeholders with equally legitimate interests. The latter might include consumers of products and services, local communities, a putative public interest, employers, the state and the natural environment. The essential requirement is that there should be a *balancing* of interests; too often institutions of worker representation are assessed solely in terms of their contribution to business performance; that is to advancing the interests of employers (e.g. Addison, 2005; Wood, 2010; see Delbridge this volume). Statutory works councils are often under a legal obligation to balance interests in this way; they must protect the interests of workers but also cooperate with employers and ensure that their activities contribute to the goals of the enterprise. Employer-sponsored systems also have a primary rationale, serving the interests of employers and, indeed, may prioritize these interests over those of workers. For their part, many CSOs are in a unique position to balance the interests of workers with those of other stakeholders because their constituencies typically are not confined to the world of work; they represent people across a range of domains, including housing, welfare, human rights and the domestic sphere (Heery et al., 2010). Unions, in contrast, are often attacked for failing to balance the interests of their members against those of other stakeholders, particularly consumers, the public and employers (e.g. Troy, 1999). However, the validity of this kind of attack is questionable. The evidence of unions damaging business is mixed (Metcalf, 2005) and, as we have seen, unions are capable of forging coalitions with community groups and groups of service users. Their primary form of representation, collective bargaining, is a process of resolution, designed to balance competing interests.

Application of this framework suggests that unions are the most effective institution for representing the interests of working people. For this reason they should remain at the centre of the system of industrial relations and their revitalization should be a priority of all who would civilize the world of work. Application also indicates, however, that there may be problematic features of union representation, possibly to do with the expression of diversity, the promotion of work quality or in balancing interests. In addition, it suggests that non-union forms can exert a beneficial influence within the system of worker representation. Thus, statutory works councils can provide additional power resources to workers, employer-sponsored participation can raise work quality and CSOs promote the interests of equity-seeking groups. In a previous section, it has already been demonstrated that all of these institutions can complement and indeed reinforce trade unionism. Given these conditions, there is surely a legitimate place for all of them, working alongside trade unionism in a multiform system of worker representation.

Conclusion

The purpose of this chapter has been to review the response of IR to the decline of trade unionism and the emergence of a more complex system of worker representation. In doing so, it has considered aspects of the debate over union revitalization and questions that have been posed with regard to the role and effectiveness of non-union institutions. Its primary conclusion is that unions should remain at the heart of our system of worker representation but that their role can be supplemented and reinforced through the activities of statutory works councils, employer-sponsored programmes and civil society organizations. In recent decades, a system of worker representation founded primarily on unions has yielded to one in which several institutions exist to provide worker voice. This change is probably irreversible now but can be welcomed; provided that non-union forms are integrated with and support trade unionism.

Underlying this conclusion and, indeed, the entire chapter is a conviction that the interests of workers *should* be represented. As Budd (2004) has argued, providing voice to workers is one of the fundamental purposes of the system of industrial relations, one incidentally that can reinforce other equally fundamental purposes to ensure equity and efficiency within the employment relationship. What is notable about the real world of work, at least in the United Kingdom, however, is the relative absence of meaningful or effective institutions of worker representation (Charlwood and Forth, 2009; Terry, 2010). Many UK workplaces are effectively despotic, in which the interests of employers and their managers hold sway. This situation is neither desirable in itself and is associated with a series of baleful consequences, perhaps prime of which has been the growth of income inequality as employers and managers have bent the economic system to their own purposes (Wilkinson and Pickett, 2010; see also Turnbull and Wass this volume). It is a situation that should not be allowed to continue.

Acknowledgements

Earlier versions of this chapter were presented at the World Congress of the International Industrial Relations Association in Sydney Australia in August 2009 and at the Annual James Connolly Memorial Seminar of the Irish Industrial Relations Association, held at NUI Galway in February 2010. I would like to thank participants at both events for helpful comments, as well as Paul Blyton and Peter Turnbull for improving the chapter in their capacity as editors.

Notes

1. There are other currents in the union revitalization literature that are not considered here, primarily because they have been propounded less forcefully in recent years. For

some, it is claimed that unions must adapt to a more reflexive and individualized worker-base by offering individual services (e.g. Legge, 2007: 51), while for others there is a belief that partnership with employers must be at the heart of union strategy (e.g. Kochan et al., 2009).

2. Coalition partners may also include political parties and politicians though typically these are located at a local level, beyond the pale of the neoliberal state (e.g. Milkman and Wong, 2001: 100).

3. A critique of the diversity position is not presented but, of course, it is possible to develop such a critique. One possible line of argument might derive from empirical findings that men, women and many other 'diverse' categories within unions seem to show the same set of preferences with regard to union representation: typically they prioritize help in case of a problem at work (Waddington and Whitston, 1997). Research findings of this kind, which stress the commonality of preferences, might be used to counter the claim that workforce change necessarily implies greater diversity in union internal and external strategies of representation; in other words that the causal (and prescriptive) link between diversity of membership and diversity of 'external' representation does not apply.

References

Abbott, B. (2004) 'Worker representation through the Citizen's Advice Bureaux', in G. Healy, E. Heery, P. Taylor and W. Brown (eds) *The Future of Worker Representation*, Basingstoke, Palgrave Macmillan: 245–63.

Addison, J.T. (2005) 'The determinants of firm performance: unions, works councils and employee involvement/high performance work practices', *Scottish Journal of Political Economy*, 52, 3: 406–50.

Bach, S. and Kolins Givan, R. (2004) 'Public service unionism in a restructured public sector: challenges and prospects', in J. Kelly and P. Willman (eds) *Union Organization and Activity*, London, Routledge: 89–109.

Baddon, L., Hunter, L.C., Hyman, J., Leopold, J. and Ramsay, H. (1989) *People's Capitalism: A Critical Analysis of Profit-sharing and Employee Share Ownership*, London, Routledge.

Behrens, M. (2009) 'Still married after all these years? Union organizing and the role of works councils in German industrial relations', *Industrial and Labor Relations Review*, 62, 3: 275–93.

Briskin, L. (2006) 'Victimization and agency: the social construction of union women's leadership', *Industrial Relations Journal*, 37, 4: 359–78.

Briskin, L. (2008) 'Cross-constituency organizing in Canadian unions', *British Journal of Industrial Relations*, 46, 2: 221–47.

Briskin, L. (2009) 'Cross-constituency organizing: a vehicle for union renewal', in J.R. Foley and P.L. Baker (eds) *Unions, Equity and the Path to Renewal*, Vancouver and Toronto, UCB Press: 137–54.

Bronfenbrenner, K. and Hickey, R. (2004) 'Changing to organize: a national assessment of union strategies', in R. Milkman (ed.) *Rebuilding Labor: Organizing and Organizers in the New Union Movement*, Ithaca and London, ILR Press: 17–61.

Brown, W., Deakin, S., Hudson, M. and Pratten, C. (2001) 'The limits of statutory trade union recognition', *Industrial Relations Journal*, 32, 3: 180–94.

Bryson, A. and Freeman, R.B. (2007) 'What voice do British workers want?', in R.B. Freeman, P. Boxall and P. Haynes (eds) *What Workers Say: Employee Voice in the Anglo-American Workplace*, Ithaca and London, ILR Press: 72–96.

Budd, J.W. (2004) *Employment with a Human Face: Balancing Efficiency, Equity, and Voice*, Ithaca and London, ILR Press.

Card, D., Lemieux, T. and Riddell, W.C. (2007) 'Unions and wage inequality', in J.T. Bennett and B.E. Kaufman (eds) *What Do Unions Do? A Twenty-First Century Perspective*, New Brunswick and London, Transaction Publishers.

Carter, B. (2003) 'Rhetoric and reality: the adoption of the organizing model in Manufacturing, Science and Finance', in P. Fairbrother and C.A.B. Yates (eds) *Trade Unions in Renewal: A Comparative Study*, London and New York, Continuum: 180–99.

Charlwood, A. and Forth, J. (2009) 'Employee representation', in W. Brown, A. Bryson, J. Forth and K. Whitfield (eds) *The Evolution of the Modern Workplace*, Cambridge, Cambridge University Press: 74–96.

Charlwood, A. and Terry, M. (2007) '21st-century models of employee representation: structures, processes and outcomes', *Industrial Relations Journal*, 38, 4: 32–337.

Cobble, D.S. (2007a) 'Introduction', in D.S. Cobble (ed.) *The Sex of Class: Women Transforming American Labor*, Ithaca and London, ILR Press: 1–12.

Cobble, D.S. (ed.) (2007b) *The Sex of Class: Women Transforming American Labor*, Ithaca and London, ILR Press.

Cockburn, S. (1983) *Brothers: Male Dominance and Technological Change*, London, Pluto Press.

Cohen, S. (2009) 'Opening Pandora's box: the paradox of institutionalised organising', in G. Gall (ed.) *The Future of Union Organising: Building for Tomorrow*, Basingstoke, Palgrave Macmillan: 28–44.

Colgan, F. (2000) 'Recognising the lesbian and gay constituency in UK trade unions: moving forward in UNISON', *Industrial Relations Journal*, 30, 3: 444–63.

Colling, T. and Dickens, L. (1989) *Equality Bargaining. Why Not?* Manchester, Equal Opportunities Commission.

Colling, T. and Dickens, L. (1998) 'Selling the case for gender equality: deregulation and equality bargaining', *British Journal of Industrial Relations*, 36, 3: 389–411.

Cornfield, D.B. and Canak, W. (2007) 'Immigrants and labor in a globalizing city: prospects for coalition-building in Nashville', in L. Turner and D.B. Cornfield (eds) *Labor in the New Urban Battlegrounds: Local Solidarity in a Global Economy*, Ithaca and London, ILR Press: 163–77.

Cox, A., Zagelmayer, S. and Marchington, M. (2006) 'Embedding employee involvement and participation at work', *Human Resource Management Journal*, 16, 3: 250–67.

Crain, M. and Matheny, K. (1999) 'Labor's divided ranks: privilege and the united front ideology', *Cornell Law Review*, 84: 1542–626.

Crouch, C. (1986) 'Conservative industrial relations policy: towards labour exclusion?', in O. Jacobi (ed.) *Economic Crisis, Trade Unions and the State*, London, Croom Helm: 131–53.

Daniels, G. (2009) 'In the field: a decade of organizing', in G. Daniels and J. McIlroy (eds) *Trade Unions in a Neoliberal World*, London, Routledge: 254–82.

Davies, P. and Freedland, M. (2007) *Towards a Flexible Labour Market: Labour Legislation and Regulation since the 1990s*, Oxford, Oxford University Press.

Dickens, L. and Bercusson, B. (1996) *Equal Opportunities and Collective Bargaining in Europe: Defining the Issues*, Dublin, European Foundation for the Improvement of Living and Working Conditions.

Duncan, C., Loretto, W. and White, P. (2000) 'Ageism, early exit, and British trade unions', *Industrial Relations Journal*, 31, 3: 220–34.

Dundon, T. and Rollinson, D. (2004) *Employment Relations in Non-union Firms*, London, Routledge.

Edelson, M. (2009) 'Confronting racism in the Canadian labour movement: an intergenerational assessment', in J.R. Foley and P.L. Baker (eds) *Unions, Equity and the Path to Renewal*, Vancouver and Toronto, UCB Press: 61–77.

Fairbrother, P. and Stewart, P. (2003) 'The dilemmas of social partnership and union organization: questions for British trade unions', in P. Fairbrother and C.A.B. Yates (eds)

Trade Unions in Renewal: A Comparative Study, London and New York, Continuum: 158–79.

Fairbrother, P. and Yates, C.A.B. (eds) (2003) *Trade Unions in Renewal: A Comparative Study*, London, Continuum.

Fine, J. (2006) *Worker Centers: Organizing Communities at the Edge of the Dream*, Ithaca and London: ILR Press.

Fine, J. (2007) 'A marriage made in heaven? Mismatches and misunderstandings between worker centres and unions', *British Journal of Industrial Relations*, 45, 2: 335–60.

Firestein, N. and Dones, N. (2007) 'Unions fight for work and family policies – not for women only', in D.S. Cobble (ed.) *The Sex of Class: Women Transforming American Labor*, Ithaca and London, ILR Press: 140–54.

Fitzgerald, I. (2009) 'Polish migrant workers in the North – new communities, new opportunities?', in J. McBride and I. Greenwood (eds) *Community Unionism: A Comparative Analysis of Concepts and Contexts*, Basingstoke, Palgrave Macmillan: 93–118.

Fletcher Jr., B. and Gapasin, F. (2008) *Solidarity Divided: The Crisis of Organized Labor and a New Path toward Social Justice*, Berkeley, University of California Press.

Foley, J.R. (2009) 'Introduction', in J.R. Foley and P.L. Baker (eds) *Unions, Equity and the Path to Renewal*, Vancouver and Toronto, UBC Press: 1–12.

Foley, J.R. and Baker, P.L. (eds) (2009) *Unions, Equity and the Path to Renewal*, Vancouver and Toronto, UBC Press.

Foster, D. and Fosh, P. (2009) 'Negotiating "difference": representing disabled employees in the British workplace', *British Journal of Industrial Relations*, doi 10.1111/j.1467-8543.2009.00748.x.

Freeman, R. (2005) 'Fighting for other folks' wages: the logic and illogic of living wage campaigns', *Industrial Relations*, 44, 1: 14–31.

Freeman, R.B., Boxall, P. and Haynes, P. (eds) (2007) *What Workers Say: Employee Voice in the Anglo-American Workplace*, Ithaca and London, ILR Press.

Frege, C.M., Heery, E. and Turner, L. (2004) 'The new solidarity? Trade union coalition-building in five countries', in C.M. Frege and J. Kelly (eds) *Varieties of Unionism: Strategies for Union Revitalization in a Globalizing Economy*, Oxford, Oxford University Press: 137–58.

Frege, C.M. and Kelly, J. (eds) (2004) *Varieties of Unionism: Strategies for Union Revitalization in a Globalizing Economy*, Oxford, Oxford University Press.

Gall, G. (ed.) (2009) *Union Revitalization in Advanced Economies: Assessing the Contribution of Union Organizing*, London, Routledge.

Gamble, A. (2009) *The Spectre at the Feast: Capitalist Crisis and the Politics of Recession*, Basingstoke, Palgrave Macmillan.

Gollan, P. (2010) 'Employer strategies towards non-union collective voice', in A. Wilkinson, P.J. Gollan, M. Marchington and D. Lewin (eds) *The Oxford Handbook of Participation in Organizations*, Oxford, Oxford University Press: 212–36.

Gregory, A. and Milner, S. (2009) 'Trade unions and work-life balance: changing times in France and the UK?', *British Journal of Industrial Relations*, 47, 1: 122–46.

Gumbrell-McCormick, R. and Hyman, R. (2010) 'Works councils: the European model of industrial democracy?', in A. Wilkinson, P.J. Gollan, M. Marchington and D. Lewin (eds) *The Oxford Handbook of Participation in Organizations*, Oxford, Oxford University Press: 286–314.

Hauptmeier, M. and Turner, L. (2007) 'Political insiders and social activists: coalition-building in New York and Los Angeles', in L. Turner and D.B. Cornfield (eds) *Labor in the New Urban Battlegrounds: Local Solidarity in a Global Economy*, Ithaca and London, ILR Press: 129–43.

Hall, S. (2003) 'New labour's double-shuffle', *Soundings*, 24: 10–24.

Heery, E. (2004) 'The trade union response to agency labour in Britain', *Industrial Relations Journal*, 35, 5: 434–50.

Heery, E. (2006) 'Bargaining for balance: trade union policy on work-life issues in the United Kingdom', in P. Blyton, B. Blundon, K. Reed and A. Dastmalchian (eds) (2006) *Work-Life Integration: International Perspectives on the Balancing of Multiple Roles*, Basingstoke, Palgrave Macmillan: 42–62.

Heery, E. (2009) 'Worker voice and reward management', in G. White and J. Druker (eds) *Reward Management: A Critical Text*, London, Routledge: 49–74.

Heery, E., Bacon, N., Blyton, P. and Fiorito, J. (2008) 'Introduction: the field of industrial relations', in P. Blyton, N. Bacon, J. Fiorito and E. Heery (eds) *The Sage Handbook of Industrial Relations*, Los Angeles, Sage: 1–32.

Heery, E., Abbott, B. and Williams, S. (2010) 'The involvement of civil society organizations in British industrial relations: Extent, origins and significance', *British Journal of Industrial Relations* doi: 10.1111/j.1467-8543.2010.00803.x.

Heery, E. and Conley, H. (2007) 'Frame extension in a mature social movement: British trade unions and part-time work', *The Journal of Industrial Relations*, 48, 1: 5–29.

Heery, E. and Simms, M. (2010) 'Employer responses to union organizing: patterns and effects', *Human Resource Management Journal*, 20, 1: 3–22.

Heery, E., Simms, M., Simpson, D., Delbridge, R. and Salmon, J. (1999) 'Organizing unionism comes to the UK', *Employee Relations*, 22, 1: 38–57.

Holgate, J. (2009) 'Contested terrain: London's living wage campaign and the tensions between community and union organizing', in J. McBride and I. Greenwood (eds) *Community Unionism: A Comparative Analysis of Concepts and Contexts*, Basingstoke, Palgrave Macmillan: 49–74.

Holgate, J., Hebson, G. and McBride, A. (2006) 'Why gender and "difference" matters: a critical appraisal of industrial relations research', *Industrial Relations Journal*, 37, 4: 310–28.

Holgate, J. and Wills, J. (2007) 'Organizing labor in London: lessons from the campaign for a living wage', in L. Turner and D.B. Cornfield (eds) *Labor in the New Urban Battlegrounds: Local Solidarity in a Global Economy*, Ithaca and London, ILR Press: 211–23.

Howell, C. (1996) 'Women as the paradigmatic trade unionists? New work, new workers and new trade union strategies in Conservative Britain', *Economic and Industrial Democracy*, 17: 511–43.

Humphrey, J.C. (2002) *Towards a Politics of the Rainbow: Self-organization in the Trade Union Movement*, Aldershot, Ashgate.

Hunt, G. and Bielski Boris, M. (2007) 'The lesbian, gay, bisexual and transgender challenge to American labor', in D.S. Cobble (ed.) *The Sex of Class: Women Transforming American Labor*, Ithaca and London, ILR Press: 81–98.

Hunt, J. (1982) 'A woman's place is in her union', in J. West (ed.) *Work, Women and the Labour Market*, London, Routledge and Kegan Paul: 154–71.

Hyman, R. (1996) 'Is there a case for statutory works councils in Britain?', in A. McColgan (ed.) *The Future of Labour Law*, London, Pinter: 64–84.

Hyman, R. (1997) 'The future of employee representation', *British Journal of Industrial Relations*, 35, 3: 309–31.

Hyman, R. (1999) 'Imagined solidarities: can trade unions resist globalization?', in P. Leisink (ed.) *Globalization and Labour Relations*, Cheltenham, Edward Elgar: 94–115.

Jacoby, S. (1997) *Modern Manors: Welfare Capitalism since the New Deal*, Princeton NJ, Princeton University Press.

Jefferys, S. and Ouali, N. (2007) 'Trade unions and racism in London, Brussels and Paris public transport', *Industrial Relations Journal*, 38, 5: 406–22.

Jenkins, J. and Blyton, P. (2008) 'Works councils', in P. Blyton, N. Bacon, J. Fiorito and E. Heery (eds) *The Sage Handbook of Industrial Relations*, London, Sage: 346–57.

Juravich, T. (2007) 'Beating global capital: a framework and method for union strategic corporate research and campaigns', in K. Bronfenbrenner (ed.) *Global Unions: Challenging*

Transnational Capital through Cross-Border Campaigns, Ithaca and London, ILR Press: 16–39.

Kaufman, B.E. (1993) *The Origins and Evolution of the Field of Industrial Relations in the United States*, Ithaca, ILR Press.

Kaufman, B.E. and Taras, D. (eds) (2000) *Nonunion Employee Representation: History, Contemporary Practice and Policy*, Armonk NY, M.E. Sharpe.

Kaufman, B.E. and Taras, D. (2010) 'Employee participation through non-union forms of employee representation', in A. Wilkinson, P.J. Gollan, M. Marchington and D. Lewin (eds) *The Oxford Handbook of Participation in Organizations*, Oxford, Oxford University Press: 258–85.

Kelly, J. (1996) 'Works councils: union advance or marginalization?', in A. McColgan (ed.) *The Future of Labour Law*, London, Pinter: 46–63.

Kessler, I. (2010) 'Financial participation', in A. Wilkinson, P.J. Gollan, M. Marchington and D. Lewin (eds) *The Oxford Handbook of Participation in Organizations*, Oxford, Oxford University Press: 338–57.

Kochan, T., Eaton, A.E., McKersie, R.B. and Adler, P.S. (2009) *Healing Together: the Labor-Management Partnership at Kaiser Permanente*, Ithaca and London, ILR Press.

Ledwith, S., Colgan, F., Joyce, P. and Hayes, M. (1990) 'The making of women trade union leaders', *Industrial Relations Journal*, 21, 2: 112–25.

Legge, K. (2007) 'The ethics of HRM in dealing with individual employees without collective representation', in A. Pinnington, R. Macklin and T. Campbell (eds) *Human Resource Management: Ethics and Employment*, Oxford, Oxford University Press: 35–51.

Logan, J. (2006) 'The union avoidance industry in the United States', *British Journal of Industrial Relations*, 44, 4: 651–76.

Luce, S. (2007) 'The US living wage movement: building coalitions for the local level in a global economy', in L. Turner and D.B. Cornfield (eds) *Labor in the New Urban Battlegrounds: Local Solidarity in a Global Economy*, Ithaca and London, ILR Press: 21–34.

Marchington, M. (2007) 'Employee voice systems', in P. Boxall, J. Purcell and P. Wright (eds) *The Oxford Handbook of Human Resource Management*, Oxford, Oxford University Press: 231–50.

McBride, A. (2001a) *Gender Democracy in Trade Unions*, Aldershot, Ashgate.

McBride, A. (2001b) 'Making it work: supporting group representation in a liberal democratic organization', *Gender, Work and Organization*, 8, 4: 411–19.

McBride, J. and Greenwood, I. (eds) (2009) *Community Unionism: A Comparative Analysis of Concepts and Contexts*, Basingstoke, Palgrave Macmillan.

McIlroy, J. (2009) 'A brief history of British trade unions and neoliberalism: from the earliest days to the birth of New Labour', in G. Daniels and J. McIlroy (eds) *Trade Unions in a Neoliberal World*, London, Routledge: 21–62.

McIlroy, J. and Daniels, G. (2009) 'Introduction: trade unions in a neo-liberal world', in G. Daniels and J. McIlroy (eds) *Trade Unions in a Neoliberal World*, London, Routledge: 1–17.

Metcalf, D. (2005) 'Trade unions: resurgence or perdition?', in S. Fernie and D. Metcalf (eds) *Trade Unions: Resurgence or Demise?*, London, Routledge: 83–117.

Milkman, R. (ed.) (2000) *Organizing Immigrants: the Challenge for Unions in Contemporary California*, Ithaca and London, ILR Press.

Milkman, R. (2006) *L.A. Story: Immigrant Workers and the Future of the U.S. Labor Movement*, New York, Russell Sage Foundation.

Milkman, R. and Wong, K. (2001) 'Organizing immigrant workers: case studies from southern California', in L. Turner, H.C. Katz and R.W. Hurd (eds) *Rekindling the Movement: Labor's Quest for Relevance in the 21st Century*, Ithaca and London, ILR Press: 99–128.

Parker, J. (2009) 'Women's collectivism in context: women's groups in UK trade unions', *Industrial Relations Journal*, 40, 1: 78–97.

Phelan, C. (2007) 'Worldwide trends and prospects for trade union revitalization', in C. Phelan (ed.) *Trade Union Revitalization: Trends and Prospects in 34 Countries*, Bern, Peter Lang: 11–38.

Piore, M.J. and Safford, S. (2006) 'Changing regimes of workplace governance: shifting axes of social mobilization and the challenge to industrial relations theory', *Industrial Relations*, 45, 3: 299–325.

Pollert, A. and Charlwood, A. (2009) 'The vulnerable worker in Britain and problems at work', *Work, Employment and Society*, 23, 2: 343–62.

Rose, F. (2000) *Coalitions across the Class Divide*, Ithaca and London, ILR Press.

Smith, P. (2009) 'New Labour and the commonsense of neoliberalism: trade unionism, collective bargaining and workers' rights', *Industrial Relations Journal*, 40, 4: 337–55.

Streeck, W. (1992) 'Co-determination: after four decades', in W. Streeck (ed.) *Social Institutions and Economic Performance*, London, Sage: 137–68.

Tattersall, A. (2005) 'There is power in coalition: a framework for assessing how and when union-community coalitions are effective and enhance union power', *Labour and Industry*, 16, 2: 97–112.

Tattersall, A. (2009) 'Using their sword of justice: the NSW Teachers' Federation and its campaigns for public education between 2001 and 2004', in J. McBride and I. Greenwood (eds) *Community Unionism: A Comparative Analysis of Concepts and Contexts*, Basingstoke, Palgrave Macmillan: 161–86.

Terry, M. (1999) 'Systems of collective employee representation in non-union firms', *Industrial Relations Journal*, 30, 1: 16–30.

Terry, M. (2010) 'Employee representation', in T. Colling and M. Terry (eds) *Industrial Relations: Theory and Practice*, Third edition, Chichester, John Wiley and Sons: 275–97.

Troy, L. (1999) *Beyond Unions and Collective Bargaining*, Armonk NY, M.E. Sharpe.

Turner, L. (2003) 'Reviving the labor movement: a comparative perspective', in D.B. Cornfield and H. J. McCammon (eds) *Labor Revitalization: Global Perspectives and New Initiatives. Research in the Sociology of Work, Volume 11*, Oxford, Elsevier: 23–58.

Turner, L. (2007) 'Introduction: an urban resurgence of social unionism', in L. Turner and D.B. Cornfield (eds) *Labor in the New Urban Battlegrounds: Local Solidarity in a Global Economy*, Ithaca and London, ILR Press: 1–18.

Turner, L. and Cornfield, D.B. (eds) (2007) *Labor in the New Urban Battlegrounds: Local Solidarity in a Global Economy*, Ithaca and London, ILR Press.

Waddington, J. and Whitston, C. (1997) 'Why do people join unions in a period of membership decline?', *British Journal of Industrial Relations*, 35, 4: 515–46.

Walsh, J. (2007) 'Equality and diversity in British workplaces: the 2004 workplace employment relations survey', *Industrial Relations Journal*, 38, 4: 303–19.

Wilkinson, R. and Pickett, K. (2010) *The Spirit Level: Why Equality is Better for Everyone*, Revised edition, London, Penguin Books.

Wills, J. (2009) 'Subcontracted employment and its challenge to labor', *Labor Studies Journal*, 34, 4: 441–60.

Wood, S. (2010) 'High involvement management and performance', in A. Wilkinson, P.J. Gollan, M. Marchington and D. Lewin (eds) *The Oxford Handbook of Participation in Organizations*, Oxford, Oxford University Press: 407–26.

The employment relationship in different work settings

16

Service work and service workers: exploring the dynamics of front-line service encounters

Emmanuel Ogbonna

Introduction

The significance of the service sector to the economies of many (ironically often called 'industrialized') countries is increasingly acknowledged. This criticality is perhaps best illustrated by recent estimates that suggest that over 75 per cent of the GDP of the United Kingdom is accounted for by service organizations (Oxford Economic Forecasting, 2006). Such domination of economic activities is also evident in the proportion of people that depend on this sector for employment opportunities, with recent data suggesting that over 80 per cent of UK (ibid.) and a similar proportion of USA employees (Rust and Chung, 2006) work in the service sector.

The growth in the importance of the service sector to economic activities has been mirrored by research contributions into a variety of issues in this area, notably but not exclusively, from marketing and employment research academies (employment research is used in this chapter to include organization studies, human resource management and employment studies). Such contributions have had a common underlying discipline-specific imperative: that the customer is key to business profitability in the marketing academy (see Pfaff, 1976; Erevelles et al., 2003), and that employees are the reason for business success in the employment research academies (see treatises on high performance work organizations, for example, the review by Harley et al., 2007). While seemingly uncontentious, the implied paradox in each discipline claiming the supremacy of their respective area is seldom discussed in the management literature. Similarly, research into the centrality of either customers or employees has tended to be function-specific, with scholars commonly exploring issues that relate to the current debates in their individual disciplines. For example, marketing scholars have focused on explicating the components of successful customer service (see Berry and Parasuraman, 1991; Rust and Oliver, 2000) while the employment research academies have tended to be preoccupied by the organization of service work and the attendant intensification of work and emotional labouring of those employees designated to provide service (see Ogbonna and Wilkinson, 1990; Sturdy et al., 2001; Korczynski, 2003a, 2004). Similarly, studies that incorporate issues of multidisciplinary concern are often conducted in ways that privilege discourses in the host discipline without a full appreciation of the current advances or contentions in the other research area. Such parallel development has been at the expense of comprehensive and inclusive analyses.

The aim of this chapter is to provide an evaluation of conceptualizations of customer service and customer service work from the marketing and employment research academies. The gaps and limitations in each area will be highlighted and this is followed by reflections on possible ways of integrating insights from the two broad research areas in order to develop more inclusive evaluations that advance research into service work and service encounters. The integration of insights from marketing conceptions of the customer and customer service in employment research is particularly important in the context where the dynamics of employer/employee relationships are increasingly mediated by an external but powerful third party (the customer) who is exerting considerable influence over management decisions and in relation to employee behaviours (for example, through the use of customer feedback and customer complaint systems). These issues clearly have implications for understanding and theorizing contemporary employment relationships and will be explored in this chapter.

While it is acknowledged that service encounters vary widely, and that service work involves a variety of groups with different levels of skills and expertise, as well as an array of organizational arrangements, it is argued that front-line, face-to-face, customer-contact service encounters involving non-professional and typically low status employees generate the most interest and controversy in both marketing and employment research academies, and it is the dynamics of such front-line service work that are explored in this chapter.

The chapter begins with an overview of conceptualizations of the role of the customer and customer service from the marketing academy. This is followed by an evaluation of service work and service workers from employment research academies. The final part of the chapter provides some reflections on the development of inclusive conceptualizations and understanding of the dynamics of service encounters.

Marketing studies of the service encounter

Marketing researchers have commonly espoused the value of their discipline by emphasizing the organizational centrality of the activities that are linked to marketing. An important aspect of this is the positioning of customer satisfaction not only as the key concept in marketing theory and practice, but also as the central element of business organizations. For example, Fournier and Mick (1999) note that businesses increasingly define their *raison d'être* and commonly design their mission statements in relation to external customers. Other researchers have gone further to argue that the satisfaction of customers is not only the dominant aspect of the marketing discipline (see Erevelles et al., 2003), but is also the ultimate objective of every market economy (see Pfaff, 1976).

The perceived importance of customers has prompted many marketing scholars to extol the virtues of customer service and customer satisfaction in the competitive positioning of organizations. For example, Harris and Goode (2004) have observed that such service can create loyal customers who not only buy more from the organization in question, but who also become loyal and enthusiastic ambassadors of the firm. Other scholars have provided more direct links between customer service/satisfaction and business performance. For instance, Anderson and Mittal (2000) concluded that on average, every 1 per cent increase in customer satisfaction results in a 2.37 per cent increase in the performance of service organizations. Similarly, Anderson et al. (1994) argue that customer satisfaction increases the overall innovativeness of product and service-based organizations. In this regard, it is perhaps instructive to note that the widely respected American Marketing Association includes customer satisfaction in its definition of marketing (Lovelock and Wirtz, 2004) and the highly acclaimed Marketing Science Institute regards customer satisfaction as a topic of the highest research priority (see Parasuraman and Grewal, 2000).

Given the belief in the fundamental value of customers to businesses, it is not surprising that customer service has emerged as one of the central tenets of marketing, and is probably the most widely researched aspect of marketing. However, interestingly, despite the exaltations, serious research interest into the concepts of customer satisfaction and service quality is relatively new in the marketing academy and can be traced to the work of a number of prominent researchers in the 1980s (for example, Grönroos, 1982; Oliver, 1980; Parasuraman et al., 1988), a development which employment researchers argue is heavily linked to broader political and ideological developments commonly characterized as the 'enterprise culture' (see du Gay, 1991; Keat and Abercrombie, 1991). Following these early studies, research into customer service has flourished and much of the interest has been in the areas of service quality and customer satisfaction where there has been no shortage of models and frameworks of both service quality (for example, Parasuraman et al., 1988) and satisfaction (see Oliver, 1980; Churchill and Surprenant, 1982).

Underpinning research into service quality and customer satisfaction is what is commonly referred to as the expectation–disconfirmation model (see Cadotte et al., 1987; Oliver, 1997). Adherents to this approach argue that consumers commonly form their expectations about a service before they purchase, and that following consumption, they evaluate the extent to which their expectations are met to determine their level of satisfaction (see for example, Parasuraman et al., 1988; Zeithaml et al., 1996). This emphasis on the perception of customers has led researchers to argue that organizations wishing to improve customer satisfaction should go beyond the standardization of services by targeting individual and idiosyncratic desires of customers (Berry and Parasuraman, 1991; Surprenant and Solomon, 1987). Others have suggested that one way of gaining advantage in an increasingly competitive environment is to develop imaginative service that caters not only for the needs that customers are aware of, but also for those needs that they do not currently know that they have but ones that they will instinctively recognize and appreciate (Lovelock and Wirtz, 2004). It is these underlying imperatives that have encouraged scholars and practitioners to call for a move from merely satisfying customers to 'delighting them', with proponents of 'customer delight' arguing that it offers a greater level of psychological experience and fulfilment to the customer (Rust and Oliver, 2000), that arises from what Gross (1994) describes as providing 'positively outrageous service'.

The objective of satisfying or delighting customers has encouraged scholars to undertake studies into the dynamics of service encounters. The service encounter is defined as the period in which a customer interacts with an organization for the provision of a service (Lovelock and Wirtz, 2004; Surprenant and Solomon, 1987). Such interaction is viewed as the most important antecedent in the evaluation of service by customers (Brown and Swartz, 1989;

Zeithaml et al., 1996), and it is at this juncture that the marketing academy interfaces with service workers who are the main organizational representatives in service encounters. It is thus no coincidence that research into service encounters has grown exponentially in the marketing field (see Gil et al., 2008). Consequently, what follows is an evaluation of the relevant marketing studies of the service encounter.

Service encounters

It is arguable that marketing studies that incorporate people into the dynamics of service encounters have developed in two main ways. The early studies tended to have an underlying rationale that organizations exist to satisfy or delight customers (see Heskett et al., 1990; Rust and Oliver, 1994), and these studies were directed to ways of achieving either or both of these objectives. Such focus on customers resulted in little emphasis on the people designated to provide the required service other than the assumption that such employees were compliant, that they shared the philosophy of their organizations on customer service and that they willingly behaved in ways that their managers espoused in relation to customers. More recently, a stream of marketing studies is emerging that is incorporating the role of employees in service encounters. However, these studies are frequently narrow in their scope, with discussions commonly focusing on the role that employees should play to improve service provision rather than exploring the philosophical and ideological underpinnings of 'customer service' and how these shape the work of service workers. These two research streams are discussed below.

Although early studies into customer service in marketing acknowledged that front-line, customer-contact service providers have the enormous responsibility of operationalizing organizational objectives in relation to customers and customer service (see Booms and Nyquist, 1981), and while some scholars have commented on the irony of front-line service providers (and supposedly the most important interface between the organization and the customer) being the least valued and rewarded members of service organizations (see Surprenant and Solomon, 1987), it is surprising that the position of employees in service encounters has not been subjected to greater scrutiny in the marketing literature. Of particular significance in this regard is that much early research in marketing conceived of employees as dispensable assets which, along with other organizational variables, could be harnessed to provide the service that is concomitant with the demands of the customers. One example of this is found in a key textbook in marketing which argues that 'marketers should be looking for opportunities to shrink a firm's productive capacity – in the form of employees, physical space, and equipment – to match predicted fluctuations in demand' (Lovelock and Wirtz, 2004: 10). However, it is arguable that a more instructive example of the general neglect of service workers in marketing research is derived from the work of two of the most highly respected marketing scholars and prominent experts in the area of customer service, who in setting the research agenda for customer service in the twenty-first century made no mention of the importance of the people who have to deliver the service (see Parasuraman and Grewal, 2000). Instead, they argued that the most important priority for the twenty-first century was to promote a greater understanding of markets in ways that helped organizations to identify more efficient ways of providing value to consumers and customers.

The focus on providing value to the customer without an assessment of the impact of the corresponding initiatives on organizational representatives at the service encounter is seen in the work of other scholars, with some comparing the level of customer service required with the TQM principle of 'zero defect' in manufacturing (Berry and Parasuraman, 1991: 15) or what has been referred to as 100 per cent defect-free service (Heskett et al., 1990). Thus, the underlying treatise is the requirement and expectation of flawless performance by those that provide service so that marketing organizations can achieve their profit imperative. Indeed, even the few studies that called for a greater acknowledgement of the role of employees in service encounters appeared more concerned with the need for organizations to exploit employees' insights on customers. For example, although Bitner et al. (1994: 95) make a strong case for the inclusion of employees in studies of service encounters, this was premised on the rationale that such a strategy will help an organization to use employees' insights to 'design processes and educate both employees and customers to achieve quality in service encounters' (see also Hartline and Ferrell, 1996; Rust and Oliver, 1994).

However, recent developments in the marketing field suggest that, to an extent, the customer service crusade of the 1980s and 1990s has given way to a more critical evaluation of service encounters. Emerging from this development have been three key themes of research: studies which have pointed to the limitations of slavishly adhering to some of the models of customer satisfaction and service quality that were developed in the last two decades, a movement towards greater acknowledgement of 'service' and customers in value creation and research that highlights the potentially disruptive role of customers in service encounters. These three themes are explored in turn.

Recent research themes

While the overwhelming imperative of marketing researchers continues to be the identification of ways of satisfying the needs and wants of customers, a number of scholars in this discipline have identified some potential problems with the extreme interpretation of this aim. For example, although researchers have urged service organizations to go beyond customer satisfaction to customer delight (see Gross, 1994), some have warned that the underlying premise of customer delight may render it financially unattractive to organizations. In this regard, it has been argued that the heightened customer expectation that arises from 'customer delight' makes it difficult to satisfy the same customer in future service encounters as the level of service required to satisfy or maintain delight will be significantly higher (Parasuraman and Grewal, 2000; Rust and Oliver, 2000). Indeed, the suggestion that the only way organizations can maintain the delight of customers is by continuing to offer 'positively outrageous service' (Gross, 1994) has encouraged employment researchers to argue that this process is likely to result in progressive intensification of the work of the people that provide such service (see below). Other critical scholars have suggested that the additional cost of such customer delight initiatives may be such that the dominant coalition in many organizations (argued to be accountants rather than marketers) may thwart such initiatives (see Knights et al., 1994).

The second stream of studies includes the work of researchers who have called for alternative conceptualizations that emphasize the important role of participants in the exchange process in co-creating value defined in terms of the ratio of inputs to outputs. Researchers promoting this approach argue that the traditional separation between manufacturing and services represents an orthodox manufacturing-dominant logic which has been insufficient in dealing with contemporary business environments (see Vargo and Lusch, 2004; Lusch et al., 2006). They propose a new paradigm (service-dominant logic), which they argue, assumes that all parties in a distribution chain (from producer to consumer) are in a collaborative and dynamic process of value creation. They go on to observe that this process requires the parties to be partners in developing the necessary systems and in generating and sharing information on the best way to improve value (Lusch et al., 2008). This perspective is increasingly gaining prominence in service research with the proponents calling for a development of 'service science' as a field of study with conceptualizations that emphasize the important role of customers as co-creators of value. One example of this approach can be seen in the number of organizations that are actively involving their customers in the creation of their own service as a way of increasing value not just for the benefits of customers but also for the organization (see Lovelock and Wirtz, 2004).

The final stream of recent marketing research on service encounters has moved from prescriptions and matrixes of service to examining the human dynamics of this process. An important aspect of this is that marketing researchers are increasingly recognizing that customers are not homogenous in terms of their interests and behaviours in service encounters. Instead, they are a diverse group of people with multiple and frequently conflicting interests and objectives, suggesting that the dynamics of service encounters may be more complex than previously assumed and more difficult to control irrespective of the best efforts of managers and their service staff. In this regard, some scholars have reported that many customers routinely engage in behaviours that are intentionally designed to harm customer service. Such customers have been categorized as 'jaycustomers' (Lovelock, 1994), 'dysfunctional customers' (Fullerton and Punj, 2003) and 'deviant customers' (Reynolds and Harris, 2006). For example, Reynolds and Harris (2005) revealed that a significant proportion of customers they studied admitted to having deliberately made complaints to organizations without prior experience of service failure or dissatisfying customer experience, a process which they described as engaging in 'illegitimate complaining'. Gregoire and Fisher (2008) uncovered examples where the dynamics of service encounters resulted in the best customers of an organization seemingly becoming the organization's worst enemies, and even engaging in extreme action to destroy the firm. Ironically, some researchers have argued that dysfunctional behaviours such as illegitimate complaining are encouraged by the obsessive pursuit of customer satisfaction and delight policies. For instance, Reynolds and Harris (2006) document the case of an illegitimate complainer who claimed that his behaviour was motivated by a desire to take advantage of a policy of one organization to reward all unsatisfied customers rather than by a genuine problem or failure in the service provided by staff:

> On checking into a hotel, I noticed that they had a 100 percent satisfaction or your money back guarantee, I just couldn't resist the opportunity to take advantage of it, so on checking out I told the receptionist that I wanted a refund as the sound of the traffic had kept me awake all night. They gave me a refund, no questions asked. These companies can be so stupid . . .
>
> (quoted in Reynolds and Harris, 2006: 326)

Others have identified different manifestations of dysfunctional customer phenomena, including, for example, shoplifting (see Piron and Young, 2000), fraudulent returning (Harris, 2008) and customer aggression and violence (Grove et al., 2004). These findings point to the existence of customer behaviours which do not fit the prevailing view of marketing and that are not integrated into mainstream marketing models and frameworks. Indeed, one implication of the growing number of dysfunctional customers is that managers may have an additional group of people (other than employees and genuine customers) that they must control in order to maintain organizational profitability, suggesting a greater necessity for the rethinking of the application and implementation of customer service initiatives.

The conclusion that can be drawn from the forgoing is that while the marketing academy may argue that the ultimate objective of any organization (Erevelles et al., 2003) or indeed every market economy (Pfaff, 1976) is customer satisfaction, there is increasing evidence that a slavish adherence to this approach represents an incomplete explanation of the exchange/relational processes in contemporary organizations. That is, the cost of providing the type of service that is commonly theorized as necessary may be prohibitive; added to this is the finding that customers are routinely behaving in ways that are detrimental to organizational profitability and to the welfare of those that are designated to provide service to them. It is the enduring marketing imperative of consumer sovereignty in the face of such insights that has contributed to the salience of the critical studies of service encounters by employment researchers, and it is to these studies that this review turns in what follows.

Employment research insights into service encounters

Although there is a plethora of research on employment-related issues concerning a variety of occupations and professions, it is arguable that the dynamics of front-line service work involving low status workers has remained relatively unexplored by employment researchers (see Rosenthal, 2004; Korczynski, 2009). Such limitation is perhaps more evident in relation to front-line, face-to-face, customer-contact service processes (for example, restaurant waiting staff and front-end retail and hotel staff) where there is a shortage of empirical evaluations (see Sturdy, 1998; Harris and Ogbonna, 2010). In this regard, although recently there have been a series of penetrating analyses of service work by employment researchers, these have typically been directed at non-customer facing roles such as back-office work (Korczynski, 2004) and call centre work (Houlihan, 2002; Korczynski, 2003a; Korczynski et al., 2000; Taylor and Bain, 2003). The discussion that follows occasionally draws from studies that have explored the general area of low status service work, although the central focus of this chapter is on front-line, face-to-face, customer-contact work. In this sense, a review of existing employment research contributions in the general area of service work finds that the dominant themes are commonly related to the organization of work, wherein the key concerns are the control and exploitation of service workers for the benefit of managements and customers, and the responses of employees to organizational arrangements designed to achieve this control.

Control

Within the broader fields of employment research, the literature on organizational arrangements to secure control is rich and diverse, and has covered a wide range of fascinating issues from the perceived desire of managements to subjugate workers (see Steiger and Form, 1991; Hodson, 1999) to the attempts by workers to resist such control (see Burawoy, 1979; Collinson, 1994; Ackroyd and Thompson, 1999; Casey, 1999). The two types of organizational control that are commonly identified by researchers (bureaucratic control and normative control) have been studied by employment researchers in relation to service encounters. For instance, scholars have argued that various aspects of customer service work embrace elements of bureaucratic control in that management strategies of generating employee compliance through Tayloristic principles of economic rationality (see Sturdy et al., 2001) or what Korczynski (2001) refers to as 'customer-oriented bureaucracy' are evident. However, of equal significance is that researchers have raised doubt about the feasibility of achieving this type of control in customer service in a manner that the marketing academy hypothesises is linked to competitive advantage. For example, Korczynski et al. (2000) have argued that the dual (and often incompatible) pursuit of customer sovereignty on the one hand and organizational efficiency on the other may hamper the extent to which managers can achieve control over the customer service process. Thus, the rhetoric of customer sovereignty is in practice often downgraded to the more important operational requirements for efficiency and cost-effectiveness. Peccei and Rosenthal (1997) raised a similar point in their contention that the conventional approach of businesses and management is to achieve maximum control of tactical and operational activities and that this is counter to marketing discourses of customer sovereignty and competitive advantage which, in theory, require a degree of flexibility and empowerment that may undermine the profit motive.

Others have explored the generation and implementation of normative forms of control through the manipulation and institutionalization of organizational cultures in ways that encourage employees to embrace management-espoused values in relation to external customers (see for example, Ogbonna, 1992). Studies of both bureaucratic and normative control practices have been critical and have commonly identified the goal of management as one of 'totalizing' employees in a manner that not only renders their behaviours visible in service encounters but that also forces them to sacrifice their own personal values and individual identities in favour of values and identities assumed to be concordant with customer service ethos (see Sturdy et al., 2001; Casey, 1999; Gabriel, 1999). For instance, Ogbonna and Wilkinson (1988, 1990, 2003) report extensive empirical examples of culture change initiatives by major British food retail organizations. They note the repressive and degrading nature of these initiatives in which a central feature was the instilling of customer care virtues in front-line employees who were required to appear and behave in highly scripted ways in relation to a variety of service encounters, from greeting customers, dress codes, body language, to offering an overall deferential treatment to the customer. A related stream of studies has presented evidence to suggest that front-line service employees are heavily regulated and controlled in their display of emotions, with managers frequently equating customer service with the requirement for various forms of emotional exhibition by front-line staff, ranging from smiling (see Sturdy, 1998) to irritation (Sutton, 1991) to compassion (O'Donohoe and Turley, 2006). Researchers have also documented examples of customer service initiatives which degenerated to abuse and even sexual harassment of front-line service employees by customers (for example, Guerrier and Amel, 2000). Collectively, these studies generally conclude that the control processes embedded in front-line customer-contact service work are repressive and that they commonly fail to achieve their management-espoused aims of internalizing organizational cultural values (see Ogbonna and Wilkinson, 1990; Sturdy, 1998).

However, as with every conception of these processes in employment research, there is commonly an opposition to control (see Mumby, 2005), and an evaluation of research into service work and service encounters will be incomplete without exploring how researchers have theorized resistance. This said, it is important to note that although resistance is theorized as an important repertoire in the employees' 'armoury' for making their workplace experience bearable (see Devinatz, 2007), it is far from being the only response of front-line workers in relation to customer care change initiatives. In this context, Sturdy (1998) provides a useful categorization of studies which have explored the responses of front-line employees to customer service initiatives.

The first category, 'smiling but not meaning it' is illustrative of what earlier work by Ogbonna and Wilkinson (1990) described as 'behavioural compliance', an outcome which is exemplified by service workers' attempts to exhibit the characteristics required by their managers but without internalizing the values that arise from them. Multiple reasons and explanations are offered for these types of reactions, ranging from the workers' desire to protect their 'sense of self' and separate their 'real identity' from management imposed identity (Kunda, 1992; Sturdy, 1998), to their attempt to mask their lack of commitment to the management cause (Peccei and Rosenthal, 2000) and to a resigned acceptance of this behavioural choice in the face of management-imposed sanctions and surveillance systems that render employee actions visible (Ogbonna, 1992).

The second category of responses identified by Sturdy (1998) is what he describes as 'smiling and sometimes meaning it'. This outcome denotes the ambivalence of front-line workers and in many ways highlights the difficulty in predicting individual responses to change initiatives, with elements of embrace and rejection often being possible in relation to the same change programme and among the same group of employees (see also Rafaeli, 1989; Kunda, 1992). In some respects, this supports the contention of Edwards et al. (1998) that employee responses to organizational change programmes are rarely linear, a viewpoint which is illustrated by the few empirical studies in this area which report evidence of multiple and differentiated responses (see Peccei and Rosenthal, 2000; Harris and Ogbonna, 1998; Ogbonna and Harris, 1998). One example here is the work of Harris and Ogbonna (1998) which concluded that the responses of front-line employees they studied to customer care change initiatives were varied and were commonly influenced by their willingness to change as well as by the strength of their existing subculture, with outcomes ranging from active participation to active rejection. A related study by Ogbonna and Harris (1998) found evidence of value commitment, although this was generally related to what they labelled 'instrumental value compliance', a finding that suggests that even the most positive outcomes of culture change efforts still involve elements of incomplete realization of management aims. Interestingly, while employment researchers have debated the ethical and philosophical aspects of these issues, the marketing academy has tended to be less concerned with the nature of the customer service behaviour generated (i.e. whether this is behavioural or attitudinal). Instead, they have commonly focused on outcome measures of organizational efficiency: initiatives are deemed to be successful where customer surveys and profit figures are positive (for example, Anderson and Mittal, 2000). However, these concerns in the employment research academy suggest the potentially contradictory nature of customer-oriented strategy. That is, the choice of a customer-oriented bureaucratic arrangement may be inevitable for reasons of profitability (Korczynski, 2001), yet this in conflict with the organizational arrangements required to achieve marketing conceptions of customer delight.

Other perspectives on employee responses go beyond investigations of the dichotomous relationship between control and resistance that has character-ized much of labour process research to the exploration of the 'subjectivity' of service workers and the ways in which such workers contribute to the dynam-ics of their employment relationships. For example, Filby (1992) demonstrates that the flirting behaviour of female service staff, which may on the surface be conceptualized as part of management-imposed control, may in fact mask the willingness of some of these employees to initiate and participate in such acts. Similarly, Rosenthal (2004) has presented an interesting evaluation and cri-tique of contemporary employment research treatises on management control and called for a greater understanding of how service employees exert some (albeit limited) control over those parties with whom they interact in the ser-vice dynamics. This mirrors earlier work by Ogbonna and Harris (2002) whose study of tipping behaviour in front-line service encounters revealed interest-ing insights on employee subjectivity. This study explored the operation of a management-initiated policy of allowing front-line staff to keep customer tips as a deliberate strategy of individualization designed to control employees and undermine their collectivism. Their findings suggest that this management strategy of involving a 'third party' (customers) in the employment relation-ship resulted in a series of unanticipated consequences. Indeed, the front-line service workers in their study reinvented the policy in a manner that enabled them to control their own earnings (for example, by varying service quality according to previously gained knowledge of customer tipping behaviour). As one waitress who earned an average tip of £50 per shift observed:

> ...I can spot the male customers with big egos...I make them feel good about themselves and the tips roll in.
>
> (Ogbonna and Harris, 2002: 742)

These illustrations lead some employment researchers to question that front-line service workers are generally unknowingly dominated by management; instead, that they may consciously and shrewdly submit to a veneer of control for purely instrumental gain, an outcome which Ogbonna and Harris (2002) label 'mutual instrumentality'.

Overall, the review of studies of the dynamics of service encounters from employment research perspectives finds that there is an underlying pessimism on the philosophical foundations of customer sovereignty and customer service. This can be seen in the over-domination of theoretical and empirical debates around concepts allied to either (or both) control or resistance (see Mumby, 2005 for a general discussion of this criticism in employment research). Here, the implied assumption is frequently one of powerless employees working with exploitative managements (for example, Ogbonna and Wilkinson, 1990; Sturdy et al., 2001; Korczynski, 2009). Even the few studies that have adopted wider frames of reference have fallen victim to the epistemological and ontological concerns of the intellectual traditions and approaches that are collectively labelled employment research in this chapter. That is, studies that uncover and discuss workers' subjectivity particularly in relation to their complicity in the construction of certain aspects of their labour processes often go on to suggest that a form of 'false consciousness' may be present and commonly argue that this confirms that the omnipotent nature of management control has been such that the workers have lost the capacity to see through such control or to resist it effectively (see Filby, 1992; Ogbonna and Harris, 2002; Sturdy, 1998). What seem to be missing are more critical evaluations of front-line workers that take the role of employees in service encounters as their starting premise rather than those that seek to document the responses of employees to management initiatives. Such studies are beginning to emerge and they commonly find that service workers are not the innocent and powerless minions of capital and managements that much employment research conceptions assume. Instead, these studies are showing that front-line customer-contact employees are active and frequently disruptive participants in the dynamics of service encounters, with the intentional dysfunctional behaviour of many front-line customer-contact employees attracting particular research attention. What follows is a review of the limited literature in this area.

Active employees

An important illustration of the active and often dysfunctional nature of the behaviour of front-line service employees is found in the limited research contributions on sabotage. While critical researchers commonly acknowledge the existence of sabotage as part of resistance activities in manufacturing sectors (see Ackroyd and Thompson, 1999), and although theorists have called for a greater understanding of employee misbehaviour in general (see Bennett and Robinson, 2003; Cullen and Sackett, 2003), an explicit recognition and study of sabotage behaviours in the service sector is relatively rare and are restricted to a few conceptualizations (see Analoui, 1995; Crino, 1994; Harris and Ogbonna, 2002, 2006). As an illustration of the widespread nature of this phenomenon, researchers have estimated that up to 75 per cent (see Harper, 1990), 85 per cent (see Harris and Ogbonna, 2002) or even 96 per cent (see Slora, 1991) of employees routinely engage in behaviours that can be described as intentionally dysfunctional. Such insights appear particularly pertinent in the context of front-line customer-contact work where the impact is not only immediate but where such actions are likely to have profound implications for the organizations and the customers concerned (see Singh, 2000). Examples include misdemeanours such as playing pranks with customers, to instances of employees that admitted to placing very hot plates into the hands of customers deliberately but apologetically (Harris and Ogbonna, 2002) and the more serious examples of front-line employees intentionally endangering and even (one would hope unintentionally) killing customers (Pitt, 1989).

Other studies of dysfunctional employee practices have documented the actions of front-line service employees who engage in behaviours that subvert formal organizational processes by concealing customer complaints, a practice which has been succinctly summarized with the aid of the ancient Japanese tale of three monkeys that deny the existence of evil by simultaneously 'seeing no evil, hearing no evil and speaking no evil' (see Homburg and Fürst, 2007). Existing studies of hiding customer complaints demonstrate that such behaviours are more prevalent in contexts where customer complaints are used to discipline employees or to control their earnings (see Harris and Ogbonna, 2010). Interestingly, this suggests that the dual and potentially contradictory aims of many customer service initiatives (to improve service while simultaneously reducing cost) have in many cases led to a failure to achieve either objective. However, it also demonstrates that such employee behaviours are counterproductive to both organizations and their customers in that the absence of customer complaint data makes it difficult for managers to recover failing service or to improve the service offered at future service encounters.

Overall, the review of conceptualizations of front-line customer-contact service work and service encounters from employment research academies find a range of studies which are commonly concerned with criticizing the ideological bases of customer service. Most studies generally provide assessments of the organizational arrangements designed to control front-line service work and workers, and the ways in which these workers respond to such systems. In this regard, with notable exceptions, employment research academics have generally conceptualized front-line employees as victims of exploitative managers and have commonly underplayed the destructive role of many customer-contact employees as well as the potential cost of their dysfunctional behaviours to customers, other employees and to the wider organization.

Similarly, both marketing and employment research academies have given insufficient attention to the role that front-line service employees can play in the creation of value and the ways in which this can benefit all parties at the service encounter. The final part of this chapter provides some reflections on the development of inclusive evaluations of the dynamics of service encounters.

Integrating research on service encounters

The foregoing discussion has demonstrated the parallel nature of research and conceptualization on service encounters wherein marketing and employment researchers have generally explored their interest in customers and service workers from their narrow research domains and have commonly treated issues of customers and front-line service employees as dichotomous, with discourses around one often being facilitated by the downplaying of the other. Such an outcome is in direct contrast to the tireless efforts of many eminent scholars from both research areas who have called for greater integration of insights as a way of advancing knowledge in the management field. For example, Edgar Schein, the renowned work and organization theorist, has urged researchers to learn from their colleagues in other management disciplines and to incorporate such knowledge in their work to improve the robustness of their conceptualizations (see Schein, 1996). Christian Grönroos, a leading scholar and one of the foremost authorities in the area of services marketing, was more specific in advising marketing researchers and practitioners to collaborate with colleagues in other disciplines such as those allied to employment research to help them to develop broader perspectives in analysing organizational issues (see Grönroos, 2001). The theoretical and practical benefits of such cross-learning and integration were previously alluded to in a different context by seminal organizational theorists who argued that a focus merely on the concerns of one organizational area (sub-system) at the expense of the others is likely to result in a state of sub-optimization, an outcome which reduces the capacity of the entire organization to function efficiently (see Trist and Bamforth, 1951).

From an employment relationship perspective, the integration of marketing insights on customers and customer service is an important step towards expanding traditional conceptions to incorporate influential actors in industrial relations systems (Bellemare, 2000), such as customers who are third-party agents with potentially pervasive influence in employer–employee relationships (Legault and Bellemare, 2008). Thus, in the context of services, the tripartite arrangement of traditional Industrial Relations Systems (Dunlop, 1958) is insufficient in explaining the dynamics of employment relationships and should be extended to include the role of customers as powerful actors whose behaviour is crucial to understanding such environments (see also Korczynski, 2003b). In this regard, rather than view customers negatively or merely as the drivers of work intensification, employment researchers should seek to identify and celebrate the mutually inter-linked nature of the interest of employees and customers, and should seize the initiative on customer service research in a manner that promotes mutual understanding. For example, scholars could explore customer–employee dynamics by demonstrating the mutual interest of customers and employees not only to provide satisfactory service but also in relation to courteous and equitable treatment in that employees who are treated fairly and who work in a positive environment are more likely to provide good quality service to customers (see Schneider et al., 1998). This also suggests the scope for investigations of customer–employee alliances and coalitions in ways that may help to undermine excessive management interference in service encounters and serve the interest of both parties. The feasibility of this in employment research and the potential impact on the employment relationship has been alluded to in other contexts (see Heery, 1993; Cutcher, 2004) but remains significantly unexplored.

Similarly, marketing and employment researchers will do well to develop their common interests in that they both focus their research efforts in exploring (and sometimes championing) the interests of people (customers and employees). Presently, the conceptualization and operationalization of issues around customer service by theorists and managers are such that it is commonly assumed that these interests are mutually exclusive (see also discussions in Knights et al., 1994; Harris and Ogbonna, 1999; Peccei and Rosenthal, 1997; Korczynski et al., 2000). However, given that customer service is an integrated activity involving an interplay of three key actors: managers setting organizational objectives, employees interpreting and implementing these objectives and customers experiencing the outcomes of these, it is arguable that closer collaboration between the intellectual 'gatekeepers' of these processes will generate alternative and potentially interesting theoretical and practical insights into these issues.

Theoretically, a strong case can be made for inclusive conceptualizations which provide equal treatment of service staff and customers. Recent developments in the marketing literature that have argued for a greater recognition that the creation of value (measured in terms of the outcomes for the parties concerned) is a collaborative process, is particularly welcome in this direction. Legault and Bellemere (2008) have equally signalled the need for theoretical development on the role of key actors in the industrial relations system in employment research through their argument that clients (customers) and project teams (employees) are co-producers of service, with each actor having the capacity (depending on the nature of the product–market) to exert a major influence not just on the outcome of service provision but also on the dynamics of employment relationships. However, unfortunately, although proponents of the 'service-dominant logic paradigm' in marketing research argue that people (customers and employees) are active participants in the value-creation process and as such are at the centre of their conception of service domination, the model is only developed in relation to the role of customers as co-creators of value (see Vargo and Lusch, 2004; Lusch et al., 2006, 2008). Similarly, while there is increasing recognition of the role of the customer as a key actor in the industrial relations system, there remains a limited number of studies in employment research that adopt a holistic view of the customer. In this regard, one possible way of achieving theoretical insights is through collaborative research involving marketing and employment researchers to develop this service paradigm in relation to exploring the role of employees in the process of value creation. Such development should adopt a wide perspective of value creation and should seek to identify and explore the multiple processes that are linked to the creation of value by front-line staff, including for example, the role of employees as co-creators of value under different employee–management relationships, the generation and harnessing of employee knowledge in value creation, the factors that contribute to employee dispositions towards value creation and the rewarding of front-line employees as co-creators of value. The inclusion of employees as central to value creation within the marketing and employment research academies will help to elevate the traditional concerns of employment researchers to a wider and potentially more organizationally central audience in ways that differ markedly from previous exaltations of employee centrality in organizations (promoted through strategic human resource management and the high performance paradigm) that have commonly failed to gain serious recognition and attention outside employment research.

There are already intersections and areas of cross-borrowing and theorizing between marketing and employment research which could be developed, and there is scope for cross-disciplinary research and collaboration in these and other areas. For example, much of the theoretical foundation of marketing conceptions of customer services is borrowed from employment research and allied fields. Significantly, the key tenet of customer service and service quality research, the 'expectation-disconfirmation paradigm' (see Cadotte et al., 1987), is pivoted on expectancy theory (see Tolman, 1951) which is a central theory in employment researchers' conceptualization of work motivation. However, instead of being selective, marketing scholars could delve into the issue of motivation more deeply by exploring not only the expectations of customers but also by examining the impact of different service expectations on employee psychological well-being, and whether and how the dynamics of this process could result in a better management of the expectations of both customers and employees. Conversely, employment researchers will benefit from a greater inclusion of marketing management concerns and issues in their conceptualizations. This is not to suggest that they should eschew their traditionally critical approaches, or that they should become functionalist in their orientations, but to argue that there is a need for a greater recognition and discussion of the transformation of organizational resources to achieve value for all stakeholders.

Furthermore, rather than focusing merely on the perspective of organizations and managers, both marketing and employment researchers should consider extending their discussions to include the practical implications of their theories on the principal parties that interact to generate outcomes in service encounters (customers, employees and managers). For example, the finding that restaurant waiters developed sophisticated insights regarding customer tipping behaviour (see Ogbonna and Harris, 2002) suggests that in some cases, employees may have more knowledge of customer behaviour than marketers and managers, and should play a more active role in developing customer service initiatives, an issue which has been mooted but not developed by marketing scholars (see Bitner et al., 1994). However, such insights should go beyond the suggestion of marketing scholars that managers should appropriate and exploit employee knowledge (Hartline and Ferrell, 1996; Lovelock and Wirtz, 2004; Rust and Oliver, 1994) to incorporate a re-examination of employment relationships, and to promote debate on why front-line workers continue to be undervalued at a time that most organizations are focusing their competitive strategy on service delivery by such employees.

Further theoretical insights could come from collaborative research involving marketing and employment researchers. Such research could provide robust, reflexive and more inclusive assessments of the role of customer service in competitive advantage that are pivoted on an evaluation of the organizational practices designed to achieve this advantage. This could also be extended to explore the impact of different competitive environments on the behaviour of both customers and service workers. Such collaboration could lead to the development of the 'dynamics of service encounters' as a research area in its own right and one which incorporates the full spectrum of relationships that characterize the processes of service and front-line service work, and that provides critical assessments of the conduct of the tripartite (customers, employees and managers) that play an important role in the construction of service encounters. A development in this direction will incorporate much-needed reflexivity in marketing research (see Harris and Ogbonna, 1999; Grönroos, 2001) and will help to promote studies into services in employment research, thereby redressing the traditional imbalance and the over-concentration of employment research on manufacturing concerns (see Harley et al., 2007).

It is also arguable that this is an area where current developments could drive theory. Indeed, the impact of the present world-wide economic recession on many long-established firms has confirmed that traditional recipes of the past may be insufficient for dealing with current problems and has forced many organizations to rethink their strategies. One example of a service sector organization that is currently rethinking its approach to generating competitive advantage is Sainsbury's. This organization has recently launched a major drive to involve front-line workers in developing and implementing initiatives that help the organization's competitive position. This initiative was led by the organization's Chief Executive who argued that:

> ... great ideas can come from anyone in any part of the company. Our colleagues are at the heart of our business and are closest to our customers. They will often see things that more senior colleagues do not and listening carefully to their ideas helps us all do a better job for our customers ....
>
> (Sainsbury's CEO, www.sainsburys.co.uk)

Employment researchers could seize the research initiative to explore and evaluate this and similar programmes to uncover the implications that such approaches may have for managing and theorizing contemporary employee relationships.

From a practical perspective, close alignment between marketing and employment researchers should present formidable partnerships that further their specific interests and concerns in a way that each field has failed to achieve alone hitherto. In this regard, both research areas should join forces in giving effective voice to front-line service employees since these jobs are disproportionately occupied by those that are typically disadvantaged in employment relationships (low skilled, feminized, ethnic minorities, new immigrants with poor language skills and the young). For example, issues that relate to the recognition of the centrality and criticality of service workers to competitive advantage and consequently the reward system of such workers, and the development of training and career paths for service workers will be taken seriously by organizations if they are pursued collaboratively and promoted by marketing and employment research academies.

Conclusion

The parallel nature of much theorizing on customer service and customer service work has proved inadequate in explaining the dynamics of contemporary service encounters. The existing theoretical gaps in these areas and the common interests of marketing and employment researchers suggest that there is a pressing need to develop inclusive conceptualizations of service work and service dynamics. Such conceptualization should be eclectic and should incorporate the reflexive and critical concerns of employment researchers but should at the same time reflect the practical concerns of marketing scholars as well as their ongoing interest in explicating the components of successful service delivery. This chapter has started the process of debating these issues by providing a review of existing studies of front-line customer-contact service encounters from marketing and employment research academies. This review finds that there is a high degree of insularity, with each area promoting particular discourses that further their traditional interests while underplaying (in the best examples) or simply ignoring (in the worst cases) the central concerns of the other. The chapter has argued that the inherent importance of both customers and employees to organizations necessitates a different approach to understanding and theorizing the dynamics of service encounters. Finally, a series of potential avenues for the development of inclusive evaluations of service encounters are presented and discussed.

References

Ackroyd, S. and Thompson, P. (1999). *Organizational Misbehaviour*, London: Sage.

Analoui, F. (1995). 'Workplace Sabotage: Its Styles, Motives and Management', *Journal of Management Development*, 14, 7, 48–65.

Anderson, E. and Mittal, V. (2000). 'Strengthening the Satisfaction-Profit Chain', *Journal of Service Research*, 3, 107–120.

Anderson, E. W., Fornell, C. and Lehmann, D. R. (1994). 'Customer Satisfaction, Market Share and Profitability', *Journal of Marketing*, 58, July, 53–66.

Bellemare, G. (2000). 'End User: Actors in the Industrial Relations System?', *British Journal of Industrial Relations*, 38, 3, 383–405.

Bennett, R. J. and Robinson, S. L. (2003). 'The Past, Present and Future of Workplace Deviance Research', in Greenberg, J. (ed.) *Organizational Behaviour, The State of the Science* 2nd edition, Mahwah, NJ: Erlbaum, 247–281.

Berry, L. L. and Parasuraman, A. (1991). *Marketing Services*, New York: Free Press.

Bitner, M. J., Booms, B. H. and Mohr, L. A. (1994). 'Critical Service Encounters: The Employee's Viewpoint', *Journal of Marketing*, 58, October, 95–106.

Booms, B. H. and Nyquist, J. (1981). 'Analysing the Customer/Firm Communication Component of the Services Marketing Mix', in Donnelly, J. H. and George, W. R. (eds) *Marketing of Services: 1981 Special Educators' Conference Proceedings*, Chicago: American Marketing Association.

Brown, S. W. and Swartz, T. A. (1989). 'A Gap Analysis of Professional Service Quality', *Journal of Marketing*, 53, 92–98.

Burawoy, M. (1979). *Manufacturing Consent*, Chicago: University of Chicago Press.

Cadotte, E. R., Woodruff, R. B. and Jenkins, R. L. (1987). 'Expectations and Norms in Models of Consumer Satisfaction', *Journal of Marketing Research*, 24, August, 305–314.

Casey, C. (1999). 'Come, Join our Family: Discipline and Integration in Corporate Organizational Culture', *Human Relations*, 52, 2, 155–178.

Churchill, G. A. Jr. and Surprenant, C. F. (1982). 'An Investigation into the Determinants of Customer Satisfaction', *Journal of Marketing Research*, 20, November, 491–504.

Collinson, D. (1994). 'Strategies of Resistance: Power, Knowledge and Subjectivity in the Work Place', in Jermier, J., Knights, D. and Nord, W. (eds) *Resistance and Power in Organizations*, London: Routledge.

Crino, M. D. (1994). 'Employee Sabotage: A Random or Preventable Phenomenon', *Journal of Management Issues*, 6, 3, 311–330.

Cullen, M. J. and Sackett, P. R. (2003). 'Personality and Counterproductive Workplace Behaviour', in Barrick, M. and Ryan, A. M. (eds) *Personality and Work*, New York: Jossey-Bass-Pfeiffer.

Cutcher, L. (2004). 'The Customer as Ally: The Role of the Customer in The Finance Sector Union's Campaigning', *The Journal of Industrial Relations*, 46, 3, 323–336.

Devinatz, V. G. (2007). 'Manufacturing Resistance: Rationalising the Irrationality of Managerial Control on the Shop Floor in a US Medical Electronics Factory', *Employee Responsibilities and Rights Journal*, 19, 1–15.

Du Gay, P. (1991). 'Enterprise Culture and the Ideology of Excellence', *New Formations*, 13, Spring, 45–61.

Dunlop, J. T. (1958). *Industrial Relations Systems*, New York: Henry Holt.

Edwards, P., Collinson, M. and Rees, C. (1998). 'The Determinants of Employee Responses to TQM: Six Case Studies', *Organization Studies*, 19, 3, 449–475.

Erevelles, S., Srinivasan, S. and Rangel, S. (2003). 'Consumer Satisfaction for Internet Service Providers: An Analysis of Underlying Processes', *Information Technology and Management*, 4, 69–89.

Filby, M. P. (1992). 'The Figures, The Personality and The Bums: Service Work and Sexuality', *Work, Employment and Society*, 6, 1, 23–42.

Fournier, S. and Mick, D. G. (1999). 'Rediscovering Satisfaction', *Journal of Marketing*, 63, October, 5–23.

Fullerton, R. A. and Punj, G. (2003). 'Choosing to Misbehave: A Structural Model of Aberrant Consumer Behaviour', *Advances in Consumer Research*, 20, 1, 570–574.

Gabriel, Y. (1999). 'Beyond Happy Families: A Critical Revaluation of the Control-Resistance-Identity Triangle' *Human Relations*, 52, 2, 179–203.

Gil, I., Berenguer, G. and Cervera, A. (2008). 'The Role of Service Encounters, Service Value, and Job Satisfaction in Achieving Customer Satisfaction in Business Relationships', *Industrial Marketing Management*, 37, 921–939.

Gregoire, Y. and Fisher, R. J. (2008). 'Customer Betrayal and Retaliation: When Your Best Customers Become Your Worst Enemies', *Journal of the Academy of Marketing Science*, 36, 247–261.

Gross, T. S. (1994). *Positively Outrageous Service*, New York: Warner.

Grönroos, C. (1982). *Strategic Management and Marketing in the Service Sector*, Cambridge, MA: Marketing Science Institute.

Grönroos, C. (2001). *Services Management and Marketing*, New York: John Wiley.

Grove, S. J., Fisk, R. P. and John, J. (2004). 'Surviving in the Age of Rage', *Marketing Management*, 13, 2, 41–46.

Guerrier, Y.-A, and Amel, S. (2000). ' "No, We Don't Provide that Service": The Harrassment of Hotel Employees by Customers', *Work, Employment and Society*, 14, 4, 689–705.

Harper, D. (1990). 'Spotlight Abuse-Save Profits', *Industrial Distribution*, 79, 10, 47–51.

Harris, L. C. (2008). 'Fraudulent Return Proclivity: An Empirical Analysis', *Journal of Retailing*, 84, 4, 461–476.

Harris, L. C. and Goode, M. (2004). 'The Four Levels of Loyalty and the Pivotal Role Trust: A Study of On-line Service Dynamics', *Journal of Retailing*, 80, 139–158.

Harris, L. C. and Ogbonna, E. (1998). 'Employee Reactions to Organizational Culture Change Efforts', *Human Resource Management Journal*, 8, 2, 78–92.

Harris, L. C. and Ogbonna, E. (1999). 'Developing and Market Oriented Culture: A Critical Evaluation', *Journal of Management Studies*, 36, 2, 177–196.

Harris, L. C. and Ogbonna, E. (2002). 'Exploring Service Sabotage: The Antecedents, Types and Consequences of Deviant Service Behaviours by Frontline Workers', *Journal of Service Research*, 4, 3, 163–183.

Harris, L. C. and Ogbonna, E. (2006). 'Service Sabotage: A Study of Antecedents and Consequences', *Journal of the Academy of Marketing Science*, 34, 4, 543–558.

Harris, L. C. and Ogbonna, E. (2010). 'Hiding Complaints: Studying the Motivations and Forms of Service Employees' Complaint Concealment Behaviours', *British Journal of Management*, 21, 2, 262–279.

Harley, B., Allen, B. C. and Sargent, L. D. (2007). 'High Performance Work Systems and Employee Experience of Work in the Service Sector: The Case of Aged Care', *British Journal of Industrial Relations*, 45, 3, 607–633.

Hartline, M. D. and Ferrell, O. C. (1996). 'The Management of Customer-Contact Service Employees: An Empirical Investigation', *Journal of Marketing*, 60, October, 52–70.

Heery, E. (1993). 'Industrial Relations and the Customer', *Industrial Relations Journal*, 24, 4, 284–295.

Heskett, J. L., Sasser, W. E. Jr and Hart, C. W. L. (1990). *Service Breakthroughs*, New York: The Free Press.

Hodson, R. (1999). 'Organizational Anomie and Worker Consent', *Work and Occupations*, 26, 3, 292–323.

Homburg, C. and Fürst, A. (2007). 'See no Evil, Hear no Evil, Speak no Evil: A Study of Defensive Organizational Behaviour Towards Customer Complaints', *Journal of the Academy of Marketing Science*, 35, 523–536.

Houlihan, M. (2002). 'Tensions amd Variations in Call Centre Management Strategies', *Human Resource Management Journal*, 12, 4, 67–85.

Keat, R. and Abercrombie, N. (eds) (1991). *Enterprise Culture*, London: Routledge.

Knights, D., Sturdy, A. and Morgan, G. (1994). 'The Consumer Rules? An Examination of the Rhetoric and 'Reality' of Marketing in Financial Service', *European Journal of Marketing*, 28, 3, 42–54.

Korczynski, M. (2001). *Human Resource Management in Service Work*, Basingstoke: Palgrave Macmillan.

Korczynski, M. (2003a). 'Communities of Coping: Collective Emotional Labour in Service Work', *Organization*, 10, 1, 55–79.

Korczynski, M. (2003b). 'Consumer Capitalism and Industrial Relations', in Ackers, P. and Wilkinson, A. (eds) *Understanding Work and Employment*, Oxford: Oxford University Press, 265–277.

Korczynski, M. (2004). 'Back-Office Service Work: Bureaucracy Challenged?', *Work, Employment and Society*, 18, 1, 97–114.

Korczynski, M. (2009). 'The Mystery of the Customer: Continuing Absences in the Sociology of Service Work', *Sociology*, 43, 5, 952–967.

Korczynski, M., Shire, K., Frankel, S. and Tam, M. (2000). 'Service Work in Consumer Capitalism: Consumers, Control and Contradiction', *Work, Employment and Society*, 14, 4, 669–687.

Kunda, G. (1992). *Engineering Culture, Control and Commitment in a High-Tech Corporation*, Philadelphia: Temple University Press.

Legault, M.-J. and Bellemare, G. (2008). 'Theoretical Issues with New Actors and Emergent Modes of Labour Regulations, *Relations Industrielles*, 63, 4, 742–768.

Lovelock, C. H. (1994). *Product Plus: How Product and Service = Competitive Advantage*, New York: McGraw-Hill.

Lovelock, C. H. and Wirtz, J. (2004). *Services Marketing-People, Technology, Strategy*, New Jersey: Prentice Hall.

Lusch, R. F., Vargo, S. L. and Malter, A. (2006). ' "Marketing as Service Exchange": Taking a Leadership Role in Global Marketing Management', *Organizational Dynamics*, 35, 3, 264–278.

Lusch, R. F., Vargo, S. L. and Wessels, G. (2008). 'Toward a Conceptual Foundation for Service Science: Contributions From Service-Dominant Logic', *IBM Systems Journal*, 47, 1, 5–14.

Mumby, D. K. (2005). 'Theorising Resistance in Organization Studies', *Management Communication Quarterly*, 19, 1, 19–44.

O'Donohoe, S. and Turley, D. (2006). 'Compasion at the Counter: Service Providers and Bereaved Consumers', *Human Relations*, 59, 10, 1429–1448.

Oxford Economic Forecasting UK Weekly Brief (2006). 'Is Manufacturing in Terminal Decline'?, 14 July.

Ogbonna, E. (1992). 'Organizational Culture and Human Resource Management', in Blyton, P. and Turnbull, P. (eds) *Reassessing Human Resource Management*, London: Sage, 77–96.

Ogbonna, E. and Wilkinson, B. (1988). 'Corporate Strategy and Corporate Culture: The Management of Change in the UK Supermarket Industry', *Personnel Review*, 17, 6, 10–14.

Ogbonna, E. and Wilkinson, B. (1990). 'Corporate Strategy and Corporate Culture: The View from the Checkout', *Personnel Review*, 19, 4, 9–15.

Ogbonna, E. and Harris, L. C. (1998). 'Managing Organizational Culture: Compliance or Genuine Change?', *British Journal of Management*, 9, 273–288.

Ogbonna, E. and Harris, L. C. (2002). 'Institutionalization of Tipping as a Source of Managerial Control', *British Journal of Industrial Relations*, 40, 4, 725–752. Ogbonna and Wilkinson, 2003.

Ogbonna, E. and Wilkinson, B. (2003). 'The False Promise of Organizational Culture Change: A Case Study of Middle Managers in Grocery Retailing', *Journal of Management Studies*, 40, 5, 1151–1178.

Oliver, R. (1997). *Satisfaction: A Behavioural Perspective of the Consumer*, New York: McGraw-Hill.

Oliver, R. L. (1980). 'A Cognitive Model of the Antecedents and Consequences of Satisfaction Decisions', *Journal of Marketing Research*, 17, 460–469.

Parasuraman, A. and Grewal, D. (2000). 'Serving Customers and Consumers Effectively in the Twenty-First Century: A Conceptual Framework', *Journal of the Academy of Marketing Science*, 28, 1, 9–16.

Parasuraman, A., Zeithaml, V. A. and Berry, L. L. (1988). 'SERVQUAL: A Multiple-Item Scale for Measuring Consumer Perceptions of Service Quality', *Journal of Retailing*, 64, 2–40.

Peccei, R. and Rosenthal, P. (1997). 'The Antecedents of Employee Commitment toCustomer Service: Evidence from a UK Context', *International Journal of Human Resource Management*, 8, 1, 66–85.

Peccei, R. and Rosenthal, P. (2000). 'Front-line Responses to Customer Orientation Programmes: A Theoretical and Empirical Analysis', *International Journal of Human Resource Management*, 11, 3, 562–590.

Pfaff, M. (1976). 'The Index of Consumer Satisfaction and Dissatisfaction: Measurement Problems and Opportunities', in Hunt, H. K. (ed.) *Conceptualization and Measurement of Consumer Satisfaction and Dissatisfaction*, Cambridge, MA: Marketing Science Institute.

Piron, F. and Young, M. (2000). 'Retail Borrowing: Insights and Implications on Returning Used Merchandise', *International Journal of Retail and Distribution Management*, 28, 1, 27–36.

Pitt, D. E. (1989). 'Tampering Suspected in Drug Doses Given to 2 Lenox Hill Patients', *New York Times*, 29, 30 April.

Rafaeli, A. (1989). 'When Cashiers meet Customers: An Analysis of the Role of Supermarket Cashiers', *Academy of Management Journal*, 32, 2, 245–273.

Reynolds, K. L. and Harris, L. C. (2005). 'When Service Failure is not Service Failure: An Exploration of the Types and Motives of "Illegitimate" Customer Complaining', *Journal of Services Marketing*, 19, 5, 321–335.

Reynolds, K. L. and Harris, L. C. (2006). 'Deviant Customer Behaviour: An Exploration of Front-Line Employee Tactics', *Journal of Marketing Theory and Practice*, 14, 2, 95–111.

Rosenthal, P. (2004). 'Management Control as an Employee Resource: The Case of Front-Line Service Workers', *Journal of Management Studies*, 41, 4, 601–622.

Rust, R. T. and Oliver, R. L. (1994). 'Service Quality: Insights and Managerial Implications From the Frontier', in Rust, R. T. and Oliver, R. L. (eds) *Service Quality: New Directions in Theory and Practice*, Thousand Oaks, CA: Sage, 1–19.

Rust, R. T. and Oliver, R. L. (2000). 'Should we Delight the Customer?', *Journal of the Academy of Marketing Science*, 28, 1, 86–94.

Rust, R. T. and Chung, T. S. (2006). 'Marketing Models of Service and Relationships', *Marketing Science*, 25, 6, 560–580.

Schein, E. H. (1996). 'Culture: The Missing Concept in Organizational Studies', *Administrative Science Quarterly*, 41, 229–240.

Schneider, B., White, S. S. and Paul, M. C. (1998). 'Linking Service Climate and Customer Perceptions of Service Quality: A Test of a Causal Model', *Journal of Applied Psychology*, 83, 2, 150–163.

Slora, K. B. (1991). 'An Empirical Approach to Determining Employee Deviance Base Rates', in Jones, J. (ed.) *Preemployment Honesty Testing: Current Research and Future Directions*, Connecticut: Quorum Books.

Steiger, T. L. and Form, W. (1991). 'The Labour Process in Construction: Control Without Bureaucratic and Technological Means?', *Work and Occupations*, 18, 3, 251–270.

Sturdy, A. (1998). 'Customer Care in a Consumer Society: Smiling and Sometimes Meaning It?', *Organization*, 5, 1, 27–53.

Sturdy, A., Grugulis, I. and Willmott, H. (eds) (2001). *Customer Service-Control, Colonisation and Contradictions*, Basingstoke: Palgrave Macmillan.

Surprenant, C. F. and M. R. Solomon (1987) 'Predictability and Personalisation in the Service Encounter', *Journal of Marketing*, 51, April, 86–96.

Singh, J. (2000). 'Performance, Productivity and Quality of Front-Line Employees in Service Organizations', *Journal of Marketing*, 64, April, 15–34.

Sutton, R. I. (1991). 'Maintaining Norms About Expressed Emotions', *Administrative Science Quarterly*, 36, 245–268.

Tolman, E. C. (1951). *Behaviour and Psychological Essays in Motivation*, Berkeley CA: University of California Press.

Taylor, P. and Bain, P. (2003). ' "Subterrranean Worksick Blues' ": Humour as Subversion in two Call Centres', *Organization Studies*, 24, 9, 1487–1509.

Trist, E. L. and Bamforth, K. W. (1951). 'Some Social and Psychological Consequences of the Longwall Method of Coal-getting', *Human Relations*, 1, 3–38.

Vargo, S. L. and Lusch, R. F. (2004). 'Evolving to a New Dominant Logic for Marketing', *Journal of Marketing*, 68, 1, 1–17.

Zeithaml, V. A., Berry, L. L. and Parasuraman, A. (1996). 'The Behavioural Consequences of Service Quality', *Journal of Marketing*, 60, 31–46.

17

Knowledge work and the employment relationship in the 'new workplace'

Tim Edwards

Introduction

The aim of this chapter is to consider the influence of the knowledge-based economy on the employment relationship. While conventional wisdom reports that industrial society has undergone major shifts, which confirm the role of new forms of 'knowledge' and the importance of 'knowledge workers' as the drivers of growth and innovation (Stewart, 1997), there remains doubt as to whether these processes have led to revisions in employment and work relations (Gospel, 1992; Thompson, 2003). An assessment of the scope and content of knowledge work and employment patterns offers the basis, in this case, to critique the paradigm shift between Fordist and post-Fordist modes of organizing and work (Jessop, 2002). Rather than suppose that changes in recent market conditions and the growing role given to intellectual capital have led to wholesale changes in extant modes of work the aim is to reflect on the nature of such transformations, highlighting their unevenness and sometimes contested reality. This analysis complements those more reflective assessments of societal change that question the validity of universalistic and 'epochal' models of industrial change (du Gay, 2003; Sturdy and Grey, 2003).

The chapter begins by outlining the background to changes associated with the emergence of the knowledge-based economy. This provides consideration of those macro features informing recent conceptualizations of the 'new' economy and the significance of 'knowledge' and 'knowledge work' in terms of the employment relationship. The subsequent section reflects on what is meant by knowledge work, the breadth of such activities and how knowledge workers are managed. This examination leads onto a discussion of the varied experiences of those individuals involved in such knowledge work. Much of the evidence presented refers to contemporary liberal economies and, in particular, the United Kingdom (UK). The final section draws on these insights in a critique of the conceptualizations that report a major shift in industrial society. Here we draw attention to the inherent contradictions between labour and capital in capitalist societies.

The emergence of a knowledge-based economy

Much current interest in the employment relationship is framed by the concept of industrial society and the assumed paradigm shift between Fordist and post-Fordist systems. Such theorization shapes debate around the employment relationship because it specifies shifts in market conditions which are connected to assumed transformations in organization and work relations (Bell, 1973; Castells, 1996; Drucker, 1969). In the case of Fordism, which at its core incorporated mass production systems, there was an attempt to develop a virtuous circle between different societal institutions to create the conditions for a sustained business and societal model. The systemic nature of Fordism was encapsulated in the link between mass production and mass consumption, underpinned by a Keynesian Welfare National State (KWNS) that supported growth through demand management (Jessop, 2002). While the Fordist model varied across capitalist societies, the social settlements that defined these arrangements confirmed a common attempt to confer mutual gains between capital and labour. This emphasized among other things a career path for workers based on a stepped progression which usually occurred in the same organization over an extended period (Brown and Hesketh , 2004). For example, in the UK the 'internalization' of the employment relationship ensured a structured approach to the screening and recruitment of white-collar workers. Every effort was given to making these workers permanent, developing internal job ladders and promotional strategies and adopting a systematic approach to providing fringe benefits (Gospel, 1992). Yet, the relationship between capital and labour altered during the Thatcher and Reagan eras when this relationship 'broke down through a combination of internal rigidities (e.g. exhaustion of productivity gains and workplace conflict) and external shocks (e.g. new competitive pressures) that undermined co-operation' (Thompson,

2003: 362; see also Jessop, 2002: 55–94; and Marinetto, 2007: 52–7). What followed has been conceptualized using a post-Fordist theory of industrial society which offers a different view of how firms and workers might react to the challenges of globalization and the failure of workplace settlements.

The response to these strictures are presented in terms of a qualitative shift in the nature of capitalism whereby the traditional factors of production – land, labour and capital – are replaced or transcended by 'knowledge' as the driver of competitiveness and innovation. This 'new reality' is linked with slower economic growth, less predictable patterns of demand, increased competition and intensified forms of product innovation based on Information and Communication Technologies (hereafter ICTs) and new forms of knowledge that have changed the process of capital accumulation (see Castells, 1996). Where once competitive advantage seemingly relied on the mass production of standardized products and services and organizations exhibited pyramidal structures, close spans of control and bureaucratic processes, the reported changes in market conditions have led to the call for flatter more flexible organizational forms with new work systems that are supposedly better able to respond to market uncertainties and discontinuous change (Heydebrand, 1989; Pascale, 1990). Coupled with these pressures and assumed organizational changes, exponents of post-Fordism argue that more traditional manual trades and blue-collar work have declined, replaced by 'knowledge work'. The characteristic feature of this 'new' work, which it is argued, is reflected in the rise of professional and managerial jobs and the growth of the service sector, is that economic value is now dependent on intangibles such as new ideas, software, services and social relationships (Leadbetter, 2000).

Knowledge work is different to manual work in so far as 'knowledge' is thought to offer the means for worker discretion and mobility which provides mutual benefit for workers and employers alike. The control mechanisms associated with mass production systems and bureaucratic processes become largely redundant because the nature of the work process relies on the inter-subjectivity of the workers involved, which is sustained through cultural (normative) co-ordination, self-discipline and internalized commitment (Jessop, 2002; Thompson, 2003). The employment relationship is, as a result, transformed reflecting a new bargain founded on the emancipatory role of 'knowledge'. For example, where once organizational loyalty was rewarded with job security and career progression, the emphasis on cerebral activities denotes a more individualistic approach to work which is said to be exciting, mobile, but also temporary (Alvesson, 2001; Scarbrough, 1999). In this respect, the employment relationship is effectively externalized with the contract between workers and capital outsourced and made increasingly sensitive (and vulnerable) to market demand (Gospel, 1992). Those individuals without such skills are disadvantaged because they cannot generate the value-added expected of them. For Brown and Hesketh (2004) this reveals a shift in work relations with employment or pre-determined work roles replaced by the idea of 'employability'. Standardized low-skilled jobs are seemingly replaced with more challenging jobs undertaken by a workforce who are increasingly engaged in their own self-development. Where organizations do look to develop their own internal knowledge assets through human resource management systems, the challenge is to adequately understand and ensure loyalty. This is not straightforward, or so it is argued, because ' "knowledge workers" ' expectations of their job extend beyond having a good salary, to include interesting work and opportunities to develop their expertise' (Newell et al., 2009: 131).

In combination, these observations reveal a number of different trends. First, relations show a gradual shift in responsibility with the individual taking on much more of the financial burden and responsibility for self-development. Second, evidence of the externalization of the labour market is associated with a shift towards outsourced knowledge work (related to a growth in the numbers of portfolio workers), while existing human resource management practices are being revised in an effort to support a more flexible employment relationship. Implicated in these various trends is the assumed belief that knowledge has both 'caring and sharing qualities' (Thompson and McHugh, 2009: 188) because 'knowledge' is positively linked with employability.

This world confirms (or so it is argued) a business model that is based on the exploitation of intellectual capital (Starbuck, 1992), which emphasizes a positive link between an individual's ability to create and share knowledge and the returns they might expect for their efforts. Such revisions infer the emergence of 'boundaryless' or portfolio careers based on marketable skills and new 'opportunities for people to use applied knowledge, initiative, and their creative energies in a wide range of occupations, including those working for small companies or in self-employment' (Brown and Hesketh, 2004: 18). Progression increasingly depends on mobility and the experiences accumulated as a feature of such mobility which is equated with shifts in the structure of work and occupations. These include the expansion of the self-employed and freelance contractors and the widespread involvement of 'flexible' labour in the service sector that, as mentioned, operates outside of the typical employment relationship (Felstead and Jewson, 1999).

While the changes in work relations are often presented as a positive outcome of the market changes just described – the new individualism is thought to reframe the relationship between labour and capital in ways that are less antagonistic – the available evidence for such claims are less certain. It remains questionable whether 'knowledge' creates a more harmonious workplace because it is not obvious how 'knowledge' can reconcile the aspirations of individuals for meaningful work with management's drive for greater efficiency and profit. While it might be assumed that organizational success depends on the 'utility of talent rather than alienated labour' (Brown and Hesketh, 2004: 20), it is unclear how this is to be achieved when knowledge work relies on expertise that is more distributed or dispersed among experts compared to standardized work (Scarbrough, 1999). It is also unclear whether the new economy and knowledge work are as widespread as is assumed (Baylies, 1998; Thompson and Warhurst, 1998) or whether achieving 'knowledge worker' status ensures ready access to the job market (Brown and Hesketh, 2004) or whether such workers are secure in a changing marketplace (Thompson, 2003). Arguably, the assumed cycle of opportunity associated with the knowledge-based economy relies on normative representations of 'knowledge' and 'knowledge work', which tend to downplay inherent tensions in the economy.

Knowledge and the knowledge-based firm

The idea of the knowledge-based economy provides a distinct interpretation of industrial society. What this interpretation assumes is 'a society organised around knowledge for the purpose of economic development, social control and institutional innovation and change' (Blackler et al., 1993: 852). Such arrangements seem to infer 'a cleverer society that will, in turn, demand cleverer services, creating cleverer jobs, to create a sort of virtuous circle of increasing enlightenment' (Lewis, 2001: 10). At the level of the firm, such ideas require a particular type of work that is 'characterised by an emphasis on theoretical knowledge, creativity and use of analytical and social skills' (Frenkel et al., 1995: 773). This 'knowledge work' is usually associated with traditional accountancy, scientific, legal and academic professions as well as more contemporary forms of professional work including consultancy, software development, advertising and public relations. It is also linked with activities related to high-performance work systems including continuous improvement and problem-solving, which cut across organization and occupational types (Huselid, 1995; MacDuffie, 1995). Of particular importance in this 'new' workplace is the idea that the worker owns the firm's primary means of production. While this has always been so, even in low-skilled work, what is different here (or so it is assumed) is the extent to which the individual is able to manipulate and apply such knowledge (see Brinkley et al., 2009).

Knowledge is no longer captured using routinized work processes or procedures as in mass production systems. Rather, knowledge workers bring their personal judgements, experiences and understanding to the workplace solving problems and creating new and improved products/services or ways of completing tasks. The constant drive for innovation ensures ongoing changes to services and products which places greater emphasis on transferable skills and mobility. The linkage between work organization and employment relations reflect the emphasis given to establishing a highly flexible workforce. The old employment rules are thought to restrict the type of worker flexibility necessary for the exploitation of expertise. Instead, the challenge is to develop human resource strategies that respond to a number of issues related to the operational autonomy of knowledge workers: their labour market power and expectations of work (Table 17.1).

Knowledge is understood as a universal good with the link between knowledge management and work relations seen as a management challenge to co-ordinate knowledge resources that are distributed among organizations and individuals (Nonaka and Takeuchi, 1995). The main challenge is in creating and transferring tacit and explicit knowledge which are seen as discrete,

Table 17.1 The challenges posed by knowledge work for HRM policy

Knowledge worker characteristics	Challenges for HRM policy
Operational autonomy in work practices	Gaining knowledge workers' commitment to the organization.
	Controlling knowledge worker behaviour.
	Designing work and reward systems that encourage required knowledge processes.
Labour market power	Recruiting and selecting employees to ensure the best fit with other staff.
	Retaining highly valued employees who are in demand from other organizations.
High expectations of work	Creating work satisfaction through interesting and challenging work.
	Developing career systems that enable knowledge workers to gain promotion and higher level jobs.

Source: Newell et al. (2009: 130).

objective, cognitive entities. Tacit knowledge represents understanding – gut feeling and experience – which resides within the individual and, which by implication, is extremely hard, if not impossible to articulate. As described by Howells (1995: 2), tacit knowledge is understood to be 'non-codified, disembodied know-how that is acquired via the informal take-up of learned behaviour and procedures' with knowledge acquisition requiring changes in the behaviour of the acquirer. Acquiring knowledge is not a passive exercise but requires developing a common understanding. For example, the activities involved in the acquisition of tacit knowledge can include 'learning by doing' (Arrow, 1962), 'learning by using' (Rosenberg, 1982) and 'learning to learn' (Stiglitz, 1987). Explicit knowledge, by contrast, is that knowledge which can be more readily codified – instructions and procedures – and forms the formal part of an organization's memory (Walsh and Ungson, 1991).

The value of knowledge workers is in their ability to draw upon and develop tacit and explicit knowledge. Nonaka and Takeuchi (1995) outline those processes whereby the tacit intuitions and local expertise of practitioners are made widely accessible for improving the innovative capacities of a firm. They state that the knowledge-creation process involves the mobilization and conversion of tacit knowledge into explicit forms which in time revert to taken-for-granted tacit understandings – what might be considered the 'nitty gritty' of knowledge work. In other words, innovation involves individuals enlisted in activities to ensure interpretive closure around the problems and solutions that are subsequently embodied (perhaps only temporarily) in a social process or technical system. From this perspective, the challenge is in being able to capture and convert tacit understanding into new forms. The means to achieving this outcome is in creating *teams* that use a broad knowledge base with both the time and space to establish a shared dialogue and trust.

In discussing their model of knowledge creation, Nonaka and Takeuchi (1995) attribute considerable importance to the idea of multi-disciplinarity. For them, multi-disciplinarity ensures reduced duplication of knowledge while autonomy is essential in allowing participants to consider multiple options to achieve optimum solutions. As explained by Nonaka and Konno (1998), an important feature of these arrangements is an enabling context that provides adequate space for individuals to interact (face-to-face or using ICTs) and to develop a shared sense of purpose and interpretative meaning. Implicit in this approach is the recognition that managers have a role in establishing a work environment to enable and shape such processes. The nature of such an enabling context has been considered by Dyerson and Mueller (1999) who argue that management have an important role in managing information flows for the purpose of building technological capability.

They describe three processes: appropriation, team working and learning. For them, 'appropriation' refers to the effective retention of knowledge (tacit and explicit) within the organization, 'team working' refers to the integration of knowledge resources while 'learning' includes the acquisition and use of knowledge held outside the firm.

Interest in understanding context has included work around the idea of 'communities of practice' which represent those social arrangements where individuals form around, and engage in, self-selecting groups to benefit from each other's experiences in solving problems (Brown and Duguid, 1991). Central to this approach is social cohesion and the situated nature of such practices. In other words, the social context helps to confirm that collaboration ensures mutual benefits, which if successful, can lead to reciprocal relationships. This is captured in the work of Orr (1990) who reported on the work of photocopier engineers. In this research, Orr describes how the technicians helped each other by sharing 'war stories' about the way they approached faulty machines. Such stories offered a way to convey the problems encountered and how these were resolved. These accounts became resources that helped other technicians orientate their future efforts to solve problems. Orr (1990) suggests that tacit insights and technical knowledge are 'mutually constituted' (Tsoukas, 1996). The technicians drew on the experience of understanding how operators used the machines as well as their expertise of the machines themselves in resolving problems. These features were brought to bear simultaneously in the process of problem-solving when the sharing of 'war stories' confirmed that the technicians shared an interest in trying to do their jobs effectively.

Such analyses have been used to convey a specific interpretation of the new workplace. This is seen in terms of flatter, less bureaucratized ways of organizing that are more akin to adhocracies. In turn, employment conditions are often described as superior, based on market value and a more flexible enabling context (Baron et al., 2001). Implicit in this formulation is the link between organic forms of organization and a revised employment relationship, which emphasizes both an 'open' contract but also new HR-approaches. These factors are thought to promote knowledge sharing, which have been identified by Cabrera and Cabrera (2005) in a recent review and comprising the following elements:

Work designs that encourage collaboration among employees, interdependency and cross-functional interactions.
Selection of employees driven by person–organization fit and the assessment of communication skills.

Extensive training programmes geared towards increasing participant self-efficacy and developing team-work skills.

Formalized orientation and socialization programmes, as well as more informal communities of practice and social events.

Developmental performance appraisals that recognize knowledge-sharing behaviours.

Incentive programmes that reward effective knowledge sharing and emphasize intrinsic rewards.

Group and firm-based compensation systems.

Value is based on the market need; job security is dependent upon the individual worker's ability to mobilize resources to problem-solve and when required to move from team to team both within and across organizations.

Critiquing knowledge work

While the picture presented provides insights into the processes through which knowledge is captured, created and shared, this work tends to focus on the enabling rather than the enabling *and* limiting features of the social and workplace context. This is because much of this work assumes a simple means–ends relationship between both knowledge creation and capital accumulation. In turn, flexible firms and mobile workers are presented as necessary features of the new economy and employment relationship. Seemingly 'the new economy is identified with a fresh pattern of work relations free from long-standing hierarchical and conflictual employment relations' (Nolan and Slater, 2003: 77). These new work relations are different because of the content of the work, which is focused on the creation and application of knowledge. Thus, not only is knowledge the means of economic value, it is also the arbiter of social cohesion. As in the work of Nonaka and Takeuchi (1995) the default assumption is that knowledge creation is a normative feature of the workplace – the legitimate outcome of extant social relations. Similarly, as in the work of Brown and Duguid (1991), the basic assumption is that community activities reveal a shared endeavour. As it is, this is an oversimplification of organizing because in each instance, it is assumed that 'knowledge work' in and of itself offers the means to solve contradictions between creativity and capital accumulation.

Such normative representations ignore the potential for conflicting interests. As argued by Tsoukas (1996), firms constitute distributed knowledge systems whereby an individual's stock of knowledge constitutes the (i) role-related normative expectations related to their job description, (ii) personal dispositions or past experiences and (iii) local knowledge of particular circumstances. An organization's knowledge is not easily managed because it is a feature of the indeterminate outcome of individuals attending to the tensions that often exist between normative expectations of the workplace, their personal dispositions and the local context (Tsoukas and Vladimirou, 2001). Arguably, knowledge work is a process that is performed in the context of individual experiences set against emerging features of the workplace and market pressures. This is not straightforward precisely because the circuit of capital accumulation and contemporary competition incorporates a number of inherent tensions (Crouch, 2005). These tensions relate to the drive for innovation when workers are faced with demands to mobilize their knowledge and those attempts to create greater value through corporate downsizing and restructuring (McKinlay, 2005).

Reference to political economy provides understanding of powerful structural tendencies that shape the context through which 'knowledge work' and 'knowledge management' processes operate (Thompson, 2003). As described by Jessop (2002), an integral feature of the knowledge-based economy is the development of greater worker discretion and new forms of employer-initiated work practices. In turn, this workplace is 'predicated on an exchange – that in return for participation in the micro-management of work and expanded responsibilities (what the managerial literature refers to as empowerment), employers will undertake commitment and trust-building measures in the employment relationship' (Thompson, 2003: 363). The outcome is a number of convergent processes that are premised on the role of 'knowledge' bringing labour and capital together. While the new workforce may need to be more mobile – portfolio-based – the common objective is to develop commitment for the purpose of improving the competitiveness of organizations (Sewell, 2005). Mobility is coupled with the expectation that knowledge workers will retain discretion over the work process, which is informed by reassurances from management that the workforce will be insulated from the vagaries of the marketplace. However, it remains unclear how such protection can be afforded to knowledge workers when demands for higher shareholder value shape corporate behaviour.

Thompson (2003) cautions us to the idea that this bargain has been embarked upon uniformly by employers, particularly in liberal market economies like the UK or US. This is because 'knowledge work' does not operate outside of the capitalist labour process: the 'contingent constraints of power structures and political choices made within particular organizations or socio-economic contexts' (364). As Jessop (2002) argues, knowledge work, like other workplace activities, is shaped by the manifestation of corporate governance structures and new forms of economic regulation in the context of specific work routines. While knowledge might be seen as a malleable and productive 'entity', such formulations tend to ignore 'knowledge' as a social phenomenon, which is shaped by broader institutional and market processes that create barriers as well as opportunities for change (Scarbrough, 1996).

In summary, the positive attributes ascribed to knowledge are often presented without due recognition of the way knowledge can become politicized and problematized by processes within and without the organization. In the next section, attention is given to considering the spread of this type of work and the experiences of such knowledge workers involved in these occupations and processes. This evidence seems to support a more cautionary view of knowledge work in terms of scope and experience.

What's it like to be a 'knowledge worker'?

Throughout the early part of this chapter reference has been made to the 'new' economy (using inverted commas). This is deliberate because while most protagonists want to report change in industrial society the reality is less clear-cut or convincing. Here we assess the nature and extent of those shifts that are assumed to have impacted the employment relationship that underpins knowledge work. The evidence informing this section derives from recent publications based on the ESRC Future of Work Programme (Nolan and Wood, 2003; White et al., 2003). This provides a useful overview to assess the post-Fordist thesis in the last section of the chapter. As will become evident, the evidence of the spread and nature of knowledge work is far from conclusive. As Nolan and Wood (2003: 165) argue: 'Change is evident, to be sure, but the shifts in the patterns and rhythms of work are not linear, pre-determined by technology or, as some writers have uncritically assumed, driven by universal trends in market globalization'. Instead, what we see is a mixed picture where changes are uneven and often partial (Baylies, 1998; Thompson and Warhurst, 1998).

According to Nolan and Wood (2003), the extant literature on the nature of work tends to provide two opposing views. These views offer different interpretations of the consequences of the same structural changes based on globalization and the role of ICTs. One version reports the collapse of work in traditional industries with higher levels of unemployment, growing levels of insecurity, the growth in low-skilled work and reductions in well paid full-time employment in highly skilled jobs (Beck, 2000). A second, more optimistic version, reports (as indicated above) a 'new' economy based on mental rather than manual labour dominated by networks and partnerships across organizations as opposed to hierarchies and bureaucratic processes (see Hamel and Prahalad, 1996; Leadbetter, 2000; Reich, 1993). This is an economy that relies on the spread of jobs related to knowledge work, which as discussed above, infers employment relations based on high trust and 'empowerment' that shape knowledge creation activities. As part of this change is the growth in *portfolio workers* in the labour market – workers who are more mobile and command higher rewards, often because of their knowledge (tacit and explicit), which includes their social skills and client relationships, is valuable and difficult to replace (Barney, 1991). This development is attributed to the idea that 'knowledge' belongs to the individual and as such the individual has greater discretion in the way they apply such expertise. In the context of a more open and harmonious economy, the idea of portfolio workers complements the vision of a virtuous system where knowledge workers are able to work simultaneously or sequentially for a number of different employees working in project teams and increasingly from home (Hamel and Prahalad, 1996; Handy, 1995; Leadbetter, 2000; Pink, 2001).

What of the evidence? According to White et al. (2004b) and Barley and Kunda (2004), there is evidence to suggest growth in skilled portfolio workers in OECD countries and especially in the USA. However, Thompson and McHugh (2009) caution us as to how such trends might be interpreted. Drawing on a number of sources they suggest that the use of high-skilled temporary workers (as with low-skilled workers) reveals an attempt to offset the costs of raising the salaries of full-time employees and those costs associated with redundancy (Houseman et al., 2003). This interpretation is extended to include the emergence of portfolio workers which they argue follows firm de-layering. Rather than reflect greater mobility such arrangements infer increased insecurity as management adopt a 'flexible' approach that suits cost-reduction as opposed to employee development; that is, flexibility for employers not workers (Burchell et al., 1999).

For the UK, Nolan and Wood (2003: 170) report that the proportion of the workforce engaged in the professions, scientific and technical occupations has increased over the 1990s from 34 to 37 per cent, in line with the predictions of those heralding the rise of a new economy. However, they also note that over the same period the total number of manual workers has been remarkably stable at around 10.5 million, or 40 per cent of total employment. When taken together with clerical and secretarial workers the non-high-skilled proportion of the workforce still remains the dominant feature. When considered in detail, the figures actually suggest higher growth in areas other than the professions that include hairdressers, sales assistants, data input clerks and also storekeepers among other groups. As they go onto argue, employment growth, in short, 'has been concentrated in occupations that are not, in the main, associated with the shift from the old to new economy' (ibid.: 170). Such findings confirm much earlier concerns over the state of vocational education and training in the UK (Finegold and Soskice, 1988). This work, which was coined as the low-skill/low-quality equilibrium debate reported that Britain was trapped in a self-reinforcing network of societal and state institutions that interacted to stifle the demand for improvement in skill levels. The findings indicated that the majority of UK enterprises were staffed by poorly trained managers and workers producing low-quality goods and services. According to Finegold and Soskice (1988), the shift to a new economy was being hindered by a confluence of features – short-term financial markets, an adversarial industrial relations system and a low supply of skills in the labour market. This is not just a question of failings in the supply side of skills training but reveals failings on the demand side of the equation as well. As noted by Edwards et al. (2004), 'the preponderance of low-specification goods manufactured using Fordist production methods is as much about industry structure as it is about the national provision of skills' (14). Such evidence confirms a significant gap between the rhetoric of the new economy and the uneven manifestation of such trends.

The gap is further supported by more recent research by the Work Foundation (Brinkley et al., 2009). This survey of knowledge work and knowledge workers in the UK confirms that while 30 per cent of the workforce might be considered 'knowledge workers' only one in ten of all workers constitute the type of high intensity knowledge worker associated with the knowledge economy. As it is, the UK workforce includes a far higher proportion of workers who utilize relatively little tacit knowledge as part of the work process. The preponderance for problem-solving and innovation is not as far reaching as is so often assumed. Part of the confusion about the state of the economy relates to how knowledge work is quantified or understood by researchers. Thus, the handling of information in the workplace is often conflated with knowledge creation when in fact they represent two distinct activities (Handy, 1995). Information handling often involves simple data storage and dissemination, which is not the same as creative thinking by experts who draw on ideas for the purpose of creating solutions to business problems. In turn, reporting the growth of a high-tech sector based on the use of ICTs or the production of technologies is not the same as reporting a high-tech workforce. In particular, the production of high-tech products is often achieved by relatively low-skilled workers. Only a small cadre of experts are required in such processes as much of this work is about the fabrication of small components (Keep and Mayhew, 1999; also see Ackroyd and Lawrenson, 1996). As noted above, this rests on a Fordist division of labour with the separation of execution from conception. The evidence does not support the new economy argument.

Another feature of knowledge work is the emergence of those work processes which are increasingly seen to require greater commitment from employees (Applebaum et al., 2000; Huselid, 1995; MacDuffie, 1995; Wood de Menezes, 1998). As discussed above, the new economy thesis not only talks about changes to employment patterns and the supposed growth of portfolio workers it also relates to the increased integration of workers to encourage high-performance practices. For example, creating self-regulating teams is thought to present opportunities for workers to capitalize on the 'knowledge and knowing capability of a social collectivity' (Nahapiet and Ghoshal, 1998: 245). Often in parallel to such activities managers use ICTs to enable data warehousing for knowledge transfer: 'the idea behind knowledge management is to stockpile workers' knowledge and make it accessible to others via a searchable application' (Cole-Gomoski, 1997: 6). Here we see knowledge as a resource that can be captured and shared through electronic means. However, recognition of the value of commitment and cooperation does not guarantee success. Similarly the adoption of ICT systems does not represent a simple solution (McDermott, 1999).

While the idea of communities of practice has, for example, become a crucial 'template' for debates about organizing for knowledge creation, such social arrangements are different to more formal teams precisely because they operate 'under the radar' of managers. Their membership is based on 'collegiality, reciprocity and influence based on expertise' and not 'efficiency, contractual relationships and influence based on formal roles' (Newell et al., 2009: 122). In turn, while ICTs seemingly offer the means to 'capture' and 'transfer' knowledge, they are subject to organizational and local circumstances that do not inevitably lend themselves to knowledge sharing precisely because such technical solutions can reinforce or create disparities between capital and labour. As argued by Boreham and colleagues (2008: 7):

> the big challenge for corporate capital is to locate, enclose and exploit new forms of intellectual property. ICTs open up greater possibilities within this search, but do not prescribe the form or content. Ownership and control of productive assets is still the central question, no matter what the array of new economy theorists say.

These insights confirm the mixed picture informing our understanding of trends in industrial society. Further evidence is provided by White et al.

(2004a: 177) who suggest that 'it seems plausible that high-commitment or high-performance management practices will have a negative impact on the private lives of workers, to the extent that they are designed to evince greater discretionary effort in pursuit of the organization's goals'. Within the literature in this area, considerable emphasis is given to the complementarities assumed between capital and labour. High-performance practices are understood to reveal complementarities between improved quality, productivity and financial returns with employee benefits such as higher wages and job satisfaction (Huselid, 1995). However, the positive reporting of such practices has also been countered by recent research. When we refer to such practices these typically incorporate a combination of both human resource management and work organization policies. These are used to encourage 'greater participation in decision making, the opportunity to learn new skills and the financial incentive to offer greater discretionary effort in the service of the employer's goals' (White et al., 2003: 178). The organization of such activities takes the form of team working, quality circles, training and career development, appraisals and performance-related pay. However, the relationship between greater discretion and capital accumulation is not readily managed. For example, the bundles of practice associated with high-performance work organization have been associated with job strain and lower pay satisfaction in the UK (Ramsay et al., 2000), while research in Canada reports that high levels of adoption are associated with low job satisfaction and self-esteem (Godard, 2001). In turn, attempts to continually improve, which include setting new targets has been attributed, elsewhere, to greater work pressure for non-manual workers (Gallie et al., 1998). Such negative experiences are not limited to the workplace as recent research has reported spill-over effects of such practices which adversely affect employees' work–life balance (White et al., 2003).

The preceding discussion provides an indication of the challenges associated with knowledge work, which demands a more conceptually robust understanding of 'knowledge'. This perspective stands in contrast to the rather formulaic and unitary interpretations of knowledge creation (Nonaka and Takeuchi, 1995). The evidence presented on the scope and nature of knowledge work also offers a less certain picture in terms of such activities in the economy. It suggests that the prescriptions attributed to the 'new' economy are overstated and overoptimistic. In the final section, these issues are considered in an attempt to caution against the assumptions informing the post-Fordist thesis that seem to neglect the potential for diverse forms of capitalism and industrial society (Crouch, 2005).

While there are more knowledge workers in the economy and while such work activities may be more demanding in the utilization of tacit knowledge

(Brinkley et al., 2009) requiring greater mobility and flexibility of those workers, this does not constitute a new economy. As indicated in the recent UK Competitiveness Report, Britain remains a low-wage, low-skill, low-productivity economy. For example, there is a considerable productivity gap between the UK and major competitors such as the US, France and Germany, which indicates that the UK has yet to make the transition to a high-value economy (Porter and Ketels, 2003). UK competitiveness has largely rested on low input costs and an efficient business environment; it has not been based on new value creation (Porter and Ketels, 2003). Arguably, the sustainability of such an economy appears to depend less on value creation and innovation and more on the nature of markets, which in recent years have become extremely volatile and unpredictable.

Epochalism and the post-Fordist debate

A central tenant of the post-Fordist debate is that the new economy has overcome many of the inherent antagonisms found in the Fordist labour process. For example, knowledge management is seen as a technical issue with concerns over the internal consistency and coherence of the labour process (antagonisms that are related to management control) effectively re-written to reflect the discretionary powers of knowledge workers. Such discretion is thought to redress the balance between capital and labour where workplace relations are premised on shared endeavour rather than more structured methods of control.[1] To ensure this, reciprocal relationship management is tasked with protecting such intellectual workers from market pressures and the fear of redundancy linked to de-layering and downsizing (Sewell, 2005; also see Thompson, 2003). Worker discretion and empowerment is complemented by reassurances from management that such worker commitment will be rewarded with greater job security. From these elements emerges (so it is assumed) a self-sustaining system which results in a *stable mode of macroeconomic growth*. Economic stability is premised on innovation as the driver of new products and processes and the full use of flexible capacity, which creates new profits and by implication the means to initiate a new cycle of developments and innovations.

Growth is tied to a specific *mode of economic regulation* that indicates a shift towards post-industrial organizational forms which are network-based, leaner, flatter and decentralized. This mode involves a move away from competition based on economies of scale in the production of standardized goods and services to one that is based on economies of scope and economies of networks that are based on knowledge-intensive processes and products and integration achieved through ever more sophisticated ICT solutions. These types of development indicate new features of competition that are based on intensified forms of creativity that are reliant on 'open' models of innovation (see Chesbrough, 2003). This infers a complex set of innovation practices ranging from research and development activities in organizations to the adoption of continuous improvement activities to encourage innovation and integration along the supply chain and, more radically a move towards discontinuous innovation based on collaborations with partners often in completely new industries (Delbridge et al., 2008). Here we see an array of models for leveraging knowledge assets in an attempt to create competitive advantage by sharing risk and knowledge as a means of realizing surplus value through the actions of knowledge workers.

However, it is also in this context of changing forms of practice and integration that we see the emergence and importance of a new money form that 'is dominated by private, rootless bank credit that circulates internationally and by proliferation of financial products, derivatives and other forms of liquid assets' (Jessop, 2002: 101). These developments are important because with the de-regulation of the money markets and financial engineering (see Froud et al., 2002; Williams, 2000) innovations in financial competition have ensured that the capital markets continue to shape and influence corporate behaviour. While workplace practices have been expressed in relation to a new bargain between capital and labour, they are also performed in the context of extant institutional rules that emphasize the 'financial circuits of capital' and the pursuit of shareholder value (see Thompson, 2003: 366, also see Lazonick and O'Sullivan, 2000; O'Sullivan, 2000) or what is coined the 'financialization of everything' (Harvey, 2005).

Innovation in the banking industry has led to the 'restoration and sustained reproduction of established structures of advantage' (Klimecki and Willmott, 2009: 2). Enduring antagonisms in the labour process re-emerge when the pursuit of shareholder value shapes management actions in ways that undermine prescribed discretionary approaches to work. Contradictions such as these tend to collapse the assumed path dependencies of the post-Fordist thesis which can be elaborated in a number of ways (Crouch, 2005). As a starting point, there is plenty of evidence to counter the view that Fordism is outdated (the foundation of epochalist arguments). Thompson and McHugh (2009), for example, draw on examples to indicate that the basic conceptual polarity between mass production and the role of flexible specialization is inherently misleading. Not only is mass production still ever-present in the economy (Pollert, 1988) but such processes can also accommodate some degree of diversification. In turn, the idea that mass markets are saturated is undermined by developments in other parts of the economy, for example, fast food and the emergence of low-cost models of servicing from airlines and other industries, which confirms the importance of mass produced homogenous products (Ritzer, 1993). While these examples do not refer to the 'knowledge economy', specifically they confirm that the assumed shift between the 'old' and 'new' economy is misplaced. The problem is in assuming broad brush changes when these changes are based on ideals – as opposed to the complexities of changing entrenched or embedded modes of economic organization.

If we assess the nature of 'knowledge work', then this is apparent in a number of other ways. For example, the idea that labour market patterns have moved towards temporary contracts and part-time work is unsustainable in the light of recent findings. For example, Nolan and Wood (2003: 168) confirm that full-time permanent employment dominates with four out of five employees working in permanent jobs. If anything, the period between 1990 and 2000 revealed a major decline in the proportion of workers employed using temporary or fixed-term contracts. Instead, Nolan and Wood (2003) argue that job tenure rates confirm the continued significance of careers as opposed to short-term arrangements often associated with portfolio workers. In terms of employment patterns, the evidence does not support the idea of a growing cadre of self-employed workers either, operating from home and holding down multiple jobs. Instead, those that hold multiple jobs are more likely to be engaged in poorly paid, low status occupations. Neither has home working increased, rather the rates of those that work from fixed premises have risen to 78 per cent of the workforce compared to 76 per cent 10 years earlier (Taylor, 2002: 12).

Such findings provide an important corrective to an 'emphasis on cohesiveness and positive connections between elements in "the system" ' (Thompson, 2003: 360). This alternative view has already been well mapped out and reveals those critiques based on continuity and constraint (Harrison, 1994; Taylor and Bain, 1998). As argued by Harrison (1994) in his book *Lean and Mean*, there is plenty of evidence to show that supposedly new forms of work organization including team working have accentuated antagonisms of the past that include, among other things, fragmented tasks, close control and work intensification. These do not reflect substantive shifts (improvements) in the labour process because the emphasis on 'knowledge' does not replace or displace the fundamental features of the employment relationship. As highlighted above, enduring features of the economy remain as the exploitation of knowledge confirms rather than overturns inherent antagonisms between capital and labour in the context of the economic circuit.

What we see (contra-epochalism) is a more fragmented set of processes rather than an instance of wholesale change. As indicated in the low-skill/low-quality equilibrium debate the link between skills provision and firm performance is, for example, not straightforward precisely because of the contradictions that exist between institutions at the industry and state levels. Despite efforts to improve skills provision, it is still necessary for industry to recognize the need to up-skill and compete on value. This is not readily achieved because of the legacy effects of past strategies (see Edwards et al., 2004) and because it is also informed by the demands of capital, which as is argued, continues to generate tensions in the employment relationship despite the move to create more flexible work practices.

Conclusions

This chapter has offered a critical review of literatures and perspectives on the employment relationship in the new, knowledge-based economy. A key objective has been to reflect on the validity of these transformations. The aim has not been to discount 'knowledge' and 'knowledge work' as unimportant. Rather, it is to confirm that the 'new' economy represents more of an ideal than a clear reality. We can make sense of this contention in a number of ways which are outlined in the discussion using UK data. Of particular importance is the way the concept of 'knowledge' is understood – my concern has been to question the simple formulation that equates 'knowledge' with social cohesion and wealth production. To this end, Scarbrough's (1996) insight that knowledge is both an enabler and barrier to change is very useful because the concept of 'knowledge' is overstated; knowledge is not a panacea it is a social process, which continues to be subject to power relations and vested interests. Knowledge and knowledge work have also to be put into a broader context, which take many forms including those processes of financialization. Such assessments provide an important corrective to the epochalist assumption of wholesale transformation. Indeed, the evidence presented paints a very different picture about the 'new' economy, especially in the UK.

The 'new' economy continues to exhibit many of the tensions found in Fordist regimes while we can also detect new strictures related to the pressures to innovate and change. While the drive for innovation has led to new opportunities for those workers able to bring their expertise to the work process, this represents only a small part of the wider picture. As is implicated by Brinkley and colleagues (2009), the workplace and the employment relationship is dominated by routine forms of work, which can be associated with limited worker autonomy, low skills and reduced opportunities to develop the existing skills base. This is the economy described by Porter and Ketels (2003) in the UK Competitiveness Report which mirrors the findings of earlier research on Vocational Education in the UK (Finegold and Soskice, 1988), and more recent work on value creation in the economy (e.g. Edwards et al., 2004). This is not the high-value economy so often prescribed by supporters of the post-bureaucratic debate rather it is an economy that continues to be wedded to low input costs with minimal forms of high intensity 'knowledge work' (Brinkley et al., 2009). This does not represent a 'new dawn' precisely because much of the economy simply does not fit the prescribed model and because 'knowledge work' does not operate outside of existing institutional rules and power relations. In particular, workers of all types remain vulnerable to the vagaries of the marketplace and uncertainties in the global economy which have been most recently associated with the financial crisis.

Note

1. Frenkel et al. (1995) refer to info-normative control as a feature of knowledge work with ICTs used to create performance indicators that structure such activities and conformance. This confirms that the means of control remain but that the form of control has subtly shifted as opposed to having been removed.

References

Ackroyd, S. and Lawrenson, D. (1996). 'Knowledge work and organisational transformation: analysing contemporary change in the social use of expertise', in R. Fincham (ed.). *New Relationships in the Organised Professions*. Aldeshot: Avebury.

Alvesson, M. (2001). 'Knowledge work: ambiguity, image and identity', *Human Relations*, 54(7): 863–86.

Applebaum, E., Bailey, T., Berg, P. and Kalleberg, A.L. (2000). *Manufacturing Advantage: Why High-performance Work Systems Pay Off*. Ithaca, NY: Cornell University Press.

Arrow, A. (1962). 'The economic implications of learning by doing', *Review of Economic Studies*, 29: 155–73.

Barley, S., and Kunda, G. (2004). *Gurus, Hired Guns, and Warm Bodies: Itinerant Experts in a Knowledge Economy*. Princeton, NJ: Princeton University Press.

Barney, J. (1991). 'Firm resources and sustained competitive advantage', *Journal of Management*, 17: 99.

Baron, J., Hannan, M., and Burton, D. (2001). 'Labor pains: change in organizational models and employee turnover in young, high-tech firms', *American Journal of Sociology*, 106(4): 960–1012.

Baylies, V. (1998). *Redefining Work: An RSA Initiative*. London: Royal Society for the encouragement of Arts, Manufacturers and Commerce.

Beck, U. (2000). *The Brave New World*. Cambridge: Polity Press.

Bell, D. (1973). *The Coming of Post-Industrial Society: A Venture in Social Forecasting*. New York: Basic Books.

Blackler, F., Reed, M., and Whitaker, A. (1993). 'Editorial introduction: knowledge workers and contemporary organizations', *Journal of Management Studies*, 30(6): 851–862.

Boreham, P., Parker, R., Thompson, P., and Hall, R. (2008). *New Technology@Work*. London: Routledge.

Brinkley, I., Theodoropoulou, S., and Mahdon, M. (2009). *Knowledge Workers and Knowledge Work*. The Work Foundation.

Brown, J.S., and Duguid, P. (1991). 'Organizational learning and communities-of-practice: towards a unified view of working, learning and innovation', *Organization Science*, 2: 40–57.

Brown, P. and Hesketh, A. (2004). *The Mismanagement of Talent: Employability and Jobs in the Knowledge Economy*. Oxford: Oxford University Press.

Burchell, B.J., Day, D., Hudson, M., Lapido, D., Mankelow, R., Nolan, J.P., Reed, H., Wichert, I.C. and Wilkinson, F. (1999). *Job Insecurity and Work Intensification*. London: Joseph Rowntree Foundation.

Cabrera, E.F., and Cabrera, A. (2005). 'Fostering knowledge sharing through people management practices', *International Journal of Human Resource Management*, 16: 720–35.

Castells, M. (1996). *The Rise of the Network Society*. Oxford: Blackwell Publishers.

Chesbrough, H.W. (2003). *Open Innovation – The New Imperative for Creating and Profiting from Technology*. Boston, MA: HBS Press.

Cole-Gomoski, B. (1997). 'Users loath to share know-how', *Computerworld*, 31(46): 6.

Crouch, C. (2005). *Capitalist Diversity and Change: Recombinant Governance and Institutional Entrepreneurs*. Oxford: Oxford University Press.

Delbridge, R., Gratton, L., and Johnson, G. (2008). *The Exceptional Manager: Making the Difference*. Oxford: Oxford University Press.

Drucker, P. (1969). *The Age of Discontinuity: Guidelines to Our Changing Society*. London: Heineman.

du Gay, P. (2003). The tyranny of the epochal: change, epochalism and organizational reform', *Organization*, 10(4): 663–84.

Dyerson, R. and Mueller, F. (1999). Learning, teamwork and appropriability: managing technological change in the department of social security, *Journal of Management Studies*, 36(5): 629–52.

Edwards, T., Battisti, G. McClendon, W. Jr., and Neely, A. (2004). 'How can firms in the UK be encouraged to create more value? A discussion and review paper', *Advanced Institute of Management Research*, ISBN-0-9546885-1-1.

Felstead, A., and Jewson, N. (1999). *Global Trends in Flexible Labour*. London: Macmillan.

Finegold, D., and Soskice, D. (1988). 'The failure of training in Britain: analysis and prescription', *Oxford Review of Economic Policy*, 4(3), 21–53.

Frenkel, S., Korczynski, M., Donoghue, L. and Shire, K. (1995). 'Re-constituting work: trends towards knowledge work and info-normative control', *Work, Employment & Society*, 9(4): 773–96.

Froud, J., Johal, S. and Williams, K. (2002). 'Financialisation and the coupon pool', *Capital and Class*, 78: 119–51.

Gallie, D., White, M., Tomlinson, M. and Cheng, Y. (1998). *Restructuring the Employment Relationship*. Oxford: OUP.

Godard, J. (2001). 'High-performance and the transformation of work? The implications of alternative work practices for the experience and outcomes of work', *Industrial and Labor Relations Review*, 54: 776–805.

Gospel, H.F. (1992). *Markets, Firms, and the Management of Labour in Modern Britain*. Cambridge: Cambridge University Press.

Hamel, G., Prahalad, C.K. (1996). 'Competing in the new economy: managing out of bounds', *Strategic Management Journal*, 17: 237–42.

Handy, C. (1995). 'Trust and the virtual organization', *Harvard Business Review*, 73(3): 40–50.

Harrison, B. (1994). *Lean and Mean: The Changing Landscape of Corporate Power in the Age of Flexibility*. New York: Basic Books.

Harvey, D. (2005). *A Brief History of Neo-liberalism*. Oxford: University Press.

Heydebrand, W.V. (1989). 'New organizational forms', *Work and Occupations*, 16(3): 323–57.

Houseman, S.N., Kalleberg, A.L., and Erickcek, G.A. (2003). 'The role of temporary help employment in tight labor markets', *Industrial and Labor Relations Review*, 57(1): 105–27.

Howells, J. (1995). 'Tacit knowledge and technology transfer', *ESRC Centre for Business Research*, WPS, 16.

Huselid, M.A. (1995). 'The impact of human resource management practices on turnover, productivity, and corporate financial performance', *Academy of Management Journal*, 38: 635–72.

Jessop, B. (2002). *The Future of the Capitalist State*. Cambridge: Polity Press.

Keep, E. and Mayhew, K. (1999). 'The assessment: knowledge, skills, and competitiveness', *Oxford Review of Economic Policy*, 15(1): 1–15.

Klimecki, R. and Willmott, H. (2009). 'From demutualisation to meltdown: a tale of two wannabe banks', *Critical Perspectives on International Business*, 5(1–2): 120–40.

Lazonick, W. and O'Sullivan, M. (2000). 'Maximising shareholder value: a new ideology for corporate governance', *Economy and Society*, 29(1): 13–35.

Leadbetter, C. (2000). *Living on Thin Air: The New Economy*. London: Viking.

Lewis, P. (2001). *Tales for the New Shop Floor: Inside the Real Jobs of the Information Economy*. New South Wales: Pluto Press.

MacDuffie, J.P. (1995). 'Human resource bundles and manufacturing performance: organizational logic and flexible production systems in the world auto industry', *Industrial and Labor Relations Review*, 48: 197–221.

Marinetto, M. (2007). *Social Theory, the State and Modern Society: The State in Contemporary Thought*. Maidenhead: OUP.

McDermott, R. (1999). 'Why information technology inspired but cannot deliver knowledge management', *California Management Review*, 41, 103–17.

McKinlay, A. (2005). 'Knowledge management', in S. Ackroyd, R. Batt, P. Thompson and P. Tolbert (eds). *The Oxford Handbook of Work and Organization*. Oxford: Oxford University Press.

Nahapiet, J., and Ghoshal, S. (1998). 'Social capital, intellectual capital and the organizational advantage', *Academy of Management Review*, 23(2): 242–62.

Newell, S. Robertson, M. Scarbrough, H. And Swan, J. (2009). *Managing Knowledge Work and Innovation*. Basingstoke: Palgrave Macmillan.

Nolan, P. and Slater, G. (2003) 'The labour market: History, structure and prospects', in P. Edwards (ed.). *Industrial Relations: Theory and Practice*, Second edition. Oxford, Blackwell Publishing: 58–80.

Nolan, P. And Wood, S. (2003). 'Mapping the future of work', *British Journal of Industrial Relations*, 41(2): 165–74.

Nonaka, I., and Takeuchi, H. (1995). *The Knowledge-Creating Company: How Japanese Companies Create the Dynamics of Innovation*. Oxford: Oxford University Press.

Nonaka, I., and Konno, N. (1998). 'The concept of "ba": building a foundation for knowledge creation', *California Management Review*, 40(3): 40–54.

Orr, J. E. (1990). 'Sharing knowledge, celebrating identity: war stories and community memory in a service culture', in D.S. Middleton, and D. Edwards (eds). *Collective Remembering: Memory in Society*. Thousand Oaks, Calif.: Sage Publications.

O'Sullivan, M. (2000). *Contests for Corporate Control: Corporate Governance and Economic Performance in the US and Germany*. Oxford: Oxford University Press.

Pascale, R. (1990). *Managing at the Edge: How Successful Companies Use Conflict to Stay Ahead*. London: Viking Press.

Pink, D. (2001). *Free Agent Nation: How America's New Independent Workers are Transforming the Way We Live*. Los Angeles: Warner.

Pollert, A. (1988). 'Dismantling flexibility', *Capital and Class*, 12(1): 42–75.

Porter, M.E., and Ketels, C.H.M. (2003). *UK Competitiveness: Moving to the Next Stage*. DTI Economics Paper No. 3 (May).

Ramsay, H., Scholarios, D. and Harley, B. (2000). 'Employees and high-performance work systems: testing inside the black box', *British Journal of Industrial Relations*, 38: 501–32.

Reich, R. (1993). *The Work of Nations*. London: Simon and Schuster.

Ritzer, G. (1993). *The MacDonaldization of Society*, Thousand Oaks: Pine Forge Press.

Rosenberg, N. (1982). *Inside the Black Box: Technology and Economics*. New York: Cambridge Press.

Scarbrough, H. (ed.) (1996). *The Management of Expertise*. Basingstoke: Macmillan Press.

Scarbrough, H. (1999). 'Knowledge and work: conflicts in the management of knowledge workers', *Technology Analysis and Strategic Management*, 11(1): 5–16.

Starbuck, W.H. (1992). 'Learning by knowledge-intensive firms', *Journal of Management Studies*, 29: 713–40.

Stewart, T.A. (1997). *Intellectual Capital. The New Wealth of Organizations*. New York: Doubleday.

Sewell, G. (2005). 'Nice work? Rethinking managerial control in an era of knowledge work', *Organization*, 12(5): 685–704.

Stiglitz, J.E. (1987). 'Learning to learn, localised learning and technological progress', in P. Dasupta, and P. Stoneman, (eds). *Economic Policy and Technological Performance*. Cambridge: Cambridge University Press, 125–53.

Sturdy, A. and Grey, C. (2003). 'Beneath and beyond organizational change management: exploring alternatives', *Organization*, 10(4): 651–62.

Taylor, R. (2002). *Britain's World of Work: Myths and Realities*. Swindon: ESRC.

Taylor, P., and Bain, P. (1998). 'An assembly line in the head: the call centre labour process', *Industrial Relations Journal*, 30(2): 101–17.

Thompson, P. (2003). 'Disconnected capitalism: or why employers can't keep their side of the Bargain', *Work, Employment and Society*, 17(2): 359–78.

Thompson, P., and Warhurst, C. (eds) (1998). *Workplaces of the Future*. London: Macmillan.

Thompson, P. and McHugh, D. (2009). *Work Organisations: A Critical Approach*. Basingstoke: Palgrave Macmillan.

Tsoukas, H. (1996). 'The firm as a distributed knowledge system: a constructionist approach', *Strategic Management Journal*, 17, 11–25.

Tsoukas, H., and Vlaimirou, E. (2001). 'What is organizational knowledge?', *Journal of Management Studies*, 38(7): 973–93.

Walsh, J.P., and Ungson, G.R. (1991). 'Organizational memory', *Academy of Management Review*, 16(1): 57–91.

White, M., Hill, S., McGovern, P., Mills, C., and Smeaton, D. (2003). 'High-performance' management practices, working hours and work-life balance', *British Journal of Industrial Relations*, 41(2): 175–95.

White, M., Hill, S., Mills, C. and Smeaton, D. (2004) *Managing to Change? British Workplaces and the Future of Work*. Basingstoke: Palgrave Macmillan.

Williams, K. (2000). 'From shareholder value to present-day capitalism', *Economy and Society*, 29(1): 1–12.

Wood, S. and de Menezes, L. (1998). 'High commitment management in the UK: evidence from the workplace industrial relations survey and employers' manpower and skills practices survey', *Human Relations*, 51: 485–515.

18

The contingent relationship between public management reform and public service work

Rachel Ashworth and Tom Entwistle

Introduction

It is a commonplace of the theory of public service employment relations to suggest a connection between the mode of public service reform and the nature of public service work. Gill-McLure and Siefert put it starkly: 'the reform of public services requires the reform of labour management' (2008: 2). In such a way it is argued that the rising tide of public service reform, apparent since at least the late 1970s, has profound implications for the nature of public service work. Kettl concludes that: 'the reforms often ended the certainty of future employment, introduced new financial rewards, and challenged managers with a new imperative to manage better. The very nature of government work fundamentally changed; and in the process, the morale of government employees often suffered' (Kettl, 1997: 453).

Although widely asserted, the reform–employment formula as rehearsed by Kettl is a little more complicated than sometimes suggested. Three contingencies moderate the translation of public management reforms into changes in public service work. First, there is more variety in the content of public management reform strategies than the outline prospectus suggests. Second, there is uncertainty about the status and duration of those reforms. Third, there are questions about the way in which public service workers themselves engage with the reform process. This chapter focuses specifically on these three considerations with a view to improving our understanding of the relationship between public service reform and the public service work.

While we want to raise questions about the reform–employment formula, we do not doubt the importance of this avenue of inquiry. The nature of public sector employment is, to a significant extent, determined by the form of governance and attempts to change it. The central planks of public service delivery – focused on the direct and permanent employment of professionals by the state – were themselves put in place by state actors focused on the governance challenges of their day (Marquand, 2004; Osborne, 1994). Barratt reports that Sir Robert Peel complained, in a letter written in 1841, 'of the excessive time that was required to devote to dealing with correspondence from relatives anxious to secure positions for their kinsfolk in the offices of government' (Barratt, 2009: 69). Northcote and Trevelyan's vision of a centrally managed, permanent meritocracy looked like a better way of running government than a system characterized by nepotism (Osborne, 1994). Just as important as Northcote and Trevelyan's prescriptions, were calls for the creation of new local government professions. Edwin Chadwick's diagnosis of the need for 'responsible officers qualified by the possession of the science and skill of civil engineers' (Chadwick, 1965: 422–42) was repeated across a range of service areas through the twentieth century (Perkin, 1989).

In such a way, the public service model – believed by many to represent an ideal form which should be defended (Du Gay, 2008) – was itself established by waves of reform through the nineteenth and twentieth centuries. Important and enduring reforms in the structures and processes of government will, in due course, translate into changes in the nature of government work. We need, therefore, to focus on the status of public management reforms and distinguish, as Hood suggests, 'surface change from deep change' (1995: 106) and then consider what these reforms mean for public employment.

In some respects this is well-trodden ground. There have been a number of important overviews of the impact of reform on the nature of public service employment and industrial relations (see, for example, Bach and Kessler, 2007; Bach and Winchester, 2003; Bach et al., 2009). Indeed, the coverage of these issues is sufficiently good to present us with a paradox, as Bach et al. express it, while 'there has been a transformation in the landscape of the public sector' these changes have not brought about a 'substantial convergence with the private sector or a transformation of the public sector model of industrial relations' (Bach et al., 2009: 331). Otherwise put, if the reforms are so great, why has the effect on employment and work been so small? The purpose of this chapter is to delve a little deeper into the sources of this paradox to develop our understanding of the nature of public service reform and its repercussions for public service work.

The chapter is divided into four main sections. First, we review the different types of reform which have been unleashed on the public services over the last three decades or so. Second, we consider the status of these reforms: has their novelty or importance been exaggerated by practitioners and academics; do they represent a consistent challenge to traditional ways of working or just a series of managerial fashions which deliver only relatively fleeting periods of reform? Third, we draw together literatures which explore the front-line experiences of public sector workers to consider the transmission of reforms into the nature of work. Finally, reflecting on the evidence considered, we argue that sociological institutional theory may prove a helpful source in improving our understanding of why public management reforms often do not deliver the desired effects in terms of radically changing the nature and organization of work in the public sector.

The content of reform strategies

The first hurdle to would-be theorists of reform and employment is presented by the challenge of defining the content of public management reform strategies. At a superficial level, at least, there is reasonable agreement. In a couple of seminal papers published in the early 1990s, Hood identifies a 'set of broadly similar administrative doctrines which have dominated the bureaucratic reform agenda in many of the OECD group of countries from the late 1970s' (1991: 3–4). He goes on to identify seven key ingredients of the New Public Management (NPM):

- Unbundling of the public services into corporatized units
- More contract based competitive provision
- Stress on private sector styles of management
- Explicit formal measurable standards of performance
- Stress on discipline and frugality in resource use
- More emphasis on visible hands-on top management
- Greater emphasis on output controls (1991: 4–5, 1995: 96).

There are of course problems with any list of this kind. Some elements – like performance management – are specified quite exactly as focused on formal, measurable, output type controls. Others – like 'private sector styles of management' – are poorly specified to the extent that it is difficult to distinguish between one style of management and another. Others still – like 'frugality in resource use' – imply, perhaps erroneously, that the public sector lacked frugality before the arrival of the new public management. Then of course there are other reform strategies – like the regulation of government – which do not even appear on the list. This, particularly, is a surprising omission given that, at least in the UK, regulation 'grew substantially over the twenty years to the mid-1990s' becoming 'more formal, complex and specialized' (Hood et al., 2000: 284–6).

Reflecting these difficulties, other commentators have sought to capture the spirit of public management reforms by identifying the themes underlying specific interventions. For Paul Du Gay, the defining features of 'recent programmes of public management reform' (337) is the emphasis on responsiveness 'to the needs of their clients' and 'political superiors' (2008: 336). Bordogna homes in on 'removing the differences between the public and private sector', and 'shifting the emphasis from process accountability towards accountability on results' (2008: 383). Gill-McLure and Seifert point to the privatization of service delivery and the 'accountingisation' of those functions that remain (2008: 2). Brunsson and Sahlin-Anderson find coherence in the attempt to construct the institutions responsible for delivering public services as more 'complete organisations' with clear boundaries, identities and objectives (2000: 736). Dunleavy et al. identify three integrating themes: disaggregation of large departments into smaller more easily managed units; injection of competition through the introduction of market testing and purchaser–provider splits; and finally, incentivization through new systems of performance management and reward (2006: 470).

Alongside these searches for coherence and integration, other commentators describe the reform agenda, captured by Hood and others, as ambivalent and conflicting. Aucoin (1990) sees public management reform as driven by the contradictory imperatives of public choice theory and managerialism. The first calls for centralization and increasing responsiveness to the political executive, the second drives decentralization and deregulation. He concludes that: 'The two prevailing paradigms of governance and management and the organizational principles which flow from them obviously introduce a measure of tension, even contradiction' (1990: 125). In a similar vein, Christensen and Laegreid describe 'a rather incoherent reform wave, consisting of a combination of ideological and instrumental elements that are partly inconsistent and contradictory' (1999: 169).

Disagreements in the definition of the reform agenda of the 1980s and 1990s have been compounded by a change of emphasis in the reform programmes of the last decade or so. In recent times, commentators have started to focus on a slightly different set of concerns. Newman and Clark, for example, claim that 'the future of public services is being shaped through arguments about new forms of governance: the rise of networks and partnerships, innovations in democratic practice, the development of co-production and choice as service models and initiatives directed towards citizenship and social inclusion' (Newman and Clark, 2009: 3).

Some parts of this agenda can be seen as the development of trends established by the new public management. In such a way, the current emphasis on the choice and personalization of public services (Cutler et al., 2007) could be said to have emerged from NPM's focus on consumerism. The interest in public service entrepreneurialism and the search for public value have identifiable roots in NPM's goal of freeing managers to manage (Moore, 1995; Osborne and Gaebler, 1993). Attempts to refocus performance regimes away from inputs and outputs towards fewer strategic outcome type indicators (Boyne and Law, 2005; Entwistle and Enticott, 2007) reflect a relatively small change in the goals of NPM's performance management regimes. Similarly – although more heroically – the push for public–private partnerships can be seen as the continuation of marketization by other means. One of us has argued, for example, that rather than seeing the market as a source of competition, the UK's New Labour Government has pointed to the complementary resources that can be realized through partial privatization (Entwistle and Martin, 2005). In such a way, the public–private partnership agenda can be understood as a development of the Conservatives' experimentation with competitive tendering and wholesale privatization.

Partnership has also been used, however, as a vehicle for improved communication between employers and employees (Bacon and Samuel, 2009), between different public service agencies (Keast et al., 2004; Ling, 2002) and between the providers and users of public services (Lowndes and Sullivan, 2004). None of these can be easily tracked back to NPM parentage. Indeed, the partnership-as-engagement agenda seems to have emerged more as a reaction to those reforms than a continuation of them. Partnership forms of employee engagement were intended to check tendencies towards adversarialism. The joining-up agenda seeks to redress the narrowly defined organizational remits which were in many ways actively advanced by NPM. While the emphasis on citizenship and co-production could be seen as an antidote to the passive consumerism of the NPM, Newman et al. observe that 'the focus of modernisation has been as much about transforming citizens in line with the requirements of neo-liberalism as with changing institutions' (Newman et al., 2008: 532).

Given the contested nature of the reform agenda, commentators need to be clear which of these instruments, or themes, matter the most. Are public service workers faced by a unified programme of reform, or an incoherent patchwork of different and perhaps conflicting initiatives? Are the reform agendas – in both the public services and industrial relations – still recognizably the neoliberal ones which emerged in the early 1980s? Or has New Labour's emphasis on partnership and co-production eclipsed these concerns and coined a distinctive third way (Howell, 2004)?

The status of management reforms

If definitions are problematic, there is even more disagreement about the status and likely longevity of public sector reform strategies. Disagreements are fed, as is often the case in the social sciences, by the strongly normative character of these debates. Critics of public management reform are often more focused on prescriptions for reform than descriptions of existing practice. Three distinctive accounts of the status of the public management reform agenda are however discernible in the literature: reforms as misdiagnosed academic obsession; as genuinely revolutionary change in the nature of public service delivery; or as a real but relatively short-lived fashion. Understanding the status and longevity of reform packages is central to understanding the relationship between reform and employment.

The first perspective suggests that the arrival of new reform paradigms has been misdiagnosed. The combined tendencies of politicians to exaggerate the novelty and scale of their achievements and of academics to pursue citations have tended to produce distorted histories of public administration in terms of epochs and paradigms. Commentators have, according to Lynn, misrepresented the 'old orthodoxy' as 'at best, a caricature and, at worst, an outright distortion of traditional thought' (2001: 145). From this perspective, public administration has always been attuned to the dysfunctions of bureaucracy, the need for cross-cutting working and responsiveness to the citizen (Lynn, 2001). According to these critics, the new public management is little more than a label applied to a bag of reforms which have 'developed through a continuous process of evolution rather than a discontinuous revolution' (Page, 2005: 723). The label 'now covers', according to Bevir et al. (2003: 2), 'all types of public sector reform; it excludes nothing.' Echoing Wildavsky's concerns about rational planning, they conclude that 'if NPM is everything maybe it's nothing' (Bevir and Rhodes, 2003: 2). Reflecting what he takes to be its shaky foundations, Lynn predicts that NPM will prove 'an ephemeral theme likely to fade for several reasons' (Lynn, 1998: 232). Its backers (both practitioners and scholars) will move on to something else and 'comparative work across countries and sectors' will mean that 'fundamental differences among reforms will begin to eclipse superficial similarities' (Lynn, 1998: 232).

If right, this perspective suggests that public service employment will be untouched by the misdiagnosed revolutions of public management. Public managers will carry on doing what they have always done – subject to a continuous process of incremental change – and continue to work in the usual way. The prediction implicit in the work of these scholars is that the enduring principles of public sector employment will be unaffected by the excitement of a few misguided commentators and practitioners: business as usual for public managers, or long live traditional public administration.

The second, and perhaps the most prominent perspective in the literature, describes a transformation in the public services wrought by application of new management techniques. Donald Kettl describes 'a truly remarkable revolution' which has swept around the world since the late 1970s (1997: 446). Supporters of this interpretation explain NPM's reach – both in terms of the countries which have adopted it and its endurance over time – by reference to a series of structural conditions which emerged in the post-war period. Increases in the fiscal burden of public services (Hood, 1995: 162–3) together with a 'shift to a more white-collar socially heterogeneous population less tolerant of statist and uniform approaches in public policy' (Hood, 1991: 7) put the public services in an unenviable position. Aucoin describes a reform movement 'driven in large part by the requirement that governments respond to the fiscal stresses brought about by changes in the international economic system on the one hand and by the unrelenting demands for government services and regulations in national political systems on the other' (Aucoin, 1990: 115). Gill-McLure and Seifert see the public service reform agenda of 'intensification, degradation and insecurity' (2008: 6) as driven by the conflicting demand for a 'stable tax regime and acceptable service standards' (2008: 2). Marquand describes how the 'public domain', where 'the public interest is defined and public goods produced' (2004: 26), has been undermined by the neoliberal emphasis on individualism.

The picture of enduring reforms rooted in fundamental structural changes in the global economy suggests that it does not matter which party is in power or how individual initiatives are evaluated; the pressures on public services – in terms of delivering value for money and increasing responsiveness – will continue. Seen as a fundamental structural change, the public management reform agenda has significant and enduring implications for the nature of public service work. The established model of public service delivery – with its emphasis on permanent and professional jobs in the public sector – will continue to come under pressure irrespective of the party in power.

The final approach, hinted at in the previous section, suggests that the evolution of the reform agenda has led to two distinct periods of public management reform. According to Newman and Clark, 'the NPM has come to be viewed as a historical phase in academic literatures and in much professional/policy political discourse' (2009: 5). Although heralding real change, NPM is portrayed by these authors as a relatively transitory phenomenon specifically associated with a particular period, a particular set of conditions and even a particular ideology. Given that many, if not all, of those conditions no longer remain, advocates of the time-bound account of NPM suggest that: 'The intellectually and practically dominant set of managerial and governance ideas of the last two decades, new public management (NPM), has essentially died in the water' (Dunleavy et al., 2006: 468).

The key question for those occupying this position is what comes next? A number of commentators have sought to label the reform agenda which has succeeded NPM. Denhardt and Denhardt describe a 'new public service' focused on citizenship, social capital and 'organizational humanism' (2000: 552–3). Stoker sees evidence of a new 'public value management' characterized by a focus on Moore's (1995) public value and the need to partner with the 'best supplier' in the new networks of governance (2006: 46–9). In a similar vein, Newman and colleagues talk about a social investment state (2005), and an emerging emphasis on 'personalisation, independence and choice' (2008: 532). For Osborne, the 'new public governance' is focused on 'enduring inter-organizational relationships, where trust, relational capital and relational contracts act as the core governance mechanisms' (2006: 384). Dunleavy et al. predict 'digital era governance' focused on the reintegration of public services, re-engineering of processes around user need and a more engaged and knowledgeable citizenry (2006: 478–88). Digital era governance 'holds out the promise of a potential transition to a more genuinely integrated, agile, and holistic government, whose organizational operations are visible in detail both to the personnel operating in the fewer, broader public agencies and to citizens and civil society organizations' (Dunleavy et al., 2006: 489).

The picture of distinct periods of reform raises important questions about the transition between reform packages. One reading suggests a gestalt-like switch from the concerns of the NPM to those of the New Public Service. Another account, from organizational sociology suggests, however, 'not so much a shift from one archetype to another, but a layering of one archetype on another' which allows for the 'persistence of values, ideas and practices, even when the formal structures and processes seem to change' (Cooper et al., 1996: 624). Newman and Clarke again put it nicely: 'The drive for efficiency and performance has by no means disappeared, but overlaid on it – in what are often deeply uncomfortable ways – are new demands that public services should empower citizens and communities, develop partnerships, collaborate with civil society groups, and foster coproduction arrangements with service users' (2009: 6).

Whether switching or layering, the implications for public service employment are much more difficult to anticipate. A switch from the old focus on efficiency and effectiveness suggests a need for public employees to develop 'therapeutic or psychological skills in order to deliver developmental and behaviour-changing strategies' (Newman and Clarke, 2009: 6). But the significance of these reforms, and their effect on employment, depends on the persistence of the reform package. If collaboration and citizen centredness are here to stay, then, yes, public managers will need to re-skill for the new priorities. If, however, the reform agenda moves on as quickly as some of these accounts suggest, then it might well be the case that each wave of reform will pass too quickly to have an enduring effect on public service employment. Rapid switching suggests the possibility of epiphenomenal reforms characterized by surface level change but only limited effects. In the extreme case it seems possible that rapidly changing initiatives will have very little effect on the nature of work at all.

Like Aucoin's (1990) account of the new public management as an incoherent and contradictory package of imperatives, the rapid switching and the layering of reforms will present public service actors with multiple competing logics of appropriateness. Rather than providing public service organizations with a clear script, reforms bequeath a series of conflicting imperatives which have to be resolved by public service organizations or individual public servants (Christensen and Laegreid, 1999). The next section considers research which explores the experiences of front-line public service employees and their responses to public management reform.

Street-level agency

Our third contingency is suggested by the way in which public service workers, both collectively and individually, respond to the reforms handed down to them. Eyeing the uneven implementation of the reform agenda across the public services (NHS, civil service, local government) and public service workers (front-line employees, management, professionals), Bach and Winchester (2003) talk of the 'impossibility' of arriving at simple summaries. In place of a summary characterization, we draw upon recent research to consider what three elements of the reform agenda – performance management, user responsiveness and partnership – mean for the nature of managerial, professional and front-line work.

The threat that public management reforms pose for public service workers is well rehearsed by those who subscribe to the transformation thesis. The emphasis placed upon performance during the 1980s and 1990s and its reinforcement and extension since 1997 (Boyne et al., 2010), it is argued, has pervaded all aspects of organization. One commonly cited consequence has been the displacement of important activities. Such displacement, it is argued by Bach (2004), has even affected public service HR departments which are less able to develop and invest in locally based initiatives as they are increasingly 'fulfilling the requirements of the audit culture' (16.) by playing their part within performance management regimes and conducting extensive staff surveys. We have also seen these trends moving beyond public service organizations and impacting on public service trade unions and their organization. This is demonstrated by Bach and Givan's (2008) study of UNISON and its attempts to incorporate key components of the public management reform agenda, such as the instigation of a target culture, within its own organization.

In contrast, little attention is devoted to the potential for agency on the part of public sector employees. Nowhere is this better exemplified than within the discussion of the development and impact of performance management regimes in the public sector. The few studies focused on the way in which public employees experience and perceive performance regimes challenge the orthodox view of prescription and displacement. Emery et al.'s (2008) study of Swiss street-level civil servants is one such example. They examine the ways in which these public employees interpret performance regimes rooted within the 'Swiss way of public management' which bears a strong resemblance to NPM (311). The authors find that their interviewees have complex and contradictory interpretations of the performance regimes to which they are subject. They describe two oppositional 'worlds' – the individualistic and functionalist industrial world – and the representative, collective and citizen-centred civic world which lead to 'a form of identity crisis experienced by civil servants confronted with contradictory orders' (318). These findings reinforce those from earlier work on the introduction of performance-related pay in the public sector which suggest that employees find the idea of PRP to be 'inappropriate' and continue to identify with the social goals of the organization (Heery, 1998). The experience of PRP in the public services, Heery suggests, is generally illustrative of the way in which public sector organizations and their employees 'absorb, deflect and modify' public service reforms (73).

In other cases it seems that, rather than constraining the activities of public employees, performance management systems have provided opportunities for public employees to advance their own agendas (Casey and Allen, 2004). A point exemplified by Rosenthal and Peccei's (2006) study of Jobcentre Plus which documents staff responding to performance management in a fairly instrumental manner by devoting more time and effort to getting lone parents and disabled people worth 12 performance points into work, rather than those on the Job Seekers Allowance only worth 2 points.

A similar debate has raged in relation to the consumer revolution in the public sector which began with a focus on 'customers' and is currently being framed within a 'citizen-centred' conceptualization of public services. In practice this has meant a much more direct relationship between the public service employee and the client or recipient of their service. Casey and Allen suggest that housing managers responded to this agenda by presenting themselves as both 'knowledgeable' and 'approachable' to clients. They document the ways in which these managers 'dress down' so as not to intimidate clients and then engage in emotional interactions, sharing information on their background, and in one case, even their experiences of depression, in order to make an 'authentic connection' between them and the user of the service (2004: 406). On occasions it seems these interactions are genuine but it seemed in other instances they had been performed on a purely instrumental basis to speed up the collection of the housing benefit application process.

The user/citizen-centred approach has led to changes in the ways that services are performed and delivered with mixed consequences for public employees. Cooke's study of 'seagull management' in the NHS (2006) suggests however that the emphasis on the Patients Charter encourages the public to expect a service that they are unlikely to receive. Cooke coins the term 'seagull management' on the basis of observing managers operating from a distance (e.g. rarely visiting wards) but adopting a hard-edged management style characterized by 'destructive criticism' and 'punitive language' (237). The research describes a highly 'defensive culture' underpinned by 'fears of litigation, complaints and adverse publicity', accompanied by trails of 'defensive documentation' with nurses spending more time 'covering their back' than delivering care (2006: 232).

In contrast, Smith et al. (2008) take the example of NHS Direct to tell a story of empowerment in exploring the nursing profession's transition from a hospital working environment to that of a call centre. They highlight the similarities between NHS Direct – which requires nurses to work in a fixed position and follow a script – and other private sector call centre work. They also emphasize, however, a process of empowerment where call centre nurses, unlike their hospital-based colleagues, operate as the dominant medical group providing a genuinely 'nurse-led service'. Overall, and contrary to gloomy expectations, the authors conclude that 'nurses have challenged the transformative feature of call centre work by mobilizing their occupational identity and power as nurses to challenge technical and managerial control pressure within NHS Direct' (593). Bolton's (2005) exploration of the role of the 'modern matron' in the NHS similarly reports a degree of empowerment but neatly captures the contradiction within the reform agenda by describing how new Clinical Nurse Managers emphasize the importance of caring for patients by reinforcing the 'enterprise' and performance culture through a discourse of quality, value for money and customer care.

There is also some evidence that public employees are engaging with service users in a highly deliberate and instrumental manner in order to better manage their work and meet performance targets. Rosenthal and Peccei (2006) demonstrate how reforms have resulted in street-level bureaucrats providing differential levels of service based upon their own classifications of their clientele. Their analysis of staff within UK Jobcentre Plus, designed to provide a user-centred, flexible and personalized service, observed 'a pervasive structuring and valorization of clients according to their attitudes to work' (2006: 1635), based largely upon interpretations of behaviours and body language. They outline the reform problematic in this case that government rhetoric has portrayed users of public services as powerful customers exerting their rights and making choices, while the practice in this context is that the users – the jobseekers – have often been perceived to be 'potential shirkers, fraudsters and aggressors' (2006: 1639). Consequently they observed staff identifying customer types such as 'twelve pointers', 'briefcase jobs', 'lazy gits', 'sad stories', 'hard core people' and 'potentially violents' who are then assessed accordingly for 'job readiness' and offered differentiated services on the basis of their manner, gratitude and level of aggression. In this case, it is argued that the work-focused structures within Jobcentre Plus encouraged front-line workers to make moral judgements about their clients and their 'deservingness' so 'sad stories' received a great deal of support while 'lazy gits' seen to be 'working the system' were given a lower priority (2006: 1649).

So it seems that even the most widely criticized aspects of public management reform, such as performance management and consumerism, leave room for employee-driven adjustments to the labour process. So what of the more widely welcomed elements of public service reform? Here too the effects are contradictory. The heavy emphasis given to the partnership agenda provides a good example of this. Inter-organizational collaboration has assumed a central role within the contemporary toolkit of public management reform. Promising the realization of goals beyond the scale or scope of the 'lonely organisation' (Hjern and Porter, 1981: 212), partnerships are now used to design and deliver a range of public services from small town refuse collection to national scale infrastructure projects. Running in parallel to the creation of these inter-organizational partnerships is the encouragement towards collaborative working within the organization between employer and employees (Bacon and Samuel, 2009).

At the *intra-organizational* level, it has been argued that the partnership agenda has been central to New Labour's attempts to re-establish public organizations as 'model employers' and create new understandings between employers and organized labour (Stuart and Martinez Lucio, 2000: 311). Early assessments of the efficacy of partnership-working by Stuart and Martinez Lucio (2000) suggest that, in practice, it had been centrally driven and top-down in nature with disappointingly few attempts being made to deliver greater involvement and communication. However, more recent reviews, such as those by Bacon and Samuel (2009), argue that there is now growing evidence to suggest that Westminster, Scottish and Welsh governments have all been investing in partnership arrangements as a means to ensure the involvement of public employees in the modernization and reform of public service organizations – although they do acknowledge that 'the increased incidence of partnership agreements in the public sector may overstate the actuality of partnership in practice' (2009: 244).

In terms of the impact that new forms of *inter-organizational* collaboration have for public employees, the evidence is patchy but again is suggestive of mixed effects, depending on context and circumstances. One of the few studies to consider the impact that changing governance systems have for public service employment comes from Hebson et al. (2003). Seeking to determine whether public service values survive the process of inter-organizational collaboration, they discuss the experiences of managers working within a health public–private partnership and an outsourced benefits office. The findings from the two cases present contrasting pictures. Public accountability and transparency are the casualties of the PPP arrangement as public sector managers begin to 'mimic private sector techniques' and engage in manipulation (498). However, among the managers in the outsourced benefits office, there is evidence of a resilient focus on the values of altruism and public interest.

Studies of the increasingly complex system of local governance have also reflected upon the implications for the work and role of the public manager. It seems that the increasing level of partnership-working has created some confusion on the ground in terms of organizational responsibilities, with public employees struggling to identify their role within a new governance framework they do not yet fully understand (Ashworth et al., 2006). An examination of nine partnership organizations in contrasting local authority areas by Skelcher et al. (2005) paints a similar picture of public managers on partnership boards negotiating their 'dual-hatted roles' as they simultaneously represent the partnership, their home organization's and the public's best interest (2005: 588).

Besides creating some confusion, the advent of partnership-working in the public sector has also created the opportunity and space for new managerial roles which necessitate a very different expertise. Within the last 10 years, we have witnessed the development of a new type of public manager – the 'boundary spanner' – a role which requires a portfolio of skills including: negotiating, networking, trust-building, communication, empathizing, listening and conflict resolution (Williams, 2002). These 'policy entrepreneurs', Williams argues, have the opportunity to deliver improved outcomes through their ability to 'connect problems to solutions and mobilize resources and effort' (2002: 121). A recent analysis of the role of boundary spanners in public–private partnerships sheds light on the ways in which these actors move from a position where they manage aspects of a single organization to one where they manage collaborative inter-organizational relationships (Noble and Jones, 2006). In the PPP cases examined by Noble and Jones (2006), public managers are described as having pre-conceived views of their private sector partners, developed through years of 'cultural socialisation', which contribute to the difficulties of generating a genuinely collaborative public–private relationship (915).

Understanding complexity and contingency

Taken alongside the overviews of changes in public service industrial relations, research into the front-line experiences of public service workers suggests that decades of public management reform have had both positive and negative effects on the nature of public service work. Even the most stringent of public management reforms – such as those witnessed in the 1980s and 1990s – did not result in the development of private sector-style working conditions in the public sector. Rather, they have contributed to the development of a hybridized and fragmented model of public service employment which sits between the traditional public and private employment model (Duncan, 2001). Reflecting on the adoption of the NPM-type reforms in Norway, Christensen and Laegreid describe 'a screening process whereby they are filtered, modified, and refined' (1999: 184). These tendencies have been confirmed by recent reforms which in some ways have provided a softer focus (better pay, more staff, more managerial opportunities for professionals) but also a harder edge particularly around performance (e.g. introduction of performance-related-pay and the zero-tolerance of poor performance resulting in intervention with severe consequences including privatization).

Clearly these reforms present challenges for those on the front-line of public service delivery. However, they have also presented staff with the opportunity to change and adapt their labour process. The evidence suggests that, despite substantial structural reform and reorganization, public servants retain elements of a public service ethos – even when working for the private sector (Allmendinger et al., 2003; Hebson et al., 2003). Moreover, it is argued that the public sector retains many of the features of a model employer, although there are important inter-sector variations (Guest and Conway, 2001; Stuart and Martinez Lucio, 2000). This has led some to conclude that 'even after 20 years of almost uninterrupted policy change the gap between the rhetoric and reality of the new public management remains so significant' (Ackroyd et al., 2007: 23).

It is worth us considering why, despite frequent attempts at reform, public service employment might maintain its distinctiveness. Certainly, the level of trade union density and representation within the public sector is a major factor, although union influence has declined over the last 20 years (Bach and Givan, 2008). There is also a question mark over the role of HR departments. They have proven to be relatively weak players within the strategic management teams of public organizations and therefore have struggled to develop the expertise and gain the legitimacy and authority to bring about major employment reform, although recent work by Truss (2008) suggests that they may be strengthening their role. Similarly, it has been argued that local-level managers within the public sector, particularly in health services, have been less able to exercise authority over employment relations than their counterparts in the private sector, resulting in the persistence of the established model of centralized personnel administration (Kirkpatrick and Hoque, 2005). It is also important to remember that public service organizations in the UK continue to provide core value goods such as education, health and social care which invoke a considerable amount of fondness and pride among the UK citizenry. Public sector employees may continue to enjoy distinctive employment conditions so long as they have the support of the wider public.

The agency of public service employees – whether exercised individually or in occupational groups – is also central. This has been discussed in the literature principally in relation to public service professionals who are largely described as successfully defending their jurisdictions and autonomy. However, even here commentators have been unable to agree on the impact of reform on the nature and extent of any consequent change to professional status. Reed documents evidence of 'fragmentation', contending that public servants – including professionals – have renegotiated and redefined their roles, not by choice but through coercion (2000). Laffin and Entwistle describe 'a host of changes in the professional environment' – from mass education to globalization – as driving the professions to 're-invent their values and strategies' (2000: 208).

The 'continuity thesis' (Ackroyd, 1996; Ackroyd et al., 2007; Laffin, 1998) asserts, however, that the public sector professions have used their resources to absorb and adapt to the changes required by the reform agenda. While acknowledging that, for some time, professionals and their organizations have 'been in remission', Ackroyd (1996) concludes that the emergent 'new model professions' will perpetuate themselves and extend their influence, as professions have in the past (617). This view is supported by Fitzgerald and Ferlie who contend that 'professionals are not inert recipients or "subjects" of change but respond actively, deciding how to mould the new situation' (2000: 733). Recent studies of public service professionals suggest levels of resistance are not abating. For example, a study of local authority social service departments uncovered 'a very strong tendency to defend the status quo amongst professional staffs and a resistance to many of the core tenets of new managerialism' (Kirkpatrick and Ackroyd, 2003: 526). Thomas and Davies (2005) forcefully reject the depiction of public service reform as a blanket discourse – 'a given, stamping its authority on the hapless professional in a highly deterministic and unidirectional way' (689). Their research demonstrates the ways in which individuals have exploited the incoherence of NPM by reinterpreting, reproducing and reinscribing the NPM discourse, a process of resistance which, they argue, results in 'low-level disturbances' which lessen and weaken the dominant discourse and create space for individuals to present a 'quiet challenge' to reform (701). Heery (1998) reminds us, public servants, even at the lowest levels, are not passive recipients of change, rather they are 'active interpreters' (92).

Reflecting on the lack of progress in reforming public service organizations, public management scholars have recently turned to sociological institutionalism to gain a deeper understanding of patterns of continuity and change. Institutional logics are defined as the values and belief systems which shape behaviour and practices within organizations and across institutional fields. Many commentators, for example, distinguish between a market and professional logic. Research on institutional logics in the public sector gives little support, however, to the suggestion that a market logic has become universally dominant as a result of public management reform. Reay and Hidings' longitudinal study of Regional Health Authorities in Alberta identifies, for example, 'accommodated logics' where 'the structure and dominant institutional logic of the field has changed, but the previously dominant logic of medical professionalism has been subdued rather than eliminated' (2005: 375). These findings, they suggest, are consistent with DiMaggio and Powell's (1983) description of an organizational field as a battlefield where actors fight one another in order to promote or resist change. There are also parallels with the local activists of Kelly's 'mobilization theory', who transform individual grievances into a greater capacity to 'create and sustain collective organization' (1998: 38).

Recent debates raise questions about the varying impact of institutional pressures and reforms across organizational fields (Ashworth et al., 2009a), suggesting that individual public servants are likely to be subject to multiple institutional logics. This indicates that displacement models of public management reform are likely to prove overly simplistic in many empirical settings (Ashworth et al., 2009b) as countervailing 'local' institutional logics moderate public management reforms in complex ways (Entwistle, 2010). Again this work highlights the scope for agency as actors appear to selectively identify with different logics under different circumstances: resisting, for example, externalization, while conforming with other elements of the market logic, such as providing user-focused services.

Conclusion

Overall, while it is evident that the public management reform agenda has impacted on public service work in real and important ways, we have demonstrated that variety in the extent and duration of that impact can only be understood through an appreciation of the three contingencies – variety, uncertainty and agency – described in this chapter. The reform agenda itself is contested, changing and subject to interpretation and contestation throughout the process of implementation. The contradictions and complexities arising from varied reform imperatives and the layering of one reform over another (Cooper et al., 1996) create tensions but also space for agency and an opportunity for public service workers to resist change or to readjust their labour processes to their advantage. Inevitably, then the effects of any one reform initiative are mixed, leaving us with hybridized rather than transformed public services (Bach and Givan, 2006). We conclude by recommending that a greater understanding of the processes of public sector institutional change and any subsequent impact on the employment relationship might be developed through a greater application of sociological institutional literature, and in particular, the study of accommodated and competing institutional logics.

References

Ackroyd, S. (1996) 'Organization Contra Organizations: Professions and Organizational Change in the United Kingdom', *Organization Studies*, 17(4): 599–621.

Ackroyd, S., Kirkpatrick, I. and Walker, R.M. (2007) 'Public Management Reform in the UK and its Consequences for Professional Organization: A Comparative Analysis', *Public Administration*, 85(1): 9–26.

Allmendinger, P., Tewdwr-Jones, M. and Morphet, J. (2003) 'Public Scrutiny, Standards and the Planning System: Assessing Professional Values within a Modernized Local Government', *Public Administration*, 81(4): 761–780.

Ashworth, R., Entwistle, T. and Skelcher, C. (2006) *The Limits of Pragmatic Legitimacy: The Theorization of Institutional Change in UK Local Government Accountability*, Paper presented at the European Group of Organizational Studies, Bergen.

Ashworth, R. E., Boyne, G.A. and Delbridge, R. (2009a) 'Escape from the Iron Cage: Organizational Change and Isomorphic Pressures in the Public Sector', *Journal of Public Administration, Research and Theory*, 19(1): 165–187.

Ashworth, R., Boyne, G. and Delbridge, R. (2009b) *Relationships between Societal and Local Institutional Logics and Innovation Outcomes: The Case of Local Government Reform in the UK*, paper presented at the EGOS Conference, Barcelona, July.

Aucoin, P. (1990) 'Administrative Reform in Public Management: Paradigms, Principles, Paradoxes and Pendulums', *Governance*, 3(2): 115–137.

Bach, S. (2004) 'Employee Participation and Union Voice in the National Health Service', *Human Resource Management Journal*, 14(2): 3–19.

Bach, S. and Winchester, D. (2003) 'Industrial Relations in the Public Sector' in Edwards, P. (ed.) *Industrial Relations: Theory and Practice*, Oxford: Blackwell.

Bach, S. and Kessler, I. (2007) 'Human Resource Management and the New Public Management' in Boxall, P., Purcell, J. and Wright, P. (eds) *The Oxford Handbook of Human Resource Management*, Oxford: Oxford University Press.

Bach, S. and Givan, R.K. (2008) 'Public Service Modernisation and Trade Union Reform: Towards Managerial-Led Renewal?', *Public Administration*, 86(2): 523–539.

Bach, S. Givan, R.K. and Forth, J. (2009) 'The Public Sector in Transition' in Brown, W., Bryson. A., Forth, J., and Whitfield, K. (eds) *The Evolution of the Modern Workplace*, Cambridge: Cambridge University Press, pp. 307–331.

Bacon, N. and Samuel, P. (2009) 'Partnership Agreement Adoption and Survival in the British Private and Public Sectors', *Work, Employment and Society*, 23(2): 231–248.

Barratt, E. (2009) 'Governing Public Servants', *Management and Organizational History*, 4(1): 67–84.

Bevir, M., Rhodes, R.A.W., Weller, P. (2003) 'Traditions of Governance: Interpreting the Changing Role of the Public Sector', *Public Administration*, 81(1): 1–17.

Bolton, S. (2005) 'Making up Managers: The Case of NHS Nurses', *Work, Employment and Society*, 19(1): 5: 23.

Bordogna, L. (2008) 'Moral Hazard, Transaction Costs and the Reform of Public Service Employment Relations', *European Journal of Industrial Relations*, 14(4): 381–400.

Boyne, G. and Law, J. (2005) 'Setting Public Service Outcome Targets: Lessons from Local Public Service Agreements', *Public Money and Management*, 25(4): 253–260.

Boyne, G.A. Entwistle, T., and Ashworth, R. (2010) 'Theories of Public Service Improvement' in Ashworth, R., Boyne, G.A. and Entwistle, T. (eds) *Public Service Improvement: Theories and Evidence*, Oxford: OUP.

Brunsson, N. and Sahlin-Andersson, K. (2000) 'Constructing Organizations: The Example of Public Sector Reform', *Organization Studies*, 21(4): 721–746.

Casey, R. and Allen, C. (2004) 'Social Housing Managers and the Performance Ethos: Towards a Professional Project of Staff', *Work, Employment and Society*, 18(2): 395–412.

Chadwick, E. (1965 [1842]) *Report on the Sanitary Condition of the Labouring Population of Great Britain*, Edinburgh: Edinburgh University Press.

Christensen, T. and Laegreid, P. (1999) 'New Public Management – Design, Resistance, or Transformation?', *Public Productivity and Management Review*, 23(2): 169–193.

Cooke, H. (2006) 'Seagull Management and the Control of Nursing Work', *Work, Employment and Society*, 20(2): 223–243.

Cooper, D.J., Hinings, B., Greenwood, R., and Brown, J.L. (1996) 'Sedimentation and Transformation in Organizational Change: The Case of Canadian Law Firms', *Organization Studies*, 17(4): 623–647.

Cutler, T., Waine, B., Brehony, K. (2007) A New Epoch of Individualization? Problems with the 'Personalization' of Public Sector Service, *Public Administration*, 85 (3): 847–855.

Denhardt, R.B. and Denhardt, J.V. (2000) 'The New Public Service: Serving Rather than Steering', *Public Administration Review*, 60(6): 549–559.

DiMaggio, P. and Powell, W. (1983) The Iron Cage Revisited: Institutional Isomorphism and Collective Rationality in Organizational Fields, *American Sociological Review*, 48(2): 147–160.

Du Gay, P. (2008) ' "Without Affection or Enthusiasm" Problems of Involvement and Attachment in "Responsive Public Management" ', *Organization*, 15(3): 335–353.

Duncan, C. (2001) 'The Impact of Two Decades of Reform of British Public Sector Industrial Relations', *Public Money and Management*, 21(1): 27–34.

Dunleavy, P., Margetts, H., Bastow, S., and Tinkler, J. (2006) 'New Public Management is Dead – Long Live Digital-Era Governance', *Journal of Public Administration Research and Theory*, 16(3): 467–494.

Emery, Y., Wyser, C., Martin, N. and Sanchez, J. (2008) 'Swiss Public Servants' Perceptions of Performance in a Fast-Changing Environment', *International Review of Administrative Sciences*, 74(2): 307–323.

Entwistle, T. (2010) 'For Appropriateness or Consequences? Explaining Organisational Change in English Local Government', *Public Administration*, forthcoming.

Entwistle, T. and Enticott, G. (2007) 'Who or What Sets the Agenda? The Case of Rural Issues in England's Local Public Service Agreements', *Policy Studies*, 28(3): 193–208.

Entwistle, T. and Martin, S. (2005) 'From Competition to Collaboration in Public Service Delivery: A New Agenda for Research', *Public Administration*, 83(1): 233–242.

Gill-McLure, W. and Seifert, R. (2008) 'Degrading the Labourer: The Reform of Local Government Manual Work', *Capital and Class*, 94: 1–30.

Guest, D. and Conway, N. (2001) *Public and Private Sector Perspectives on the Psychological Contract*, CIPD.

Hebson,G., Grimshaw, D. and Marchington, M. (2003) 'PPPs and the Changing Public Sector Ethos: Case Study Evidence from the Health and Local Authority Sectors', *Work, Employment and Society*, 17(3): 481–501.

Heery, E. (1998) 'A Return to Contract? Performance Related Pay in a Public Service', *Work, Employment and Society*, 12(1): 73–95.

Hjern, B. and Porter, D. (1981) 'Implementation Structures: A New Unit of Administrative Analysis', *Organization Studies*, 2(3): 211–227.

Hood, C. (1991) 'A Public Management for All Seasons', *Public Administration*, 69(1): 3–19.

Hood, C. (1995) 'The New Public Management in the 1980s: Variations on a Theme', *Accounting, Organizations and Society*, 20(2/3): 93–109.

Hood, C., James, O. and Scott, C. (2000) 'Regulation of Government: Has it Increased, Is it Increasing, Should it be Diminished?', *Public Administration*, 78(2): 283–304.

Howell, C. (2004) 'Is There a Third Way for Industrial Relations?', *British Journal of Industrial Relations*, 42(1): 1–22.

Keast, R., Mandell, M.P., Brown, K. and Woolcock, G. (2004) 'Network Structures: Working Differently and Changing Expectations', *Public Administration Review*, 64(3): 363–371.

Kelly, J. (1998) *Rethinking Industrial Relations: Mobilization, Collectivism and Long Waves*, London: Routledge.

Kettl, Donald F. (1997) 'The Global Revolution in Public Management: Driving Themes, Missing Links', *Journal of Policy Analysis and Management*, 16(3): 446–462.

Kirkpatrick, I. and Ackroyd, S. (2003) 'Transforming the Professional Archetype?: The New Managerialism in UK Social Services', *Public Management Review*, 5(4): 511–531.

Kirkpatrick, I. and Hoque, K. (2005) 'The Decentralisation of Employment Relations in the British Public Sector', *Industrial Relations Journal*, 36(2): 100–120.

Laffin, M. (1998) *Beyond Bureaucracy: The Professions in the Contemporary Public Sector*, Aldershot: Ashgate.

Laffin, M. and Entwistle, T. (2000) 'New Problems, Old Professions? The Changing National World of the Local Government Professions', *Policy and Politics*, 28(2): 207–220.

Ling T. (2002) 'Delivering Joined-up Government in the UK: Dimensions, Issues and Problems', *Public Administration*, 80(4): 615–642.

Lowndes, V. and Sullivan, H. (2004) 'Like a Horse and Carriage or a Fish on a Bicycle: How Well Do Local Partnerships and Public Participation Go Together?', *Local Government Studies*, 30(1): 51–73

Lynn, Laurence E. (1998) 'The New Public Management: How to Transform a Theme into a Legacy', *Public Administration Review*, 58(3): 231–237.

Lynn, Laurence E. (2001) 'The Myth of the Bureaucratic Paradigm: What Traditional Public Administration Really Stood For', *Public Administration Review*, 61(2): 144–160.

Marquand, D. (2004) *The Decline of the Public: The Hollowing Out of Citizenship*, Cambridge: Polity Press.

Moore, M. (1995) *Creating Public Value: Strategic Management in Government*, Cambridge MA: Harvard University Press.

Newman, J. and McKee, B. (2005) 'Beyond the New Public Management? Public Services and the Social Investment State', *Policy and Politics*, 33(4): 657–674.

Newman, J. and Clarke, J. (2009) *Publics, Politics and Power: Remaking the Public in Public Services*, London: Sage.

Newman, J., Glendinning, C. and Hughes, M. (2008) 'Beyond Modernisation? Social Care and the Transformation of Welfare Governance', *Journal of Social Policy*, 37(4): 531–557.

Noble, G. and Jones, R. (2006) 'The Role of Boundary-Spanning Managers in the Establishment of Public-Private Partnerships', *Public Administration*, 84(4): 891–917.

Osborne, T. (1994) 'Bureaucracy as a Vocation: Governmentatlity and Administration in Nineteenth-Century Britain', *Journal of Historical Sociology*, 7(3): 289–313.

Osborne, D. and Gaebler, T. (1992) *Reinventing Government*, Reading MA: Addison-Wesley.

Page, S. (2005) 'What's New about the New Public Management? Administrative Change in the Human Services', *Public Administration Review*, 65(6): 713–727.

Perkin, H. (1989) *The Rise of Professional Society in England since 1880*, London: Routledge.

Reay, T. and Hinings, C.R. (2005) 'The Recomposition of an Organizational Field: Health Care in Alberta', *Organization Studies*, 26(3): 351–384.

Rosenthal, P. and Peccei, R. (2006) 'The Social Construction of Clients by Service Agents in Reformed Welfare Administrations', *Human Relations*, 59(12): 1633–1658.

Skelcher, C., Mathur, N., Smith, M., (2005) 'The Public Governance of Collaborative Spaces: Discourse, Design and Democracy', *Public Administration* 83: 573–596.

Smith, C., Valsecchi, R., Mueller, F. and Gabe, J. (2008) 'Knowledge and the Discourse of Labour Process Transformation: Nurses and the Case of NHS Direct for England', *Work, Employment and Society*, 22(4): 581–599.

Stoker, G. (2005) 'Public Value Management: A New Narrative for Networked Governance?', *American Review of Public Administration*, 36(1): 41–57.

Stuart, M. and Martinez Lucio, M. (2000) 'Reviewing the Model Employer: Changing Employment Relations in the Health and Private Sectors', *Journal of Management in Medicine*, 14(5/6): 310–325.

Thomas, R. and Davies, A. (2005) 'Theorizing the Micro-Politics of Resistance: New Public Management and Managerial Identities in the UK Public Services', *Organization Studies*, 26(5): 683–706.

Truss, C. (2008) 'Continuity and Change: The Role of the HR Function in the Modern Public Sector', *Public Administration*, 86(4): 1071–1088.

Williams, P. (2002) 'The Competent Boundary Spanner', *Public Administration*, 80(1): 103–124.

Author index

Baylies, V., 405, 411
Becker, B., 99, 101
Beck, T., 240
Beck, U., 149, 412
Beer, M., 107
Behrens, M., 354, 356
Bell, D., 402
Bell, M., 125, 324–325
Bellemare, G., 390
Belussi, F., 207
Beniger, J. R., 44
Bennett, R. J., 388
Benwell, B., 156
Bercusson, B., 348–9
Berg, P., 305
Bergström, O., 161–2
Berkley, J. D., 58
Berle, A. A., 125–6
Berman, E., 274
Berry, A. J., 41
Berry, L. L., 376, 378, 380
Beveridge, W., 212
Bevir, M., 429
Bhabha, H., 157
Bhattacharya, C., 112
Bhatt, E. R., 202
Bitner, B. B. H., 380, 393
Bittman, M., 6
Black, B., 238
Blackaby, F., 278
Blackler, F., 405
Blair, T., 253, 254, 275, 290, 324
Blanchflower, D. G., 273
Blau, F. D., 79
Blundell, R., 259
Blyth, M., 177
Blyton, P., 1–15, 91n5, 128, 161, 207–8, 299–314, 342, 354, 365
Bognanno, M., 237
Böheim, R., 309–10
Boltanski, L., 149
Bonney, N., 300, 307
Booms, B. H., 379
Bordogna, L., 427
Boreham, P., 414
Boris, M. B., 348
Bosch, G., 175
Boselie, P., 21, 26, 100, 103–4, 109
Boston, S., 320–1
Bowles, S., 292
Boxall, P., 26, 33–5, 107, 358
Boyer, R., 183
Boyne, G., 428, 433

Bradley, H., 88
Bradley, K., 225
Brady, D., 291
Braverman, H., 46
Brewer, M., 274–5
Brinkley, I., 406, 413, 416, 419–20
Briskin, L., 149, 334, 348–9
Bronfenbrenner, K., 345–6
Brown, A., 201, 207, 209–10
Brown, J. S., 408–9
Brown, P., 86, 402, 404–5
Brown, S. W., 75, 77, 81, 378
Brown, W., 3, 6–7, 75, 77, 81–2, 86, 91, 172, 176, 187–8, 226, 238, 353
Brunsson, N., 427
Bryson, A., 99, 102, 358, 362
Budd, J. W., 8, 129–30, 134, 276, 365
Bullock, S. S., 212
Bunting, M., 307
Burawoy, M., 23–6, 27, 30–2, 35, 41, 45, 384
Burchell, B. J., 412
Burkett, L., 129
Burns, M., 207
Burrell, G., 43–4, 50, 53, 64, 150, 160
Butler, J., 157, 160

C

Cabrera, A., 408–9
Cabrera, E. F., 408–9
Cadotte, E. R., 378, 392
Campbell, J. L., 173
Canak, W., 348
Cappelli, P., 5–6, 187
Card, D., 275
Carley, M., 91n3
Carr, C., 235
Carter, B., 351
Casey, C., 45–8, 53, 153, 161, 384–5
Casey, R., 434
Castells, M., 42–3, 52, 55, 57–8, 61, 63, 149, 402–3
Castle, B., 320
Causer, G., 154
Chadwick, E., 425
Chandler, A., 240
Chaney, P., 328
Charlwood, A., 342, 356, 365
Chesbrough, H. W., 417
Child, J., 44–5, 48, 55
Christensen, T., 427, 432, 437
Chung, T. S., 375
Churchill, G. A. Jr, 378

Holgate, J., 85, 91n2, 149, 346, 348, 361–2
Hollingsworth, J. R., 173
Holmer-Nadesan, M., 157, 161
Holt, H., 304
Homburg, C., 389
Hood, C., 425–7, 430
Hooker, H., 311–12
Hoque, K., 83, 333, 438
Horton, S., 151–2
Houlihan, M., 383
Houseman, S. N., 300, 412
Howard, E., 324, 326–7
Howell, C., 7, 290, 350, 429
Howells, J., 407
Humphrey, J. C., 348
Hunt, G., 348
Hunt, J., 348
Hurley, J., 198, 207, 209
Huselid, M. A., 99, 102–3, 405, 414–15
Husserl, E., 136
Hutchinson, J., 201, 207, 209–11
Hutton, W., 126, 231, 275
Hyman, J., 63, 342
Hyman, R., 197, 199, 226, 342, 344, 356–8, 361

I
Ichniowski, C., 100
Innes, M., 42

J
Jabko, N., 174
Jackall, R., 142
Jackson, G., 233, 242
Jackson, M., 89
Jackson, S., 110
Jackson, S. E., 184
Jacobides, M. G., 187
Jacoby, S., 6, 179, 231, 355
Jacques, R., 44, 53
Jaffe, M., 89
James, O., 292
Janssens, M., 26, 35–7, 40, 107, 112
Jefferys, S., 348
Jenkins, J., 11, 91n5, 171, 181, 195–220, 274, 299, 301, 342, 354
Jenkinson, T., 240
Jermier, J. M., 29, 32, 152, 163
Jessop, B., 250, 401–3, 410–411, 417
Jewson, N., 404
Johnson, P., 57
Jones, C., 134, 152–4, 185

Jones, R., 198, 207, 209, 211, 437
Jones, T., 108
Juravich, T., 345

K
Kahn-Freund, O., 3
Kahn, L. M., 79
Kaler, J., 132–3
Kallinikos, J., 27–8
Kant, I., 131–2
Kanter, R. M., 43
Kaplan, D., 105
Kärreman, D., 47–8, 154
Katz, H. C., 183
Kaufman, B. E., 127–8, 355, 358
Kaysen, C., 125–6
Keast, R., 428
Keat, R., 47–8, 378
Keegan, A., 21, 26, 109
Keenoy, T., 21, 26, 29–30
Keep, E., 414
Keim, G., 114
Kelly, E., 80
Kelly, J., 204, 229–30, 288, 290n2, 343, 355, 358
Keltner, B., 185
Kemeny, M. E., 292
Kersley, B., 7, 176, 289n3, 300, 305, 312
Kessler, I., 355, 425
Ketels, C. H. M., 416, 420
Kettl, D. F., 424, 430
Keynes, J. M., 177
Kierkegaard, S., 135
Kindleberger, C. P., 258
King, A., 113
Kinnie, N., 102–3
Kirkpatrick, I., 438–9
Kirton, G., 323, 334
Kleiner, M. M., 251
Klein, N., 110
Klimecki, R., 417
Knetter, M., 229
Knight, K. G., 82
Knights, D., 44–5, 48–9, 161–2, 381, 391
Kochan, T., 127–8, 141, 353n1
Kondo, D., 53, 157
Konno, N., 407
Korczynski, M., 48, 50, 376, 383–4, 387–8, 391
Kuhn, T., 128
Kunda, G., 48, 153, 386, 412
Kurdelbusch, A., 187

Milner, S., 7, 348, 350
Minford, P., 74–5
Mittal, V., 377
Moberg, D. J., 142
Monks, R., 225
Moody, K., 171, 196
Moore, M., 132, 428
Morgan, G., 44, 48, 161, 182
Morgan, P., 159
Morris, G., 71–3
Morris, J., 55, 152, 156
Morrison, E. W., 4
Morton, G., 253
Moss, P., 304
Mueller, F., 183, 187, 407
Mulgan, G., 61
Mulholland, H., 153
Mumby, D. K., 385, 388
Munro, A., 334
Musson, G., 153
Myconos, G., 198

N

Nahapiet, J., 414
Nash, D., 7, 11–12, 77–8, 81, 225–68
Neal, A., 71
Newell, A., 285
Newell, S., 404, 406, 414
Newman, J., 49, 55, 59, 154, 427–8, 431–2
Newton, T., 161
Nichols, T., 125
Nickell, S., 274
Nietzsche, F., 135
Niskanen, J., 113
Niven, B., 329
Njoya, W., 3
Noble, G., 437
Nohria, N., 58
Nolan, P., 88, 409, 411–12, 418
Nonaka, I., 58, 406–7, 409, 415
Noon, B., 105
Noon, M., 83, 306–8, 323, 333
Norton, R., 105
Norton, W. W., 105
Nye, J. S., 61
Nyquist, J., 379

O

O'Brien, M., 304
O'Brien, N., 328–9
O'Brien, R., 199, 304, 328–9
O'Cinneide, C., 325

O'Donohoe, S., 385
Ogbonna, E., 14, 323, 375–9, 385–7
Ohmae, K., 195
Oikelome, F., 92n7
Oi, W., 74
Oliver, M., 321–2
Oliver, R. L., 376, 378–81, 393
Orlitzky, M., 110
Orr, J. E., 408
Orton, M., 291
Osborne, D., 428
Osborne, T., 425
O'Sullivan, M., 231, 417
Oswald, A. J., 273
Ouali, N., 348
Oxenbridge, S., 77

P

Paauwe, J., 26, 35–6, 97, 99–100, 104, 107, 112
Pagel, M., 321–2
Page, S., 429
Pahl, R., 290
Pangsapa, P., 209–10
Parasuraman, A., 376–8, 380–1
Parker, J., 348
Parker, M., 46
Parker, P., 176, 185
Park, Y., 292, 299
Pascale, R., 403
Paton, N., 261, 268n24
Patterson, M. G., 99, 101–2, 104
Pearce, F., 51
Peccei, R., 384, 386, 391, 435
Peck, J., 58
Peden, G., 278
Peel, R., 425
Peiperl, M., 257, 259
Pendleton, A., 187, 231–3, 235, 237–8
Percival, J., 63
Perkin, H., 425
Perlow, L. A., 305, 308
Perrow, C., 44, 62
Persson, T., 289
Peters, M., 92n6
Peters, P., 313
Petrova, M., 110–114
Pettigrew, A. M., 48, 55, 57
Pfaff, M., 375, 377, 383
Pfeffer, J., 34, 98–9, 102
Phelan, C., 346
Phelps, R. A., 259–60, 268n20
Phillips, N., 47

Subject index

accreditation
  elite business qualifications of, 259–60
  as form of regulation, 257–8
  as institutional intermediation, 258–9
  mission of, agencies, 260–3
  principal, agencies, 260
  see also business school accreditation
active behaviour of employees, 388–90
affirmative action, 321
American Marketing Association, 377
Americans with Disabilities Act (ADA), 322
AMO framework, 100
Amsterdam Treaty, 324
analytical HRM, characteristics of, 34
Annual Survey of Hours and Earnings
  (ASHE), 293
anti-discrimination, as employment
  right, 87
anti-discrimination law, British, 319–26
  approach to politics/labour markets and,
  322–6
  social/labour movements role, 319–22
appropriation, 408
Asia Floor Wage Alliance, 211–2
Asia Pacific Economic Cooperation
  (APEC), 197
Association of MBAs (AMBA), 260–1
Association to Advance Collegiate Schools
  of Business (AACSB), 260
average growth rates, 277t

Bangladesh Independent Garment
  Workers' Union (BIGU), 210
Bank of America, 132
behaviour studies, working time, 310–1
Being and Nothingness (Sartre), 137, 138
Being and Time (Heidegger), 135, 140
benchmarking, as standardized work tool,
  182–3

best practice/fit perspectives, 102–3
bilateral/multilateral trade agreements,
  174–5
Birth of the Clinic, The (Foucault), 52–3
Bolkestein Directive, 217
bottom-up control, 52
boundary spanner, public manager, 437
British anti-discrimination law, 319–26
  approach to politics/labour markets and,
  322–6
  social/labour movements role, 319–22
British Employment Tribunals (ETs), 335
British Sex Discrimination Act 1975, 326
broken society, 273–4
brokerage, 204
Burberry, 208
business case for equality, 323
Business in the Community, 106, 114
business school accreditation, 249–65
  employment relations and, 251–6
  labour market effects of qualifications
  and, 256–63

capillary control, 50–7
capital, fixity of, 196
capitalism
  disconnected, 230, 243
  employment relationship and, 123–5,
  226–30
  ethics/philosophy and, 123–5
  fast, 64
  industrial relations and, 123–5
  labour management and, 226–30
  managerial, 123
  new, 149–50
  varieties of, (VoC) model, 72, 226–30
Capitalism: A Love Story, 132
capitalistic relations, new configurations of,
  149–50

456

diversity
  interests of workers and, 362
  management, 334
  in trade union revitalization, 344*t*,
    347–50
  unions and, 344*t*, 347–50
Diversity Champions programme, 84, 87
dominance effects, 183
dualistic control strategy, 63
Dynamics of the Employment Relationship,
  The (Blyton and Turnbull), 128–9

earnings inequality, employment and,
    273–95
  data sources/measures of, 293–4
  explained by occupation, 285*t*
  in labour market, 276–87
  markets/institutions and, 287–91
  Standard Occupational Classification
    and, 294–5
economy
  emergence of knowledge-based, 402–5
  Fordism in knowledge based, 402–3
  globalization and, 199–200
  knowledge-based firms and, 405–9
effort-biased technical change, 6
egotistical calculation, 258
embedded liberalism, 174
emerging market economies (EMEs), 230
emotional labour, 50
Employment Agencies Standards
    Inspectorate, 85
Employment Equality Directive (EED),
    324–5
employment ethicists, employment
    relationship and, 129–36
employment law, 71–91
  efficacy of, 77–81
  mediating, 82–7
  see also juridification
Employment Relations Act 1999, 77–8
employment relationships
  accreditation and, 249–65
  business school accreditation and,
    249–65
  capitalism and, 123–5, 226–30
  changes in context of, 5–8
  company level practices of, 186–8
  contextual influences shaping, 171–265
  control in work organizations and, 41–64
  defined, 2–5
  in different work settings, 375–440
  earnings inequality, 273–95

employment ethicists and, 129–36
ethics/philosophy and, 122–44
evolving nature of, 238–42
existentialism and, 137–43
future of HRM and, 21–39
globalization and, 195–219
governance impact and, 225–45
identity research and, 147–63
intersectionality problems as, 318–38
juridification and, 71–91
knowledge-based economy and, 401–20
labour management and, 234–8
market influences and, 171–89
markets and, reassessing, 171–89
market segmentation of, 184–6
performance, HRM and, 97–118
perspectives on, 21–163
product markets and, 179–84
public service and, 424–40
reassessing, introduction to, 1–2
service sector, 375–95
strategies used in, 184–5
substantive developments in, 273–365
worker representation and, 342–65
work-life balance and, 299–314
employment research, into service
    encounters, 383–8
  control and, 384–8
  response categories, 386
employment rights regime, 87–90
  recombination thesis of, 89–90
End of History, The (Fukuyama), 123
Enron, 122
enterprise culture, 378
epochalist theories, 356
epochalism, post-Fordist debate and, 416–9
Equalities and Human Rights Commission
    (EHRC), 318, 331
equality
  concepts/theories of, 326–32
  as employment right, 87
  laws, changes in, 328–32
  workplace, future of, 332–7
Equality Duties, 328
equality laws, changes in, 328–32
Equal Pay Act 1970, 78–9, 320
Equal Value Amendment Regulations,
    320–1
Equinet, 326
ethical turn, 123

ethics/philosophy and employment
relationship, 122–44
capitalism and, 123–5
corporate governance and, 126–9
employment ethicists and, 129–36
existentialism and, 137–42
post-2/12 world, 122–3
EU Acquired Rights Directive, 241
European Community Shipowners'
Association, 216, 218
European Foundation for Management
Development, 260
European Network of Equality, 326
European port transport industry, 212–8
European Quality Improvement System
(EQUIS), 260
European Sea Ports Organisation (ESPO),
216
European Sector Social Dialogue
Committee, 217
European Transport Workers' Federation
(ETF), 213, 214–5
European Union (EU), 174–5
globalization and, 197, 198
European Union (EU) Amsterdam Treaty
European Works Council Directive, 236
Excellence and Ethics (Solomon), 133
existentialism
employment relationship and, 137–43
ethics/philosophy and, 133–6
Existentialism and Humanism (Sartre), 136,
139
exit, as shareholder strategy, 234
expectation–disconfirmation model, 378,
392–3
ExxonMobil, 110

Fair Employment Enforcement Board, 86
Fairness at Work, 253–5
fast capitalism, 64
Federation of European Private Port
Operators (FEPORT), 216
Federation of Transport Workers' Unions,
214
flags of convenience (FOC), 215
flexible labour markets, 58
Ford, Dagenham plant strike, 320–1
Fordism, knowledge based economy and,
402–3
Ford Motor Company, 126, 186
foreign direct investment (FDI), 198–9
formal equality, 326
formula of humanity, 131

foundation hospitals, 59
Fruit of the Loom, 211
Future of Work Programme, 411

Gangmasters Licensing Authority, 85
Garment and Textile Workers' Union
(GATWU), 210
garment industry, race to the bottom, 203
Gender Equality Duty (GED), 328
Genealogy of Morality (Nietzsche), 135
General Agreement on Tariffs and Trade
(GATT), 203
general labour inspectorate, 86
General Motors, 182, 186–7
GERPISA, 183
globalization
employment relationship and, 195–219
European port transport industry and,
212–8
foreign direct investment (FDI) and,
198–9
gross domestic product (GDP) and,
199–200
international clothing industry and,
205–12
International Labour Organisation (ILO)
and, 201–2
regional *vs.* global economy, 199–200
social institutions and, 198–205
governance
capitalism and, 226–30
caveats of, 238–43
defined, 52
employment relationship and, 230–4
evolving nature of, 238–42
impact on employment relationship and,
225–45
labour management and, 234–8
neo-Weberian control and, 55
panopticon control and, 54–5
governance mechanisms, markets and,
173–6
governmentalists, 52
panopticon control and, 55
grand campaigns, 210
greedy organisations, 6
Gross Value Added, 114
Groundwork of the Metaphysics of Morals
(Kant), 131
growth rates, 277*t*
Grundlegung zur Metaphysik der Sitten
(Kant), 131
Guinness, 124

harassment, 324
hard regulation, 250, 255–6
Health and Safety Executive, 85
hegemonic system, 123
high involvement management (HIM), 102
high performance work practices (HPWP), 102
high performance work systems (HPWS), 58, 99, 102
high trust/low control employment systems, 55
HM Revenue and Customs, 85
HRM, *see* human resource management (HRM)
Human Development Index (HDI), 111
human resource management (HRM)
  Burawoy on, 23–6
  conceptualization of, 102–3
  concerns with, 21–2
  critical management studies (CMS) and, 26–33
  future of, 21–39
  key developments/debates, 99–107
  multidimensional organizational measures and, 107–18
  performance and, 97–118
  plurality and, 33–8
  research, impact of, 25
human resource management/performance link
  conceptualization of HRM and, 102–3
  methodological limitations in, 100–1
  organizational performance and, 103–7
  theoretical underpinnings of, 99–100
hybridization, process of, 57
hygiene factors, 103
hyper-competitive environments, 57

ICI, 124
identities-turn, 149, 157
identity anchors, 150
identity control, 153–6
identity research, employment relations and, 147–63
  relevance of, 160–3
  uncertainty in, 149–60
identity uncertainty, 149–60
  identity control at work and, 153–6
  managerial-inspired discourses and, 156–60
  social work professionals and, 154–6
Imperial Tobacco, 124

Independent High-Level Study Group, 290–1
indirect discrimination, 327
Inditex, 211
Industrial Relations (IR)
  as academic field, 72
  efficacy of employment law and, 77–81
  employment rights regime and, 87–90
  mediation and, 82
  New Deal system of, 87
  see also employment relationships
Industrial Relations Act 1971, 77
inequality measures, 281*t*
Information and Consultation of Employees (ICE) Regulations, 78, 236
insider system, 234
institutional appropriation, 205
instrumentalism, critical management studies and, 30–1
interests of workers
  balancing of, 363–4
  cooperative-conflicting, 363
  depth of, 359, 361
  diversity of, 362
  levels of, 362–3
  range of, 361–2
international clothing industry, 205–12
International Dockworkers' Council (IDC), 214
International Framework Agreement, 211
International Labour Organisation (ILO), 201–2
  Convention 110 of 1951, 320
  Declaration of Philadelphia of 1944, 132
  hard regulation and, 255–6
International Ladies' Garment Workers' Union (ILGWU), 206
International Monetary Fund (IMF), 175
International Textile Garment and Leather Workers' Federation (ITGLWF), 211
International Transport Workers' Federation (ITF), 214
  Directive, 215
intersectionality, problems of, 318–38
  British equalities policy/law and, 319–26
  equality concepts/theories, 326–32
  future and, 337–8
  workplace equality agendas, 332–7
isomorphism, product-market-driven, 181–4

jobbers, Union and, 206
job creep, 6
John Lewis Partnership, 225
J & P. Coats, 124
juridification
  deregulation as, 73
  efficacy of, 77–81
  employment rights regime, 87–90
  mediating law, 82–7
  opposition to, 73–6
  responses to, 71–91

Keynesian Welfare National State (KWNS),
  402
Kinder, Lyndenberg and Domini
  Research & Analytics, Inc. (KLD),
  106, 111
knowledge-based economy, employment
  relationship and, 401–20
  assessment of, 411–6
  critiquing knowledge work, 409–11
  emergence of, 402–5
  knowledge-based firms and, 405–9
  new economy and, 411–6
  post-Fordist debate, epochalism and,
    416–9
knowledge-creating companies, 58
knowledge work, 50
  challenges posed by, for HRM policy,
    406t
  critiquing, 409–11
  in new economy, 411–6
  organizations and, 53

Labour Behind the Label (LBL), 211
Labour Government, 77, 277–9
labour management, governance and,
  234–8
labour market, earnings inequality in,
  276–87
  institutions and, 287–91
laissez faire solutions, 323
Lean and Mean (Harrison), 418
learning, knowledge and, 408
L'Etre et le Neant (Sartre), 136
liberalism, embedded, 174
liberal market economies (LMEs), 228, 232
licensing, as form of regulation, 257
liquid modernity thesis, 150
Lisbon Strategy, 324
living wage, 212
London Stock Exchange (LSE), 124, 234

managerial capitalism, 123
managerial-inspired discourses, identity
  uncertainty and, 156–60
managerialist thinking, critical
  management studies and, 27–30
manufacturing of subjectivity thesis,
  161
market-driven management, basics of,
  184
marketing research themes, 381–3
  customer categories, 382
Marketing Science Institute, 377
market mechanisms, 173–6
markets and employment relations,
  reassessing, 171–89
  company level of, 186–8
  governance mechanisms and, 173–6
  market segmentation and, 184–6
  neo-liberal ideologies and, 176–9
  product-market-driven isomorphism
    and, 181–4
  scope of product markets and, 179–81
Market to Book Ratio (MBR), 114
Masters of Business Administration (MBA)
  degrees, 259–60
mauvaise foi concept, 138
maxims, 131
McDonald's, 182
McPherson Inquiry, 328
measurement of performance, 114–8
mediating employment law, 82–7
  government enforcement agencies and,
    85–6
  HR managers and, 84
  non-union actors and, 83–7
  unions and, 82–3
  voluntary sector of, 84–5
Mercado Común del Sur (MERCOSUR),
  197
methodological limitations, in
  HRM/performance literature,
  100–1
Michigan Business School model, 131
mixed market economies (MMEs), 230
modelling, 205
Modernising Company Law, 109
mono-organizational forms, 59
moral heteronomy, 139
Moral Mazes (Jackall), 142
moral-suasion, 250
motivators, 103
multi-agency partnerships, 59
Multi-Fibre Agreement (MFA), 203, 207

National Minimum Wage Act 1998, 74–5
National Minimum Wage, Britain, 74,
   85, 86
negative mediation, 82
neo-liberal ideologies, markets and, 176–9
neo-Weberian control, 44
network-based control, 52
network production/distribution
   systems, 58
new capitalism, 149–50
New Earnings Survey (NES), 293
New Public Management (NPM), 151
   key ingredients of, 426
NHS and Community Care Act 1990, 152
Nike, 185
non-governmental organizations (NGOs),
   202
   unions and, 210–1
non-meeting, 217
non-union actors, mediating employment
   law, 83–7
non-union representation, 353–64
   assessing forms of, 359–64
   relationship to unions and, 354–7
   relative effectiveness of, 358–9
   types of, 353–4
Nordic countries, employment rates in,
   288–9
North-American Free Trade Agreement
   (NAFTA), 174, 197
Northern City study, 125

occupational log wage differentials,
   283t
Office for National Statistics (ONS),
   293
Operating and Financial Review
   (OFR), 109
organizational control, 41–2, 384–8
   hybridized forms of, 52
organizational forms, 58–9
organizational performance, 103–7
   outcome indicators of, 104
   Performance Information Market and,
      105–6
   see also performance measures
Organizing Academy, 346
Organizing Institute, 346
Organizing Works, 346
outcome focused approach, 331
outsider system, 234, 236, 239
Oxford Handbook of Human Resource
   Management (Boxall et al.), 34

panopticon control, 54–5, 59
paradigm revolution, 128
part-time working, work-life balance and,
   311–3
pass through provision, 206
Performance Information Market (PIM),
   105–6
performance measures
   business strategies/time frames and,
      109–10t
   financial performance and, 107–8
   measurement of, 114–8
   multidimensional, 107–18
   stakeholders and, 111–4
   subjective, 104–5
performative intent, critical management
   studies and, 30–1
plurality, opportunities of, 33–8
politics/labour markets, approach to, 322–6
Porsche, 185
portfolio workers, 412
position, as market-driven management
   basic, 184
positive mediation, 82
post-Fordist debate, epochialism and,
   416–9
post-2/12 world, business ethics in, 122–3
power, unions and, 344t, 345–7
primary care networks, 59
principal accreditation agencies, 260
process-based approach, 331
production, vertical disintegration of,
   187–8
productivity coalitions, 178–9
product markets, scope of
   benchmarking and, 182–3
   employment relations and, 179–81
   isomorphism, product-market-driven,
      181–4
psychological contract, 4
public management reform strategies
   content of, 426–9
   status of, 429–32
   street-level response to, 432–7
public–private partnerships, 59
Public Sector Equality Duties, 335–6
public service work/management,
      relationship between, 424–40
   complexity/contingency and, 437–40
   management reforms and, 429–32
   public service workers response to, 432–7
   reform strategies and, 426–9